Think AND **DISCUSS**

As directed by your instructor, discuss the following questions in class or in groups.

1. Why do you think a basic truth in computing is that one never has enough storage space? What factors contribute to this situation? As hard disks get larger and larger, do you think we will reach a point where the standard desktop computer has more than enough storage space for the average user's needs? Have we reached that point already?

2. Do you think that using a spell checker and a grammar checker for all your final documents is a sufficient substitute for proofreading? Explain why.

 Think & Discuss is your opportunity to hone your critical thinking skills, going deep into a computing topic in each lesson.

WITHDRAWN

Some business projects are completed by one person, but many others are built piece-by-piece by several people, each adding expertise at the appropriate stage of the process. In this exercise, you will try the kind of teamwork that includes independent effort during each of three separate phases. Each team member will try each phase.

Divide into teams of three students. Each team will use presentation software such as PowerPoint to create a slide displaying the national estimates for the median annual wages of computer systems analysts. To find the most recent data, go to the Occupational Employment Statistics page of the Bureau of Labor Statistics Web site (www.bls.gov/oes/), and click on "Multi-Screen Data Search." Select "One occupation in multiple industries"—the occupational code for systems analysts is 151051. Obtain data for all industries or at least 10. When you have the data, each team member follows these steps:

1. Starting with a blank slide, enter the industry names and median wages. Format this information in whatever way you find effective, but do not add any text, titles, colors, or artwork. Save your work in a file you can share with your teammates.

2. Exchange your file with another member of the team. U̶s̶i̶n̶g̶ ̶t̶h̶e̶ ̶s̶l̶i̶d̶e̶ ̶you received, add titles, explanations, and any other words needed to make the inform̶a̶t̶i̶o̶n̶... data in the slide, but you can adjust the placement of...

Team EXERCISE
Reading/Writing/ Verbal

Team Exercises bring your class together to incorporate computing into your lives and solve the latest problems in technology today! >>

Fact Check questions save you study time! We know your time is valuable—these strategically-placed questions give you the chance to pause and evaluate your own progress through each chapter and reinforce your understanding of the Learning Objectives as you go. >>

Fact Check

1. What is a bitmap?
   a. A diagram of where to find data on a hard drive
   b. A series of interconnected line objects
   c. A grid, whose cells are filled with one or more colors
2. What are draw programs?
   a. Programs that require an underlying bitmap to function properly
   b. Vector-based graphics programs
   c. Programs that can only show straight-line objects

LEARNING OBJECTIVES

After reading this chapter, you will be able to:

3.1 Summarize the ways in which an operating system works with the computer and user, p. 84.

3.2 Describe the way data are moved around the computer, and the basic concept of the machine cycle, p. 87.

3.3 List and describe the major PC operating systems, p. 93.

3.4 Explain how the Windows file system organizes its files, p. 97.

3.5 Identify four ways to acquire software, p. 106.

3.6 Describe three kinds of formatting you can perform with word processing software, and define types of data that can be used by spreadsheet software, p. 110.

3.7 Identify four ways to load graphic files into a computer, and compare the types of graphics software and their uses, p. 120.

 Learning Objectives provide a plan for the chapter material. Each Learning Objective is tied directly to a main heading in the chapter, as well as to a chapter summary point, to help reiterate important topics throughout. Each **Learning Objective** is also given a page number of the main heading it is tied to, for easy, searchable reading.

CHAPTER CONTENTS

 Chapter Tables of Contents show immediately what the student can expect, and tie directly into the Learning Objectives above.

Computing Now

VICE PRESIDENT/DIRECTOR OF MARKETING *Alice Harra*
PUBLISHER *Scott Davidson*
SPONSORING EDITOR *Paul Altier*
DIRECTOR OF DEVELOPMENT *Sarah Wood*
DEVELOPMENTAL EDITOR II *Alaina Tucker*
EDITORIAL COORDINATOR *Allison McCabe*
MARKETING MANAGER *Tiffany Russell*
LEAD DIGITAL PRODUCT MANAGER *Damian Moshak*
DIGITAL DEVELOPMENT EDITOR *Kevin White*
DIGITAL PRODUCT MANAGER *Thuan Vinh*
DIRECTOR, EDITING/DESIGN/PRODUCTION *Jess Ann Kosic*
PROJECT MANAGER *Jean R. Starr*
SENIOR BUYER *Sandy Ludovissy*
SENIOR DESIGNER *Anna Kinigakis*
SENIOR PHOTO RESEARCH COORDINATOR *Keri Johnson*
DIGITAL PRODUCTION COORDINATOR *Brent dela Cruz*
OUTSIDE DEVELOPMENT HOUSE *Ingrid Benson, Debbie Meyer, Amber Allen, Integra-Chicago, Inc.*
TYPEFACE *11/13 Minion Pro*
COMPOSITOR *Integra-Chicago, Inc.*
PRINTER *Quad/Graphics*

COMPUTING NOW

Published by McGraw-Hill, a business unit of The McGraw-Hill Companies, Inc., 1221 Avenue of the Americas, New York, NY, 10020. Copyright © 2013 by The McGraw-Hill Companies, Inc. All rights reserved. No part of this publication may be reproduced or distributed in any form or by any means, or stored in a database or retrieval system, without the prior written consent of The McGraw-Hill Companies, Inc., including, but not limited to, in any network or other electronic storage or transmission, or broadcast for distance learning.

Some ancillaries, including electronic and print components, may not be available to customers outside the United States.

This book is printed on acid-free paper.

1 2 3 4 5 6 7 8 9 0 QDB/QDB 1 0 9 8 7 6 5 4 3 2

ISBN   978-0-07-351685-1
MHID   0-07-351685-6

Library of Congress Cataloging in Publication Data

Library of Congress Control Number: 2011944709

The Internet addresses listed in the text were accurate at the time of publication. The inclusion of a Web site does not indicate an endorsement by the authors or McGraw-Hill, and McGraw-Hill does not guarantee the accuracy of the information presented at these sites.

www.mhhe.com

ComputingNow APP

New with this text, try the *Computing Now* app, which includes:

▶ Key term flash cards
▶ Quizzes
▶ Game, Over the Edge

Scan with your smartphone to access more…anytime, anywhere:

Mobile App Review key concepts through interactive quizzes, flashcards, & games

for Apple®

for Android™

Android is a trademark of Google, Inc.

Extra Resources
Additional digital resources & news

DID YOU KNOW that by purchasing this book you also purchased the FREE *Computing Now* app? Visit the Apple or Android app stores to download, or scan the code below to access immediately!

www.mhhe.com/computingnow

ACKNOWLEDGMENTS

Thank you to everyone who helped us develop *Computing Now!*

Bamkole Adeleye *Passaic County Community College*
Lancie Affonso *College of Charleston*
Doug Albert *Finger Lakes Community College*
Rosalyn Amaro *Florida State College at Jacksonville*
Tim Anderson *Western International University*
Wilma Andrews *Virginia Commonwealth University*
Tom Ashby *Oklahoma City Community College*
Ijaz Awan *Savannah State University*
Tahir Aziz *J. Sargeant Reynolds Community College*
Carolyn Barren *Macomb Community College—Center*
Richard Beebe *Buena Vista University*
Rocky Belcher *Sinclair Community College*
Paula Bell *Lock Haven University of Pennsylvania*
Jessica Blackwelder *Wilmington College of Delaware*
Barbara Buckner *Lee University*
Lynn Byrd *Delta State University*
Sandy Carriker *North Shore Community College*
Tricia Casey *Trident Technical College*
Maureen Cass *Bellevue University*
Jim Chaffee *University of Iowa*
Paulette Comet *The Community College of Baltimore County*
Ronald Conway *Bowling Green State University*
Lee Cottrell *Bradford School Pittsburgh*
William Crosbie *Raritan Valley Community College*
Spring Davidson *University of Delaware*
Phillip Davis *Del Mar College*
Jennifer Day *Sinclair Community College*
Ralph De Arazoza *Miami Dade College*
Charles DeSassure *Tarrant County College—SE Campus*
Russell Dulaney *Rasmussen College*
Annette Easton *San Diego State University*
Deb Fells *Mesa Community College*
Jean Finley *Asheville-Buncombe Technical Community College*
Barbara Fogle *Trident Technical College*

Brian Fox *Santa Fe College*
Susan Fuschetto *Cerritos College*
Rachelle Hall *Glendale Community College*
John Haney *Snead State Community College*
Andrew Hardin *University of Nevada Las Vegas*
Ranida Harris *Indiana University Southeast*
Shohreh Hashemi *University of Houston—Downtown*
Terri Helfand *Chaffey College*
Kristen Hockman *University of Missouri Columbia*
Terri Holly *Indian River State College*
Bobbie Hyndman *Amarillo College*
Valerie Kasay *Georgia Southern University*
Jan Kehm *Spartanburg Community College*
Darenda Kersey *Black River Technical College*
Annette Kerwin *College of DuPage*
Kurt Kominek *Northeast State Community College*
Jeanette Landin *Empire College*
Kevin Lee *Guilford Tech Community College*
Kate LeGrand *Broward Community College*
Mary Locke *Greenville Technical College*
Howard Mandelbaum *John Jay College of Criminal Justice*
Daniela Marghitu *Auburn University*
Richard Martin *Missouri State University*
Prosenjit Mazumdar *George Mason University*
Roberta McClure *Lee College*
Sue McCrory *Missouri State University*
Gary McFall *Purdue University*
Beverly Medlin *Appalachian State University*
John Mensing *Brookdale Community College*
Mike Michaelson *Palomar College*
Shayan M. Mirabi *American Intercontinental University*
Jeffery Mobley *Pitt Community College*
Kathleen Morris *University of Alabama*
Carol Y. Mull *Greenville Technical College*
Shirley Nagg *Everest Institute*
Melissa Nemeth *IU Kelley School of Business Indianapolis*
Eloise Newsome *Northern Virginia Community College—Woodbridge*

Brenda Nielsen *Mesa Community College*
George Nolasco *Harper College*
John Panzica *Community College of Rhode Island*
Lucy Parakhovnik *California State University—Northridge*
Angie Parker *Anthem College Online*
Robert Peery *Columbia College—Marysville*
Andrew Perry *Springfield College*
Teresa Peterman *Grand Valley State University*
Julie Pettus *Missouri State University*
Jeremy Pittman *Coahoma Community College*
Herbert Rebhun *University of Houston—Downtown*
Laura Ringer *Piedmont Community College*
Marlene Roden *AB Tech Community College*
Diane Santurri *Johnson & Wales University*
Karen Scott *University of Texas at Arlington*
Pat Serrano *Scottsdale Community College*
MaryJo Slater *Community College of Beaver County*
Candice Spangler *Columbus State Community College*
Gary Sparks *Metropolitan Community College*
Diane Stark *Phoenix College*
James Stephenson *Western International University*
Lynne Stuhr *Trident Technical College*
Denise Sullivan *Westchester Community College*
Lo-An Tabar-Gaul *Mesa Community College*
Kathy Tamerlano *Cuyahoga Community College Western*
Margaret Taylor *University of Southern Nevada*
Jay Tidwell *Blue Ridge CTC*
Dennis Walpole *University of South Florida*
Billie Jo Whary *McCann School of Business and Technology*
Melinda White *Seminole Community College*
Diana Wolfe *Oklahoma State University Oklahoma City*
Mary Ann Zlotow *College of DuPage*
Laurie Zouharis *Suffolk University*

iii

ComputingNow TABLE OF CONTENTS

CHAPTER 3
Operating Systems and Application Software 82

CHAPTER 4
Meeting Your Computing Needs 136

CHAPTER 5
Bringing the World to You 178

CHAPTER 8
Your Future in Computing 338

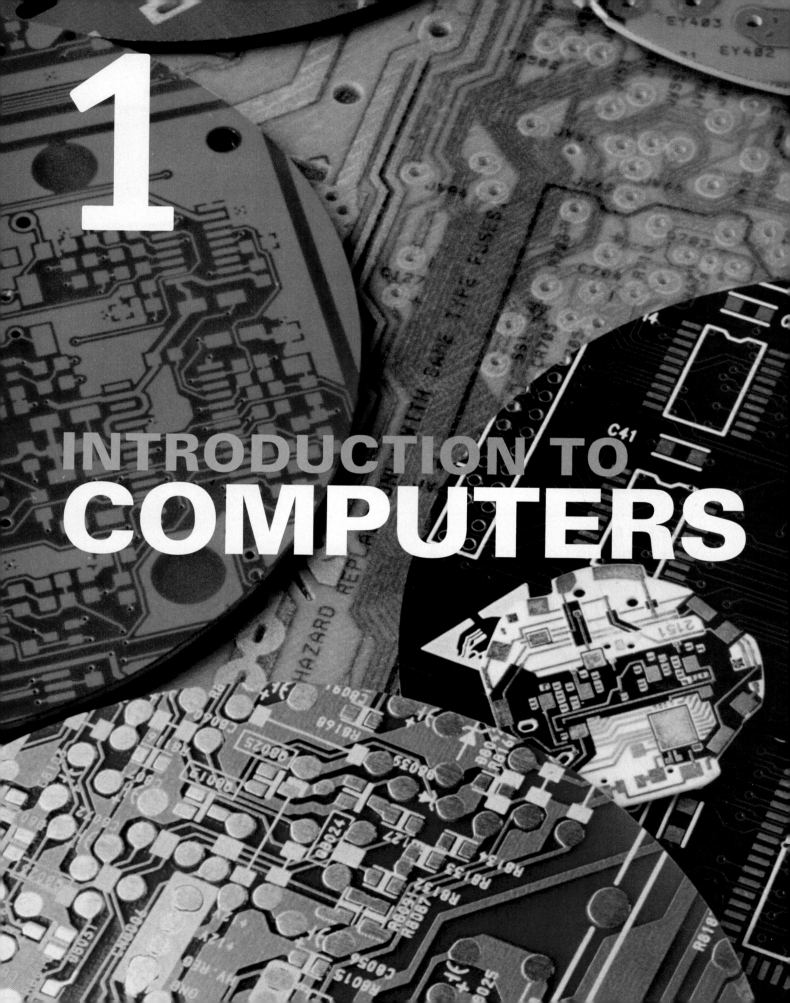

1

INTRODUCTION TO
COMPUTERS

Chapter Overview

This chapter introduces you to the computer, inside and out. You'll learn about the types of computers that are in use today, and you'll get an overview of different ways that computers are used in our society. You will take a look inside a computer and see some of the parts used to construct it, and you'll learn how the machine, the software programs, and users all work together to transform a computer from a calculating engine to a data-processing marvel. Where have you already used a computer? How would you like to use computers in the future?

LESSON 1A:
Computers and Their Uses

Computers are everywhere!

From office desks to kitchen tables, from library tables to people's laps in coffee shops, the screen and keyboard combination is a familiar sight. But if you look more carefully, you'll discover that computers exist in even more places than you first realize. Cash registers in stores have computers inside that calculate prices and help manage inventory. Most cars produced today have diagnostic computers to help find problems and improve performance. Cell phones contain computers, and wristwatches often rely on simple computers for stopwatch and calendar functions.

Since the 1970s, computers have rapidly reshaped personal and business life as we know it. Factories and industrial companies often use computer-controlled machinery. Professional occupations such as law, engineering, medicine, and finance use computers almost universally. Many workers who once had little use for technology now interact with computers almost every minute of the workday.

At home, people use computers to read the news, play games, and keep in touch with family and friends. News from around the world is instantly available. More and more people have international friends and colleagues, and they can use computers to communicate.

1.1 What Is a Computer?

In the simplest terms, a **computer** is a machine that accepts some kind of input, performs actions and calculations according to a set of instructions, and returns the result of its calculations. All computers, regardless of their size, purpose, or type, follow this definition.

The computer in a stopwatch, for example, accepts a command to start (a person pressing the button), counts the passing of time, and shows the time on a screen to the person holding the stopwatch. A personal computer accepts input from a person via the keyboard, runs programs like word processors or games, and displays the results on the screen. A diagnostic computer in a car accepts input from engine parts, sorts the data, and stores performance information for a mechanic to retrieve when a problem occurs.

Computer design is separated into two categories: analog and digital. You don't hear much about analog computers anymore, and that's because they've been largely replaced by digital computers.

Analog computers, which have been around in one form or another since ancient times, are usually mechanical. For input, they rely on some kind of fixed starting point, like fluids at certain levels or wires connecting electrical components together. As they operate, their physical state changes—fluid levels rise and fall, for example—to indicate solutions or new input. Analog computers can be very complex and may employ thousands of parts to construct, but in spite of all that complexity, each analog computer will solve only one specific kind of problem. An analog computer designed to calculate a differential equation cannot also be used to calculate where a bomb will land when dropped from an airplane.

The computers discussed in this book and found throughout the world are known as digital computers, because they work by processing sequences of numbers. Digital computers convert their input and operating instructions into numeric codes and perform calculations with those codes. The calculations are performed in strict, single steps; however, because they use numbers, digital computers can execute their instructions extremely fast. Unlike their analog counterparts, digital computers rely on electrical components rather than heavy gears. Digital computers are also flexible. The same digital computer can run programs to calculate differential equations, determine where a dropped bomb will fall, store recipes for tonight's dinner, and show you a map with the best route to the airport.

Figure 1.1 Computers have become so commonplace that sometimes we hardly notice people carrying them.

1.2 Types of Digital Computers

While some computers are designed to work with many people at the same time, most computers are meant to be used by only one person at a time. Those computers are known as **personal computers (PCs)**. It's common for personal computers to have separate work spaces and storage for several different users (those in a computer lab are probably set up that way), but only one user can work with the machine at a time.

Personal computers are also called **microcomputers** because they are among the smallest computers created for people to use. Although personal computers are used by individuals, they can be connected together to create **networks**, allowing users to share information from computer to computer. In fact, networking—the process of connecting to and sharing data between devices and locations—has become one of the most important jobs of personal computers, and even tiny handheld computers can now be connected to networks. You will learn about computer networks in Chapter 7.

Some computers, while still following the same fundamental design of all digital computers, are specially created to handle the needs of many users at the same time. These powerful systems are most often used by businesses or schools, and are commonly found at the heart of an organization's network. Each user interacts with the computer through his or her own input and output hardware, freeing people from having to wait their turn at a single keyboard and monitor. The largest organizational computers support thousands of individual users at the same time, from thousands of miles away. While some of these large-scale systems are devoted to a special purpose, enabling users to perform only a few specific tasks,

Figure 1.2 The same technology that helps us build bridges and airplanes is also a great fit for family game night.

many organizational computers are general-purpose systems that support a wide variety of tasks.

Six primary types of computers are designed to be used by one person at a time:

- Desktop computers
- Workstations
- Notebook (or laptop) computers
- Tablet computers
- Handheld computers
- Smart phones

There are four main types of multi-user computers:

- Network servers
- Mainframe computers
- Minicomputers
- Supercomputers

DESKTOP COMPUTERS

The most common type of personal computer is the **desktop computer**—a PC that is designed to sit on (or more typically under) a desk or table.

Today's desktop computers are powerful and versatile, and they are used for an amazing array of tasks. Not only do these machines enable people to do their jobs with greater ease and efficiency, but they can be used to communicate, produce music, edit photographs and videos, play sophisticated games, and much more. Used by everyone from preschoolers to nuclear physicists, desktop computers are indispensable for learning, work, and play.

As its name implies, a desktop computer is a full-size computer that is too big to be easily carried around. The main component of a desktop PC is the **system unit**, which is the case that houses the computer's critical parts, such as its processing and storage devices.

WORKSTATIONS

A **workstation** is a specialized, single-user computer that typically has more power and features than a standard desktop PC. These machines are popular among scientists, engineers, and animators who need a system with greater-than-average speed and the power to perform sophisticated tasks. Workstations often have large, high-resolution monitors and accelerated graphics-handling capabilities, making them suitable for advanced architectural or engineering design, modeling, animation, and video editing.

NOTEBOOK COMPUTERS

Notebook computers, as their name implies, approximate the shape of a writing notebook and easily fit inside a briefcase. Because people frequently set these devices on their lap, they are also called **laptops**. Notebooks have a "clam-shell" design; during use, the notebook's lid is raised to reveal a thin monitor and a keyboard. When not in use, the device folds up for easy storage.

Notebooks are fully functional microcomputers; the people who use them need the power of a

Figure 1.4   Notebook computers help people get their work done no matter where they are.

Figure 1.3   The screen, keyboard, and system unit of a desktop computer is a familiar sight practically everywhere.

full-size desktop computer wherever they go. Along with the monitor and keyboard, notebooks also typically contain a mouse, DVD player, and wireless networking capability.

Notebook computers come in a variety of sizes, with different sets of features and hardware to accommodate a wide range of user preferences. Notebook computers can operate on either an AC adapter or special batteries. They generally weigh less than eight pounds, and some even weigh less than three pounds.

Some notebook systems are designed to be plugged into a **docking station**, which allows the notebook to hook up to devices and services like full-sized keyboards, large monitors, and local networks.

Recent arrivals to the notebook scene are small and inexpensive computers referred to as **netbooks**. Netbooks are small, compact computers with reduced processing power and often without extra devices such as DVD drives. They are designed both for notebook shoppers with a very low budget and for users who only need a computer for casual use.

Figure 1.5 A tablet PC.

Because of their portability, notebook PCs fall into a category of devices called **mobile computers**—systems small enough to be carried by their user.

TABLET PCS

The **tablet PC** is the newest development in portable, full-featured computers. Tablet PCs offer all the functionality of a notebook PC, but they are lighter and can accept input directly from a special pen—called a **stylus** or a **digital pen**—or even the user's fingers. Some of the newer models can display an image of a keyboard on the screen and allow the user to type.

Many tablet PCs also have a built-in microphone and special software that accepts input from the user's voice. A few models even have a fold-out keyboard, so they can be transformed into a standard notebook PC. Tablet PCs run specialized versions of standard programs and can be connected to a network.

The popularity of tablet PCs has exploded in recent years both for business and personal use. The combination of portable size and friendly interface makes them ideal in a wide range of circumstances for note-taking, document sharing, and online communication.

HANDHELD PCS

Handheld personal computers (or just **handheld PCs**) are computing devices small enough to fit in your hand. Though they can be indispensable tools for many types of

users, their small size and limited processing power puts them in a different category from notebook and tablet computers. Handheld PCs are typically used for applications that help connect mobile users to online resources; provide portable entertainment in the form of games, music and video; and assist with mobile computing tasks such as taking notes and managing address books or task lists. Many users rely heavily on their handheld PC to stay current all day long with the latest news from the world and their friends.

As handheld PCs became widely popular in the 1990s and early 2000s, they were commonly known as **personal digital assistants (PDAs)**. Early PDAs had a limited set of software programs that they could run, many of which were targeted toward note-taking, small spreadsheets, and appointment management. Input to the PDA was commonly accomplished via tapping and drawing on a touch-sensitive screen with a stylus. Now, handheld PCs often have intuitive and shortcut-rich user interfaces with colorful displays, and touch screens that can accept various kinds of fingertip taps and swipes for input.

The term **smart phone** was coined as manufacturers of cellular telephones began including PDA features and programs in their telephones. The combination of PDA and cell phone produced a convenient multi-function device that proved

Figure 1.6 Smart phones provide communication, computing power, and more.

highly popular not only with business and technical PDA users, but also with cell phone consumers. Not every handheld PC user prefers to combine their phone and handheld computer together, so sales of devices both with and without phones are increasing. The concept of the PDA is alive and well, even though the "PDA" term itself is rapidly becoming a thing of the past.

Manufacturers of handheld PCs have made rapid advances in their products as a result of this widespread acceptance and demand for mobile computing devices. While the PDA of the past provided a limited set of business-oriented software programs for their users, vast libraries of programs are now available for download that support business and entertainment interests alike.

NETWORK SERVERS

Today, most organizations' networks are based on personal computers. Individual users have their own desktop computers, and those computers are linked together in a network to allow convenient file and information sharing between users. In cases where all the people use their computers for a common purpose (for example, running e-mail programs or working on documents), a special, central computer called a **network server** is added to the network.

A network server is a powerful personal computer with special software and equipment that enable it to function as the primary computer in the network. Though their exact functions are different from organization to organization, network servers all have the basic task of making documents, programs, and in some cases other computer hardware available to others.

For example, a network server might run the e-mail services for a company. Rather than having each employee run his or her own mail program, employees simply access the central e-mail program running on the server to retrieve their messages.

Network servers are also responsible for sending Web pages to users who are browsing the Internet; a single server can send its Web pages to thousands of people visiting the site that it hosts.

Often, the requests from the network grow so large and complex that a single PC cannot handle the job by itself. In such cases, network server computers are linked together to share the load. In some cases, dozens or even hundreds of individual servers work together to manage data processing requests. When set up in such groups—sometimes called *clusters* or *server farms*—network servers may not even resemble standard PCs. The big case that holds the typical PC system unit is reduced to a thin unit called a "blade," which can slide in and out of a rack that holds many of its companion servers. In these large networks, PC groups are often serving different purposes, such as supporting a certain set of users, handling printing tasks, enabling Internet communications, and so on.

Depending on how the network is set up, users may be able to access the server in multiple ways. In an office, users might have a standard desktop PC on their desk that is permanently connected to the network. Mobile users may be able to connect a notebook PC or a handheld device to the network wirelessly.

Figure 1.7 Blades are full PCs in a narrow box suitable for side-by-side installation.

MAINFRAME COMPUTERS

Mainframe computers are large, powerful systems used in organizations such as insurance companies and banks, where many people frequently need to use the same data.

In a traditional mainframe environment, each user accesses the mainframe's resources through a device called a **terminal**. There are two kinds of terminals. A dumb terminal does not process or store data; it is simply an **input/output (I/O) device** that functions as a window into a computer located somewhere else. An intelligent terminal can perform some processing operations, but it usually does not have any storage. In some mainframe environments, however, workers can use a standard personal computer to access the mainframe.

The largest mainframes can handle the processing needs of thousands of users at any given moment. But what these systems offer in power, they lack in flexibility. Most mainframe systems are designed to handle only a specific set of tasks. In your state's Department of Motor Vehicles, for example, a mainframe system is probably devoted to storing information about drivers, vehicles, and driver's licenses, but little or nothing else. By limiting the number of tasks the system must perform, administrators preserve as much power as possible for required operations.

Figure 1.8 Mainframe computers are often housed alone in special rooms, away from their users.

MINICOMPUTERS

First released in the 1960s, **minicomputers** got their name because of their small size relative to other computers of the day. The capabilities of a minicomputer are somewhere between those of mainframes and personal computers. For this reason, minicomputers are often called **midrange computers**. Like mainframes, minicomputers can handle much more input and output than personal computers. Although some "minis" are designed for a single user, the most powerful minicomputers can serve the input and output needs of hundreds of users at a time. Users can access a central minicomputer through a terminal or a standard PC.

SUPERCOMPUTERS

Supercomputers are the most powerful computers and physically they are some of the largest. These systems can process huge amounts of data, and the fastest supercomputers can perform nearly two quadrillion calculations per second.

Fact Check

1. What is the most common type of single-user computer?
   a. Desktop computer
   b. Minicomputer
   c. Analog computer
2. List the four types of multi-user computers.

Figure 1.9 Supercomputers like Cray's XT5 Jaguar are massive machines, integrating hundreds of thousands of smaller processors together.

Some supercomputers link together hundreds of thousands of processors. Supercomputers are ideal for handling large and highly complex problems that require extreme calculating power. For example, supercomputers are actively used in the mapping of the human genome, forecasting weather, and modeling complex processes like nuclear fission.

1.3 Computers in Society

How important are computers to our society? People often talk in sweeping terms about computers and their impact on our lives, with expressions like "computers have changed our world" or "computers have changed the way we do everything." Such statements may strike you at first as exaggerations, but if you stop and really think about the effect computers have had on our daily lives, they may not be so far off the mark.

To better gauge the impact of computers, think of the impact of other inventions. Can you imagine, for instance, the many ways in which American life changed after the introduction of the automobile? Consider a few examples:

- Because of the car, people were able to travel farther than ever before, and this created huge opportunities for businesses to meet the needs of the traveling public.

- Because vehicles could be mass-produced, the nature of manufacturing and industry changed, and throngs of people began working on assembly lines.

- Because of road development, suburbs became a feasible way for people to live close to a city without actually living in one.

- Because of car travel, motels, restaurants, and shopping centers sprang up in places where there had previously been nothing.

Think of other great inventions and discoveries, such as electricity, the telephone, or the airplane. Each, in its own way, brought significant changes to the world and to the ways people lived and spent their time. Today, still relatively soon after its creation, the digital computer is beginning to make its mark on society.

WHY ARE COMPUTERS SO IMPORTANT?

People can list countless reasons for the importance of computers. For someone with a disability, for example, a computer may offer freedom to communicate, learn, or work without leaving home. For a sales professional, a PC may mean the ability to communicate whenever necessary, track leads, and to manage an ever-changing schedule. For a researcher, a computer may be the workhorse that does painstaking and time-consuming calculations.

But if you took all the benefits that people derive from computers, mixed them together, and distilled them down into a single element, what would you have? The answer is simple: information.

Computers are important because information is so essential to our lives, and information is much more than the stuff you see and hear on television. Facts in a textbook or an encyclopedia are information, but only

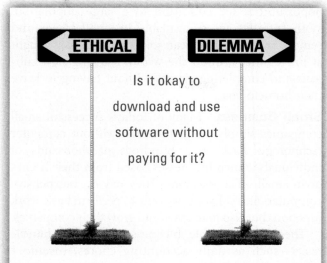

ETHICAL DILEMMA

Is it okay to download and use software without paying for it?

Yesterday, you and your friend Tracy were looking at family photos on her computer. Tracy showed you a hilarious picture of her little nephew that had been altered to make it look like he was dancing with penguins. You asked her where she'd found the thousand dollars to buy fancy photo-editing software.

"I found this great site on the Web where you can download old versions of software for free," she replied. "The photo software company doesn't support this version anymore, but it works perfectly."

Looking through the site Tracy mentioned, you see that you could easily get the photo software and lots of other programs. The download site is safe, virus-free, doesn't track who accesses the site or downloads programs, and contains only software versions that are out of date and no longer supported.

QUESTIONS

1. Would it be ethical to download and use the program even though you're not paying for it?
2. Is this situation different from finding a copy of this same software at a garage sale and paying the person in the driveway a few dollars to take it home? If so, how?

that ready access to information has created some ethical gray areas along with learning opportunities. For an example of one such gray area, see the "Ethical Dilemma" feature.

When you consider the importance of computers in our society, think about the importance of information. As tools for working with information, and for creating new information, computers may be one of humanity's most important creations.

Let's take a look at where computers are found in our society and what they do there.

Home In many American homes, the family computer is nearly as important as the refrigerator or the washing machine. In fact, a growing number of families have multiple PCs in their homes; in most cases, at least one of those computers has an Internet connection. Why do home users need their computers?

- **Communication.** Electronic mail (e-mail) allows family members to communicate with one another and to stay in contact with friends and coworkers. Social networking programs such as Facebook help extended families and groups of friends stay in touch and share their lives. Services like Twitter take the "keep in touch" idea even further, allowing people to broadcast quick updates, thoughts, and items of interest throughout the day. It's more common than ever for computer users to meet and make friends with people all over the world, no matter where they live.

- **Business work done at home.** Thanks to computers and Internet connections, more people are working from home than ever before. It is possible for many users to connect to their employer's network from home. Computers also are making it easier for people to start their own home-based businesses.

- **Schoolwork.** Today's students are increasingly reliant on computers, and not just as a replacement for typewriters. The Internet is replacing printed books as a reference tool, and easy-to-use software makes it possible for even young users to create polished documents.

- **Entertainment.** Computers and video game consoles are intensely popular, with an endless variety of games from solitaire to simulating your own living room rock band. People can play games alone, with a family member, or go online to play with tens of thousands of others in a single, massive fantasy or sci-fi world. PCs can also serve as

one kind. Mathematical formulas and their results are information, too, as are the plans for a building, or the recipe for a cake. Pictures, songs, addresses, games, poems, menus, shopping lists, résumés—the list goes on and on. All these things and many others can be thought of as information, and they can all be stored and processed digitally by computers. In fact, media centers, storing music, videos, and movies for on-demand playback on other computers, consoles, and televisions throughout the home.

- **Creativity.** Poetry, music, painting, essays on the state of the world, funny stories—these once required publishers and marketing efforts to produce. Now, with blogs, personal Web pages, and Web sites for sharing pictures and video clips, people can create anything to their hearts' content and share it with an audience.

- **Finances and Shopping.** Computers and personal finance software can make balancing your checkbook an enjoyable experience. Well, almost. At any rate, they certainly make it easier. Home users rely on their PCs for bill paying, investing, and other financial chores. They also use computers to spend what they earn, shopping online for everything from cars to collectibles.

Computer technology has also brought more opportunities for education to a large population. With Internet access available in small towns and remote areas, students can join online classes taught at universities around the world, learning new subjects and completing classes without having to leave their hometowns.

Small Business Many of today's successful small companies simply could not exist without computer technology. Each year, hundreds of thousands of individuals launch businesses based from their homes or in small-office locations. They rely on inexpensive computers and software not only to perform basic work functions but also to manage and grow their companies.

These tools enable business owners to handle tasks—such as daily accounting chores, inventory management, marketing, payroll, and many others—that once required the hiring of outside specialists. As a result, small businesses become more self-sufficient and reduce their operating expenses.

> ❝Many of today's successful small companies simply could not exist without computer technology.❞

Education More and more schools are adding computer technology to their curricula, not only teaching pure computer skills, but also incorporating those skills into other classes. Students may be required to use a drawing program, for example, to draw a plan of the Alamo for a history class, or use spreadsheet software to analyze voter turnouts during the last century's presidential elections. Educators see computer technology as an essential learning requirement for all students, starting as early as preschool. Even now, basic computing skills such as keyboarding are being taught in elementary schools, and kids are taught how to search online for information at an early age.

Businesses both small and large can also benefit from using computers and networks to allow their employees to work from home, or to support satellite offices away from the main corporate site. Workers who would face a prohibitive commute or who want to live in a remote location can still be productive, connected employees via their computers.

Industry Today, enterprises use different kinds of computers in many combinations. A corporate headquarters may have a standard PC-based network, for

Figure 1.10   Users of all ages at home can use computers for work, creative expression and play.

example, but its production facilities may use computer-controlled robotics to manufacture products. Here are just a few ways computers are applied to industry:

- **Design.** Nearly any company that designs and makes products can use a computer-aided design or computer-aided manufacturing system in their creation.

- **Shipping.** Freight companies need computers to manage the thousands of ships, planes, trains, and trucks that are moving goods at any given moment. In addition to tracking vehicle locations and contents, computers can manage maintenance, driver schedules, invoices and billing, and many other activities.

- **Process control.** Modern assembly lines can be massive, complex systems, and a breakdown at one point can cause chaos throughout a company. Sophisticated process-control systems can oversee output, check the speed at which a machine runs, manage conveyance systems, and look at parts inventories, with very little human interaction.

Government Not only are governments big consumers of technology, but they help to develop it as well. As you will learn in Chapter 4, the U.S. government played a key role in developing the Internet. Today, computers play a crucial part in nearly every government agency:

- **Population.** The U.S. Census Bureau was one of the first organizations to use computer technology, recruiting mechanical computers known as "difference engines" to assist in tallying the American population in the early 20th century.

- **Taxes.** Can you imagine trying to calculate Americans' tax bills without the help of computers? Neither could the Internal Revenue Service. In fact, the IRS now encourages taxpayers to file their tax returns online via the Internet.

- **Military.** Some of the world's most sophisticated computer technology has been developed primarily for use by the military. In fact, some of the earliest digital computers were created for such purposes as calculating the trajectory of missiles. Today, for tasks including

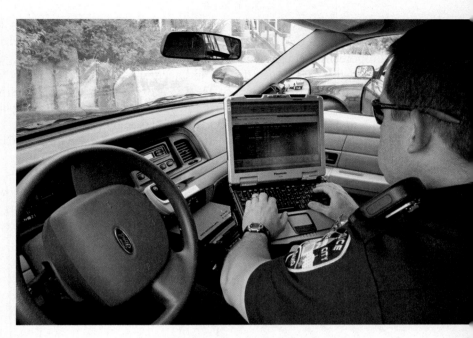

Figure 1.11 Police officers use computers to quickly access vital information on the job.

everything from payroll management and weapons control to games and simulations that teach combat skills, the armed forces use the widest array of computer hardware and software imaginable.

- **Police.** When it comes to stocking their crime-fighting arsenals, many police forces consider computers to be just as important as guns and ammunition. Today's police cruisers are equipped with laptop computers and wireless Internet connections that enable officers to search for information on criminals, crime scenes, and procedures.

Fact Check

1. The common element that makes computers so important throughout society is
   a. the central processing unit
   b. information
   c. flexibility
2. List four things a home computer might be commonly used to accomplish.
3. List three types of government agencies that use computers.

Health Care Pay a visit to your family doctor or the local hospital, and you'll find yourself surrounded by computerized equipment. Computers, in fact, are making health care more efficient and accurate while helping providers bring down costs.

Many different health care procedures now involve computers, from ultrasound and magnetic resonance imaging to laser eye surgery and fetal monitoring. Surgeons now can use robotic surgical devices to perform delicate operations and even to conduct surgeries remotely. New virtual-reality technologies are being used to train new surgeons in cutting-edge techniques, without cutting an actual patient.

But not all medical computers are so high-tech. Clinics and hospitals use standard computers to manage schedules, maintain patient records, and perform billings. Many transactions between physicians, insurance companies, and pharmacies are conducted by computers, saving health care workers time.

Green Computing Environmental impact is a familiar topic in business and personal life. Companies, governments and individuals around the world are considering the influence that their choices and actions have on the health and well-being of our planet. Green computing refers to the efforts made

Focus on the Issues

Controlling Computers with the Mind

The idea that humans could control computers with little more than their thoughts is the stuff of science fiction. Or is it?

A team of doctors, scientists, and programmers has developed a device that does exactly that. For the first time, a severely paralyzed—or "locked-in"—patient has the ability to control a computer directly with his or her thoughts.

The device, called the Brain Communicator, was created by Neural Signals, Inc., and allows a locked-in user (who is alert and intelligent but unable to move or speak due to stroke, disease, or injury) to control his or her personal computer without the need for a manual keyboard, voice recognition system, or other standard means of control. No voluntary movement is necessary.

Neural interface devices (NIDs) such as the Brain Communicator allow users to take advantage of small electrical signals generated spontaneously in the body. These signals can be obtained either directly or indirectly. Direct methods of collecting the signals involve surgical implantation in the user's body; indirect methods can utilize the user's muscle movements, eye movements, or EEG brain waves.

With NIDs, simply by imagining movement, locked-in patients can use a word processor or speech synthesizer, surf the Internet, or access environmental controls such as lights, music, and TV. Medicine and computer technology combine to open the horizons of their locked-in world.

Even as the future looks bright, the field of neural interfacing technology is still in its infancy, and the practical applications of the technology have yet to be realized. Perhaps, someday soon, personal computers will come bundled with biological signal sensors and thought-recognition software just as commonly as the word processing and educational programs of today.

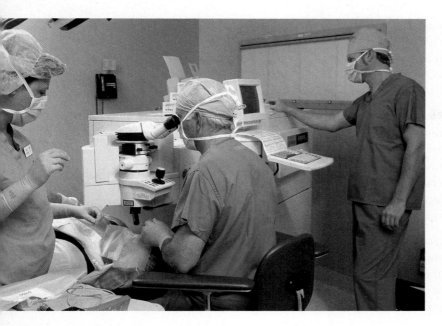

Figure 1.12 Computers help in nearly all aspects of health care, from billing to controlling machines for surgeons.

toward reducing the environmental impact in the manufacture, use, and disposal of computers.

Like many products, the manufacture of computers of any size can use or produce hazardous materials. But properly handling and reducing the use of those materials is just the beginning for green computing.

The "green" philosophy includes looking at ways to reduce waste when replacing computers. Underperforming computers could be simply replaced, of course, but then the old computers are completely discarded. Instead, upgrading components as needed (for example, increasing the amount of memory or data storage capacity) may allow a computer to keep up with demand, reducing the amount that is thrown away in the process.

Computers can generate a great deal of heat, and a lot of power is used to keep them cool; fans in the case and attached to individual parts use a lot of energy, and in large computer installations air conditioning plants may be required to keep room temperature low. Green computing solutions can combine more power-efficient computer hardware with improved cooling techniques such as liquid-cooled components and improved air flow to significantly reduce power use. Even home users can reduce power usage by keeping the fans and airways of their home computers free of dust.

There are many other ways that green computing advocates work to find ways to improve the condition of our planet, from designing software programs to run more efficiently, to encouraging businesses to let some of their employees work from home, leave the car in the driveway, save gas and reduce pollution. With computers in such heavy use all around the world, even small improvements in computer efficiency can make a big difference to the pressure we place on the environment.

Social Communication As you've seen in this lesson, computers have become familiar tools in many different parts of our society. But computer technology is also having a profound effect on society itself by changing the ways we communicate. The way we interact with others, the people to whom we're connected, the frequency of communication, and the methods we now use are all startlingly different than they were twenty, ten, or in some cases just one or two years ago.

Once, if we wanted to contact a friend or colleague, we called their telephone number. If they weren't home or at their desk, we'd just have to call them back later and in the meantime, chances were good that we didn't know for sure where they were.

Now, mobile computers and smart phones provide instant access to people. Send a text message and it instantly requests attention from the receiver. Call someone's cell phone, and you rarely get silence in return.

Services have also sprung up that encourage people to constantly share their whereabouts and thoughts. Foursquare is a social software program that allows you to alert the world that you just walked into Jim's Fabulous Bakery. Twitter will help you tell your friends and followers that the place is packed, and you're going to be in line forever. Facebook lets your friends know that chocolate croissants are simply the best thing in your life right now.

In the past, you might tell a small handful of people about your divine croissant, but on Facebook and Twitter you might have dozens, hundreds, or even thousands of connections, and every one of them gets your news. On the receiving end, you get a steady stream of similar updates from everyone with which you have a connection.

Computers allow us to create and maintain intimate social connections with far more people than had ever before been possible, no matter where in the world they live. Whatever changes this may bring to our local and global cultures, computers will certainly continue to play a major role in our rapid evolution of communication.

IN *Summary*

- A computer is an electronic device that processes data, converting it into information that is useful to people. The two basic types of computers are analog and digital. The computers commonly used today are all digital computers.

- Computers designed for use by a single person include desktop computers, workstations, notebook (or laptop) computers, tablet computers, handheld computers, and smart phones. Other types of computers—such as network servers, mainframes, minicomputers, and supercomputers—are commonly used by organizations and support the computing needs of many users at once.

- Computers have changed the way we work, communicate, create, and play. Computers are important because information is so essential to our lives, whether that information takes the form of a news report, song, X-ray, mathematical formula, or recipe. All these kinds of information can be stored and processed by computers. As tools for working with information, and for creating new information, computers may be one of humanity's most important creations.

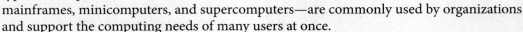

Key Terms

computer, 4
desktop computer, 6
digital pen, 7
docking station, 6
handheld personal
   computer, 7
input/output (I/O) device, 9
laptop computer, 6
mainframe, 9
microcomputer, 5

midrange computer, 9
minicomputer, 9
mobile computer, 7
netbooks, 6
network server, 8
networking, 5
networks, 5
notebook computer, 6
personal computer (PC), 5

personal digital assistant
   (PDA), 7
smart phone, 7
stylus, 7
supercomputer, 9
system unit, 6
tablet PC, 7
terminal, 9
workstation, 6

Key Terms QUIZ

Complete each statement by writing one of the terms listed under "Key Terms" in each blank.

1. The general name for a single-user computer is a(n) _____.

2. A computer designed to handle the needs and requests of thousands of users at a time is known as a(n) _____.

3. When not in use, a(n) _____ computer folds up for easy storage.

4. _____ PCs are flat computers that have a touch-sensitive screen that can accept input from a special pen or finger.

5. Though it may look like a desktop computer, a(n) _____ is a device that provides access to a mainframe computer.

6. A(n) _____ combines a cellular phone with computer programs in a single device.

7. A(n) _____ is similar in function and appearance to a smart phone, but lacks the telephone capability.

8. The special pen used with touch-sensitive computer screens is known as a(n) _____.

9. Computers can be connected together with wires or wireless technology to create a(n) _____.

10. _____ are the most powerful computers ever created, linking hundreds of thousands of smaller computer processors together.

Review QUESTIONS

In your own words, briefly answer the following questions or respond to the statements.

1. What is a computer?

2. List six types of computers designed to be used by one person at a time.

3. List four types of computers that are designed to support many users and can be accessed by multiple people at the same time.

4. What are four ways that computers can be used in a typical home?

5. How can computers improve education for people who live in remote areas where local colleges and schools are not available?

6. Describe two ways that computers can help people running small businesses.

7. In addition to helping doctors perform surgery, what are two functions in the health care industry that are aided by computers?

8. Explain what the term "green computing" means.

9. List three ways that computer technology or users can reduce the harm done to the Earth's environment.

10. Describe three ways that computers have affected the way we communicate with each other.

Complete the following exercises as directed by your instructor.

LESSON LAB

1. During the course of a normal day, keep a list of your encounters with computers of various kinds. Your list should show the place and time of the encounter, the type of interaction you had with the technology, and the results of that interaction. (Remember, computers can take many sizes and forms, so be alert to more than just PCs.) Share your list with the class.

2. Learn more about green computing. Start your computer's browser and go to Google at http://www.google.com/. Search on the term "green computing" and follow search result links to at least two of the related sites. Then, take a look at Google's own statistics for their data center efficiency at http://www.google.com/corporate/datacenter/efficient-computing/index.html and see how they compare the energy they use for searches to other common activities.

Team EXERCISE
Critical Thinking

This lesson identified many different types of computers that are used in the world today, from handheld PCs to giant, room-sized supercomputers. In this exercise, you'll revisit that topic by applying an important workplace ability: *critical thinking*, which brings together skills such as observation, interpretation, and evaluation to understand and apply information. In this case, you'll be paying closer attention to the part that computers play in the world around you and your classmates.

Before your next class session, note three different types of computers (for example, handheld, tablet, or desktop PCs) that you see being used, either by yourself or by people around you. For each type of computer, identify and record the basic tasks that are being performed.

Back in class, divide into groups of three or four. First, compare notes on commonality. Were there some types of computers that all of you found in use? Was there a kind of computer that only one person identified? If everybody found at least one type in common, was the same type of activity being performed?

Then, have each person choose one computer task that they noted and discuss whether the computer itself is a requirement to perform that task. Could the task still be accomplished without a computer, or is this a type of activity that simply did not exist before digital computers were made readily available? Create a list of these tasks and findings to share with other groups when the exercise is complete.

Ask Andy Yother what the best part of his job is, and his answer comes quickly: "I get to play with million-dollar toys," says this lead hardware and support engineer at Norcross, Georgia-based Canvas Systems, a reseller of certified, pre-owned IT equipment. Those toys span a wide range of technology systems and manufacturers, making Yother's job both challenging and fulfilling at the same time.

"I handle any piece of equipment that a manufacturer like Sun Microsystems or IBM would make," says Yother. "It's neat to know that during any given week I'm going to build, configure, test, and prepare for sale a wider variety of equipment than most folks will see in their entire careers."

Yother, who is currently completing his bachelor's degree in business administration at Shorter College, has racked up career experience working for PC makers and circuit board manufacturers. He started in an entry-level position at Canvas Systems, handling low-level testing and identification of systems. Today he oversees a team of six auditors and five engineers who build bare-metal assembly orders to customer specifications.

"Our customers contact us, tell us what they need, and we start with the bare bones and work up from there," says Yother, whose typical workday starts at 8 a.m. and ends at 7 p.m. or later, depending on the time of year and level of demand. "We configure the machines, test them, and prepare them for customer use."

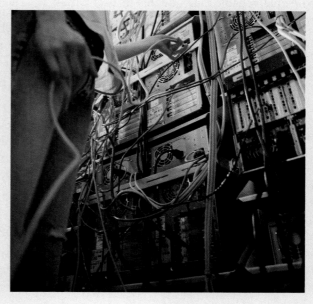

Keeping up with changing technology is no easy task for Yother, who must know how to break down and rebuild both older systems and the newest, state-of-the-art systems available on the market. To keep up, he reads trade and technology magazines, visits manufacturers' Web sites, and subscribes to online mailing lists. "It's about trying to find the best sources of accurate information and digesting it all," says Yother. "Some days, my brain just aches from information overload."

Yother sees hardware technicians' roles increasing in the future. "We wouldn't have an IT field without the circuits, memory, and processors to back it up," says Yother, who advises all aspiring technicians to learn the computer inside and out, and to truly understand how it processes information and accomplishes tasks. Whether they're working for a company like Canvas Systems or within a firm's IT department, hardware maintenance technicians are responsible for the following kinds of tasks:

- Installing and configuring new computer hardware. Installing peripherals.

- Upgrading computers (installing updated cards, memory, drives, etc.).

- Dealing with network-related hardware issues (installing network interface cards, working with cabling, installing hubs or routers, etc.).

- Troubleshooting and repairing hardware of all types.

Many companies rely on their hardware maintenance technicians for input when planning for new system development, expansion, or acquisitions. Their input is important because technicians are in daily contact with end users and develop a good understanding of their needs. A significant advantage of the hardware technician's job is that it is a great springboard to other, more advanced careers in technology. Entry-level technicians typically earn $30,000 to $35,000, with pay scales increasing with experience to levels of $50,000 a year or more.

Looking Inside the Computer

Most people believe computers must be extremely complicated devices because they perform such amazing tasks. To an extent, this is true. The complexity of a central processor's circuitry, layering millions of connections together in a space the size of your fingernail, is one of humankind's greatest technological triumphs. No less of a feat is the lightning-fast coordination of all the different subsystems in a computer to produce a flexible, reliable machine that its user barely notices as he or she performs tasks with it.

Yet like any machine, a computer is still a collection of parts, which are grouped according to the kinds of work they do. Although there are many, many variations on the parts themselves, there are only a few major categories. If you learn about those families of computer components and their basic functions, you will have mastered some of the most important concepts in computing. As you will see, the concepts are by and large simple and straightforward.

This lesson gives you a glimpse inside a standard desktop computer and introduces you to its most important parts. You will learn how these components work together and allow you to interact with the system. You also will discover the importance of software, without which a computer could do

nothing. Finally, you will see that the user is (in most cases, at least) an essential part of a complete computer system.

1.4 The Parts of a Computer System

As you saw in Lesson 1A, computers come in many varieties, from the tiny computers built into household appliances to the astounding supercomputers that have helped scientists map the human genome. But no matter how big it is or how it is used, every computer is part of a system. A complete **computer system** is much more than just the box on the floor at your feet and the monitor on your desk. The term encompasses the four broad categories that make the machine fully useful: hardware, software, data, and the user (see Figure 1.13).

HARDWARE

The physical devices—both electronic and mechanical—that make up the computer are called **hardware**. Hardware is any part of the computer you can touch. Input and output devices, the system case, cables, and networking devices are all examples of hardware.

SOFTWARE

Software is a set of instructions that makes the computer perform tasks. In other words, software tells the computer what to do. The term **program** refers to any piece of software. Some programs exist primarily to help the computer and its subsystems perform tasks and manage their own resources. Other types of programs exist for the user, enabling him or her to perform tasks such as creating documents, playing games, using the Internet, or even writing other programs. Thousands of different programs are available for use on personal computers.

DATA

Data consist of individual facts or pieces of information. Data are specific to the task at hand and often make sense only in their intended context. For example, if you were writing a proposal to lower the speed limit on a neighborhood street, you might include facts about the average speed of cars on that road and statistics about auto speed and serious injuries. Those facts are data, and while they are relevant for your proposal, they might not be useful data when

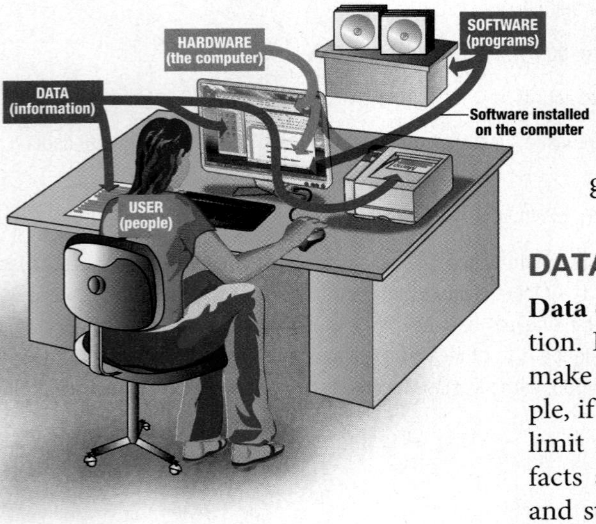

Figure 1.13   A complete computer system.

Figure 1.14 Software turns a generic computer into just the right tool for each user.

A computer can still have users without a person sitting in front of it at every moment. A car's diagnostic computer normally doesn't have an attentive user, but the information it saves and provides is certainly put to use at the repair shop. The repair technician is that computer's user, even though he or she is rarely present.

A direct user can also be other computers or computer components acting on behalf of people. For example, a network server (whose sole job is to route network traffic from one PC to another) communicates with client computers instead of directly with people. Even so, those client computers are ultimately there at the request or intention of people, so no useful computer is completely isolated from human contact.

planning recipes for this weekend's dinner party. Choosing the right data to examine and process is a big part of making the computer an effective tool.

There is a difference between information and data. Information describes concepts, facts, and ideas that people find useful. Data are raw materials that we use in the creation of information. For example, you could think of the letters of the alphabet as data. By themselves, the letters mean little; they are merely symbols. But when we put them together to form words and sentences, we produce information. Others can read the words and gain understanding of concepts and ideas.

Information can also be used as data, as you can see in the example above about auto speed and injuries. Data about speeds can produce statistical information, and that information could itself be used as data when creating presentation pictures for the proposal.

Computers require data in order for their programs, their processing tasks, to take on meaning. A program that simply adds numbers together for no purpose isn't very useful. A program that adds a list of auto speeds together in order to calculate an average is producing value for the user by helping the user create a proposal.

USERS

People are the computer operators, also known as **users**. One might argue that some computer systems are complete without a person's involvement; however, no computer is totally autonomous. Without a user, a computer would have no data to use in its calculations, and its results would be of no value because no person would put those results to use.

THE INFORMATION PROCESSING CYCLE

Using all its parts together, a computer converts data into information by performing various actions on the data. For example, a computer might perform a mathematical operation on two numbers and then display the result. Or the computer might perform a logical operation, such as comparing two numbers, and display that result. These operations are part of a process called the **information processing cycle**, which is a series of steps the computer follows to receive data, process the data according to instructions from a program, display the resulting information to the user, and store results (see Figure 1.15).

Each step in the information processing cycle involves one or more specific components of the computer:

1. **Input.** The computer accepts data from some source, such as the user, a program, or some sort of hardware, for processing.

2. **Processing.** The computer's processing components perform actions on or with the data, based on instructions from the user or a program.

3. **Output.** The computer provides the results of its processing. Typically, the results appear as text, numbers, or a graphic on the computer's screen or as sounds from its speaker. The computer also can send output to a printer or transfer the output to another computer through a network. During the information processing

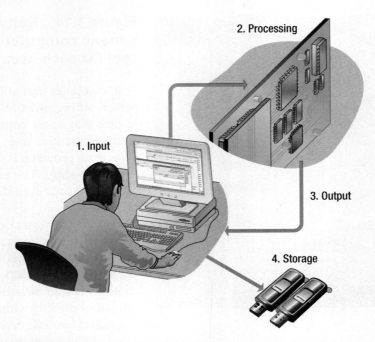

Figure 1.15 The information processing cycle.

cycle, the computer will always produce some form of output, but that output will not necessarily be noticeable for its user. Output may be stored, held for later, or used as input for new tasks without the user being aware of it.

4. **Storage.** The computer stores the results of its processing. If the computer stores output in its memory, it is usually considered temporary storage because information in memory can be lost when the computer shuts down. To store

information permanently, the computer will save its output to a hard drive or some other kind of storage medium. Storage is optional and may not always be required by the user or program. (The next section discusses memory and storage devices.)

1.5 Essential Computer Hardware

Electronic parts and subsystems in a computer are generally installed on a **circuit board**, which is commonly a thin, rigid piece of plastic or other material that provides a convenient way to mount, organize, and connect parts together. Circuit boards are usually rectangular, come in a wide variety of sizes, and have at least one kind of connector so they can be conveniently linked to other parts of the computer.

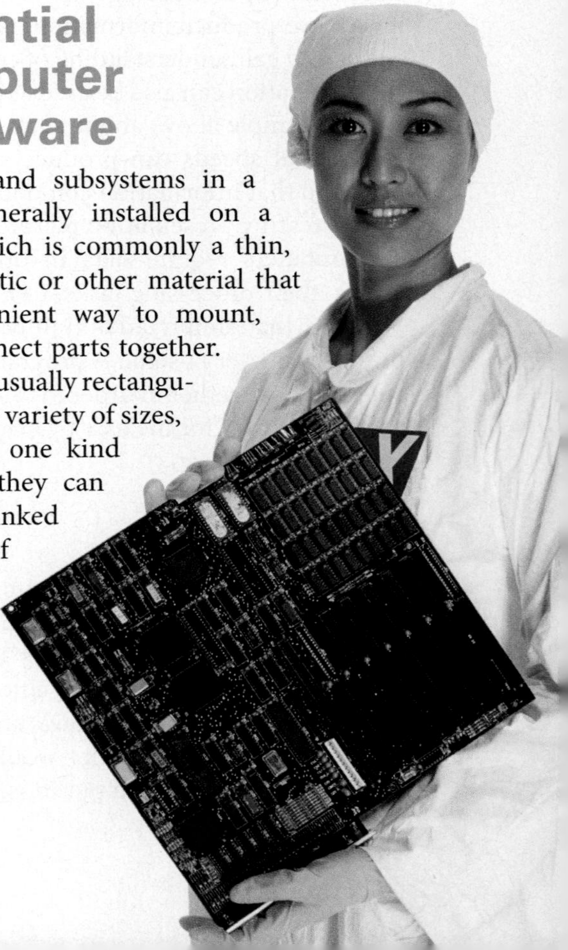

Figure 1.16 A circuit board with sets of chips installed.

Fact Check

1. A complete computer system includes
   a. hardware, software, data, and users
   b. CPU, hard drive, keyboard, and mouse
   c. windows, Web windows, Web browser, e-mail, and word processor

2. Computer hardware
   a. is only contained within the system unit
   b. must never be plugged in when the computer is turned on
   c. is any part of the computer you can touch

3. The specific components involved in each step of the information processing cycle are
   a. hardware, software, data, and users
   b. input, processing, output, and storage
   c. hard drive, optical disk, and tape

Circuit boards that are used to provide a specific ability (like sound or video capability) in the computer are also commonly called **cards**.

MOTHERBOARD

A computer has several hardware subsystems that perform its required tasks. While it's common to refer to the CPU as the central part of a computer system, there is a less-mentioned hardware component that truly serves to connect everything else together: the **motherboard**. Sometimes called a mainboard, a motherboard is the largest circuit board in a personal computer. It contains connectors and ports for hooking up all the other parts of a computer, from the CPU to the webcam on top of the monitor. It also contains its own set of electronic components to help regulate power to different subsystems and manage the flow of data from one hardware subsystem to another. In some cases, the motherboard contains its own electronic subsystems that years ago were only stored on separate circuit boards, handling tasks such as video and sound output and network communication.

To be fully functional, a computer requires a set of hardware components that are connected to the motherboard. These hardware devices fall into one of four basic categories:

- Processors
- Memory
- Input and output
- Storage

While any type of computer contains these four types of hardware, this book focuses on them as they relate to the PC.

PROCESSORS

The procedure that transforms raw data into useful information is called **processing**. Logically, the computer components responsible for this procedure are called **processors**. Processors are complex electronic circuits etched into slivers of silicon.

The main processor for the computer is known as the **central processing unit (CPU)**. The CPU is like the brain of the computer; it organizes and carries out instructions that come from either the user or the

software. In a personal computer, the CPU consists of a specialized chip, called a **microprocessor**, which integrates several different processing functions into a single chip.

The CPU is plugged into a special socket on the computer's motherboard. CPUs come in a wide variety of designs and processing power. By designing the CPU as an installable unit, manufacturers allow users more flexibility; computer makers can select different combinations of motherboards and CPUs, which would not be possible if CPUs were preinstalled on each motherboard.

Modern CPUs generate a great deal of heat when they operate. Without cooling, the heat would quickly damage a CPU and cause it to stop functioning. CPUs are therefore installed with cooling units that consist of large blocks of heat-conducting metal pressed tightly against the CPU and cooling fans to whisk the heat from the metal. Between the cooling unit and the mounting circuit board with dozens of tiny copper pins, the CPU looks like a very large unit, yet the chip itself is just a thin wafer a fraction of an inch across.

Figure 1.17 The motherboard provides connections for many different devices and subsystems.

MEMORY

In a computer, **memory** is one or more sets of chips that store data and/or program instructions, either temporarily or permanently. Memory is a critical processing component in any computer. Personal computers use several different types of memory, but the two most important are called random access memory (RAM) and read-only memory (ROM). These two types of memory work in very different ways and perform distinct functions.

The most noticeable type of memory for a PC user is called **random access memory (RAM)**. As a result, the term *memory* is typically used to mean RAM. Like many computer components, RAM consists of a set of chips mounted on a small circuit board. Those circuit boards are plugged into sockets on the motherboard so that various subsystems can access the memory.

RAM is like an electronic scratch pad inside the computer, allowing the computer to store and retrieve

Figure 1.18 RAM for a PC comes in modules ready to be installed into the motherboard.

data and instructions very quickly. Accessing RAM is far faster than reading and writing from storage media like hard drives or DVDs. When a program is launched, it is loaded into and run from RAM. As the program needs data, it is loaded into memory for fast access.

RAM is **volatile**, meaning it loses its contents when the computer is shut off or if there is a power failure. Because RAM needs a constant supply of power to hold its data, it is not considered to be a form of permanent storage.

RAM has a tremendous impact on the computer's operating efficiency. Generally, the more RAM a computer has, the more it can do and the faster it can perform certain tasks. If the computer needs data but doesn't have enough RAM to hold what it needs, it must store some of what is in RAM already onto its hard drive in order to make more room. Storing and retrieving chunks of data on disk is very time consuming, and if the computer is following this process frequently, programs run slowly. Adding RAM to a computer system to improve its performance is one of the more common system upgrades people perform.

The most common measurement unit for describing a computer's memory is the **byte**—the amount of memory it takes to store a single character, such as a letter of the alphabet or a numeral. When referring to a computer's memory, the numbers are often so large that it is helpful to use terms such as **kilobyte (KB)**, **megabyte (MB)**, **gigabyte (GB)**, and **terabyte (TB)** to describe the values; these terms are defined in Table 2.1. Today's personal computers commonly require at least one gigabyte of memory to comfortably function for light-duty use. Many users choose to add more (four to eight gigabytes) for better performance.

RAM cards are not all created equal. Different models of RAM may have different speeds at which they store and retrieve data, different methods for data storage and retrieval, and even different physical layouts.

Each PC motherboard requires a specific type and speed range of RAM. Many older styles of RAM cannot even be physically installed on newer motherboards because their connectors are a different size and shape. But even if a RAM card can be plugged in, an incompatible data transfer speed or method can result in terrible performance or—more likely—a completely nonfunctional computer. Whether building a computer from scratch or upgrading an existing system's RAM, it is critically important to match the RAM card's specifications to the requirements provided by the motherboard manufacturer. When adding extra RAM to a system, it's also important to make sure the existing and new RAM modules match in speed in order to avoid poor performance (or no performance at all).

Read-only memory (ROM) permanently stores its data, even when the computer is shut off. It is used not for programs and user data but, rather, to store computer instructions and hardware information that rarely changes. Though ROM's contents can be changed, the

TABLE 1.1 UNITS OF MEASURE FOR COMPUTER MEMORY AND STORAGE

Unit	Abbreviation	Approximate Value (bytes)	Actual Value (bytes)
Kilobyte	KB	1,000	1,024
Megabyte	MB	1,000,000 (1 million)	1,048,576
Gigabyte	GB	1,000,000,000 (1 billion)	1,073,741,824
Terabyte	TB	1,000,000,000,000 (1 trillion)	1,099,511,627,776

process is much slower than for altering RAM, and that makes ROM unsuitable for storing temporary or rapidly changing information. ROM is called **nonvolatile** memory because it never loses its contents.

INPUT AND OUTPUT DEVICES

A personal computer would be useless if you could not interact with it, because the machine could not receive instructions or deliver the results of its work. *Input devices* accept data and instructions from the user or from another computer system. Examples include keyboards, mice, and digital cameras. *Output devices*, including the monitor, printer, and speakers, return processed data to the user or to another computer system. The computer sends output to the monitor (the display screen) when the user needs only to see the output. It sends output to the printer when the user requests a paper copy—also called a *hard copy*—of a document.

Some types of hardware can act as both input and output devices. For users, a touch screen displays output in the form of text or icons you can touch, and it accepts input via special sensors on the screen to detect the touch of a finger. Between two computers, the most common types of devices that can perform both input and output are **communications devices**. These devices connect one computer to another—a process known as networking. Such hardware devices typically are one of two types (both of these will be discussed in greater detail later in this chapter):

1. A **modem** converts in both directions between digital data the computer understands and analog signals that are transmitted over telephone or cable television wires.

2. **Network interface cards (NICs)** are digital-to-digital hardware components that both allow communication and can uniquely identify the computing device on the network.

STORAGE DEVICES

A computer can function with only processing, memory, input, and output devices. To be really useful, however, a personal computer also needs a place to keep program files and related data when they are not in use. The purpose of **storage** is to hold data permanently, even when the computer is turned off.

Figure 1.19   A peek inside a hard drive shows a round platter and one of the read/write heads.

You could think of storage as an electronic file cabinet and RAM as an electronic worktable. When you need to work with a program or a set of data, the computer locates it in the file cabinet and puts a copy on the table. After you have finished working with the program or data, you put it back into the file cabinet. The changes you make to data while working on it replace the original data in the file cabinet (unless you store it in a different place).

The main types of computer storage are magnetic, optical, and flash memory. The most common type is the **magnetic disk**. A disk is a round, flat object that spins around its center. (Magnetic disks are almost always housed inside a case of some kind, so you can't see the disk itself unless you open the case.) **Read/write heads**, which work in much the same way as the heads of a tape recorder or VCR, read data from the disk or write data onto the disk. The complete device that holds a disk is called a **disk drive**.

In addition to magnetic storage, nearly every computer sold today includes at least one form of **optical storage**—devices that use lasers to read data from or write data to the reflective surface of an optical disc. For a time, the **CD-ROM drive** was the most common type of optical storage device, but it has lately been surpassed by the use of DVD drives, which in turn are rapidly losing ground to the new Blu-ray optical storage format. **Compact discs (CDs)** are a type of optical storage, identical to audio CDs. Data CDs can hold varying amounts of data up to nearly 900 MB. **CD-Recordable (CD-R)** disks allow you to create your own CDs, but CD-R disks cannot be erased and reused. A **CD-ReWritable (CD-RW)** disk allows you to write and erase data multiple times on the same disk.

The **digital video disc (DVD)**, which is familiar if you rent movies for home viewing, is used not just for home theaters but personal computers as well. Using sophisticated compression technologies, the typical single-sided DVDs can hold anywhere from 4.7 GB to 8.5 GB of data. Though this capacity is still far less

than the capacity of a hard disk, DVDs are popular for permanent, removable storage.

Modern DVD drives for computers are combination units, capable of reading from and writing to both DVDs and CDs, freeing the user from the need to purchase different drives for each type of disk. With just one drive, users can install programs and data from their standard DVDs and CDs as well as listen to music and watch movies on their personal computers.

The latest advance in optical storage technology is called the **Blu-ray disc**, named after the blue-spectrum laser that the drive uses. Though the disc's diameter is the same as for CD and DVD drives, switching to a blue light laser and improving the design of the disc itself have resulted in a storage format that can store 25 to 50 GB of data depending on whether one or two storage layers are in use. The newest Blu-ray storage formats allow for more than 100 GB to be written to a single disc. Blu-ray drives are rapidly becoming the new standard for both home entertainment media and permanent data storage and are included in many home theater, game console, and computer systems. Most Blu-ray devices can also read CD and DVD disks.

The future of data storage may well be the **solid state drive (SSD)**, a memory subsystem that relies on special kinds of ROM to permanently store data. Since SSDs use memory chips for storage, they have no moving parts like hard disks; consequently, they have no risk of losing data due to mechanical failures, and they generally use less power in their operation. Their lack of mechanical parts also results in a smaller size, which along with reduced power requirements makes them an ideal match for mobile computing devices like notebook computers.

Though most PCs still use a hard drive, you may very well have recently been using an SSD without using the term. **Flash drives**, commonly found as the little storage sticks that plug into a USB port, are a regular staple of many computer users. Once used to transfer occasional files between computers, flash drives are now produced with enough storage to rival hard drives, with recent models providing 256 GB of storage. This allows users to store entire music and video libraries in one small package, or back up their PC's hard drive to a device that can be easily secured in a different location.

Also included in the SSD category are the small, thin memory cards used to store data in portable devices such as digital cameras and phones. The two major formats currently in use for these devices are **CompactFlash (CF)** and **Secure Digital (SD)**, and manufacturers for each of those formats produce a

Figure 1.20   Solid state drives have no moving parts; perfect for small devices with limited power.

range of cards in different sizes and storage capacities. It's common to find SSD cards that provide anywhere from 2 to 32 GB of storage, but both CF and SD formats are expanding to support storage amounts into the terabytes and beyond.

CF and SD cards require little power to run, which makes them ideal choices for storage in devices that rely on limited battery capacity to operate. They can be easily removed from their home device and transferred to a special reader on a PC, to allow the quick transfer of images or video from the mobile device to the PC.

Though SSD technology has been commercially available since the 1970s, it is rapidly evolving. Costs are

Fact Check

1. What is the purpose of storage?
   a. Ensuring the user's workspace is kept neat and tidy
   b. Holding data permanently, even when the computer is turned off
   c. Freeing up resources for the CPU
2. A microprocessor
   a. must be isolated from the other hardware subsystems
   b. integrates several different processing functions into a single chip
   c. is actually surprisingly large

falling even as design improvements are increasing the efficiency of the devices. It may not be long before hard drives cease to be a common component of desktop PCs and notebooks.

1.6 Software Brings the Machine to Life

The set of instructions that enable a computer to perform specific tasks is generically called a program or software. These instructions tell the machine's hardware components what to do; without a program, a computer could not do anything at all. When a computer uses a particular program, it is said to be **running** or **executing** that program.

Most programs that run on a computer are not built directly into the computer system. This allows different users to customize their computer to ideally suit their needs. To make software available to the computer, it is **installed**, which means that the program is written into the computer's permanent storage. For all but the simplest of programs, installation also usually includes adding references to the new program into the computer's operating system, so that the operating system will know where to find the program, and how to start it.

Installation may also include many other tasks, such as the creation and placement of data files for the program to use, establishing connections to devices such as printers for the new software to use, and updating software modules in other programs that are required by the new software. With few exceptions, the installation of software for consumer devices such as PCs and smart phones is automatic, requiring little else from the user than permission to perform the installation.

Although the array of available programs is vast and varied, most software falls into two major categories: system software and application software.

System software is any program that controls the computer's hardware or can be used to maintain the computer in some way so it runs more efficiently. There are four basic types of system software:

1. **Firmware** is used to directly control hardware devices, such as keyboards, hard drives, and memory cards.[1] Firmware can also be found outside of a personal computer; the programs that control your TV remote and cell phone would be considered firmware as well. Firmware is embedded on microchips and placed on the device that it controls.

2. An *operating system* tells the computer how to use its own components. An operating system is essential for any computer, because it acts as an interpreter between the hardware, application programs, and the user. Three of the most common operating systems are Microsoft's Windows, Apple Computer's Mac OS X, and Linux.

3. A **network operating system** allows computers to communicate and share files and device resources across a network while controlling network operations and overseeing the network's security.

4. A **utility** is a program that makes the computer system easier to use or performs highly specialized functions. Utilities are used to manage disks, troubleshoot hardware problems, and perform other tasks that the operating system itself may not be able to do.

Application software tells the computer how to accomplish specific tasks, such as word processing or drawing, for the user. Thousands of applications are available for many purposes and for people of all ages. Table 1.2 identifies major categories of applications and describes how they are most commonly used.

Though application software performs user-oriented tasks, it must still be created with hardware and the operating system in mind. A game designed for an Apple computer, for example, will not run on Sony's Playstation 3 game console without significant modification. Not only are the operating system and hardware completely different, but the fundamental way that people use the two machines are also worlds apart. A game console user typically controls the software's actions through a small set of buttons or by simply moving a controller pad through the air. A desktop computer substitutes a keyboard and mouse

Fact Check

1. Which type of software is a word processor program?
   a. An operating system
   b. Firmware
   c. Application software
2. List the four types of system software.

---

[1] R. Kayne (2010), What is firmware? *WiseGEEK*. Retrieved May 22, 2010, from http://www.wisegeek.com/what-is-firmware.htm

TABLE 1.2 MAJOR CATEGORIES OF APPLICATION SOFTWARE

Type	Purpose
Document publishing	Creating text-based documents such as newsletters, reports, articles, and brochures
Spreadsheets	Creating numeric-based documents such as budgets or balance sheets
Database management	Building and manipulating large sets of data, such as the names, addresses, and phone numbers in a telephone directory
Presentation	Creating and presenting electronic slides
Graphics	Designing illustrations or manipulating photographs, movies, or animations
Multimedia authoring	Composing music and building digital movies that incorporate sound, video, animation, and interactive features
Business software	Managing inventories, client contacts, sales databases, and accounting
Education software	Teaching subjects to children and adults, groups or individual learners
Internet applications	Designing Web sites, surfing the Web, sending e-mail, and much more
Games	Playing single-player or multiplayer games ranging from the simple to dazzlingly complex strategic games hosted on the Internet

for joysticks, triggers and colored buttons, and may assign commands and controls to a wide array of keys that the controller simply doesn't have.

As hardware changes, software may also need to adapt in order to operate efficiently. For example, when manufacturers began producing multi-core processors—microprocessors containing more than one CPU—application software could not take advantage of the extra computing power without making changes to distribute the program's work to the different CPUs.

It is not always necessary for all application software to reside on the user's machine. It is common today for part or all of a program to be provided to users via a local network or the Internet. For example, Google's Google Docs service allows users to create documents such as letters and spreadsheets using online editors, and store the data on Google's servers instead of their own computers. This allows many users to access and update those documents in real time, and collaborate and coordinate their work at a central location without the need to buy software and maintain special servers. It's an ideal solution when

team members for a project may participate from all around the world.

1.7 Data and Users

Hardware and software together create a functional computer, but all computers require data in order to become useful. Without data to process and information to create or deconstruct, a computer has no value. Data serves as the computer's raw material for performing every task.

Personal computers are designed to work with a human user. In fact, the user is a critical part of a complete computer system, especially when a personal computer is involved. This may seem surprising, since it's easy to think of computers as intelligent devices that can do practically anything. People also sometimes believe computers can think and make decisions, as humans do, but this is not the case. Even the most powerful supercomputers require human interaction—if for no other reason than to get them started and tell them which problems to solve.

COMPUTER DATA

The computer is a tool that aids in that process of converting data to information. A computer processes and manipulates everything as data. All letters, numbers, sounds, pictures, and even its software are reduced to strings of digits; hence the terms "digitize" and "digital." It accepts the data it has been given, processes its instructions in a strict sequence, modifies or replaces data as required by the instructions, and returns its result to the user. The computer's software is ultimately responsible for completing the conversion from data to information by displaying the results of the computer's activity in a way that is meaningful for the user.

Within the computer, data is organized into **files**. A file is simply a set of data that has been grouped together and given a name. A file that the user can open and use is often called a **document**. Although many people think of documents simply as text, a computer document can include many kinds of data. For example, a computer document can be a text file (such as a letter), a group of numbers (such as a budget), a video clip (which includes images and sounds), and so on. Programs are organized into files as well; these files contain the instructions and data that a program needs in order to run and perform tasks.

THE USER'S ROLE

When working with a personal computer, the user can take on several roles, depending on what he or she wants to accomplish:

- **Setting up the system.** Have you ever bought a new PC? When you got it home, you probably had to unpack it, set it up, and make sure it worked as expected. If you want to change something about the system, you will likely do it yourself, whether you want to add a new hardware device, change the way programs look on your screen, or customize the way a program functions.

- **Installing software.** Although your new computer probably came with an operating system and some applications installed, you need to install any other programs you want to use. This may involve loading software from a disk or downloading it from a Web site. Either way, it is usually the user's responsibility to install programs, unless the computer is used at a school or business. In that case, a system administrator or technician is more likely to do the job.

- **Running programs.** Whenever your computer is on, several programs are running in the background, including the software that runs your mouse, network connections, and anti-malware protection. Such programs do not need any user input; in fact, you may not even be aware of them. But for the most part, if you want to use your computer to perform a task, you need to launch and run the software that is designed for the task, and work with it to make sure it gives you the results you want.

- **Managing files.** As you have already learned, a computer saves data in files. If you write a letter to a friend, you can save it as a file, making it available to open and use again later. Pictures, songs, and other kinds of data are stored as files. But it is the user's job to manage these files. Managing files means setting up a logical system for storing them on the computer and knowing when to delete files, move them, or copy them to a storage device for safekeeping.

- **Maintaining the system.** System maintenance does not necessarily mean opening the PC and fixing broken parts, as you would repair a car's

Figure 1.21 Computers display data in ways that help viewers learn new things.

Figure 1.22 Users put together their own choices for hardware and software to build a computer tailored to their needs.

Fact Check

1. What is the difference, if any, between data and information?
   a. Data is the raw material used in the creation of information.
   b. Data is smaller than information.
   c. Data and information are essentially the same.
2. What is the relationship between data and a computer file?
   a. Files can only hold information, not data.
   b. A file is the smallest unit of data on a computer.
   c. A file is a set of data that has been grouped together and given a name.
3. Which of the following is a role of the user?
   a. Auditing firmware
   b. Installing software
   c. Processing data

engine. But it could! In that case, you might call a qualified technician to do the job or roll up your sleeves and tackle it yourself. In most cases, however, PC maintenance generally means running utilities that keep the disks free of clutter and ensure that the computer is using its resources efficiently.

"USERLESS" COMPUTERS

Many kinds of computers require no human interaction once they have been programmed, installed, and started up. For example, if you own a car built within the past decade, it almost certainly has an on-board computer that controls and monitors engine functions. Many new home appliances, such as washers and dryers, have built-in computers that monitor water usage, drying times, balance, and other operations. Sophisticated

userless computers operate security systems, navigation systems, communications systems, and many others.

Userless computers are typically controlled by their operating systems. In these devices, the operating system may be installed on special memory chips rather than a disk. The operating system is programmed to perform a specific set of tasks. These systems are not set up for human interaction, except as needed for system configuration or maintenance.

But even without a person directly controlling and receiving output from them, these systems still have users. A computer that monitors the temperature in a refrigerator has an indirect user in the owner who is counting on the milk staying fresh for as long as possible. No useful computer is completely separated from human users.

Figure 1.23 Newer cars contain onboard computers designed to monitor and control the engine with only occasional user contact.

- A complete computer system includes hardware, software, data, and users. To manipulate data, the computer follows a process called the information processing cycle, which includes data input, processing, output, and storage.

- A computer's hardware devices fall into four categories: processing, memory, input and output (I/O), and storage.

- The set of instructions that enable a computer to perform specific tasks is generically called a program or software. There are four basic types of system software: firmware, operating system, network operating system, and utility.

- There is a difference between information and data. The computer is a tool that aids in that process of converting data to information. Personal computers are designed to work with a human user. In fact, the user is a critical part of a complete computer system.

Key Terms

application software, 27
Blu-ray disc, 26
byte, 24
cards, 23
CD-Recordable (CD-R), 25
CD-ReWritable (CD-RW), 25
CD-ROM drive, 25
central processing unit (CPU), 23
circuit board, 22
communications devices, 25
compact discs (CDs), 25
CompactFlash (CF), 26
computer system, 20
data, 20
digital video disc (DVD), 25
disk drive, 25
document, 29
executing, 27

file, 29
firmware, 27
flash drives, 26
gigabyte (GB), 24
hardware, 20
information processing cycle, 21
installed, 27
kilobyte (KB), 24
magnetic disk, 25
megabyte (MB), 24
memory, 23
microprocessor, 23
modem, 25
motherboard, 23
network interface cards (NICs), 25
network operating system, 27
networking, 25
nonvolatile, 25

optical storage, 25
processing, 23
processors, 23
program, 20
random access memory (RAM), 23
read-only memory (ROM), 24
read/write heads, 25
running, 27
Secure Digital (SD), 26
software, 20
solid state drive (SSD), 26
storage, 25
system software, 27
terabyte (TB), 24
users, 21
utility, 27
volatile, 24

Key Terms QUIZ

Complete each statement by writing one of the terms listed under "Key Terms" in each blank.

1. A complete _____ refers to the combination of hardware, software, data, and people.

2. A(n) _____ is a set of data or program instructions that has been given a name.

3. A(n) _____ is the complete device that contains a disk.

4. Electronic instructions that tell the computer's hardware what to do are known as _____.

5. A rectangular card containing microchips is known as a(n) _____.

6. Data and program instructions are temporarily held in _____ while the processor is using them.

7. The _____ includes four stages: input, processing, output, and storage.

8. One _____ is roughly equivalent to 1 million bytes of data.

9. Operating systems fall into the category of _____ software.

10. In a magnetic disk drive, a special device called the _____ reads data from and writes data to a disk's surface.

Review
QUESTIONS

In your own words, briefly answer the following questions or respond to the statements.

1. List the four parts of a complete computer system.

2. What are the four phases of the information processing cycle?

3. Identify four categories of computer hardware.

4. Describe the basic purpose of the central processing unit (CPU).

5. List four units of measure for computer memory and storage, not including the byte.

6. Name and differentiate the three main categories of storage devices.

7. Name and differentiate the two main categories of computer software.

8. What is the difference between data and information?

9. What is a fundamental difference between data and programs?

10. List five tasks a user may be responsible for when working with a personal computer.

Complete the following exercises as directed by your instructor.

LESSON
LAB

1. What type of computer system do you use in class or in the lab? If your computer is running Windows 7, you can access this information from the Start Menu. Select "Control Panel," and from that window double-click the "System" icon. From that window, you can see the type of processor, its speed and the number of cores it has. You'll also see the amount of RAM installed in the computer, and the version of Windows 7 that is installed.

Then, in the bottom left corner of that "System" window, click on the link that says, "Performance Information and Tools." You will see a rating provided by Windows of the relative power of the computer's main subsystems, using a scale of 1.0 to 7.9. What subsystems received the lowest and highest values on your computer?

2. What kind of software is installed on your computer? To find out, all you have to do is turn on your computer. After it starts, you should see a collection of icons—small pictures that represent the programs and other resources on your computer. List the icons that appear on your screen and the names of the software programs they represent.

Team
EXERCISE
Diversity

Most workplaces bring together people of varying ages and physical abilities. For example, even in a workplace where no one would meet the definition of "disabled," there are likely to be individuals who wear glasses or contact lenses, and perhaps some older workers who don't read small type as well as they once did. Fortunately, today's computers typically can be customized to meet the needs of a physically diverse workforce. In this exercise, you will explore some of these capabilities.

Divide into groups of three or four. Each group will work on this exercise at one shared computer. On a sheet of paper, list the group members' names, ages, and whether or not they use glasses, contact lenses, or some other vision correction.

Using your computer and an Internet connection, visit the Web site of the Bureau of Labor Statistics (www.bls.gov). From the list of Economic News Releases, choose a news release about major economic indicators to download in PDF format. When the document is displayed, notice the zoom feature in the toolbar of icons above the document: a button with a minus sign, one with a plus sign, and a percentage. Give each group member a turn to read a paragraph of the text and adjust the document size by clicking on the plus and minus buttons or changing the display percentage. Record the preferred display percentage for each person.

Option: If you are able to save the document you downloaded and open it with Adobe Reader, do that, and then use the software's document-reading function. Highlight a paragraph of the document with your cursor. Then, in the toolbar, click on "View," and select first "Read Out Loud" and then "Activate Read Out Loud." Listen to the computerized voice read the paragraph. On your list, note whether each group member found listening helpful or unhelpful. Then deactivate "Read Out Loud," using the same drop-down menu.

Were the preferences the same for all group members? If not, what variations did you observe? Be ready to compare your group's experience with that of the other groups in a class discussion.

[*Chapter* LABS]

1. The race to build a faster computer is never ending. Find out who is currently making the world's fastest supercomputer. Open your computer's Web browser, visit a search engine site such as Google (http://www.google.com) or Bing (http://www.bing.com) and search for the phrase *world's fastest supercomputer*. Look through the search results for recent news stories, and follow links to news or encyclopedia sites that have the latest information. If your search results contain too many stories about old computers, try including the current year in your search phrase *(world's fastest supercomputer 2011*, for example). Read the article and compare how much more processing power the new computer provides over the previous record holder.

2. Explore some free services that help you use computers and the Internet to share information and creativity.

   a. Learn more about starting your own blog. Using a Web browser, navigate to http://www. blogger.com/. From the front page, click the *quick tour* link to read information about the service and what it does. You can also follow the *video tutorial* link to a YouTube video that gives you details about how to set up and start posting to a blog.

   b. Read about starting a new Web site. Use your browser to visit http://www.webs.com/. Near the bottom of the front page, follow the *View Features* button to learn more about what services are offered for free and for a fee, and get a feel for the different ways that Web sites can quickly be constructed for new users.

   c. Investigate wiki software to see how people with a common interest can share information about that subject. Go to http://www.wikia.com/ and explore some of the wiki sites that have been created. You can do this either by clicking the Random Wiki button near the top of the screen to jump to one of the thousands of wikis that Wikia hosts; or you can type a subject (for example, a favorite TV show, computer game or hobby) in the nearby search box and search for a wiki on that subject. Look through a couple of wikis to see how information is organized, and how thoroughly or superficially the subject is covered.

3. Replacing or adding RAM modules is a common operation that many home users do themselves. Learn more about this process by watching a tutorial online. With a browser, visit http://www.youtube.com/ and search on the phrase *install ram desktop*; you will most likely see a long list of results for this query. Pick one or two videos from the list to watch. If you pick a tutorial that was posted within the last year or two, you'll probably see the inside of a computer that is similar to what you might purchase today. But older demonstrations still show the same basic concept; the process of installing RAM has been the same for many years.

[*Think* AND DISCUSS]

As directed by your instructor, discuss the following questions in class or in groups.

1. Home computers are used more extensively than ever for tasks such as banking, investing, shopping, and communicating. Do you see this trend as having a positive or a negative impact on our society and economy? Do you plan to use a computer in these ways? Why or why not?

2. With the exploding popularity in tablet and handheld PCs, do you think those devices are likely to replace (or at least greatly reduce the number of) desktop PCs being used in the future? Why or why not? What factors would contribute to the desktop PC's demise; or, what factors will ensure its future survival?

[*Fact Check* ANSWERS]

1A:

LO1.1 What Is a Computer?

1: **b.** analog and digital
2: **b.** they process all their data and instructions as numbers

LO1.2 Types of Digital Computers

1: **a.** Desktop computer
2: network servers, mainframes, minicomputers, supercomputers

LO1.3 Computers in Society

1: **b.** information
2: Communication; business work at home; schoolwork; entertainment; creativity; personal finances; shopping; education.
3: Census bureau; Internal Revenue Service; military; police

1B:

LO1.4 The Parts of a Computer System

1: **a.** hardware, software, data, and users
2: **c.** is any part of the computer you can touch
3: **b.** input, processing, output, and storage

LO1.5 Essential Computer Hardware

1: **b.** Holding data permanently, even when the computer is turned off
2: **b.** integrates several different processing functions into a single chip

LO1.6 Software Brings the Machine to Life

1: **c.** Application software
2: firmware, operating system, network operating system, utility

LO1.7 Data and Users

1: **a.** Data is the raw material used in the creation of information.
2: **c.** A file is a set of data that has been grouped together and given a name.
3: **b.** Installing software

2

THE INS AND OUTS OF COMPUTING

Chapter Overview

Computers are versatile tools, in large part because there are so many ways that the data-processing core of the computer can receive input and deliver output. In this chapter, you'll learn details about some of the more common forms of input devices, and you'll explore a variety of devices for communicating output to users. Think of a computer you've recently seen; did you notice hardware that you could use to send data or commands to the computer? What kinds?

LESSON 2A:
Input Devices

Computers are data processing marvels, but they need to receive data from the outside world in order to transform it into something useful. Sounds, colors, air speeds, the density of iron, user commands and everything else a computer might process must first be delivered to the machine before the computer can use it.

Two main challenges exist with regard to an input device. The first is the process of collecting the input from its source. A beautiful sunset destined for a digital photo album must first be captured in some way. A sound recording device is needed in order to receive a wailing guitar solo that will someday be shared across the Internet with fans around the world. The letters that will form the words of the next blockbuster spy novel must be collected one by one.

However, collection is just the first step. We all know what cameras, microphones, and keyboards are, but in order to make those collection devices useful to a computer, the input must be converted to a digital format. Only when sights, sounds, words and commands are represented digitally can the computer make use of them.

2.1 User Interfaces

Before discussing input and output devices in detail, let's take a moment to get an overview of two software subsystems that sit in the middle between input devices, output devices, and the user: the operating system and the user interface.

OPERATING SYSTEM BASICS

An **operating system (OS)** is a software program, but it is different from word processing programs, spreadsheets, and all the other software programs on your computer. The OS is an example of system software—software that controls the system's hardware and that interacts with the user and application software. The OS ensures that the results of program and user actions are displayed on screen, printed, and so on. The operating system also acts as the primary controlling mechanism for the computer's hardware.

The operating system performs the following functions:

- Displays the on-screen elements with which you interact—the **user interface**
- Loads programs into the computer's memory so that you can use them
- Coordinates how programs work with the computer's hardware and other software
- Manages the way information is stored on and retrieved from disks

As you can see, the operating system acts as the manager and activity coordinator for almost everything that goes on in a PC, even though most users are rarely directly aware of its presence.

The most direct experience users have of an operating system is with its user interface. These on-screen elements may take the form of a graphical user interface or a command-line interface.

GRAPHICAL USER INTERFACES

Most current operating systems, including all versions of Windows, the Macintosh Operating System, OS/2, and some versions of UNIX and Linux, provide a **graphical user interface** (**GUI**, pronounced GOO-ee). Graphical user interfaces are so called because you launch programs and make choices with graphical objects such as windows, menus, icons, buttons, and other tools. These graphical tools all represent different types of commands; the GUI enables you to issue commands to the computer by using visual objects instead of typing names of commands.

Windows is one of several GUIs that use the **desktop metaphor**, in which the background of the GUI is said to be a desktop on which you have your graphical tools and within which you can store your work. Figure 2.1 shows the Windows 7 desktop. The small pictures on the desktop—called **shortcuts**—represent links to resources on the PC or network. Although shortcuts are often called icons, an **icon** actually is only the tiny picture that represents an object. Using your mouse or other pointing device, you can move the pointer and choose (or **activate**) a shortcut, telling Windows you want to use the resource that the shortcut represents.

The items that appear on the desktop depend on the contents of the computer's disks, the resources it can access, and the user's preferences; therefore, any two Windows desktops can look different.

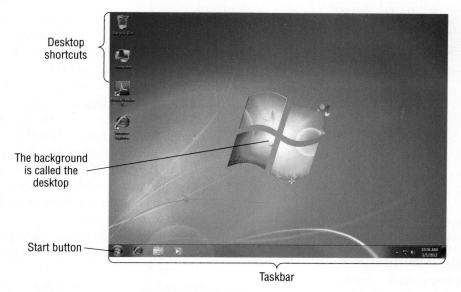

Desktop shortcuts

The background is called the desktop

Start button

Taskbar

Figure 2.1 The Windows 7 GUI has several standard features, including the desktop, taskbar, and Start button.

Certain elements always appear on the Windows desktop. As shown in Figure 2.1, the **taskbar** appears at the bottom of the Windows desktop; it is used to launch and manage programs. The **Start button** is a permanent feature of the taskbar; click it to open the Start menu. The **Start menu** contains shortcuts for launching programs and opening folders on a computer (see Figure 2.2). Shortcuts can be added to the desktop, the Start menu, and other areas. When you start a program in Windows, a button representing it appears on the taskbar.

You also can launch programs by clicking icons on the **Quick Launch bar**, a special section at the left end of the taskbar where you can add icons for the purpose of quickly starting programs. Once you start a program, a button appears on the taskbar. When you have several programs on the desktop, one way in which you can switch between them is to click the program's button on the taskbar.

When you right-click an object in Windows, a small menu usually appears containing the most common commands associated with that object. Depending on the version of Windows you are using, and whether you are using a specific application, this type of menu may be called a **shortcut menu** or a **context menu**. Either way, its function is the same: to provide quick access to commonly used commands related to the item you have right-clicked.

When you launch a program, it is loaded into memory and begins to run. A running program may take up the whole screen, it may appear in a rectangular

frame called a **window**, or it may appear only as a shortcut on the taskbar.

You access all the resources on your computer through windows. For example, you can view the contents of a disk in a window, run a program and edit a document in a window, view a Web page in a window, or change system settings in a window. A different window appears for each resource you want to use.

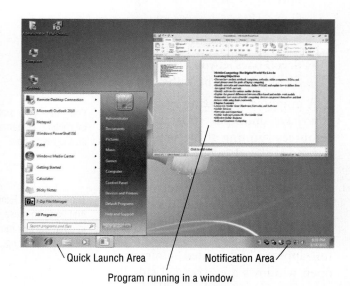

Quick Launch Area   Notification Area

Program running in a window

Figure 2.2 The Start menu contains shortcuts to programs and folders. After a program is launched, it will have a button on the taskbar.

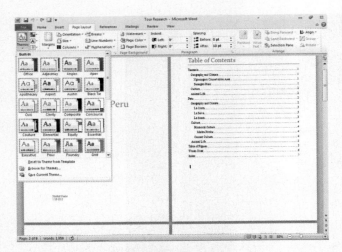

Figure 2.3 Most Windows applications feature the tools shown here.

Figure 2.3 shows Microsoft Word running in a window. Some menus and buttons, such as the ones shown here, appear in nearly every window you open. In the Windows GUI, programs share many of the same features, so you see a familiar interface no matter what program you are using. Several GUI features are common:

- The **title bar** identifies the windows' contents, and it also contains the Minimize, Restore, and Close buttons, which let you hide the window, resize it, or close it altogether.

- The **menu bar** provides lists of commands and options for this specific program.

- **Toolbars** contain buttons that let you issue commands quickly.

- **Scroll bars** let you view parts of the program or file that do not fit in the window.

A graphical operating system lets you have multiple programs and resources running at the same time, but you can work in only one window at a time. The window that is currently in use is called the **active window**; its title bar appears in a deeper color shade than that of other visible open windows, and its taskbar button appears highlighted. Unless all open windows are arranged side by side, the active window will appear on top of any inactive windows.

You must select the window you want to use before you can access its contents. The process of moving from one open window to another is called **task switching**. You can either click

an open window to activate it or click an open program's taskbar button to activate its window.

You initiate many tasks by clicking icons and toolbar buttons, but you also can perform tasks by choosing commands from lists called menus. In most program windows, you open menus from a horizontal list called the menu bar. Many programs feature a File menu, such as the one shown in Figure 2.4, which typically contains commands for opening, closing, saving, and printing files. To execute or run one of the menu commands, you click it. In many cases, you can also issue menu commands by using keyboard shortcuts instead of the mouse.

Different programs may use different styles for GUI elements such as menus. For example, while the traditional menu style is a list of vertical choices as shown in Figure 2.4, some newer programs favor a **ribbon** style, where choices and options in a menu are displayed horizontally across the top of the work area, as shown in Figure 2.5. More traditional menus are displayed only when the user wants to make a selection from them, while ribbons are typically always visible.

Dialog boxes are special-purpose windows that appear when the OS or application needs to give you some status and possible choice of actions or you need to tell a program (or the operating system) what to do next. A dialog box is so named because it conducts a "dialog" with you as it seeks the information it needs to perform a task. A dialog box can even have more than one page, in which case the pages are made available through tabs and look like a stack of tabbed

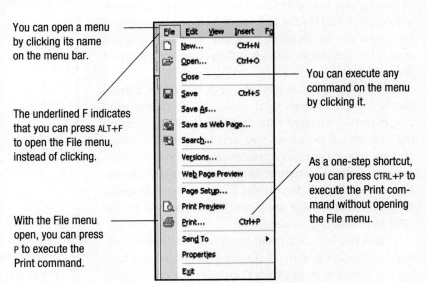

You can open a menu by clicking its name on the menu bar.

The underlined F indicates that you can press ALT+F to open the File menu, instead of clicking.

With the File menu open, you can press P to execute the Print command.

You can execute any command on the menu by clicking it.

As a one-step shortcut, you can press CTRL+P to execute the Print command without opening the File menu.

Figure 2.4 A typical File menu.

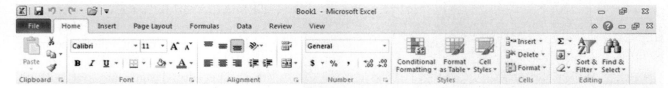

Figure 2.5 A ribbon style menu in Microsoft Excel.

pages. Figure 2.6 shows a dialog box from Microsoft Word and describes some of the most common dialog box features.

COMMAND-LINE INTERFACES

Some older operating systems (such as MS-DOS), some current versions of UNIX and Linux, and many mainframe operating systems feature a **command-line interface**, which uses typewritten commands rather than graphical objects to execute tasks. A command-line interface displays in character mode—using only alphanumeric and other simple symbols. Users interact with a command-line interface by typing commands and requests at a **prompt** on the screen. In DOS, the prompt usually includes the identification for the active disk drive (a letter followed by a colon), a backslash (\), and a greater-than symbol (>), as in C:\>.

As much as people prefer to work in a GUI, a command-line interface gives you a quick way to enter commands, and even now Windows has an optional command-line interface, called the Command Prompt. This command prompt is most often used

Fact Check

1. A graphical user interface is so named because
   a. the screen graphics are amazing
   b. the user performs operations primarily with graphical objects
   c. it was originally intended for use by graphic designers
2. What is a GUI's "desktop"?
   a. The main workspace where shortcuts to files and programs are displayed
   b. The area immediately underneath the computer's monitor on the desk
   c. A table of programs and files waiting to be processed by the CPU
3. Command-line interfaces typically provide
   a. a prompt for entering commands and no graphic elements to select
   b. a comprehensive and intuitive interface
   c. menus of commands to select

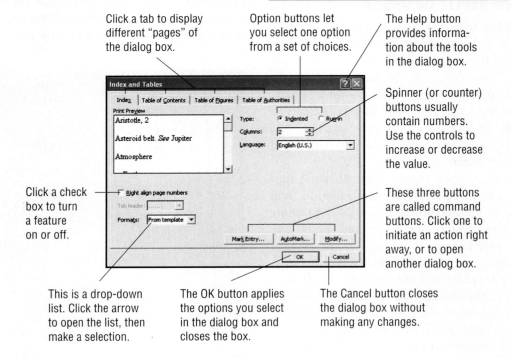

Click a tab to display different "pages" of the dialog box.

Option buttons let you select one option from a set of choices.

The Help button provides information about the tools in the dialog box.

Spinner (or counter) buttons usually contain numbers. Use the controls to increase or decrease the value.

Click a check box to turn a feature on or off.

These three buttons are called command buttons. Click one to initiate an action right away, or to open another dialog box.

This is a drop-down list. Click the arrow to open the list, then make a selection.

The OK button applies the options you select in the dialog box and closes the box.

The Cancel button closes the dialog box without making any changes.

Figure 2.6 This dialog box includes multiple tabs and a variety of methods for selecting options.

Figure 2.7 A command line interface provides a simple way to type text commands.

by administrators to run non-GUI programs for managing and troubleshooting Windows, but any program that can be run in Windows can be launched from here, opening its own GUI window, if necessary.

2.2 Common Input Devices

Now that you have an overview of a computer's user interface, let's look at some of the common devices used to provide input to the computer.

OVERVIEW: INPUT DEVICES

You might think of a computer's central processing unit (CPU) as its brain because it is the central data-processing hardware (for details about CPUs, see Chapter 2). Extending the analogy, you might think of the input devices as the computer's sensory organs—the eyes, ears, and fingers. After you buy and set up the computer, you may take the CPU for granted because you interact directly with input devices and only indirectly with the CPU.

An input device does exactly what its name suggests: It enables you to enter information and commands into the computer. The most commonly used input devices are the keyboard and the mouse. If you buy a new personal computer, it will include a keyboard and mouse unless you specify otherwise. Other types of input devices are available as well, such as variations of the mouse and specialized "alternative" input devices such as microphones and scanners.

While many input and output devices have a standard look and function, some types of computers use devices that do not exactly match what is typical. For example, computers made by Apple Computer use keyboards that do not exactly match the keys found on a common PC's keyboard, and Apple mice do not follow the more usual right and left button design. Though these specialty designs are not without advantages, this lesson will focus only on the layout and use of the more universal PC hardware.

PORTS

All input and output devices need a way to hook into the computer, so that information can be transmitted between the computer and the user. In personal computers, each device connects to the computer via an interface socket called a **port**.

If you look at the back of a desktop PC (on notebook computers, check both in the back and along the sides), you'll notice an array of sockets into where things can be plugged. They come in all different shapes. Some have holes for rows of pins, some are circular or flat, and some are just big square holes with the connection wires all the way inside.

These various openings are all ports, and each one normally has a specific piece of hardware to which it is designed to connect.

Many devices such as cameras, printers, and some models of keyboards and mice connect to the computer via **USB ports** (which stands for Universal Serial Bus). Unlike other ports that are designed for one specific kind of hardware, USB ports are made to accept any kind of input or output device, so long

Figure 2.8 A port accepts a plug or connector from an external device.

as it makes use of the USB connector. A custom piece of software is usually supplied along with the device to ensure that the computer recognizes and understands how to use the device when it is first plugged in.

THE KEYBOARD

Despite the arrival of touch sensitive screens and other new input devices, the keyboard is still the primary input device for entering text and numbers. A standard keyboard includes about 100 keys; each key sends a different signal to the CPU. The skill of typing, or **keyboarding**, is the ability to enter text and numbers with skill and accuracy.

Keyboards come in many styles. The various models differ in size, shape, and feel; except for a few special-purpose keys, most keyboards are laid out almost identically. They have about 100 keys arranged in five groups, as shown in Figure 2.8.

1. The **alphanumeric keys**—the area of the keyboard that looks like a typewriter's keys—are arranged the same way on almost every keyboard. Sometimes this common arrangement is called the QWERTY (pronounced KWER-tee) layout because the first six keys on the top row of letters are Q, W, E, R, T, and Y. Along with the keys that produce letters and numbers, the alphanumeric key group includes four keys having specific functions: TAB, CAPS LOCK, BACKSPACE, and ENTER.

2. The SHIFT, ALT (Alternate), and CTRL (Control) keys are called **modifier keys** because they modify the input of other keys. In other words, if you hold down a modifier key while pressing another key, then you are changing the second key's input in some way. For example, if you press the J key, you input a small letter j. But if you hold down the SHIFT key while pressing the J key, you input a capital J.

3. The **function keys**, which are labeled F1, F2, and so on, are usually arranged in a row along the top of the keyboard. Most keyboards have 12 function keys. They allow you to input commands without typing long strings of characters or navigating menus or dialog boxes. Each function key's purpose depends on the program you are using. For example, in many programs, F1 is the help key. When you press it, a special window appears to display information about the program you are using.

4. Most standard keyboards also include a set of **cursor-movement keys**, which let you move around the screen without using a mouse. In many programs that display what you type, a mark on the screen indicates where the characters you type will be entered. This mark, called the **cursor** or **insertion point**, appears on the screen as a blinking vertical line, a small box, or some other symbol to show your place in a document or command line. Figure 2.9 shows an insertion point in a document window.

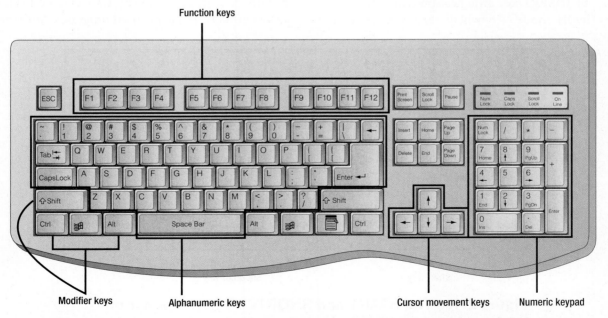

Figure 2.9 Nearly all standard PC keyboards include the keys shown here.

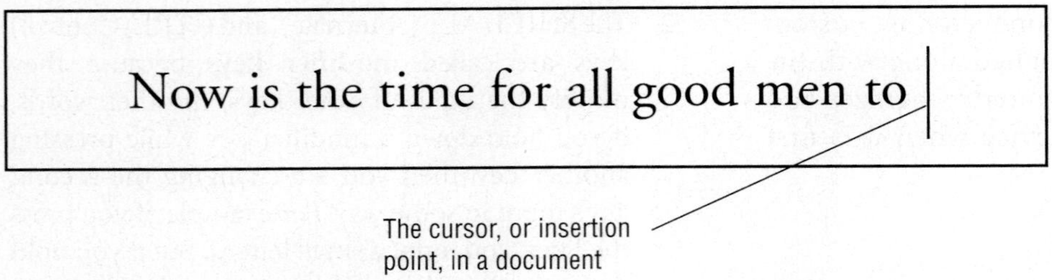

Now is the time for all good men to |

The cursor, or insertion
point, in a document

Figure 2.10 The cursor, or insertion point, shows where the next letter typed will appear.

5. The **numeric keypad** is usually located on the right side of the keyboard, as shown in Figure 2.9. The numeric keypad looks like a calculator's keypad, with its 10 digits and mathematical operators (+, –, *, and /). The numeric keypad also features a NUMLOCK key, which switches the meaning of the keys between digits and cursor control.

Sometimes, especially on smaller notebook models, the numeric keypad is not present. In those cases, you'll often find that some of the alphanumeric keys have been given extra alternate values so that they can function in a similar way.

In addition to the five groups of keys described earlier, PC keyboards feature six special-purpose keys:

- DELETE is typically used to remove objects in the currently running program.

- ESCAPE is often used to cancel the appearance of a dialog box, or in some other way "move back" one level in a multilevel environment.

- The INSERT key switches some programs from "insert mode" (in which text is inserted into the document at the cursor, pushing the existing text forward) to "overtype mode" (in which new text is typed over existing text, erasing the text that was there before), and vice versa.

- The PRINT SCREEN key allows the user to capture whatever is shown on the screen into an image file.

- Typically, SCROLL LOCK causes the cursor to remain stationary on the screen, and the document's contents move around it.

- PAUSE can be used to stop or pause execution of a command in some programs.

Nearly all PC keyboards include two additional special-purpose keys designed to work with the Windows operating systems (see Figure 2.11):

- The START key, which features the Windows logo, opens the Windows Start menu on most computers. Pressing this key is the same as using the mouse to click the Start button on the Windows taskbar.

- The SHORTCUT key, which features an image of a menu, opens an on-screen shortcut menu in many Windows-based application programs.

Some manufacturers add Internet and multimedia controls to their keyboards. For example, you can use the buttons to launch a Web browser, check e-mail, and start your most frequently used programs. Multimedia

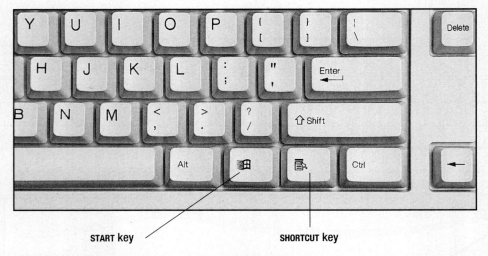

START key   SHORTCUT key

Figure 2.11 The START and SHORTCUT keys appear on keyboards sold with Windows-based computers.

buttons let you control the computer's CD-ROM or DVD drive and adjust the speaker volume.

Every key's exact function and purpose depends entirely on the program you are running. Word processing software will treat the letter keys as letters, but a game may use letter keys for moving around or performing actions within the game. Not every program will use every key on the keyboard, and there is no restriction as to which keys may be used for any given purpose by a program.

THE MOUSE

GUI users need a way to select specific graphical objects that they wish to activate or change. In most PC GUIs, this is accomplished with a **pointer**. The pointer is an on-screen object, usually an arrow, that is used to select text; access menus; and interact with programs, files, or data that appear on the screen.

In order to move the pointer and issue commands at the pointer's location, every PC includes a pointing device as standard equipment. Full-size PCs usually include a mouse as the **pointing device**. By sliding the mouse on a flat surface, users are able to manipulate the pointer and interact with the computer.

Mice usually have at least two buttons on the top, arranged so that your first two fingers rest on them. Many mice also contain additional controls, such as a wheel between the two top buttons, and sometimes additional buttons along the side of the mouse.

Mice are either mechanical or optical. A **mechanical mouse** contains a small rubber ball that protrudes through a hole in the bottom of the mouse's case. As the user slides the mouse back and forth, sensors attached to the ball detect the speed and direction of its rotation, and the computer adjusts the location of the pointer on the screen accordingly. Though you can still find mechanical mice in use, they are rapidly being replaced by optical mice.

An **optical mouse** is non-mechanical. It emits a beam of light from its underside to illuminate the nearby surface and uses a sensor and special image processor to track the motion of the mouse. Like its mechanical relative, the optical mouse calculates the speed and direction of its motion and relays that data to the computer so the mouse pointer's position can be updated.

Mice transmit their data either through a cord that plugs into the computer, or via a wireless transmitter to a small receiver that is plugged into a computer's USB port.

Wireless mice are great for reducing the clutter of wires on your desk, and for eliminating the hassle of the cord getting stuck underneath papers or your monitor stand.

However, that convenience comes at a price. While wired mice draw their operating power through their cord from the computer, a wireless mouse requires batteries. Along with the extra cost, the user must keep spare batteries handy for when the mouse runs out of power.

In addition, many models of wireless mice can interfere with each others' operation. More than a couple of wireless mice near each other can cause hiccups in their functioning, making a combination of wired and wireless more desirable.

The mouse offers two main benefits. First, the mouse lets you position the cursor anywhere on the screen quickly without using the cursor-movement keys. You simply move the pointer to the on-screen position you want, press the mouse button, and the cursor appears at that location.

Second, instead of forcing you to type or issue commands from the keyboard, the mouse and mouse-based operating systems let you choose commands from easy-to-use menus and dialog boxes (see Figure 1.5). The result is a much more intuitive way to use computers.

USING THE MOUSE

Moving the pointer to a location on the screen with your mouse is a process called **pointing**. As you push the mouse across your desk, the pointer on the screen moves in relation to the mouse. Push the mouse forward, and the pointer moves up. Push the mouse to the left, and the pointer moves to the left.

Almost everything you do with a mouse is accomplished by combining pointing with these techniques that make use of the mouse's buttons:

- Clicking
- Double-clicking
- Dragging
- Right-clicking
- Scrolling

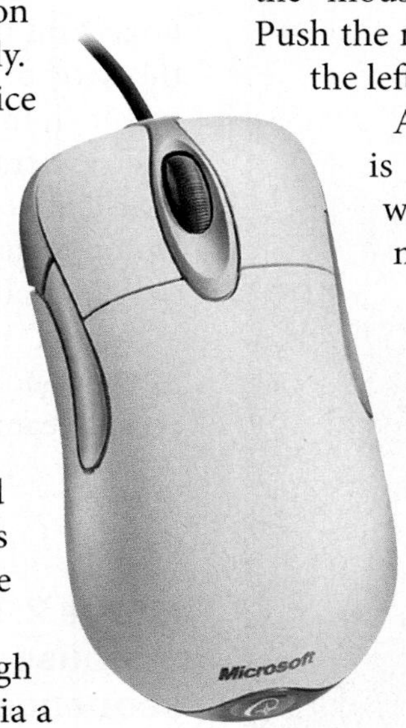

Figure 2.12 A wired, optical mouse for a PC.

Techniques such as clicking, double-clicking, and dragging are usually carried out with the left mouse button, which is commonly designated as the "primary" mouse button on multi button mice.

To **click** an item with the mouse, you move the pointer to the item on the screen. When the pointer touches the object, press and quickly release the primary mouse button once.

Double-clicking an item means pointing to the item with the mouse pointer and then pressing and releasing the primary mouse button twice in rapid succession.

Typically, single-clicking is used to select objects on the screen, and double-clicking is used to request some kind of extra action to be taken with what you're selecting.

Dragging an item means positioning the mouse pointer over an item, pressing the primary mouse button, and holding it down as you move the mouse. As you move the pointer, the item you selected is "dragged" along with it across the screen. You can then drop the item in a new position on the screen by releasing the mouse button. This technique is also called **drag-and-drop editing**, or just **drag and drop**.

Windows and many Windows programs support **right-clicking**, which means pointing to an item on the screen and then pressing and releasing the right mouse button. Right-clicking usually opens a shortcut menu that contains commands and options related to the item you right-clicked.

Some programs may support **scrolling**, which is the action of moving a list of information up and down on the screen. A mouse may have a wheel between the two top buttons, and the wheel can be used to scroll through the information.

As with keyboards, the actual results of every mouse action is determined by the application software being used.

If your mouse has a wheel between the two top buttons, some programs may support **scrolling**, which is the action of moving a list of information up and down. Not all applications and operating systems support the use of the wheel, and the specific actions each program performs may be different.

Figure 2.13   A trackball can be useful when there's no room to move a mouse around.

TRACKBALLS

A **trackball** is a pointing device that works like an upside-down mouse. You rest your index finger or thumb on an exposed ball, then place your other fingers on the buttons. To move the pointer around the screen, you roll the ball with your index finger or thumb. Because you do not move the whole device, a trackball requires less space than a mouse. Trackballs gained popularity with the advent of laptop computers, which typically are used on laps or on small work surfaces that have no room for a mouse. However, non-mechanical devices such as the touchpad have largely replaced trackballs in recent years.

Figure 2.14   The buttons and wheel on a mouse make it quick and easy to issue sequences of commands.

Trackballs come in different shapes, sizes, and configurations. Some trackballs are large and heavy with a ball about the same size as a cue ball. Others are much smaller. Most trackballs feature two buttons, although three or more buttons are also available on some models. Trackball units also are available in right- and left-handed models.

TOUCHPADS AND POINTING STICKS

The **trackpad** (also called a **touchpad**) is a stationary pointing device that many people find less tiring to use than a mouse or trackball. The movement of a finger across a small touch-sensitive surface is translated into pointer movement on the computer screen. The touch-sensitive surface may be only 1.5 or 2 inches square, so the finger never has to move far. The trackpad's size makes it ideal for a notebook computer, and most notebooks now contain one in front of the keyboard. Some notebook models feature a built-in trackpad as the only pointing device (see Figure 2.15).

Trackpads usually include two or three buttons that perform the same functions as mouse buttons. Trackpads are also "strike sensitive," meaning you can tap the pad with your fingertip instead of using its primary button.

Many portable computers now feature a small **pointing stick** positioned near the middle of the keyboard, typically between the G and H keys. The pointing stick is controlled with either forefinger,

Pointing stick

Touchpad

Figure 2.15 Some notebook computers and desktop keyboards feature a built-in trackpad.

and it controls the movement of the pointer on screen. Because users do not have to take their hands off the keyboard to use this device, it can save a great deal of time and effort. Two buttons that perform the same function as mouse buttons are just beneath the spacebar and are pressed with the thumb. Several generic terms have emerged for this device; many manufacturers refer to it as an **integrated pointing device**, while others call it a 3-D point stick. On the Lenovo ThinkPad line of notebook computers, the pointing device is called the **TrackPoint**.

TOUCH SCREENS

Touch screens accept input by allowing the user to place a fingertip directly on the computer screen. Most touch screen computers use sensors on the screen's surface to detect the touch of a finger, but other touch screen technologies are in use as well.

Computers and terminals with a single purpose, like ticketing kiosks at an airport and order-entry screens for waiters in restaurants, provide touch screens so users can make a selection from a menu of choices. Smart phones and tablet PCs have a much more sophisticated use of touch screens, allowing users to drag items around the screen with their finger, double-tap to open programs, and make windows larger or smaller by moving their thumb and forefinger apart or together.

Figure 2.16 Touch screen interfaces are common where most commands can be made by one-tap selections.

Touch screens work well in environments where dirt or weather would render keyboards and pointing devices useless, and where a simple, intuitive interface is important. As well as smart phones and tablet PCs, they have become common in restaurants, department stores, drugstores, and supermarkets, where they are used for all kinds of purposes, from creating personalized greeting cards to selling lottery tickets.

2.3 Inputting Data in Other Ways

Although the keyboard and the mouse are the input devices that people use most often, there are many other ways to input data into a computer. Sometimes the tool is simply a matter of choice. Some users just prefer the feel of a trackball over a mouse. In many cases, however, an ordinary input device may not be the best choice. In a dusty factory, for example, a standard keyboard or mouse can be damaged if it becomes clogged with dirt. Grocery checkout lines would slow down dramatically if cashiers had to manually input product codes and prices. In these environments, specialized input devices tolerate extreme conditions and reduce the risk of input errors.

Alternative input devices are important parts of some special-purpose computers. Tapping a handheld computer's screen with a pen is a much faster way to input commands than typing on a miniature keyboard. Sometimes a specialized device can give new purpose to a standard system. If you want to play action-packed

games on your home PC, for example, you may have more fun if you use a joystick or game controller than a standard keyboard or mouse.

This section examines several categories of alternative input devices and discusses the special uses of each. You may be surprised at how often you see these devices, and you may find yourself relying on one of these devices for your own computer work in the future.

DEVICES FOR THE HAND

Most input devices are designed to be used by hand. Even specialized devices like touch screens enable the user to interact with the system by using his or her fingertips. Unlike keyboards and mice, many of these input devices are highly intuitive and easy to use without special skills or training.

Pens Pen-based systems—including many tablet PCs, personal digital assistants, and other types of handheld computers—use a pen for data input. This device is sometimes called a stylus. You hold the pen in your hand and write on a special pad or directly on the screen. You also can use the pen as a pointing device, like a mouse, to select commands by tapping the screen.

Because handwriting recognition is so complex, pen-based computers are not used to enter large amounts of text, although they are used frequently for taking notes, creating short messages, and writing annotations on electronic documents. PDAs and tablet PCs are popular for these kinds of tasks, which do not require keyboarding.

Artists who create images on a computer often use special graphics tablets like the Wacom Cintiq, which combine extra-sensitive touch screens and pens that allow the artist to create both quick sketches and intricate images.

Pen-based computers are commonly used for data collection, where the touch of a pen might place a check in a box to indicate a part that must be ordered or a service that has been requested. Another common use is for inputting signatures or messages that are stored and transmitted as a graphic image, such as a fax. When delivery-service drivers drop off packages, they often have recipients sign their names on such a computer-based pad. In some cases, the input pen is also the computer. The Livescribe Echo Pen is a pen that writes with real ink on special dotted paper. As the user writes, a computer in the pen stores both the writing motions and nearby sounds, saving a spoken lecture along with the written notes. The notes and audio can be reviewed together, and can be transferred from the pen to a PC, searched for keywords, and shared with others.

Game Controllers Personal computers are widely used as gaming platforms, challenging dedicated video game units like the Sony PlayStation and others. If your computer is connected to the Internet, you can play games with people around the world. A game controller can be considered an input device because a computer game is a program, much like a word processor. A game accepts input from the user, processes data, and produces output in the form of graphics and sound. As computer games have become more detailed and elaborate, more specialized **game controllers** have been developed to take advantage of their features.

If you have ever used a video gaming system, you are familiar with **game pads**. A game pad is a small, flat device designed to be held with both hands. Newer game pads provide an array of buttons, triggers and thumb-driven joysticks that enable the user to send complex commands to the game system.

In recent years, game systems such as the Nintendo Wii have introduced support for wireless controllers that transmit input based on their location as well as through buttons on the controller. The system tracks the position of the controller as the user moves it through the air, translating that motion into actions within the game.

OPTICAL INPUT DEVICES

For a long time, futurists and computer scientists have had the goal of enabling computers to "see." Computers may never see in the same way that humans do, but optical technologies allow computers to use light as a source of input. These tools fall into the category of optical input devices.

Bar Code Readers **Bar code readers** are one of the most widely used input devices. The most common type of bar code reader is the flatbed model, which is commonly found in supermarkets and department stores. Workers for delivery services, such as FedEx, also use handheld bar code readers in the field to identify packages.

Figure 2.17   Game console controllers provide many different types of controls on a single input device.

These devices read **bar codes**, which are patterns of printed bars that appear on product packages. The bar codes identify the product. The bar code reader emits a beam of light—frequently a laser beam—that is reflected by the bar code image. A light-sensitive detector identifies the bar code image by recognizing special bars at both ends of the image. These special bars are different, so the reader can tell whether the bar code has been read right-side up or upside down.

After the detector has identified the bar code, it converts the individual bar patterns into numeric digits that the computer can understand. The reader then feeds the data into the computer, as though the number had been typed on a keyboard.

A new format for storing data visually is called the **QR Code**. Short for Quick Response, the code appears as a square filled with dots and lines. Different kinds of optical scanners—even a smart phone with a camera and the right software will work—can read and interpret these codes. They are used for a wide variety of purposes, including tracking items in a business or directing a cell phone to open a specific web address in a browser.

Figure 2.18   Bar codes appear on practically anything that needs to be tracked and counted.

Figure 2.19 A QR Code reader on a smartphone can take you to a Web site or provide additional information.

Image Scanners and Optical Character Recognition (OCR) The bar code reader is a special type of image scanner. **Image scanners** (also called scanners) convert any printed image into electronic form by shining light onto the image and sensing the intensity of the light's reflection at every point. Figure 2.20 illustrates the scanning process.

Color scanners use filters to separate the components of color into the primary additive colors (red, green, and blue) at each point. Red, green, and blue are known as primary additive colors because they can be combined to create any other color. Processes that describe color in this manner are said to use RGB color.

The image scanner is useful because it translates printed images into an electronic format that can be stored in a computer's memory. Then you can use software to organize or manipulate the electronic image. For example, if you scan a photo, you can use a graphics program such as Adobe Photoshop to increase the contrast or adjust the colors.

If you have scanned a text document, you might want to use **optical character recognition (OCR) software** to translate the image into text that you can edit. Despite the complexity of the task, OCR software has become quite advanced. Today, many programs can decipher a page of text received by a fax machine. In fact, computers with fax modems can use OCR software to convert faxes directly into text that can be edited with a word processor.

Scanners come in a range of sizes from handheld models to flatbed scanners that sit on a desktop. Handheld scanners are more portable but typically require multiple passes to scan a single page because they are not as wide as letter-size paper. Flatbed scanners offer higher-quality reproduction than do handheld scanners and can scan a page in a single pass. (Multiple scans are sometimes required for color images, however.)

Biometric Scanners Scanners can be used for more than just processing coded patterns of ink. **Biometric scanners** are used to analyze physical patterns in humans.

One common form of biometric scanner is the fingerprint scanner. The scanner is able to detect the print pattern of a finger that is pressed against the scanner, and relay a digital representation of that print to a computer. Banks, private companies and even notebook computers may use fingerprint scanners to grant access to accounts, buildings and data. Passwords and security cards can be forgotten or stolen; a fingerprint does not have those liabilities.

Biometric scanners can be used in a variety of ways for research as well as security. Human faces can be scanned both for their physical properties and for emotional expressions and responses, aiding behavioral scientists. Marketing, military and medical researchers also use eye-tracking scanners, which use scanner hardware both on a subject's head and in the room to identify precisely where the subject is looking.

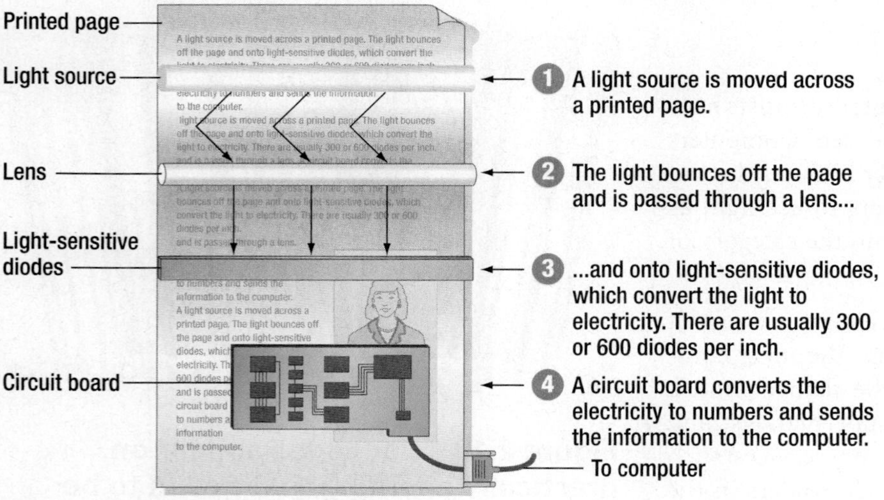

AUDIO INPUT DEVICES

Today, many new PCs are equipped with complete multimedia capabilities. Computers have features that enable them to

Printed page
Light source
Lens
Light-sensitive diodes
Circuit board

1 A light source is moved across a printed page.

2 The light bounces off the page and is passed through a lens...

3 ...and onto light-sensitive diodes, which convert the light to electricity. There are usually 300 or 600 diodes per inch.

4 A circuit board converts the electricity to numbers and sends the information to the computer.

To computer

Figure 2.20 How an image is scanned.

Figure 2.21 Keyboards and other electronic instruments can be connected together—and to a computer—by using the MIDI interface.

use a microphone to record your voice and create files on disk. You can embed these files in documents, use them in Web pages, or e-mail them to other people. There is also a demand for translating spoken words into text, much as there is a demand for translating handwriting into text. Translating voice to text is a capability known as **speech recognition** (or **voice recognition**). With it, you can dictate to the computer instead of typing, and you can control the computer with simple commands, such as Open or Cancel.

Speech recognition software and hardware have applications beyond simple commands. Users who are blind or have mobility disabilities can use special computers that combine speech recognition hardware and software, such as Dragon's NaturallySpeaking, to control their computer's activity. Combining the computer with hardware to control lights, heating and other environmental systems allows disabled users to take control of those systems simply by speaking.

Microphones vary greatly in quality and design. The sensitivity and quality of the audio pickup are major factors in the microphone's performance, as is the method by which sound is transmitted to the computer.

In a microphone, physical sound waves are converted to electrical impulses. However, since all computer data is digital, those electrical signals must be further converted to the zeroes and ones that the computer can use.

Higher quality microphones often incorporate a digital converter in the microphone's design, reducing the chances for the sound data to be adversely affected as it travels to the computer. Lower grade microphones may simply transmit the analog electrical information to

record audio and video input and play it back. Now that sound capabilities are standard in computers, microphones are becoming increasingly important as input devices to record speech. Spoken input is used often in multimedia, especially when the presentation can benefit from narration.

There are many chat networks, like Skype and Microsoft's MSN Messenger, that support audio and video communication. If you have a microphone and speakers (or a headset with an attached microphone), you can use your PC for chatting and to place telephone calls.

Using simple audio recording software that is built into your computer's operating system, you can

Figure 2.22 Microphones from tabletop models to tiny headsets can be used for audio input.

Figure 2.23   By transmitting full-motion video to viewers, PC video cameras let people stay in touch and communicate over long distances.

the computer's sound subsystem for conversion, risking a loss in sound quality in the analog signal before it is converted to digital data.

As with most hardware and software, the user's needs factor heavily in selecting a microphone. Chatting with friends online can be done with practically any microphone, while speech recognition or broadcasting applications may require a better—and more expensive—model.

INPUTTING MUSIC

With the right kind of computer hardware, you may be able to input music from a CD, a tape player, or MP3 player.

If your computer has a built-in musical instrument digital interface (MIDI) port, or if you have a dedicated MIDI adapter, you can connect many kinds of electronic musical instruments to your computer. MIDI-based instruments can communicate with and control one another, and any PC can be used to control MIDI instruments and to record their output. MIDI is extremely popular among musicians of all stripes, who use it to write, record, and edit music, and even to control instruments and effects during performances.

VIDEO INPUT DEVICES

With the growth of multimedia and the Internet, computer users are adding video input capabilities to their systems in great numbers. Applications such as video conferencing enable people to use full-motion video images, which are captured by a **PC video camera**, and transmit them to a limited number of recipients on a network or to the world on the Internet. Videos are commonly used in presentations and on Web pages where the viewer can start, stop, and control various aspects of the playback. Social Web sites such as YouTube host millions of professional and amateur video clips for anyone to view.

A popular and inexpensive type of PC video camera—called a **webcam**—can sit on top of a PC monitor or be placed on a stand, so the user can "capture" images of himself or herself while working at the computer. This arrangement is handy for videoconferencing, where multiple users see and talk to one another in real time over a network or Internet connection.

Notebook computers contain a built-in video camera as standard equipment, typically mounted inside the case just over the top of the screen. Appearing as a tiny opening in the case, just a fraction of an inch across, the embedded camera is able to produce excellent video quality.

Using a **video capture card**, the user also can connect other video devices, such as DVD players and camcorders, to the PC. This enables the user to transfer images from the video equipment to the PC, and vice versa. Affordable video capture cards enable home users to edit their video footage like professionals.

DIGITAL CAMERAS

Digital cameras are portable, handheld devices that capture still images. Whereas film cameras capture images on specially coated film, digital cameras capture images electronically. The user can then copy the picture data to a PC, where the image can be edited, copied, printed, embedded in a document, or transmitted to another user.

Most digital cameras can store dozens to hundreds of high-resolution images at a time. Moving digital images from a digital camera to a computer is a simple process that uses standard cables, disks, or even infrared networking capabilities.

Digital cameras have become standard equipment for designers of all kinds. In the field of Web page design, for example, digital cameras enable designers

Fact Check

1. A touch screen typically identifies the position of the user's finger via
   a. sensors on the surface of the screen
   b. laser triangulation
   c. analog triangulation
2. Speech-recognition software relies on small individual sounds called
   a. vowels
   b. phonemes
   c. consonants
3. Digital cameras designed to work directly as video input for computers are called
   a. webcams
   b. single-pass scancams
   c. image scanners

to shoot a subject and quickly load the images onto their computers. Designers can update a Web site's illustrations quickly and regularly using digital cameras. Graphic designers can edit and enhance digital photographs in innumerable ways, using photo-editing software. For example, a landscape designer can use a digital camera to take a picture of a house, and then use landscape design software to modify the image to show how the house might appear with different landscaping.

2.4 Ergonomics and Input Devices

Any office worker will tell you that working at a desk all day can be extremely uncomfortable. Sitting all day and using a computer can be even worse. Not only does the user's body ache from being in a chair too long, but hand and wrist injuries can result from using a keyboard and mouse for long periods. Eyes can become strained from staring at a monitor for hours. Such injuries can be extreme, threatening the user's general health and ability to work.

Much is being done to make computers easier, safer, and more comfortable to use. **Ergonomics**, which is the study of the physical relationship between people and their tools—such as computers—addresses these issues. Now more than ever before, people recognize the importance of having ergonomically correct computer furniture and using proper posture and techniques while working with computers. (The term *ergonomically correct* means that a tool or a workplace is designed to work properly with the human body and thus reduces the risk of strain and injuries.)

REPETITIVE STRESS INJURIES

The field of ergonomics did not receive much attention until a certain class of injuries began appearing among workers who spend most of their time entering data on computer keyboards. These ailments are called **repetitive stress injuries (RSIs)** or repetitive strain injuries, and they result from continually using the body in ways it was not designed to work. One type of RSI that is especially well documented among computer users is **carpal tunnel syndrome**, a wrist or hand injury caused by using a keyboard for long periods of time.

AVOIDING KEYBOARD-RELATED INJURIES

If you use a computer frequently, you can avoid RSIs by adopting a few good work habits, and by making sure that your hardware and workspace are set up in an ergonomically friendly way.

When setting up your workspace, make it a priority to choose a comfortable, ergonomically designed chair. Your office chair should

- Allow you to adjust its height.
- Provide good lower-back support.
- Have adjustable armrests.

Your desk also should be well suited to computer use, like the one shown in the photo. The desk should hold your keyboard and mouse at the proper height, so that your hands are at the same height as your elbows (or a few inches lower) when you hold them over the keyboard.

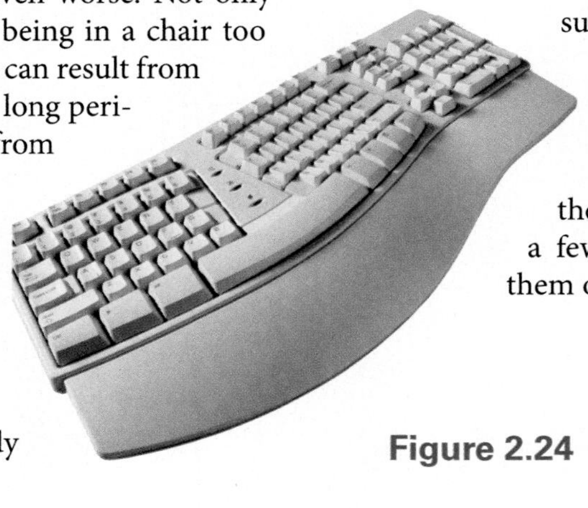

Figure 2.24 An ergonomic keyboard.

Here are some other tips that can help you avoid RSIs while working with your keyboard and mouse:

- **Use an ergonomic keyboard.** An ergonomic keyboard allows you to hold your hands in a more natural position (with wrists straight, rather than angled outward) while typing.

- **Use a padded wrist support.** If you type a lot, a wrist support can be helpful by allowing you to rest your hands comfortably when you are not typing. Remember, however, that you should never rest your wrists on anything—even a comfortable wrist support—while you type.

- **Keep your wrists straight.** When typing, your hands should be in a straight line with your forearms, when viewed either from above or from the side. Keeping the wrists bent in either direction can cause muscle fatigue.

- **Sit up straight.** Avoid slouching as you type, and keep your feet flat on the floor in front of you. Avoid crossing your legs in front of you or under your chair for long periods.

- **Learn to type.** You will use the keyboard more efficiently and naturally if you know how to type. If you "hunt and peck," you are more likely to slouch and keep your head down while looking at the keyboard. That not only slows you down, but it leads to fatigue and stiffness.

- **Take frequent breaks.** Get up and move around for a few minutes each hour, and stretch occasionally throughout the day.

Figure 2.25   A properly designed computer desk properly and safely positions the input and output hardware, and the user.

Fact Check

1. What is ergonomics?
   a. An exercise program designed to help you avoid injuries
   b. The study of efficient, cost-effective computer use
   c. The study of the physical relationship between people and their tools
2. List three behaviors that can help avoid repetitive stress injuries.

Key Terms

alphanumeric keys, 43
bar code reader, 49
bar code, 49
biometric scanners, 50
carpal tunnel syndrome, 53
click, 46
cursor, 43
cursor-movement keys, 43
digital camera, 52
double-clicking, 46
drag and drop, 46
drag-and-drop editing, 46
dragging, 46
ergonomics, 53
function keys, 43
game controller, 49

game pad, 49
image scanner, 50
insertion point, 43
integrated pointing device, 47
keyboarding, 43
mechanical mouse, 45
modifier keys, 43
numeric keypad, 44
optical character recognition
   (OCR) software, 50
optical mouse, 45
PC video camera, 52
pointer, 45
pointing device, 45
pointing, 45
port, 42

QR Code, 49
repetitive stress injury
   (RSI), 53
ribbon, 40
right-clicking, 46
scrolling, 46
speech recognition, 51
touch screens, 47
touchpad, 47
trackball, 46
trackpad, 47
TrackPoint, 47
USB port, 42
video capture card, 52
voice recognition, 51
webcam, 52

Key Terms QUIZ

Complete each statement by writing one of the terms listed under "Key Terms" in each blank.

1. Most personal computers use a(n) _____, which allows the user to interact with the computer by selecting graphical objects such as windows, menus, icons and buttons.

2. Many computer devices such as mice, digital cameras, and printers connect to the computer via a(n) _____.

3. The _____ are the collection of letter and number keys on a keyboard.

4. The row of command keys across the top of a keyboard (typically labeled F1, F2 and so on) are known as _____.

5. A(n) _____ uses a beam of light from its underside and an image processor to track its motion across a flat surface.

6. Computers use a(n) _____ to accept input by allowing the user to place a fingertip directly on the computer screen.

7. Scanners and smart phones can recognize and decode special square bar codes known as _____.

8. The image of a page of text can be translated back into editable text in a computer by using a type of program called _____.

9. Special optical scanners called _____ are used to analyze physical patterns in humans.

10. _____ is the study of the physical relationship between people and their tools.

Review QUESTIONS

In your own words, briefly answer the following questions or respond to the statements.

1. What are the four primary functions that an operating system performs?

2. List two main differences between a traditional and ribbon style of menu.

3. Why are most standard keyboards called QWERTY keyboards?

4. What does the CTRL key do?

5. What is the purpose of the mouse pointer?

6. How does an optical mouse work?

7. Identify three different places where you might see a touch screen being used.

8. Explain how a bar code reader reads a bar code and what it does with the information from a bar code.

9. Describe how a biometric fingerprint scanner can be more secure than using a password to guard against unauthorized use of your notebook computer.

10. List three things you can do to avoid repetitive stress injuries while using a computer.

Complete the following exercises as directed by your instructor.

LESSON LAB

1. Use your online help system to learn more about Windows. Click the Start button (in Windows Vista or System 7, it will be the button with just the Windows logo in the bottom left corner of the screen), and then choose **Help and Support** from the Start menu. Explore the Help window to learn more about the tools provided by the help system in your particular version of the operating system. (The exact features vary from one version of Windows to another.) When you are comfortable with the Help window, use any method you prefer to search for information on these topics: *operating system, GUI, command, dialog box, menu, and multitasking.* When you are finished, close the Help window.

2. Test your typing skills in Notepad. Click the Start button, point to All Programs, click Accessories, and then click Notepad to open the Notepad text-editing program. Notepad opens in a window. Have a classmate time you as you type a paragraph of text. The paragraph should be at least five lines long and should make sense. (For example, you could type a paragraph of text from any page in this book.) Do not stop to correct mistakes; keep typing until you are finished typing the selection. Trade places with the friend, and see how long each of you took to type the paragraph; compare the number of errors as well.

This lesson introduced the subject of ergonomics, the study of work design that minimizes the risk of injury. In this lesson, you'll revisit that topic by applying an important workplace ability: *critical thinking,* which brings together skills such as observation, interpretation, and evaluation to understand and apply information. In this case, you'll be learning about particular work settings—the places where you and your team members study—and applying what you know about ergonomics to help one another create environments where you can work more comfortably, effectively, and safely.

Divide into groups of two or three people. In your group, take turns describing the environment where you typically study. Using words, sketches, and demonstrations, give the others in the group enough information to help you evaluate the ergonomics of your work area. You might include information about furniture, computers and other equipment, location of supplies, and your posture while you work. Help each other think of ways to improve the worksites and avoid ergonomic injuries.

For each group member, create a list of three or more things that each person can do to improve his or her work area or behavior. Be prepared to share that list during class discussion.

LESSON 2B:
Output Devices

The computer is a tool that is built to serve its users, and arguably the most critical thing a computer can do is to provide a solution or an answer. We give computers input because we want a result. We give it image data so we can see a picture. We give it numbers and instructions so it can fill out our tax forms correctly. We provide it with digital representations of sound so we can listen to music.

It's no surprise, then, that output devices are evolving in variety and sophistication just as rapidly as the computer itself. Computer monitors have grown from small black squares with simple green letters to vivid, rich-colored widescreen displays providing images in fine detail. Sound systems evolved from a single, small onboard speaker suitable for little else than tinny beeps into surround-speaker configurations with full stereo support. Printers, originally just typewriters connected to a computer, now smoothly deliver full color documents at high speed.

In this lesson, you'll explore some of the latest versions of common output devices that help a computer to produce audio and visual information. You'll also learn a bit more about some of the less common, yet still important, ways that a computer can communicate with its user.

2.5 Monitors

Two important hardware devices determine the quality of the image you see on any monitor: the monitor itself and the video controller. A monitor has a display screen that is divided up into tiny dots, called **pixels** (a contraction of the term *pic*ture *el*ement). Each pixel has a unique address, which the computer uses to locate the pixel and control its appearance.

In general, two types of monitors are used with PCs (see Figure 2.26). The first, a **cathode ray tube (CRT)** monitor (named for the large vacuum tube that powers it), was once the typical monitor that came with most desktop computers. Though they are relatively low cost and their pictures are bright and sharp, CRT monitors have fallen out of favor because they are heavy and bulky and consume far more power than other display devices. They have been largely replaced by the **flat-panel display**, a much lighter-weight and thinner alternative. Notebook computers, as portable devices, have naturally always used flat-panel monitors.

Whether they have CRT or flat-panel displays, all monitors can be categorized by the way they display colors:

- **Monochrome monitors** display only one color (such as green, amber, or white) against a contrasting background, which is usually black. These monitors are used for text-only displays where the user does not need to see color graphics. Such monitors are rarely found in use with PCs.

- **Grayscale monitors** display varying intensities of gray (from a very light gray to black) against a white or off-white background and are essentially a type of monochrome monitor. Grayscale flat-panel displays, when used at all, are found in low-end portable systems—especially handheld devices—to keep costs down.

- **Color monitors** can display between 16 and 16 million colors, and if needed many color

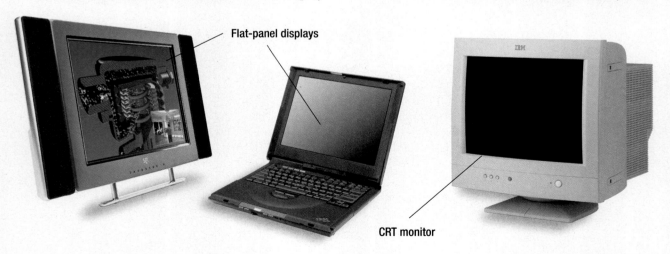

Flat-panel displays

CRT monitor

Figure 2.26 Types of monitors used with personal computers.

monitors can be set to work in monochrome or grayscale mode. Color monitors are by far the most commonly encountered display device on PCs today.

TYPES OF MONITORS

A CRT monitor works by shooting beams of electrons onto a glass screen coated with phosphors, chemicals that glow when struck by the electrons. Images are rendered by switching the beams on and off as they scan across the surface of the monitor, illuminating patterns of phosphor dots. The thick glass display, magnets for controlling the electron beam, and the distance required to properly produce and aim the beam, all contribute to a CRT monitor's heavy weight and bulky footprint.

There are several types of flat-panel monitors, but the most common is the **liquid crystal display (LCD)** monitor. An LCD monitor contains a light source, and a screen of special crystals placed in the monitor between the user and the light source. By default, the crystals do not allow light to shine through them; however, the crystals shift when electricity is applied to them, allowing light to pass through. By switching on specific pixels of crystals, patterns can be drawn on the monitor. LCD monitors use transistors to control the display of each pixel on the screen. The way transistors are used is determined by the type of LCD display:

- The **passive matrix LCD** relies on transistors for each row and each column of pixels, thus creating a grid that defines the location of each pixel. The color displayed by a pixel is determined by the electricity coming from the transistors at the end of the row and the top of the column.

- The **active matrix LCD** technology assigns at least one transistor to each pixel, and each pixel is turned on and off individually. Active matrix displays use **thin-film transistor (TFT)** technology, which employs as many as four transistors per pixel.

One disadvantage of LCD monitors is that their images can be difficult to see in bright light. For this reason, laptop computer users often look for shady places to sit when working outdoors or near

windows. A bigger disadvantage of LCD monitors, however, is their limited viewing angle. With most CRT monitors, you can see the image clearly even when standing at an angle to the screen. In LCD monitors, however, the viewing angle can shrink; as you increase your angle to the screen, the image can become fuzzy or dark, especially in older and very low-end models. Technological improvements have extended the viewing angles of flat-panel monitors over those older models, and many new LCD monitors show relatively little distortion or darkness even at a sharp angle.

Because LCD monitors employ a constant source of light behind the crystals—usually a fluorescent light bulb—some monitors may not display with consistent brightness across their entire surface. The farther from the bulb's position, the darker the monitor's display may become.

A new monitor design, called an **LED monitor**, works to correct this problem. LED monitors use the same liquid crystal design found in LCD monitors, but instead of a single electric light source, LED monitors are lit by a grid of tiny electronic lights called light emitting diodes (LEDs). By spreading the LED grid

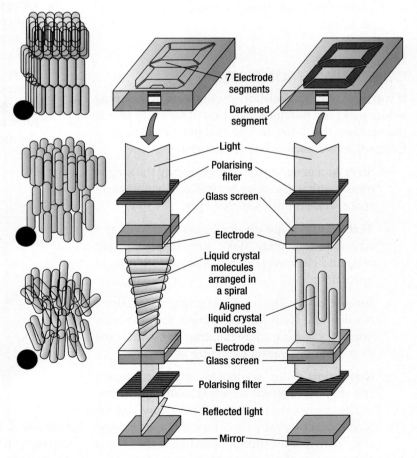

Figure 2.27   How an LCD monitor creates an image.

across the entire back surface of the monitor, a more consistent brightness can be achieved.

While flat-panel and CRT monitors are the most frequently used types of displays in PC systems, other kinds of monitors use specialized technologies and have specific uses:

- **Paper-white displays** are sometimes used by document designers such as desktop publishing specialists, newspaper or magazine compositors, and other persons who create high-quality printed documents. A paper-white display produces a very high contrast between the monitor's white background and displayed text or graphics, which usually appear in black.

- **Electroluminescent displays (ELDs)** are similar to LCD monitors but use a phosphorescent film held between two sheets of glass. A grid of wires sends current through the film to create an image.

- **Plasma displays** are created by sandwiching a special gas (such as neon or xenon) between two sheets of glass. When the gas is electrified via a grid of small electrodes, it glows. By controlling the amount of voltage applied at various points on the grid, each point acts as a pixel to display an image.

COMPARING MONITORS

If you need to buy a monitor, go comparison shopping before making a purchase. The best fit for every user is the monitor that looks best to that person's own eyes. Even so, several factors bear considering:

- **Size.** As a general rule of thumb, buy the largest monitor that fits your budget and your workspace, and still pleases your eyes.

- **Text display.** Open a document and look at a screen full of text. Make sure the letters are crisp and clear, without any trace of fuzziness or distortion.

- **Image display.** Open a photograph of something familiar and see if the colors meet your expectations. Try surfing some familiar Web sites if the store's demonstration computer allows it.

- **Resolution.** Your computer's video controller can support different screen **resolutions**, meaning the number of pixels that are displayed on the screen. Check what your computer supports, and make sure that the monitor you like in the store is compatible with the resolution you want to use.

- **Response rate.** The **response rate** of a monitor is the amount of time in milliseconds that it takes for a pixel to change from black to white. If you're playing graphically-intense games or watching movies, you'll want a faster response rate than if you're just surfing the web or chatting with friends.

- **Contrast ratio.** The liquid crystals in LCD monitors aren't able to completely shut off light on a "black" pixel, nor are they completely able to display pure light on a "white" pixel. The **contrast ratio** measures how close the monitor can get to perfect black and white. The bigger the ratio, the better.

- **Viewing angle.** LCD monitors produce the best picture when viewed from straight ahead. The **viewing angle** measures how far to the side a user can be before the picture fades or blurs.

- **Refresh rate.** The **refresh rate** identifies the number of times per second that the monitor draws its visible image. Most monitors are able to support at least 60Hz (refreshing the display 60 times each second), which is a common rate produced by video cards.

- **Dot pitch. Dot pitch** is the distance between the like-colored phosphor dots of adjacent pixels. In other words, if you measure the distance between the red dots of two adjacent pixels, you are measuring the monitor's dot pitch. Dot pitch is measured as a fraction of a millimeter (mm). As a general rule, the smaller the dot pitch, the finer and more detailed images will appear on the monitor.

Figure 2.28 With the right hardware, computers can use multiple monitors to create a single display.

VIDEO CARDS

The quality of the images that a monitor can display is defined as much by the **video card** (also called the *video controller* or the *video adapter*) as by the monitor itself. The video controller is an intermediary device between the CPU and the monitor. It contains the video-dedicated memory and other circuitry necessary to send information to the monitor for display on the screen. In many newer computers, the video circuitry is built directly into the motherboard, eliminating the need for a separate card. When users need high-end video capability for image editing or playing complex games, they typically use a separate higher-powered graphics card that plugs into a motherboard socket.

In the early days of personal computing, PC screens displayed only text characters and usually only in one color. These displays took little processing power because there were only a couple hundred or so characters to display in a limited area. But in order to support modern computing needs with high-resolution, high-quality color images, animations, and video, a large and dedicated amount of memory and processing power is required. Video controllers contain their own dedicated microprocessors and memory in order to free the CPU and system RAM from having to manage the millions of calculations and storage required to produce video output. The combination of the graphics processing unit (GPU)—the video card's microprocessor—and the amount of video RAM (or VRAM) available determines the relative power of the video controller.

Video cards now commonly provide more than just output for a single monitor. Most cards support at least two displays, allowing the computer to combine the display area and treat the two physical monitors as if they were a single device.

Though digital output is standard to match the digital signal that LCD monitors expect, many video cards also come with a digital-to-analog converter so that they can also drive older, analog displays. Many cards also support the high-definition HDMI output standard.

For very intense graphics—for example, video games that have a complex and fast-moving picture—

Figure 2.29 A video card supporting two monitors and HDMI output.

some video cards are designed to be linked together, allowing the user to install and connect multiple cards to share the processing load.

ERGONOMICS AND MONITORS

As you saw in Lesson 2A, a number of health-related issues have been associated with computer use. Just as too much keyboarding or improper typing technique can lead to hand or wrist injuries, too much time at a monitor can endanger your eyesight. Protecting your eyesight means choosing the right kind of monitor and using it correctly.

Eyestrain is one of the most frequently reported health problems associated with computers, but it is also one of the most easily avoided. Eyestrain is basically fatigue of the eyes, caused by focusing on the same point for too long. When you look at the same object (such as a monitor) for too long, the eye's muscles become strained. Think of how your arms would feel if you held them straight out for several minutes. Your shoulders and upper arms would soon begin to ache and feel weak; eventually you would have to rest your arms, or at least change their position. The same kind of thing occurs in eyestrain.

Experts say that eyestrain does not pose any long-term risks to eyesight, but it can lead to headaches. It also can reduce your productivity by making it

Figure 2.30 By positioning your monitor as shown here, you can avoid eyestrain and neck fatigue.

harder to concentrate on your work. Luckily, you can take several steps to reduce eyestrain when using a computer:

- If you work with a CRT monitor, choose a monitor that holds a steady image without flickering.

- Position your monitor so it is 2 to 2½ feet away from your eyes, with the screen's center a little below your eye level. Then, tilt the screen's face upward about 10 degrees, as shown in Figure 2.11. This angle will enable you to view the monitor comfortably without bending your neck. If you have vision problems that require corrective lenses, however, ask your optometrist about the best way to position your monitor.

- Place your monitor where no light reflects off the screen. If you cannot avoid reflections, use an *antiglare screen* to reduce the reflections on the screen.

- Keep your screen clean.

- Avoid looking at the monitor for more than 30 minutes without taking a break. When taking a break from the monitor, focus on objects at several different distances. It is a good idea to simply close your eyes for a few minutes to give them some rest.

- Do not let your eyes become dry. If dryness is a problem, ask your optometrist for advice.

Portable computers have all but replaced old-fashioned slide projectors and overhead projectors as the source of presentations. Instead of using photographic slides

Figure 2.31 Computer speakers can range from tiny ones included in a monitor to full surround-sound systems.

or overhead transparencies, more and more people are using software to create colorful slide shows and animated presentations. These images can be shown directly from the computer's disk and displayed on the PC's screen or projected on a wall or large screen.

2.6 Sound Systems

Microphones are important input devices, and speakers and their associated technologies are key output systems. Today, nearly any new multimedia-capable PC includes a complete sound system, with a microphone, speakers, a sound card, and a DVD/CD-ROM drive. Sound systems are especially useful to people who use their computer to create or use multimedia products, watch videos or listen to music, or participate in online activities such as videoconferences or distance learning. Sound systems also may support certain types of research, as described in the "Focus on the Issues" feature.

Speakers are common features on today's multimedia PCs. Top-of-the-line PC audio systems include premium sound cards and tweeters, midrange speakers, and subwoofers for sound quality that rivals home stereo systems.

Many computer users prefer listening to audio through headphones or a headset, rather than using speakers. These devices are helpful when using computers without high-quality speakers, when playing audio might disturb other people, or when the user wishes to better isolate the sound output from environmental noise. Headphones and headsets (which add a microphone to the unit) can be plugged directly into the sound card, and many desktop speaker systems also include a convenient jack to accept a headset plug.

The most complicated part of a computer's sound system is the sound card. A computer's **sound card** is a circuit board that converts sound from analog to digital form, and vice versa, for recording or playback. Analog signals are accepted from microphones or devices like MP3 players and converted into digital data for the computer to process. Inside the computer, digital data representing music can be sent to the sound card and converted to electrical current that speakers can play.

Similar to video cards, many new computers provide a sound subsystem directly on the

Focus on the Issues

Call of the Wild: Bioacoustic Research

Using high-tech hardware and software to "bug" the Earth's wild places from the African savannah to the ocean floor, scientists are gaining a better understanding of the secret lives of animals. Bioacoustics research gives scientists and researchers new insight into animal biodiversity by recording animal vocalization. This valuable statistical information yields a wealth of data about the health and behavior of indigenous animal populations.

Those listening to the calls of the wild hear sounds including clicks, rumbles, squawks, and whines as they try to interpret and analyze the sounds the creatures they study make. These bioacoustics researchers use sound to understand everything from the spawning habits of fish to the migratory path of herons to the social behaviors of humpback whales.

The Bioacoustics Research Program (BRP) at Cornell University is one of the world's leading bioacoustics programs. The computer software, techniques, and equipment developed at BRP for recording and analyzing sounds are used by scientists both at Cornell and around the world to study animal communication.

One of the key tools used by the Cornell team is an ARU—an autonomous acoustic recording device—which consists of a microphone (or hydrophone), amplifier, frequency filter, programmable computer, and specially developed software that schedules, records, and stores the acoustic data. The crucial features of the ARU are its small size, low power consumption, and large storage capacity (an ARU can collect up to 60 gigabytes of digital recordings).

One exciting application of the technology is the ongoing study of whale communication. BRP has several projects under way, recording ocean sounds in locations ranging from Southern California to the North Atlantic to the southern ocean. Subjects include the study of blue, finback, bowhead, minke, humpback, and the highly endangered North Atlantic right whale.

For the collection of whale sounds, researchers use a special ARU device, called a "pop-up," for undersea deployment. The pop-up is carried out to sea by ship or small boat and released, sinking to the ocean floor, where it hovers like a balloon tied to a brick. It contains a computer microprocessor, enough hard disks for up to six months of data storage, acoustic communications circuitry, and batteries, all sealed in a single 17-inch glass sphere. An external hydrophone is connected to the internal electronics through a waterproof connector. At the conclusion of a mission, the sphere separates itself from its anchor and "pops up" to the surface where it is recovered. Scientists then extract the data and process it to quantify ocean noises, detect endangered species, and describe the densities and distributions of different whale species.

Back on land, the computer workstation used by Cornell is powered by RAVEN, a software application for the digital acquisition, visualization, measurement, manipulation, and analysis of sound. RAVEN was developed by BRP with support from the National Science Foundation to provide a low-cost, user-friendly research and teaching environment tailored to the needs of biologists working with acoustic signals.

Together, this combination of technologies has given scientists some of "the best profiles of any endangered species yet," according to BRP.

motherboard and do not require a separate sound card for audio output. Separate sound cards are primarily used in newer computers by users who require specialized or premium sound output.

Some sound cards can also process digital signals to and from other digital devices such as DVD players and game consoles. Instead of electrical connectors, digital transmission is commonly done via fiber optic wire. Unlike analog transmissions, digital sound data does not degrade in quality as it travels through wires and connections, so unless the digital wire or transmitter is broken, the sound data at the receiving end is just as complete as what was sent.

With the appropriate software, you can do much more than simply record and play back digitized sound. Sound editing programs provide a miniature sound studio, allowing you to create, mix, and edit everything from single sound waves to complex multichannel orchestrations.

2.7 Printers

Over the past decade, the variety of available printing devices has exploded, serving both the needs of the average home and office user and the requirements of special applications such as banner and sign output, and extremely accurate color production.

Generally, printers fall into two categories: impact and nonimpact. An **impact printer** creates an image by striking an inked ribbon against paper with some physical instrument such as metal pins or hammers. A simple example of an impact printer is a typewriter, which uses small hammers to strike the ribbon. Each hammer is embossed with the shape of a letter, number, or symbol; that shape is transferred through the inked ribbon onto the paper, creating a printed character. **Nonimpact printers** use other means to create an image, applying ink to the page without physically striking a ribbon on the page.

At home and in businesses, three types of printers have become the most popular: dot matrix, inkjet, and laser. Within those three groups, consumers have hundreds of options, ranging widely in price and features.

TYPES OF PRINTERS

Dot matrix printers are impact printers commonly used in workplaces where physical impact with the paper is important, such as when the user is printing to carbon-copy or pressure-sensitive forms. As home and small office document printers, they are nowadays quite rare. A dot matrix printer creates an image by using a mechanism called a **print head**, which contains a cluster (or *matrix*) of short pins arranged in rows and columns. By pushing out pins in various combinations, the print head can create shapes and alphanumeric characters. With the correct pins pushed outwards, the print head strikes an ink ribbon against the paper to transfer the shape or character.

Inkjet printers are nonimpact printers that create an image directly on the paper by spraying ink through tiny nozzles (see Figure 2.33). The nozzles are mounted on a carriage that slides back and forth across the page, applying in the desired pattern as the page is fed through the printer. Color inkjet printers have four ink nozzles: cyan (blue), magenta (red), yellow, and black. For this reason, they are sometimes referred to as **CMYK printers**. These four colors are used in almost all color printing because it is possible to combine them to create any color. Inkjet printers

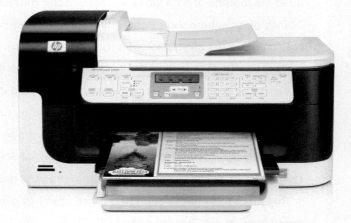

Figure 2.32   A multifunction printer.

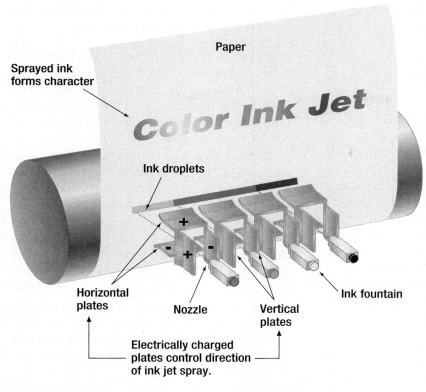

Figure 2.33 How an inkjet printer creates an image.

A **laser printer** is a nonimpact printer that relies on a laser to accomplish its printing. A CPU and memory are built into the printer to interpret the data that it receives from the computer and to control the laser. Figure 2.34 shows how a laser printer works. Just as the electron gun in a CRT monitor can target any pixel, the laser in a laser printer can aim at any point on a drum, creating an electrical charge. **Toner**, which is a powder composed of tiny particles of ink, sticks to the drum in the places the laser has charged. Then, with pressure and heat, the toner is transferred off the drum onto the paper. A color laser printer works like a single-color model, except that the process is repeated four times and a different toner color is used for each pass. The four colors used are the same as in the color inkjet printers: cyan, magenta, yellow, and black.

Several printer makers now use inkjet or laser printers as the basis for **all-in-one peripherals** (also called **multifunction peripherals**). These devices combine printing capabilities with scanning, photocopying, and faxing capabilities (see Figure 2.32). Small, lightweight, and easy-to-use all-in-one devices are popular in home offices and small

typically use one cartridge for each color and one black-only cartridge for black-and-white printing. This feature saves money by reserving colored ink only for color printing, and for allowing ink cartridges to be replaced individually as they are used.

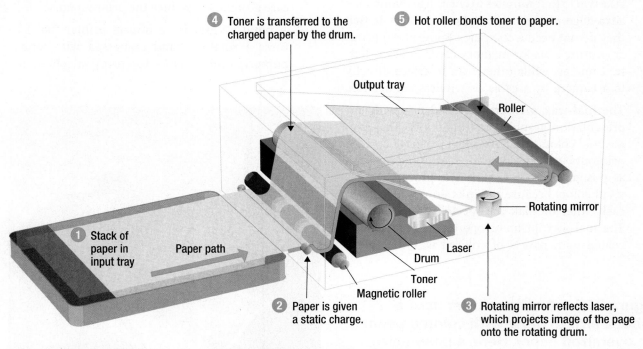

Figure 2.34 How a laser printer creates a printed page.

businesses, since they remove the need for filling up an office with several separate pieces of printer-related equipment.

Although most offices and homes use inkjet or laser printers, other types of printers are used for special purposes:

- Desktop publishers and graphic artists get realistic quality and color for photo images using **dye-sublimation (dye-sub) printers**. In dye-sublimation technology, a ribbon containing panels of color is moved across a focused heat source capable of subtle temperature variations. The heated dyes evaporate from the ribbon and diffuse on specially coated paper or another material, where they form areas of different colors. The variations in color are related to the intensity of the heat applied. Dye-sub printers create extremely sharp images, but they are slow and costly.

- With digital cameras and scanners becoming increasingly popular, users want to be able to print the images they create or scan. While the average color inkjet or laser printer can handle this job satisfactorily, some people are investing in special **photo printers**. Some photo printers use inkjet technology, and some use dye-sublimation technology. The best photo printers can create images that look nearly as good as a photograph printed using traditional methods. Photo printers work slowly; some can take two to four minutes to create a printout. One advantage of the newest photo printers is that they do not need a computer. Some photo printers feature slots for memory cards used by digital cameras, while others can interface directly to a camera by a cable or wireless connection.

- **Thermal-wax printers** are used primarily for presentation graphics and handouts. They create bold colors and have a low per-page cost for printouts with heavy color requirements, such as posters or book covers. The process creates vivid colors because the inks do not bleed into each other or soak the specially coated paper. Thermal-wax printers operate with a ribbon coated with panels of colored wax that melts

and adheres to plain paper as colored dots when passed over a focused heat source.

- A **plotter** is a special kind of output device. It is like a printer because it produces images on paper, but the plotter is typically used to print large-format images, such as construction drawings created by an architect. Table plotters use robotic arms, each of which holds a set of colored ink pens, felt pens, or pencils, for drawing on a stationary piece of paper. A variation on the table plotter is the roller plotter (also known as the drum plotter), which uses only one drawing arm but moves the paper instead of holding it flat and stationary. The drawing arm moves side to side as the paper is rolled back and forth through the roller. Working together, the arm and roller can draw perfect circles and other geometric shapes, as well as lines of different weights and colors. In recent years, mechanical plotters have been displaced by thermal, electrostatic, and inkjet plotters, as well as large-format dye-sub printers.

- A **line printer** is a special type of impact printer. It works like a dot matrix printer but uses a special wide print head that can print an entire line of text with a single strike. Line printers do not offer high resolution but are incredibly fast; the fastest can print 3,000 lines of text per minute. In addition to being fast, they can also be extremely noisy and sometimes are housed in a case designed to reduce the printing noise.

- A **band printer** is an impact printer that features a rotating band embossed with alphanumeric characters. To print a character,

Figure 2.35   A roller plotter uses a robotic arm to draw with colored pens on oversized paper. Here, a poster-size photograph is being printed.

the machine rotates the band to the desired character, and then a small hammer taps the band, pressing the character against a ribbon. Although this sounds like a slow process, band printers are very fast and very robust. Depending on the character set used, the fastest band printer can generate around 2,000 lines of text per minute.

COMPARING PRINTERS

As with monitors and most other kinds of computer hardware, the perfect printer for you is the one that best fits your needs and meets your expectations. If you only print letters and documents, you probably don't need a laser printer. If you need extremely crisp printing without a trace of soaking ink on the paper, an inkjet printer is the wrong choice. When you've decided on the style of printer that meets your needs, here are a few factors to consider when comparing models:

- **Image quality.** Image quality, also known as print resolution, is usually measured in **dots per inch (dpi)**. The more dots per inch a printer can produce, the higher its image quality. For example, typical inkjet and laser printers can print around 600 dots per inch, which is fine for most daily business applications. If a printer's resolution is 600 dpi, this means it can print 600 columns of dots and 600 rows of dots in each square inch of the page. High-quality laser printers, and professional printers used for creating colorful presentations, posters, or renderings, offer resolutions of 1,800 dpi and higher.

- **Speed.** Printer speed is measured in the number of **pages per minute (ppm)** the device can print. Most printers have different ppm ratings for text and graphics because graphics generally take longer to print. As print speed goes up, so does cost. Most consumer-level laser printers offer print speeds of 6 or 8 ppm, but high-volume professional laser printers can exceed 50 ppm. Be careful when comparing page-per-minute rates. Printer manufacturers often quote both the speed for draft printing (a lower quality, lower-resolution way of printing text) and full-quality output. A printer might be able to print 35 to 40 pages per minute in draft mode but only 5 or 6 per minute at full quality.

- **Initial and maintenance cost.** The cost of new printers has fallen dramatically in recent years, while their capabilities and speed have

improved just as dramatically. It is possible to buy a decent-quality inkjet or laser printer for personal use around $100. Check the price of the printer's ink or toner and how often you'll likely have to replace parts and ink. Consider the higher cost of color supplies, too, and any specialty paper you might need. Make sure you're aware of the full cost of a printer, not just the sale price.

2.8 Other Output Devices

Monitors, speakers and printers are far and away the most common devices used to deliver computer output to a user. There are many other devices, however, that can provide output for more specialized applications.

PROJECTORS

Overhead and movie projectors have been used for decades in business, education, and entertainment to display slides and moving images. Up until recently, all of those have been analog display devices; the image to be shown is placed on a transparent film, which is held in front of a bright light source, and a lens focuses and directs the light output onto a screen or wall.

Computers can easily show images on a monitor, but image projection is another matter. Digital computers cannot store and retrieve analog images. Every picture on your cell phone and desktop PC is

Fact Check

1. What does the term *CMYK printers* refer to?
   a. They were invented by a scientist named Joseph Cimyk.
   b. They perform their printing with four different-colored lasers.
   c. They use the colors cyan, magenta, yellow, and black for printing.
2. What is toner?
   a. An ink powder used in laser printing
   b. A spray applied to color printing to keep the color from fading
   c. Specially treated printer paper

Figure 2.36   A portable digital projector.

stored as binary data, so for a projector to work with a computer, it must be able to somehow convert that data to an analog image our eyes can see.

One early method for projecting digital images was made possible with the arrival of LCD monitor technology. As you've learned earlier in this chapter, an LCD monitor pairs a light source with a film that selectively allows light to pass through. If an LCD monitor minus its light source is placed on an overhead projector, the projector can serve as the light source and display the image just as if an ordinary slide transparency had been used. Though overhead-ready products were manufactured for a time, this method of digital image display is now more popular with do-it-yourselfers; you can easily find helpful how-to videos on the Internet for converting an LCD monitor to a computer-connected projector.

Digital projectors that can accept data directly from computers and display images first began to appear in the late 1980s. Many of these devices use a display method called **digital light processing (DLP)**, developed by Texas Instruments. DLP projectors use a special chip on which are mounted a grid of thousands—or in some cases millions—of microscopic mirrors. The mirrors can be individually shifted back and forth to either reflect the source light through a lens for projection, or away from the projection lens.

The mirrors correspond to the pixels of a monitor. Just as an LCD monitor can activate specific crystal dots on the screen in order to display a pattern, a DLP projector can flip specific mirrors toward the lens and project a pattern. Since mirrors can be switched on and off several thousand times each second, the brightness of each pixel can be increased or reduced by changing the amount of time the mirror is switched on. Because the human eye cannot detect such rapid changes, no flickering is perceived as the mirrors switch back and forth.

Color can be added to a DLP projector in a couple of ways. By passing light through a filter to create red, green, and blue light, and then timing each color with the mirror switching, the projector can blend bursts of colored light together at each pixel to create different color shades. Some projectors simply use three DLP chips dedicated to red, green, and blue light, and combine the output together to create the image.

Digital projectors can be placed on a table or permanently mounted on a wall or ceiling. They can accept data to output in a variety of ways. Nearly all digital projectors can serve simply as a monitor for the computer, hooked up with an ordinary digital monitor cable and projecting what would normally show up on the screen. More advanced models can accept output via a local network or multiple computers, and some can retrieve images and video from a USB flash drive.

Some projectors come with their own limited user interface, allowing users to directly configure the projector's options and issue display commands. Some, such as the InFocus IN3900, come with a digital wand that viewers can use to highlight and annotate an image, bringing digital projectors full circle to

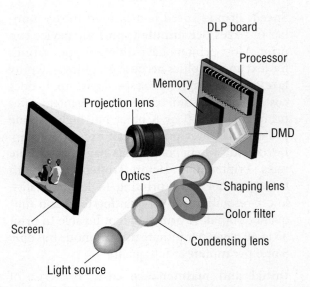

Figure 2.37   How a DLP projector works.

the days when a teacher or presenter could draw on analog overhead slides to highlight or demonstrate ideas.

SMART BOARDS

Even though image projectors can in some cases provide pointers to highlight and annotate, there are times when that isn't an effective substitute for scrawling on a white board. Teachers, business presenters, programmers, creative designers and many others rely on whiteboards to teach and rapidly create pictures and words to share with others in the room.

To meet that need, a company called SMART Technologies created the **SMART Board**, a digital version of the analog whiteboard. The latest models combine an array of input and output devices to create a whiteboard that seems more like a wall-sized smart phone or tablet computer than a chalkboard from the past.

SMART Boards are attached to the wall in the same manner as an ordinary whiteboard. The board itself is a touch-sensitive input device, similar in concept to the touch screen on a smart phone. A digital **short-throw projector** (a projector designed to be used very close to the display area) is installed at the top of the board. Special pens and an eraser are included in a tray at the board's bottom. The

Figure 2.38 SMART Boards can display pictures, respond to touch, and digitally save whatever users draw on them.

SMART Board connects to a computer that collects input from the board and provides output to be displayed.

A SMART Board user can draw on the white board with one of the provided pens, a finger, or practically anything else. As the user draws and writes, the touch-sensitive board transfers that input to the computer, which updates a digital image that it transmits to the projector for display. The board appears to fill with text and drawings, even though no actual ink is being used.

Because all the writing and drawing is digitally stored, the SMART Board and its software programs can do things that no ordinary whiteboard can accomplish. Presenters and teachers can explain and illustrate concepts on the board, and then later send images of their writing to others directly from the computer via email or a local network, removing the need for others to copy or transcribe the writing. The computer can provide background images and shapes, and allow users to drag and place those shapes by fingertip on the whiteboard. The computer can also provide command icons at the edge of the whiteboard, giving users the ability to issue commands to the computer simply by tapping the appropriate icon on the board.

HAPTIC TECHNOLOGY

All the output devices you've learned about so far have been concentrated on sight and sound. Monitors and projectors provide visual output. Speakers provide sounds. But what about the sense of touch?

In limited ways, computers provide touch feedback as well. The communication of vibration, motion or physical resistance to a user is called **haptics** or **haptic feedback**. Haptic devices can enhance other kinds of feedback and output from computers to make them more relevant or noticeable.

One of the most common devices using haptic technology is the handheld smart phone or PC. Many cell handheld devices contain a little vibrator that can buzz not only for incoming calls, but can also be triggered at appropriate moments when running a software program. For example, a user's experience watching a boulder fall to the bottom of the screen in a game can be enhanced by having the phone give a little shake as it hits.

Game controllers for consoles and PCs commonly have similar mechanical motion generators, to increase the sense of immersion for users who are driving, flying or shooting things on the screen.

Figure 2.39 Haptic feedback provides resistance to simulate the pressure of holding an object.

The application of motion to a controller in conjunction with a visual event (for example, giving the steering wheel controller a bump when your car goes off the road in a computer game) is known as **force feedback**.

Beyond the gaming world, haptic feedback is found in many places. In both modern aircraft and flight simulators, haptics are sometimes used in digital control systems like joysticks to provide feedback to pilots that could once be felt in the analog controls of older airplanes. Hardware systems that remotely control robots and robotic arms, for example to handle radioactive or toxic materials, may contain

haptic technology to let operators feel resistance as they move controls to twist, squeeze and lift with the remote machines.

COMPUTER-AIDED MANUFACTURING

Sometimes, computer output involves more motion that just the sensory nudge provided by haptic technology.

Computer output is used to drive industrial machinery and robot production in many different industries and manufacturing. Auto assembly factories, once filled with lines of people welding and installing parts, are now in many areas staffed by rows of robots. Robotic arms and welders, controlled by computer output, retrieve automotive parts, position them, and weld them into place. Computer

Figure 2.40 Computer controlled robotic arms creating automobile frames.

Fact Check

1. Digital light processing
   a. uses a chip containing millions of microscopic mirrors to project images.
   b. can only display black and white images, because it is a binary system.
   c. employs a special video card called a Light Processing Unit (LPU).
2. A SMART Board combines a whiteboards and a computer in order to
   a. allow people to write on the board by speaking out loud.
   b. support video games that require the user to hit a moving target.
   c. simulate the use of a wall-sized tablet computer with touch input and digital output.
3. Haptic devices are
   a. special video cards that also provide audio support.
   b. devices that use vibration or motion to enhance the user's experience.
   c. virtual-reality systems, commonly including a headset that fits over the user's eyes.

instructions coordinate and control several differ-ent motors in a robotic arm to position it in exactly the right place at exactly the right time to perform its operation. So long as no malfunctions occur, the robot arm will perform its task exactly the same way every time, ensuring that all of the products are assembled to the same level of quality.

That same style of manufacturing can be found everywhere, from factories creating ready-to-assemble furniture with the right holes drilled in the right place for each piece, or metal fabrication shops where sheets of metal are cut and bent to create precise and consis-tent parts. Computers—even the ones we use to pro-gram and control the manufacturing machines—have many parts that are created by computer-controlled manufacturing. The process of creating computer chips out of silicon wafers is far too complex for humans to accomplish on their own.

IN Summary

- Modern computer monitors are most commonly flat-panel displays that activate grids of tiny crystals to form patterns through which a light shines. Older CRT monitors relied on beams of electrons to activate glowing phosphors on a heavy, glass screen. Video cards provide extra processing power to run the monitor; the quality of the image is typically a combination of the design of the monitor and the detail in the output data.

- Sound systems are especially useful to people who use their computer to create or use multimedia products, watch videos or listen to music, or participate in online activities such as videoconferences or distance learning.

- The two most commonly used types of printers are inkjet, which sprays tiny jets of ink onto the page to form letters and shapes; and laser, which uses a laser to direct the placement of toner, and pressure and heat to apply the toner to the page.

- Less common output devices include digital projectors, which project their image onto a wall; SMART Boards, which use a touch-sensitive white board both to accept input and display projected output; haptic devices that provide vibration and other forms of motion feedback; and robotic machinery used in computer-aided manufacturing tasks.

Key Terms

active matrix LCD, 61
all-in-one peripherals, 67
band printer, 68
cathode ray tube (CRT), 60
CMYK printers, 66
color monitor, 60
contrast ratio, 62
digital light processing
  (DLP), 70
dot matrix printers, 66
dot pitch, 62
dots per inch (dpi), 69
dye-sublimation (dye-sub)
  printers, 68
electroluminescent displays
  (ELDs), 62
eyestrain, 63

flat-panel display, 60
force feedback, 72
grayscale monitor, 60
haptic feedback, 72
haptics, 72
impact printer, 66
inkjet printers, 66
laser printer, 67
line printer, 68
LED monitor, 61
liquid crystal display (LCD), 61
monochrome monitor, 60
multifunction peripherals, 67
nonimpact printer, 66
pages per minute (ppm), 69
paper-white displays, 62
passive matrix LCD, 61

photo printers, 68
pixels, 60
plasma displays, 62
plotter, 68
print head, 66
refresh rate, 62
resolution, 62
response rate, 62
short-throw projector, 71
SMART Board, 71
sound card, 64
thermal-wax printers, 68
thin-film transistor (TFT), 61
toner, 67
video card, 63
viewing angle, 62

Key Terms QUIZ

Complete each statement by writing one of the terms listed under "Key Terms" in each blank.

1. The smallest area on a monitor that can be accessed and changed is a dot called a(n) _____.

2. The _____ measures how close an LCD monitor can get to perfect black and white colors.

3. In most PCs, a device called the _____ sends information to the monitor for display on the screen.

4. A computer's _____ is a circuit board that converts sound from analog to digital and vice versa.

5. Color inkjet printers that use the four colors cyan, magenta, yellow and black are known as _____ printers.

6. Laser printers use a black powder called _____ to create letters on a page.

7. A _____ is a large-format printer that uses a robotic arm to draw with a set of colored pens or pencils.

8. Digital projectors often use a technology called _____, which shines light on a special computer chip containing thousands or millions of microscopic, individually controlled mirrors.

9. A(n) _____ combines input and projected output on a touch-sensitive white board.

10. Game console controllers sometimes employ _____ to vibrate the controller in concert with events happening in the computer game.

Review QUESTIONS

In your own words, briefly answer the following questions or respond to the statements.

1. Describe how an LCD monitor controls each pixel.

2. Explain the difference between an LCD and an LED monitor.

3. What is an LCD monitor's *response rate*, and how does a monitor's response rate affect someone playing an intense video game or watching an action movie?

4. Explain a benefit of transmitting sound data digitally between devices, rather than using analog electrical signals.

5. In what general situation would a dot-matrix printer be an ideal choice to use?

6. Describe the printing process used by an inkjet printer.

7. List three factors to consider when shopping for a printer.

8. Explain how digital light processing (DLP) works to project an image onto a screen or wall.

9. How does a SMART Board combine input and output to allow a user to draw on a digital image?

10. List at least three places where haptic technology can be found.

Complete the following exercises as directed by your instructor.

1. Print a test page for your computer's default printer. (Note: This exercise assumes you are using Windows 7. If you have a different operating system, ask your instructor for specific directions.)

   a. On your Windows desktop, click the Start button. On the right side of the Start menu, click *Devices and Printers*. This will open a window showing the various devices that are connected to the computer.

   b. In the device window, find the default printer in the *Printers* and *Faxes* section. The default printer will have a check-marked green circle over its picture. Right click the default printer, and select *Printer properties* (this is not the same as simply *Properties*, which will be at the bottom of the popup menu).

   c. The printer's properties window should open with the *General* tab visible. Click the button in that window that says, *Print Test Page*.

   d. This should print a fact sheet to the printer. Though it does not show off any of the printer's fancy features, the test page verifies that the printer is working properly.

   e. Collect the test page from the printer, and look it over. Note your computer's name, the printer's name, and the type and model of the printer on that sheet.

   f. When you are done, close all of the windows opened during this lab.

2. Examine your computer's monitor.

   a. First, look at the monitor attached to your computer. What brand and model is it? What other information can you get from the monitor by looking at its exterior? (Remember to look at the back.)

   b. Next, measure the monitor. What is the diagonal measurement of the monitor's front side? What is the viewing area, measured diagonally?

   c. Visit the manufacturer's Web site and see if you can find any additional information about your specific monitor.

One way or another, businesses run on information, so workers in all fields must be able to communicate clearly and accurately. Part of getting the message across is to choose your mode of communication—speech, writing, and pictures, for example. You want to put your message out there in a way that will generate the necessary attention, interest, and understanding.

This exercise tests the impact of different modes of communication. Start by dividing into pairs. Your instructor will direct you whether to continue this exercise during the next class or by meeting with your partner before the next class session.

Before you meet with your partner, choose a place you have lived in or visited that your partner might not be familiar with. Your location can be on campus or halfway around the world; it can be famous or known only to you. What matters is that you know some details about the place and can describe it. Find or draw a picture and/or a map of the place.

During your meeting with your partner, one of you begins by using words to describe your place. Invite questions, and continue describing the place in words until the partner says he or she can understand what you are describing. Then share your picture and map, showing information about the place. Next, switch roles, and repeat the process.

Discuss how well you understood the description without pictures. Did the pictures clarify the description? What if the presenter had used words and pictures at the same time—would that have been easier to understand, or would the pictures have been a distraction from the words? How well would you have learned from just pictures and no words? After your discussion, write a brief paragraph recommending the combination of words, pictures, and/or other media you would post on a Web site promoting a city or resort to tourists.

[*Chapter* LABS]

Complete the following exercises using a computer in your classroom, lab, or home.

1. Check your keyboard's repeat rate. You can control the length of time your keyboard "waits" as you hold down an alphanumeric key before it starts repeating the character. You also can set the repeat speed. In this exercise, check the repeat settings, but do not change any settings without your instructor's permission.

   a. Click the Start button on the Windows taskbar to open the Start menu.

   b. Click **Control Panel**, and then double-click the **Keyboard** icon in the Control Panel window. If you are using Windows Vista or System 7, you can single-click the Keyboard icon or link (if you don't see a list of icons in the Control Panel window, try changing your **View by** setting near the upper right corner of the window).

   c. Click the **Speed** tab at the top of the **Keyboard Properties** window that appears. Drag the **Repeat delay** and **Repeat rate** indicators all the way to the right, then to the left , and in different combinations. Test the repeat rate at each setting by clicking in the test box and then holding down an alphanumeric key.

   d. Drag the **Cursor blink rate** indicator to the right and left. How fast do you want your cursor to blink?

   e. Click **Cancel** to close the dialog box without making changes.

2. Mouse practice. Perform the following steps:

   a. Click the Start button on the Windows taskbar to open the Start menu.

   b. Point to **All Programs**, click **Accessories**, and then click **WordPad**. The WordPad program will open in its own window. (WordPad is a "lightweight" word-processing application.) Notice the blinking insertion point in the window.

   c. Type: **Now is the time for all good men to come to the aid of their country.**

   d. Using your mouse, click in different parts of the sentence. The insertion point moves wherever you click.

   e. Double-click the word *good*. The word becomes selected: the letters change from black to white, and the background behind the word changes color.

   f. Right-click the selected word. A shortcut menu appears.

   g. Choose the Cut option. The highlighted word disappears from your screen.

   h. Click in front of the word *country* to place the insertion point; right-click again. When the shortcut menu appears, choose Paste. The word good reappears.

   i. Double-click the word *good* again to select it. Now click on the selected word and drag it to the left while holding down the mouse button. (A little mark appears on the mouse pointer, indicating that you are dragging something.) When the mouse pointer arrives in front of the word *men*, release the mouse button. The word *good* is returned to its original place.

   j. Continue practicing your mouse techniques. When you are finished, close the WordPad program by clicking the CLOSE button (the button marked with an X) in the upper right corner of the window. The program will ask if you want to save the changes to your document; choose **No**.

3. What is your resolution? Like the color setting, your system's screen resolution can affect the quality of your computing experience. If your resolution is set too high, text and icons may be too small to view comfortably, and you may strain your eyes. If the resolution is too low, you will spend extra time navigating to parts of your applications that do not fit on the screen. Try different settings to find what works best for you.

   a. Click the Start button to open the Start menu. Next, click Control Panel. The Control Panel window opens.
   b. Double-click the Display icon. The Display Properties dialog box opens.
   c. Click the Settings tab. Note the current setting in the Screen resolution box and write it down.
   d. Click the Screen resolution slider control, and drag it to the lowest setting. Then click Apply. Follow any instructions that appear on your screen. (Your computer may restart.)
   e. Open a program or two, and look at the screen. How does it look? Note your impressions.
   f. Repeat steps (a) through (e), this time choosing the highest setting. Again, note your impressions.
   g. Repeat steps (a) through (e), and select the system's original resolution setting.

[*Think* AND DISCUSS]

As directed by your instructor, discuss the following questions in class or in groups.

1. Despite the rapid advancements being made with handwriting-recognition software, do you think that the keyboard will continue to be the preferred input device for generating text? Why or why not? If you could invent the ultimate method for computer input, what would it be? Handwriting or speech recognition? Something else?

2. The mouse is a standard staple of most desktop and notebook systems. Touch screens, however, are used almost exclusively for handheld devices and newer tablet PCs. Do you think that touch screens might some day replace the traditional monitor and mouse for desktop PCs? Explain your reasoning. Make a list of three advantages or obstacles that touch screens could present for desktop PC users.

[*Fact Check* ANSWERS]

2A:

LO2.1 User Interfaces
1: **b.** the user performs operations primarily with graphical objects
2: **a.** The main workspace where shortcuts to files and programs are displayed
3: **a.** a prompt for entering commands and no graphic elements to select

LO2.2 Common Input Devices

1: alphanumeric, modifier, function, cursor-movement, numeric keypad
2: **c.** Opens the Windows Start menu on Windows-based computers
3: **c.** opens a menu of choices related to the object that was right-clicked
4: **a.** left-clicking

LO2.3 Inputting Data in Other Ways

1: **a.** sensors on the surface of the screen
2: **b.** phonemes
3: **a.** webcams

LO2.4 Ergonomics and Input Devices

1: **c.** The study of the physical relationship between people and their tools
2: use an ergonomic keyboard; use a padded wrist support; keep your wrists straight; sit up straight; learn to type; take frequent breaks

2B:

LO2.5 Monitors

1: **b.** Flat-panel
2: **a.** the graphics processing unit of a video card

LO2.6 Sound Systems

1: **b.** typically includes a microphone, speakers, a sound card, and a DVD/CD-ROM drive
2: **a.** converts sound from analog to digital form and vice versa

LO2.7 Printers

1: **c.** They use the colors cyan, magenta, yellow, and black for printing.
2: **a.** An ink powder used in laser printing

LO2.8 Other Output Devices

1: **a.** uses a chip containing millions of microscopic mirrors to project images.
2: **c.** simulate the use of a wall-sized tablet computer with touch input and digital output.
3: **b.** devices that use vibration or motion to enhance the user's experience.

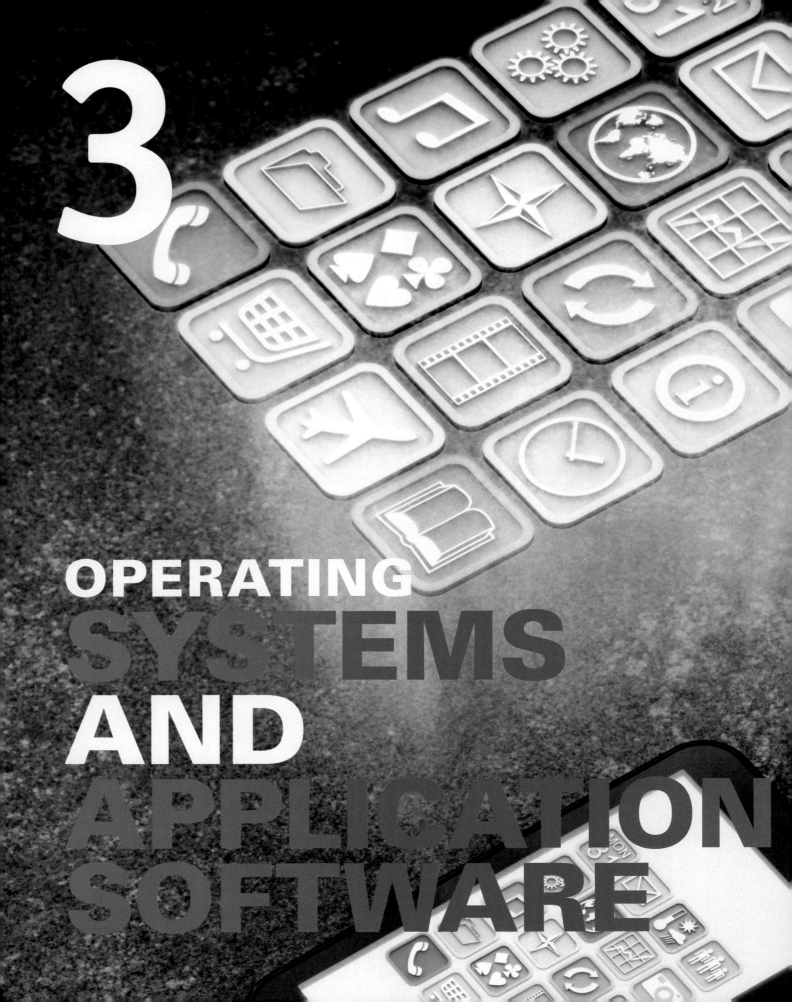

3

OPERATING SYSTEMS AND APPLICATION SOFTWARE

Chapter Overview

This chapter provides more detail about the methods a computer uses to move data between its hardware subsystems in order to produce information that is meaningful to the user. You'll also gain an understanding of how the computer stores data in files, and you'll learn about a selection of software you might use with computers, including the operating system, productivity software and graphics programs. What kinds of software (if any) have you already purchased or used for a home computer, smart phone, or game system? What would you like to try using?

LESSON 3A:
Operating System Basics

Hardware and software work together in a computer to create a useful machine. As data flows between the hard disk, memory, input and output devices, and the microprocessor, the computer's hardware is what actually transmits and stores the data. But the methods with which data are transferred are determined by software. The computer's operating system plays a critical role in determining where and when data are sent in the computer.

There are many different designs of operating system software. Sometimes, a computer's operating system is designed to fit within certain limitations (for example, it must use only a small amount of space to store itself in the computer). Other times, an operating system's design reflects a practical requirement, such as the ability to handle requests from multiple users at the same time. In some cases, new operating systems are designed to match new technology, like smart phones. And occasionally, a new OS is created simply because the designer believes that a better implementation of an existing design is possible.

Regardless of design, however, an operating system's basic purpose is the same: to manage the flow of data between hardware subsystems as well as between the computer and the user. Let's look at different categories of operating environments in which operating systems need to manage data flow.

3.1 Operating System Types and Functions

Operating systems can be organized into four major types: real-time, single-user/single-tasking, single-user/multitasking, and multi-user/multitasking.

REAL-TIME AND EMBEDDED OPERATING SYSTEMS

A **real-time operating system** is a very fast, relatively small OS. Its "real-time" name is given because it is designed to respond to hardware and program requests almost instantly. Real-time operating systems are designed not to handle a wide variety of tasks, or for the ability to process millions of requests in a short time, but simply to guarantee that, when a request is given from its user or hardware, the OS will respond right away. Real-time OSs are often also embedded OSs, which means they are built into the circuitry of a device and are not loaded from a disk drive. Embedding the OS directly into the hardware improves its response time.

Real-time applications are needed to run medical diagnostics equipment, life-support systems, machinery, scientific instruments, industrial systems, and other programs or hardware where instant response to input is required.

SINGLE-USER/SINGLE-TASKING OPERATING SYSTEMS

An operating system that allows a single user to perform just one task at a time is a **single-user/single-tasking operating system**. MS-DOS is one example of a single-tasking OS, and the Palm OS, used on the Palm handheld computers, is another. To a user, a "task" is a function such as printing a document, writing a file to disk, editing a file, or downloading a file from a network server. To the operating system, a task is a process, and small and simple OSs can only manage a single task at a time. The vast majority of desktops and notebooks no longer use this type of OS. In many types of jobs, a single user can be more productive when working in a multitasking operating system.

SINGLE-USER/MULTITASKING OPERATING SYSTEMS

A **single-user/multitasking operating system** is one that allows a single user to perform two or more functions at once. The most commonly used personal computers usually run such OSs, including Microsoft Windows and the Macintosh Operating System. The multitasking features of these OSs have greatly increased the productivity of people in a large variety of jobs because they can accomplish more in a shorter period of time. For instance, to an office worker, it is important to be able to send a large document to a printer and be able to do other work on his or her computer while it is being printed. It is also helpful for many types of workers to be able to have two or more programs open, to share the data between the two programs, and to be able to instantly switch between the two programs.

MULTI-USER/MULTITASKING OPERATING SYSTEMS

A **multi-user/multitasking operating system** is an operating system that allows multiple users to use programs that are simultaneously running on a single network server, called a **terminal server**. This is not at all the same as connecting to a network server for the sake of accessing files and printers. As you will learn in Chapter 2, when a computer is connected to a server to access document files to edit, the client computer performs the processing work locally. Not so with a multi-user OS, which gives each user a complete environment, called a **user session**, on the server. Each user's applications run within their user session on the server separate from all other user sessions. The software that makes this possible is called a **terminal client**. In a multi-user/multitasking operating system environment, all or most of the computing occurs at the server (see Figure 1.8). Examples of multi-user OSs include UNIX, VMS, and mainframe operating systems such as MVS.

SUPPORTING PROGRAMS

The operating system provides a consistent interface between application programs and the user. It is also the interface between those programs and other computer resources such as memory, a printer, or another program. Programmers write computer programs with built-in instructions—called **system calls**—that request services from the operating system. They are known as "calls" because the program has to call on the operating system to provide some information or service. For example, when you want your word-processing program to retrieve a file, you use the Open dialog box to list the files in the folder that you specify. To provide the list, the program calls on the operating system. The OS goes through the same process to build a list of files whether it receives its instructions from you (via the desktop) or from an application. The difference is that, when the request comes from an application, the operating system sends the results of its work back to the application rather than to the desktop.

In addition to listing files, an operating system provides several other services to programs:

- Saving the contents of files to a disk
- Reading the contents of a file from disk into memory
- Sending a document to the printer and activating the printer
- Providing resources that let you copy or move data from one document to another, or from one program to another
- Allocating RAM among the running programs
- Recognizing keystrokes or mouse clicks and displaying characters or graphics on the screen

SHARING DATA BETWEEN WINDOWS AND PROGRAMS

Many types of applications let you move chunks of data from one place to another. For example, you may want to copy a chart from a spreadsheet program and place the copy in a document in a word processing program (see Figure 3.1). Some operating systems accomplish this feat with a feature known as the **Clipboard**. The Clipboard is a temporary holding space (in the computer's memory) for data that is being copied or moved.

If you want to move a paragraph in a word processor document, for example, you select the paragraph and choose the **Cut command**; the data is removed from the document and placed on the Clipboard. (If you want to leave the original data in place, you can use the **Copy command** instead; a copy is made of the data, and it is stored on the Clipboard but is not removed from the document.) After selecting the point in the document where you want to place the paragraph, you choose the **Paste command**; the data on the Clipboard is then moved into the document. The Clipboard also can be used to move data from one document to another within a program.

The real versatility of the Clipboard, however, stems from the fact that it is actually a part of the operating system and not a particular application. As a result, you can use the Clipboard to move data from one program to another. The versatility of between-application transfer using the Clipboard has been extended further with a feature known in Windows as **OLE**, which stands for **Object Linking and Embedding**.

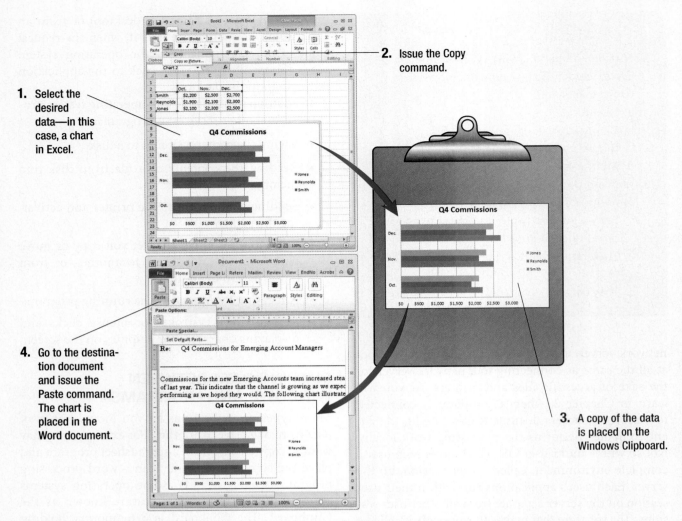

1. Select the desired data—in this case, a chart in Excel.

2. Issue the Copy command.

3. A copy of the data is placed on the Windows Clipboard.

4. Go to the destination document and issue the Paste command. The chart is placed in the Word document.

Figure 3.1 Using the Clipboard to copy a chart from an Excel document to a Word document.

A simple cut and paste between applications results in object embedding. The data, which is known as an object in programming terms, is embedded in a new type of document. It retains the formatting that was applied to it in the original application, but its relationship with the original file is destroyed; that is, it is simply part of the new file. Furthermore, the data may be of a type that the open application cannot change. Therefore, if you want to edit embedded data, simply double-click the embedded object, and the original application that created the data is started to allow editing of the embedded data.

Object linking adds another layer to the relationship: the data that is copied to and from the Clipboard retains a link to the original document so that a change in the original document also appears in the

> **"The operating system is the intermediary between programs and hardware"**

linked data. For example, suppose the spreadsheet and memo shown in Figure 3.1 are generated quarterly. They always contain the same chart updated with the most recent numbers. With object linking, when the numbers in the spreadsheet are changed, the chart in the report will automatically reflect the new figures. Of course, object linking is not automatic; you need to use special commands in your applications to create the link.

MANAGING THE COMPUTER HARDWARE

When programs run, they need to use the computer's memory, monitor, disk drives, and other devices, such as a printer. The operating system is the intermediary

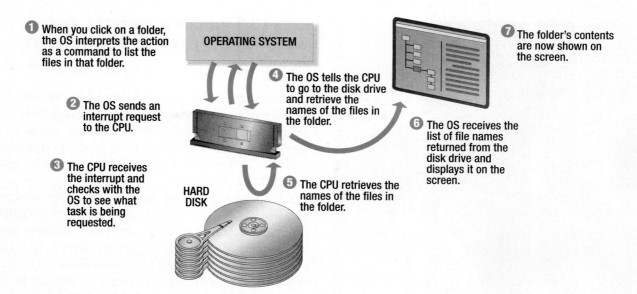

1 When you click on a folder, the OS interprets the action as a command to list the files in that folder.

OPERATING SYSTEM

4 The OS tells the CPU to go to the disk drive and retrieve the names of the files in the folder.

7 The folder's contents are now shown on the screen.

2 The OS sends an interrupt request to the CPU.

6 The OS receives the list of file names returned from the disk drive and displays it on the screen.

3 The CPU receives the interrupt and checks with the OS to see what task is being requested.

HARD DISK

5 The CPU retrieves the names of the files in the folder.

Figure 3.2   How the operating system uses interrupts to work with the CPU.

between programs and hardware. In a computer network, the operating system also mediates between your computer and other devices on the network.

Programs and hardware subsystems rely on **interrupts** to work in a harmonious way with each other. A computer interrupt is a request for attention by some part of the system. While the computer processes tasks, it keeps a lookout for interrupts that are higher priority than whatever it happens to be doing. Whenever it notes an interrupt request that is more important than its current task, it saves its work, handles the new request, and then continues with its previous task.

The operating system responds to interrupt requests to use memory and other devices; keeps track of which programs have access to which devices; and coordinates everything the hardware does so that various activities do not overlap, causing the computer to become confused and stop working. The OS may also generate its own interrupts to ensure that the computer's CPU can process important system functions at appropriate times.

The operating system uses interrupt requests (IRQs) to help the CPU coordinate processes. For example, Figure 3.2 shows what happens if you tell the operating system to list the files in a folder.

WORKING WITH DEVICE DRIVERS

In addition to using interrupts, the operating system often provides programs for working with special devices such as printers. These programs are called **drivers** because they allow the operating system and

other programs to activate and use—that is, "drive"—the hardware device.

In general, software you buy and install will work with your printer, monitor, and other equipment without requiring you to install any special drivers. Most add-on pieces of hardware like webcams, drawing tablets, and printers will either use drivers already present in the operating system or will come with a disk containing drivers to be installed.

3.2 Moving Data Around the Computer

It often seems as though computers must understand us because we understand the information they produce. Computers produce answers to complex questions, and a computer's output may interest, challenge, and delight us.

However, computers cannot actually understand anything. Underneath the face of what we can take as knowledge, computers are simply machines that recognize two distinct physical states produced by electricity, magnetic polarity, or reflected light. If they are capable of any kind of understanding, it is for just one thing: whether a switch is on or off. In fact, the computer's CPU, which acts like the "brain" of the computer, consists of millions of tiny electronic switches, called **transistors**, that are in either an on or off state. The CPU follows its instructions strictly as directed by the people who wrote them, without thought or creativity or insight. A computer

In our familiar decimal system, when we want to add to a value of 9, we add a second digit to get 10. The "1" in that number represents the number of tens, and the "0" represents the number of ones. As numbers continue to become larger, we add more digits: 100, then 1,000, and so on.

Computers also have their own number system, but instead of our decimal system or an irregular counting system that clocks and tape measures use, a computer uses the binary system. In a binary (or base 2) system, there are only two values (*bi* means *two* in Latin): zero and one. Using zeroes and ones, any number can be represented by adding more digits, just as with the decimal system. The value of zero and one are represented as 0 and 1. If we want to add one more to get two, we have to represent it as "10" because those are the only symbols available. The "1" represents the number of twos, and the "0" represents the number of ones. Just as with the decimal system, more digits are added to express larger numbers, as shown in Table 3.1.

It's easy to see that, in binary, numbers require many more digits to represent than in decimal. A decimal value of 35, for example, translates into a binary representation of 100011. Why, then, did computer designers settle on binary, if it requires so many digits?

The reason is that binary counting has two states (zero and one). Electricity also has two values: off and on. Binary is an ideal companion for an electronic machine because its switches (transistors) are either on or off. Six electronic switches together can make on-off-off-off-on-on, or, written more simply, 100011, neatly capturing the value of 35 in an electronic circuit.

In a computer, a single binary digit is called a **bit**. Bits are grouped together to represent larger numbers, as Table 3.1 illustrates. Eight of those bits grouped together form one byte, which is generally used to represent a single text character of information to a user.

TEXT CODES: ASCII VERSUS UNICODE

To a computer, everything is a binary number because every function it performs is done via on-and-off electronic circuitry. Numbers are numbers; letters and punctuation marks are numbers; sounds and pictures are numbers. Even the

appears to understand information only because it operates at such phenomenal speeds, grouping its individual on/off switches into patterns that become meaningful to us.

In this section, you will learn more about the ones and zeroes that are used to build all data inside of a PC, and how that data moves through and is stored within the computer as it builds information that is useful to its users.

BINARY: THE COMPUTER'S NUMBER SYSTEM

Counting is a natural thing people do, starting at a very early age. As we grow, we almost universally begin to use the decimal **number system,** a term that describes any regular structure for counting, most likely because we have 10 fingers. The decimal number system is sometimes also called "base 10" because we use 10 symbols to represent all numbers.

The decimal system is not the only way that counting is possible. A clock, for example, counts time without using the decimal system. Clocks have 24 hours, each composed of 60 minutes, and each minute is composed of 60 seconds. Distance is sometimes counted in a decimal system (meters and kilometers are decimal-based), but in the United States, we still measure distances in miles, which are made up of 5,280 feet, and feet each have 12 inches.

TABLE 3.1 COUNTING IN BASE 10 AND BASE 2

Base 10	Base 2
0	0
1	1
2	10
3	11
4	100
5	101
6	110
7	111
8	1000
9	1001
10	1010
11	1011
12	1100
13	1101
14	1110
15	1111
16	10000

so that input and output of those characters would be the same across all computers. In such a system, numbers would represent the letters of the alphabet, punctuation marks, and other symbols. While several different standards were developed, three have broad acceptance today in personal computers:

- **ASCII.** ASCII (pronounced AS-key) stands for the **American Standard Code for Information Interchange**. Today, the ASCII character set is by far the most commonly used in computers of all types. ASCII is an eight-bit code that specifies characters for values from 0 to 127.

- **Extended ASCII.** Extended ASCII is an eight-bit code that specifies the characters for values from 128 to 255. The first 40 symbols represent pronunciation and special punctuation. The remaining symbols are graphic symbols.

- **Unicode.** The **Unicode Worldwide Character Standard** provides up to four bytes—32 bits—to represent each letter, number, or symbol. With four bytes, enough Unicode codes can be created to represent more than 4 billion different characters or symbols. This total is enough for every unique character and symbol in the world, including the vast Chinese, Korean, and Japanese character sets and those found in known classical and historical texts. In addition to world letters, special mathematical and scientific symbols are represented in Unicode. One major advantage that Unicode

computer's own instructions are numbers. When you see letters of the alphabet on a computer screen, you are seeing just one of the computer's ways of representing numbers.

Early programmers realized that they needed a standard **text code**, a list of text characters and an associated number for each character. That would allow computers to translate text characters into binary numbers and back again in a standard way,

Figure 3.4 The Unicode character set includes support for symbolic languages around the world, including the characters for the Korean language.

has over other text code systems is its compatibility with ASCII codes. The first 256 codes in Unicode are identical to the 256 codes used by the ASCII and Extended ASCII systems. Some software developers are now modifying their older programs to support Unicode and the global community.

HARDWARE AND PROCEDURES FOR MOVING DATA

As you've already seen, computers process data, perform input and output functions with users, and store data both in memory and in permanent storage devices. Each of the steps in the information cycle (input, processing, output, and storage) requires specific hardware and procedures that the computer follows. The remainder of this section will follow the flow of binary data through various hardware subsystems in a PC.

The Bus To complete its tasks, the computer spends a great deal of its time shuttling data from place to place, whether to be stored, to be used elsewhere, or for communicating with the user. The electronic path in a computer that is used to transfer data between components is known as a **bus**. Buses sometimes use more than one wire at a time to transmit electronic data in order to speed up the transfer. While one wire can transfer a bit of data for each processing cycle, eight wires can transfer eight times as much data in that same cycle (see Figure 3.5). A bus sending its information in parallel lines across multiple wires is known as a **parallel bus**. A bus may also send its information one bit at a time in series, and is then referred to as a **serial bus**.

Although a wider parallel bus can transfer more bits of data per processing cycle, some newer bus designs actually favor a serial approach. As improving technology continues to decrease the processing cycle time, a parallel bus may not be able to deliver all the required bits at the same instant, causing the computer to miss data bits or wait extra cycles to get it all. By using groups of serial buses instead of a single parallel bus, large amounts of data can be delivered without risking a loss of data because the bits for each piece of data are delivered in series.

There are two main buses in a computer: the internal bus and the external bus. The **internal bus** (sometimes called the system bus) connects the CPU to memory modules and subsystems that reside directly on the motherboard. An **external bus** (or expansion

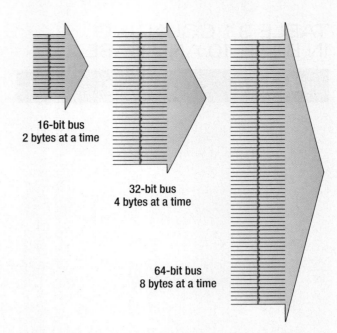

16-bit bus
2 bytes at a time

32-bit bus
4 bytes at a time

64-bit bus
8 bytes at a time

Figure 3.5 With a wider bus containing more wires, the computer can move more data in the same amount of time.

bus) connects external devices, such as hard drives, keyboards, mice, video cards, printers, and so on, to the CPU. Devices are connected to an expansion bus by plugging them into an external port or to a connector directly attached to the motherboard.

External Bus Standards Standards have been created for bus technology to ensure that hardware manufacturers and software designers have a common and predictable way to transfer data to and from the CPU. As PC technology has evolved to encompass new ideas and meet demands for higher performance, bus design has similarly evolved and changed. Many bus standards have already come and gone, while still others are familiar, universal, and probably here to stay for a good while longer. Unless you have a very old PC on your desk, you will probably not encounter many of the older bus standards. Some of the common bus standards currently in use include the following:

- **IEEE 1394** is a bus standard commonly known as **FireWire**. It is a serial bus that is typically used to transfer video and audio data. Developed in the late 1980s, it is one of the older bus standards still in use. Firewire originally supported a transfer rate of up to 400 megabits per second; the latest standard, FireWire 800 (or more formally, IEEE 1394b) doubles that support to 800 megabits per second.

TABLE 3.2 EXTERNAL BUS CAPACITIES

Bus Standard	Bit width	Maximum transmission rate
Firewire	Serial, 2 pairs of data wires	800 Mbits/second (Firewire 800)
PCI	Parallel, 32 bits	Approximately 1 Gbit/second
PCIe	Serial, 4 data wires per lane	128 Gbits/second (PCIe 3.0)
SATA 3.0	Serial, 2 pairs of data wires	6 Gbits/second
USB 2.0	Serial, 1 pair of data wires	480 Mbits/second
USB 3.0	Serial, 8 data wires	5 Gbits/second

- The **Peripheral Component Interconnect (PCI) bus** is a type of bus designed by Intel to integrate various hardware devices into a computer. Many types of hardware interfaces—for example, sound cards and network interface cards—use the PCI bus standard. Video cards once used the PCI bus, but the demands of video output long ago outstripped the effectiveness of the PCI interface, and video cards now either sit directly on the motherboard or connect via the PCI-E bus, described next. Though faster bus designs are in use throughout the modern personal computer, PCI connectors are still commonly included. The parallel PCI bus has a 32-bit interface, and has a peak transfer rate of just over 1 gigabit per second.

- **PCI Express (PCIe)** was created as a replacement technology for the PCI bus. Its data transfer design is more efficient than its predecessor and offers scalability, meaning that, as demands on the bus increase, the standard allows for the addition of more data pathways, called **lanes**, to support the increased needs. PCIe 3.0, the latest version of the standard released at the end of 2010, allows for a data transfer rate of 8 gigabits per second for each data lane, twice the transfer rate of the prior version. For a 16-lane device, the most that is typically used at present, this provides a 128 gigabit per second transfer rate. New video cards now routinely use the PCIe interface instead of older technologies.[1]

[1]R. Kayne (2010), What is PCI Express? *WiseGEEK*. Retrieved June 2, 2010, from http://www.wisegeek.com/what-is-pci-express.htm

- **Serial ATA** (or **SATA**; ATA stands for Advanced Technology Attachment) is the current bus standard for connecting hard drives to the computer. It uses a small, 7-pin connector; supports features such as hot swapping, meaning that hard drives can be plugged into and unplugged from a computer without first switching it off; and can achieve transfer rates of up to 6 gigabits per second under the most recent SATA 3.0 standard.

- The **Universal Serial Bus (USB)** is a common, popular bus found on all modern computers and is supported by a host of devices including keyboards, mice, webcams, flash drives, and digital cameras. The familiar 4-pin connector houses a single pair of data transmission wires, and supports transmission rates up to 480 megabits per second. USB supports up to 127 devices connected to one computer, and also allows convenient hot swapping of devices. USB 3.0, the new transmission standard that is now appearing in newer computers, uses eight data wires to achieve a 5 gigabit per second transfer rate.

Cache Memory To process its instructions as quickly as possible, the CPU must be able to efficiently store and retrieve its data. RAM memory is far faster and more efficient for a CPU to use than a hard drive, but even RAM takes so long to provide data to the CPU that a special, closer memory system was designed.

A **cache** is a smaller, faster memory subsystem than the main RAM in a computer. It is generally located

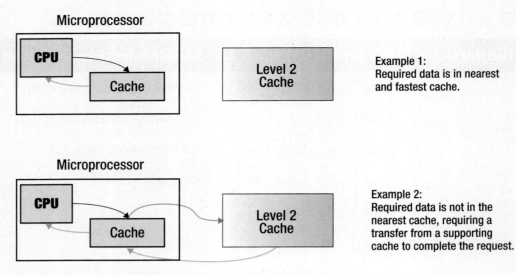

Example 1:
Required data is in nearest and fastest cache.

Example 2:
Required data is not in the nearest cache, requiring a transfer from a supporting cache to complete the request.

Figure 3.6   Retrieving data from a cache.

physically closer to the part of the computer that uses it, which reduces the time it takes the data to travel along the bus. A modern CPU has more than one cache at its disposal. The most immediate ones are included in the microprocessor unit that plugs into the motherboard.

The computer loads data into a cache in chunks from another, usually slower, source, such as a cache that is farther away, the computer's RAM, or permanent storage like the hard drive. Loading the data into a cache in chunks generally increases the chances that a chunk containing data for one request may also have data for subsequent requests, reducing the number of retrievals from a slower source.

As shown in Figure 3.6, when the CPU needs data, it requests it from its nearest and fastest cache. If the data it needs is present in that cache, then it can very quickly receive and process that data. If the fastest cache does not contain what is requested, then one of the slower supporting caches will provide the requested data for the CPU.

Processing Data with the CPU Every piece of software is ultimately a detailed list of instructions for the CPU and other hardware subsystems to perform. For each and every instruction a CPU executes, it must be told exactly what action is required and what data it needs to

process. The CPU follows a specific and consistent set of steps in order to fetch, process, and return data to other computer subsystems. Regardless of its construction, every CPU has at least two basic parts: the control unit and the arithmetic logic unit.

All the computer's resources are managed from the **control unit**. Think of the control unit as a traffic signal directing the flow of data through the CPU, as well as to and from other devices. The control unit is the logical hub of the computer. The CPU's instructions for carrying out commands are built into the control unit. The instructions, or **instruction set**, list all the operations that the CPU can perform. Each instruction in the instruction set is expressed in **microcode**—a series of basic directions that tell the CPU how to execute more complex operations.

Because all computer data is stored as numbers, much of the processing that takes place involves comparing numbers or carrying out mathematical operations. These steps are normally performed in the **arithmetic logic unit (ALU)**. In addition to establishing ordered sequences and changing those sequences, the computer can perform two types of

Figure 3.7   A microprocessor's case houses the CPU, cache, and ALU. The grid of pins on the underside transfers instructions and data.

operations: arithmetic operations and logical operations. **Arithmetic operations** include addition, subtraction, multiplication, and division. **Logical operations** include comparisons, such as determining whether one number is equal to, greater than, or less than another number.

Many instructions carried out by the control unit involve simply moving data from one place to another—from memory to storage, from memory to the printer, and so forth. When the control unit encounters an instruction that involves arithmetic or logic, however, it passes that instruction to the ALU.

Each time the CPU executes an instruction, it takes a series of steps. The completed series of steps is called a **machine cycle**. A machine cycle itself can be broken down into two smaller cycles: the **instruction cycle** and the **execution cycle**. At the beginning of the machine cycle (that is, during the instruction cycle), the CPU takes two steps:

1. **Fetching.** Before the CPU can execute an instruction, the control unit must retrieve (or fetch) a command or data from the computer's memory.

2. **Decoding.** Before a command can be executed, the control unit must break down (or decode) the command into instructions that correspond to those in the CPU's instruction set.

At this point, the CPU is ready to begin the execution cycle:

1. **Executing.** When the command is executed, the CPU carries out the instructions in order.

2. **Storing.** The CPU may be required to store the results of an instruction in memory (but this condition is not always required).

Although the process is complex, the computer can accomplish it at an incredible speed, translating millions of instructions each second.

Even though most microprocessors execute instructions rapidly, newer ones can perform even faster by using a process called **pipelining** (or pipeline processing). In pipelining, the control unit begins a new machine cycle—that is, it begins executing a new instruction—before the current cycle is completed. Executions are performed in stages: when the first instruction completes the fetching stage, it moves to the decode stage, and a new instruction is fetched. It is helpful to think of a pipeline as an assembly line. Each instruction is broken up into several parts. Once the first part of an instruction is done, it is passed to the second part. Because the first step in the line is now idle, the pipeline then feeds

a new step one. Using this technique, newer microprocessors can execute more than two dozen instructions simultaneously.

3.3 Common Operating Systems

When computer users interact with the operating system, it is usually for the purpose of accomplishing a task they find noticeable and meaningful. We normally use the operating system for tasks like starting programs or moving or deleting files. It's a rare person who will sit at the keyboard and request that the operating system move data from one part of memory to the other.

But as you've seen in this and previous chapters, the operating system is responsible for more than just a pretty background image on the monitor and a collection of program icons to click. Its many layers help manage the transfer of data to and from different hardware subsystems, including across network lines. It helps the CPU manage certain processes. It provides a file system structure both to aid users in organizing their information and to provide a standard and predictable way for the computer to store and retrieve data at a lower level. Even so, the perception that the operating system's main job is to provide a user interface is not entirely wrong. The operating system is instrumental in facilitating the conversion between data and useful user information.

CONCEPTS AFFECTING ALL OPERATING SYSTEMS

There are many different operating systems in use today in the various PCs, smart phones and large computers in our world. Before reviewing some of the more common operating systems you might see or use, let's consider a couple of concepts that can affect any operating system: bit size and backward compatibility.

Bit Size You may have seen discussions or advertising about 32-bit and 64-bit operating systems. Some operating systems offer both versions; others offer one or the other, or simply don't mention a bit size.

The bit size refers to the number of bits the operating system uses to represent values. A 32-bit operating system uses 32 bits to create numbers; a 64-bit operating system uses twice as many.

Consider that when the computer needs to store and retrieve data from RAM, it must be able to say exactly where the data should be stored, and it must be able to retrieve exactly and only the data it requires. This requires that every byte of a computer's RAM have its own unique numeric identifier, called an **address**. When the computer requires certain data from RAM, it uses the address of the memory it needs to ensure that it gets the right data.

Memory addresses, like all other computer data, are groups of binary digits. As you learned earlier in this lesson, the more bits a computer uses to represent a number, the larger the number it can process. For example, a 3-bit number can be used to represent values up to 7 (see Table 3.1). By adding a fourth bit, numbers up to 15 can be used.

If a computer only has 15 bytes of RAM available, a four-bit number will work just fine to make addresses for each of those bytes. However, most computers today have many millions of times more RAM bytes than that, requiring many more bits than just four in order to make addresses big enough for all the memory locations.

The biggest number that a 32-bit operating system can store is 4,294,967,295. This allows the operating system to manage data storage and retrieval for up to four gigabytes of RAM. While that was once considered to be a very large amount of storage, that amount is not only common in today's PCs, but is in some cases inadequate for tasks that users want to perform. 32-bit operating system cannot take advantage of more than four gigabytes of RAM, even if more is physically installed in the computer, because it simply cannot make addresses for the extra amount.

64-bit operating systems remove this restriction. A 64-bit operating system can make addresses well over 18 quintillion in value, which in theory could support computers with many exabytes (billions of gigabytes) of RAM. There are many other restrictions that prohibit computers from actually using that much storage, not the least of which is the physical space required for all those chips and hardware cards. But from a practical perspective, using a 64-bit operating system at least allows users to put dozens of gigabytes of RAM to use if their tasks require it.

Different bit sizes can also be used by CPU subsystems. Different microprocessor designs may employ different bit sizes for their instruction sets, as well as for storing and retrieving data. If a CPU can receive 64 bits of data at a time, it can receive more data to process with each operating cycle than a 32-bit CPU can.

Similar to including extra RAM that a 32-bit operating system cannot access, running a 64-bit CPU with a 32-bit operating system can be made to work, typically by having the CPU change to a 32-bit mode, but a 32-bit operating system cannot make use of 64-bit CPU functions.

Backward Compatibility One of the challenges facing operating system designers is the concept of compatibility. Because a computer's operating system works so closely with every aspect of hardware and software, many software applications from games to spreadsheets are written to work with specific parameters and behaviors in the operating system. If the operating system makes fundamental changes to the way it handles hardware and software requests, some or all of the applications may simply stop working because the operating system no longer understands the applications' requests, or it may deliver unexpected results to the applications for the requests that it still understands.

The conversion from a 32-bit architecture to a new 64-bit design is a good example of this problem. A software application requesting memory resources from the operating system will expect to get a 32-bit address telling it where to find the data; however, if the operating system provides the application with a 64-bit address, the program may misunderstand the returned value and attempt to store or retrieve data from the wrong address.

Operating system designers cannot realistically tell all application developers to re-write their software to fit the new operating system, and then tell consumers that along with the new operating system, they will have to buy new copies of all their application software. They are therefore faced with the challenge of making their new operating system **backward compatible**, meaning that it has been designed to work with most or all of the programs that were created for the old version.

There are various ways to achieve backward compatibility. Sometimes, designers of the new operating system provide translation functions so that the new program can convert input and output to an old format when communicating with older software. In other cases, the operating system may provide an **emulator**, which are software programs that are designed to re-create the exact environment of the older program. For example, Windows can run a DOS emulator as a separate program, providing a command prompt and all the expected input and output functions. Programs run within that emulator think they are communicating with the DOS operating system, even though the emulator is just a program being run by the actual operating system.

Now, let's review some of the common operating systems that are in use in computers made for consumers.

WINDOWS

Microsoft's Windows operating system continues to thrive on PCs all over the world and has the largest market share of any competitor, with one version or another of Windows appearing on roughly 90 percent of personal computers.

Figure 3.8   The Windows 7 desktop.

are designed to better protect users from malware attacks. Windows 7 also provides a 64-bit operating system version to support larger amounts of memory, and 64-bit CPU and other hardware subsystems.

MAC OS X

Mac OS X is the operating system used for computers sold by Apple Inc. "Mac" refers to the Macintosh brand name of computer, first introduced by Apple in 1984. Mac OS X, whose most recent version is named Snow Leopard, is a graphical operating system based on the Unix operating system, described next. Apple

> **"**The operating system is responsible for more than just a pretty background image on the monitor and a collection of programs to click**"**

Windows has undergone dramatic transformations since its first introduction in the 1980s, when it was released as a graphic extension of Microsoft's MS-DOS operating system. Many versions have come and gone as Microsoft has changed both the user interface and the internal processes and features. The latest version for new computers is Windows 7, which is intended to replace the previous two PC versions, Windows XP and Windows Vista.

Windows 7 adds many new features for productivity and safety. It provides improved support for multicore processors (a microprocessor design that includes multiple CPU units in the same microprocessor), a user interface that is intended to be simpler and more intuitive, and security management tools that

produces versions of the operating system not only for its desktop and notebook computers but also for its other consumer devices such as the iPhone smart phone and iPad tablet PC.

The Snow Leopard version of Mac OS X provides many upgrades over previous versions, including improved desktop support, voice and video handling improvements, and a substantially smaller amount of disk space required to store its own files.

Though Mac OS X and Microsoft's Windows operating system share similar features and functions that are visible to the user, Mac OS X has a distinctly different style and operation. Information is presented with a different style of graphics and animation, and program options and flow are in some ways unique to the operating environment. For several years, Mac OS X has appeared on approximately 5 percent of the personal computers in use; its adoption has been limited in part by the licensing restriction that it only be run on Apple-manufactured computers.

Mac OS   Snow Leopard

Figure 3.9   The Mac OS X Snow Leopard desktop.

LINUX FOR DESKTOP PCS

Even though Linux is considered a "freeware" operating system, industry experts have been impressed by its power, capabilities, and rich feature set. Based on the Unix operating system, Linux is a multitasking operating system that supports multiple users and multiple processors. Linux can run on nearly any computer and can support almost any type of application. Linux uses a command-line interface, but windows-based GUI environments, called *shells*, are available.

The biggest nontechnical difference between Unix and Linux is price. Anyone can get a free copy of Linux on the Internet, and disk-based copies are often inserted in popular computer books and magazines. Commercial versions of Linux, which are inexpensive when compared with the cost of other powerful operating systems, are also available from a variety of vendors who provide the Linux code for free and charge for the extras, such as utilities, GUI shells, and documentation.

For all these reasons, Linux has become a popular OS in certain circles. Students and teachers have flocked to Linux not just for its technical advances but to participate in the global community that has built up around the operating system. This community invites Linux users and developers to contribute modifications and enhancements, and it freely shares information about Linux and Linux-related issues. Although Linux is typically considered to be a server platform, an increasing number of software companies are writing new desktop applications or modifying existing ones for Linux.

OTHER OPERATING SYSTEMS

Many other operating systems for PCs have come and gone over the last few decades, though a couple of those legacy operating systems continue to exist in specialized or older environments. New operating systems are springing up in the handheld PC market, and there is stiff competition among several companies to become the dominant handheld operating system provider. Since the technology and utility of a handheld device is fundamentally different from that of a full-size PC, new operating systems are necessary to optimally run those devices. These other operating systems include:

- **DOS.** DOS, which is an acronym for *Disk Operating System*, came into widespread use in the 1980s with the appearance of the IBM PC, the first personal computer to catch on with consumers and businesses. DOS is a command-line interface with very limited support for hardware and networking, and can support only small amounts of memory and system resources compared to today's computer. It is still in use here and there, sometimes embedded in devices that run simple, single tasks, and sometimes running custom applications for small businesses, where no modern alternatives are available or desired.

- **Unix.** Unix, another command-line interface, predates DOS. It was created in 1969, and its multi-user, multitasking design made it the operating system of choice for many mainframes and supercomputers. Some derivatives of Unix, for example the Linux operating system, are fairly popular today for both businesses and single-user computers, and Unix itself is still in limited use in academic or scientific environments.

- **iOS.** iOS, or iPhone OS as it was originally known, is Apple's operating system for its mobile devices such as the iPhone and iPad. First released in 2007 along with the iPhone, iOS is gaining rapidly in popularity, though that increase is due only to increased sales of its devices; like its Mac OS for desktop computers, Apple does not license iOS for use on non-Apple devices. iOS is a multitasking operating system that provides a user interface based on fingertip taps, swipes and pinches. iOS is also able to respond to sensor input that registers when a user shakes or rotates the handheld device.

- **Android.** At the opposite end of the licensing spectrum from iOS is Google's Android operating system. In 2007, Google along with other companies in the mobile computing sector formed the Open Handset Alliance to promote publicly available standards and software for mobile hardware devices. The Android operating system, a mobile OS based on Linux, was made available to the public in 2008. Android supports a multi-touch interface and a host of mobile and smart phone features from calling and messaging to allowing the device to act as a wireless Internet connector for a PC. As of mid-2011, Android had established itself as the most widely used smart phone operating system among its competitors.

- **Chrome OS.** Another Google operating system called Chrome OS is making its way onto netbooks. Based on Linux, Chrome OS boots the computer straight to a web browser interface. Unlike more common PC operating systems like Mac OS and Windows, Chrome OS relies on the browser interface and computing done largely by servers on the Internet to provide user services. This fits the needs of netbook machines, which can lack the computing power to run a full operating system and complex software. Though Chrome OS is sold on machines manufactured by Google partners, Google provides a version of the operating system to the public under the name Chromium OS.

3.4 Data, Files, and Utility Programs

ORGANIZING DISK STORAGE: TRACKS AND SECTORS

The operating system is responsible for determining the exact layout of data on a permanent storage disk. The drive itself contains a surface that is able to store data, but it is up to the operating system to determine how to use it.

Before the computer can use a hard disk to store data for the first time, the disk's surface must be magnetically mapped so the computer can go directly to a specific point on it without searching through data. The process of mapping a disk is called **formatting** or **initializing**. Drives that have already been used can be reformatted, which has the effect of erasing all the files from the disk.

During formatting, a disk drive creates a set of concentric rings, called **tracks**, on each side of the disk. Each track is a separate circle, like the circles on a bull's-eye target. In the next stage of formatting, the tracks are divided into smaller parts, called **sectors**. Sectors are where binary data is physically stored on the disk. All the sectors on a disk are numbered in one long sequence, so the computer can access each small area on the disk by using a unique number. Figure 3.10

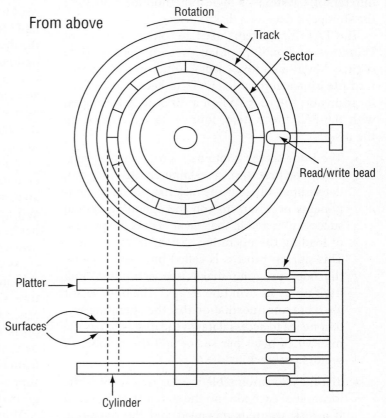

Figure 3.10   Tracks and sectors on a hard disk.

shows a basic diagram of the track and sector layout on a hard drive.

A sector is the smallest unit with which any magnetic disk drive can work; the drive can read or write only whole sectors at a time. Regardless of physical size, a hard disk's sectors hold the same number of bytes; that is, the shortest, innermost sectors hold the same amount of data as the longest, outermost sectors. Hard drives may sometimes place extra sectors on the outer area of the disk to avoid wasting space.

Note that other kinds of permanent storage, like CD and DVD optical drives, use a different physical method for laying out sectors and storing bits of data. Even so, the basic idea of tracks and sectors remains consistent in those media.

HOW THE OPERATING SYSTEM FINDS DATA ON A DISK

A computer's operating system can locate data on a disk because each track and each sector are labeled, and the location of all data is kept in a special log on the disk.

Different operating systems can format disks in different ways. Each formatting method configures the disk's surface in a different manner, resulting in a different **file system**—a logical method for managing the storage of data on a disk's surface.

The FAT file system, used by older versions of Windows and still popular in some places (like digital camera memory cards), relies on a standardized **file allocation table (FAT)** to keep track of file locations on the disk. When a diskette is formatted with the FAT file system, four areas are created on the disk:

- The **boot sector** contains a program that runs when you first start the computer. This program determines whether the disk has the basic components necessary to run the operating system successfully, and in that event begins the process of loading the operating system from the disk. This startup process is called **booting,** because the boot program makes the computer "pull itself up by its own bootstraps." The boot sector also contains information that the operating system needs to access data on the disk, such as the number of bytes per sector and the number of sectors per track.

- The file allocation table is a log that records the location of each file and the status of each sector. If a disk sector is damaged and the operating system cannot read from or write to it, it marks the sector as bad on the table so it can avoid using it in the future.

- The **root folder** is the "master folder" on any disk. A **folder** (also called a **directory**) is a tool for organizing files on a disk. Folders can contain files or other folders, so it is possible to set up a hierarchical system of folders on your computer, just as you can have folders within other folders in a file cabinet. The topmost folder is known as the *root* but may also be called the *root folder* or *root directory*. This is the folder that holds all the information about all the other folders on the disk.

- The **data area** is the part of the disk that remains free after the boot sector, the file allocation table, and the root folder have been created. This is where data and program files are actually stored on the disk.

The **New Technology File System (NTFS)**, introduced for Windows NT and used with the current Windows versions, was a leap forward from FAT, offering better security and overall performance. NTFS also allowed Windows computers to use long file names (file names longer than eight characters) for the first time.

When the operating system receives a request to read from the hard drive, it checks the file allocation table to identify the physical location of the data on the drive. It then directs the disk controller (a combination of hardware and firmware normally attached as a circuit board to the hard drive case) to retrieve the contents of the required sectors. When the data has been retrieved, the operating system sends the data to the subsystem making the request (typically, the RAM in the computer).

When writing new data to the disk, the operating system checks the file allocation table to find an open area, stores the data, and then logs the file's identity and its location in the table. If the operating system has been told to replace the contents of a disk sector, it overwrites what was originally there.

As a general rule, each operating system employs its own unique file system design, though many of them now share common elements. For example, Apple's Mac OS X has a file system called **HFS+**, which supports the same directory structure that a Windows user might expect, but provides a different method from NTFS for finding data within its directories, and supports the Macintosh file design of separating program data and visual element data.

While an OS's file system provides both the user-visible structure for storing files and the functions for storing and retrieving individual blocks of data from the hard drive, a file system can sometimes focus only on managing files that users see. **The WebDAV file system, which stands for Web-based Distributed Authoring and Versioning**, describes a structure for managing access and changes to files stored on the Web that are created and modified by multiple users in different locations. A number of operating systems, including Windows, Mac OS X, and Linux, have added support for WebDAV so that their users can access shared files on the Web as if they were using files and folders on their own system.

THE FILE SYSTEM IN THE USER INTERFACE

Not coincidentally, the file system structure used by Windows is the same one that the user sees in the user interface. A disk drive's root folder is represented as the drive itself (for example, the main hard drive is commonly referred to with the letter C). Windows Explorer shows all the files and folders directly in the root directory as being at the top level of the drive. Folders within folders, and files within folders, are all represented graphically.

Windows also provides a few other user conveniences that are not reflected in the disk's actual file structure. A **shortcut** in Windows is an object that points to another file. For example, you might create a shortcut to a program you run frequently and put that shortcut on your desktop. The program file is still sitting in its original place on the disk; the shortcut is simply a way to run it from a different location. The shortcut

itself is not the file. Shortcuts, because they are not actually disk files, are maintained by the operating system and not stored as files on the hard disk. The desktop itself, with its icons and files, is maintained as part of the file system (because you can store files on the desktop), but its contents are managed a bit differently on the drive than the way it appears to the user. To learn about another convenience available in the most recent versions of Windows, see the "Ask the Expert" feature.

OPTIMIZING DISK PERFORMANCE

The efficiency with which the operating system stores and retrieves data on a hard drive can have a substantial impact on the overall execution of the system. For example, if a hard drive is cluttered with thousands and thousands of file fragments to the point where there are no large areas of empty space available, and the operating system needs to write a large file, it must separate the large file into smaller parts and potentially write the various parts in sectors all across the disk surface. Reading a file that is fragmented in that manner similarly takes extra time. Reading and writing data from the disk surface occurs far more quickly than the time it takes to reposition the read/write head of the drive to a new location.

The operating system makes a limited effort to clean up temporary data from the hard drive, but the user has a role in keeping the hard drive running efficiently. Periodically, users should perform the following actions, assuming they own the machine or are responsible for maintaining it:

- **Remove unnecessary files.** If your computer has programs that you no longer use (and likely never will again), consider uninstalling them. If you have many gigabytes of TV show episodes you don't watch and audio books you don't care about, consider deleting them. The more empty space on the hard drive, the easier it is for the operating system to efficiently organize the data.

- **Compress your data.** If you have very large media files, consider using a utility that will compress those files into a significantly smaller size.

- **Defragment your drive.** Windows contains a disk defragmentation utility, which will reorganize data sectors to place related ones nearer to each other, reducing the amount of moving around

Figure 3.11   Computer file systems have things in common with files stored in a doctor's office, but colored tabs aren't one of them.

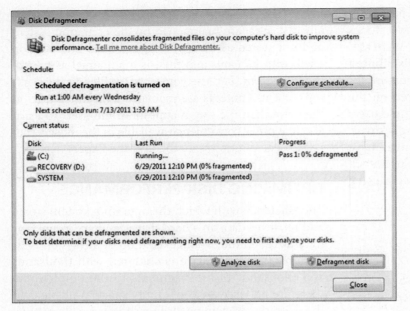

Figure 3.12 The disk defragmentation utility in Windows 7.

required by the read/write heads. The more free space available, the more effective the defragmenter can be, so if you have things to remove, do that first.

ENHANCING AN OS WITH UTILITY SOFTWARE

Operating systems are designed to let you do most of the tasks you normally would want to do with a computer, such as managing files, loading programs, printing documents, and so on. But software developers are constantly creating new programs—called **utilities**—that enhance or extend the operating system's capabilities, or that simply offer new features not provided by the operating system itself. As an operating system is improved and updated, the functionality of popular utilities is included with subsequent releases of the OS.

While it is difficult to give a definitive list of utility software categories, the most common types that ordinary people use are disk and file management, Internet security, and OS customization tools. To complicate matters further, there are many packaged utility suites that combine two or more utilities into one bundle. The following sections describe a small selection of popular utilities.

Backup Utilities For safekeeping, a **backup utility** can help you copy large groups of files from your hard disk to another storage medium. Many newer operating systems feature built-in backup utilities, but feature-rich backup software is available from other sources. These utilities not only help you transfer files to a backup medium, but they also help organize the files, update backups, and restore backups to disk in case of data loss.

Anti-Malware **Malware** is a generic term that describes various kinds of software programs that are designed to harm a computer's data or operating system, or compromise the security of a computer. If you've seen references to viruses, worms, Trojans, or adware, those are all different types of malware; they have different characteristics and behaviors, but they are all designed to harm computer systems. Malware can be anywhere from slightly annoying, showing you popup advertising now and then, to extremely dangerous, destroying your computer's data files or stealing passwords and sensitive information.

As you will learn in Chapter 5, malware can be transmitted in numerous ways, and users should be especially vigilant when downloading files over the Internet or receiving e-mail attachments. An anti-malware utility can examine files, memory, and parts of the operating system to look for traces of infection,

Figure 3.13 Screen saver utilities are still popular even though modem monitors don't need their protection.

require highly trained people to manage them.

Much simpler software and hardware firewall solutions are available for the home consumer. If you have a home network with one or more computers hooked up to a broadband router, the router will have the ability to perform firewall functions. PC operating systems, including Windows, also contain a firewall utility that you can activate.

and it can remove the intruder software. Some anti-malware products also include real-time guarding and monitoring, scanning new files that you receive and warning you about suspicious Web sites that are risky to visit.

Firewall   Your Internet service provider and most corporations employ specialized computers and hardware on their Internet connections that are dedicated to examining and blocking traffic coming from and going to the Internet. Such hardware is called a **firewall**, and manufacturers such as Cisco, 3COM, and others offer these products. These firewalls also

Screen Savers   **Screen savers** are popular utilities, although they serve little purpose other than to hide what would otherwise be displayed on the screen. A screen saver automatically appears when a keyboard or pointing device has not been used for a specified period of time. The screen saver remains active until the keyboard or pointer is used again.

Screen savers display a moving image or a sequence of pictures on the screen and were originally created to prevent a single, unmoving displayed image from "burning" into the monitor. Today's monitors do not suffer from this problem, but screen savers remain popular because they can add personality to the user's system.

IN Summary

- An operating system is system software that acts as a master control program, controlling the hardware and interacting with the user and application software. It displays the on-screen elements with which the user interacts (the user interface), loads programs into the computer's memory, coordinates how programs work with the computer's hardware and other software, and manages the way information is stored on and retrieved from disks. The four major types of operating systems are real-time operating systems, single-user/single-tasking operating systems, single-user/multitasking operating systems, and multi-user/multitasking operating systems.

- Computer data and instructions are moved between storage and the CPU via electronic pathways called buses. The CPU follows a set of steps for each instruction it carries out. This set of steps is called the machine cycle. Within the CPU, program instructions are retrieved and translated with the help of an internal instruction set. By using a technique called pipelining, many CPUs can process more than one instruction at a time.

- The most common PC operating systems are Windows, Apple Mac OS X, and Linux. Mobile computing operating systems such as iOS and Android are rapidly increasing in popularity as handheld PCs become more common.

- The Windows file system organizes its files in a hierarchical system, using a series of nested folders to contain and organize files. The root folder (or root directory) on the hard drive holds all other folders.

Key Terms

address, 94
arithmetic logic unit (ALU), 92
arithmetic operations, 93
American Standard Code for Information Interchange (ASCII), 89
backup utility, 100
backward compatible, 94
bit, 88
boot sector, 98
booting, 98
bus, 90
cache, 91
Clipboard, 85
control unit, 92
Copy command, 85
Cut command, 85
data area, 98

directory, 98
drivers, 87
emulator, 95
execution cycle, 93
Extended ASCII, 89
external bus, 90
file allocation table (FAT), 98
file system, 98
firewall, 101
FireWire, 90
folder, 98
formatting, 97
HFS+, 98
IEEE 1394, 90
initializing, 97
instruction cycle, 93
instruction set, 92
internal bus, 90

interrupts, 87
lanes, 91
logical operations, 93
machine cycle, 93
malware, 100
microcode, 92
multi-user/multitasking operating system, 84
New Technology File System (NTFS), 98
number system, 88
Object Linking and Embedding, 85
OLE, 85
parallel bus, 90
Paste command, 85
PCI Express (PCIe), 91
Peripheral Component Interconnect (PCI) bus, 91

Key Terms QUIZ

Complete each statement by writing one of the terms listed under "Key Terms" in each blank.

1. The most widely used text code system among personal computers is _____.

2. A(n) _____ is a high-speed memory location built near or directly into the CPU that holds data for fast retrieval and storage.

3. The operating system records the location of a new file in the _____ before writing it to a hard disk.

4. The computer's ALU is used for processing _____.

5. Binary and decimal are examples of a(n) _____.

6. _____ replaced PCI as a fast and efficient interface for video cards.

7. A disk drive is formatted into _____, which are then broken down into a series of _____.

8. The pathway on a motherboard that shuttles data back and forth between subsystems is called a(n) _____.

9. Erasing and setting up a fresh data map on a hard disk is called _____.

10. The CPU contains a list of codes it can execute; this list is known as the _____.

Review QUESTIONS

In your own words, briefly answer the following questions.

1. Why do computers use the binary number system?

2. Explain the basic concept of the machine cycle.

3. What is the purpose of the arithmetic logic unit (ALU)?

4. Which PC operating systems are widely used? What are their major differences?

5. What steps can a user take to optimize the performance of a PC's hard drive?

6. How does the Windows file system organize its files?

7. What is a bus?

8. How does the CPU use a cache to store and retrieve data?

9. Why is it important to have a standard text code?

10. What is the purpose of the external bus in a PC?

LESSON LAB

Complete the following exercises as directed by your instructor.

1. Use your operating system's search tools to find files on your computer's hard disk. Note that the following steps apply if you are using Windows 7. If you use a different version of Windows or a different operating system than Windows, ask your instructor for directions.

   a. Open the Windows Explorer window by clicking the folder icon near the Start button on the toolbar (note that this is not the same as the Internet Explorer browser program).

   b. Explorer will show you a list of folders and locations on the left side of its window. Click the "Computer" location in that list (it will have a small, blue computer icon next to the name).

   c. In the large area to the right of the location list, you'll see a list of hard disk drives and devices. Double click your main hard disk drive to select it. It is probably labeled with a name and then "(C:)". If you do not see this name, ask your instructor for help.

   d. In the upper right corner of the window, you'll see a text box with a magnifying glass icon. Type ".txt" in that box to search your main hard disk drive for text files. The computer will begin its search, adding file names to the main part of the window as it finds them. Note that the location bar at the top of the window gradually turns green as the computer completes its search.

   e. You can change how the output looks by right-clicking on the list of files. In the pop-up menu that appears, move your mouse over "View", and then select a new type of display.

   f. When the search is done, repeat the search using the text ".doc" and ".gif". When you are finished, close the Windows Explorer window.

2. Explore the contents of your computer's hard disk. Start Windows Explorer and select your computer's main hard drive as shown in Lesson Lab 1. The strip along the bottom of the Explorer window will give you statistics about the object you currently have selected. How many items (folders and files) are in the root directory of your main drive? Click several folders and review their contents in the main part of the Explorer window. When finished, close Windows Explorer.

Teams sometimes achieve greater insight into problems than individuals can. Effective groups may answer questions faster than an individual working alone, and the dialogue among team members can spark provocative questions and creative answers. See if you can participate in that kind of team problem solving in this exercise.

Divide into groups of three or four. Work as a team to make sense of the following simple coded text message:

89   111   117   32   115   111   108   118   101   100   32   105   116   33

Your group's task is to decode this message. The code is very familiar to any personal computer, so you might first discuss what forms of encoding might be used, based on what this lesson said about how computers represent data to users. Once you have selected a type of code to test, discuss how you could convert the numbers and discover the text of the message. Might there be Internet resources that could help? Whatever method or methods you decide to use to decode the message, work as a team to complete the decoding.

Evaluate the team experience: Did the involvement of more than one person make it easier or harder to arrive at a solution? What strengths or knowledge did group members bring to the task? Did your group use information or assistance from any of the other groups to speed up the completion of your task? How could your group have improved the way it worked?

Hint: This is a simple ASCII representation of the string *You solved it!* Unicode also supports these number-characters. Tables of ASCII codes are readily available online. See, for example, http://www.simotime.com/asc2ebc1.htm; www.asciitable.com; and www.pcguide.com.

LESSON 3B:
Application Software

By itself, the hardware of a computer doesn't do much of anything. Under the control of the operating system, a computer becomes a functional machine, ready to perform tasks for a user. But the operating system's activity is focused less on the user's needs and far more on the business of running the computer.

Application software shifts the focus from the computer to humans. There are as many different types of application software as there are different tasks to accomplish on a PC, covering a near-endless spectrum from business and industry to entertainment and personal development.

This lesson introduces you to some of the most commonly used types of application software that are used to make people more productive (hence the term *productivity software*) and discusses some of the applications and data formats used to create graphics and animation.

3.5 Acquiring and Installing Software

As there are hundreds of different types of software applications, there are various ways for users to obtain the software they need. Sometimes individuals create the special software they need, but the vast majority of people use commercial products. These products

are designed to perform the work, teach, or provide the entertainment that people require.

COMMERCIAL SOFTWARE

The term **commercial software** refers to any software program that requires or requests payment. Commercial software programs come in several different forms:

- **Stand-alone programs.** A **stand-alone program** is an application that performs only one type of task, such as a word processing program, a graphics program, or an e-mail program. Of course, such a program might have many tools and features, but it basically focuses on one type of task or a range of related tasks.

- **Software suites.** Software programs that are very commonly used—such as word processing software, spreadsheets, Web-authoring tools, and e-mail programs—are often packaged together and sold as **software suites**. A software suite is a set of carefully integrated tools that are designed to work together seamlessly. This includes the popular Microsoft Office family of products—Word, Excel, Outlook, PowerPoint, Access—as well as more special-purpose suites, like the Corel family of graphics software. Privacy and security utilities are also often sold as a suite, with one package providing anti-virus, anti-advertising and firewall protection.

- **Shareware programs.** One very popular type of commercial software is called **shareware**. Shareware gets its name from the fact that its developers encourage users to share it with one another and to try out the software before purchasing it. Some shareware authors ask for payment, but others only require the user to register the program. Sometimes shareware is delivered with a module that displays advertising to the user, and the advertising display is disabled when the user buys a copy of the software. Though many commercial programs offer free trials and demo copies, this is not the same as shareware. Demo software is either limited in function (for example, you cannot save your work, or some features are not available) or is provided for a limited time, after which payment is required to continue using the program. Shareware does not place those same limitations on the user.

Figure 3.14 Application software makes the computer useful to people.

FREEWARE AND PUBLIC DOMAIN SOFTWARE

A close cousin to shareware is **freeware**. Freeware is any software that is made available to the public for free; the developer does not expect any payment from users. As with shareware, the original author of freeware maintains an ownership interest in the product, even though the software may be given away at no charge. If you use shareware or freeware programs, you must abide by the terms of a license that prohibits you from making changes to the software or selling it to someone else. (For more on software licenses, see the "Focus on the Issues" feature.)

Because you don't pay for it, freeware may sound like **public domain software**, but it is not. Not only can users obtain public domain software for no charge in many cases, but the *source code* is free for anyone to use for any purpose. (Source code is the list of program instructions for an application.) You may be familiar with the concept of public domain from literature. If a publisher determines that a market exists for a new book of nursery rhymes, there is no need to hunt down the heirs of Mother Goose to negotiate a royalty or to get permission to change the poems, because those stories are freely available for anyone to use and modify. It is the same with public domain software.

OPEN-SOURCE SOFTWARE

Sometimes software is designed for users who need to customize the programs they use. This special need is often met by **open-source software**.

Open-source software is software whose source code is available to users. Source code is available

Figure 3.15   Firefox is an example of freeware, software that can be downloaded and installed for free by users.

in editable formats, as are the many development libraries that are used to create applications. Some Web sites, such as SourceForge (at http://sourceforge.net/), provide hundreds of source libraries and complete programs for many types of programs, including e-mail and word processing programs, network software, and games. Software developers can modify this code and customize it, within certain guidelines set forth by the application's creator.

Open-source developers sometimes sell their programs commercially, and sometimes they make it available for free. A company may release an open-source version of a product it is developing to build interest in the product before it is sold. The developer also may benefit from the comments and experience of many users who don't work for the company but freely give their thoughts in an informal exchange for the software being available. The increasingly popular OpenOffice suite of business programs is an example of open-source software that is freely given to the public, in an effort to build interest in an alternative to the market-dominant Microsoft Office suite.

WEB-BASED APPLICATIONS

People who work on the same tasks from different computers—for example, writing documents at work and then working on them in the evening from home—need to have the same software on each computer, and they need to make sure the latest version of the document is brought with them wherever they go. This multi-computer scenario only grows more complicated if more than one person needs to participate in the work.

Some people have simplified this process by using software and document storage that is hosted on the Internet rather than on their own, personal computer. By storing documents on the Web, a user can access the same document no matter what computer is being used, in the same way that a Web site can be accessed from any computer. Web-based storage also allows more than one person to access and update the same document. Similarly, Web-based software that can create and change those documents removes the need for users to have purchased and installed a copy of the software on each computer they use.

Users are generally required to create an account, and in exchange for registering an email address and in some cases paying a monthly or annual fee, they are provided with access to the software and document storage. For example, Google provides the Google

Docs service, which gives users both document storage and Web browser-based programs to edit document files, spreadsheets and calendars.

This kind of hosting, part of a service structure known as *cloud computing*, will be covered in greater detail in Chapter 6.

INSTALLING SOFTWARE

For very basic programs, the user might be able to simply place the program on a computer's hard drive and execute it. Most of the time, however, programs are built to work closely with the operating system and hardware subsystems in order to make them more efficient. This often requires that information about the program be provided to the operating system. So that all of a program's pieces are in the correct place and properly recognized by the operating system, software is placed on a personal computer through a process called installation.

During installation, a special program called a **script** is run to place files in various folders on the hard drive as required by the software being installed. With the files in place, the script also adds entries to a special file called the **registry**, which contains detailed information for the operating system about the locations and purposes of programs, files, and utilities. The exact locations of the files, and the exact information placed in the registry, are entirely dependent on the purpose and structure of the application software.

Software can sometimes be intended to be portable from computer to computer. Commercial software is not typically designed this way (after all, the software company wants to sell as many copies of their programs as possible), but it is not uncommon for shareware or freeware to have a portable design. Portable software can sometimes be installed onto a USB flash drive rather than a computer's hard drive, so that the user can unplug the flash drive and easily bring the program and whatever data it needs or produces to a new computer. Depending on its purpose and complexity, software installed on a flash drive may only provide a subset of features that can be installed on a computer's main hard drive, especially if some features require modification of the computer's registry.

When you want to remove software from a PC, unless the program is extremely basic, simply deleting the executable file on the hard drive will not fully remove the application. Most of the time, when software is installed, an "uninstall" script is included in the package. Running the uninstall script properly

Figure 3.16 Whether purchased online or on a DVD, software must usually be installed before a computer can put it to use.

deletes all related files and folders, and removes file and program information from the registry.

For most commercial software, the installation process relies on program and data files contained on a DVD drive. However, some software companies allow new users to download those program and data files from the Internet once the purchase is made, both to control production costs and provide software to online shoppers who don't want to wait for the delivery of a package in the mail. In some cases,

Fact Check

1. What is commercial software?
   a. Software that requires or requests payment
   b. Software that displays commercial advertising
   c. Software that automates commerce
2. What is open-source software?
   a. Software whose author is unknown
   b. Software whose source code is available to users
   c. Software that can be run on any operating system
3. What is software installation?
   a. The building where computers are housed
   b. A special program called a script
   c. The process of placing software on a personal computer

Focus on the Issues

Who Really Owns the Software on Your PC?

Once you start using a computer, it doesn't take long to learn that software can be expensive. If you use your PC a lot, especially if you use it for work, you can easily spend hundreds or even thousands of dollars on software. But even though you pay a lot for the software, you do not necessarily *own* the programs on your PC.

What happens, then, when you pay for a piece of software? That depends on the software maker, but very few developers grant you actual ownership of a program, even after you "purchase" it. Legally speaking, instead of buying the software itself, you really pay for a license that grants you permission to install and use the software.

WHY A LICENSE?

In simple terms, a license is an agreement between you and the software's maker. Under most software license agreements, the developer grants you a few rights to the program but keeps all the remaining rights.

Most licenses allow the user to install the program on a single computer. If you want to install the software on a different computer, the agreement may require that you uninstall it from the first computer. If you install the program on multiple PCs or make multiple duplicates of it, you may be violating the terms of the license. If the software developer catches you, it can take the software away from you and even press charges under applicable laws.

Software developers have good reasons for licensing software instead of selling it outright:

- **Piracy.** Software piracy is the act of copying software without the developer's consent and then using, selling, or giving away the copies. If developers sell their products outright, rather than license them, they may forfeit their legal recourse against pirates.

- **Modifications.** Most license agreements state that you cannot make modifications to a program's instructions. If developers allowed this, it would be easy for others to change a program and then try to claim the modified program as their own.

WHERE WILL I FIND THE LICENSE?

Typically, the license agreement will be displayed during the software installation process. This means that, when you install the program, the agreement appears on the screen so you can read it. You then can click a button to indicate whether you accept or decline the agreement. If you accept, the installation continues. If you decline, the installation will not continue.

Read the license agreement carefully. Much of the time, the agreements are standard documents, but you need to review them to ensure there are no terms that would cause you to decline to use the software.

such as for Blizzard's World of Warcraft game, rather than requiring endless hours of waiting to transfer the game's many gigabytes of data to the new player, the user receives just enough of the game so that it can be installed and started. The software company then continues to gradually send and install more and more parts of the game while the user plays, until the complete application is installed.

3.6 Productivity Software

Productivity software includes some of the most popular programs that help businesses efficiently carry out tasks such as writing letters, preparing invoices and receipts, creating sales presentations, and scheduling meetings. The same software helps students prepare reports for class and keep track of exam schedules. People also use productivity software in their homes to organize their time and keep in touch with family and friends.

WORD PROCESSING PROGRAMS

A **word processing program** (also called a **word processor**) provides tools for creating all kinds of text-based documents. Word processors are not limited to working only with text; they enable you to add images to your documents and design documents that look like products of a professional print shop. Using a word processor, you can create long documents with separate chapters, a table of contents, an index, and other features.

A word processor can enhance documents in other ways; you can embed sounds, video clips, and

Figure 3.17   Word processors create all sorts of text-based documents, from simple notes to photo-rich newsletters.

animations into them. You can link different documents together—for example, link a chart from a spreadsheet into a word processing report—to create complex documents that update themselves automatically. Word processors can even create documents for publishing on the World Wide Web, complete with hyperlinked text and graphics.

The word processor's main editing window displays a document and several tools. In addition to a **document area** (or **document window**), which is where you view the document, a word processor provides tools such as the following:

- A **menu bar or ribbon**, which displays titles of menus (lists of commands and options)
- **Toolbars**, which display buttons that represent frequently used commands
- **Rulers**, which show you the positions of text, tabs, margins, indents, and other elements on the page
- **Scroll bars**, which let you scroll through a document that is too large to fit inside the document area
- A **status bar**, which displays information related to your position in the document, the page count, and the status of keyboard keys

You create a document by typing on the keyboard—a process known as entering text. In a new document, the program places a blinking cursor (see Chapter 1) in the upper-left corner of the document window. As you type, the cursor advances across the screen, showing you where the next character will be placed. The cursor can be moved anywhere in the document by selecting its new location with a mouse click or by using the cursor control keys to move it to the new location. When you type, new text will appear wherever the cursor is positioned.

Word processing software lets you change any amount of text already in the document; you retype only the text that needs to be changed. Changing an existing document is called **editing** the document.

The word processor's real beauty is its ability to work with blocks of text. A **block** is a contiguous group of characters, words, lines, sentences, or paragraphs in your document that you mark for editing or formatting. To mark text, you **select** it by dragging across it, by clicking with the mouse, or by using keyboard combinations—or all of these. When you select text, it changes color—becoming highlighted—to indicate that it is selected. The highlighted area will replace the cursor; the word processor will not use both a blinking cursor and a block selection at the same time.

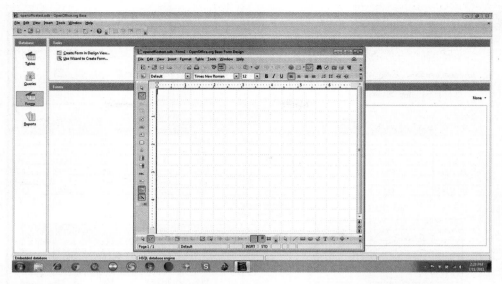

Figure 3.18 OpenOffice Writer's main editing window.

Once a block of text is marked, you can delete the block by using the backspace or DELETE key, replace the block by typing something new, move it to a new location in the document by dragging with the mouse, or change the appearance of the selected block (for example, changing the font size or type). To **deselect** a block without changing it, you simply click elsewhere in the document with the mouse or use a cursor key. The text's appearance will return to normal, and the cursor will reappear in the document.

The process of **formatting** a document includes controlling the appearance of text, the layout of text on the page, and the use of pictures and other graphic elements. Most formatting features fall into one of three categories:

- **Character formatting** includes settings that control the attributes of individual text characters such as fonts, font size, and type style. A **font** is a named set of characters that have the same characteristics. Popular fonts include Courier, Times New Roman, and Arial, but popular word processors feature dozens of different fonts. A font's size (its height) is measured in **points**. One point equals 1/72 of an inch, so 72 points equal one inch. **Type styles** are effects applied to characters such as boldface, underline, or italic.

- **Paragraph formatting** includes settings applied to one or more entire paragraphs, such as line spacing, paragraph spacing, indents, alignment, tabs, borders, or shading. In a word processor, a **paragraph** is any text that ends with a special character called a paragraph mark. You create a paragraph mark when you press the ENTER key.

- **Document formatting** includes the size of the page, its orientation, and headers or footers. Word processing software also lets you apply special formats, such as columns, to documents. You also can divide a document into sections and give each section its own unique format.

These same data-entry and data-editing concepts apply to many other types of programs, including spreadsheets, databases, presentation programs, and others. If you can enter, edit, and select text in one program, then you know how to do it in many other programs.

SPREADSHEET PROGRAMS

A **spreadsheet** program is a software tool for entering, calculating, manipulating, and analyzing sets of numbers. Spreadsheets have a wide range of uses—from tracking family finances to statistical analysis and producing corporate earnings statements. You can set up a spreadsheet to show information in different ways, such as the traditional row-and-column format (the format used in ledger books) or a slick report format with headings and charts. One of a spreadsheet's most powerful purposes is to answer "what if" questions that users pose. For example, a spreadsheet can be used to calculate mortgage payments for a house, using a loan amount, interest rate and duration of loan as input values. A user can ask, "What happens to the monthly payment if the interest rate is six percent instead of four?" and by changing input values on the spreadsheet, answers to that and other "what if" questions are immediately calculated.

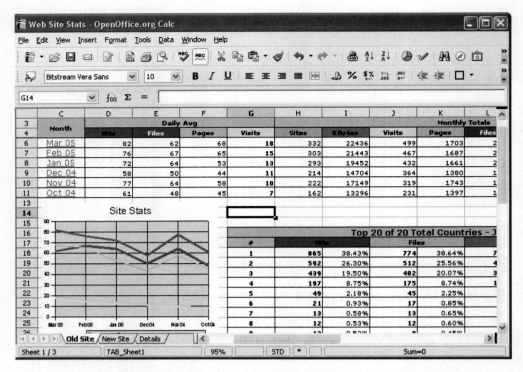

Figure 3.19　An example of a spreadsheet in OpenOffice Calc.

Like a word processor, spreadsheets provide a document area, which is where you view the document. In a spreadsheet program, you work in a document called a **worksheet** (or simply sheet), and you can collect related worksheets in a **workbook** (called a notebook in some programs). Worksheets can be named, and a workbook can contain as many individual worksheets as your system's resources will allow.

A typical spreadsheet interface provides a menu bar or ribbon, toolbars, scroll bars, and a status bar, as shown in Figure 3.19. Spreadsheet programs also display a special **formula bar**, where you can create or edit data and formulas in the worksheet. An empty worksheet (one without any data) looks like a grid of rows and columns. The intersection of any column and row is called a **cell**. A cell holds data in the form of text, numbers, formulas for calculation, or images. Simple spreadsheets may use a handful of cells; complex ones can use thousands.

Entering data in a worksheet is simple. Using the mouse or arrow keys, you select a cell to make it active. The active cell is indicated by a **cell pointer**, a rectangle that makes the active cell's borders look bold. To navigate the worksheet, you need to understand its system of cell addresses. All spreadsheets use row and column identifiers as the basis for their **cell addresses**. If you are working in the cell

where column B intersects with row 3, for example, then the active cell has the address B3.

When you have selected a cell, you simply type the data into it. When a cell is active, you also can type its data into the formula bar. The formula bar is handy because it displays much more data than the cell can. If a cell already contains data, you can edit it in the

Figure 3.20　Spreadsheets neatly track expenses and give users a way to test future forecasts with "what-if" scenarios.

formula bar. A worksheet's cells can hold several types of data, but four kinds are most common:

1. **Labels.** Worksheets can contain text—called **labels** (names for data values)—as well as numbers and other types of data. In spreadsheets, text is usually used to identify a value or series of values (as in a row or column heading) or to describe the contents of a specific cell (such as a total). Labels help you make sense of a worksheet's contents.

2. **Values.** In a spreadsheet, a **value** is any number or text that is considered spreadsheet data, not a label. Values can be data entered by the user, or they can be the result of a calculation that the spreadsheet has been directed to perform. Spreadsheets can work with whole numbers, decimals, negative numbers, currency, and other types of values, including scientific notation. Spreadsheets can also perform text-based operations, such as searching through strings of characters and building new lines of text.

3. **Dates.** Dates are a necessary part of many worksheets, and spreadsheet programs can work with date information in many ways. A date may be added to a worksheet simply to indicate when it was created. Spreadsheets also can use dates in performing calculations, as when calculating late payments on a loan. If the spreadsheet knows the payment's due date, it can calculate late fees based on that date.

4. **Formulas.** The power of the spreadsheet lies in **formulas**. Formulas are special cell contents that perform calculations or logical tests, using the values in other cells as input for their tasks. Formulas can range from simple (for example, producing a sum of all the numbers in a column) to very complex, involving calculus or trigonometry and hundreds or thousands of other cells as input. Often, the values produced by formulas are themselves used by other formulas. For example, a spreadsheet might have columns of sales figures arranged by calendar quarter. Each column could have a formula at the bottom that would total the sales for the quarter. Another formula could be created to add together the results of each total, to get a complete, annual sales amount. Formulas can also contain logical tests; for example, a formula can be created to only display a result if one cell's value is greater than another cell's value.

Cells also can hold graphics, audio files, and video or animation files. To the spreadsheet program, each type of data has a particular use and is handled in a unique manner.

PRESENTATION PROGRAMS

If you have ever attended a class or other lecture where the presenter used slides or overhead transparencies projected on a wall screen or displayed on a computer screen or video monitor, then you probably have seen the product of presentation software. Presentation programs enable the user to create and edit colorful, compelling presentations that can be displayed in various ways and used to support any type of discussion.

Presentation programs allow the user to design **slides**—single-screen images that contain a combination of text, numbers, and graphics (such as charts, drawings, or photos) often on a colorful background. A series of slides, displayed in a specific order to an audience, is called a **presentation**. Usually, the person showing the slides (the presenter) speaks to the audience while the slides are being displayed. The slides themselves show unique, specific pieces of information; the presenter fills in the details with his or her speech.

Slides can be simple or sophisticated. Depending on your needs, you can turn a basic slide show into a multimedia event using the built-in features of many presentation programs.

Figure 3.21 Presentation programs let users create appealing and informative visual aids.

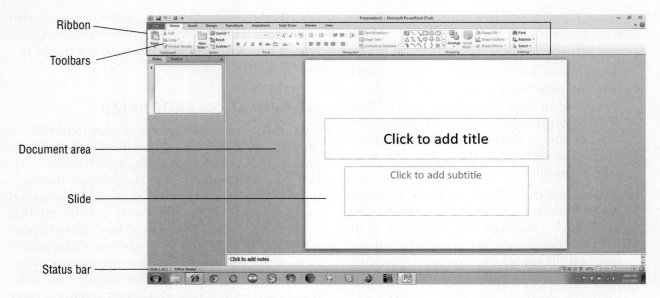

Ribbon

Toolbars

Document area

Slide

Status bar

Figure 3.22 A slide in Microsoft PowerPoint.

The typical presentation program displays a slide in a large document window and provides tools for designing and editing slides. Presentation programs offer many of the features found in word processors (for working with text), spreadsheets (for creating charts), and graphics programs (for creating and editing simple graphics). You can add elements to the slide simply by typing, making menu or toolbar choices, and dragging. As you work on the slide, you see exactly how it will look when it is shown to an audience.

Figure 3.22 shows a slide in Microsoft PowerPoint, a popular presentation program. Note that the status bar says that the presentation contains five slides. A presentation can contain a single slide or hundreds. Presentation programs let you save a group of slides in one file so you can open the related slides and work with them together.

A presentation program includes a menu bar or ribbon, one or more toolbars (for managing files, formatting, drawing, and doing other tasks), rulers, slide-viewing or navigation buttons that let you move from one slide to another, a status bar, and other tools.

Creating a basic presentation is simple; just choose the type of slide you want to create, and then start adding the content. A complete presentation usually includes multiple slides arranged in a logical order. As you go, you can insert new slides anywhere, copy slides from other presentations, and reorder the slides.

You can create a slide format from scratch (building a background of images and colors to appear on every slide), but it is easier and faster to work with one of the presentation program's many templates. A **template** is a predesigned document that already has coordinating fonts, colors, a layout, and a background. Presentation programs often provide dozens of built-in templates.

After you select a template, you can quickly assemble a presentation by creating individual slides. To create a slide, you choose a layout for it. Presentation programs provide many slide layouts that hold varying combinations of titles, text, charts, and graphics. You can choose a different layout for any slide in your presentation, if you want.

After you select a layout, the blank slide appears in the document window, ready for you to add text, charts, or graphics. The program provides special **text boxes** and **frames** (special resizable boxes for text and graphical elements, respectively) to contain specific types of content. These special boxes often contain instructions telling you exactly what to do. To add text to a text box, simply click in the box and type your text. The text is formatted automatically, but you can easily reformat the text later, using many of the same formatting options that are available in word processors.

Adding charts, tables, or other graphics is nearly as easy. When you choose a slide layout that contains a chart, for example, you enter the chart's data in a separate window, called a *datasheet* (see Figure 3.23).

The program uses the data to create a chart. To insert another type of graphic in a slide, you can select an image from your software's collection of graphics or import an image file such as a drawing you have scanned or a photograph you imported from your camera to your computer. Built-in paint tools also enable you to draw graphics and add them to your slides. These tools are handy if you want to add callouts to specific elements of a slide.

Presentation programs can also animate the appearance of slide elements, so the slide updates its contents over time until the final effect is visible. Tools are provided to simplify the process of choosing elements and the manner in which they are to be displayed.

You can present slides directly from your computer's disk, along with any audio or video files you embed in your slides. Your audience can view slides in several ways:

- **On the PC's screen.** If you are presenting slides to a few people, your PC's monitor might be adequate for an informal slide show. Of course, the larger the monitor, the more clearly your audience can see the slides.

- **On a large-format monitor.** Large-format CRT and plasma monitors can display your slides at the proper resolution and large enough for a sizable audience to view comfortably. These devices are expensive and more difficult to transport than a standard monitor, but they may be the best solutions for some presentation settings.

- **On a television screen.** Older computers or televisions need a PC-to-TV converter in order to view the PC's video output on the television screen, or a PC video card that can output television-specific signals. The latest computers and televisions can work in a high-definition video mode, allowing presentation delivery using a television connected to the PC with a DVI or HDMI cable.

- **From a data projector.** Portable, high-resolution data projectors can display slides to a large audience. These projectors plug into one of the PC's ports and accept the system's video output.

Regardless of the method you use to project your slides, navigating a slide show is a simple process. You can move from one slide to the next by clicking the mouse button or pressing ENTER. Or you can automate the presentation by setting a display time for each slide. Presentation programs allow you to take slides out of sequence or rearrange slides during a presentation. You can even use the program's drawing tools to draw on a slide while it is being displayed. When using these and other tools, be sure they are enhancing the presentation's value from the audience's standpoint.

DATABASE MANAGEMENT SOFTWARE

With or without computers, people accumulate data, store it, and then use it to produce information. For

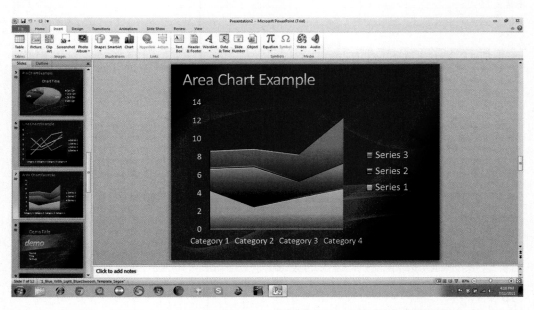

Figure 3.23 PowerPoint uses a separate datasheet to store and organize data for a chart on a slide.

example, people who have a stamp collection often have more than a book filled with stamps; they also record details about each stamp, including where it was found, how much it cost, its relative quality, and so on.

It can be fairly simple—though time consuming—to store data like this without a computer. Notebooks and a pen can do a decent job of recording information about a stamp collection of any size, but it can be difficult and time consuming to retrieve information. What is the oldest stamp in the collection? How many stamps come from China? How many American stamps cost more than $100 to acquire? These types of questions, which transform the raw data into useful information, may not be quickly obtainable by searching through notebooks of handwritten notes. Creating a database on a computer provides a way to retrieve and analyze that information in an instant.

A computer database is simply an organized method for storing information. Very simple databases do not even require specialized software. A Microsoft Excel spreadsheet can do a satisfactory job of storing data for an upcoming school bake sale, for example. Creating columns for each person's name, phone number, and the item they're planning to bake provides organized data, as you can see in Figure 3.24.

Often, however, a database tracks far more than just a few columns of names and phone numbers. For example, an online store selling cell phones has many different things about which they need to store data: customers, vendors, business partners, employees, inventory, and sales data are only a partial list, and each of those categories has different types of associated data. Customer data would include several items, including each person's name, address and payment information. Data for each cell phone in inventory might include such attributes as model number, manufacturer, purchase and retail price, and quantity on hand.

In addition to organizing and storing the data items, the phone store may need to create relationships between data. When a phone is purchased, for example, the store needs an efficient way to link the specific phone and the specific customer together in the database. Those relationships allow database users to answer more complex questions than two-dimensional databases can easily provide. The cell phone store can use related data to find out how many Brand X pink cell phones are being sold in California, even though phone inventory and customer locations are organized separately.

Creating tables and relationships, filling them with data, and answering complex questions require software assistance in order to make those tasks easy to accomplish. To help accomplish these tasks, many users employ a **database management system** (or **DMBS**). Microsoft Access, part of the Microsoft Office software suite, is a popular DBMS choice for many businesses and individuals.

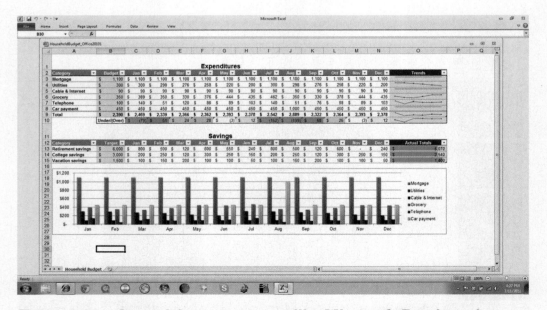

Figure 3.24 Spreadsheet programs like Microsoft Excel can be used to create a simple database.

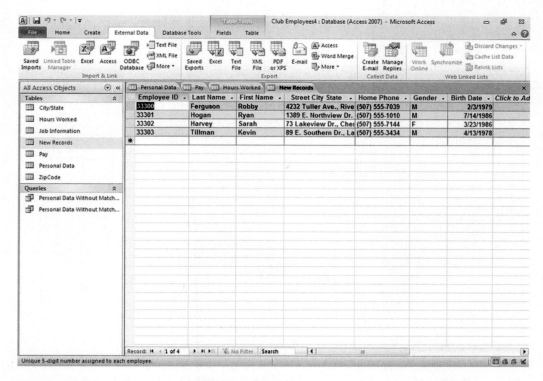

Figure 3.25   A table in Microsoft Access.

Users build an Access database by creating one or more **tables,** which are two-dimensional row and column sheets. Tables are usually created to hold data for a single concept like a customer or an employee. The columns of the table define the types of data to be stored for each concept, so columns for a "customer" table might include their name and address, and the "employee" table might contain columns for an employee's name, address, employee number and hourly rate of pay.

Though a table looks very similar to a spreadsheet, Access and Excel treat their data differently. In Excel, individual cells are treated independently, no matter how the rows or columns might be labeled. In Access, each column must hold the same type of data; if the column is defined as holding a purchase date, then all values in that column must be dates. In addition, all of the values on each row are associated with each other and are called a **record.**

Access becomes even more powerful by helping users create relationships between tables. An Access user defines one column in every table to be that table's **key;** the key column uses its values to uniquely identify each record in the table. When the contents of one table are related in some way to a second table, Access can use that key column to form that relationship in the database.

Consider Figure 3.26, which shows the relationship design window in Access. Two tables now exist in the database; along with the *Customers* table, a second table called Purchases has been created. As you can see, *Purchases* contains the columns Order Num, Item Purchased, and Customer ID. The user has created a relationship between the Customer ID key column in *Customers* and the Customer ID column in *Purchases,* as shown by the line connecting those two column names. This means that when a purchase is made, the user simply needs to enter the purchasing customer's id number into the *Purchases* table, and the database is able to follow that unique id number to *Customers* and look up the purchaser's name and address.

Access also allows the user to formulate questions or information requests called **queries,** which specify data to be retrieved from the database. A query could be simple, for example requesting a list of the first and last names from all the records in the *Customers* table. Queries can also be more complex and involve multiple tables, such as requesting the first and last name fields from *Customers,* for every customer that has purchased a specific item in the *Purchases* table.

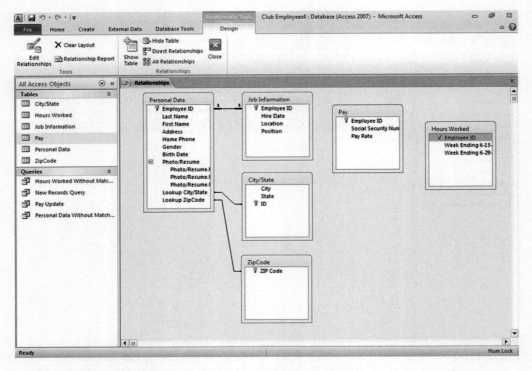

Figure 3.26 Key columns in one Access table can be used to create relationships to other tables.

PERSONAL INFORMATION MANAGERS

It's harder than ever to keep track of contact information for all the people in our lives. You probably know several people who have a home phone number, a cell phone number, one or two e-mail addresses, an instant messenger address, a Facebook page, and Twitter ID, all in addition to their home mailing address. To make matters more difficult, some people also have a Web page, more online contact modes, and maybe even a second mailing address.

It is very common for businesspeople to have multiple contact points. Of course, these many means of

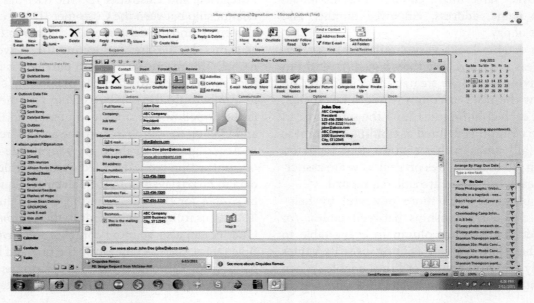

Figure 3.27 Entering contact information in Microsoft Outlook.

Figure 3.28 PIM software can help manage the ever-increasing complexity of personal networking and communication.

contacting people are supposed to make it easier to reach them. But keeping track of all those names, numbers, and addresses—called contact information—can be frustrating.

The explosion of contact information has given rise to a special type of software, called the **personal information manager (PIM)**. A personal information manager is designed to keep track of many different kinds of contact information, for many different people. PIMs are sometimes referred to as **contact managers** or **contact-management software**. One of the most popular PIMs is Microsoft Outlook (see Figure 3.9).

PIMs make contact management easy because they provide special placeholders for all kinds of contact information—everything from phone numbers and e-mail addresses to Web pages and regular mail addresses. To manage contact information for a person, you add the person's name to your contact list.

(Most PIMs store and arrange contacts by first name or last name, according to your preference.) Then you simply type all the contact points into the appropriate boxes in that person's contact sheet.

Like many other PIMs, Outlook stores much more than just contact information. You can use a PIM to manage your schedule, create reminders, and set up to-do lists. Outlook also provides e-mail program that you can use to send messages to anyone in your contact list. Contact lists are often called **address books** in e-mail programs and PIMs.

Many professionals, especially salespeople, use a PIM as their primary software tool. This is because they can manage their calendar and associate specific events with specific contacts. For example, if you schedule a meeting, you can place it in your PIM's calendar; note the time, place, and purpose of the meeting; and create a list of attendees from your contact list. This capability not only lets you manage your schedule down to the last detail, but it also gives you a permanent record of your activities.

Many businesses have invested in software suites that include and extend beyond PIM programs. Called **customer relationship management (CRM)** software, this type of integrated tool includes PIM-style features like contact data for customers and meeting calendars, and adds a host of other features for managing ongoing customer relationships. The software can track customer purchases, forward customer inquiries to sales agents for follow-up, log complaints and requests for support, and provide management with analysis tools for tracking the company's performance with regard to customer satisfaction and behavior. As personal information grows to include the ever-changing updates and thoughts posted via social applications such as Facebook, LinkedIn and Twitter, applications such as TweetDeck allow you to collect and distribute social media updates from a central location. TweetDeck can organize and display the ongoing status updates from different social media networks on a single screen, and allows users to make a single update and broadcast it to multiple social services at once.

Fact Check

1. Which of the following is an example of formatting a document in a word processor?
   a. Erasing and completely remapping the data
   b. Controlling the appearance of text
   c. Correcting misspelled words
2. Microsoft Outlook is an example of what kind of software?
   a. Personal Internet mail
   b. Productivity inference metrics
   c. Personal information manager

3.7 Graphics Software

OVERVIEW: GRAPHICS, GRAPHICS EVERYWHERE

Many of the images you see are created on a computer. From postage stamps to magazine illustrations, from billboards to television programs, all kinds of graphics are created and edited using computers and graphics software. Graphics programs—and the designers who use them—have become so polished that it is often impossible to tell a photograph or hand-drawn illustration from a computer-generated or computer-altered graphic. In fact, the capabilities have grown so powerful that sometimes ethical quandaries arise, as described in the "Ethical Dilemma" feature.

With the computer's capability to mimic traditional artists' media, graphics software allows artists to do with a computer what they once did with brushes, pencils, and darkroom equipment. Similarly, architects and engineers now do most of their design and rendering work on computers—although many were trained in traditional paper-based drafting methods. By using the computer, they produce designs and renderings that are highly accurate and visually pleasing.

Graphics software has advanced a great deal in a short time. In the early 1980s, most graphics programs were limited to drawing simple geometric outlines, usually in one color. Today, graphics software offers advanced drawing and painting tools and almost unlimited color control. You can see the products of these powerful tools everywhere you look. Their results can be subtle or stunning, obviously artificial, or amazingly lifelike.

UNDERSTANDING THE STRUCTURE OF GRAPHICS FILES

Computers can create many, many kinds of graphics—from simple line drawings to three-dimensional animations. But all graphics files fall into one of two basic categories, known as bitmaps and vector files:

1. Graphics files may be made up of a grid, called a **bitmap**, whose cells are filled with one or more colors. The individual cells in the grid can all be filled with the same color, or each cell can contain a different color. Bitmaps also may be referred to as *bitmapped images*. The easiest way to imagine how bitmaps work is to think of your computer's monitor. It displays images as collections of individual colored pixels. Each pixel is a cell in the grid of a bitmapped image.

Is there an ethical line when using photo-editing software?

With photo-editing software, amateur and professional photographers can touch up and improve the visual quality of their pictures, but that's not all. Skilled software users can alter the content of the images they capture with their camera. They can change the shape, size, and color of buildings and scenery, add and delete objects, and even place people in scenes they never visited or situations that never happened.

Photo-manipulation programs can seamlessly alter and combine pictures to create striking effects.

This capability can be fun and even artistic, but is there an ethical line between creativity and falsehood? For example, should users alter photographs to show people in situations that didn't actually occur? Does your answer depend on whether the photo is hung in an art gallery, posted on Facebook, or presented as news in a newspaper or magazine? Does it depend on whether the image shows famous people, unnamed subjects—or you? When you look at a photograph in a print or online newspaper, do you trust that the image is showing exactly what the photographer saw? Would you accept alterations to make the photo more dramatic if the publisher included a statement that it had been altered?

Figure 3.29 Vector graphics are ideal when resizing and repositioning an object are required.

2. Graphics files may be made up of a set of **vectors**, which are mathematical equations describing the size, shape, thickness, position, color, and fill of lines or closed graphical shapes.

Some types of graphics programs work with bitmaps, some work with vectors, and some can work with both.

Each type of graphics file has its own advantages and disadvantages. Whether you use a bitmap- or vector-based program depends on what you are trying to do. For example, if you want to be able to retouch a photo, create seamless tiling textures for the Web or for 3-D surfaces, or create an image that looks like a painting, you will choose bitmap-based software. Vector-based software is your best choice if you want the flexibility of resizing an image without degrading its sharpness, the ability to reposition elements easily in an image, or the ability to achieve an illustrative look as when drawing with a pen or pencil.

Vector-based software can use mathematical equations to define the thickness and color of a line, its pattern or fill, and other attributes. Although a line on the screen is still displayed as a series of blocks (because that is how all monitors work), it is an equation to the computer. Thus, to move the line from location A to location B, the computer substitutes the coordinates for location A with those for location B. This substitution saves the effort of calculating how to change the characteristics of thousands of individual pixels.

FILE FORMATS AND COMPATIBILITY ISSUES

A **file format** is a standardized method of encoding data for storage. File formats are important because they tell the program what kind of data is contained in the file and how the data is organized.

File formats may be proprietary or universal. The structure of a proprietary file format is under the sole control of the software developer who invented the format. Universal file formats are based on openly published specifications and are commonly used by many different programs and operating systems. Many programs that have their own proprietary format can also save files in one or more universal formats, to allow graphic work to be shared to other programs that also support those universal formats.

Nearly all bitmap-based graphics programs can use any of the file formats listed in Table 3.2. For this reason, these formats are said to be **compatible** with such programs. For example, most bitmap-based programs can open, read, and save a file in GIF format.

Most vector-based programs create and save files in a proprietary file format. These formats either are **incompatible** with (cannot be used by) other programs or are not totally supported by other programs. The problem with incompatibility led developers to create universal file formats for vector-based programs. Only a handful of common file formats, such as DXF (Data Exchange Format) and IGES (Initial Graphics Exchange Specification) exist for vector graphics.

GETTING IMAGES INTO YOUR COMPUTER

Nearly all graphics programs let you create images from scratch by building lines and shapes into complex graphics. But artists and designers do not always start from scratch; they often begin with an existing image and then edit or enhance it by using graphics software. There are several ways to load images into a computer for editing, but the most common methods are the following:

- **Scanners.** An image scanner is like a photocopy machine, but instead of copying an image onto paper, it transfers the image directly into the computer. A scanned image is usually a bitmap

TABLE 3.2 STANDARD FORMATS FOR BITMAP GRAPHICS

Format	Description
BMP	BitMaP: A graphics format native to Microsoft Windows, BMP is widely used on PCs for icons and wallpaper. Some Macintosh programs also can read BMP files. The BMP file format supports up to 24-bit depth color, or over 16 million different colors.
PICT	PICTure: This is the native format defined by Apple for use on Macintosh computers. It is widely used on Macs but is not usually used on PCs.
TIFF	Tagged Image File Format: TIFF is a bitmap format defined in 1986 by Microsoft and Aldus (now part of Adobe) and widely used on both Macs and PCs. This format is usually the best to use when exchanging bitmap files that will be printed or edited further.
JPEG	Joint Photographic Experts Group: JPEG is often abbreviated as JPG (pronounced JAY-peg). This bitmap format is common on the World Wide Web and is often used for photos and other high-resolution (24-bit or millions of colors) images that will be viewed on screen.
GIF	Graphic Interchange Format: Like JPEG images, GIF images are often found on World Wide Web pages. Unlike JPEG images, GIF images can contain only 256 or fewer unique colors.
PNG	Portable Network Graphics: This format was created to improve upon the GIF format. PNG files support more color options than GIF, and in many cases can compress images to a smaller size. Though PNG is not as efficient as JPEG at compressing images, PNG does not suffer the loss in quality that JPEG can create during compression.
EMF	Windows Enhanced Metafile: This format was originally developed for the Microsoft Office suite of applications. It uses the Windows built-in graphics device interface, or GDI, to create images that can be scaled to display at the highest-possible resolution on any device selected—screen or printer. This technology creates something of a hybrid between the vector graphics and bitmap types, since EMF bitmaps can be resized without any loss of quality.

file, but software tools are available for translating images into vector format.

- **Digital cameras.** A digital camera stores digitized images for transfer into a computer. The resulting file is generally a bitmap.

- **Digital video cameras.** A digital video camera captures and stores full-motion video on small tapes or optical discs. You can copy the content onto a computer for editing or transfer to another storage medium, such as DVD.

- **Clip art.** The term **clip art** originated with large books filled with professionally created drawings and graphics that could be clipped from the pages and glued to a paper layout. Today, clip art provides an easy way to enhance digital documents. Many software programs (especially word processors) feature built-in collections of clip art, and collections are also available on DVD/CD-ROM and the Internet. Clip art can be in either bitmap or vector format.

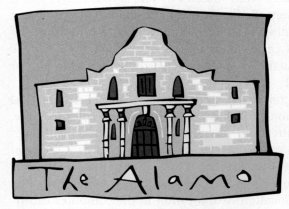

Figure 3.30   Example of clip art.

TYPES OF GRAPHICS SOFTWARE

Creating a digital image or manipulating an existing image can involve a complex array of processes. Because even the most sophisticated graphics program cannot perform all the operations that may be required for some types of graphics, designers frequently achieve their goals by using more than one of the five major categories of graphics software:

1. Paint programs

2. Photo-editing programs

3. Draw programs

4. Computer-aided design (CAD) programs

5. 3-D modeling and animation programs

Of the five, the first two are bitmap-based paint programs; the remaining three are vector-based draw programs (although 3-D programs commonly work with vectors or bitmaps).

Paint programs are bitmap-based graphics programs. You already may be familiar with a paint program, like Windows Paint. Paint programs range from the very simple (with only a handful of tools) to the very complex, with tools that have names such as paintbrush, pen, chalk, watercolors, airbrush, crayon, and eraser. Because paint programs keep track of each and every pixel placed on a screen, they also can perform tasks that are impossible with traditional artists' tools—for pixel or changing every pixel in an image from one color to another color.

Paint programs provide the tools for creating some spectacular effects. More sophisticated paint programs can make brush strokes that appear thick or thin, soft or hard, drippy or neat, opaque or transparent. Some programs allow you to change media with a mouse click, turning your paintbrush into chalk or a crayon or giving your smooth "canvas" a texture such as rice paper or an eggshell.

Draw programs are vector-based graphics programs that are well suited for work when accuracy and flexibility are as important as coloring and special effects. You see the output of draw programs in everything from cereal box designs to television show credits. Simply by clicking and dragging in a draw program, you can change a shape into a different shape, move it, or copy it. Paint programs don't provide this flexibility because they do not recognize lines, shapes, and fills as unique objects. Draw programs are sometimes referred to as *object-oriented programs* because each item drawn—whether it is a line, square, rectangle, or circle—is treated as a separate and distinct object from all the others. All objects created in draw programs consist of an outline and a fill. The fill can be nothing at all, a solid color, a vector pattern, a photo, or something else.

Cousins to paint programs, **photo-editing programs** now take the place of a photographer's darkroom for many tasks. Because photo-editing programs (like paint programs) edit images at the pixel level, they can control precisely how a picture will look. They also are used to edit non-photographic images and to create images from scratch. Photo-editing programs are often used for simple jobs such as sharpening focus, adjusting contrast, or removing flaws from digitized images. But photo-editing programs are also used to modify photographs in ways far beyond the scope of a traditional darkroom—for example, by combining elements from two or more photos into one image. See the "Ethical Dilemma" feature, earlier in the chapter, for more on some implications of this capability.

Computer-aided design (CAD), also called *computer-aided drafting* or *computer-aided drawing*, is the computerized version of the hand-drafting process that used to be done with a pencil and ruler on a drafting table. CAD is used extensively in technical fields such as architecture and in mechanical, electrical, and industrial engineering. CAD software also is used in other design disciplines, such as textile and clothing design and product and package design.

Vector-based CAD drawings are usually the basis for the actual building or manufacturing process of houses, engine gears, or electrical systems, for example. To satisfy the rigorous requirements of manufacturing, CAD programs provide a high

Figure 3.31   An image scanner can digitize a picture of anything that can be placed on the scanning surface.

No two workdays are alike for Corby Simpson, senior programmer at Toronto-based Creative Post Inc., a post-production facility offering creative solutions for broadcast television and interactive media.

When he's not developing video content, designing distribution labels, authoring a DVD, or creating content for use on a PDA, he's updating his skills and learning about new technologies.

"Keeping up with the new trends can be a full-time job in itself," says Simpson, who completed a three-year media arts program and a one-year interactive multimedia postgraduate program at Sheridan College.

For Simpson, the multimedia field is most enjoyable for the creative outlet it provides. "It's one of the only industries where you can invent things with no cost attached to them, just time," says Simpson. "You can also invent other people's ideas, and if they're successful, you get a piece of that pie too."

Sometimes, the creative aspect also can pose challenges for Simpson, who recently was under pressure to learn how to change the way 50,000 lines of computer code worked. "The application was our own invention, so we couldn't outsource it," says Simpson. "Under normal conditions somebody would go to school for three years to learn what we did in less than a month." Simpson sees opportunities in the multimedia field as growing, thanks to an increase in Web-based applications and wireless development.

Careers in multimedia are as varied and as numerous as multimedia products, with the workload typically shared by a team and led by a creative director who is responsible for developing and refining the overall design process from start to finish. The creative director is also responsible for integrating that design process into the developmental process of the company. The team members of a multimedia project usually include some or all of the following:

- **Art director.** Directs the creation of all art for the project.

- **Technical lead.** Ensures that the technological process of a project works and that it accommodates all project components and media.

- **Interface designer.** Directs the development of the user interface for a product, which includes not only what users see but also what they hear and touch.

- **Instructional designer.** Designs the instructional system for the product, which determines how material is taught, if the product is educational.

- **Visual designer.** Creates the various art forms, usually within a specialized area.

- **Interactive scriptwriter.** Weaves the project's content among various media and forms of interactivity.

- **Animator.** Uses 2-D and 3-D software to create animation and effects.

- **Sound producer.** As a manager, creative artist, and programmer, a sound producer designs and produces all the audio in a product.

- **Videographer.** Creates the video footage that interfaces with the interactive technology of the product.

- **Programmer/software designer.** Designs and creates the underlying software that runs a multimedia program and carries out the user's commands.

The Bureau of Labor Statistics reported a median annual earnings estimate of salaried multimedia artists and animators at $58,250 in 2009.

degree of precision. If you want to draw a line that is 12.396754 inches long or a circle with a radius of 0.90746 centimeter, a CAD program can fulfill your needs. In fact, CAD programs are so precise that they can produce designs accurate to the micrometer—or one-millionth of a meter.

You are constantly exposed to elaborate 3-D imaging in movies, television, and print. Many of these images are now created with a special type of graphics software, called **3-D modeling software**. Fast workstations or PCs coupled with 3-D modeling programs can lend realism to even the most fantastic subjects. Digital 3-D objects can be modified to any shape using electronic tools much like those used in woodworking. For example, holes can be drilled into computer-based 3-D objects, and corners can be made round or square by selecting the appropriate menu item. Three-dimensional objects also can be given realistic textures and patterns, or they can be animated or made to fly through space.

An outgrowth of the 3-D explosion, **computer-generated imaging (CGI)** has changed the world of animation in many ways. Since the creation of filmmaking, animation was possible only through a painstaking process of hand-drawing a series of images (called cels) and then filming them one by one. Each filmed image is called a frame. When the film is played back at high speed (usually around 30 frames per second for high-quality animation), the images blur together to create the illusion of motion on the screen. The process of manually creating a short animation—even just a few seconds' worth—can take weeks of labor.

Although computer animation works on the same principles as traditional animation (a sequence of still images displayed in rapid succession), computer animators now have highly sophisticated tools that take the drudgery out of the animation process and allow them to create animation more quickly than ever. Computer animators also have the advantage of being able to display their animation on the computer screen or output them to CD-ROM, videotape, or film.

An added bonus of computer animation is the ability to animate three-dimensional characters and create **photorealistic** scenes. (The computer-generated image looks so realistic that it could be mistaken for a photograph of a real-life object.) These capabilities make computer-generated characters difficult to distinguish from real ones. Some examples are the character Gollum in *The Lord of the Rings: The Two Towers* and the eerie landscapes of *The Matrix* series of movies. Using computers and special animation software, artists and designers can create many types of animation, from simple perspective changes to complex full-motion scenes that incorporate animated characters with real-life actors and sound.

MULTIMEDIA SOFTWARE

For much of history, information was presented via a single medium at a time. A *medium* is simply a way of sharing information. Sound, such as the human voice, is one type of medium; for centuries before written language came into widespread use, speech was the primary way of sharing knowledge. People also told stories (and left a record of their lives) through drawings and paintings. The creation of written language gave people yet another medium for expressing their thoughts.

Figure 3.32   Because they provide the user with multiple forms of information and many options for affecting the output, both computer games and reference programs are highly interactive.

Today, people commonly combine different types of media (the term *media* is the plural of *medium*), such as speech, sounds, music, text, graphics, animation, and video, to convey information. People discovered that messages are more effective (that is, the audience understands and remembers them more easily) when they are presented through a combination of different media. This combination is what is meant by the term **multimedia**—using more than one type of medium at the same time.

The computer has taken multimedia to a high level by enabling us to use many different media simultaneously. A printed encyclopedia, for example, is basically pages of text and pictures. In a multimedia version, however, the encyclopedia's pictures can move, a narrator's recorded voice can provide the text, and the user can move around at will by clicking hypertext links and using navigational tools. By combining different types of media to present the message, the encyclopedia's developer improves the chances that users will understand and remember the information.

Though television programming also produces content using more than one medium, computer technologies enable PC-based multimedia products to go one step further. Because the computer can accept and respond to input from the user, it can provide multimedia events that are **interactive**, involving the user unlike any book, movie, or television program.

Most television programs require the viewer only to sit and observe, creating a passive, receive-only experience. Computers make it possible to create interactive media, which enable people to respond to—and even control—what they see and hear. By using the PC to control the program, the user can make choices, move freely from one part of the content to another, and in some cases customize the content to suit a specific purpose. Interactive media are effective because they provide this give and take with the user. You will find this level of interactivity in practically any popular multimedia product, whether the program is a video game, a digital reference tool, an electronic test bank, or a shopping site on the Web.

As the complexity of multimedia productions has increased, more powerful creative software tools have been designed to keep pace. Multimedia software can often be acquired as a large suite of tools, but some producers of those suites also sell single parts of their multimedia offerings. Many designers specialize in just one aspect of a multimedia production, such as sound or animation, and prefer to avoid the extra monetary and hard drive storage costs associated with a complete multimedia suite. The following overview explores some of the multimedia tools that are available.

Audio editing and production. While almost any personal computer can be configured to accept and store audio input, professional audio production requires far more than just a microphone and a computer to store a sound data file. Music and sound effects often require the blending and balancing of multiple individual sound tracks to create the final desired result. Software suites such as Sony Sound Forge provide a set of tools for recording and digitizing sound; mixing tracks together; editing individual sound tracks; applying effects and filters to the sound; and creating master recordings ready to be transferred to CDs for sale. Such programs may also allow the editor to match sound to digital video, coordinating a soundtrack frame by frame to the video. For sound editors on a budget, free sound editing software such as Audacity provides a solid set of features for recording and editing sound.

Video editing and production. Millions of people share their own movies and video clips via online services such as YouTube. In some cases, no editing is required; the video capture device can output a movie clip as a file that can simply be uploaded. However, many people prefer to do at least some basic editing, for example cutting out irrelevant footage at the start or end of the clip, or adding a music soundtrack. Programs such as Windows Live Movie Maker or iMovie for Apple computers provide a consumer-friendly interface and a host of production

Fact Check

1. What is a bitmap?
   a. A diagram of where to find data on a hard drive
   b. A series of interconnected line objects
   c. A grid, whose cells are filled with one or more colors
2. What are draw programs?
   a. Programs that require an underlying bitmap to function properly
   b. Vector-based graphics programs
   c. Programs that can only show straight-line objects

shortcuts to make this editing job simpler. Both of those programs help users easily edit footage, build scenes and add soundtracks, and even provide pre-constructed templates for users who want to add graphics and visual themes. For more professional efforts, programs like Sony Vegas Pro support greater video quality, more detailed editing control for both video and audio, a wide range of video data formats, and even the ability to create Blu-ray DVDs.

Multimedia authoring software. Often, multimedia content is created not just for its own sake, but to improve the communication of ideas. Presentations and online courses often benefit from the inclusion of audio and video components, but a program developed only for audio or video editing may not be ideal for producing the complete multimedia presentation. Numerous software suites provide a variety of solutions for producing multimedia products. Programs like Adobe Director supply tools to create and publish interactive games, simulations and online courses (commonly called eLearning courses). Director provides the ability to integrate and customize audio and video, including the creating of 3-D graphical images and environments. Another company, Articulate, provides tools especially for eLearning course creators, helping users to create presentations, quizzes and surveys. Articulate also provides online services to publish eLearning courses on the Web, and additional online tools to track course users' participation in quizzes, surveys and interactive parts of the presentation.

- There are four basic ways to acquire software. Commercial software, which requires or requests payment, comes in the form of stand-alone programs and software suites. Shareware is software that is freely distributed with the request that users voluntarily compensate the developer in some way for its use. Free software, known as freeware, may be acquired without purchasing it. Open-source software allows the users to obtain the program's source code, or instructions, and modify it for their own use subject to conditions.

- Word processors allow the user to format documents by altering the appearance of characters, paragraphs, and the layout of the entire document.

- Spreadsheets work with four basic kinds of data: labels, values, dates, and formulas.

- Database management programs collect and organize data into tables, and allows the user to define relationships between various data elements in different tables. Users can employ queries to request sets of data from the database.

- Graphics files can be loaded into the computer via scanners, digital cameras, video cameras, and clip art files found on optical storage and the Internet.

- Paint programs provide tools for the user to create and manipulate bitmap images. Draw programs use vector graphic objects to create line and shape drawings. Photo-editing programs also work with bitmaps and are primarily used to adjust and alter photographs. Computer-aided design programs produce detailed, highly accurate drawings for engineering and scientific applications. 3-D and animation software generates three-dimensional pictures and animations for engineering and entertainment.

Key Terms

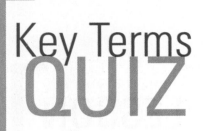

Key Terms QUIZ

Complete each statement by writing one of the terms listed under "Key Terms" in each blank.

1. You can try out a(n) _____ program before you must purchase or register it.

2. _____ is software of any type whose source code is available to users.

3. Changing an existing document is called _____ the document.

4. A spreadsheet column letter and a row number combine to form a(n) _____.

5. A spreadsheet program uses _____ to calculate numbers based on the contents of a worksheet's cells.

6. A(n) _____ provides tools for creating databases and managing their contents.

7. If a program can use a specific file format, the two are said to be _____.

8. Users create _____ to request specific sets of data items from a database.

9. The term _____ refers to the use of more than one medium at a time to present information.

10. If a multimedia program can accept and respond to input from the user, it is said to be _____.

Review QUESTIONS

In your own words, briefly answer the following questions.

1. In what ways do software developers make their programs available to users?

2. Describe three kinds of formatting you can perform with word processing software.

3. What are the types of data that a user can enter and manipulate with spreadsheet software?

4. Suppose you want to create computer files to store images for a school project. What four ways can you consider to load your images onto your computer? Which do you think would be easiest to use? Why?

5. What are the basic types of graphics software? Name an application for each.

6. Describe the two primary categories of graphics files.

7. Where does the term *clip art* come from? How is this type of art used?

8. Explain in a basic way how relationships can be created between groups of data in a database.

9. What does the term *multimedia* refer to? Where have you encountered it in your own experience?

10. What is interactivity, in the context of multimedia?

LESSON LAB

Complete the following exercises as directed by your instructor.

1. Explore cloud-based software on Google Docs. Using a browser, visit the Google Docs Web site at http:/docs.google.com/. If you do not already have access to Google Docs, click on the button that says, "Try Google Docs Now".

   a. Google Docs will allow you to experiment with three different types of document editors: text, spreadsheet and drawing. You can switch between types of editors by selecting them near the top of the screen.

   b. Spend a few minutes with each type of document. How easy is it to add, delete and modify information in the document? View the list of tools and functions that are available for each type of document. If you have used similar programs installed on your PC, such as Microsoft Word or Excel, how do the Google Docs features compare to those other programs. Are the features offered by Google Docs sufficient for you to work with these kinds of documents?

   c. With your instructor's permission, break into pairs. Have one person share the link in the demo's top box with their partner, so that both people can access the same document. Experiment with making changes now that two people are collaborating. What parts of the shared-work experience do you find attractive or frustrating?

2. Explore how multimedia collections can be used to educate, fascinate and sometimes simply share raw information on the Web. Point your browser to NASA's Multimedia Page at http://www.nasa.gov/multimedia/. Note the various collections of pictures, audio and video that are available from the main page, as well as links to companion information hosted on social media sites such as Flickr and YouTube. Browse through links, pictures and video as time permits. Do you find this site's organization and layout easy to navigate? Do you find the wide variety of topics and multimedia modes confusing, or does it provide a rich experience for you?

Some business projects are completed by one person, but many others are built piece-by-piece by several people, each adding expertise at the appropriate stage of the process. In this exercise, you will try the kind of teamwork that includes independent effort during each of three separate phases. Each team member will try each phase.

Divide into teams of three students. Each team will use presentation software such as PowerPoint to create a slide displaying the national estimates for the median annual wages of computer systems analysts. To find the most recent data, go to the Occupational Employment Statistics page of the Bureau of Labor Statistics Web site (www.bls.gov/oes/), and click on "Multi-Screen Data Search." Select "One occupation in multiple industries"—the occupational code for systems analysts is 151051. Obtain data for all industries or at least 10. When you have the data, each team member follows these steps:

1. Starting with a blank slide, enter the industry names and median wages. Format this information in whatever way you find effective, but do not add any text, titles, colors, or artwork. Save your work in a file you can share with your teammates.

2. Exchange your file with another member of the team. Using the slide you received, add titles, explanations, and any other words needed to make the information clear. Do not edit, change, or correct the data in the slide, but you can adjust the placement of that information. Save your work.

3. Share the file with the member of the team who has not yet worked on that slide. This third person adds whatever colors, formatting, and artwork will make the slide appealing, interesting, and clear.

Compare the slides your team created. Which slide is the easiest to understand? Which slide is the most accurate? Which slide is the most visually appealing? Do the slides look like the result of teamwork or more like the work of three separate people? How could you improve the way your team collaborated?

[*Chapter* **LABS**]

Complete the following exercises using a computer in your classroom, lab, or home.

1. **Watch those files grow.** The concept of bits and bytes may seem unimportant until you begin creating files on your computer. Then you can begin to understand how much memory and storage space your files take up (in bytes, of course). Create a file in Notepad, save it to disk, and take the following steps to add to the file to see how it grows:

   a. Launch Notepad. The steps to launch the program vary, depending on which version of Windows you use. If you need help, ask your instructor for directions.

   b. Type two or three short paragraphs of text. When you are done, click the "File" menu, and then click the "Save As" command.

   c. In the "Save As" dialog box, choose a drive and folder in which to save the new file, and give the file a short name you can remember easily, such as "size-test.txt."

   d. With Notepad running, launch Windows Explorer. If you need help, ask your instructor for directions.

   e. Navigate to the drive and folder where you saved your Notepad file. When you find the file, look for its size in the "Size" column, and write down the size. Close the "Exploring" window.

   f. Return to the Notepad window and add two or three more paragraphs of text. Then, click the "File" menu, and click the "Save" command to resave the file under the same name.

   g. Reopen Windows Explorer and look at the file's size again. Has it changed? By how much?

2. **Create a file system.** Suppose that you work for a soft drink company. Your manager has asked you to create a business proposal for a new product—a fun, caffeine-free soda for kids under the age of eight. The proposal will be about 50 pages long and will include several supporting documents, such as reports, memos, budgets, customer lists, research on the product's safety, focus group results, taste tests, and so on. These different documents will be created in several forms, including word processing documents, spreadsheet files, databases, presentations, and so on.

   Your first task is to create a file system on your computer's hard disk where you can store and manage all these files. Using a piece of paper, design a set of folders (and subfolders, if needed) to store all the files in a logical manner. Be prepared to share your file system with the class and to discuss the logic behind your file system.

3. **Check out some audio/video players.** Several audio and video players are available for use on the PC, and each provides a unique set of features in addition to supporting various multimedia file types. Visit these Web sites for information on a few players, but do not download any software without your instructor's permission:

   - **Real Networks, Inc.** For information about the RealOne Player, visit http://www.real.com.

   - **Microsoft.** For information about Windows Media Player, visit http://www.microsoft.com/windows/windowsmedia.

   - **Apple Computer, Inc.** For information on the QuickTime player, visit http://www.quicktime.com.

[*Think* AND DISCUSS]

As directed by your instructor, discuss the following questions in class or in groups.

1. Why do you think a basic truth in computing is that one never has enough storage space? What factors contribute to this situation? As hard disks get larger and larger, do you think we will reach a point where the standard desktop computer has more than enough storage space for the average user's needs? Have we reached that point already?

2. Do you think that using a spell checker and a grammar checker for all your final documents is a sufficient substitute for proofreading? Explain why.

[*Fact Check* ANSWERS]

3A:

LO3.1 Operating System Types and Functions

1a: medical diagnostics equipment, life-support systems, machinery, scientific instruments, industrial systems
1b: old operating systems, such as MS-DOS or Palm OS.
1c: most consumer-oriented computers; PCs; Macs; tablets and smart phones.
1d: network computers; mainframe computers
2: a. They allow the computer's user to do multiple things at the same time.

LO3.2 Moving Data Around the Computer

1: a. Moves data from one hardware subsystem to another
2: c. Cache
3: b. arithmetic logic unit

LO3.3 Common Operating Systems

1: b. Windows
2: b. Only computers made by Apple

LO3.4 Data, Files and Utility Programs

1: b. bringing a computer from power-up to fully operational
2: a. The name of the file system used with current versions of Windows
3: b. remove unnecessary files, compress data,and defragment drive
4: The more efficiently data is stored on a hard drive, the faster the computer can retrieve what it needs. Faster data retrieval and storage means overall better performance for the computer.

3B:

LO3.5 Acquiring and Installing Software

1: b. Software that requires or requests payment
2: b. Software whose source code is available to users
3: c. The process of placing software on a personal computer

LO3.6 Productivity Software

1: b. Controlling the appearance of text
2: c. Personal information manager

LO3.7 Graphics Software

1: c. A grid, whose cells are filled with one or more colors
2: b. Vector-based graphics programs

4

MEETING YOUR COMPUTING NEEDS

Chapter Overview

Computers are the ultimate exception to the "one size fits all" rule. The vast array of available hardware and software choices mean that users often achieve their ideal computing experience by customizing their computer environment to match their exact needs. In this chapter, you'll learn about many factors to consider when buying, setting up, and using a new computer, whatever form it may take. When you think of acquiring a new computer, what is the first necessary decision that comes to mind?

LESSON 4A:
Choosing the Right Computer

Chances are good that you were using a computer of some kind even before you began this course. Computers are common objects at home, work, and on the go. If you've used a desktop or mobile computer recently, you may not have given much thought to the components inside it, but when the time comes to buy a new computer, the details of those components suddenly become much more important.

You may find, especially if shopping for a new desktop computer, that you are faced with a dizzying assortment of decisions and choices to make. The simple question, "What computer should I buy?" becomes a seemingly endless discussion about speed, capacity, cost, and personal preference. Fortunately, with a bit of planning and organization, it's easy to transform the process of shopping back into a straightforward and fun experience.

4.1 Determining Your Computing Needs

As you explore your computing requirements, you may very well find that you need a computer for more than just one primary task. Some people use their computer for a wide variety of functions, from games to work, socializing to writing in solitude.

Figure 4.1   New computer buyers face many choices when they shop; basic prioritizing can simplify the experience.

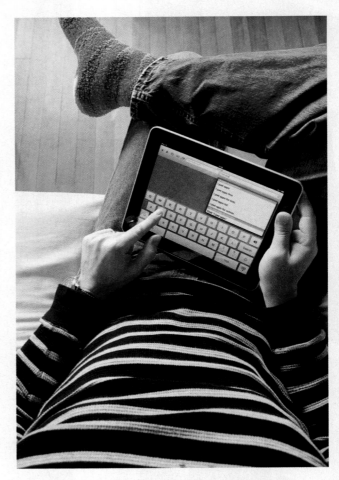

Figure 4.2   Computers are not always ideal for every application. You may find that more than one type is required to meet all your needs.

You may also discover that you have requirements that seem to conflict. For example, you may be a gamer with very high performance standards, yet you also want the freedom of chatting online with friends while at the bistro down the street because it has free wireless Internet access. A tablet computer like an Apple iPad might be the perfect choice for the bistro table, yet you would likely find it underpowered and completely unsuitable to run high-intensity games, if those games could even be found for that type of computer.

Strictly from the perspective of matching computers with needs, your ideal solution may require buying more than one computing device. A high performance computer and large monitor on your desk at home can be your best friend whether you find yourself slaying dragons, solving crimes, or defending a base against incoming soldiers. When it's time to head out with friends, an iPad or smart phone is small and easy to use, perfect for staying in touch on the go and in a crowd. By owning both those devices, you provide yourself with an ideal computing experience no matter where you are and what you want to do.

Of course, budget is a big factor for most people, and it may not be possible to purchase a different computer for every circumstance in your life. Compromise may be required if your lifestyle calls for owning more than one device, either in the quality of what you buy or buying one of the devices later after extra money can be saved. Even so, it is important to create the best match between your requirements and the hardware so you can make the best possible choices and plan future purchases more effectively.

UNDERSTANDING YOUR CURRENT TECHNOLOGY SETUP

The first necessary step in selecting the right computer to purchase is to understand your current computing environment and estimate your future needs. To select the right tool for the job, you have to first understand the job. As you consider your computing needs, take the time to note down requirements on paper as you go. There are enough factors to consider that a list may help you prioritize and focus on what is most important.

Begin with a broad, basic evaluation of yourself as a computer user. Are you a casual computer user, turning it on only now and then to perform a specific task; or do you find yourself relying on your computer heavily for work, play, or staying in touch? Do you use a computer for "a little bit of everything," playing games, chatting, surfing the Web, watching TV shows, and writing a letter now and then? Or are you a power user in some ways, playing intense games, composing music, or creating movies from raw footage? Are you a business user more than a home user, working with spreadsheets, databases, document-sharing systems, or inventory tracking software?

Having thought over the role that a computer plays (or soon will play) in your life, consider the computer technologies that might already be in use in the environments where you will use the computer. Do you need access to a wireless network that's already in place? Will you need to receive and deliver information on DVD disks to customers or friends? Will you be frequently transporting data from place to place via USB flash drive? Is your computer-based work so time-critical that you must be able to recover immediately from a hard drive failure instead of taking the extra time to reinstall your programs and data from backups?

Finally, determine whether there are any existing devices and programs in your computing environment with which you must be compatible. Are there printers already in place that you plan to use? Will you

Figure 4.3 Knowing what devices will connect to your computer will help make sure you have the right interface connections.

be transferring data back and forth between a video camera that uses FireWire? Will you need to connect your computer to external hard drives that use the eSATA interface? Do you have several USB devices that may all need to connect simultaneously, such as a keyboard, mouse, flash drive, digital camera, and/or music player? Do you need to connect to a local network or the Internet via a wired connection rather than Wi-Fi? Do you require software suites and applications that are available only for one computer operating system or type of hardware?

REVIEWING SYSTEM AND SOFTWARE REQUIREMENTS

As you explored the things you most need a computer to do, if you discovered that you have a small set of requirements, you may find that a conventional PC (desktop or mobile) is not your best choice. There may be more specialized computers that better fit your needs.

If virtually all of your computer time will be spent playing games, you might want to consider purchasing a game console. Sony's PS3, Microsoft's XBOX 360, and Nintendo's Wii all provide a different approach to gaming systems, and each hardware platform has its own exclusive software titles in addition to many that are shared across all of them. PCs can, of course, serve as outstanding game devices in their own right, and PCs provide access to styles of games that are not generally available on consoles, such as online role-playing games like World of Warcraft or strategy games like Starcraft and Civilization. However, the cost of the best console system is still beneath the budget you'll need to purchase a solid PC gaming system and far less than the money required to build a top-of-the-line gaming computer.

If your top priority is to be able to use a computer to stay in touch 24/7 with others, everywhere you go, then you should first consider a mobile device. If you need to carry your computer everywhere, a desktop PC simply won't work. If you need to immediately access text messages and e-mails, a conventional notebook PC is probably not the best choice because they are bulky and cannot be opened, activated, and easily used at an instant's notice. Tablets and handheld PCs provide a range of features and processing power. Lesson 4B will cover mobile devices in greater detail.

If mobility is essential, but only in the sense that you need to bring your work environment from place to place, then some form of notebook is probably a good fit, especially if you prefer an interface and processing power that is similar to the more traditional desktop environment. However, if you prefer a tablet interface and your tasks can be properly handled by the processing power that a tablet provides, then there is every reason to choose one.

Software can also create hardware requirements. If your requirements specifically include Apple's operating system, then you are also required to purchase an Apple computer; Apple does not license its operating system to run on PCs built by other manufacturers. Windows and Linux, however, can all be installed on a desktop or notebook PC whether the hardware is assembled by Dell or in your own garage.

Beyond the operating system, you may have software requirements that force your choice of type of computer or operating system. Some software developers create their software only for Windows, Mac OS, or a mobile platform, and if such software is a must-have for you, then your computer must match what is required.

If a specialized computer is not required, then the next step is to begin building a specific list of hardware requirements for your new computer. The degree to which you can customize your computer will depend both on the type you buy and the way you plan to acquire it.

Tablets and handheld computers are quite limited in terms of their configuration options; manufacturers

Figure 4.4   Specialty computers like game consoles are not versatile, but they are a cost-effective way to meet a single computing need.

decide on a set of features and components for each model, and then simply let consumers choose the model they prefer. The amount of permanent storage and RAM can vary from model to model, but there is little else a user can change.

Notebooks and desktops are much more flexible, providing options for processing and graphics power in addition to storage and RAM. Different manufacturers of notebooks also commonly offer different options for the size of the monitor and for various external connections and services like USB, FireWire, flash memory cards, television, and networks.

Desktop systems are the most flexible of all. Retail stores, whether they are national chains such as Best Buy, online manufacturers like Dell, or local computer stores, allow each customer to tailor the specifications of each hardware subsystem in their computer. Those who plan to build their own computer can choose the manufacturer and precise specifications for each component and shop around for vendors who provide the best deals on the components.

To begin the process of choosing the components for a new computer, create a list of components and assign them either a low, medium, or high priority given the ways you will use your computer and given the following considerations.

Operating System Unless your requirements have already decided your choice of operating system, your choice will ultimately depend on personal preference. The desktop and notebook PC market is dominated by the Microsoft Operating System. Apple's Mac OS and Linux run a distant second and third place in comparison respectively. As a consequence, more software programs exist for Windows-based PCs, and you can choose from a wide array of competing sources for hardware purchases and repair services. Nevertheless, the other operating systems each have their advantages; if you are so inclined, you can try out various user interfaces and do research online to select your preference.

Some operating systems, such as Windows 7, are available as both a 32-bit and 64-bit version. As you learned in Chapter 3, this affects both the amount of memory a computer can use and the rate at which it can internally transfer data. Unless you are buying or building a very low-powered computer for occasional use, a 64-bit operating system is a medium- to high-priority. A 32-bit operating system won't provide deep savings in the cost, but it will limit your ability to add more memory later if needed, and you will miss out on any performance gain from the larger bit size.

CPU The CPU is a high priority if you will be playing very intense games (for example, Crysis or Mass Effect), doing detailed work with art or sound that involve multiple audio tracks or complex images, or performing very complex statistical or database calculations. You probably should consider it a medium priority if you are running business applications such as Microsoft Office and a range of other programs. If you are a casual user—writing an e-mail, checking the news on the Web, posting to Facebook and Twitter, and maybe writing a letter now and then—the CPU is a low priority.

RAM Memory for the computer can make a vast difference in a computer's performance. Insufficient memory can cause the operating system to swap program data back and forth between RAM and the hard drive as the user switches between programs or even simply uses different features in the same program. The swapping process is extremely time-intensive, and users of computers without enough memory frequently find themselves sitting and listening to the hard drive chatter while they wait for the computer to catch up to their latest request. RAM is always a high priority when building a system, though as you'll see in the next section, the "more is better" rule of thumb is only true up to a point.

Figure 4.5 **Determining the importance of each computer subsystem helps ensure that the most important performance needs are met first.**

Storage Permanent storage is required for the operating system, all the programs you will install, and all the data that you will use. Typically, computers use a hard disk for primary permanent storage, though other technologies may soon change that. In Learning Objective 4.2, you'll learn more about the various storage options that are available for today's computers, but at this point you can still consider the relative importance of storage in your new computer. Storage capacity is a high priority for people who want to build their own libraries of TV shows, movies, and music for viewing and listening, and for people who store large numbers of high-resolution digital photos. It is also a high priority for die-hard gamers who regularly buy and install the latest high intensity games, each of which can consume many gigabytes of disk space. For most other people, disk storage is a medium-priority consideration; average users will probably not need to spend the extra money on extra-large storage solutions for their PC. For basic, casual users who don't plan to install much software or save many files, storage space is a low priority.

Graphics Unsurprisingly, video power and performance for a computer is most important to those whose tasks involve complex visual output. The graphics processor is a high priority for gamers, photo or video editors, and anyone who plans to attach multiple monitors to the same computer. If you are not a user of graphic-intensive applications but want to watch full-screen movies and TV shows, then video is probably a medium priority for you. Users focused on creating documents and surfing the Web do not require much graphic power; for those people, graphics support is a low priority.

FINE-TUNING YOUR PURCHASE: NEEDS VERSUS WANTS

More details are needed in order to finalize your new system's requirements, but these basic priorities will make selecting specific components easier. Having reviewed your overall needs and requirements for a computer, you can use those requirements to define what you'll need for each hardware component. Fine-tuning what you need for each component serves the dual purpose of ensuring that the computer has the performance and capacity you require as well as keeping expenses under control.

Make a list of the hardware components in the computer you will target for purchase, using this section as a guide along with your priorities that you set in the last section.

CPU CPUs today increase their performance in part by combining multiple microprocessor cores together in one unit, so that

Figure 4.6 Video cards improve performance for high-end graphics software; for more casual users, motherboards often provide on-board video at a lower cost.

processing tasks can be distributed between the cores. If the CPU was one of your high priorities, look for a high-end CPU with at least four cores (commonly called a **quad-core processor**). Six to eight core processors are available; however, unless you have extreme processing needs, a quad-core processor will probably get the job done at a fraction of the cost of a CPU with more cores. Dual-core processors are a good choice as a medium priority. If the CPU is a low priority, there are many single-core models available, often based on older designs, that are very economical and reliable.

The electric frequency of the processor, measured in gigahertz or GHz, is also a measure of its relative speed. For medium- and high-priority choices, consider the fastest CPU that your budget allows. While 3.4 GHz will certainly improve your processing throughput over a 3.0 GHz model, many people find the cost increase to be prohibitive for the fastest processors. Speed is less of a consideration for low-priority choices.

There are two major processor manufacturers, AMD and Intel, and each company produces similar CPU products. If you are a careful shopper and like to do lots of research, you can find many online resources that exhaustively compare performance and price between each of the models that the two companies produce; each company's CPUs behave a bit better or worse compared to the other depending on what is being measured. However, a quad-core processor from either company will do a fine job of running a game or a spreadsheet, so users who are not concerned with every detail of their new system can pay less attention to the manufacturer of their CPU.

RAM The most casual of users should probably run with no less than two gigabytes of RAM, since the Microsoft Operating System takes approximately a gigabyte for its own operation. Bargain-basement computers are commonly sold with a single gigabyte of memory, but these systems are best upgraded or avoided if at all possible, even if RAM is a low priority. Four-gigabyte configurations are fine for most medium- and high-priority requirements, including users who play intense video games. It is fairly unusual for consumer software to be designed to load many gigabytes of data into RAM, and extra memory will not speed up the computer by sitting unused. If your programs only use a gigabyte or two of RAM, a 12-gigabyte system won't run any faster than a computer with only four. For users who need to actively run many programs at the same time, or do video and movie editing, 10 to 16 gigabytes is a better target. As stated earlier, if you plan to use more than four gigabytes of RAM, you must have a 64-bit operating system.

RAM modules can vary a great deal in terms of how fast they read, write, and transfer data; the delay between the request and the completed task is called **latency**. If either your RAM or your CPU is a high priority, consider investing in faster RAM models with lower latency if your budget allows it. RAM modules also run at different electrical frequencies, so it is important to match your RAM's frequency to the correct value specified by the motherboard manufacturer. Both online and retail shopping sites can help ensure you are purchasing RAM to match the rest of your system.

Graphics. Most motherboards today contain a basic video processor right on the board, along with an expansion slot that can accept a video card. If graphic performance is a low priority, you can simply use the video output from the on-board processor and save the cost of buying a video card. Medium-priority users may find that the on-board graphics are sufficient for them as well, but it is worth checking the cost of a basic video card to see if the video processor can be upgraded within budget. Make sure that the basic video card has more video memory and a faster graphics processor than the on-board module before buying it.

High-priority graphics require at least one video card to handle the processing load. There is a wide selection of manufacturers, chipsets, and performance ratings for video cards, so you may need to read reviews and comparisons online to find a video card that has an acceptable price tag but also produces the performance you need. If you have gaming friends, you can check with them for advice, as well. For the most intense performance requirements, you may need to link two graphics cards together. This can be a costly solution, but it provides

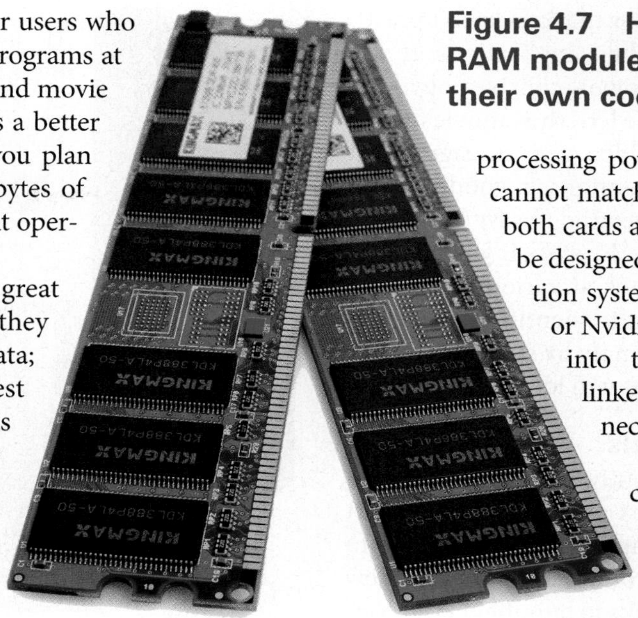

Figure 4.7 Higher performance RAM modules often come with their own cooling systems.

processing power that a single video card cannot match. In order to use two cards, both cards and the motherboard must all be designed to use a special communication system, such as AMD's CrossFire or Nvidia's SLI. The cards are plugged into the motherboard and then linked together with another connector on the top of the card.

As a special consideration for consumers evaluating notebook computers, be aware that it is common for manufacturers to build notebooks that share the computer's system RAM with the video processor. The advertisement may declare that the graphics processor has two gigabytes of RAM, but the fine print may explain that the graphics system has only a small amount of its own memory and that it will use available system RAM for the rest of its needs. This may be an acceptable design for low- and medium-priority users, but if you need fast graphics in a notebook, look for a model that does not borrow RAM for video memory. Dedicated video memory is more expensive, but the video output will run more smoothly, and the rest of the computer's operations will have all the RAM it needs.

Monitor. If you will be buying a new monitor along with the computer, then now is a good time to select the features and quality you want. Video and photo editors should place a high priority on both the image quality and the size of their monitor. Monitor size is a high priority for gamers, but gamers should probably focus on the response rate more than other factors, such as true color representation, in order to

Figure 4.8 Visiting a computer store to evaluate a monitor purchase will help you compare models better than shopping online.

make sure they have a monitor that can keep up with the fast-changing video in their applications. If you plan to watch full-screen movies, consider buying a widescreen monitor, since the letterbox movie format may fit it more closely. If video is not a significant priority for you, then the monitor is a good place to keep the size and quality lower and to save money for more important components. Even so, if you have the ability to visit a store and look at various models in action, it will be much easier to identify models that are acceptable to you than simply by shopping online and guessing what the output will look like.

Networks and Peripherals. Almost every desktop and notebook PC currently manufactured contains a built-in Ethernet port and controller as part of the motherboard, allowing a wired connection to the Internet via a local network. Virtually every new mobile device, from notebooks to handheld PCs, contains wireless networking hardware and support. But if you are buying a desktop computer and will need to connect to a wireless network, you will need to add wireless capability to the computer. This can either be added either with an internal card that plugs into the motherboard or with an external USB antenna.

If you plan to frequently plug in and remove USB devices, such as cameras or flash drives, you may want to make sure that the computer case provides USB ports on the front. As an alternative, you can purchase a USB hub device that can plug into the computer and then be placed on a desk for easy access.

If you identified other types of peripheral interfaces that you require, such as eSATA for external hard drives or FireWire for video devices, make sure those are included and supported in the computer.

Case. When considering your budget and the computer's performance, the case containing your desktop PC's components is always a low priority. If you are buying a brand-name PC such as Dell or Hewlett-Packard, you may not even get a choice regarding the appearance and features of the computer's case. But if you are building your own computer or ordering parts from a local computer store so they can build it for you, you have a wide array of choices when it comes to the case, including its appearance, the features and connections it provides, and its price.

If budget is a big concern, then spend as little as possible on the case and allocate the money to more critical system components. You should be able to find a basic model for your computer for $50 or less. As the cost rises, manufacturers add more features such as extra front-panel connectors, a speaker so the motherboard can send audio output during its startup

Figure 4.9 Some gamers invest extra money in their computer case to make their machines eye-catching.

self-test, and more room to accommodate extra storage devices, accessory cards, and cooling fans.

If you have the money and the inclination, you can buy cases that are stylish and artistic, complete with futuristic lines, see-through panels, and sets of LED lights to make it glow. Some gamers spend hundreds of dollars to buy and customize a case to turn their computer into a showpiece. But for most people, the case is just the simple, black box that sits on the floor next to the desk.

Power Supply. As with the case, the power supply for your computer is likely to simply be provided without options by the manufacturer, unless you are building your own system or having a local store build it for you. Unlike the case, however, your computer's power supply is one of the most critical components in its operation, at least when it comes to running reliably. The power supply, which sits in the corner of the case, is responsible for converting the AC power from the wall into precise amounts of direct current for the computer to use. It must carefully monitor and regulate the power it provides because varying amounts of electricity can affect computer performance and damage the electronics over time. When a power supply burns out, it may simply stop providing power to the computer, but it can also deliver a burst of electricity to the rest of the computer that can ruin the motherboard, CPU, and other subsystems.

If you are buying your computer components individually, look for a power supply that can adequately power your system and is also highly rated

Fact Check

1. RAM is a high priority primarily for which type of users?
   a. All users, and especially those who will be editing video or image data
   b. Any user who doesn't plan to include a hard drive in their system
   c. Users who need to run both Windows and Linux simultaneously
2. Using graphics support on the motherboard instead of a separate video card is ideal for
   a. users who do not have a widescreen monitor because on-board video cannot support them
   b. users who do not plan to spend time playing high-intensity games or performing other graphic-oriented tasks
   c. users who watch movies on DVDs because the on-board graphics chip is physically closer to the DVD drive in a computer

for its reliability. Online reviews can help determine the amount of power you need, as well as the manufacturers who are well known for producing high-quality power supplies.

Motherboard. You need to consider the computer's motherboard only if you are buying components individually. If the motherboard is on your purchase list, you must ensure that it is compatible with the CPU you have selected; an AMD CPU cannot be installed on a motherboard designed to support an Intel processor. You should also make sure that the motherboard supports all the features you have determined that you need, including support for SATA hard drives and optical devices, USB support, onboard video, or multi-card graphics support. There are many different manufacturers of motherboards, each providing many different models, so look for online reviews and suggestions to help with the selection process.

4.2 Storage Devices and Options

Every computer needs permanent storage for its programs and data. Today, there are many different types of hardware used for various kinds of data storage. While you'll most likely use a hard disk as your computer's primary storage device, there are many other devices (or at the very least, support for those other devices) that you may want to consider adding to your new computer.

HARD DISK DRIVES FOR PERMANENT STORAGE

The most common consideration for hard disks is the amount of data they can hold. If storage is a high priority for you, look for the biggest hard drive you can reasonably afford. One- to three-terabyte models should be sufficient for the needs of most users. If storage is a less critical issue, then models storing 500 gigabytes to a single terabyte should provide plenty of storage at a lower cost. For casual users, hard drives under 500 gigabytes are available, but pay close attention to the balance between financial savings and reduced capacity. You may find that you won't save much money by reducing your capacity below 500 gigabytes, and in such a case, you may prefer to stay with the greater capacity.

Along with capacity, you may want to consider the rotation speed of the device. The faster the device spins, the less time the drive will spend waiting for the needed sectors to arrive at the read/write head. Consumer hard drives typically have a rotation rate of either 5400 or 7200 rpm. From the perspective of the user waiting for data, either of these spin rates will likely seem acceptable; the slower drive might wait an extra millisecond for its sector to arrive. For applications that rely heavily on the hard drive, such as large database programs, a faster rotation can help improve performance.

If you are interested in green computing, you can also consider hard drives like Western Digital's Caviar GP that reduce power consumption by varying their spin rate. When the hard drive is not in demand, it

Figure 4.10   Hard disk drives can provide rapid access to terabytes of data.

Figure 4.11 Solid state drives offer greater reliability and similar storage to hard disks but are still much more expensive for the same capacity.

slows rotation and therefore consumes less power. The power savings comes at a limited performance cost, so this may not be the best choice for high-performance applications; nevertheless, it is a reasonable option when consistently fast response is not a requirement.

If your budget allows it, you may want to purchase two drives and divide the storage between them. Your primary drive can house the operating system and all of your programs, while the secondary drive can be used to store large libraries of audio, video, or other kinds of data. This allows you to use each drive to store backups of the other, providing a convenient way to keep your data backed up regularly.

Solid state drives are rapidly increasing in popularity, and in time they might become a viable replacement for the ubiquitous mechanical hard drive. They use less power than a hard drive and operate silently because they have no mechanical parts. For some operations, they store and retrieve data more quickly than a conventional hard disk drive. The main obstacle to their acceptance is currently cost. For the same amount of storage, SSDs can cost several times as much as mechanical drives, especially as storage approaches a terabyte or more.

OPTICAL DRIVES FOR MULTIMEDIA, SOFTWARE INSTALLATION, AND BACKUP

Optical storage drives have been common in computers since the 1990s. Since the first CD reader was fitted into a computer, there has been a steady parade of improvements and format changes. Today's computers almost always include an optical device, which is far more versatile and capable than its CD ancestor.

All optical drives have the same basic function: they use a laser to write to and read from the familiar plastic disks we use for music and movies. Unlike a hard disk, which is a self-contained unit that holds the data media as well as the drive hardware, optical drives have, which means that the user can insert and remove the data-holding medium while leaving the drive in place.

If properly cared-for, optical disks do not lose the data that they store, so optical disks are an ideal medium for permanently archiving old information. They also serve as simple playback devices, too, so users can play music CDs and movie DVDs in the same device that can back up the contents of their hard drive. Though they are used to read and write data, they are far slower than hard disks and SSDs, making them unsuitable for use as the primary storage device for the computer.

Originally, optical drives supported the Compact Disc data format. As CD technology matured, different formats were created for writing and reading, in order to increase the amount that each CD could hold without abandoning the storage standard, and in order to allow the data on a CD to be erased and replaced with new data.

DVD drives were developed and largely replaced CD-only drives. They, too, provided the ability to read, write, and rewrite the data on their disks, but they were able to store far more data on a single disk than a CD could. In addition, most DVD drives supported the reading and writing of older CD formats as well, removing the need to have both a DVD and a CD drive in a computer in order to work with older media.

DVD disks were for some years the primary means for storing data and distributing software, but the recent arrival

Figure 4.12 Blu-ray optical drives can read and write the latest high-capacity data disks, and they often still support older DVD and CD formats.

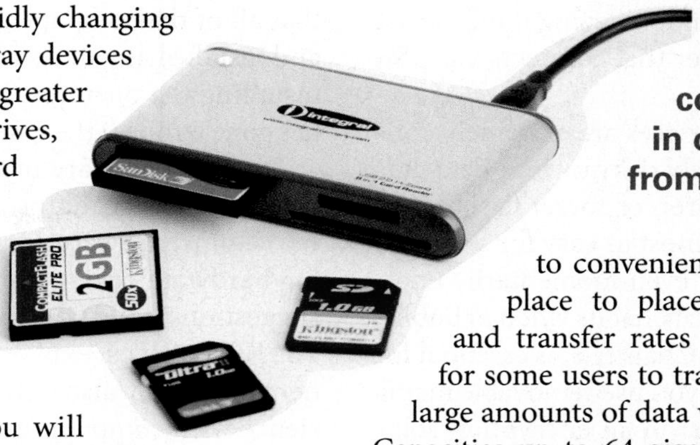

of Blu-ray technology is rapidly changing that dominance. While Blu-ray devices provide a faster response and greater data density than DVD drives, they continue to be backward compatible with DVD and CD disk formats both for reading and writing.

Choosing the right optical drive for your new computer is one of the simpler decisions you will make. If you can afford to include a Blu-ray writer, you should do that, provided that the manufacturer declares that the drive is capable of both reading and writing older DVD and CD formats; not every manufacturer of optical devices will promise backward compatibility. With just that one optical device, your new computer will be able to read and write the new-format disks, yet still accept and produce older formats if required.

If your budget simply won't accommodate the extra expense for a Blu-ray drive, then include a DVD read/write drive instead, again making sure that the manufacturer supports reading and writing both DVD and CD formats. Though they are still manufactured, selecting a CD drive for your computer is unlikely to be your best choice because so many users and major software companies have abandoned the CD format.

REMOVABLE MEDIA FOR PORTABILITY AND BACKUP

While optical drives provide a way to make data portable, they don't do a very good job of making that portable data quickly available. In addition, DVD and even Blu-ray disks cannot store hundreds or thousands of gigabytes of data, limiting their effectiveness as mass storage devices.

Other devices, however, fill that gap. External hard disk drives are hard disk drives that are contained within a case designed to sit on a desk rather than inside a computer case. The external drive's case provides a plug for standard AC power rather than the direct current provided by the computer's power supply and a port to access the computer via an eSATA, FireWire, or USB connection. External hard drives can be removed and carried, making large amounts of data portable. They can also simply be used as a way to extend a computer's permanent data storage capacity without installing the new disks into the computer.

USB flash drives are found in shirt pockets and on key chains practically everywhere. Once used simply

Figure 4.13 Your new PC may need a compact card reader in order to accept data from smaller devices.

to conveniently transfer a few files from place to place, their increasing capacity and transfer rates make them a popular way for some users to transport entire programs and large amounts of data with them wherever they go. Capacities up to 64 gigabytes are now common for flash drives, and at a higher cost even 256 gigabyte models are now available.

Though not commonly used for data storage for a computer, many users need the ability to read compact solid state memory cards like CompactFlash and SDHC cards. Some computer manufacturers, especially for portable computing devices, provide built-in readers that can accept these cards for reading and writing. If you use these cards frequently, you can add this type of connection to your shopping list for a new computer. However, if you find that the need for a compact card reader makes it difficult to find

Fact Check

1. Why do many users still favor hard disk drives instead of the newer flash drive technology for their permanent storage component?
   a. Flash drives spin more slowly than hard drives, providing a much slower data retrieval rate.
   b. Flash drives cannot store as much data as a hard disk drive in the same physical area.
   c. Flash drives are still substantially more expensive for the same amount of storage space.

2. Assuming you are not on an extremely strict budget, what is an ideal optical drive configuration for a typical user's new desktop computer?
   a. One CD, one DVD, and one Blu-ray drive, so that any type of optical disk that can be used.
   b. A single Blu-ray drive that can read and write Blu-ray and all older optical formats.
   c. A Blu-ray drive and a DVD drive because Blu-ray drives are good for data storage, but the laser can distort the picture from DVD movie disks.

the computer you want, consider leaving it off the list and buying an external reader that connects via USB adapter to the computer.

Though portable media devices are extremely convenient, they are also extremely risky to your data. It is extremely easy for users to drop or forget flash drives in a careless moment, and almost as easy for a thief to steal when a computer is left even momentarily unattended. Practicing good security habits when in public, as you'll learn more about in Chapter 6, is essential for keeping your data safe, but if you use removable media it is also worthwhile to invest in an encryption solution. Some portable media products, such as Seagate's FreeAgent line and IronKey flash drives, contain built-in data encryption so that even if the portable device is stolen, the data cannot be easily obtained from it.

4.3 Selecting a Manufacturer and Vendor

With the requirements for your new computer complete, it's time to shop. There are a number of ways that you can acquire your new computer. Since there is no single way to buy a computer that is ideal for everyone, your best choice is the one that most closely matches your budget and preferences.

DECISION TO MAKE, BUY, OR CUSTOMIZE

One of the least expensive ways to buy your new computer is to purchase all the components and build it yourself. Building your own computer also gives you the greatest control over the exact components that are used. Though it is uncommon for consumers to build their own, it is an interesting project if you have the time and a little bit of mechanical skill. Most of the time, building a computer requires no tools other than a screwdriver, and the assembly tasks themselves are less complex than the learning required to know exactly what must be done.

When building your own computer, you alone are responsible for deciding what parts to include. You must ensure that the motherboard, CPU, and memory are all compatible with each other, that the power supply is sufficient for everything you will include, and

Figure 4.14 Building your own computer can be fun and less expensive than buying a brand-name system, but it's not a job for everyone.

that all of the components and accessories are present and installed as you wish. You are also on your own for installing the operating system and figuring out what has gone wrong if the computer does not work properly.

Even so, there are many resources online that can help you. For example, Tom's Hardware at http://www.tomshardware.com is an excellent Web site for hardware reviews and comparisons, component suggestions, and diagnosing problems. There are YouTube videos explaining how to install components. You may also have a friend who has some experience with computer building and may be willing to help you through the process.

If you decide to build your own system, you can pick and choose your component supplier from a variety of online and locals sources. As with any other kind of product, different retailers may offer deals and specials that can help you lower costs. Some online stores may offer kits for sale, selling you a complete set of components that you can put together yourself.

If you want to choose all the components for your new computer but find the prospect of building it to be daunting, check with a local computer shop for assistance. You may find that they are more than willing to order the parts you require and build your system for you, adding their labor costs to the total purchase price.

At the other end of the spectrum from "building your own box," are already-built computers sold at major electronics chains, local computer stores, and online shopping sites. You can usually find brand-name

Figure 4.15 Buying a pre-built computer gets you a PC right away, but make sure it matches your requirements.

retailers like Dell encourage shoppers to select a basic range of capability for a new computer, and then customize their system by upgrading, downgrading, and adding or eliminating features and components. Each component choice during the process explains the extra or reduced cost to the user, and the price of the system changes with each selection so the customer can gauge the financial impact of each decision.

The end result of the process is a system that closely or exactly matches the features and performance that customers need, without requiring the customer to be especially knowledgeable about the technical details of each component. With the system properly configured, the user can add peripheral devices such as keyboards, printers, and monitors and then order the entire system to be delivered to their home or office. Qualified buyers can even apply for and arrange financing at the same time for more expensive purchases, if needed.

computers built by manufacturers such as Hewlett-Packard and Sony, as well as **white box computers**, which are computers constructed by the store instead of by a major manufacturer.

Purchasing a pre-built system from a store gives you the advantage of immediately purchasing a working, tested computer. If the contents of the computer meet your requirements, then there is no need to search for components and wait for delivery. If you are purchasing a white box system, the store will often list the exact components they used to build it, allowing you to review the suitability of what they have included.

The risk of buying a pre-constructed computer is primarily that it may not be a good match for your needs. If you required a certain kind of video card, the pre-built system may not include one that is up to the task for your planned uses. If you had specified a full terabyte of storage and the one on the shelf has half as much, you may find yourself wishing you had made a different purchase a few months later.

If you decide to purchase a pre-built computer that is not ideal for your needs, at the very least check to see if it can be upgraded in the future. If you might want more RAM, find out the maximum that the system will support. If you plan to add more hard disk space, verify that both the case and the motherboard are able to support more drives.

In between the do-it-yourself computer and the off-the-shelf model is the customizable system. Online

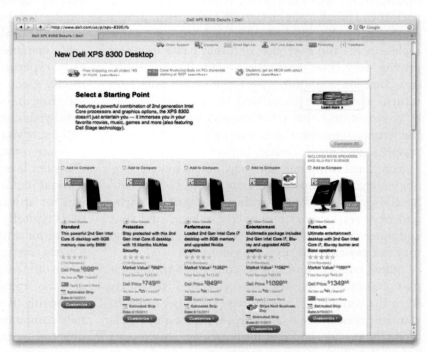

Figure 4.16 Companies like Dell allow shoppers to configure a system online and have it built and delivered.

Manufactured computers, whether customized from Dell or purchased through a retail chain like Best Buy, give the new owner no say in the exact components that are used in the machine. While it is by no means a given, there is nevertheless a risk that a manufacturer may use sub-par parts that may be more likely to break down quickly, or run at a lower degree of performance than the new owner is expecting, in order to save money on the cost of the unit. If you have strict, high performance requirements for your computer, you may want to forego the ease of buying a manufactured computer in favor of working with a local shop that will help you find top-quality parts.

POST-PURCHASE SUPPORT AND MAINTENANCE

There is always a risk, no matter how and where you buy your new computer, that its hardware will fail in the future. Different stores have very different rules for support, warranties, and repair. The best time to investigate their policies and procedures is before you have purchased their computer.

If you buy components in order to assemble your own computer, you will probably receive only a limited manufacturer's warranty for each part that only covers manufacturing defects. If your power supply fails and destroys your motherboard, the motherboard manufacturer will most likely refuse to replace the part. If you break a pin on the CPU when installing it on the motherboard, you will probably not get a free replacement. You may also find that parts suppliers provide very short warranties; one to three months is a common duration. Check the store's policy on returns and exchanges, as well, in case you discover at assembly time that you have accidentally ordered the wrong component. You may be required to pay a restocking fee at one retailer but not at another.

Your local computer store may have a more generous policy for computers they build on your behalf. Small businesses often provide a combination parts-and-labor warranty as part of the package, so if your computer breaks in the first year of operation, you may not pay anything extra to get it fixed.

Major retailers and online configuration companies commonly sell warranty packages separately from the computer. Though these packages can substantially raise the cost of purchase, thoroughly investigate the process and cost for basic-warranty repairs before deciding against warranty upgrades. You may discover that the manufacturer's policy requires extensive amounts of your time talking to a telephone call center to make an initial diagnosis. You may be

Figure 4.17   If you bought your computer from a major manufacturer, the first step to repairing it is probably a phone call.

required to box up your broken computer, mail it to a repair center, and then wait several weeks for it to return. You may also be told that your data may not be preserved during the repair, meaning you could lose all programs and saved data on your hard drive even if your hard drive has not failed.

More expensive warranty programs sometimes provide for the on-site repair of your system and may not require that you first diagnose the problem via extended telephone sessions. You may decide that buying a warranty upgrade to gain a faster response is worth the extra expense. You may also discover that the extra money spent on a brand-name PC's warranty is about the same amount a local store will charge to custom-build your computer and quickly repair it if it breaks. Make sure you are comparing your options completely.

Some stores offer long extended warranties. Consider that most of the time, if your computer runs without incident for a month or two, it will probably run for at least the next couple of years; electronic parts typically either fail soon after they are installed, or not for a long time. You may not need to pay for a parts warranty that lasts for many years, though a labor-only extended warranty may be useful. Consider also that computer technology is ever-changing and improving; if a five-year warranty is half the cost of a new computer, you might be better off just buying a new computer in three years if it breaks.

Ultimately, your best warranty decision takes into account the relative impact a broken computer will have in your life and what you can reasonably afford to protect your purchase.

TAKING YOUR COMPUTER HOME

Whether you are building or buying, at some point all the effort you put into research and shopping will result in the delivery of your new computer. If you are constructing it yourself, you will need to make sure you have all the components you ordered and proceed through the steps required to assemble the hardware and configure your operating system. If you bought an already-assembled computer, then your job of unpacking and setting up the system is simpler.

Regardless of the way your computer is assembled, there are a few considerations to address to ensure the new computer's environment is properly prepared. You can accomplish much of this setup before the computer is sitting in a box in your hallway, waiting to be used.

First, ensure you have a proper place to use the computer. Review the section in Chapter 2 on ergonomics, and if at all possible, set up a workspace that will allow you to use a computer without risk or damage to your body.

Next, make sure you have adequate, clean power for your computer to use. Standard AC electricity from your wall is never guaranteed to be completely consistent and steady. Surges and drops in the electrical current are relatively common. Even when minor, such fluctuations are unhealthy for electronic equipment. The internal components of your computer rely on the power supply to deliver precise amounts of electricity, but the power supply can be damaged over time by inconsistent incoming power. In addition, other components such as printers, monitors, and network routers are also vulnerable to deviations in electrical service.

To protect your equipment, at the very least ensure that you have surge-protecting power strips available for all of your computer-related components. Note that stores commonly sell inexpensive power strips that do not protect against power problems, so make sure that your power strips are rated to actually protect against surges.

If you can afford it, consider buying an **uninterruptable power supply**. These units contain a battery backup system along with power delivery that is much more consistent than a simple surge protecting power strip. It will provide clean electricity to all devices it supports and allow those devices to continue to function for a limited time, even if your building loses its power completely. If you provide a backup power unit for your monitor and network hardware as well as your system unit, then a power interruption in your home or office won't interrupt any of your immediate computing activity.

Setting up your computer is a straightforward process. Be patient as you plug your various devices and components into the system unit, especially the monitor cable. Though it is not delicate, haste and pressure can bend the connector's pins if they are not properly lined up. When assembling a computer and connecting devices, the general rule of thumb is that if the connection cannot easily be made, then a closer look is warranted to ensure that everything is properly positioned.

Once the computer is in place, fully connected, and plugged in, you are ready to turn it on and begin using it for its intended purposes. If you purchased a brand-name computer, you will probably discover when starting it for the first time that the manufacturer has loaded your new system with a variety of small programs that offer to sell you Internet access subscriptions, security and protection utilities, and free trials for assorted software suites. It is entirely up to you whether you accept or ignore any or all of these solicitations; any trial software and

Figure 4.18   An uninterruptable power supply provides clean, consistent electricity and a battery backup if your house loses power.

free offer applications that you don't want can be switched off or uninstalled, especially in cases where the software slows down the computer or interferes with your use of the system.

Whether your computer is new or old, its primary enemy is dust, and unless you use your computer in an industrial clean room, the accumulation of dust inside your computer is inevitable. If you or others in your computing environment are smokers, you will accumulate dust and grime inside the system unit even more quickly. Dust can interfere with airflow needed to keep your computer cool, which can reduce the operating life of its components as well as increase the computer's power consumption as it runs its fans faster to compensate for the higher heat. In extreme cases, grime and dust can create short circuits between components and cause them to fail.

Focus on the Issues

Keep it Cool

Heat is a major enemy of every PC. Heat can warp and damage the delicate electronic components inside any device, so it is critically important that the computer be able to draw heat away from its parts. Most computers have multiple ways to solve the heat control problem.

CPU and video card microprocessors usually have large aluminum and copper-tube cooling towers firmly attached to the top of the chip to quickly draw heat away. High-performance RAM units may come with a metal jacket attached to the chips to reduce heat. Sometimes, smaller chipsets on the motherboard will also have little cooling towers attached to them.

Though the cooling towers generally do a decent job of drawing heat away from the chip, the towers themselves will become too hot to act as effective heat sinks unless air circulation can take heat away from those towers. Most desktop PCs are studded with a selection of cooling fans to move air through the towers, and in and out of the case. The CPU's cooling tower is usually shipped with its own attached fan, and high-performance video cards will also have one or two fans on board. Power supply units almost always have one fan facing the outside of the case to exhaust hot air, and larger power supplies contain a second fan facing the PC's motherboard to improve air flow. A PC case commonly comes with as many as a half-dozen areas that are designed to accept cooling fans, allowing users to direct air flow both in and out of the case to keep all of the parts at optimal temperatures.

High-performance PC users may discover that with all those fans, their computer makes an unpleasant amount of noise, and such cooling systems may still be inadequate to match the heat output of a quad-core or heftier processor. Both noise and efficiency issues can be addressed by shifting to a liquid cooling solution. Once the domain of the risk-taking do-it-yourselfer, sealed and well manufactured liquid cooling systems can now be installed in practically any PC. Simple solutions for consumers often replace the entire cooling tower and fan assembly on the CPU with a liquid-filled tower. Hoses transport the liquid back and forth from a radiator mounted on the PC case, where a single fan is used to cool the liquid as it passes through the radiator.

Because the system transfers and sheds heat more efficiently, fewer fans are often required in order to cool the system. If the PC is able to run its fans at variable speeds, it may spin the fans more slowly - and therefore quietly - because it requires less air flow to achieve the same temperatures.

Regardless of how components are cooled, every PC owner should ensure that every cooling component is dust-free and working as intended in order to ensure the computer's long and healthy life.

To keep dust under control, periodically unplug your system unit, remove the side panel, and use a can of compressed air to clear dust from the CPU fan, front and rear air ports, the power supply, and anywhere else that it has accumulated. Do not use a vacuum cleaner to remove dust from electronic components; if you are concerned about the cloud of dust that will appear when you clean the computer, move it outside. If you have enough dust in the system that a can of air doesn't remove most of it, call around to your local computer store and see if they have a higher-pressure air system available to use.

Another computer component that requires frequent cleaning is the monitor. They, too, accumulate dust over time, along with occasional fingerprints and little dots of material, until the monitor's display doesn't seem as vibrant as it once did. If you have a flat-panel monitor, it can be cleaned, but it must be cleaned with extreme care. The membrane surface of the monitor is very delicate, and scrubbing at it with window cleaner on a paper towel will scuff and ruin it over time.

To clean a flat-panel monitor, gently wipe the dust from it with a microfiber cloth. Household tissue and paper towel of all sorts contain sharp wood fibers that will damage the screen, no matter how many softness claims are made about them in advertising, so avoid those altogether. The cloth should pick up all the dust

Fact Check

1. There are many places to go to buy a new computer. Typically, shoppers do best when
    a. they buy computers online because they always get the lowest price
    b. they buy computers at a national retail chain because the quality at such stores is generally higher than when buying online
    c. they consider factors such as price, post-purchase repair and support, and the degree to which they want to choose their components; and then buy in whatever manner best fits their needs
2. An uninterruptable power supply unit is a valuable accessory, both because it provides backup power and because
    a. it provides consistent, carefully regulated electricity to the computer
    b. it provides a noticeable boost to the speed and performance of the computer
    c. it provides a noticeable boost to the speed of the computer's Internet connection

and smudges, even with gentle wiping. Don't scrub at the little spots and dots. If they refuse to come off, dab at them with a moist corner of the cloth until they loosen and come free or disappear. Though it seems fussy, treating the monitor's surface with care will ensure that it provides optimal output for a long time.

Though dust cannot creep into the operating system and software environment, your computer's operating performance can be compromised by the introduction of unwanted software. You will learn more about safe computing in Chapter 6, but consider adding basic malware protection to your system as soon as you acquire it. No malware protection system will keep you totally safe from intrusion, but even a free protection system such as Alwil's Avast will catch most of the threats you might encounter.

Utilities that you intentionally install are not malware, but they may nevertheless impact the way your system runs. Pay close attention to your system's performance whenever you install a utility, including malware protection. If you notice that your system suddenly becomes sluggish after installing software, you may want to review the decision to use that utility.

Figure 4.19 Setting up a new computer is a straightforward and easy process.

As customer relationship management (CRM) supervisor for Jenny Craig Inc. in Carlsbad, California, Jon Kosoff starts his day when he clicks on his e-mail box in the morning to check his messages and then prioritizes the day's projects. After that, it's anything goes, and Kosoff wouldn't have it any other way.

"My job is very project-oriented, so no two days are ever the same," says Kosoff, who holds a degree in economics from the University of California at Santa Barbara. He says the technical training he's learned along the way, combined with a solid financial foundation, has helped him not only to use technology but also to understand the return on investment that his employer gains from its use.

Kosoff oversees Jenny Craig's e-mail and Web site as well as the integration of customer data into the company's database and marketing efforts. That means using the Internet in conjunction with the firm's internal database to reach customers worldwide. "When I started here four years ago, we were sending out 4,000 text-based e-mails a month," says Kosoff. "Today we send out about 700,000 flash and HTML messages a month."

Other key duties include updating Jenny Craig's Web site content to ensure that it represents the firm's current business objectives. That's not as easy as it sounds, says Kosoff, who explains that the firm has gone through a number of leadership changes over the past few years. Such changes lead to business objective changes and can have a profound effect on a firm's overall Web site and marketing strategy.

Perhaps the most satisfying aspect of working with the Internet, Kosoff adds, is the instant gratification that it provides. "You can see what you've done almost instantly and share it not only with the company," he says, "but also with your friends and family 24/7."

Salaries vary depending on the exact nature of the job, but the Bureau of Labor Statistics reports a national median 2009 income for network and systems administrators as a whole at approximately $68,000.

In the Internet age, there is a growing demand for network administrators, information system professionals, and data communication managers. Aside from careers that focus on architecture and administration of the Internet, many other professions require not only a working knowledge of the Internet but also a mastery of the tools used to create and distribute content across it. Here are a few such careers:

- **Web designers and webmasters**. Corporate Web, intranet, and extranet sites are developed, designed, and maintained most often by teams of professionals. At the helm of such teams are experienced designers and webmasters.

- **Multimedia developers**. As more people connect to the Internet, companies face increasing competition to provide highly visual, interactive content that enables them to capture and retain visitors to their Web sites.

- **Programmers**. Programmers are finding all sorts of opportunities in Internet development because Web sites are commonly used to support high-level functions such as interactivity, searches, data mining, and more.

- To decide what computer is best for you to buy, first examine the ways that you plan to use the computer; then, consider and note any existing technology and devices that your new computer will need to access. Once you are clear about the intended tasks your new computer will perform, assess the relative importance of the operating system, CPU, RAM, data storage, and graphics subsystems. Finally, identify the requirements for each computer subsystem based on priority and budget, listing those requirements as you go in order to simplify the shopping process.

- The three basic categories of data storage devices are hard disk drives and their solid state counterparts (SSDs), optical drives, and removable or portable media. Hard disks and SSDs are used as primary storage devices for the computer. Optical drives are used to play optical disk-based media, such as music and movies, and can be used to write data disks both for transferring data to another computer or as part of a data backup system. Removable media are used both for easily transferring files from one computer to another and creating portable sets of programs that can be run on different computers.

- Computer shoppers have three basic ways they can acquire a new computer. They can shop for and purchase their own components and build their own computer (or hire a local store to build it for them); they can shop at a retail or online store and purchase a computer that is already assembled and ready to start up; and they can shop online at a manufacturer's site to configure specific features and have the manufacturer assemble a computer to match those requirements.

- The decision to purchase a computer should include considerations of price and performance, as well as factors such as warranty coverage and the convenience provided for repairing the system if it breaks.

- Once a computer is purchased, occasional simple maintenance and protection tasks such as providing a stable power supply, cleaning the dust from the computer case, and keeping anti-virus protection updated and active can improve the chances of a long life for the machine.

Key Terms

latency, 143
quad-core processor, 142

removable media, 147
uninterruptable power supply, 151

white box computers, 149

Key Terms
QUIZ

Complete each statement by writing one of the terms listed under "Key Terms" in each blank.

1. _____ refers to the amount of time that passes between a request to perform a RAM operation and the completion of the requested operation.

2. To provide both consistent power to a computer system as well as backup power if the electrical service fails, a(n) _____ can be used.

3. A(n) _____ is a CPU unit that contains four separate microprocessors, or cores, that can be used simultaneously to increase the processing power of the computer.

4. Computer stores sometimes sell _____, which are computer systems that have been assembled at the store rather than by a separate manufacturer.

5. Computer storage devices sometimes have _____, which means that the stored data can be removed and carried away from the computer.

Review QUESTIONS

In your own words, briefly answer the following questions or respond to the statements.

1. What are the first issues for a new computer shopper to consider, even before deciding on components to purchase?

2. How much RAM would a typical computer user probably require for their new system? What factors might raise or lower that amount?

3. What options for video processing hardware are available for users who want low, medium, and high performance graphics?

4. Provide one reason why you might include a solid state drive in your new computer and one reason why you might stay with a conventional hard disk drive instead.

5. What are two main benefits from choosing a Blu-ray optical disk over either a DVD or CD drive?

6. Explain how you can make your computer compatible with CompactFlash and other solid state minicard media.

7. List at least two benefits and two risks associated with assembling your own computer.

8. What primary advantages do system configuration companies like Dell provide to their customers shopping for a new PC?

9. Discuss two alternatives for providing power conditioning to reduce the chance of damage to your computer from inconsistent AC power.

10. Describe the steps to take and avoid when cleaning a flat-panel monitor.

Complete the following exercises as directed by your instructor.

LESSON LAB

1. Do price comparison shopping on internal hard disk and solid state drives for a new computer. Use your Web browser to visit the price comparison site http://www.mysimon.com. In the top bar of the site, mouse over the *Computers* tab and select *Hard Drives & Storage*. The sidebar on the left of the site allows you to choose various filters for your search. Refine the search to include only 500 GB and higher hard drives, with at least 7200 rpm speed. Note various prices for a few different 500 GB and one TB models of drives. Then clear the search and in the top search bar enter the words "solid state drive." Browse through the list of available drives, and note prices for a few of the 500 GB drives you find. Pay attention to the typical capacity of the SSD units—are there many at 500 GB or more?

2. Shop for a complete computer system at Dell. Point your browser to http://www.dell.com. At the top of the main page, select the option *For Home*, and on the sidebar of the resulting page, select *Desktops & All-in-Ones*. From there, pick your favorite category of computer, view its details, and proceed through the process of customizing your components. When you have completed the configuration process, print the summary of the computer you have created, but do not proceed to the checkout and purchasing section.

Team
EXERCISE
Critical Thinking

Many companies today aggressively control costs in order to stay profitable. Budgets and spending proposals are often reduced, and employees must find creative ways to accomplish their intended goals with less money. In this exercise, you will work as a team to acquire new computers at a price less than an original estimate.

Divide into groups of three or four students. Your team has been told to buy 10 new desktop system units for the company. Your instructor will provide you with the exact specifications of the computer that was chosen for purchase. Divide the list of components to purchase between the team, and then use online stores like Amazon.com to get prices for all the components. When finished, remember to multiply by 10 to get the total purchase cost. Note your first price for future reference.

Now, imagine that your vice-president has told you that you must still buy 10 new computers, but you must cut the total cost by 30 percent. Meet as a team and explore cost-cutting measures, including buying from different sources, changing brand names, or reducing the performance of certain components. Once you have solutions, divide up the shopping chore again, and have each team member find new prices. Record prices, and calculate the total savings you were able to achieve.

Be prepared to share and discuss your experience with the rest of the class. Were you able to achieve your 30 percent goal? What solutions did you find that allowed you to cut costs? Were you able to retain most or all of your system's performance capabilities, or did you have to make so many sacrifices that the budget-conscious machines would be unlikely to meet the needs of the employees?

LESSON 4B:
Mobile Gear

Early digital computers were so big they required an entire room to house them. As the decades passed, new innovations in computer design resulted in both increased processing speed and decreased machine size. Eventually, computer makers introduced the personal computer, small enough to sit on the user's desk.

Once the computer became desktop-sized, computer users began to look for ways to take their computer with them from place to place. Unhooking wires from a PC and lugging heavy boxes and monitors to and from the car were possible but not practical as a daily exercise. One early answer was the creation of **portable computers**—self-contained units, with keyboard, monitor, and system unit combined. However, they were called "luggable" computers for a reason. Even with their more compact design, portable computers were (and still are) based on making a full-sized computer transportable, rather than providing computing power in a small package. The first smaller computers using the familiar flip-screen notebook style arrived in the early 1980s, around the same time as the portable computer.

Even as hardware engineers were innovating with smaller and smaller computers, microchip technology was being put to a wide array of uses not directly tied to traditional computing tasks. Companies introduced digital sound players, digital home movie machines, digital cameras, and cellular telephones. Citywide transmission networks were created to serve cellular phones, and cable television networks began to provide digital signals for television.

Computer designers found ways to integrate these new applications even into some of their smallest (and therefore most portable) products.

**Figure 4.20
Smart phones and notebooks share some features but overall serve very different functions.**

Today's notebook computers often include onboard digital cameras, as well as hardware for connecting to the Internet. Cell phones added digital cameras and Internet capabilities. The technology and ideas in mobile computing are arriving so quickly now that we are probably seeing just the beginning of significant **convergence**, the process where devices or applications with very different initial purposes become more and more alike as they share features.

4.4 Mobile Devices

Although mobile computing involves far more than hardware, it always requires some form of computer. This section covers mobile computing devices in greater detail than the quick overview in Chapter 1. The convergence of features and technologies in notebooks and smart phones have produced an array of in-between products such as tablets and music players. Even so, both notebooks and smart phones continue to be popular choices for many users.

NOTEBOOKS: FULL COMPUTERS FOR ALMOST EVERYWHERE

Mobile computers have the desktop PC as their most obvious ancestor. The goal of laptop computing is to provide users with all the programs and functions of a desktop environment in a package they can comfortably carry and open to use at a moment's notice almost anywhere.

The modern notebook computer (as you learned in Chapter 1, the terms *notebook* and *laptop* are interchangeable) does a good job of meeting most aspects of that goal. A laptop can provide the user with a full-size keyboard, monitor, and an external mouse. It can run any software that a desktop can run, since it uses the same operating systems and the same basic hardware technology. Notebooks can be expanded with external devices (such as printers and digital cameras) in the same way as desktops. They can also access networks just as effectively as a desktop PC.

Notebooks have a couple of advantages over desktop PCs, even in the office or at home. First, and most obviously, they are easily portable. Weighing in at a handful of pounds (and lighter, for the smallest models), notebooks can be easily moved from place to place. They also include batteries, allowing for use when a power outlet isn't handy; the battery also doubles as a built-in uninterruptible power supply (see Chapter 5), so if the power goes out, your laptop keeps running.

Notebooks provide several features specifically for the mobile user, in addition to their compact size and one-piece design. Newer laptops come with a variety of network connection ports:

Figure 4.21 Notebook computers are ideal for meetings on the go, even if you're just meeting your kids at the library.

- *Wired.* They typically have an Ethernet port, for wired connections. Though it's not common to find Ethernet wires in your local coffee shop, some hotels provide wired Internet access, and businesses that provide visitor desks may sometimes include a wired connection.

- *Modem.* Though the use of telephone modem connections has become far less popular with the advent of faster and more reliable methods, many new laptops still include a modem for telephone connections during those times when a broadband connection is down or unavailable and a nearby phone is ready and waiting.

- *Wireless.* Wireless networking has become a common form of notebook connection to the Internet. Older laptops may require additional hardware, commonly plugged into the USB port or PCMCIA slot, in order to make wireless connections; but new laptops have all the necessary hardware included commonly support some kind of convenient way to connect to various networks. As you'll see later in this chapter, Windows provides a way to save connection information, automatically log on to certain networks when they are in range, and change security settings depending on where you are connected.

Notebooks also provide extra ports to make input and output more flexible, to meet the needs of a variety of users. For input, laptops often provide at least a couple of specialty connections for video or digital memory card connections. For output, many laptops provide a **High-Definition Multimedia Interface (HDMI)** port for sending a signal to a digital television, a port for an analog monitor, and audio ports for plugging in a headset. Notebooks also provide one or more USB ports to connect all manner of other devices, from mice and printers to digital cameras and cell phones.

POWER MANAGEMENT FOR NOTEBOOKS

One of the main concerns for any laptop user is power; without power, the computer isn't useful for much more than holding down papers in an outdoor café. Notebooks usually are usually designed to run from a single battery; it is possible but unusual to find a notebook that contains more than one battery. Notebook batteries come in different sizes and capacities, measured in **cells**, which are the sections in the battery that hold power to be distributed. The more cells in a battery, the longer it will last, at a cost of extra money, a larger size, and more weight.

If the laptop is plugged into the wall, the computer will charge the battery until it is full. If you have spare batteries to charge, you can usually **hot swap** the

Figure 4.22 The digital HDMI interface allows you to transfer your notebook's video output to a digital television, to share presentations or to play games or movies.

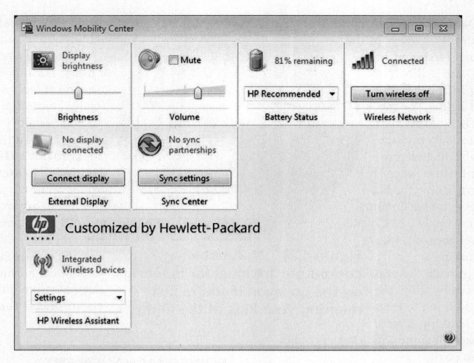

Figure 4.23 A power plan lets you reduce the power your computer uses when running from a battery, extending the amount of time you can use it before recharging.

batteries, meaning you can remove and replace them while the computer is running and active. This allows you to charge one, then remove it, and charge another. Check with the computer's manufacturer before hot swapping, to make sure the system is designed to allow it. If the computer is running on battery power, you must shut down your computer completely before swapping batteries; otherwise, you will lose your work session when you unplug the battery.

While a greater number of cells means a longer battery life, the specific life of the battery will depend on your hardware configuration, your power management settings, and what you are doing with the computer. Bigger monitors and higher-performance CPUs, for example, will draw more power than smaller models. Writing a document will use far less power than playing a high-detail, 3D online game; you might find that a four-cell battery can last for a couple of hours when you are writing in a word processor program but can run down after just a half hour of playing a high-performance game.

Computer buyers often place more importance on minimizing the weight they have to carry than on getting extra operating time—most laptops ship with relatively small batteries and no capacity to add extra batteries. Users who have the budget and need to run their computer for many hours at a time

between charging sessions can invest in one or more large-capacity batteries. The smaller one is ideal for shorter sessions, and the larger one can be left charged and ready for long road or airplane trips.

Notebooks usually have ways for you to manage various power consumption settings on your computer. Microsoft Windows, for example, displays a battery icon at the far right side of the toolbar that shows how much power remains in the battery and whether wall power is present. Right-clicking that icon and selecting "Power Options" will bring up a power management screen.

A laptop comes with at least one **power plan**, which allows you to list various settings for the computer to use depending on whether it is on battery or wall power. If you wish, you can create your own power plans by selecting "Create a Power Plan" from the list on the left of the power management screen (this example uses Windows 7; the exact details may be different if your computer uses a different operating system). Figure 4.23 shows an example of the options available, including how long to allow a fully lit display, when to put the screen and the computer to sleep, and how bright to make the screen. Users typically make more conservative power settings for battery use than for wall power, allowing the computer to function at its best performance when power is not an issue.

Figure 4.24 Netbook computers have the same basic configuration as notebooks, but they are smaller and have more limited processing power than their larger cousins.

NETBOOKS: NEARLY NOTEBOOKS

For users who want the traditional structure of a notebook computer—keyboard, vertical monitor, integrated mouse—but don't need the full power or size they typically provide, a netbook may fit the bill. In terms of size, processing power, features, and cost, netbooks resemble their larger notebook relatives. Where a full notebook's screen may measure diagonally anywhere from 13 to 22 inches, netbook screens are commonly 9 or 10 inches. Netbooks often use a CPU that is less powerful but designed to consume significantly less electricity than its counterparts. Their memory and hard-drive amounts are typically smaller than in notebooks, and they usually lack DVD drives and some of the extra input/output ports that the larger machines possess.

Windows-based netbooks run a reduced-feature version of the Windows 7 operating system, called **Windows 7 Starter**, in order to consume less of the limited system resources. Windows 7 Starter lacks many of Windows 7's personalization features, as well as support for some of the higher-end multimedia abilities, such as running multiple monitors and certain kinds of streaming video.[1]

[1]Keith Ward, What is Windows 7 Starter Edition? About.com. Retrieved June 27, 2010, from http://windows.about.com/od/windowsosversions/a/Win7Starter.htm

In exchange for the smaller feature set and processing power, netbooks cost about half of the price for a basic, entry-level notebook. Netbooks consume less electric power, so they can generally last for more hours before charging is required. While the operating system and hardware have somewhat reduced functioning, they can handily run familiar software for Internet browsing, e-mail, and business office tasks.

Netbooks are ideal not only for users with a limited budget or computing needs but also for those who want to use a computer where work space is difficult to find. Owners of notebooks with 17-inch screens might not unpack them on a crowded airplane, for example, but a netbook user can spend hours with the computer, even when the person in front of him or her pushes back the seat to sleep.

One of the areas where netbooks have not cut features is in wireless connectivity. Most netbooks have a wired Ethernet port and support the latest wireless transmission standards. Mobile users who emphasize convenience over computing power may find netbooks to be a more ideal match than notebooks.

Google's Chromebook is an alternative form of netbook that relies heavily on cloud services for both its applications and its underlying operation. Rather than a conventional operating system like Windows or Mac OS X, Chromebooks come with

Fact Check

1. Which of the following statements reflects a basic, accurate comparison between desktop and notebook PCs?
   a. Notebook PCs are portable, wireless network devices, while desktop PCs rely on a faster wired connection because they are stationary.
   b. Desktop PCs always have bigger monitors and full-sized keyboards, which notebooks cannot support.
   c. Notebooks are easily portable PCs that in most cases can run the same software as a typical desktop PC.
2. Some notebooks support the hot-swapping of batteries, which
   a. is essential to prevent them from overheating.
   b. allows the user to swap in fresh batteries without first shutting down the computer.
   c. provides a CPU speed boost.

a special, limited operating system that boots in seconds and places the user directly into a Web browser. From there, users can navigate to Internet sites and launch applications.

Programs and file data reside on Google's cloud servers rather than on the user's hard drive. When editing a document, for example, the user runs the program, opens and changes the document, and saves the changes on Google's server. This allows the netbook itself to provide solid performance with less powerful hardware, because the Chromebook itself is not loading and operating the application software.

While this creates an inexpensive and innovative solution for mobile computing, it is ideal only for users who can always access the Internet, and whose application needs match those that Google and its partners provide. Frequent travelers may find that they are too often out of reach of the Internet, or that the connection and roaming fees at airports, hotels, and on airplanes negate the low-budget aspect of the computing model. Users who require specific software programs may find themselves unable to use them on a Chromebook. Even so, users who spend virtually all of their time in Google's domain already may find a Chromebook to be the perfect tool.

4.5 Handheld Devices

Though handheld computers have been around for decades, recent innovations have made them the favorite choice for more consumers than ever before. As handheld sales outpace those of stationary PCs, new hardware and software continue to redefine the purpose and community for these devices.

TABLET COMPUTERS

Not everyone prefers using a keyboard and mouse to interact with the computer. Tablet computers were created as a way to provide alternative to that interface. Tablet computers provide a touch-sensitive screen that responds to contact with fingers or, in some cases, a stylus. Where a mouse would be used to click and drag, a tablet screen allows users to tap icons with their fingers to start programs and drag objects around on the screen by moving them with a fingertip. Some models also support more complex touch-based operations, such as expanding

and shrinking windows by moving the thumb and forefinger apart and together on the screen, or scrolling rapidly along a list of menu options or icons by swiping at it with a finger.

Touch screens on tablets can also be used to interpret motions as letters and numbers. The user draws the shape of a letter or number on the screen, and the tablet makes its best guess at a letter or number match and adds it to the current document or sends it as input to the current program.

While the newest tablets are surprisingly good at guessing letters, entering large amounts of information this way is slow in contrast to using a keyboard because you have to wait for the computer to match the motion before beginning each new letter. Tablets have addressed this liability in a couple of ways:

- Some tablets provide a "virtual keyboard" as part of their operating environment, displaying a picture of keys on the touch screen. Users type on the screen by tapping on the displayed letters. Some people find this to be natural and intuitive, but others still prefer the mechanical response of a real keyboard.

- Tablets often have a port that allows the connection of an external keyboard, but users who still want a one-piece computer may prefer a convertible model. **Convertible tablets** are tablet computers that contain a keyboard attached by a special hinge. The tablet screen can be rotated and flipped up, effectively turning the tablet into a notebook shape. Convertibles allow people to use the computer as a more traditional notebook or as the hands-on tablet, depending on what they are doing.

Tablet computers use processors, memory, and hard drives that are similar to the components found in notebooks. The main difference in the hardware involves the touch screen and video output. The operating system must be extended to handle touch input as well. New Windows-based tablets typically ship with a version of Windows 7. The popular iPad tablet from Apple Computer runs a version of iOS, the company's operating system designed specifically for its mobile devices.

**Figure 4.25
Convertible tablet PCs provide a touch screen for intuitive input and an attached keyboard when conventional data entry is more appropriate.**

Figure 4.26 Shopping for a tablet PC ideally involves trying out different models to see which one fits best.

Of course, because tablets are designed specifically to be mobile computing devices, they also have the hardware and software necessary to support wired and wireless communication.

There are a number of companies that produce competing versions of tablets; Apple's iPad, Motorola's Xoom and Hewlett-Packard's TouchPad are three examples of very different designs for the same type of product. Each manufacturer configures its hardware options differently, but not dramatically; one might use a better camera than another, for example, or provide more storage space than their competitors. As companies release new versions of their products, they pay close attention to the reaction and demands of the marketplace, so hardware choices tend to stay close together between companies in order to match features and prices that are popular.

Ultimately, what differentiates tablets most is the user experience that they provide. As with other types of computers, each tablet operating system provides its own unique methods for common tasks. One operating system might allow users to select a program by providing them with a simple list of names, while another might accomplish the same task with a set of pictures showing the programs in use. Different operating systems and hardware also support different sets of programs. The number and type of programs available for users will vary from system to system.

If you are considering purchasing a tablet PC, it is important to take the time to test out various models. There is simply no way to know what you will like best in a tablet until you are able to try at least a couple of different options. You may find selecting programs by picture to be immensely helpful, or it might be a tedious and annoying exercise. An ultra-thin tablet could feel perfect in your hands, but it could also feel unstable and overly delicate. Evaluate the size and sensitivity of the various touch screens, and the type of touch interactions they support.

Along with the hardware, look into the various applications that are available. If you absolutely must have specific programs or services that are supported on only one operating system, then tablets based on other operating systems must be ruled out. Do consider the variety of programs available, but don't necessarily simply base a decision on raw numbers. The platform with 50,000 applications is not necessarily better than the one with 20,000, if some of the ones you need aren't available.

Cost can also be a factor in deciding which tablet to purchase. Of course, each manufacturer will charge a different amount for their computer, but consider other charges or savings as well. Some tablets, like RIM's Playbook, allow users to access their existing cellular or data subscriptions for their BlackBerry phone, blurring the line between smart phone and tablet but also allowing a BlackBerry user to move to a larger device while retaining their phone service. Applications may cost different amounts on different platforms, and you may find that music and video libraries on a device you already own may not be portable to another.

SMART PHONES

While notebook computers were created as a way to make the desktop computer easily portable, the handheld PC was born from a different—though not completely unrelated—perspective on computing. From the beginning, handheld computers, including the smart phone and the personal digital assistant (PDA) from which it evolved, have focused on mobile computing.

The ancestor of the PDA, the Psion Organiser, was released in 1984 and marketed as "the world's first practical pocket computer."[2] It was a tough, durable plastic brick that looked more like a calculator. It had a narrow, one-text-line display and an alphabetic keyboard, and it provided an extremely basic clock and simple database so the user could enter information for later retrieval. Psion's Organiser II, first released in 1986, provided up to four lines of text, a telephone dialer, and the ability to use simple software such as a word processor and spreadsheet.[3]

Though the Organiser hardly resembles the smart phone of today, the concept of a battery-run pocket organizer fueled a new way of thinking about computing. While the notebook designers were working to find a way for users to take a full-featured computer wherever they went, PDA development focused more on what could be accomplished with a computer that fits into a coat pocket or belt holster.

The next major development in this direction was Apple Computer's release of the Newton MessagePad in 1993. Though much larger than the PDAs of today, the MessagePad had a large screen and no keyboard, relying on stylus input on the screen. Later versions and products in the Newton platform added keyboard support and interesting features such as the ability for the device to reorient its display to **landscape** mode, meaning horizontally across the longest dimension.

PDAs have evolved considerably since their introduction, with perhaps their most significant change being the convergence with cellular telephones to create the now-ubiquitous smart phone. Small screen areas and miniature or alternative input methods were common to both devices, and designers of both devices needed to link them in some way with other computers and networks. By combining cell and PDA technology and function, companies enabled consumers to carry just one pocket-sized mobile device, and the concept quickly became popular. Though older-style PDAs

[2]Steve Litchfield (2005), The history of Psion, *3-Lib*. Retrieved June 28, 2010, from http://3lib.ukonline.co.uk/historyofpsion.htm
[3]Centre for Computing History, Psion Organizer II XP. Retrieved June 28, 2010, from http://www.computinghistory.org.uk/det/3489/Psion-Organiser-II-XP/

Figure 4.27 The BlackBerry manages to pack a QWERTY keyboard into a very small space.

can still be found, the market for those models is dwarfed by the sale of smart phones that combine a cell phone with Internet access and an array of software programs to run. Two models of smart phones commonly found today are the BlackBerry, by Research in Motion (RIM), and Apple Computer's iPhone. Each device takes a very different approach to working with the user.

Most BlackBerry models provide a small, curved QWERTY keyboard, a tiny trackball, and selector buttons for user input. It has a wide array of software applications that it can run, but its primary function since its creation has been the efficient delivery of e-mail. Corporate accounts set up e-mail relay software, which forwards new e-mail messages to a RIM data center, which in turn passes the e-mail to the local cellular provider for delivery to the BlackBerry user. Whereas other smart phone e-mail programs require the user to check via the Internet for new messages, BlackBerry users have the mail arrive on their units shortly after the messages are received at the users' place of work.

The iPhone is designed more with the multimedia user in mind. It provides a touch screen and has no physical keyboard for input (it does provide a virtual keyboard via the touch screen). Input is accomplished via a touch screen that specifically requires finger touch; a stylus will not cause the unit to respond. It provides Internet software that receives e-mail and allows Web browsing, and it also provides audio and video media support. The iPhone's software application library contains hundreds of thousands of downloadable titles, ranging from social networking programs and games to reference and business-style programs.

Despite their small size, smart phones are adopting a number of technology advances found on their larger and more powerful full-size relatives. Some devices now sport dual-core processors to increase speed, and **active-matrix organic LED (AMOLED)** screens that use significantly less power than conventional LED screens. Though their screens are small, the screen resolution continues to increase, providing high-detail viewing for games and movies.

Along with PC-style components, smart phones contain a number of features that notebook computers do not generally provide, such as motion and proximity sensors, gyroscopes and compasses, all of which support and provide information to software on actively mobile devices.

Smart phones also provide a wide range of accessories, many of which are based on the **Bluetooth** wireless protocol, which provides short-distance radio communication between devices. Many governments have passed laws mandating hands-free cell phone operation while driving a car, and there are many wireless earpieces, microphones, speakers and voice-activated dialers that remove the necessity of holding the phone while talking.

As with tablets, there are a number of competing smart phone manufacturers that provide different combinations of hardware, power, features and user interfaces. Several different operating systems—Android, Symbian, iOS and Windows, to name four—each provide access to different applications and a different user experience. Apple's iOS is proprietary and runs only on Apple hardware, but others, like Android, are available on devices from many different manufacturers. Some Android-based manufacturers have customized the operating system beyond what Google provides, further separating their products' behavior from that of other Android-running devices. If you are shopping for a new phone, you'll need to try out different types to see which one best fits your budget, style and preferences as a user.

CHOOSING THE RIGHT TOOL FOR THE JOB

If you look closely at mobile computing devices, you'll see that the features of mobile products overlap somewhat. For example, smart phones contain small, efficient calendar and appointment systems, which you can also find on a notebook computer. Notebooks allow the user to make telephone calls via **Voice over**

Figure 4.28 Bluetooth communication enables the convenient use of wireless devices such as this hands-free cell phone headset.

Internet Protocol (VoIP) programs like Skype, and cellular telephone service is, of course, available on all smart phones. This overlap is not just redundant; it gives users flexibility in choosing the technology they like best. Some people love smart phones and view notebooks as clunky. Others are reluctant to leave their desktop environments and have a hard time envisioning what they would do with a handheld device. Thanks to the variety of hardware choices, users can select what they prefer.

Think about your favorite ways to use computers or mobile devices, and see what works best for you. A handheld system is great if your preferred uses emphasize light-duty mobile computing tasks such as these:

- Managing your schedule on a daily or hourly basis, via calendar and schedule-management capabilities
- Managing a list of contacts
- Making notes on the fly, via keyboard, screen, or microphone
- Receiving and sending e-mail messages
- Responding immediately to incoming text messages and online status updates
- Spending time online no matter where you are

If your job requires you to travel but you still need a full-featured computer, you may consider using a notebook computer, which provides the functions of a smart phone if you need them, plus the following services that handhelds alone cannot support:

- You can carry your desktop data, programs, and work environment with you as you travel.
- The same computer that holds data and programs can be used to produce presentations.
- You can run complex and processor-intense software and connect your notebook to a larger monitor.

Of course, if your mobile needs simply involve the ability to make a phone call now and then when you're out of the office, and your idea of a useful computer requires a 24-inch monitor and a curved ergonomic keyboard, then you can keep your cell phone with you at your desk and enjoy all the benefits that a desktop computer can provide.

4.6 Mobile Networks and Communications

Putting your notebook computer on a table at your local coffee shop certainly qualifies as mobile computing. But, increasingly, people sitting at the Half-Full Mug are there to do more than just write a chapter of a book or fix a business spreadsheet. Mobile users routinely want to share information, stay in touch, and find new information of their own. Networks provide the means to make that happen.

You will learn more about networks and networking hardware in Chapter 7, but even so, let's examine mobile networking a little more closely. By and large, mobile devices share data via wireless networks. Notebook and netbook computers are the main exception to the rule; they can just as easily connect to networks with an Ethernet wire as with a wireless interface. Even with that dual capability, however, many notebook users do not find themselves in a place where wired connections are especially convenient to use, so they rely exclusively on the wireless mode.

NETWORK PROVIDERS

Wireless networking for mobile users is divided between user and provider. The provider is the entity that makes network access available, either free or for a fee. The user is the person who has the mobile computing device.

Cellular service providers for mobile phones use their own network of cell sites, which are collections of antennas and transmission and reception equipment mounted throughout their coverage area on towers and atop buildings and other structures. Unlike wireless Internet hardware, the transmitters and receivers themselves are not sold to consumers as individual items.

Cellular service providers commonly provide deals and discounts to new subscribers to persuade them to join as customers. In return, service providers will often place restrictions on users designed to keep them from jumping quickly from provider to provider. They may impose contract terms that fine or penalize users who discontinue their service before a certain amount of time (typically one or two years) has passed.

Providers often **lock** the cell phones that they sell to customers, meaning that they disable the phone's ability to connect to networks other than the one owned by the provider. This way, if a customer discontinues their service, they cannot use their existing phone with a new provider. Many people find that early termination fees plus the cost of a new phone to be a prohibitive factor against frequently switching services.

Some phones can be unlocked after an initial subscription period, and not all phones are locked by the service providers. Users can purchase certain brands of unlocked phones from an electronics retailer and then bring them to a compatible service provider for activation. Some phones, however, such as the Apple iPhone, are never unlocked, forcing subscribers to stay with Apple-approved service providers for as long as they use that phone.

Smart phone buyers should be aware and very careful of the terms required to use various models of phones that they are considering. Sometimes, finding just the right hardware is easier than finding an ideal service provider, connection plan, and contract terms.

Most cell phone providers that support Internet access via phones do not provide direct Internet access. Rather, they make the connection between the Internet and cell phone network at a central location, and they communicate Internet data to the user via the cell network hardware.

Some Internet service providers (ISPs) have begun to provide area-wide wireless plans for consumers, using a rapidly emerging telecommunications protocol called **Worldwide Interoperability for Microwave Access (WiMAX)**. WiMAX-based services support a data transfer rate competitive with other broadband methods and can provide wireless coverage across a much wider area than a Wi-Fi antenna.[4] (Wi-Fi signals typically extend no more

---

[4]Prashant Sharma (June 20, 2009), Facts about WiMAX and why is it "the future of wireless broadband," *TechPluto*. Retrieved June 29, 2010, from http://www.techpluto.com/wimax-in-detail/

than a few hundred feet from the point of origin at best, while WiMAX signals can be received at least a few miles away, and in some cases more.) WiMAX subscribers must use a special antenna to connect to the service, as the standard Wi-Fi antennas receive a different frequency of signal.

While the term *Internet service provider* refers to companies that are in business specifically to provide the infrastructure necessary to connect to the Internet, these days that term could also be extended to a second group: individuals and small businesses that purchase a connection to the Internet through a traditional ISP and then elect to share that connection with others.

The local coffee shop or restaurant that has a "free Wi-Fi" sign in its window is effectively taking on the role of a limited ISP, as a courtesy to its customers. People who install personal wireless networks may choose to share their connection with nearby neighbors. In some cases, improperly installed home networks that are unsecured turn the homeowners into unwitting ISPs as they unknowingly share their open connection.

The typical hardware for sharing an Internet connection with others in the immediate area is simple: The provider connects a wireless traffic-directing device called a **router** to its local network, or directly to the hardware that provides Internet service. The router creates and manages connections with the local wireless users, and communicates data between the users and the Internet.

Some smart phones have the capability to use their cellular Internet connection to serve the same function as a router. The phone can be connected to one or more local computers, and allow those computers to access the Internet via the cellular connection. Users have Internet access when either type of network is available, and if both can be accessed, the user can select the more reliable or cost-effective connection according to their preference.

A wireless router has several settings that affect network safety and availability. The exact method for configuring a router depends on the manufacturer. Most new routers are configured via the browser of a computer within its network. Typically, to look up and edit router settings, you start a Web browser and enter the router's **IP address**—a unique set of numbers that identifies the router on the network—as provided by the manufacturer in the installation and startup instructions. The IP address is in the form of a URL and is usually http://192.168.1.1/ or something similar. The router requests a password and then displays a convenient interface for reviewing the router's status and changing settings as needed.

To install your own wireless router, you need to be prepared for several possible considerations (the details may vary by manufacturer):

- **Router password**. Routers are designed to have their configuration and status screens protected by a password. Typically, all routers are shipped by a manufacturer with the same default IP address, account name, and password. Therefore, if you completely reset your router to its default state and can't remember how to log in to the router, you can look up the information easily on the Web—and so can anybody else in your city. When you install a router and log in, change the user name and password to something other than the default.

- **SSID broadcast**. A wireless router can continuously broadcast its **service set identifier (SSID)**, which is a name that identifies it to the nearby area. This makes it convenient for visitors to find and connect to your network; for example, customers sitting in the Half-Full Mug's lounge area will easily know which network to use if it is named "Half-Full Mug WiFi." You can turn off this broadcast, in which case the router will announce its presence without its name. For visitors to gain access to the network, they will need to find out the name from someone hosting the wireless service. Turning off the router's SSID is a security measure to guard against only the most casual of intruders. Discovering a router's SSID is a fairly simple matter even if the device is not broadcasting it, so any motivated network hacker will be undeterred by a lack of SSID broadcast. Unless you have a network name that would be embarrassing or inconvenient if seen by nearby wireless users, turning it off is probably not worth the effort.

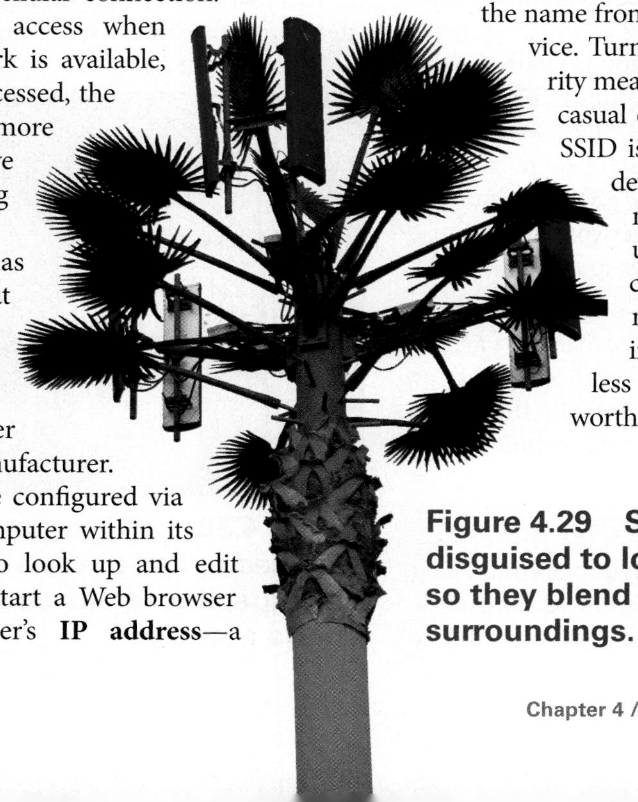

Figure 4.29 Some cell phone sites are disguised to look like trees or statues, so they blend in better with their surroundings.

- **Network access password.** Providers that are offering their Internet connection to visitors often provide an **unsecured** connection, meaning anyone within range of the router can simply connect his or her mobile device and gain access. With the router properly installed and configured, this can safely allow visitors to access the Internet without seeing any of the other computers that might be present at that location. If the wireless connection is to be available for specific visitors and not the general public, then the connection must be secured with a password. Secured router connections are encrypted to keep them safer. One encryption method, called **Wired Equivalent Privacy (WEP)**, is included in router setup to support old networks, but its encryption is fatally flawed and can be defeated in minutes. Nowadays, routers should use a method called **WPA2**, for **Wi-Fi Protected Access**, which provides better protection. The router owner gives the router a passphrase to require, and network users must know that passphrase in order to log in.

Placing a router may be a trial-and-error process based on how well the signal is received in various places. You may need to try different locations, or install a signal extender that retransmits the signal with a separate antenna in a different location.

NETWORK USERS

As mentioned earlier, if you have a mobile computing device that uses a cellular connection to send messages, files, and access the Internet, you don't likely have much to think about for hardware once you have chosen your smart phone. Your signal (or lack of it) and connection services depend on the coverage provided by cell network companies.

If you want to connect a mobile device to a specific type of service, the device needs some kind of antenna, receiver, and adapter to translate the incoming data into a form the device can use. Cell phones typically contain receivers and transmitters compatible with the network protocols used in their region or country. Some may contain the ability to receive in multiple countries or continents, making them good choices for international travelers who want to stay in touch. Many cell phones support Bluetooth, and a few models even have direct Wi-Fi connections and the ability to switch from the cell network to Wi-Fi Internet; in those cases, subscription plans may allow the user to pay less or nothing at all for calls made over the Internet connection.

New notebook computers commonly contain a Wi-Fi adapter and antenna of some kind, but not all computers are built to internally support Bluetooth and other communication methods. USB adapters are now commonly used to provide wireless access for mobile computers (and even desktop models when the owner wants to connect them in that manner). Using an unobtrusive adapter about the same shape and size as a flash storage stick, users can add the ability to connect to Bluetooth devices, WiMAX networks, and Wi-Fi Internet connections.

Network connections of any type typically involve some kind of initial setup for safeguarding the security of the network, its provider, and its users. Bluetooth devices that transfer certain kinds of data need to register with each other (sometimes by having the user

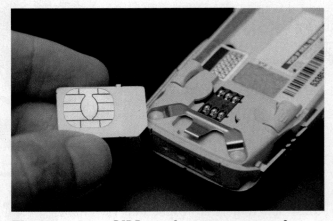

Figure 4.30   SIM cards are separately installed in cell phones, and are used to hold specific details about a subscriber's phone account.

enter the same personal identification number on both devices). Cell phones contain **subscriber identity module (SIM)** cards that identify the user and subscription owner of the phone; these are usually provided and configured by the company that provides the user with cellular service. Secure Wi-Fi connections require that the user know both the SSID and the passphrase in order to log in and access the network. With notebooks and each Wi-Fi connection you make, you usually have the option of saving your connection information for the next time you log in, and you can also typically specify whether you want your computer to connect to that network automatically.

Once these connections are established, however, most wireless devices connect seamlessly for routine use. Your cell phone connects to its closest compatible cell site, no matter where in town, the country, or in some cases the world you happen to be. Notebooks running WiMAX service connect in much the same way. If your notebook is near a Wi-Fi connection that it has been told to join automatically, then as soon as it detects the network, it will connect your computer. Bluetooth devices recognize each other when they are in range and create a connection without requiring user intervention.

4.7 Mobile Access to Your Data

Many people either own or use multiple computing devices on a regular basis. A person may have a desktop computer at work, and carry a tablet with them when they are away from their desk. Some people use a home computer to store movies for playback on their living room TV, and they also carry a smart phone to access online video clips and streaming shows.

Eventually, many people confront the challenge of storing data that they can use in more than one place. When someone switches from their desktop PC to their tablet, there may be documents or information on the desktop computer that they want to bring along. When someone leaves home with their smart phone in hand, there may be new songs, video clips or other files on the home media center that would be good to have. Sometimes, users also want to provide multiple people with access to the same information, so that people can collaborate on creating documents and ideas.

Users can, of course, rely on USB flash drives to store files, or copy data from one device to another and maintain multiple copies on different machines. But USB devices are in most cases insecure and easy to misplace, making them less than ideal as a primary storage solution. Maintaining separate copies of documents can become a support nightmare, especially if many files or people are involved, and duplicating large amounts of data increases the cost of each device by increasing the amount of storage that must be purchased.

USING YOUR HOME NETWORK FOR STORAGE

Users who have a small set of computers at home or work can implement centralized data storage as a way to cut down on storage costs, increase access to data and improve data security. With documents, music files and other data stored in one place, and with a local network up and running, any computer participating in that network can access the data. Since users simply reach across the network to access the data, only one copy of a given file needs to exist, removing the concern over which computer has the latest version of the data. When considering large amounts of data, for example video clips and movies, storing only one copy of the data can significantly reduce the amount of storage needed by every device that will view the video files. Each device need only have the viewing program installed, and the data is transmitted as needed to the requesting computer for viewing.

Centralized storage can provide a safer place to keep user data, regardless of whether the data is sensitive or simply important to the owner. Centralized storage units can also be combined with automatic backup systems so data files are periodically saved. In the event of a drive failure, most or all of the data can be recovered from backup.

Products such as Drobo provide complete solutions for data storage ideal for a small office or home network. A Drobo unit allows the user to plug in sets of hard disk drives for storage. The unit monitors the available space on the drives that are installed, and notifies the user to add more storage when space is running low. The unit can also spread or duplicate data

Figure 4.31   A Drobo storage solution allows users to add extra storage when needed, and provides backup and data recovery services.

across hard drive devices for critical data, so if one drive fails, the data on that drive can still be accessed on other devices. Large Drobo units can store as much as 24 terabytes, far more than a typical home or office user would require, but owners may provide the unit with only as much storage as they need.

While Drobo provides centralized storage for a network, it is just that: storage. As an alternative for users who want to do more, Microsoft has created the Windows Home Server (WHS), a program that runs on a Windows-based computer. With the computer properly connected to an Internet-accessible network and data saved to the server's hard drives, Windows Home Server performs automatic backups and manages data on the drives, and also provides ways for users to access their data across the Internet.

USING THE INTERNET FOR CLOUD-BASED STORAGE

Storage solutions like Drobo and Windows Home Server can provide powerful, convenient ways to centrally store data, but extra hardware is required. Buying the hard drives and storage unit (or a separate computer for running WHS) may create an extra cost that the user or small business doesn't want to pay. Plus, even though data may be accessible from remote locations, it is up to the user to make sure the server stays up and running whenever data may be needed.

Cloud service companies provide alternatives that do not require up-front hardware purchases, because users transfer data to the service company's servers for storage instead of their own central storage hardware. Some services provide limited data storage for free, while others provide their services for a monthly or annual fee.

Carbonite is an online company that primarily provides automatic data backup. Once installed, the software automatically makes backup copies of your data files and transmits the copies via an Internet connection to Carbonite's array of storage servers. If you need to recover lost files or download them to a different device if you are away from your main computer, you can log into their web site and retrieve the data.

This makes data sharing simple, and also provides valuable disaster recovery features that can be especially useful for a small business or self-employed user. Most people, if they make backup copies at all, store their backups on disks or flash drives in the office where they work. Unfortunately, if the office burns down, floods or experiences some other devastating circumstance, both the computer and the backups will likely be destroyed. By using an offsite backup service, only the local data will be lost if a disaster strikes, and the company or user can move to a safer location and restore all their data.

Carbonite does not provide much depth when it comes to collaboration, however. For users who want to store their data in the cloud and allow multiple people to access and make changes to files, services like Windows Live SkyDrive, Dropbox and Google Docs all provide variations on the sharing theme. These services allow you to upload documents from your computer

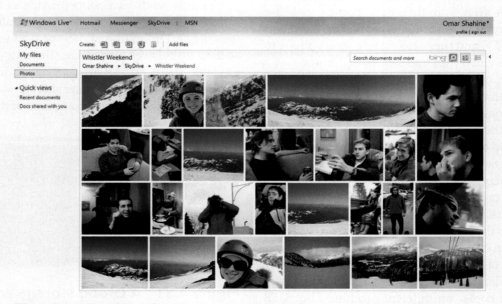

Figure 4.32   Cloud storage services often provide online programs for viewing and editing the documents that they store for users.

to their central storage facility, and then they manage access and changes that are made to the documents.

Dropbox maintains a list of devices and users that are connected to a subscriber's account. Every time a change is made, the changes are delivered immediately to all the participating devices as a way to keep all devices synchronized. The system is a good way for a single person with multiple devices such as a desktop, notebook, and handheld PC to easily distribute new and changed data to all devices, though the service does not actually save storage space on any of the devices. It may also not be ideal for active organizations where many people are making changes offline; because an Internet connection is required to receive changes from others, an offline user could make changes to their copy of the document that others will not see until that user restores their Internet connection.

Windows Live SkyDrive and Google Docs are more focused on collaboration. They both provide ways for users to upload, store, and change documents, where both the data and the programs that change them are hosted by the service company rather than the user. Both services provide ways for users to keep documents private and also to grant viewing and editing permission to sets of other users.

Every cloud storage solution can add convenience, flexibility and efficiency to a user's task of storing, retrieving and sharing data. Many users will find that the subscription cost to accomplish their task is very reasonable given the help that cloud storage can provide.

Even so, it is critically important to remember that every time your data leaves your computer, it is placed at risk of theft. Cloud companies have a vested interest in providing a secure storage facility for their users, but it is impossible to be absolutely certain that data you store in external servers will be completely unavailable to intruders. A number of companies, including cloud service companies, have had security lapses or successful hacker attacks that compromised sensitive customer information. If you are storing ordinary documents, you may not need to be extra careful about your choice of cloud storage company; but if you are working with extremely sensitive information, you should take great care to evaluate the best way to store your data that properly balances cost, convenience and security.

Fact Check

1. File servers and centralized storage devices provide
   a. Guaranteed availability to your data no matter where you are.
   b. A way to store, back up and provide a single copy of data for multiple devices or users on the network.
   c. A higher degree of data compression than conventional storage.
2. Cloud-based storage
   a. provides a special kind of software known as "vaporware."
   b. is always a lower-cost alternative to storing data locally.
   c. allows users to store, retrieve and change data on the service-provider's computer instead of their own hard drive.

IN Summary

- The goal of laptop computing is to provide the user with all the programs and functions of a desktop environment in a convenient, portable package that can be used practically anywhere. Modern notebook computers can provide full-sized keyboards, monitors, and mice; access to much of the same software found on desktop PCs; and access to the same networks and types of peripheral devices as for desktop PCs. They do this in a package that is much smaller and lighter than a desktop computer.

- A notebook computer's power plan specifies the way the computer and operating system should balance performance and power consumption. The user can choose how much power to use depending on whether the power is provided by a battery or electrical service.

- Many mobile devices, including smart phones and tablet computers, do not provide traditional keyboards for input. On a tablet computer, the user typically enters text tapping, swiping or writing with their fingers. Some of those devices provide virtual keyboards, which are pictures of a keyboard displayed on their screen, and they simulate typing by allowing the user to tap the screen over the desired keys that are displayed. The device also may include a port into which the user can connect a keyboard for entering large amounts of text.

- Tablets and smart phones are produced with a wide assortment of operating systems, hardware features and available software titles. Shoppers for these types of products should take the time to try out different models to make sure that their needs and preferences are met by the device's behavior.

- WiMAX is a telecommunications protocol used by Internet service providers to provide wireless Internet service over wide areas. Whereas Wi-Fi can be received reliably only within dozens of yards of the antenna, WiMAX can be reliably used for a few miles or more around a broadcast point.

- To eliminate the extra time and space required to store the same files on multiple devices in order to share the data, users can create a central data storage system on their home or office network. The file server or storage hardware can provide access to a single, central copy of the data for multiple users on different devices; periodically back up the data; and guard against data loss in the event of a limited hardware failure.

- Cloud-based storage service companies allow users to store their data on servers that are owned by the service companies rather than the user. The data can be kept safe from loss by the user, and in many cases the cloud storage service allows multiple users to access and change documents from within a Web browser.

Key Terms

active-matrix organic LED (AMOLED), 164
Bluetooth, 165
cells, 159
convertible tablets, 162
convergence, 158
High-Definition Multimedia Interface (HDMI), 159
hot swap, 159
IP address, 167

landscape, 164
lock, 166
portable computers, 158
power plan, 160
router, 167
service set identifier (SSID), 167
SSID Broadcast, 167
subscriber identity module (SIM), 169
unsecured, 168

Voice over Internet Protocol (VoIP), 165
Wi-Fi Protected Access (WPA2), 168
Worldwide Interoperability for Microwave Access (WiMAX), 166
Windows 7 Starter, 161
Wired Equivalent Privacy (WEP), 168

Key Terms QUIZ

Complete each statement by writing one of the terms listed under "Key Terms" in each blank.

1. A(n) _____ port is used to send video output to a digital, high-definition television.

2. Many notebook computers allow you to _____ the battery, changing it while the computer is running.

3. Some cellular phone service companies may _____ the phones that they sell, preventing subscribers from using their phone on a competing service's network.

4. When video or graphic output is shifted so that the long side of its rectangle is horizontal rather than vertical, it is said to be in _____ mode.

5. A(n) _____ is a network device that helps provide wireless Internet service by managing data traffic between multiple wireless users and the Internet.

6. One of the newer protocols for delivering Internet service that is gaining in popularity is called _____.

7. A wireless router can broadcast its _____ to the nearby area, to make it easier for users to find and connect to it.

8. The current encryption standard used by Wi-Fi routers is called _____.

9. _____ is a short-distance radio communication standard to link mobile devices.

10. The process of different styles of hardware devices becoming more and more alike is known as _____.

Review QUESTIONS

In your own words, briefly answer the following questions.

1. Describe two advantages that notebook computers have that make them more suitable for mobile computing than a desktop model.

2. What network connections do notebook computers typically support?

3. Describe some of the factors that can extend or reduce the amount of time a battery can supply power for a notebook computer. If you own a notebook computer, what measures can you use to make the best use of your battery power?

4. What sort of services do smart phones provide to the user?

5. Describe a major difference between the user interfaces of a BlackBerry and an iPhone. What type of user is each device designed for?

6. How can the owner of a wireless router configure it to change the degree of security protecting the router and its network?

7. Compare three types of network connections that cell phones can support.

8. How do WiMAX and Wi-Fi compare with regard to signal coverage?

9. How can central data storage reduce the cost of owning multiple computing devices?

10. Explain how cloud computing services help people share and collaborate on changes to documents without requiring that each person have their own document copy.

Complete the following exercises as directed by your instructor.

1. Learn more about the ways that cloud services provide security for the data that they host. Visit the Web sites of Carbonite at http://www.carbonite.com/, Dropbox at http://www.dropbox.com/ and Windows Live SkyDrive at http://explore.live.com/windows-live-skydrive. Find the pages on each site that explain how user data are kept secure, and note the basic methods that are used. Do they encrypt user data? What kinds of passwords are required? Do they archive changes so old versions of a document can be recovered in case an intruder damages the current file's contents? Which site, if any, seemed like they provided better data protection? Explain your reasoning.

2. Look for wireless hotspots in your area. Start your computer's browser, and navigate to Google at http://www.google.com. Click the Maps link at the top of Google's page to bring up the map interface. In the search box, type **wireless hotspots** and your zip code (for example, **wireless hotspots 97202**), and press Enter to search. Review the list of hotspots, and note their location, along with the type of establishments that are providing the service. When you are done, close your browser.

At many workplaces, employees have to schedule time for meetings and conferences, and they have to manage their time so they are prompt and prepared for each appointment.

Divide into groups of three or four. Schedule a half-hour meeting to take place between now and your next session of this class. What day will it be? What time? Where? Try to plan a meeting that everyone can attend in person, but if that's impossible, decide what technology you will use to include the person who cannot be there.

At your meeting, discuss the following questions:

• Did everyone show up at the scheduled time? If not, why not? How did that affect the group? If so, how did they keep track of the appointment and plan to be prompt?

• Did everyone participate in person? If not, how did it affect the group to have someone connected by phone, computer, or other means? Were the remote people still able to participate effectively?

• Were all the meeting attendees able to stay for the entire meeting? If interruptions or early departures occurred, how did these affect the group?

Be prepared to discuss your experiences in class and share your ideas for successfully scheduling and organizing your time.

[*Chapter* **LABS**]

1. Learn more about what a computer really costs. Many people buy more than just the system unit when they buy or upgrade their desktop PC. Think about all the things you would need if you were buying a new computer, and make a list of whatever items that come to mind. Do you need a new monitor, keyboard and mouse? What about a webcam? Do you need external storage like a USB flash drive or an external hard drive? Will you need software; serious programs, games or utilities? What about an antivirus subscription?

    Once you have a list of a few to several items, depending on your needs or wants, go online and find out what your shopping list will cost you. When you are done, calculate your total. Be prepared to compare your list and total cost to others in the class. If you are aware of how much a new desktop PC might cost you, how does that system unit price compare to the cost of everything else?

2. Investigate things you can do with a tablet or smart phone. Pick a device name or operating system that interests you, like iPad or Android. In your favorite Web search engine such as Google or Bing, enter the phrase, *best apps for iPad or best apps for Android*. You should receive many links to reviews and recommendations for applications that people like on the platform you selected.

    Look through the top ten or so recommendations on a few different review sites. Is there any consensus; in other words, do multiple sites recommend the same programs, or does everyone have a completely different list of favorites? Of the applications that are listed, do you find yourself intrigued or interested by the entire list, a few programs, or none at all? Are there types of programs that interest you more than others (for example, games more than schedulers, or schedulers more than location-reporting programs)? Note your findings and be prepared to discuss them with the class.

3. Explore the lighter side of cloud services. With a browser and an environment that courteously supports sound, visit the OnLive service's Web site at http://www.onlive.com/. OnLive allows subscribers to play a wide variety of games, including graphically-intense action and sports games, on TVs and computers, even if the computers are not ideal gaming systems. The service hosts the game on its own fast-processing servers, and uses a network connection to deliver the video and receive commands from the players. The service also allows non-players to log in and watch others play.

    On the Web site, click the Service tab at the top of the screen, and view the marketing videos that describe the service and cloud gaming in general. Note the prices advertised on the site, and compare those prices to the cost of renting movies or individual games at a local movie outlet. If you buy or rent games, would this service change your spending habits? Why or why not?

[*Think* AND DISCUSS]

1. We often make shopping decisions simply by price, buying our products at whatever store provides them at the cheapest cost. Local computer stores cannot generally compete with online high-volume manufacturers solely on the basis of cost, so they often advertise advantages they provide that online retailers cannot, such as fast repairs and personal service. What advantages and disadvantages can you think of when comparing online and local computer sales? If you prefer either online or local shopping, can you think of anything your non-preferred retailer could do to change your buying habits?

2. The degree of popularity or acceptance for smart phone platforms is sometimes measured by the number of applications that are available (for example, one manufacturer might list 200,000 apps for use, while another might have only 75,000). Do you find this to be a good way to measure popularity? Does the larger number of apps make it more likely that the type of smart phone will have the programs you need? What other factors might contribute to one phone platform having more applications than its competitors?

[*Fact Check* ANSWERS]

4A:

LO4.1 Determining Your Computing Needs

1: a. All users, and especially those who will be editing video or image data.

2: b. users who do not plan to spend time playing high-intensity games or performing other graphic-oriented tasks.

LO4.2 Storage Devices and Options

1: c. Flash drives are still substantially more expensive for the same amount of storage space.

2: b. A single Blu-ray drive that can read and write Blu-ray and all older optical formats.

LO4.3 Selecting a Manufacturer and Vendor

1: c. they consider factors such as price; post-purchase repair and support; and the degree to which they want to choose their components; and then buy in whatever manner best fits their needs.

2: a. it provides consistent, carefully regulated electricity to the computer.

LO4.4 Mobile Devices

1: c. Notebooks are easily portable PCs that in most cases can run the same software as a typical desktop PC.

2: b. allows the user to swap in fresh batteries without first shutting down the computer.

LO4.5 Handheld Devices

1: b. a touch-sensitive screen

2: c. A small, curved QWERTY keyboard

LO4.6 Mobile Networks and Communications

1: b. By connecting a wireless router to its LAN

2: a. Cellular network, Wi-fi, and Bluetooth

LO4.7 Mobile Access to Your Data

1: b. A way to store, back up and provide a single copy of data for multiple devices or users on the network.

2: c. allows users to store, retrieve and change data on the service-provider's computer instead of their own hard drive.

5

BRINGING THE WORLD TO YOU

LEARNING OBJECTIVES

CHAPTER CONTENTS

Chapter Overview

Just as the personal computer revolutionized the way the world solves problems and completes tasks, the Internet has changed how the world communicates. This chapter provides basic information about the structure of the Internet network; discusses an array of services that the Internet provides to its users; and describes software solutions and good habits that can make the mobile computing experience safe and pleasant both for users and the people around them. Have you spent time on the Internet? What activities can you think of already that people can do online?

LESSON 5A:
The Internet

Even if you have not had a lot of experience with computers, it wouldn't be surprising to learn that you have been on the Internet. Year after year, millions of users access the Internet for the first time, and some of them probably used to believe they would never have a reason to use a computer. Indeed, many Internet enthusiasts buy computers just so they can go online to shop, keep in touch with friends, or play games.

But what is the Internet? Simply put, the **Internet** is a network of networks—a global communications system that links together thousands of individual networks. Thanks to the Internet, virtually any computer on any network can communicate with any other computer on any other network. These connections allow users to exchange messages, communicate in real time (seeing messages and responses immediately), share data and programs, and access limitless stores of information.

The Internet has become so important that its use is considered an essential part of computer use. Mastering the Internet is one of the first things you should do if you want to get the most from your computing experience. In this lesson, you will get an overview of the Internet by reviewing its history and structure. You'll also learn about some of the services available on the Internet and examples of how the Internet can be used at home.

Figure 5.1 The Internet provides a network to help connect people around the world, and sometimes even in the same room.

5.1 The Internet's History and Structure

No introduction to the Internet is complete without a short review of its history. Even though today's Internet bears little resemblance to its forebear of 30-plus years ago, it still functions in basically the same way.

Figure 5.2 Before it became known as the Internet, ARPA's network served universities, defense contractors, and a few government agencies.

THE BEGINNING: A "NETWORK OF NETWORKS"

The seeds of the Internet were planted in 1969, when the Advanced Research Projects Agency (ARPA) of the U.S. Department of Defense began connecting computers at different universities and defense contractors. The resulting network was called **ARPANET**. The goal of this early project was to create a large computer network with multiple paths—in the form of telephone lines—that could survive a nuclear attack or a natural disaster such as an earthquake. If one part of the network were destroyed, other parts of the network would remain functional, and data could continue to flow through the surviving lines.

ARPA had a second important reason for creating such a network: it would allow people in remote locations to share scarce computing resources. By being part of the network, these users could access faraway systems—such as governmental mainframes or university-owned supercomputers—and conduct research or communicate with other users.

At first, ARPANET was basically a large network serving only a handful of users. (Figure 5.3 shows the extent of the network as of 1971.) However, it expanded

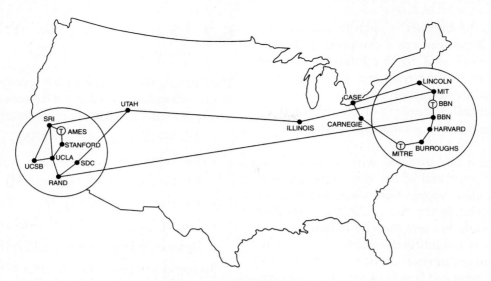

Figure 5.3   The reach of ARPANET in 1971

rapidly. The network jumped across the Atlantic to Europe in 1973, and it never stopped growing.

In the mid-1980s, another federal agency, the National Science Foundation (NSF), joined the project after the Defense Department stopped funding the network. NSF established five "supercomputing centers" that were available to anyone who wanted to use them for academic research. The NSF expected the supercomputers' users to use ARPANET to obtain access, but the agency quickly discovered that the existing network could not handle the load. In response, the NSF created a new, higher-capacity network, called **NSFnet**, to complement the older and by then overloaded ARPANET. The link between ARPANET, NSFnet, and other networks was called the Internet. The name comes from the term for the process of connecting separate networks. That process is called **internetworking**, and a collection of "networked networks" is described as being *internetworked*.

NSFnet made Internet connections widely available for academic research, but the NSF did not permit users to conduct private business over the system. Therefore, several private telecommunications companies built their own central network structures, called **backbones**, that used the same set of networking protocols as NSFnet. These private portions of the Internet were not limited by NSFnet's "appropriate use" restrictions, so it became possible to use the Internet to distribute business and commercial information.

The original ARPANET was shut down in 1990, and government funding for NSFnet was discontinued in 1995, but the commercial Internet backbone services replaced them. By the early 1990s, interest in the Internet began to expand dramatically. The system that had been created as a tool for surviving a nuclear war found its way into businesses and homes. Now, personal conversations are far more common online than collaborations on physics research.

TODAY AND TOMORROW: STILL GROWING

Today, the Internet connects thousands of networks and hundreds of millions of users around the world. It is a huge, cooperative community with no central ownership. This lack of ownership is an important feature of the Internet, because it means that no single person or group controls the network. Although there are several organizations (such as The Internet Society and the World Wide Web Consortium) that propose standards for Internet-related technologies and guidelines for its appropriate use, these organizations almost universally support the Internet's openness and lack of centralized control.

The lack of ownership of the Internet is a continual source of confusion in classrooms and the halls of government alike. The concepts of free expression and censorship are hot topics around the world, as populations struggle with the need to gain information they want and the desire to eliminate information that seems harmful or inappropriate. Governments and businesses would love to own the keys to the Internet gates, but it is precisely its independence—frustrating as it can be—that makes the Internet the universally powerful tool it has become.

As a result, the Internet is open to anyone who can access it. If you can use a computer and if the computer is connected to the Internet, you are free not only to use the resources posted by others but also to create resources of your own; that is, you can publish documents on the World Wide Web, exchange e-mail messages, and perform many other tasks.

This openness has attracted millions of users to the Internet. By the end of the year 2000, approximately 360 million people were using the Internet around the world. By the end of 2009, that number had grown fivefold to more than 1.8 billion users. In the United States, roughly three-quarters of the country's population are Internet users. With the Internet evolving as an open and largely unregulated resource, some members of the education and research communities found that the Internet could not provide them with sufficient network speed or reliability for their communication and collaboration. In 1997, the Internet2 Project was founded to design and distribute a more powerful private network.

Despite its name, the purpose of the Internet2 project is not to replace the existing Internet, but rather to create a controlled, reliable high-speed network for the participants; and to encourage the development and installation of improved technology into the public Internet. Though there is no public connection between the Internet and Internet2 networks themselves, many network improvements in the Internet flow from research and ideas enabled by the Internet2 Project.[1]

[1] *Internet World Stats* (2010), Internet usage statistics. Retrieved June 9, 2010, from http://www.internetworldstats.com/stats.htm

5.2 Overview of Internet Services

The Internet acts as a carrier for several different services, each with its own distinct features and purposes. Several Internet services are most commonly used:

- The World Wide Web (WWW)
- Electronic mail (e-mail)
- Chat and instant messaging (IM)
- File transfer protocol (FTP)
- Peer-to-peer (P2P) data transfer services
- Voice over Internet Protocol (VoIP) service

To use any of these services, you need a computer that is connected to the Internet in some way. Most individual users set up an account with an Internet service provider (ISP), a company that provides local or regional access to the Internet backbone, and connect with some manner of wired or wireless interface. Many other users connect to the Internet through a school, business, or public network.

To use a specific service, you also need the right type of software. Some programs enable you to use multiple Internet services, so you do not necessarily need separate applications for each service.

THE WORLD WIDE WEB (WWW)

The **World Wide Web** (also known as the Web or WWW) was created in 1989 at CERN, a research laboratory in Geneva, Switzerland, as a method for incorporating footnotes, figures, and cross-references into online documents. The Web's creators wanted to create a simple way to access any document that was stored on a network, without having to search through indexes or directories of files, and without having to manually copy documents from one computer to another before viewing them. To do this, they established a way to "link" documents stored in different locations on a single computer or on different computers on a network.

If you imagine a collection of billions of documents, all stored in different places but all linked together in some manner, you might imagine them creating a "web" of interconnected information. If you extend that collection of documents and their links to cover the entire globe, you have a "worldwide web" of information. This concept is where the Web gets its name. As with all computer technology, the Web has been evolving since its creation. Though its evolution is continuous, with new ideas and uses coming into being year after year, terms for describing the basic purpose of the Web have been created for its past, present, and future.

The term **Web 1.0** (a shorthand of "The Web, version 1.0") refers to the state of the World Wide Web from its creation through the early 2000's. Web 1.0 focused on providing information to users. Universities, research facilities, governments, companies, and individuals created Web sites and filled them with documents so that Web users could travel to those sites and view what was provided. The distinction between the site owner, who provides all the content, and the site visitor, who receives the information, was fairly strongly enforced.

Web 2.0 identifies the state of the Web from about the middle 2000's into the short-term future, probably around the middle 2010's. The owner–provider, visitor–receiver model of Web 1.0 is still very much present and popular for all manner of information, of course, whether to download a tax form or find answers to medical questions. Web 2.0 sites primarily feature user-generated content; instead of the owner providing documents, the owner simply provides a place for others to share their own material with others. YouTube, Wikipedia, and Facebook are examples of Web 2.0 sites; each of those sites hosts material that is created and supplied almost entirely by the community of visitors to the sites.

Beyond the sites themselves, the Web 2.0 label also applies to new behaviors that have arisen with the concept of the hosted sharing of information. A significant component to social sites involves tagging pieces of information with "like" and "dislike" labels. People share videos on YouTube, and they also share their opinions of the videos they watch. People can write restaurant reviews on a review-hosting Web site, and then others can like, dislike, or even post follow-up responses to those reviews. The labels and expressions of preference are targeted partly at the poster of the video or review; but they are also a way for people to share their opinions with everyone else who participates on that site.

Web 3.0 designates the next phase of activity that is expected to occur in the way that people use the Web. In Web 3.0, users will increasingly receive information based on their ongoing expression of preferences, interests, and activities.

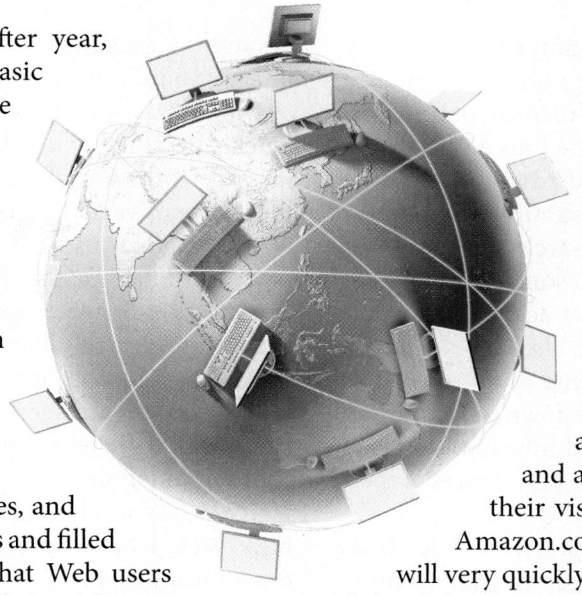

Figure 5.4 The World Wide Web is just what its name suggests: billions of documents and information sources linked together around the world.

Some forms of Web 3.0 behavior are already well established. For example, many advertisers and online shopping sites are already customizing offers, deals, and ads based on the past behavior of their visitors. If you buy video games at Amazon.com, you'll note that the Web site will very quickly begin to suggest new game titles that might interest you whenever you visit the site. The more types of things you buy, the better the site should become at identifying your preferences.

Much more sophisticated forms of this type of information tailoring are actively being designed, in some cases combining information from many different sources and types. For example, a user's search engine results may highlight sites that the user's friends have chosen in their own similar searches. Online retailer information about a user's purchasing habits could be combined with "like" and "dislike" opinions, which the user and their friends have expressed in various social networking formats, to promote certain brand names or products that are popular.

Beyond sales and advertising, Web 3.0 concepts could be applied in a wide variety of ways. Data on restaurant preferences and travel plans could be combined so that when a user plans a road trip, a travel service might suggest a route that provides access to food, sights, and attractions that the user likes, rather than simply showing the shortest distance on a map. As data becomes available not just from computers but also from cars and home appliances, a user might receive an email from a referral service suggesting local repair shops for the user's refrigerator, which has just notified the service that its cooling system has broken down.

In the future, designers envision an even greater degree of information customization, distilling the almost limitless raw data on the Internet to closely match the needs and wishes of individual users, greatly reducing the time we spend sifting through irrelevant information and uninteresting requests for our attention.

Already in Web 2.0, users are faced with complex choices between information customization and the privacy of their personal information and lives. Many people post details of their lives and thoughts on Facebook, but they occasionally run into trouble when their Facebook-published ideas are found by a disapproving employer. While targeted advertising can be useful, some people find such customization to be an unwelcome reminder that their purchasing decisions are being monitored and tracked, sometimes without their specific approval. Still others decline to participate in the tagging of sites and businesses because they do not want their movements to be tracked as they drive from place to place in town, and they are uncomfortable having Web-based information being featured or restricted based on the preferences of their friends.

Going forward, it is likely that Web 3.0 facilities will simply be another set of tools available to those who choose to embrace it. Users who provide large amounts of personal information and allow many sources and devices in their environment to report data will be able to use the information-tailoring features to their greatest advantage. Users who find information tracking and customizing to be intrusive and uncomfortable should be able to avoid the tracking and participation in exchange for managing their own filtering of data.

ELECTRONIC MAIL (E-MAIL) SERVICES

The only Internet service used more frequently than the Web is **electronic mail**. Electronic mail, more commonly called **e-mail**, is a system for exchanging messages through a computer network. Most often, people use e-mail to send and receive text messages, but depending on the software you use, you may be able to exchange messages containing graphics, images, sound, and video.

E-mail was one of the first uses of the Internet and quickly became popular because it lets users exchange messages from anywhere in the world. Further, e-mail is less expensive than using the telephone because there is no charge for using it, beyond the regular fees you pay your ISP. E-mail is also a faster way to communicate than postal mail because e-mail messages typically reach their destination in seconds rather than days.

Another reason for e-mail's popularity is that e-mail services are very easy to access. You can manage e-mail through a typical ISP account and a desktop computer or use a Web-based e-mail service, which lets you check your messages wherever you have Web access. Many cellular telephones provide e-mail features, too.

Many users also take advantage of the ability to attach data files and program files to e-mail messages. For example, you can send a message to a friend and attach a digital photograph to the message. Or you can attach a résumé to a message seeking a job with a company in your neighborhood or across the country. The recipient then can open and use the document on his or her computer.

E-mail is not a real-time communications system. In other words, after you send a message to someone, you must wait until he or she reads it and sends you a reply. This delay, however, doesn't stop people from exchanging billions of messages each year. As discussed in the Focus on the Issues box, some of those messages are more welcome than others.

CHAT AND INSTANT MESSAGING (IM)

Because e-mail is not a real-time system, other services have been created to allow people to communicate across the Internet without delivery delays. **Internet Relay Chat (IRC)** was one of the early methods used to **chat**, or communicate in real time via software. Using special software, users can join a chat channel, where all participants' communication is shared. As each user enters a sentence, it appears on the screens of the other participants in that channel. People read the messages and respond with thoughts of their own, creating an ongoing conversation. Chat channels are typically created by topic, and people join them because of the topic being discussed.

The popularity of public chat rooms created a huge demand for a way to chat privately, so that a limited number of invited people could exchange real-time messages on their screens without being seen or interrupted by anyone else online. This demand led to the

Figure 5.5 Email programs provide a digital way to write letters and messages, and deliver them to a specific audience.

Focus on the Issues

Slogging through Spam

In a society almost as dependent on e-mail as on the U.S. Postal Service, junk e-mail—better known as "spam"—has become more than a mere annoyance. For Internet-connected individuals, it's a persistent, time-consuming, and offensive aggravation. In the business world it's a crisis, draining resources and bandwidth and laying networks vulnerable to numerous security hazards.

During the past several years, the volume of unsolicited e-mail has grown steadily. Today, unsolicited e-mail accounts for nearly a staggering 80 percent of worldwide e-mail traffic. The vast majority of the spam messages being sent are advertisements for products of dubious origin (for example, off-market medicines and drugs, and replica watches) or attempts to steal personal information such as passwords and financial account numbers.

Among the many problems caused by unsolicited e-mail, spam consumes significant time and resources. One estimate placed the cost of spam in 2009 at $42 billion in the United States, spent to pay for blocking hardware and software and to pay people to sift through suspected junk mail and monitor e-mail systems. In addition to the cost of dealing with spam, a heavy price is paid by users who sort through and delete messages that bypass filters, accidentally install spam-delivered malware on their systems, or are tricked into divulging sensitive personal information to identity thieves.

Because of spam, about three-fourths of e-mail users now avoid giving out their e-mail addresses, more than half say they trust it less, and one in four uses it less, according to a recent study by the Pew Internet and American Life Project. Some are even returning to more traditional forms of communication: the telephone and U.S. Postal Service.

Efforts are ongoing to stem the tide, with limited and inconsistent success. Some companies invest in complex and expensive hardware and software filtering tools to keep out unwanted junk. Internet service providers spend large sums of money each year to filter and block spam at the source and to collaborate with anti-spam organizations. Some countries have created laws that prohibit spam, allowing spammers to be prosecuted when caught.

Ultimately, though, the battlefield is ever-changing. As one form of spam is successfully blocked, new methods for message construction are invented to renew the assault. As large spam-sending domains are identified and shut off from the Internet, new avenues are found to introduce the spam. Convictions for spamming are rare, fines are often not paid, and the problem is compounded by cases where spam originates in countries that do not prosecute the senders.

Most Internet experts agree that spam will probably never be eradicated. Ultimately, a consensus approach that coordinates legal and high-tech responses is likely to provide the best defense against the unrelenting flood of junk e-mail.

Sources: Dan Fletcher (November 2009), A brief history of spam, *Time*. Retrieved June 10, 2010, from http://www.time.com/time/business/article/0,8599,1933796,00.html; Commtouch Software (2010), *Internet Threats Trend Report: Q1 2010*, retrieved June 10, 2010, from http://www.commtouch.com/download/1679; and Ferris Research (2010), Industry statistics, retrieved June 10, 2010, from http://www.ferris.com/research-library/industry-statistics/.

Figure 5.6   Modern chat systems work in different modes and can include text typing, file sharing, and live video.

development of **instant messaging (IM)**, a type of chat software that restricts participation to specific users.

Using one of these programs, you can create a **buddy list**—a list of other users with whom you would like to chat. Whenever your IM program is running and you are online, the software lets you know when your "buddies" are also online, so you can chat with them. IM software can be configured to allow only your buddies to send you messages; spammers are just as present in IM systems as they are in e-mail, and many people find the unsolicited advertising and scam attempts from spammers to be just as unwelcome in their chat system.

As IM software has evolved, IM systems have tacked on features that once required separate software. IM programs now commonly allow users to send live video and audio signals, transfer images and data files, and share links to locations on the Web. IM modules can be stand-alone programs, as with AOL's Instant Messenger and Microsoft's MSN Messenger. They can also be bundled with other programs that have a different primary function, such as the social media site Facebook or the Internet-telephone program Skype. Web sites that have a customer support function commonly provide a real-time chat system, which lets customers ask questions via chat with a customer service representative.

FILE TRANSFER PROTOCOL (FTP)

Besides sending and receiving messages, Internet users may want to share files on the Internet. To do this, they can attach a file to an e-mail message,

or they can copy files from one computer to another by using an Internet service called **file transfer protocol (FTP)**. An FTP site is a collection of files, including data files and/or programs, housed on an FTP server. FTP sites, which are often called *archives*, may contain thousands of individual programs and files. FTP sites can be private or public. Private sites require a specific user ID and password in order to gain access to the files. Public FTP archives permit anyone to make copies of their files.

Files can be retrieved either with special client software (see Figure 5.7) or with a common Web browser like Microsoft's Internet Explorer. (Some browsers, like Mozilla's Firefox, require a free piece of extension software in order to support FTP.) FTP client programs have many features that add convenience to moving files back and forth between the PC and the FTP server, and these are ideal for users who frequently retrieve or send files to multiple FTP sites.

In the past, Internet users who wanted to find files around the world to download needed to use specialized search programs and servers with extensive catalogs of available documents. Nowadays, however, search

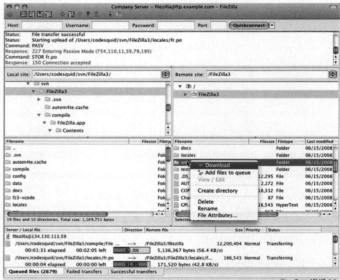

Figure 5.7   An FTP client allows users to see files on the local computer and file server, and move files between systems by dragging them between windows.

engines like Google and Microsoft's Bing have rendered those specialized archive list servers obsolete. The search engines provide the same search capabilities for FTP documents as they do for Web pages.

FTP sites provide access to many different types of files. You can find information of all kinds, from weather maps to downloadable software. FTP is often used to distribute shareware and freeware PC software (TUCOWS is a long-established site for this purpose), and computer hardware and software developers frequently host their own FTP sites, where you can copy program updates and new versions of software.

Figure 5.8 The NOAA daily weather map is released on FTP sites for more convenient downloading.

PEER-TO-PEER (P2P) DATA TRANSFER SERVICES

FTP's ability to transfer files is dependent on a single connection. The requesting computer establishes a connection to the FTP server and then receives the file from that one source. This kind of transfer is vulnerable to problems between server and requester: If the server or the Internet connection is busy and slow to respond, the transfer can take a very long time. Another transfer design, called **peer-to-peer (P2P)**, addresses this issue by using a distributed network (individual computers, which may be miles apart, that are connected by a network) that does not require a central server, such as a Web server, to manage files. Instead, specialty software allows an individual's computer to identify other computers in the distributed network and access them directly and independently.

Peer-to-peer services are popular because they allow people to share files of all types directly from the peer connections available via the peer software. Users within the network can make files available to others. Requesters seeking a specific file may find multiple copies within the peer-to-peer network and request a copy from a participating computer with the most efficient connection. Corporations have adopted P2P technology as a quick means of transporting information without having to have all the information stored in a centralized location.

The BitTorrent protocol has recently become very popular for sharing large files, such as software programs or full-length videos and movies. BitTorrent uses a P2P design that makes large numbers of peer connections and requests small pieces of the desired file from each of them. This allows a large amount of data to be transferred to the requesting machine without relying on just one connection to one sender. It also allows requesters to become senders and aid others in their downloads, even before a requester has downloaded the entire large file. As soon as a data piece has been downloaded to the requester's computer, that piece is made available to others who need it.

P2P networks are used both for the legitimate sharing of bulk data, and also for illegally sharing copyrighted copies of movies, books, music, and software. The software companies claim, with limited success, that they cannot be held accountable for users' illegal activities if the software also has a legitimate purpose. Copyright owners argue, also with limited success, that P2P data sharing software and networks exist primarily to share data illegally, and that their creators should be punished.

A few companies such as Napster and LimeWire have been forced to cease operations by copyright owners, but many other services around the world continue to provide both legal and illegal access to data. Along with complex questions regarding accountability, jurisdiction is also a factor because the Internet itself is not governed by one set of rules. A network and software produced and hosted in one country may be immune from the laws of another country. What is legal on the Internet in the United States may be a crime in China, and vice versa.

VOICE OVER INTERNET PROTOCOL VOIP SERVICE

Besides sharing written information, today's Internet users often communicate directly via the spoken word. **Voice over Internet Protocol (VoIP)** is an excellent example of how the Internet can merge with old-style technology (in this case, the telephone) to create a

Figure 5.9 Contemporary Web pages, especially pages of news sites, provide a rich variety of images, colors, and choices.

Fact Check

1. What is the World Wide Web?
   a. A document-linking and -sharing system accessible via the Internet
   b. Another term for the Internet
   c. A system that can only be accessed from a university computer
2. What is the purpose of file transfer protocol (FTP)?
   a. Displaying files that Web browsers do not support
   b. Allowing users a convenient way to transfer files
   c. Protecting users against unwanted spam
3. What does VoIP stand for?
   a. Variably Oscillating Independent Power
   b. Voice over Internet Protocol
   c. Very old Internet Programs

valuable new service. VoIP translates analog voice signals into digital data and uses the Internet to transport the data. VoIP systems can connect to telephone networks as well as to digital sources like PCs. Therefore, a VoIP user on a computer can direct the system to place a call to a telephone on the wall of somebody's home or a cell phone in somebody's pocket. PC-to-PC connections also are possible.[2] Some services, such as MagicJack, go even further and provide a VoIP system that can work with traditional telephones. MagicJack provides a USB adapter that connects a telephone to a computer, so the analog handset can be used to make digital calls.

Besides providing a calling service that allows inexpensive (and in some cases free) communication, VoIP providers like Skype also offer the ability to lease a telephone number in countries around the world. People who call that number think they are calling a local telephone, but the user's Skype program running on his or her computer is what allows them to answer the call. That allows users to answer "local" calls from anywhere in the world they can access the Internet.

The quality of VoIP calls depends on the quality of the network connection. If the Internet connection is consistent and of high quality, then the call is as clear as (if not more clear than) an analog telephone-to-telephone call. If Internet access is inconsistent, the call may be garbled or may disconnect in mid-conversation.

5.3 The Internet at Home

Though the Internet's roots are in the military and academia, a large proportion of the traffic now carried by the Internet serves the home user. From TV programs and movies to online games, the Internet is providing a unique and powerful connection to the world beyond the walls where we live.

BROWSER BASICS

To access the Web, you need a special software program called a Web browser, such as Microsoft's Internet Explorer, Mozilla's Firefox, or Apple Computer's Safari. Internet Explorer is included on every Windows-based PC (and Safari is similarly bundled with Apple computers running the Mac OS X operating system); Firefox is free software that can be downloaded and installed from the Internet. A Web browser is launched by double-clicking its program icon on the desktop (or by selecting it from the Start menu), just as you would launch any other PC program. Once running, it will display its **start page**, a document on the Web that the user has selected as the first one to load upon being launched.

Documents for Web browsers are commonly known as **Web pages**. Web pages are used to distribute news, interactive educational services, product information, catalogs, live audio and video, and other kinds of information. Web pages permit readers to consult databases, check the flight status of an airplane in real

---

[2] Robert Valdes and Dave Roos, How VoIP works, *How Stuff Works.* Retrieved June 10, 2010, from http://communication.howstuffworks.com/ip-telephony.htm

time, shop and pay for products, and much more. Web pages, once mostly text, now typically display a wide array of colors, images, and choices for the user.

What sets Web pages apart from other documents is that they contain a special kind of text called **hypertext**, which is document text that is able to respond to user input and link to other objects. Hypertext is organized in Web pages using a formatting language called **hypertext markup language (HTML)**. HTML contains special text flags and instructions for browsers to interpret. The text flags, called tags, identify links to other documents; display information such as font types and colors; display structures for laying out the page, such as headings and tables; and incorporate many other elements.

As you read a Web page on the browser screen, you can click a word or picture encoded as a **hypertext link** (or simply **hyperlink**) and immediately jump to another location within the same document or to a different Web page. The destination page may be located on the same computer as the original page or anywhere else on the Internet. Because you do not have to learn separate commands and addresses to jump to a new location, the World Wide Web organizes widely scattered resources into a seamless whole.

Hyperlinks on the Web use a specific format called a **uniform resource locator**, or **URL**. (The acronym is pronounced either by spelling its letters out, as in "U-R-L," or, less commonly, by saying it as "Earl.") If you've ever used a browser, you're familiar with the URL's structure, for example:

http://www.apple.com/iphone/features/

A URL is a way to uniquely identify every single object on the Web, as well as the manner in which it should be retrieved. When a browser requests the document specified by the URL above, the Internet service provider looks up the server hosting the Web page, requests the specific page from the server, and delivers the data to the browser for display. Thankfully for the user, all of the lookup and fetching is completely transparent; the typical user only sees that, when a link is clicked in the browser, a new page appears.

Figure 5.10 Search engines are one way to look up information online

Users may access Web pages both by clicking hyperlinks in documents and by typing or pasting a URL into the browser's address field. Figure 5.10 shows these two ways to access Web pages, along with a third way to find information, described next.

The first part of a URL (before the colon) defines the type of data transfer that will take place between the user's browser and the Web server. It typically begins with "http," which stands for **HyperText Transfer Protocol (HTTP)**. HTTP is a detailed standard of electronic communication defining an exact way that data is formatted and transferred back and forth between browser and server. While it is an effective standard, it is not secure, meaning that intruders can in certain circumstances eavesdrop on the data that is passing back and forth between the user and the Web site.

This lack of security makes HTTP very undesirable for transmitting financial and other sensitive data to a Web server. For those transactions, many online retailers use a protocol called **HyperText Transfer Protocol Secure (HTTPS)**. This communication standard adds data encryption and Web site identity verification to the rules for transmitting data. Secure Web sites obtain a digital certificate from a certificate authority such as Microsoft or VeriSign. When you first access a secure site, the browser requests the certificate from the site, and then verifies the certificate with its authority. If the received certificate matches the authority's copy, then the browser continues with the transaction using encrypted data; if not, the browser displays a warning to the user that the certificate does not match, and the site may not be secure.

If you are buying products online, it is common to see the start of the URL shift from "http" to "https" when you begin the purchasing process. The browser may also change the color of the browser's title bar, display a key icon, or provide some other kind of notification that it has begun transmitting data in a secure format.

FINDING WHAT YOU WANT

Without some help, finding what you're looking for on the Web is a daunting prospect. More than 1 trillion unique URLs were found on the Web back in 2008, and the number has no doubt continued to grow since then.[3] Humans simply cannot process that much information, so once again, computers come to our rescue.

Search engines are complex and sophisticated combinations of hardware and software that constantly crawl through the Web's contents, finding new sites and information and verifying the contents of what was previously known. In some cases, search engines can identify new information (for example, news stories from online newspaper sites) within a few minutes of it being published. Even changes to less visible sites (your own personal Web site, perhaps) can be spotted by the major search engines within a handful of days or less.

There are several different major search engines, but two currently vie for first place. Google (at http://www.google.com) has firmly established itself as a leader both in finding new information and in delivering relevant results to users. Bing (at http://www.bing.com), developed by Microsoft to compete with Google, is a worthy alternative for finding what you need on the Web.

Searching is simple, though finding the information you need can require a little persistence. To search for information, enter a word, a name, or even a phrase in the search engine's text field, for example:

- Hewlett-Packard
- Applebee's restaurant
- Funny cat pictures
- How many documents are there on the Web

Figure 5.10 shows the text field of Google's search engine where such a phrase could be entered.

In a matter of a second or two, you'll get a list of results that the search engine has selected as the

Figure 5.11 Search engines can help find any information on the Web, whether you need documents, auto parts or pictures of cute cats.

most relevant match for what you've requested. The results typically are presented as the Web page title, a brief description, and a link that shows where the information is contained. For example, a recent search for "Applebee's restaurant" returned results that included the Applebee's corporate Web site, the Web page for applying for jobs at Applebee's, and a map showing nearby Applebee's restaurant locations. A search for "funny cat pictures" returned several amusing photographs (and links to more), Web sites that collect humorous photos, and videos featuring cats.

Search engines typically display 10 or so results to review. If you don't find what you need, you can move forward to new pages of results, 10 at a time, by clicking on an appropriate link.

If you notice that the results being returned are not even close to what you had hoped to get, you may need to change your search text to be more or less specific, or closer to what you had intended. If you wanted to find the lyrics to a piece you just heard on the radio titled "Love Song," you might discover that just entering the song's title will return a wide variety of things you didn't want. Changing your search phrase to "lyrics to love song by the grey orchids," adding the name of the band and the keyword "lyrics," you are much more likely to get links that are useful.

RADIO AND TELEVISION

First, there was television, and when it was time for our favorite shows, we sat down and watched. Then came the VCR, allowing us to record our favorite shows to tape, so we could play them whenever we

---

[3] *The Official Google Blog* (July 2008), We knew the web was big . . . . Retrieved June 10, 2010, from http://googleblog.blogspot.com/2008/07/we-knew-web-was-big.html

wanted. VCR tapes were nice but unwieldy at times, not of the highest quality, and if the power went out, erasing the recording instructions, we missed the episode on TV.

Next on the scene were digital video recorders (DVRs), which allowed programs to be saved to the unit's hard drive. The DVRs automatically downloaded program schedules, simplifying the process of picking what shows to watch. Even so, a power failure could cause missed recording sessions.

Now, with high-speed Internet access readily available, people are going online to watch their favorite shows. Networks are routinely saving past episodes online, allowing people to log in and download them to watch. Any PC can now show television content, rendering the heavy living room hardware much less necessary than it once was. Shorter clips of news and talk show programs are also commonly available, both directly from the networks and sometimes from private parties.

Radio channels also are available online. Many local radio stations are simultaneously broadcasting their signals over the Internet, so people with a PC instead of a radio can receive their favorite stations' offerings.

Many people, professionals and amateurs alike, are creating their own radio and video broadcasts and saving them as online files for people to download. **Podcasts** are radio broadcasts suitable for downloading to a portable music player. (The term *podcast* combines part of "iPod"—Apple's popular music player—and "broadcast.") Video essays and shows are commonly uploaded to the YouTube video hosting site at http://www.youtube.com.

SOCIAL MEDIA

With the advent of the Web, it didn't take long for home users to figure out that they could create their own Web pages with photos, thoughts, and details about their ongoing lives. But because creating a Web page requires a certain amount of design knowledge, that option excluded a lot of people who may have had something to say but didn't have the desire to learn to use HTML tags. Also, people who did create their own pages and Web sites had a daunting task in gaining an audience; they were just one page in a pile of billions of others.

The interest in sharing the details of our lives and ideas led to the development of **social media software**, which are programs and utilities that make it simple for people to share common interests and information. As you learned earlier in this chapter, the current state of the Web—Web 2.0—is based on the concept of encouraging user communities to build and share their own information collections. **Social networking** Web sites, which are designed to connect people directly together, provide their users with a standard structure for Web page organization, so it is easy for anyone to create a personal information layout, or **profile**. People can add pictures, music clips, poems and essays, links to Web pages of interest, and details of events in their lives. They can also easily search for and link up with friends, coworkers, and family who also participate in the site. New users are typically allowed to join major social network sites for free, to encourage participation.

Facebook (at http://www.facebook.com) is one of the most popular of these sites, with more than 500 million profiles in its system. Many users frequently update a *status* field, sending out messages to their network of friends and family multiple times a day with news and happenings. LinkedIn has fewer participants (but still quite a few at around 100 million) and is established as a business networking site for people to connect with colleagues, write recommendations for coworkers, collaborate to share expertise, and search for new professional opportunities. Using these sites makes it so easy to share information about ourselves that sometimes social networking raises etiquette and ethics challenges. For an example, see the Ethical Dilemma box.

In contrast to most other social network services, which provide a

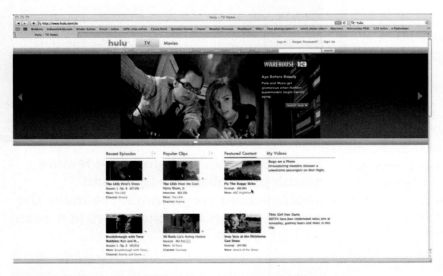

Figure 5.12   Online services such as Hulu offer access to full-length episodes of favorite television shows.

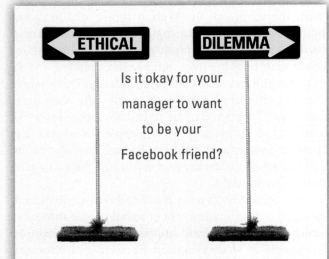

Twitter enjoys a wide following, from celebrities and sports figures to private citizens. Businesses of all sizes also use Twitter as a way to instantly alert their customers to new offerings and information. Some social media sites, such as YouTube, emphasize the site content over the social networking aspect. Users upload video clips for others to see, and the site encourages visitors to leave comments and feedback for the posters. The site provides a way for users to create profiles and chat with other users, but many site users visit YouTube simply to watch the video clips without forming relationships with the contributors.

GAMES

Games have been a part of the world of computing since even before the first personal computer was invented. The first graphical computer game was a tic-tac-toe game made back in 1952.[4] Since that time, games have continuously evolved in complexity and visual appeal. Thousands of games are available to the modern PC and game console user, covering a range of subjects from simple solitaire games to visually stunning world exploration games that feel more like an interactive movie than a video game.

The Internet has provided a new twist to game technology by enabling people to play with or against each other. Web sites exist to pair up people who want to play traditional board games like Scrabble or chess in an online setting. Many people play poker and other

Figure 5.13 Video games can feature startlingly realistic imagery and sophisticated programming to make the game world and the characters in it seem almost lifelike.

[4] Mary Bellis, Computer and video game history, *About.com*. Retrieved June 11, 2010, from http://inventors.about.com/library/inventors/blcomputer_videogames.htm

wide array of forms of expression, Twitter (http://twitter.com) is a social networking tool that specializes only in the sharing of micro-status messages. The Twitter service allows people to transmit messages, called *tweets*, up to 140 characters in length. The messages they send go only to the list of people who have signed up to receive them (known as *following* in Twitter), and each user receives messages as they are posted from all of the various people that he or she follows. Though Twitter maintains a central Web site, tweets are generally sent and received by simple programs that run on PCs and mobile devices.

Computer gaming is a favorite pastime for a big slice of the world's population. Whether they prefer playing on a home computer or using console hardware designed specifically for games, millions of people spend at least part of their leisure time playing some kind of computer game.

Joining a game software studio team is high on the list of career dreams for a number of gamers. "I could totally write games like this," is a common refrain in homes around the world. But as Jon Shafer of Firaxis Games can tell you, there's a lot more to working at a game company than playing.

"People think it's all fun playing games all day," says Shafer. "A lot of it is really hard work and long hours, with very little vacation." Game production is a serious business; a major game title can require dozens of people and require many millions of dollars in funding. Game studios must heavily market their titles in order to generate interest, and that can lead to intense pressure to complete high-quality programs as deadlines near.

As lead designer for Firaxis's Civilization V game, Shafer—the company's youngest lead designer to date—has to draw on a varied background pairing knowledge of world history and games. He picked up an early interest in history from his mother, a schoolteacher. He fell in love with many of the early computer games related to history, including the original Civilization game. He participated in beta tests for new games, and his gaming experience combined with persistence finally got him noticed at Firaxis. "I kept pestering them until they finally acquiesced. They said they didn't have any full-time positions, but they could make a programming internship for me."

Shafer's strategy to combine wide interests, gaming experience, and dedication is echoed by others in the game development industry. Lars Gustavsson of Sweden's game maker EA DICE advises, "Get educated, start up your own project/portfolio to show that you can perform, and keep going after jobs. Don't give up."

Games today are often rich and complex multimedia programs, combining sound, visual effects, and compelling writing along with programming for strategy, physics, and artificially intelligent companions or opponents. This provides a unique opportunity for a beginning designer to be involved both in the larger development of the system and also participate in some way in many detailed functions.

Salaries for game designers in 2009 averaged just over $69,000; salaries for gaming programmers had a higher average, at $80,320 that same year.

Sources: Dennis Nishi (June 29, 2010), Intern to Civilization leader, *The Wall Street Journal*, retrieved July 30, 2010, from http://online.wsj.com/article/SB10001424052748703964104575334890003927342.html?mod=WSJ_hps_sections_tech; John Keefer (May 13, 2009), How to develop a gaming career, *Crispy Gamer*, retrieved July 30, 2010, from http://www.crispygamer.com/blogs/post/2009/05/13/How-to-Develop-a-Gaming-Career.aspx; and Julian Murdoch and Jason Wilson (April 30, 2010), Civilization 5, *GamePro*, retrieved July 30, 2010, from http://www.gamepro.com/article/features/215018/civilization-5/.

Fact Check

1. How does a Web browser find a Web page?
   a. By using the information in a URL
   b. By connecting with Skype
   c. By creating hyperlinks
2. Google and Bing are examples of
   a. router firewalls
   b. search engines
   c. social networking Web sites
3. Twitter is a social networking application that sends and receives tweets, which are
   a. one-word concepts
   b. messages up to 140 characters in length
   c. sounds that play primarily on smart phones

card games online at virtual tables. On game consoles, people can join with others to play music and dance simulation games together. PCs and consoles alike provide many games where people can adopt a soldier's persona and play together to defeat computer enemies or fight against each other in Internet-supported arenas.

Perhaps the most substantial use of the Internet for gaming is known by its abbreviation MMORPG, which stands for *massively multiplayer online role play game*. Creators of these games provide vast worlds to explore and conquer, allowing many thousands of people to play the same game at the same time, interacting with each other or following their own path as they choose. The largest of these is Blizzard Corporation's World of Warcraft, with millions of subscribers around the world playing as mythical creatures in a fantasy setting. Along with the game play itself, MMORPGs provide many different ways for people to interact, chat, and develop friendships and rivalries, regardless of where in the world they live.

5.4 The Internet at School

From grade school to universities and beyond, the Web and the Internet can help students succeed in their pursuits.

THE INTERNET AS EDUCATION HELPER

Many children now have their first experience with computers during their first year of school, if not sooner at home. Many **edutainment** programs— programs that attempt to be both educational and entertaining—have been written over the last couple of decades. They target different age groups in school by varying the degree of difficulty and sophistication in the lessons and by including skill tests and learning exercises appropriate for each age. For example, the *Reader Rabbit* software series, first published in 1993 by The Learning Company, is a familiar sight in elementary schools and students' homes, using puzzles, animated characters, voices, and opportunities for self-expression to encourage children to read and write.

Kids often begin to take their learning online in elementary school as well. At more and more schools, computers in labs or right in the classrooms are connected to the Internet. Schools provide filtered, limited access to the Web to ensure that students are surfing to relevant and safe information sites.

Some school districts provide standardized testing for their students via Web-based test programs.[5] By the end grades of elementary school, many children are being encouraged to seek help with homework in online forums and at Web sites that connect students with tutors. Teachers sometimes use news sites (like Google News or MSN.com) to add depth to discussions of current events. As students begin learning to write research reports, they are often taught to combine library sources and online resources for completing their research.

Tutor services have become a hot item on the Web in recent years. Many Web sites provide access to a stable of tutors across a wide variety of subjects. Students can ask for help for free, or they can offer to pay a commission for the service, ranging anywhere from a dollar or two up to two hundred or more. The free questions are posted to a general forum, and the commission questions are offered directly to tutors. As tutors answer questions and receive positive feedback, they gain a higher reputation and greater visibility, thereby improving their chances to work for commissioned questions. Answers, especially for more advanced subjects, are often detailed and complete.

ONLINE RESEARCH: HOW DO YOU KNOW WHAT IS RIGHT?

Online research is an everyday thing, whether you're a student in school or you are looking for tips on safely cooking up a batch of beef jerky. Every researcher, no matter how scholarly or casual, has the same dilemma: How do you know your information is accurate? There are helpful and useful Web sites around the world, but there are also many sites that either are designed to be maliciously wrong or are simply put together carelessly.

People looking for information often rely on Web sites that are generally considered to be trustworthy, but not everyone agrees about what meets the standard of trustworthiness. For example, some people swear by the online encyclopedia Wikipedia (http://en.wikipedia.org) as an information source, while many others decry it as unreliable. Both sides have a lot of statistics and stories to back up their points of view. Rather than ignoring a disputed source outright, you might consider using it as a starting point.

Figure 5.14 Children begin using computers at a very young age to have fun and to enhance their education.

[5] Juan Antonio Lizama (April 13, 2009), Schools turn to online testing for Standards of Learning, *Richmond (Va.) Times-Dispatch*. Retrieved June 12, 2010, from http://www2.timesdispatch.com/rtd/news/local/education/article/SOLS13_20090412-221912/254987/

Figure 5.15 Library books may be out of date, and online information may not be reviewed; always verify source material, whether online or in print.

Wikipedia articles almost always list information sources at the end; following the citations to the source material may help you verify what you've read. Try to include sources whose writers and publishers are expected to meet professional standards:

- Professional journalists are expected to meet standards for information gathering and fact checking, so look for general-interest and industry- or interest-specific newspapers and magazines.

- Most academic journals require that articles be reviewed by the researchers' peers. Ask your school's library or an instructor for guidance about which journals in a particular field are highly respected. (Articles in most academic journals are available online either directly or through database services.)

- The major encyclopedias and dictionaries obtain their information from subject-matter experts. Again, a librarian can guide you to the best references in your field of interest, and many of these publish online editions.

- Government agencies hire experts in statistics and other fields to gather accurate data. The Census Bureau and NASA are just two agencies offering a wealth of reliable information online.

The reliability and professionalism of information sources is important, but don't mistake dependability for accuracy. Even the best research sources can make a mistake. Your best bet is to check with multiple high-quality sources and compare the information they have.

ONLINE CLASSES AND UNIVERSITIES

High-speed Internet access has prompted a wave of new technologies and services based on the ability to effectively deliver multimedia content around the world. Schools at all levels are taking advantage of classes delivered online.

Some classes are designed to supplement classroom education. School districts that cannot afford to hire language instructors can subscribe to online classes that deliver a full series of lessons. The language lessons can be integrated into the rest of the classroom instruction. The students gain the opportunity to learn the language without a special teacher for each school and without requiring that the main classroom teacher be fluent in the language.

Individual classes in many different subjects are available to students who cannot conveniently attend a school and want to learn more about a certain subject. High schools, community colleges, and universities all offer classes to allow students to take a course in creative writing, sample a course in a new area of study, or finish that last math or English course in order to earn their degree.

Some universities offer accredited online degree programs in a limited set of subjects. Both bachelor's and master's degree programs may be available. Students view online lectures and submit coursework via e-mail or FTP sites for review and grading. Instructors may be available to answer questions via e-mail or chat systems. Some universities are traditional brick-and-mortar institutions (meaning they have physical buildings as opposed to just an online presence) that offer online courses, while

Fact Check

1. To ensure that online research material is accurate, it is a good idea to
   a. check with multiple trustworthy sources
   b. call the author of the article or Web site
   c. make sure the article was written in the past 12 months
2. List three reasons that someone might take an individual online class.

Figure 5.16   This woman is learning sign language through an online course.

several others offer their services exclusively over the Internet. Universities are also experimenting with blending classroom and online components, and studies show that this can be a highly effective form of teaching.

For students who simply want to learn and do not require course credit or a recognized degree, the Massachusetts Institute of Technology offers a facility called MIT OpenCourseWare. OpenCourseWare provides large portions of both graduate and undergraduate lectures in documents and videos via their Web site at no cost to the user. The use of OpenCourseWare does not result in a degree from MIT, but it nevertheless provides access to a large amount of educational materials to anyone with a Web browser.

Online degrees have had something of a dubious reputation, with not every online university meeting college accreditation standards. Studies have recently shown an increase in employer satisfaction with employees who received online degrees, but despite this trend, many employers still prefer candidates with degrees from universities with an established reputation and a long history.[6]

---

[6] Lianting Tu (September 4, 2009), Online schooling picks up students—and respect, CNBC. Retrieved June 13, 2010, from http://www.cnbc.com/id/32663024

- The Internet was created for the U.S. Department of Defense as a tool for communications. Today's Internet is a global network of interconnected networks, created to serve both public and private communication needs.

IN Summary

- The Internet provides a wide array of different services to its users. Some of the major ones likely to be seen by a household or business user include the World Wide Web (WWW), electronic mail (e-mail), file transfer protocol (FTP), Voice over Internet Protocol (VoIP), chat and instant messaging (IM), and peer-to-peer (P2P) data transfer services.

- Browsers are programs used to view pages and navigate from site to site on the World Wide Web. Browsers request documents from Web servers and display the contents for the user. Hyperlinks embedded in the documents allow the user to quickly navigate from site to site, and document to document, without requiring knowledge of the exact Web location of each document or site.

- Web pages and information on the Web can be found via search engines, which are specialized catalog services provided to users via search engine Web sites. Users can enter keywords or phrases, and the search engine delivers a list of results containing those terms.

- Social networking is the process of using social media, types of Internet software that promote connections and exchanges among people, to stay in touch with others. Facebook and LinkedIn are examples of social networking Web sites. Twitter is an example of a simple broadcast application for keeping in touch with others throughout the day. YouTube is a site that encourages users to upload and share video clips, creating a massive online video library for all visitors.

- The Internet provides students access to research and information sites. States and school districts sometimes provide standardized tests on the Web. The Internet allows students in remote areas to view video lectures and submit coursework for review. Some universities provide free courseware for students who want to learn without participating in a degree program.

Key Terms

ARPANET, 180
backbones, 181
buddy list, 186
chat, 184
edutainment, 194
electronic mail, 184
e-mail, 184
file transfer protocol (FTP), 186
hyperlink, 189
hypertext, 189
hypertext link, 189
hypertext markup language (HTML), 189

HyperText Transfer Protocol (HTTP), 189
HyperText Transfer Protocol Secure (HTTPS), 189
instant messaging (IM), 186
Internet, 180
Internet Relay Chat (IRC), 184
internetworking, 181
NSFnet, 181
peer-to-peer (P2P), 187
podcasts, 191
profile, 191

search engines, 190
social media software, 191
social network, 191
start page, 188
uniform resource locator (URL), 189
Voice over Internet Protocol (VoIP), 187
Web 1.0, 183
Web 2.0, 183
Web 3.0, 183
Web pages, 188
World Wide Web, 182

Key Terms QUIZ

Complete each statement by writing one of the terms listed under "Key Terms" in each blank.

1. The _____ is the name of the massive global network of networks.

2. Browsers are programs used to retrieve information on the _____.

3. The first ancestor network of the Internet was called _____.

4. _____ is a system of sending electronic letters and messages from one person to one or more recipients.

5. A Web file designed to be displayed by a browser is called a _____.

6. The special kind of text in a Web page is called _____.

7. A(n) _____ is a program or Web site designed to help people connect with each other.

8. People can chat via a real-time message system called _____.

9. The tags used to direct browsers in displaying Web pages are in a language called _____.

10. Files and documents intended for download rather than browser viewing are often transferred via _____.

Review QUESTIONS

In your own words, briefly answer the following questions.

1. What were the original uses for which the Internet was created?

2. List six types of services you can access via the Internet. Which of them have you tried?

3. Summarize the similarities and differences of an e-mail message and an instant message.

4. Give an overview of how the BitTorrent protocol functions.

5. How does a computer user navigate to different Web sites with a Web browser?

6. Describe what a hyperlink does.

7. Explain what HTML stands for and what it does.

8. Suppose you want to use the Web to find the location of restaurants in your town. How could you search for that information? How could you narrow your search if you wanted great ice cream? How could you narrow your search if you wanted only restaurants near your campus?

9. What are three Web sites or programs you can use for social networking? Compare the features of these sites.

10. What is an MMORPG? How does it differ from other kinds of games played on or with computers?

Complete the following exercises as directed by your instructor.

1. Practice using your browser. Launch your browser, and practice navigating the Web. Try using URLs based on the names of people or companies you want to learn more about. For example, if you type **http://www.cheerios.com** in your Address box, what happens? Make up five different URLs from company, product, or individual names, and see where they lead your browser. As you visit different sites, look for hyperlinked text and graphics; click them, and see where they lead.

2. Pick a topic and search the Web for information about it. Pick a keyword to use in your search, and then visit three search engines, and use each of them to conduct a search using your chosen keyword. Use Yahoo! (http://www.yahoo.com), Bing (http://www.bing.com), and Google (http://www.google.com) for your searches. What similarities and differences did you see in the first page of results from each search engine?

Team **EXERCISE** Communication

There are many ways to communicate on the job—speeches and closed-door meetings, lengthy reports and hastily scribbled notes. To this mix, the Internet has added e-mail, blogs, text messages, and much more. Of course, not every communication channel is right for every situation. Some situations call for the instant feedback and emotional cues of a face-to-face encounter. At other times, the determining factor is efficiency, privacy, or the creation of a permanent record. Savvy businesspeople know not just *what* to say, but also *how* to say it.

To prepare for this exercise, read the following list of work situations, and identify the communication channel you think would get the best results. (Some possibilities are face-to-face meeting, personal blog, Facebook wall, e-mail, text message, written report, telephone call, and a note slipped under the boss's office door.)

1. Quarterly sales figures

2. Your reaction to being denied a promotion

3. Two new ideas you have for the latest software release your company is developing

4. Suggestion that people not leave dirty dishes lying around the company's lunchroom

5. A conversation you overheard between two employees about their latest successful theft of memory cards from office computers

Divide into groups of four to six students. Between class sessions or for a predetermined time (say, 15 minutes) during class, record your votes for which communication mode to use in each situation. Then discuss your reasoning and try to reach a consensus on a best answer for each situation. Vote changing is allowed! As a class, tally the final votes to determine whether the groups found similar best answers for each situation.

LESSON 5B:
The Mobile User

A quiet movie theater, a dramatic moment . . . and in the middle of the crowd, a cell phone suddenly, shrilly comes to life. The disapproval of the audience deepens as seconds later the phone's owner actually answers it and begins to talk.

If you haven't experienced this, you've likely heard a tale from a friend about this kind of event. Mobile computing and being available 24/7 creates a certain amount of social risk. While smart phones and notebook computers themselves are fairly unlikely to cause you any physical harm—unless you drop a laptop on your foot, perhaps—mobile devices can definitely contribute in a major way to damaging yourself, your job, your relationships, and the privacy of your personal information.

Using your cell phone while driving can place you in significant danger. Wandering away from your home office computer to make a sandwich in the middle of a boring videoconference with your vice president can be toxic to your career. Texting your friends during a romantic dinner is a good way to hurt feelings and start a fight. Loudly reading off your credit card number into your phone in a crowded area invites you to become a victim of fraud.

The missing element in all these scenarios is a sense of awareness, being able to see ourselves from the outside and determine whether our behavior is appropriate for our surroundings. We can do all kinds of things with our mobile devices without really being aware of the personal risk and without really thinking about how our actions affect others. The cell phone talkers in movie theaters probably aren't malicious; it simply doesn't occur to them just how much their mid-movie conversations ruin our experience.

Awareness is a key factor in being an effective mobile user. You need to be aware of where you are, what you are doing, and who is around you, just like for any other activity. If you are alert, you are more likely to stay safe, see opportunities, and be a savvy mobile user without annoying or endangering the other people around you.

5.5 Mobile Software

Before discussing mobile business and social computing topics, let's first look at the final component needed to make the mobile experience complete. Along with mobile devices, networks, and network connections, software completes the list of gear commonly required for mobile computing. (You might want a carrying case for your laptop and a custom-colored faceplate for your cell phone, but those are not necessities.) Much of the software related to mobile computing is for smart phones and PDAs, and that software can be grouped into three basic categories: software to support or enhance the mobile device's operating environment, software to assist in mobile computing tasks, and software for general use.

SOFTWARE FOR NOTEBOOKS, TABLETS, AND NETBOOKS

Software for mobile devices by and large excludes notebooks, tablets, and netbooks. Since they are full-featured PCs running a full operating system (or, in the case of netbooks, nearly full-featured), software for those machines

Figure 5.17 Effective mobile computing requires a good device, the right software, and a healthy supply of courtesy.

is limited only by what the hardware and operating system are capable of running. Even so, a couple of operating-system-related items are worth mentioning.

As already discussed, you should set a power plan for your system when it is on and off battery power. Practice the habit of checking your power type, battery level, and power plan every time you begin to use your computer in a mobile setting. You wouldn't be the first person to dutifully plug your notebook into the wall at the airport, only to lose power (and your work) because the wall outlet wasn't actually producing electricity and you hadn't verified that the battery was charging.

Checking your settings will vary by operating system. In Windows 7, you can simply look at the battery icon in the lower right corner of your desktop and then use the mouse to hover over that icon. You will see the power remaining, a plug if the notebook is on wall power, and charging animation if the battery is recharging. You may also get a pop-up window that shows the current power plan and power plan choices. You can also check the quality of your wireless network connection in Windows by hovering over the wireless icon in the same lower-right desktop area as the battery symbol. You will see the name of the network you are using, a quality rating, your connection speed, and its basic status.

Occasionally, you may temporarily lose your connection to either the local network or the Internet. If that happens, the computer will try to reconnect and normally will succeed so long as the network is still available. However, if your computer persists in an offline state while others can access the network, you may be able to reset your connection by specifically telling the computer to disconnect and then reconnect. In Windows 7, you can click on the wireless icon to bring up a list of connections, click on the network you are currently using, select "Disconnect," and once that operation is complete, reconnect by selecting "Connect."

SOFTWARE TO SUPPORT MOBILE DEVICES

Some of the most popular types of software (or simply data, in many cases) for smart phones are designed to customize or enhance the use of the device itself. For example, you can use software to choose the way your phone signals you that you have received a text message or the picture displayed when you open it up to use it.

Cell and smart phones have a number of conditions where they are directed to play a sound (for

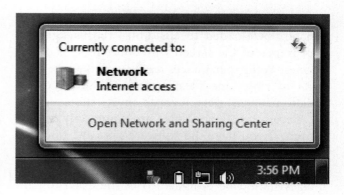

Figure 5.18 Hovering your mouse over the wireless connection icon on your taskbar will give you a quick status of the condition of your connection.

example, when it rings for an incoming call or text message), and those sounds, called ring tones, can be chosen by the user. Most phones come with an assortment of **ring tones**. Not long after smart phones hit the market, downloadable ring tone files became widely available. Ring tone files play sound effects, snippets of speeches, songs, sayings by TV characters, and just about anything else that has been recorded. You can obtain ring tones from a variety of sources:

- Cell phone service providers often have a wide selection of extra ring tones you can browse through online. You can select your favorite and pay a small fee to have it sent directly to your phone.

- If you're handy with sound editing and can make short music files, there is a good chance that you can load your custom-created sound files into your cell phone via a data wire or Bluetooth. The exact method for loading the files depends on the phone's manufacturer.

- Many Web sites advertise free ring tones or free customization services. While not all of these sites are hosts for malware or hackers, keep in mind an important rule of thumb: *there is no such thing as a free lunch.* It may be tempting to save a few bucks by downloading a cool new ring tone from a free Web site, but one way or another, the chances are very good that you will ultimately pay for that ring tone via a malware invasion or some manner of invasion of your privacy. Even if the site is not hosting malware, you may be asked to provide your name, cell phone number, e-mail address, or other information that can be sold to spammers.

Along with ring tones, files called **wallpaper** can be downloaded to customize the background appearance of the screen with some models of cell phones. Wallpaper images are as varied as the contents of ring tone files; options include scenery, artistic patterns, pets, favorite sports shots, and so on. Because wallpaper files are commonly in JPG format, if you have the software on a PC to create JPG files, you can move those files to your cell phone to create your own custom wallpaper. Wallpaper images should be designed to fit the exact dimensions of your cell phone screen, so if you are purchasing wallpaper files or making your own, be sure that the size of the file matches what the phone is expecting. And, of course, the same cautions apply to free wallpaper files from the Web as with free ring tone files: they probably aren't truly free, so it's best to avoid them.

SOFTWARE TO ASSIST WITH MOBILE COMPUTING

Another category of software, while useful to the user, concentrates more on the function of the mobile device than on services and information for the user. Mobile utility software, like most computer software, serves many different needs and purposes. Some device manufacturers may provide basic programs for some of these categories, but there are many additional programs available even for the types provided with the device. Here is a very basic list:

- **Anti-malware programs.** Privacy attacks against smart phones are increasing in frequency and sophistication, so you need anti-malware software for your smart phone, just as you do for your PC.

- **File browsers.** This type of software provides improved ways to view, add, and delete files on your phone and transfer them to and from other devices.

- **Mobile phone number information.** These programs attempt to identify and display the source of any unknown number that has called you (numbers in your own phone list are identified by the phone when they call).

- **Synchronizing programs.** This software transfers information between the same or compatible programs on different devices, making sure calendars, appointment books, and other frequently changing sets of data are the same on both devices.

- **Wi-Fi scanning software.** For Wi-Fi-enabled devices, this software makes it easy to find and connect to open Wi-Fi networks.

One type of application combines the hardware and software of a smart phone. A **QR code** is a two-dimensional bar code, created by the Denso Wave Corporation that encodes Web addresses and other information. Companies are increasingly using these QR codes as a way to provide users with quick access (QR stands for Quick Response) to Web sites and Web pages.

Smart phone owners can use the digital camera in their phone to take pictures of QR codes found in magazines and on billboards, or they can use the browsers in their phones to show QR codes that appear on Web pages. With the picture of a QR code visible, the smart phone user activates a scanner app on the phone, which reads the QR code and translates it into a Web address that you can access on the phone.

QR codes are easy for everyone to create. The QRStuff Web site at http://www.qrstuff.com/ provides a simple and free interface that converts text, URLs, e-mail addresses and many other types of data into QR codes. Users can make their own QR codes for printing and e-mailing, and can even have them transferred to t-shirts, coffee mugs, and other marketing products. Because they are so easily transferred to and decoded by smart phones, QR codes can be a more effective way to generate interest in a Web site or company than with a text-based representation.

QR codes are being used by companies to market their goods or enhance the shopping experience for customers. Some supermarkets, for instance, use QR codes on shopping baskets that lead customers to a Web page listing specials and coupons. They can also place them to provide information; for example, a store might place a QR code near the fruit department that links to a Web video describing how to choose a ripe melon.

Figure 5.19 QR codes can be captured and translated on a smart phone.

Figure 5.20 Mobile software can transform your smart phone into a compass or GPS device.

SOFTWARE FOR GENERAL USE

The available software for smart phones and PDAs is seemingly endless. Apple's App Store, which hosts programs for the iPhone, iPod, and iPad products, reported more than 225,000 titles in its catalog as of mid-2010.[7]

The exact programs vary depending on the brand of device; because many different operating systems are used on mobile devices, software must be written specifically for each operating system. Some developers write software for more than one operating system, but if you change from using one device to another, you may find that the software you are familiar with is not available with your new phone. Fortunately, with so many applications being developed across all platforms, there is still a good chance you will be able to find a program that provides comparable functions.

Some of the available software will make your online experience better, providing applications that help you browse the Web, read the latest news, and send e-mail. There is also a hefty list of titles available to provide access to online social services. For example, most phones provide Facebook and Twitter access, and you can also add any of several custom

[7] AppleInsider staff (June 7, 2010), Apple says App Store has made developers over $1 billion, *AppleInsider*. Retrieved June 30, 2010, from http://www.appleinsider.com/articles/10/06/07/apple_says_app_store_has_made_developers_over_1_billion.html

chat and dating-site programs. It's worth being careful in this category; consider checking the advertised sites independently (for example, use search engines on the Web to see who is using the program, and what they think of it) to make sure they are legitimate forum providers, not malware servers.

Other applications support particular interests. You can buy apps related to hobbies, music, and travel, as well as programs that send you up-to-the-minute sports scores for your favorite teams. One fast-growing category of mobile app is games, with a large assortment of ways to have fun with humorous, challenging, or relaxing themes.

Business and productivity software is common as well. Much of this software treats the pocket mobile device as a helper rather than a replacement for the full computer. Applications let people record business card and contact information, maintain a calendar or appointment book, and even let their smart phone control the pace of a slide presentation being run from a personal computer.

This overview is just that; there is no practical way to list all the categories or types of mobile software here. If you have a smart phone, your best bet is to start exploring and see what you find that interests you.

CHOOSING SOFTWARE TO DOWNLOAD

Choosing software for your smart phone or PDA can be a daunting and frustrating task, primarily because there are so many sources for software, a vast and constantly growing array of titles to choose from, and no coherent source of information for many of the titles. If you use Google or Bing to search for "mobile software" or "mobile apps," you'll retrieve dozens of Web site listings, few of which have recognizable names. Even if you are feeling cautious and rule out all the sites with names like *www.superfreemobile.com* or *www.amazingfreeapps.com*, you still have a seemingly endless supply to choose from.

Most Web sites providing software for download organize them by keyword or category, so you can search for games or social media helpers that way. Within those categories, however, the search can again become tedious and inconclusive because there are so many to choose from, and so many whose only description is terse and nearly unreadable, along the lines of "Your best awesome browser."

Ways to narrow the search results present their own problems: If you search by "top rated" applications, the list is likely to include five-star ratings based on the responses from only one or two people (that even could have been provided by the developer). The "most popular" (meaning the most frequently downloaded) applications could include programs that have just been around a long time, persisting in spite of errors or even malware.

Four suggestions may improve your chances at finding useful software for your mobile device:

1. Start with the application stores provided by the manufacturer of the phone or operating system. If you have an Apple iPhone or iPad, you can visit http://www.apple.com/iphone/apps-for-iphone/ and http://www.apple.com/ipad/from-the-app-store/. If you have an Android device, you can find apps at https://market.android.com/. If you have a RIM BlackBerry, you can visit http://appworld.blackberry.com/webstore/.

2. If you bought your mobile device from a store with knowledgeable salespeople, check with them. Ask where they go for their apps. The store or mobile company may have a corporate site that provides trusted software, or it may have specific sites that it recommends.

3. Think of your most sensible and computer-savvy friend with a similar mobile device, and ask that person where he or she goes to download applications. Talk to your friend about his or her experiences to verify that your friend is aware of the free-lunch and malware problems.

4. Visit a trusted download site for PC programs such as TUCOWS (http://www.tucows.com/), and see if it links to a mobile application partner or has a mobile section of its own. The Web site should have information about the programs indicating that the site owner is actually paying attention to what is being added for download. Recommendations of titles by specific people—not anonymous commenters—provide added confidence that the software is useful and malware-free. For example, Butterscotch's mobile page (http://mobile.butterscotch.com), which is linked by the main TUCOWS site as its source for mobile apps, has a staff of contributors that describe and recommend various applications for a variety of mobile platforms.

5.6 Effective Mobile Business

The traditional model for business involves a central office or industrial site. Employers create the work space, and managers organize and direct the work that goes on there. Employees dress for work, come to the central location, perform their job functions, and go back home until their next workday. This model is consistent across many types of businesses, from factories to restaurants to architectural firms.

When computers first arrived in the business world, they were simply added as components of the company. They were installed in the central location as tools to increase productivity in some manner. But with the advent of mobile computing tools, and the flexibility these brought to communication, the central business office model was challenged to change. Deskbound employees looked at the nature of their work and realized they could transport their desk to another location, and their work routines wouldn't change much because of their network and cell phone connections. Employers began to consider the possibility of hiring new employees in other parts of the country without the expense of relocating them to a central place.

The ability to create **virtual teams**—teams whose members are geographically dispersed and use technology to communicate and collaborate in real

Figure 5.21 An effective employee in a home-based office can be a valuable asset no matter where the company is located.

time—had never before been possible, and businesses and employees had to invent the rules for the new game as they went. Today, those rules are still in flux. Different industries and individuals have different requirements, and employees have different capabilities. Many mobile business experiments have failed, and others have been a rousing success. Many more have found results that were in between those extremes. But just as with mobile computing technology itself, mobile business is here to stay, and the chances are good that service and professional companies will increasingly look to mobile solutions to improve productivity, reduce costs, and contribute to employee well-being.

MOBILE CONSIDERATIONS FOR BUSINESSES

Not all occupations are suitable for mobile work. Factory employees who use heavy machinery can't really do that work anyplace else but at the factory. Restaurant workers cannot be mobile chefs and waiters and still serve at the central location. In contrast, some workers, such as salespeople who travel extensively, were already mobile employees before the advent of computers, and mobile technology has simply made them more effective.

Figure 5.22 Jobs that require over-the-shoulder management—or managers that require it—may not be a good match for mobile employees.

Businesses in the middle—those with employees who could potentially work remotely but currently are central office workers—may find themselves evaluating the possibility of supporting mobile employees.

Though you may not be a business owner, you may find yourself in that position in the future, or you may become a manager with the responsibility for making decisions about **telecommuting**—the practice of having employees work remotely. You may also choose the dual role that comes with being a freelancer or independent contractor: in business for yourself, shouldering all the responsibilities while enjoying the freedom of being your own employee.

For those reasons, it is worth thinking about some of the considerations that businesses have when deciding to set up and manage remote employees and work groups. It is also good to be aware of a company's perspective as an employee, if only to better understand the corporate perspective on mobile employees.

Business owners and managers may first balk at the idea of mobile office workers. On the surface, there appears to be a lack of accountability when employees are not sitting at a desk in the office. Traditionally, employees are only absent when sick or on vacation, so it is not much of a stretch to understand why an empty desk for an employee on the clock can make a manager nervous. To make a reasonable decision about the introduction of mobile working, a few factors deserve a pragmatic, honest look:

- **Management style.** For mobile computing to succeed at work, managers must be able to walk a fine line between constant control and

> "Managers should have a way (other than by listening for the sound of typing fingers) to measure performance."

benign neglect. If a supervisor must oversee hour-by-hour activity by physically watching or spot-checking employees, this management style may clash with the trust and empowerment typically required for mobile computing. Nevertheless, managers need to find ways to keep abreast of the progress and accomplishments of their mobile workers, to make sure that any problems are being addressed and that all employees are focused on their work goals.

- **Performance measurement.** Managers should have a way (other than by listening for the sound of typing fingers) to measure performance. Short- and long-term goals, regular delivery dates, and some kind of consistent visibility of the offsite workers to management and other team members are all important. Workplaces that already cultivate collaboration and goal-oriented schedules will probably have an easier time with remote employees.

- **Costs.** Offsite employees may need hardware and software to set up their mobile environment, and they may need to subscribe to new or faster Internet services. Companies may need to provide the funds to set up and support the remote employee. On the upside, there may also be savings associated with telecommuting. Some companies that have embraced telecommuting are able to operate much smaller facilities, so they save on rent and utilities. If most of an organization's workforce is mobile, it may set up a **virtual office**, a work arrangement in which the company sets up minimal office services—such as several cubicles, a conference room, and a receptionist—so employees can visit the space as needed for meetings with managers and colleagues. Employees are not assigned to a particular workspace but use available space as needed. Other companies reduce travel expenses by working with mobile employees who live close to key customers.

- **Information risk.** Companies may need to consider whether there is a risk to the company's **intellectual property**—that is, the ideas, trade secrets, patents, and confidential operating practices of the company—by having employees work outside a central office. If you allow employees to lug software instruction listings, contracts, proposals, hardware prototypes, and other sensitive information back and forth between home and office, the risk of loss becomes higher. Organizations should incorporate security concerns into their plans for telecommuting (for example, setting up an FTP site so documents can be stored at the company and accessed from home with no carrying required).

SPECIFIC TIPS FOR BUSINESSES

Whether a company wants to use mobile workers so it will be closer to customers, will be able to attract employees who demand flexibility, or be in a position to cut office expenses, it can create processes that improve the odds of success. Actions a business can take to manage effective mobile employees will vary greatly from company to company, but the following basic ideas apply to many situations:

- **Manage by goal, not by typing time.** Telling an employee, "Deliver the PowerPoint slides by Thursday at noon," provides a clear goal and a simple, no-nonsense way to measure productivity. Either the slides are in your e-mail inbox by lunchtime on Thursday, or they aren't. What the employee was doing on Wednesday at 3 p.m. is irrelevant, as long as you get those slides.

- **Make at least some of the work goals very short term.** Make sure that some of an employee's tasks can be completed daily, or at least every few days. Managers can request a brief status report. This regular reporting not only helps uncover problems while there is still time to resolve them, but it also keeps the mobile worker visible, so the worker gets credit for accomplishments and builds stronger working relationships.

- **Establish when and how workers should be available to their supervisor, colleagues, and customers.** If mobile employees need to be available and at their screens during specific hours, those requirements should be clear. An instant message system such as AOL's AIM is useful for creating a method for communicating. AIM, like other instant messaging software, can be set to post an "away from keyboard" flag when the computer is left idle for a few minutes.

- **Supervisors should have guidelines for when not to contact employees.** In some lines of work, employees need to be on-call; in other cases, salaried employees may routinely work long hours. Nevertheless, it is important for supervisors to respect boundaries outside of work hours. Mobile employees, especially those who work at home, need to be able to separate their personal and work lives.

- **Set up proper, reliable access to any internal networks and online material that mobile workers need to access for success at work.** Salespeople may need to quickly look up sales histories or product information. Call-center employees may need to be able to reach a supervisor quickly with questions. Difficulty sharing work directly with others can reduce productivity and increase security risks, especially if employees save confidential information on flash drives because it's hard for them to look it up on the company's secure network.

CONSIDERATIONS FOR MOBILE WORKERS

When business owners and managers think about mobile-computing scenarios, they might imagine anything from lazy, drifting employees taking weeks to complete daily tasks to dynamic, creative work teams spread across the country, working 16-hour days together from their homes to produce brilliant product designs. When mobile employee candidates envision working outside an office, their expectations can vary just as much. Some people just want to get away from the distractions of a noisy office so they can better concentrate on their tasks, while others envision half the work day spent in pajamas and the other half spent on a park bench.

Just as businesses and managers need to be aware of the risks, plan for clear communication, and set specific goals, the mobile employee needs to be similarly aware of his or her responsibilities, strengths, and weaknesses as a worker.

Mobile workers fall into two basic categories: remote employees and self-employed workers. Although there

Figure 5.23   Instant messaging systems such as AOL's AIM can help mobile employees stay connected throughout the work day.

are a few differences between those two groups, there is a great deal more in common. A remote employee has goals set by a manager and must conform to the company's performance requirements. A self-employed person is responsible for determining how to accomplish his or her work, but even that work must live up to the expectations set by his or her clients.

For the self-employed worker, the employee who wants to try telecommuting, or the supervisor whose team includes mobile employees, certain considerations need to be evaluated, to make sure the employee is prepared to work effectively offsite:

- **Preferred environment.** Where do you do your best work? Do you like silence and a distraction-free environment, or does a quiet room make you stir-crazy? Are you energized by bustling coworkers, or is every person you see a kind of distraction? Whether you are considering mobile work or considering a candidate to hire for this type of work, some self-knowledge will help you match personal qualities with the job requirements.

- **Active communication.** Some jobs set up mobile work time to be free of interruptions (for example, "I am working on the new software design every Wednesday from home, and I will be unreachable until Thursday"). Often, however, mobile work requires a communication balancing act. You need to stay in touch with managers, clients, and coworkers enough that people understand what you are doing, yet not so often that you are constantly interrupting them. Mobile workers must be flexible enough to respond to reasonable inquiries during the workday. Also, mobile workers should ask about or experiment with the kinds of communication that would be most welcome: phone calls, text messages, e-mail, teleconferencing, or face-to-face meetings.

- **Consistent focus.** Every worker experiences interruptions, equipment breakdowns, and a variety of other setbacks. The mobile computing environment doesn't change that. Even so, if you are working without direct and constant supervision, you need to have a mind-set and work environment that support getting back on track quickly. Also, you should be clear about the kind of support you can expect: If your notebook computer crashes, will you get help from your company's IT department, or is it your responsibility to repair or replace it? If you have a question about job requirements, who should you contact? Being well prepared will help you stay focused.

Figure 5.24   Mobile work environments must suit the job and worker; productivity is a good measure of that match.

- **Appropriate tasks.** Management and employees share the responsibility for ensuring that tasks assigned for mobile completion can be reasonably done that way. Tasks that require private resources (files or databases that cannot be accessed outside of the office, for example) and work that requires a lot of setup before and afterward (for example, a lot of time required to copy files to a notebook before starting, and then hours to put everything back when the task is done) are not ideal choices for offsite work.

WHEN AND WHERE TO WORK

One of the most striking changes about today's mobile computing is that it opens up many new options of when and where to work. With a cell phone and laptop computer, you don't have to be tied to a large workspace or a telephone landline. This freedom requires some choices about which options will do most to enhance your productivity and effectiveness.

From creative advertising messages, you might think mobile work looks like the images you have seen of contented and relaxed workers sitting on a park bench and sharp, independent people sitting in coffee shops. To be sure, some people may thrive by working in those places, but to be effective at many jobs, you need to find a quiet place where you can avoid distractions and unimportant interruptions.

Therefore, one of your first decisions in planning mobile work is to find an appropriate location for meeting job requirements. Many people prefer to work from a specific area in their home that they can reserve (at least during work hours) for themselves, and ensure that their necessary connections to the outside world (typically, phone and Internet) are readily and consistently available. This approach is common among employees who perform part of their jobs while away from the office. Many companies that employ telecommuters require that they establish a quiet location such as this.

The home can be both a sanctuary and a trap, however. Some people who try telecommuting from home become distracted by chores and children, while others find it impossible to *stop* working when work tasks are always close at hand. One alternative to working at home is a concept called **co-working**, a central workplace that provides a desk, phone, and copier access; meeting rooms; and a community feeling, all for a daily or monthly fee.[8] This is designed much more for the self-employed worker than an employee of a company. Most of the time, mobile employees already have an office they can go to if needed.

When evaluating a work space, make sure that your surroundings allow you to use all of the tools you require for working remotely. If you need to make frequent calls, choosing a library or other quiet zone is ill-advised. If you have folders full of papers to reference, an outdoor location may not be ideal. If you need room to spread out, a desk or table might work better than the liv-

---

[8] Kerry Miller (February 26, 2007), Where the coffee shop meets the cubicle, *Bloomberg BusinessWeek*. Retrieved July 4, 2010, from http://www.businessweek.com/smallbiz/content/feb2007/sb2007 0226_761145.htm

ing room couch. If you need to be online when you work, make sure there's a strong Internet connection available. Consider everything you need, and then try to make your work area compatible.

Wherever you work, most mobile workers follow some kind of schedule. A predetermined schedule may be set by an employer, or the schedule may be self-designed as a way to be organized and productive. Any schedule should consider the needs of employers, clients, and coworkers. Some common software applications available on notebook computers and cell phones can help you set up and follow a schedule.

That sense of discipline should also extend to interactions with the outside world. When you take phone calls and participate in meetings, make sure you can give your full attention to the conversations you're having. Listen and participate as actively as you would if you were sitting at a table with the person or work group. Chances are you wouldn't be doing laundry in that setting, so resist the temptation to add distracting tasks along with business meetings.

5.7 Safe and Courteous Computing

Mobile computing is about more than getting a job done. Computer users have an impact on all the people they interact with—and often on friends, coworkers, and strangers around them as well. Mobile computing requires the same attention to courtesy as every other activity. It is such a new phenomenon (never before in all of human history have people been able to carry on multiple conversations simultaneously with others around the globe while waiting for a bus) that in many cases the rules for safety and courtesy are still being sorted out. Even so, in the absence of long-standing rules, some common sense can go a long way to making you a modern, mobile computer user who doesn't earn the contempt of others. Common sense also can help keep you out of harm's way.

KEEPING YOURSELF AND YOUR HARDWARE SAFE

Safe computing is perhaps a simpler issue than courtesy. Staying alert and aware while in high-risk activities will go a long way to reducing the risk of injury to yourself and others. Common sense should help you decide when it is safe while scaling a steep rock face to stop and snap a picture with the camera on your cell phone; your sense of awareness should help you refrain from texting friends in the middle of that climb when you discover your phone is still connected to the network way out where you are climbing.

One of the most controversial and prevalent risks in mobile computing is the danger of using cell phones while driving. We spend so much time behind the wheel of a car, and so much time staying in touch on our phones, that the combination of those two activities is understandable. It's easy to feel that since one is sitting in one seat and looking out one set of windows, driving doesn't occupy our brains, and a phone conversation is the perfect thing to fill the time. However, driving does require attention, and the risk of an accident is greatly elevated with the use of cell phones. Many states have passed or are considering laws banning the use of cell phones while driving.

Some states and countries have already passed laws restricting cell phone use to hands-free hardware, which allows the cell phone user to place calls without typing numbers and holding the handset. Unfortunately, despite these laws, studies have shown that there is no effective increase in safety by calling with hands-free hardware; the risk lies in our lack of attention because of our focus on the phone call,

---

[9]Suzanne P. McEvoy et al. (July 12, 2005), Role of mobile phones in motor vehicle crashes resulting in hospital attendance; a case-crossover study, *BMJ Publishing Group*. Retrieved July 5, 2010, from http://www.bmj.com/cgi/content/abstract/bmj.38537.397512.55v1; and Donald A. Redelmeier and Robert J. Tibshirani (February 13, 1997), Association between cellular-telephone calls and motor vehicle collisions, New England Journal of Medicine. Retrieved July 5, 2010, from http://content.nejm.org/cgi/content/abstract/336/7/453

not because of the hardware we use for the call.[9] Even though it is legal in some cases to use hands-free cell phones, consider whether this is really a wise choice. A car accident can ruin much more than just the paint job on the car.

Beyond your own safety, you need to consider the safety of the equipment you use as well. Most people who actively use cell phones are accustomed to keeping the phone in a pocket or purse that keeps it available but safe from scratching or being dropped.

Most mobile device manufacturers declare that excessive moisture (for example, from being left out in the rain, or falling into a swimming pool) will void the warranty, so it is wise to keep your cell phone somewhere that will protect it from being sprayed or soaked. If you carry a notebook computer, consider investing in some kind of case; even just a lightweight sleeve case can make a difference in keeping it dry and clean.

Losing your equipment is another risk to its safety, not to mention the security of the information it contains. Cell phones are arguably easier than notebooks to leave behind somewhere, just by virtue of their size. If you are the kind of person who leaves your car keys behind in a store now and then, you might consider strategies for not holding your phone in your hand while you shop. Stow it in a pocket when you get ready to pay for merchandise, and check around you when you leave any place where you were sitting and working.

STAYING SECURE ON THE GO

The threats to your mobile hardware and data are by and large the same as for what is on your desktop. Malware and online invasions of privacy, hardware theft, and low-tech security threats are all common.

Low-tech security threats probably pose a greater threat to the mobile user than to a home or office user, simply because these users take their devices out in public. Just by being in public, you expose yourself to greater risk of losing your privacy. As with other kinds of precautions, awareness of your actions and surroundings can go a long way to making you and your data more secure. Here are some guidelines for

Figure 5.25 The risks in public computing are not always visible; awareness of your surroundings is vital.

protecting your security when you use mobile computing devices:

- **Know where your screen faces.** If you sit with your back to a window, a busy sidewalk, or a crowded restaurant, a steady stream of people may see what you are doing. While the vast majority of passersby will not care, you are definitely more vulnerable to snooping, especially if you are a creature of habit and occupy that same back-facing chair day after day. Consider moving so that your screen shares its output with no one but you.

- **Do less confidential work in public places.** Working on your monthly finances, with spreadsheets containing account numbers, is probably not your best choice for close quarters on an airplane or in a busy coffee shop, nor is work that displays sensitive client information.

- **Be extremely cautious about what you say on a cell phone in public.** It may seem obvious not to give out sensitive credit card and Social Security numbers (including the "last four of your social" that so many companies now ask us to repeat for them). There are other, less-obvious dangers as well. Discussing your vacation plans and how you haven't found a house-sitter seems like a harmless tale of anticipation and frustration, until somebody follows you home and marks the location and time for a robbery.

- **Install malware protection on your cell phone, if you spend time online.** It's easy to forget that your smart phone isn't just a cell phone; it's more of a computer with cell capability. Malware does exist to sift through your contact database and other personal information on your smart phone. If you download apps and connect to the Internet with your phone, you are vulnerable to an infection, and you should guard against it.

- **Be extra-careful to make sure that, when you bring papers and flash drives to a location for work, you bring the same papers and flash drives back home or to the office.** Leaving behind a flash drive filled with company account information could be devastating.

- **If you are not interested in having your phone filled with ads and company images, be wary of providing your phone number to potential advertisers.** Though the practice is still in its infancy, technologies and services are being developed to serve advertising to cell phone customers—not just to the owner's screen but perhaps to a second screen designed to show mini-billboards to nearby people when the cell phone is in use—possibly as a way to reduce the cost of the phone service. If this idea is a concern to you, be vigilant in monitoring the terms of new cell phone plans and programs in the future. In the not-too-distant future, you may need to treat your cell phone number as you do your e-mail address, providing it only to trusted people who will not spam your phone.

ACCESSING PUBLIC WI-FI SPOTS SAFELY

Mobile computing usually involves some sort of network connection in order to send and receive information. Mobile devices and networks alike have made it convenient to quickly connect, but you should be very cautious about joining open wireless networks. When you can see the network, the network can see you. If you are not protected against intrusions, other computers on the local network may be able to install malware on your system. It is also easy for other systems to monitor your Internet traffic, detect when you are accessing insecure Web sites, and hijack your login or user information for those sites.

Your best bet is to join open networks only at businesses that specifically set up the network as a service (hotels, restaurants, bars, and coffee shops, for example) and make sure your computer is configured to be as private as possible while using those networks. While a legitimate Wi-Fi network is not guaranteed to keep you safe, you are at the very least not joining a network that exists specifically to hack into the computers of unsuspecting mobile users.

To increase the security of your network connection, even if you are accessing unsecured Web sites, you

Figure 5.26   Some threats to your mobile gear are as low-tech as a split-second grab when you leave your hardware unattended.

can use a private, secure connection called a **virtual private network (VPN)**. As shown in Figure 5.27, a VPN employs a method called **tunneling**, in which each piece of data, called a **packet**, from the sending computer is encapsulated within another packet before being sent over the Internet. A VPN is often made more secure by adding encryption of the data within each encapsulated packet.

When you use a VPN, all of your regular Internet-based activities, such as sending emails or surfing Web sites, first will pass through the secure connection between your device and the VPN server before traveling out to the Internet. While the VPN cannot protect you from malware that you might encounter in your Internet activities, it does effec-

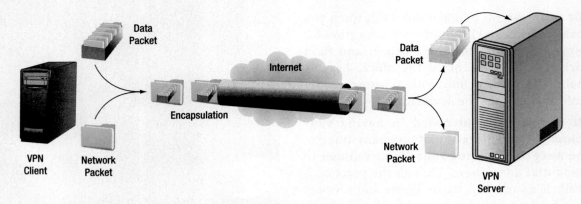

Figure 5.27 A VPN encapsulates data within a network package—called a packet—to increase security during transmission.

tively shield your data traffic from nearby hackers who would otherwise be monitoring your unsecured communication.

In order to use a VPN, you need to have a small piece of software on your system that handles the secure data communication, and you need to have access to a VPN server. Some companies provide VPN access for their remote employees, but few of them are generous about allowing employees to use that secure business connection for unrestricted personal surfing. If you don't already have unrestricted access to a VPN, or would prefer to keep your personal Internet activities separate from the server that your employer monitors, you can subscribe to a **personal VPN**.

Personal VPNs are services that, for a monthly or annual fee, provide users with access to a VPN server that allows them to securely connect to the Internet. StrongVPN, at http://www.strongvpn.com/, is an example of a Personal VPN service. Along with the secure connection, StrongVPN also provides the ability to surf the Internet with a degree of anonymity; anyone checking your IP address when you visit their Web site will be given StrongVPN's IP address rather than your own.

COURTEOUS MOBILE COMPUTING

While personal and equipment safety are fairly straightforward concepts, the same cannot be said about courtesy to others when using mobile computing equipment. Rudeness to one person might be a socially acceptable norm for another, and as with all other aspects of social behavior, some people simply don't care whether they behave politely in a given situation.

If you are one of the people who would like to be not just a modern mobile user but a mobile user who is unusually pleasant for those around you, the following guidelines will help:

- **Don't divide your attention between cell phone and circumstances.** If you're at dinner with a friend or about to buy bread at the bakery, don't use your phone. Mixing a phone call with a face-to-face interaction signals a lack of interest in the person you are with, and it makes a person's job difficult if the person is supposed to be communicating with you. Either wait to answer the call, or step out of line at the store so you can concentrate on the call.

- **Keep private conversations private.** One-sided phone conversations are often far louder and more noticeable than talkers think. Unless you would normally include everyone in the coffee shop in your conversation, take it outside. Even outside, dramatic or emotional conversations are probably best reserved for a time when you are alone. And do you really know who is listening when you are sharing details about that exciting new product you're developing or that big sale you hope to close by the end of the day? Could an employee of your biggest competitor be nearby?

- **Mind your beeps.** Cell phones let you customize your ring tones. Chat programs on a notebook computer can be customized to play alert sounds when people send you messages or log in and out of the system. This can make for a pleasant little social symphony, but only to your ears. The repeated *blink! blink! blink!* sounds of your chat messages goes from annoying to nearly

Not everyone can get work done in a coffee shop, but you certainly can. Your home office is good for administrative work, but your best creative time is spent amid the sounds of hissing steam and the conversation of others.

Yesterday, as you worked away at the Half-Full Mug in the middle of a busy Saturday afternoon, you heard an exasperated comment from another patron as they headed for the door: "You can't ever find a chair in this place anymore; it's getting to where I'd rather go someplace else for coffee."

Looking up, you realize that, of the dozen or so tables, more than half of them are taken up by people just like you, notebook open and engrossed in whatever was on the screen. Even though the coffee shop provides free Wi-Fi access, it isn't clear that they really intended for the store to become an office building.

Do you feel that it's reasonable to take up a table for three or four hours at a time, if the coffee shop doesn't tell you otherwise? Should you have to make way for others if you're following the rules and simply got there first? Explain your reasoning.

◄ ETHICAL   **DILEMMA ►**

Is it ok to take up a table for three or four hours at a time, if the coffee shop doesn't tell you otherwise?

"Don't poach a wireless signal, even if it's in the clear."

unbearable in a surprisingly short amount of time. If you are going to sit in one place for a while, turn your sound way down, or just mute your device.

- **Don't make the coffee shop your new office unless you've been invited.** If you sit down at the Half-Full Mug and spread your notebook computer, stacks of papers, and your cell phone across a four-person table, you're occupying a lot of real estate that the owners may have hoped could be used by more than a single person (see the "Ethical Dilemma" feature). If you plan to occupy that table for hours, consider whether that four-dollar cup of coffee is adequate rent for the office space you are using. If the Half-Full Mug has a sign that says, "Welcome wireless office-ers, make yourselves at home!" then no worries, but in the absence of that invitation, consider checking with the management about your plans to spend your weekdays in their store. If you get uncomfortable looks and a hesitant response, then you have been politely told to reduce the square footage and length of your stay.

- **Don't poach a wireless signal, even if it's in the clear.** Security risks aside, simply because the paint store hasn't learned to password-protect its wireless network doesn't mean you should punish the owners by slowing down the network they are paying for. If they don't have a "Free Wi-Fi" sign

Figure 5.28 Splitting your attention isn't polite to either of the people you're talking to.

in the window, at least check with the business to see if the owners meant to leave the network open.

- **Don't disappear in mid-conversation.** If you are chatting online with someone and need to go (or have run out of things to say), take the time to say good-bye. A graceful end to a conversation will make you far more popular with friends, coworkers, and fans of your company than an abrupt disappearance.

- **Don't send e-mail or write Web comments when you are furious.** Most of us would avoid yelling at someone face to face, and when it does happen, we would agree it isn't polite. Somehow, it feels safer to write e-mails that attack others. To spare hurt feelings, reduce your reputation risk, and give yourself a second chance to think clearly, simply use a different button when you are done writing a message while you are angry. Rather than triumphantly clicking "Send," click the "Save" button. Do something else for an hour or two, and then review what you wrote. Chances are good that parts of the message can be more constructive.

Fact Check

1. Which of the following guidelines will *not* protect you against safety risks associated with mobile computing?
   a. Avoid using a cell phone while driving, so you can avoid collisions.
   b. Be aware of your surroundings, so you can avoid theft and accidents.
   c. Write your Social Security number on your laptop, so you can identify it if you lose it.

2. What is a wise practice for communicating online about a situation that angers you?
   a. Write a message, but save it for a while before reviewing and sending it.
   b. Use text messages to get your point across quickly and quietly.
   c. Say whatever you want as long as your message is anonymous.

- Software to support mobile devices includes software for adding personalized ring tones (sound files played by mobile devices to announce certain events, such as incoming calls and messages, or to announce an alarm or appointment time) and wallpaper (background images for the phone's display screen). Software to assist with mobile computing includes anti-malware programs, file browsers, mobile phone number information, synchronizing programs, and Wi-Fi scanning software. Software for general use includes programs designed to improve the user's experience, support hobbies or other special interests, and manage business activities, such as keeping track of appointments and business contacts. Mobile devices usually provide some way to acquire new files for use, typically by downloading them from the Web or transferring them from another computer or mobile device.

- A traditional business model includes a central office or industrial site. Employees travel to that central location, perform their work under the direct supervision of management, and then go home until the next work day. The mobile business model reduces or eliminates the use of a central office. Employees are more autonomous, selecting their own work location and in some cases their own work hours. Meetings and other communication are done via phone and computer connectivity.

- Several factors affect the success of telecommuters and other workers using mobile technology. The manager needs to be able to give employees some autonomy and be able to accept mobile work. The organization needs a way to effectively measure the performance of these employees, and the costs and cost savings must be acceptable. The company must also prepare to manage the risks of allowing people to work outside the office, particularly risks to data security. Businesses can improve the likelihood of success by measuring performance in terms of goal achievement; including short-term goals in performance measures; establishing when and how employees are to be available, including when not to contact them; and setting up reliable access to networks and data.

- Candidates for mobile work should realistically assess their ability to adapt to the more flexible circumstances and should determine the type of environment in which they work best. They should be able to communicate actively but not constantly with coworkers, clients, and supervisors, and they must be able to consistently focus on their work goals. They must ensure that the tasks they are expected to do will be suitable for mobile computing. Important decisions for mobile workers include when and where to work; these decisions must be made in the context of any guidelines laid down by the employer, as well as customers' requirements.

- Using mobile equipment involves risks. One of the most significant is the threat of collisions when a user is driving while using a cell phone or other mobile device. Mobile computing equipment also is vulnerable to a number of threats. Moisture, whether in the form of rainfall, spilled drinks, or a swimming pool, is a common hazard for mobile devices and may void their warranty. Another common threat is loss of the equipment when users leave it behind while moving about. Other precautions—such as positioning screens to avoid public display, using malware on mobile devices, guarding private data, and being selective about wireless networks—are aimed at protecting mobile users' data.

- For extra security, mobile users can make use of a virtual private network, or VPN, which encrypts and shields communication between the mobile device and a secure server. Personal VPN services provide VPN access to consumers, typically for a fee.

- Mobile workers can practice courtesy in a variety of ways. One guideline is to avoid conducting cell phone conversations while also trying to interact with others face to face. Phone users should avoid conversations in situations that could be embarrassing or invasive or that could disclose private information to the public. They should respect others around them by reducing the noise produced by mobile devices and by not taking over large areas in public or retail areas for long periods without first verifying that such camping is welcome. Courteously ending online conversations builds goodwill, and refraining from sending messages while angry can prevent damage to relationships.

Key Terms

co-working, 208
intellectual property, 206
packet, 211
personal VPN, 212

telecommuting, 205
tunneling, 211
virtual office, 206

virtual private network
  (VPN), 211
virtual teams, 204

Key Terms QUIZ

Complete each statement by writing one of the terms listed under "Key Terms" in each blank.

1. A(n) _____ is a package of data that is transmitted across a network.

2. Self-employed mobile users who need a more formal office setting than a home office can consider a shared-space environment called _____.

3. _____ is the practice of employees working from home rather than traveling to an office.

4. The _____ of a company includes its ideas, patents, trade secrets, and company processes.

5. Companies with many mobile workers can use a(n) _____ to provide a desk and conference room in a central building, along with receptionist support.

6. People who work together on a project, yet work from different parts of town or the country, form a(n) _____.

7. Users who want to connect to unsecured Web sites in a secure and encrypted manner can make use of a(n) _____.

8. A(n) _____ provides consumers with secure, shielded mobile data transmissions.

9. A VPN protects data transmitted between a mobile device and a secure server via a process known as _____.

Review QUESTIONS

In your own words, briefly answer the following questions.

1. Describe an example of a time when you noticed someone who was using a mobile device and seemed unaware that he or she was using it in a way that was risky or annoying. How could that person have used the device in a safer or more appropriate manner?

2. Suppose you work for an organization's information technology department and were asked to participate in a team of employees investigating whether to allow the accounting employees to telecommute two days per week. What are some of the issues the company should consider?

3. Would you prefer to work at a company's workplace, at home, or on the road traveling to customer or construction sites? Which of the qualities of a successful telecommuter do you have?

4. At some organizations, for an employee to work from home, the employee has to set up a workplace that meets certain standards set by the employer. What conditions do you think would be important for a home-based workplace for an employee whose job involves handling calls from customers?

5. If you are driving somewhere, what is the safest way to use your cell phone?

6. Explain how a personal VPN can help protect you from hacking and data theft.

7. How can you use a notebook computer in a way that protects you from common threats to your security?

8. How can users avoid annoying others with noise related to using their mobile devices?

9. Describe a good way to end an online conversation, and how people might feel if you simply disappeared or drifted away without a final word.

10. Why is it important to hold back on sending angry messages until you have cooled down? What are some possible consequences of sending angry messages?

Complete the following exercises as directed by your instructor.

1. Take a tour of Google Docs. Google has created a set of document processing tools that allow people to store, work on, and share a variety of document types. Take a tour of Google Docs, a set of document-processing tools that allow people to store, work on, and share a variety of document types. Many companies rely on Google Docs and similar services to keep documents in a central place for their telecommuting employees to share. Visit http://docs.google.com/, and use the links on that page to look up explanations and examples of the types of documents and editing that are supported. When you have investigated the service's set of features, write a brief description of the two features you think would be most valuable to a telecommuter, and explain your reasons for choosing them.

2. Working with another classmate or on your own, identify three types of situations (preferably in your own experience) where mobile device users annoyed you with their online or cell phone behavior. Role-play or write a positive response for each situation. Your role-play or report should identify alternative behaviors that allow the mobile user to access his or her device without bothering others.

Business communication is different from social communication. In our instant messages and on our cell phones with friends, we might use lots of abbreviations, like LOL, sux 2bu, and so on. But in work-related writing, your colleagues or customers might think of you as unprofessional if your language veers far from Standard English. Still, even in the business world, shorthand writing can be a useful skill for communicating via Twitter or SMS, as long as you keep in mind when it is appropriate.

Divide into pairs. Near the top of a sheet of paper, work independently to write a sentence or two about any topic, such as a place you recently went or an activity you enjoy. But instead of writing in Standard English, write the message as if you were texting it: use shorthand and abbreviations as much as possible. If you are unfamiliar with common texting abbreviations, just do your best, and make the words as short as possible while still being understandable.

Trade papers with your partner. Under your partner's message, write a translation of the message into proper, complete English. Then write a reply, again using as much shorthand as you can. Switch papers again. Check your partner's translation, and then translate your partner's reply.

Finally, in pairs or as an entire class, discuss the experience. How easy was it for everyone to write in shorthand? What misunderstandings occurred? When might employees want to use this kind of shorthand in work situations? How could you prevent misunderstandings in those situations?

[*Chapter* LABS]

Complete the following exercises using a computer in your classroom, lab, or home.

1. Learn how food carts combine mobile computing and social media to attract and retain customers. First, read a background article to learn more about the subject in general. Use a browser and navigate to http://www.sfgate.com/. In the search box, search on **street food carts twitter**, and read the article titled "Street food carts rely on Twitter and Facebook." Then, navigate to the Google search engine at http://www.google.com/ and search for **food cart twitter**. Pick a search result that lists food carts using Twitter, and review the list. Visit two of the business Web sites for types of food that look interesting.

2. Design a co-working facility, where self-employed people could work on an occasional or daily basis. Create a plan to include:

   - The types of office services the facility would offer (both people-based and hardware-based services, if applicable)
   - The layout for individual work areas
   - The number of work areas to provide and how they should be organized
   - Ways that participants could have private meetings with clients
   - Types of common areas that could be shared by all users
   - Ways for people to pay for the time they spend at the facility

3. Investigate anti-malware solutions for smart phones. Visit three different security software providers of your choice (for example, Kaspersky at http://www.kaspersky.com/, McAfee at http://home.mcafee.com/ or Avast! at http://www.avast.com/). For each company, list the mobile operating systems that it supports, the types of protection it offers, and the cost for the software. Choose your favorite of the three, identify the reasons for your choice, and be prepared to share those reasons with the rest of the class.

[*Think* AND DISCUSS]

As directed by your instructor, discuss the following questions in class or in groups.

1. Even though a clear link between cell phone use and greater risk of auto accidents has been established, many states continue to allow their use by drivers (including states that allow hands-free sets, which do not appear to significantly reduce the risk of accidents). What (if any) restrictions do you think would be appropriate regarding cell phones and driving? How would those restrictions be enforced? If you are a cell phone user, would it be easy for you to obey laws and restrictions to stay off your phone while driving?

2. Some people consider it to be rude to talk on a cell phone while checking out at a supermarket or department store. In what way would a cell phone conversation in that situation be different from talking to a friend who is standing next to you? How do social interactions in general change between two people when one of them is talking on a cell phone? What does each person do?

[*Fact Check* ANSWERS]

5A:

LO5.1 The Internet's History and Structure

1: b. A military network
2: a. No one

LO5.2 Overview of Internet Services

1: a. A document-linking and -sharing system accessible via the Internet
2: b. Allowing users a convenient way to transfer files
3: b. Voice over Internet Protocol

LO5.3 The Internet at Home

1: a. By using the information in a URL
2: b. search engines
3: b. messages up to 140 characters in length

LO5.4 The Internet at School

1: a. check with multiple trustworthy sources
2: Students can gain access to classes not offered at their school; students in a remote region can take classes even if they cannot attend the school; online classes may fit better with a work schedule for working students.

5B:

LO5.5 Mobile Software

1: a. It should fit the exact dimensions of your cell phone screen.
2: c. Trusted online stores, the mobile phone store and sensible friends.

LO5.6 Effective Mobile Business

1: a. manage by goal, not by typing time
2: b. The needs of employers and clients

LO5.7 Safe and Courteous Computing

1: c. Write your Social Security number on your laptop, so you can identify it if you lose it.
2: a. Write a message, but save it for a while before reviewing and sending it.

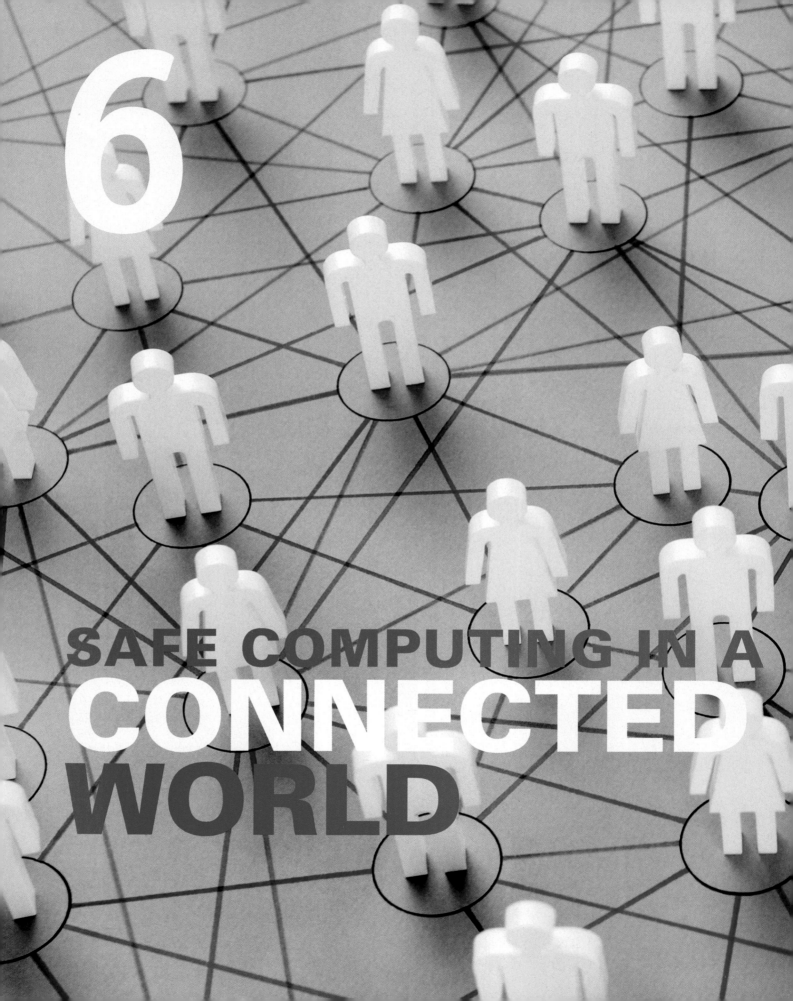

6

SAFE COMPUTING IN A CONNECTED WORLD

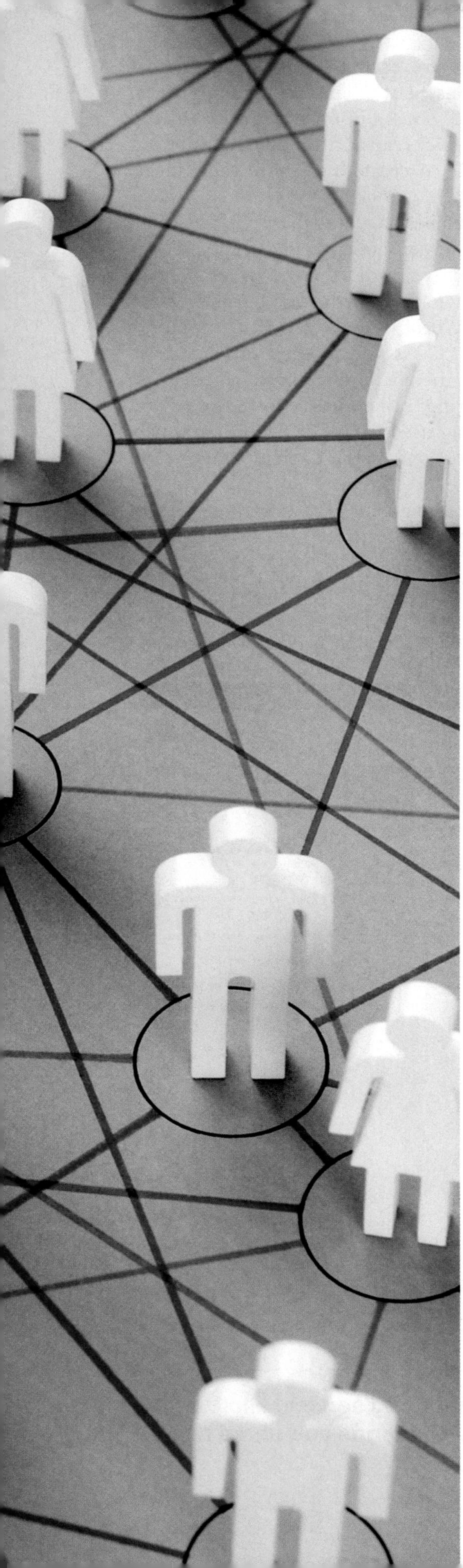

LEARNING OBJECTIVES

After reading this chapter, you will be able to:

6.1 Explain the various types of social media that exist on the Web, including social networking, social bookmarking, blogging, and wikis, p. 224.

6.2 Define business-to-consumer and business-to-business e-commerce, and discuss how businesses can use social media and the Internet to reach their customers, p. 240.

6.3 Describe ways that businesses and individuals can use cloud-computing services, p. 248.

6.4 Define the terms *threat*, *vulnerability*, and *countermeasure* in the context of computer security, p. 259.

6.5 Identify the kinds of threats that can damage computer hardware and ways to prevent that damage, p. 260.

6.6 Summarize types of threats to your computer data and ways to protect against those threats, p. 263.

6.7 Define *identity theft*, and explain ways that it can be avoided, p. 272.

CHAPTER CONTENTS

Chapter Overview

Every day around the world, people go online to collaborate with business colleagues and share details of their personal lives with friends and relatives. That constant sharing of ideas and information can put people at greater risk, whether from social errors that cost them their reputation or job, or from a loss of privacy that leads to financial or physical harm. In this chapter, you will take a closer look at the world of social media and ways you might participate; you will also learn about some of the risks involved in computing and techniques for reducing your exposure to those risks. Have you already shared thoughts, photographs, or personal information online? What tools or Web sites have you used for that purpose?

LESSON 6A:
Social Media and E-Commerce

6.1 Making Your Mark on the Web

Whether you run a business or are an individual, the Internet provides you with unique and powerful forms of self-expression. You can completely control the look and feel of what you produce by creating your own Web site. You can join social media sites and use those services to share your thoughts and creativity. You can use the Internet to promote your business and process transactions. You can even use services on the Internet to store data and run programs that in the recent past had to reside on your own computer.

and services that are used to create and support those interactions, such as text, photographs, maps, sound, and video. Put together, social media includes the services and sites on the Internet that allow people to create and share their ideas, thoughts, and lives.

The desire people have to share information, along with the Internet's unsurpassed ability to connect people together around the world, led both to the development of social media and to the ongoing evolution of the World Wide Web that is commonly known as Web 2.0. As you learned in Chapter 5, Web 2.0 doesn't merely support social media and information sharing; rather, user contributions and opinions are being used to create, change, and personalize large portions of the content available on the Web.

Social media contains several sub-categories of services. Though each form may be very different from the others in terms of the exact type or manner in which information is shared, the concept of sharing is critical and central to each one of them.

SOCIAL MEDIA IS EVERYWHERE

If you have spent much time online, chances are good that you have used or at the very least read about some kind of social media program or Web site. The popularity of using the Internet for sharing personal information has skyrocketed in recent years, and new programs and methods regularly join those that are already heavily used.

The term *social media* encompasses far more than Facebook and Twitter, even though those programs might be the first ones to come to mind. The "social" part of the term refers to interactions between people, like collaboration, communication, building relationships, and sharing information; and "media" refers to the methods

Figure 6.1   Facebook is a social networking service, allowing people and businesses to connect with friends and share news.

None of these sites and services would exist in any meaningful form if the user community were not also the major content contributors. Social media genres include:

Social Networking. Facebook, LinkedIn, and the new arrival Google+ are examples of social networking sites. These sites thrive not only on the information its participants post, but also on the connections that are made between participants. Users are encouraged to invite people to create connections so that personal information and ideas can be shared between connected participants.

Social Bookmarking. Services such as Digg, Delicious, and StumbleUpon provide a way for participants to tag articles and Web pages that they find interesting. The bookmarking service keeps track of all the bookmarks that its users make, and reports the relative popularity of Web pages based on the opinions continuously being expressed by the service's community.

Blogging. Blogging sites, like Blogger and TypePad, provide a way for participants to produce anything from brief thoughts to long essays, and then publish their work for others to read. Blogs commonly provide a place for readers to leave comments and participate in discussions about what the blogger has written. Blog readers can sign up as followers of the writer, and it is not unusual for bloggers to both write and follow the work of others. Beyond the more traditional blog format, micro-blogging services, like Twitter and Tumblr, provide easy ways for people to broadcast small, quick updates to their followers. Geo-blogging sites, like Foursquare and Gowalla, let people broadcast their location instead of written updates, so followers can see the places that the poster visits throughout his or her day.

Wikis. A wiki is a collaborative information site that collects and displays text pages in a standard, easy-to-edit format. Wiki services like Wikia and Wikispaces host sites filled with information about practically any subject, including video games, comic books, movies, finance, gardening, cooking, and more. Wikis encourage people with subject knowledge to contribute at their convenience, adding to or fixing pages where information is missing or incorrect. The ongoing process of collaborative contributing and editing is designed to produce increasingly accurate and rich content over time.

Media Sharing. Many sites exist for sharing non-text media. YouTube encourages users to upload videos of everything from a funny accident caught on cell phone to serious, professionally-produced presentations. SlideShare and Scribd provide services for

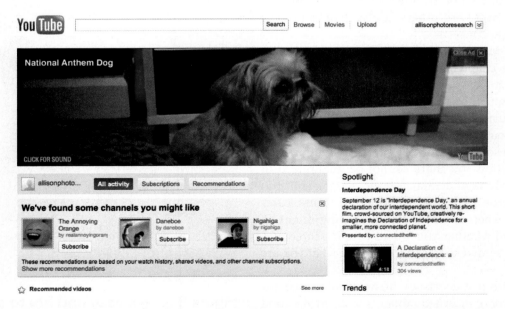

Figure 6.2 Media sharing services like YouTube provide a single site for users to contribute audio and video clips, and to see what others have shared.

sharing documents and slide shows. Photos can be shared on Flickr and Photobucket, and DeviantArt provides both cutting-edge artists and amateur sketchers with a place to showcase their work. Music can be shared on LastFM and Grooveshark, and sites like CanadaPodcasts create a place to find and share podcasts.

Social Reviews.   Review sites are quickly gaining popularity for researching restaurants, hotels, service companies, and much more. Some review sites like TripAdvisor focus on travel-related services and companies, while others such as Yelp provide reviews for a wide assortment of businesses, organized by major city. Contributors provide reviews and ratings of a business based on their experience. Readers can research the best-reviewed places to eat or get a car repaired; they can also search for reviews of a specific business that interests them.

Social Events.   Sites such as Meetup bridge the gap between social interaction online and in-person interaction. Meetup encourages people with a common hobby or interest to join an online group with other people in their area, and then use the online group to organize and promote in-person meetings. Singles, scuba divers, hikers, quilters, and many others can meet and stay in touch through the site with others who are actively pursuing their interest.

Social media provides a rich variety of ways that people can share their lives with others. While this new communication frontier provides fascinating ways to connect with others, it also creates privacy and copyright concerns.

You will learn more about privacy and security later in this chapter, but specifically with regard to social media there is a critical lesson that cannot be repeated often enough: you cannot completely control the security and privacy of what you share with others. No matter whether you are sharing something via e-mail, a social networking site, or an online store, the information you share cannot be guaranteed to be completely confidential forever. Before you join any service or share any information, think carefully about whether what you are sharing might be sensitive and whether you would care if people outside your intended audience were to see what you are sharing.

Along with privacy issues, many people and organizations are concerned about social media and copyright violations. Simply put, people love to share information whether or not they own the legal rights to share it. YouTube and music sharing site users sometimes post copyrighted songs and videos without permission. Images owned by photographers and artists can be copied and shared by social networking users who find the images interesting or relevant. Bloggers may reprint entire articles from newspapers, columnists, or other bloggers without proper credit to the writer.

Sometimes, people willfully distribute copyrighted material without permission; other times, copyright violations occur simply through carelessness. Social media sites make it easy to share what you like with others; if one sees a friend post an interesting sketch on their Facebook page, it takes only a couple of mouse clicks to forward that sketch to one's own friends list, without even a passing thought about whether the artist had given permission for everyone to share his or her work.

Given the relatively unregulated nature of the Internet, and with social media still in its infancy, the battle between copyright owners and online social media participants is bitter but so far inconclusive. Copyright owners have had limited success taking action against individuals who share their images or text without permission. However, there is little evidence that occasional successful lawsuits are having much overall effect on the practice of illegal sharing.

Further complicating the legal sharing issue, there are many works of writing, music, and video that are

Figure 6.3   It's easy and fun to share information on the Internet, but be aware that what you share may not always stay private.

legitimately in the public domain and may be shared without permission. In addition, numerous musicians and artists release some of their work on YouTube or other social media sites with conditional or unconditional permission to share the items, in some cases to reach more fans and in others specifically to counter what they perceive to be a heavy-handed approach to copyright enforcement.

As a social media user, your best bet is to be as aware as possible of the copyright status of what you share, whether it is text, images, music, or video. If you are caught sharing copyrighted materials without permission, the copyright owner could sue you for damages, even if you were unaware that your actions were illegal.

If you are a producer of original writing or art, you need to be aware that what you create may not be effectively guarded by a simple copyright declaration. One alternative to a traditional and contentious copyright is to license your work for conditional distribution online. Creative Commons (at http://www.creativecommons.org) is an organization working to find common ground between the producers are social media community by creating licenses that are designed to be more flexible than the traditional copyright license.

Their goal is to create a licensing structure and culture that can work effectively with the new global sharing model that now pervades the Internet. Licenses typically grant receivers the right to distribute the artist's work, as long as proper credit is given and certain conditions specified by the artist are met. This allows artists to participate in sharing that would probably take place even with a more rigid copyright in effect, while reaching out to encourage their fans to share legally and respectfully.

CREATING YOUR OWN WEB SITE

Facebook pages are fabulously simple to create, and they allow you to express a variety of creative ideas, from essays to photographs and quick thoughts, but there are significant limitations. For one, your Facebook page uses a standard layout and structure, and you cannot change it. Many people also dislike the advertising content that appears; they do not want to see ads for weight-loss pills appearing next to their latest poem. Finally, social media sites may, as part of their terms of use, declare that they have a license to use whatever you put on your page, for as long as you maintain it. Giving away the control over your creative products just to have them on a Web site is unacceptable to many people.

If you are up for the challenge, there are a few ways you can create a Web site of your own, depending on how much control over the process you want. But first, before you open a file and type your first HTML tag or visit a create-your-own service, you need to stop and think about what you want to do.

An effective, appealing Web site does not happen by accident; it requires some design work, even for simple, personal sites. A good design need not take weeks or require complex tools. Grab a pad of paper (or a word processor if you type faster than you write) and make an outline. What is the main purpose of your site? What is the first thing you want people to see when they arrive? With that in mind, list the specific items you would like to include. Look at your information, and group items together in a way that makes sense; those groupings will likely become their own Web pages.

If, for example, you wanted to make a travel Web site, you might decide that your main page should feature a picture of your most recent trip, followed by a brief description of who you are and where you've been in the world. Along with that, you could offer descriptions of each of your trips, complete with pictures and anecdotes. Each trip could be its own separate Web page, so the main page might (underneath your introduction) simply list your trips and provide links to the detail pages.

As you define and organize your information onto pages, also consider how to make it easy for people to navigate through the site. In the travel example, you'd probably want your front page to have links to all your trips, rather than just a single link to your first trip (see Figure 6.5). If visitors can only read through one page after another in order to find the trip they want to see, many will lose interest long before they get to the end. At the end of each trip's page, you might put a link that says, "Back to the trip list" (which sends them to the front page) and another one that says, "Next stop—Singapore!" (which takes the reader to the next trip on the list). The more easy choices you provide, the more likely it is that you will anticipate what visitors to your site want to do.

Having decided what to produce and how to organize it, you're ready to create the site. If you have little interest in the details of building your site by hand, look into a site creation service. Many service companies have templates and automated tools ready to help you fill in the blanks and create a site from scratch with little effort. You'll give up some control over the exact appearance of the site, but you won't have to learn as much about HTML.

Some hosting and creation companies charge you to create your site; some will create the site for free if you agree to let them host your site for a monthly fee; and some offer you fully free setup and hosting, but be careful. Unless your free service is specifically offered by a nonprofit or charitable organization, it may not be entirely free. By signing up to use the hosting company's service, you may be agreeing to have advertising posted on your site, or to allow the service company to provide you with offers from other vendors. You may also want to investigate creating your own domain to host your Web site. When you register a domain name, you gain the exclusive ability to use that name as a URL. So long as no one has already reserved it, you can register and use "jackstravels.com" for your new travel Web site, for example.

There are many services that can register and host your domain name; most Web site hosts also provide domain hosting services as well. For as little as a few dollars per month, you can register and host a domain, and some companies will host one or two domains for free as part of a package deal.

Web sites are sets of files that contain both the visible information and instructions on how to format and display the information for the user. Though complex sites may also contain many files to run programs and databases related to the site's contents, simpler Web sites commonly have two types of files.

HTML files contain the information to display and HTML markup tags that identify headers, paragraphs, images, and links within the information. Each file usually corresponds to one page of the Web site.

Cascading Style Sheets (CSS) are files that provide detailed formatting instructions to the browser regarding fonts, colors, and how to lay out text on the screen. Simpler Web sites commonly have just one CSS file that contains the formatting instructions for the whole site.

If you are ready to take the plunge into site creation and the world of HTML, there are good software packages that can help you create your new site. While it is possible to type HTML tags directly into a text file and build a site by hand, construction programs make the process far simpler. Many provide **WYSIWYG (what you see is what you get**, pronounced "whizzy-wig") **editors** that show you how a Web page actually looks while you build it. They also provide convenient ways to lay out page information, create links to other pages and Web sites, and test that links are properly functioning. Some site builder software packages also come with templates, so you can find a basic layout you like and customize it, if you're not interested in the process of creating a complete new look from scratch.

Given the large number of Web creation programs, there is sure to be one to fit your needs and budget. You might consider one of the following titles, but be sure to investigate features to make sure your needs are met, and read independent software reviews as part of your research:

- *Expression Web* from Microsoft Corporation is a fairly technical tool and possibly not the best choice for a budding Web designer's first software assistant. It provides page creation tools with an emphasis on visual elements and provides support for a number of industry programming standards.

- Adobe Systems Inc.'s *Dreamweaver* is the heavy-hitter in the Web design software category. Not intended to be a beginner's tool, Dreamweaver provides a full complement of Web design and layout tools and adds many extra features such as a way to test your site's performance on multiple browsers and operating systems. Dreamweaver can operate on its own but is created to be part of a full suite of creative development software for creating and integrating all kinds of multimedia, social media, and e-commerce elements.

An even simpler alternative to building and hosting your own Web site is a **Web content management system (WCMS)**. A WCMS is a software service that

Figure 6.4   With Web site development software, you can create a site that's just right for your organization.

Figure 6.5 **Designing a page layout for a Web site can greatly improve the delivery of information to users.**

provides storage, usually in a database, of the information to be displayed on a Web site, and a set of predefined display templates for the user. The user chooses their preferred style for display and adds information to the database. The WCMS software creates Web site pages for visitors and allows the site owner to quickly add new content and make any necessary changes to what already exists.

Some WCMS systems, like Drupal and WordPress, are free to use; many bloggers appreciate the quick setup and easy maintenance that WordPress provides. Other systems require paid subscriptions or licenses to use.

BUILDING RELATIONSHIPS THROUGH SOCIAL NETWORKING

Unlike Web sites that people create, social networking sites provide little or no control over the appearance and layout of the site, leaving users free to produce information for sharing and to maintain and manage the connections they create with each other.

Some social networking sites are all-encompassing services that encourage you to share anything and everything with as many people as you care to have in your personal network. Other tools are more specialized, providing networks for specific purposes like career-building, professional networking, or school reunions, and excluding many types

of information and connections that more generic systems provide.

Facebook is an example of an open-ended service that invites users to share practically every aspect of their lives with others. New users create a free account and are then prompted to provide a wide range of personal data and preferences, including their name; contact information; favorite movies, books and music; affiliations with organizations, churches, and political parties; and relationship status and preferences. Along with personal data, Facebook provides users with a convenient way to upload pictures and to write notes and essays that can be viewed by others. None of the information is required, and many people gradually add and subtract details over time as their lives and interests change.

Facebook encourages people to make connections with others. Facebook calls connected people friends, and refers to the group of connected people as a user's **friends list**. Users can find friends by searching the system for names of people that they know. Facebook also provides its users with suggestions for new connections based on the personal information a user gives Facebook, and on "friends of friends," which are the friends lists that a user's friends have built. In all cases, a friend link is established only by mutual consent; one person must ask another to be Facebook friends, and the other person must agree before the connection is made.

The concept of friends serves both to solidify relationships and restrict access to sensitive information. Facebook allows users to determine how private they wish to keep their information to a certain degree. One can allow all visitors (whether Facebook members or not) to see certain things; restrict some kinds of data to be visible only to friends and friends of friends; and allow only specific people (including no one but the posting user) to see some items.

If Facebook's purpose was simply to compile personal data, then the service would be little more than a static profile site, and it wouldn't have the central role it currently enjoys in the online world. In addition to storing user profiles, Facebook provides an easy method for sharing information of all kinds with others. Users can quickly post a joke, opinion, or idea; add a photograph; or broadcast a Web link. Every time a user posts something, it appears in a list called a **news feed** that their friends can see. Each participant can watch their news feed throughout the day and see the sum of the ideas and activities in which their friends are involved.

To make the sharing concept more powerful, Facebook added the ability to approve of and comment on the items that users and their friends post. Users who see a comment, status message, or other piece of information that they like can click a **like button**, which is a Facebook-generated link that tags the item with that user's approval. The original poster, and all the people who can see the item, will see that the user likes that item; it provides a near-instant way to transmit a quick sense of approval and connection to the poster. Users who want to react in more detail to an item of any kind can add their own comments or thoughts underneath the item; those comments, in turn, may be "liked" or generate comments of their own, creating brief conversations.

Facebook provides other services, such as an instant messaging system, a direct-message system similar to e-mail, and voice communication via Skype. Facebook also supports a programmatic interface for software developers so that programmers can write apps that Facebook users can run from within Facebook. Zynga's FarmVille is one of the more famous of these programs, providing a fun way for Facebook users to grow and sell crops, and to share resources with others who play the game. Along with games, programmers write surveys, trivia challenges, and interactive adventure stories. The games and alternate forms of communication all enhance and extend Facebook's underlying mission of creating networks of people who actively share information with each other.

In contrast, the LinkedIn service provides a much narrower focus than Facebook. LinkedIn provides the same concepts as Facebook of building a profile and creating a network of associates by invitation, but LinkedIn is designed with a strictly business-oriented focus. The lion's share of profile data is related to education, professional experience, and other items one would typically find on a resume. Casual observations, vacation pictures, links to funny or controversial Web sites, and details about relationship problems are largely considered inappropriate by the user community.

Along with a profile page, LinkedIn makes it easy to organize and display travel plans; post notifications of upcoming events such as conferences and online seminars; and participate in conversation forums organized by topic, where people can discuss news and ask questions with others who share a specific professional interest or expertise.

LinkedIn encourages participants to provide recommendations for others in their network. Recommendations are free-form notes, usually a paragraph or two in length, that identify something exceptional about the subject based on the writer's experience as a co-worker, employee, or manager of the subject. Participants can request recommendations from people in their network, or they may be provided without solicitation. Recommendations can serve as a significant set of professional references for job seekers looking within their online network for new employment.

Figure 6.6 The Facebook friends list provides the critical links for sharing and receiving information about the people you know.

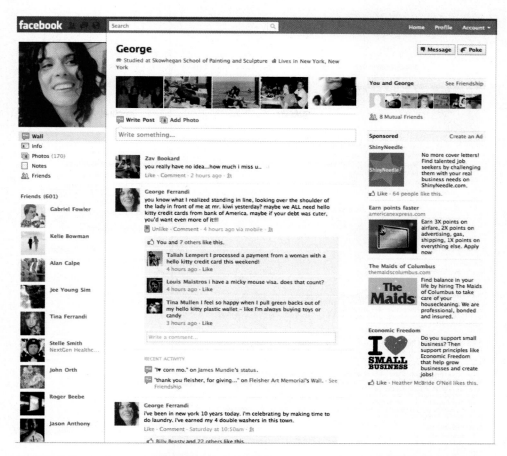

Figure 6.7   Facebook's news feed provides continuous updates about friends' activities.

Consistent with its business theme, LinkedIn makes it easy to search for people not only by name but also by employer, allowing users to scan lists of names for people they recognize at a former company. As with Facebook, LinkedIn makes suggestions to users about people they might know, taking past employers, types of employment, and region into consideration along with the user's existing network of connections.

SHARING LINKS THROUGH SOCIAL BOOKMARKING

Many forms of social media involve groups of users creating and sharing content with each other. Social bookmarking is a bit different in that bookmarking users do not create much content; rather, they express their likes and preferences to collectively identify the things that the bookmarking community find interesting.

The mechanical concept of social bookmarking is simple. All over the Web, participating sites provide clickable links for various bookmarking services, as shown in Figure 6.9. When Web surfers come across a page they particularly like, they simply click the link for their bookmarking service, and the Web page is marked. In that perspective, social bookmarking is not much different than saving your own page bookmarks in your browser, but bookmarking services provide several other features to add the "social" part of the experience.

In order to use a service like Delicious, people must create a free account. Delicious requires only a name and e-mail address from its users in order to create the account, and other than taking the time to fill out the short questionnaire, no extra steps are needed. Requiring individuals to create accounts allows Delicious to create social links that go beyond simple lists of bookmarks; it also reduces simpler forms of bookmarking abuse, such as a Web site owner creating a program to submit bookmarks thousands of times to make their site appear popular.

When a user bookmarks pages, the service accumulates those bookmarks in a list for the user. By

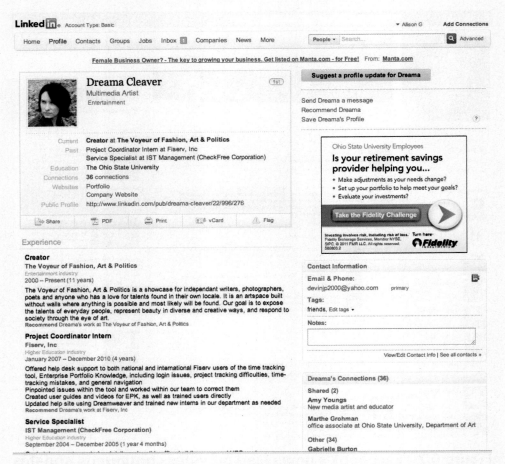

Figure 6.8   LinkedIn provides a business and professional networking service, discouraging after-hours personal data and topics.

visiting the main Delicious site, each user can review their list of saved bookmarks. In addition, the site accumulates bookmark requests from all users and maintains ever-changing lists of bookmarked pages that show the most popular and most recently discovered pages by the Delicious community. Each user's preferences and interests are expressed by bookmarking, and each user influences what the community as a whole thinks is popular.

Delicious tracks and displays the name of the subscriber who first submitted each link, encouraging users to actively bookmark new items; users can get a little boost to their pride by seeing their name as the first submitter of a topic that became extremely popular. You can click on any user's name in one of the lists and view their list of bookmarks. When you find people that bookmark pages you consistently find interesting, you can add their user name to a personal network so you can easily follow their links.

To organize and identify links for themselves and others, users will commonly add keywords called tags to their bookmarks. Tags are simple labels (for example, "cycling" or "low-carb" for fitness or diet enthusiasts) that help identify the subject of a bookmark. You can search for tags in your own list or throughout the entire Delicious service to find bookmarks that are related to that topic. If you want to be notified whenever someone adds a new bookmark for a specific tag, you can create a subscription for it; when a new bookmark with that tag is submitted to Delicious, the service alerts you of the new arrival, making it easy to stay current with the topics that interest you most.

Over time, the stand-alone social bookmarking services have seen increased competition from more comprehensive social media sites like Facebook. Facebook encourages its users to mark web pages and news stories with recommendation tags using its "like" system. Though Facebook does not provide a separate system for organizing and tracking bookmarked pages, it does post links to sites and services on users' news feeds as they make recommendations.

BLOGGING AND MICRO-BLOGGING

Creating a Web site is a great way to share business concepts or details about your personal interests, but you might think of yourself as more of a journalist or creative writer. Perhaps you've got strong political views and want to share them, or maybe you love movies and have friends who always ask you what you think about them, so it would be natural to write reviews for your friends to read online. If you want to publish your thoughts on a regular or semi-regular basis, you might not want to bother with all of the bells and whistles of a Web site.

If you find yourself with a lot to say, a blog may be just the thing for you. Blogs allow you to write whatever is on your mind, short or long, scholarly or silly, and make it quickly available for others to read. You can post three times a day or once a month—however your needs are best served. People who read your posts can leave thoughts of their own in a comment section.

Many people use blogs as an ongoing personal or professional journal. Most blog services provide either automatic or convenient methods to date and archive posts as the months and years pass. Users can associate tags and keywords with each entry, making it easy to retrieve sets of posts that are related to a specific topic no matter when they were written.

Why not just put your thoughts on your Web site? A conventional Web site can indeed be used to create blog-style posts, but extra effort may be needed to produce in a Web site what a blog service can do much more efficiently. It can be cumbersome to add new essays to a conventional Web page, move older posts to an archive page, and assign keyword tags to each post so readers can find various topics easily. A blog, however, is designed to be periodically updated with essays and ideas in a fairly linear way. Readers of a blog can search past posts by keyword, but more often posts are viewed chronologically, starting with the latest one.

As with Web sites, you can use a service provider to create and maintain your blog, or you can do it yourself. Many people use Blogger.com (http://www.blogger.com) or TypePad (http://www.typepad.com) to create and host their blogs. Blogger is a free service that provides a variety of layout templates and customization templates, and

makes getting started a quick and easy process. TypePad, after a free trial period, requires a monthly subscription. It also provides templates and layout customization, and it adds domain hosting, linking to social media sites, and other features for its subscribers.

If you'd rather create your own blog rather than work with a blog provider, you can do that, too. Many domain and service host companies that allow you to create and maintain a domain and Web site also provide you with blog development software. WordPress (http://wordpress.org/) is a popular blog development program. It is free to download and use, and it provides convenient tools for creating, customizing, and administering your blog site. You can dig deep into the features and functions of a blog site with WordPress, or you can also simply rely on the default settings and layouts provided by WordPress and produce a simple, high-quality blog site with minimal effort.

Figure 6.9 Web sites hosting practically any kind of information often provide a quick way to share bookmarks of their pages.

Regardless of the specific software package used to produce a blog, the creation process is fairly consistent. The user directs the site to create a new post, which produces an editing template that includes a window for the new entry's text and fields to accept keywords and other identifiers used to aid in the post's archiving. The user can type the new entry into the editing window or simply copy and paste text from a PC editor or browser if the new entry has already been written elsewhere. When complete, the user can preview the new post to check for formatting problems, then tag the post with keywords and publish it. Blog posts can appear for public viewing either immediately after being published or at a specific time determined by the user. If errors are found

Figure 6.10   Blogs can serve as a professional journal; archiving searches by date and keyword make it easy to find specific entries.

after publishing, the user can simply start the blog editor, make changes, and update the published post with the new version.

While a traditional blog enforces no practical limits on how small or large a post can be, nor on the particular format or form of expression used in the blog, the micro-blogging service Twitter takes the opposite approach. Twitter is designed specifically to encourage people to make short, frequent posts about news, thoughts, and events, both in the life of the poster and in the world in general. The service restricts posts to a maximum of 140 characters, requiring people to become more concise in expressing themselves.

Some people broadcast links to interesting news stories; other people send out titles of songs they are listening to; still others post about rush hour traffic and long lines at the supermarket. Many celebrities and politicians use Twitter to send messages to their fans, and news columnists and bloggers use the service to express opinions on current events in between longer pieces they publish on their main sites.

Businesses use Twitter to announce anything from corporate information to daily discounts and menu changes.

Using Twitter is even simpler than maintaining a traditional blog. A new user can quickly create a Twitter account, load a small piece of software on their computer or smart phone to manage the incoming and outgoing messages, and immediately begin participating. Each user chooses a set of people from which they wish to receive messages; establishing that request for messages is known as **following**. Users can find people to follow either by searching the Twitter site or by finding invitations in other places on the Web. Many bloggers, businesses, and others active in social networking have "follow me on Twitter" messages in their profiles and e-mail signatures. Unlike Facebook, following someone does not require the consent of both people; the service by default simply adds the new follower.

Whenever a user sends a message, called a **tweet**, all their followers (and only their followers) receive the message. Twitter apps on phone or PC provide ways to filter and organize tweets, so people who follow many active posters can keep track of what is being said. Building a list of followers is normally a much

Figure 6.11   Twitter allows users to broadcast short status updates, and follow the thoughts and activities of others.

more gradual process than building a list of people to follow. Friends, family, and close colleagues already on Twitter will often follow a new user, but beyond that an audience is built primarily by broadcasting interesting tweets. The community is fairly quick to stop following posters who are boring or excessively chatty, and users who almost never post are simply not visible enough to gain followers.

COLLABORATING WITH WIKIS

Wiki software (*wiki* means "quick" in the Hawaiian language) provides a simple, standard way to collect, organize, and update information. Though the wiki concept has been on the Internet since 1995, it so far has not achieved universal recognition. You may have heard of or browsed Wikipedia, the online encyclopedia, but you may not have known that there are thousands of other wikis, public and private, that are actively in use.

Along with special software that allows the site to collect and store information, a wiki site also contains formatting instructions, called a **skin**, that create a standard browser layout for displaying the information. Each page on the site contains information about a single, specific topic; for example, at a wiki dedicated to collecting information about fruit, each wiki page would be a description of one kind of fruit.

A wiki has two major components that make it powerful as an information-sharing tool. First, its editing tools use very simple commands, so no knowledge of HTML is required for people to make effective, proper-looking entries. Second, it provides a simple way to link to other pages within the wiki and gracefully handles links to pages that do not yet exist. Contributors can create links to pages for related topics without concern for whether those pages exist. When a page is displayed, the wiki software checks all the links on the page, and links to any nonexistent pages are shown in red (see Figure 6.12). If you click on a red link, you are usually taken to a page that encourages you to create that page and enter new information for it.

Wiki sites excel at rapidly building information in a collaborative style. Unlike a typical Web site, where all content is controlled (and in many cases conceived and created) by one person or workgroup, a wiki's content is developed over time by a community of people who have expertise and an interest in the subject.

For example, imagine visiting a conventional travel Web site and reading a fellow traveler's description of Mt. Fuji in Japan. You might notice that no picture of Mt. Fuji exists on the Web page, and you remember that you have a very nice picture from a trip you made there last year. To help the site and add the picture, you'd have to send it (or an inquiry) to the webmaster of the site; even if your picture was well received, weeks might pass before it appeared, and if the webmaster didn't want to be bothered with posting the picture, it might never appear at all. But if you visited a travel wiki site, you could easily upload the image to the wiki and place it on the appropriate page yourself, immediately improving the quality of the information for other users.

The main risk for a wiki lies in preserving the integrity of its information. Allowing anyone to freely add and modify the information in a wiki leaves the door open for making maliciously incorrect modifications (called **vandalism**) or adding mistakenly wrong information. Though undoing vandalism is a simple process (wiki software can easily return a page to a previous version), fully public wikis are tempting enough targets for vandalism in some cases that undoing the damage is a full-time effort. Undoing

Figure 6.12 **Blue words and phrases are links to existing wiki pages; red words and phrases refer to pages that have not yet been created.**

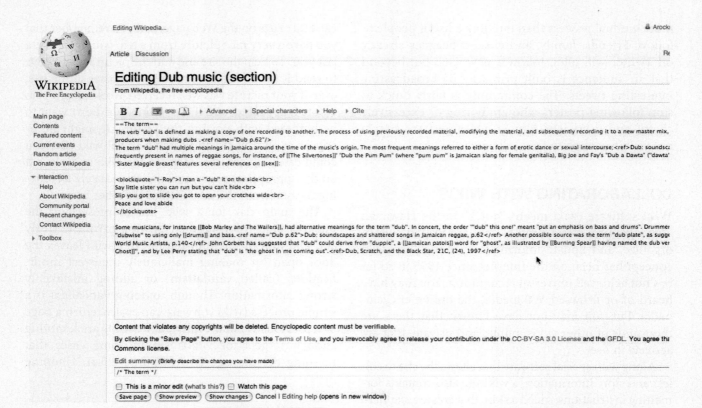

Figure 6.13   Users can edit wiki pages to immediately correct errors, add new information or improve the quality of what's already there.

well-intentioned mistakes can be tricky, because it requires an editor who has sufficient expertise to know a mistake is present.

To combat vandalism, some wiki owners require that users register in some way before being allowed to make changes. To reduce unintentional errors, some wiki communities regularly review all changes in some manner.

Wiki communities can be public or private. Private wikis are often found in businesses and other organizations, which use them as a way to build catalogs of policies and procedures to aid in sustaining and improving company practices. Public wikis exist to gather information about a rich variety of topics. People have created wikis for computer games to compile tips and strategies, for long-running TV shows to track the various characters and plot twists, and for a long list of scholarly and hobby interests.

If you find yourself in a group or company engaged in an effort to centralize and improve ways to build information about a subject, you might consider creating a wiki. There are different methods for establishing and maintaining a wiki to fit different levels of technical expertise and requirements for controlling the appearance, contents or access to the information.

If the information is to be public, you could create the wiki at a free hosting company such as Wikia (http://www.wikia.com). Wikia will allow you to immediately create a fully functional wiki site accessible as a subdomain of wikia.com, and the company will support and maintain the servers. In exchange, Wikia adds advertising boxes to your site over which you have little or no control; and because Wikia owns and maintains the servers and software, upgrades to new versions of the wiki software occur on their schedule, not yours.

If you have your own domain and site at a Web hosting company, you might be able to easily set up the wiki software on your Web site via tools provided by your domain hosting company. Many hosting companies provide a wiki software package, such as MediaWiki, as part of the standard Web tool package they give their customers. In that circumstance, creating the wiki is as easy as filling basic information in an online form (such as what to call it and what URL to use) and submitting the form to an automatic software process that sets the wiki up for you to use.

Lacking some kind of automatic setup, many people choose to install a wiki themselves on a home or business network. The project is normally straightforward and fairly simple, with a basic understanding of how to unpack and move files from place to place. MediaWiki, which is the software suite that runs Wikipedia and many other wiki sites, has a complete installation script that will successfully install a wiki in most situations. Be aware, however, that while installation of the wiki software is well automated and normally straightforward, if problems arise, you may quickly find yourself required to troubleshoot complex Web systems. Consider having an expert lined up to help if things go wrong.

As a supported alternative, PBWorks (http://pbworks.com) provides wiki software and site hosting as a business service. The most basic version of PBWorks software is free for non-commercial users. Businesses, schools and users who want extra security, sharing, and data management features pay an annual license to use the software. Similar to Wikia, PBWorks provides hosting and software support, but PBWorks does not add advertising to your site. PBWorks does, however, provide extra tools, such as a WSYWIG editor, for intuitive page creation that Wikia does not have. PBWorks gives site administrators control over security, passwords, user accounts, and page access, so the site can be more fully customized and controlled than it would be if you were using a strictly free hosting service.

SHARING DOCUMENTS AND MEDIA

Blogs, wikis, and bookmarking sites can combine text and visual elements together, but the greatest concentration of audiovisual information sharing takes place on specialty sites designed primarily to serve those types of media.

For video, YouTube is unparalleled in its capacity and variety. Founded in 2005, the service offered ordinary users a convenient way to store and share their video clips. Within months of the official start of the site, tens of thousands of videos were being uploaded every day. By 2010, more than 13 million hours of video had been uploaded. Billions of video views are watched around the world each day.

In its simplest form, YouTube provides a library of user-contributed video clips to watch. The clips cover almost any topic you might think of, including music videos and snippets of TV shows, family backyard

Figure 6.14   YouTube hosts video clips, amateur and professional, covering almost any subject you can think of.

scenes, tips on how to play an instrument or repair a computer, and an endless variety of people saying something important while looking into a video camera. Beyond the homespun videos and clips sampled from other productions, YouTube is also host to a rising number of business videos; many companies upload Web seminars, product announcements, and speeches given by company executives, and then refer interested parties to those clips. Some musicians and artists use YouTube as the primary method for airing new songs.

Given the vast number of clips that have been uploaded, the idea of browsing through the video catalog unaided is unimaginable. There are several different ways that people navigate the service's contents. Many people visit YouTube seeking a specific title or concept, and they can find videos by searching for words and phrases. The service also provides lists of recommended and most popular videos as determined by visitor ratings and a user's past viewing history.

As with other forms of social media, YouTube provides ways for users to customize their environment and experience. Users can create a free account on YouTube, which enables features such as the ability to "like" or "dislike" posted videos to show approval or disapproval; attach comments to video clips; and track what has been viewed, liked, and disliked in the past. Registered users can create a profile page, which includes basic information about the poster, recommendations of favorite videos, and easy access to the videos that the user has uploaded for viewing. Viewers who like a user's video clips can create a connection to that user, which YouTube calls subscribing to their channel, and receive automatic updates on their home page when new videos are added.

YouTube requires that its hosted videos be played with its own player, but the service has created a simple way for people to embed a mini-player in Web pages on other sites. Rather than simply publishing a link to a YouTube video that someone must follow, the user creates a clickable window on his or her own page that will play the video without leaving the original Web page. This feature makes it easy to share video clips directly inside Facebook, from wiki pages, and within blog entries.

While YouTube is the primary location for viewing video clips, other services and sites specialize in still photographs and art images. Flickr (http://www.flickr.com) is one of the major sites that provides hosting and sharing services for pictures.

Any Web site can host and display photographs, and all-encompassing sites like Facebook encourage users to upload pictures and create photo albums. As with other forms of social media, specialty sites often provide extra features that the general sites do

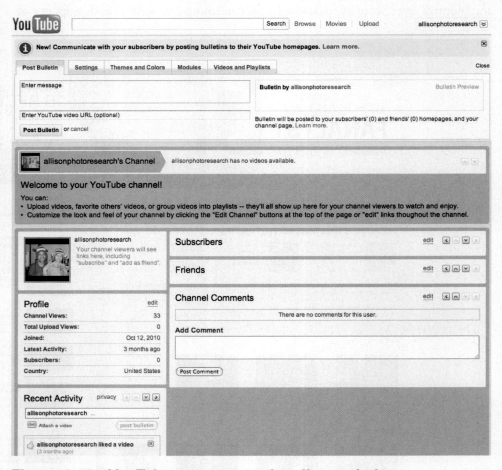

Figure 6.15   YouTube users can subscribe to their favorite video uploaders' channels, and keep track of new videos when they arrive.

Figure 6.16 Flickr provides many features for organizing and sharing photographs with friends and the general public.

vacation trip, for example), Flickr allows the poster to associate pictures with a map location, so viewers can get a better idea of where the pictures were taken. Viewers can leave comments, questions, and reactions for the user. Flickr has ways to edit photos within the site using an editor called Picnik, and users can connect with printing apps and services that can make paper prints of photographs.

not; and sometimes their attraction lies in the omission of features that its user community simply does not want. Users whose sole interest is photography may prefer Flickr specifically because it does not contain chat boxes, news feeds, and community game requests.

For the uploading user, Flickr's service follows the familiar social media pattern: create a free account, provide basic identifying information, upload pictures to the service, and create structures to organize and limit access to the pictures according to the poster's wishes. Flickr provides several different ways to upload pictures to the service, including Web browser, smart phone app, and e-mail. It makes organizing easy and effective by allowing the user to group pictures together into named sets and collections; security options are similarly straightforward, allowing the user to define groups of people and then declaring which groups are allowed to see which pictures or sets.

Flickr also provides extra features to make the presentation of pictures more interesting and effective for viewers. Keyword tags, titles, and descriptions can be added to pictures to help viewers find them. If pictures are related to a location (pictures from a recent

Fact Check

1. One of the first steps to making an effective, engaging Web site is
   a. to make an outline of the information to include
   b. to buy Web design software
   c. to create a new domain
2. In which situation would a blog be most appropriate?
   a. For telling consumers about a company's services
   b. For regularly sharing a person's thoughts about a particular subject
   c. For collecting and sharing many people's knowledge
3. What is a wiki site?
   a. A formal name for Wikipedia
   b. A Web site that collects information and uses a standard format for displaying it
   c. A Web site that publishes reference books such as dictionaries and encyclopedias

6.2 Online Income and E-Commerce

As you have already learned, professional, industrial, and retail companies rely heavily on computers and networks to improve their efficiency and reliability. The Internet is a valuable tool for providing access to corporate Web sites, delivering videoconferencing feeds to employees and customers, allowing collaboration between remote employees, and much more.

But the Internet can also be used to make money in a more direct fashion. The Web has become a global vehicle for **electronic commerce (e-commerce)**, creating new ways for businesses to interact with one another and their customers. E-commerce means doing business online, such as when a consumer buys a product over the Web instead of going to a store to buy it.

E-commerce technologies are rapidly changing the way individuals and companies do business. You can go online to buy a book, lease a car, shop for groceries, buy insurance, and rent movies. You can get pizza delivered to your door without picking up the phone and even check the status of your order while you wait.

But these kinds of transactions are only the tip of the e-commerce iceberg. In fact, the vast majority of e-commerce activities do not involve consumers at all. They are conducted among businesses, which have developed complex networking systems dedicated to processing orders, managing inventories, and handling payments.

E-COMMERCE: BUSINESS TO CONSUMER (B2C)

Tens of thousands of online businesses cater to the needs of consumers. These companies' Web sites provide information about products and services, take orders, receive payments, and provide on-the-spot customer service. Consumer-oriented e-commerce Web sites take many forms and run the gamut of products and services, but they can be divided into two basic categories: shopping sites and sites for managing personal finances and home services.

Online shopping is the process of buying a product or service through a Web site. Even if you have never shopped online, you have probably heard of Web sites such as Amazon.com and eBay.com. They are just two of many popular Web sites where consumers can buy all sorts of things.

What can you buy online? The list is almost limitless but includes cars and appliances, electronics and jewelry, clothes and books, fine wines, and rare collectible baseball cards. You can also buy the services of a lawyer, subscribe to newspapers and magazines, rent a car, book a hotel room, and order T-shirts to support your favorite online comic strip artist.

There are thousands of consumer Web sites, and each has its own look, feel, and approach to customer

Figure 6.17   Online stores commonly provide ways to easily select options such as colors and sizes.

Figure 6.18   B2C sites provide complete shopping services, from product selection to customer care.

satisfaction. But effective online shopping sites share a few essential features:

- **A catalog of the products and services that are for sale.** This can be a simple description of the product, or it can be a complex set of information that includes specifications, reviews, availability, and more. Some stores may have a single page of items to buy, and others may have millions.

- **A convenient way to pay for and arrange shipping for the purchased products.** Many sites provide multiple payment options, including credit cards, direct bank debits, and payment services that specialize in online sales. Shipping costs and methods are commonly provided at the time of purchase. Some of the larger retailers have formed arrangements with major shipping companies so that the customer can purchase a product and then track the shipment without having to find and enter shipping numbers.

- **Customer support.** Many retailers provide telephone, e-mail, and online chat services to answer questions, aid in purchasing, and resolve customer complaints and billing problems.

Shopping sites often have other features to make the shopping experience more convenient and pleasant for the online consumer. A **shopping cart** is an electronic holding bin where consumers can place items they want to purchase while they shop. The Web site's server keeps track of what has been placed in (or removed from) the shopping cart, so users are free to browse, choose items, and change their mind as they shop.

When you visit e-commerce sites, many of them store snippets of information about which parts of their sites you have visited. The information is stored in small files on your system known as **cookies** (short for "magic cookies," a networking term used to describe a special kind of data packet). Critics contend that cookie files are an intrusion because they can be used to track your browsing choices. However, legitimate e-commerce sites use them to make your shopping experience more efficient. By storing data about the products you've viewed or information you've requested during previous visits, the Web site can in some cases anticipate your needs or provide shortcuts for searching and viewing.

Sites with more than a few items for sale often provide search tools. Amazon.com, for example, provides the ability to search categories of products. Also, along with the search results, Amazon provides product suggestions based on similar searches and what other customers using your search criteria have purchased. Search tools are also available at Web sites that have established themselves as price comparison engines. These are a major part of the online shopping experience, even though they do not actually sell any products. For example, at MySimon.com, you can search for a wide variety of products by category or by specific model number. Users select the products that interest them, and MySimon lists the best prices currently offered at various online retailers.

To make shopping easier for repeat customers, Web vendors encourage shoppers to create accounts. This allows the retailer to securely store shipping and billing addresses as well as payment information, so that when consumers return for repeat purchases, far less clerical work is involved. Some sites even offer a **one-step checkout**, an option to purchase the contents of your shopping cart simply by clicking on a button on the screen, bypassing the need to fill out and confirm shipping and payment options.

The most common way to pay for an online purchase is to enter a credit or debit card number. In addition, many businesses of all sizes also accept funds from **online payment companies**. The largest of these is PayPal, a well-established payment company. PayPal handles both credit card processing for merchants and credit card payments for consumers. It also links to bank accounts to transfer funds directly to and from consumer and merchant accounts. If you run an e-commerce site and someone pays you via PayPal, your PayPal account is updated. You can move the money to your bank account or leave it in the PayPal system. When you pay someone else or buy goods of your own, money is debited from your PayPal account. If the PayPal account doesn't have sufficient funds for the transaction, PayPal contacts your bank to approve and process the payment.

Auction sites offer a twist on the traditional shopping experience. A familiar example is eBay, a large and comprehensive auction site that allows sellers to auction an endless variety of new and used goods. The site also provides an avenue for selling unusual services; for example, celebrities sometimes auction lunches or dinners with themselves to raise money for charity. Sellers post a starting price and length of time to run the auction, along with a description of the item to be sold and any special terms for the sale. EBay provides a system for buyers to bid on the items until the auction ends. It also uses a feedback system for rating buyers and sellers. As transactions are completed, buyer and seller each enter a one-line description of the selling experience for others to see. Sellers who deliver damaged goods and buyers who disappear without completing the transaction are quickly identified and banned from using the Web site. Repeat buyers and sellers jealously guard their reputation and generally strive to show they are reputable and reliable.

Many retailers that have already established a chain of stores in the real world use an online presence as a companion to their brick-and-mortar outlets. If you need office supplies and are far away from a city center, you can shop online at OfficeDepot.com and have the items shipped to your location. If you are near one of the Office Depot stores in your town, you can use the company's Web site to search for products, buy items, and have those items sent to your local store for you to pick up. This allows you to eliminate the extra shipping costs, in cases where you are willing to go to the store yourself, while still enjoying the convenience of shopping from your desk.

Online retailers have a huge advantage over brick-and-mortar stores when controlling costs. Warehouses can be located in extremely inexpensive parts of the world, while the local store has to pay far more rent for prime locations. Online retailers often have such high sales volumes that they can negotiate lower wholesale prices than local stores are able to receive. Many forms of Internet advertising are cheap or free, in contrast to the price of more traditional radio, TV, and print advertising. This places intense pressure on the storefront operation, and many businesses in direct competition with e-commerce companies go out of business because they cannot match the online prices.

Those that survive often do so by exploiting a niche that the online store cannot match: personal customer service. You can buy a great cordless screwdriver online, but the online store's customer support people won't be able to give you advice on how to install the drywall for your new bedroom. You can order pet supplies from a Web site, but the site probably won't help you teach your finicky cat how to like her new brand of food. Chat systems and tips on Web pages can address some customer issues, but many consumers prefer face-to-face conversations.

The efficiency of online transactions has been an attractive way for banks to reduce costs and add services. With **online banking**, customers can log in to bank Web sites, check rates and balances, and perform financial transactions. From the bank's perspective, maintaining a Web site is cheaper than paying enough tellers to serve all its customers face to face. From the customers' perspective, online banking lets them pay bills, order checks, and transfer money anytime around the clock, anywhere they have an Internet connection.

This type of mutually beneficial arrangement appears more and more frequently in the e-commerce world. A variety of service companies, including cable TV,

Figure 6.19 Many brick-and-mortar companies sell products online, and then deliver the products to your door from a local store.

phone companies, and other utilities, encourage their customers to establish regular **automatic payments**. Once the customer creates an online account and provides required information—typically their service account number, contact information, and bank account number—the companies can automatically deduct each month's bill from the customer's bank account, eliminating the hassle of making payments and the penalties for missing payments.

E-COMMERCE: BUSINESS TO BUSINESS

Beyond individual consumer transactions, e-commerce has given companies an entirely different way to conduct business. Using powerful Web sites and online databases, companies not only sell goods to individual consumers, but they also track inventory, order products, send invoices, and receive payments. Using e-commerce technologies, companies are rapidly forming online partnerships to collaborate on product designs, sales and marketing campaigns, and more. By giving one another access to their private networks, corporate partners access vital information and work together more efficiently.

Although millions of consumer transactions take place each day on the Web, **business-to-business (B2B) transactions** actually account for most of the money spent online. As its name implies, a business-to-business transaction is one that takes place between companies; consumers are not involved.

The concept of B2B transactions did not arrive with the Internet. In fact, companies were doing business electronically long before the rise of the Web, by using private networks and computer systems to handle transactions. But Internet technologies have made the process easier, more efficient, and available to virtually all businesses. Any financial transaction between two companies can be considered a B2B transaction and probably can be handled over the Internet. Consider some examples:

- A store orders an out-of-stock product from a distributor.
- A car manufacturer orders parts from a wide range of suppliers.
- A stock broker buys shares for a client by using an electronic exchange.
- A bank requests credit information from a major credit-reporting agency.

Figure 6.20 Online B2B connections help both a garden store and its suppliers manage inventory and ship products.

You can probably think of other examples, too. In any case, the transaction occurs whether it is handled on paper, through a private network, or via the Internet. It does not necessarily have to take place on the Web. However, Web-based technologies are making it easy for companies to handle huge volumes of transactions.

ADVERTISING ON THE INTERNET

You can't sell a product or service without customers, and you won't get customers if they don't know about what you are offering. That's true of traditional businesses, and it is just as true of companies using e-commerce technologies. Many tools are available for Internet-based companies to use in advertising.

One of the earliest types of advertising was simply the process of sending e-mails containing advertisements as their content. Such ads normally contain information about products and services, plus a link to a Web page to further explain the product or arrange for a sale. Advertisers would either create their own mailing lists based on e-mail addresses they discovered or were given, or they would purchase lists of e-mail addresses from list companies. E-mail continues to be used heavily for advertising, both to reach new customers and to market new offerings to existing customers. Legitimate

companies work to ensure that their mailings comply with legal requirements for spam prevention.

One of the common methods of advertising on Web pages is the use of **banner ads**, thin rectangular advertising boxes commonly placed across the top of a Web page. All visitors to the Web page are greeted with the advertising message as one of their first visual impressions. The ads can contain simple text, artwork, or even animation to gain visibility.

Web browsers can open new windows to display information without changing what is showing in the current browser window. This ability eventually created a form of advertising called a **pop-up ad**, where Web site owners would create an advertisement window that "popped up" to cover the content of the Web site, forcing the site visitor to view the ad.

Pop-up ads became the bane of the Web surfer's existence for a time, as many sites on the Web began displaying the intrusive advertising. Abuse of the technology further developed to where an attempt to close a pop-up ad would spawn a new one for the user to contend with. Surfing was becoming a strange video game of "kill the pop-up window," as users tried to close all the advertising windows before new ones could appear. Independent software developers, along with the browser companies, created utilities called **pop-up blockers**, which intercepted and denied the requests to create pop-up windows. Back under control, Web surfing once again became useful, and advertisers had to look to new technologies to gain visibility.

Many Web sites are experimenting with other forms of direct advertising. One of these is a softer take on pop-up advertising that is meant to be more appealing: when a visitor first arrives at a Web site, an advertising screen is loaded and displays the ad's content along with an option for the user to close the window to bypass the ad and proceed to the requested page. While this method forces the user to see the ad rather than the requested Web page, bypassing the ad is easy, and the ads are displayed only once, rather than at every new page provided. Other sites provide alternative forms of banner ads, integrating the advertisements in various places on the Web pages and using multimedia advertising content to make the ads more visible and appealing.

While early advertising agreements often relied on the traditional practice of charging a certain amount of money for placement of the ad, advertisers quickly moved to a payment model called **pay-per-click**. Web browsers and servers, working together, can log and count the number of times pages and ads are accessed. Pay-per-click means the advertisers pay for their ads only when a Web site visitor clicks on the ad to go to the advertiser's site.

Google created a new form of advertising called AdWords, which combines the company's popular and comprehensive search engine with advertising to create a pay-per-click advertising model that advertisers can customize. AdWords users create lists of keywords and search phrases relevant to their product or service offering; for example, an insurance agent in Portland, Oregon, might define search phrases like "insurance agent Portland" and "good life insurance Portland." Whenever Google processes a search request, it places a list of advertisements along the side of the list of search results, where the ads directly correspond to what the user requests. Advertisers pay per click, but they determine the amount per click they want to pay. Higher amounts give them better visibility by placing them closer to the top in the list of advertisements; very low amounts have the opposite effect. Google estimates, based on the popularity of the search term, how much the advertiser needs to allocate per click in order to have an ad appear in the first page of search results. Advertisers using the same search term in effect begin to bid against each other for more favorable placement. Advertisers can also set a maximum number of clicks per day they will fund; if enough visitors click on an advertisement to reach that threshold, Google simply stops displaying the ad for the rest of the day.

Advertising is a natural fit with the social media practice of sharing large amounts of personal information and activity. If you are at least an occasional shopper on sites like Amazon.com, you may have noticed that when you visit the site, you are greeted with ads and suggestions for products that match the types of products you have shopped for in the past. For example, if you buy a lot of computer games from Amazon, you will very likely see ads for the latest release of several game titles when you visit the store's site.

Amazon, Facebook, Google, and many other sites regularly use your personal data and information about your online habits to provide you with matching advertisements that you are more likely to notice and act upon. Most of the time, the information they use for targeting their advertising comes directly from the user, either unwittingly or eagerly. Shopping sites track the products you browse and the search terms you use, and then attempt to guess your interests by combining

> **"Many Web sites are experimenting with other forms direct advertising."**

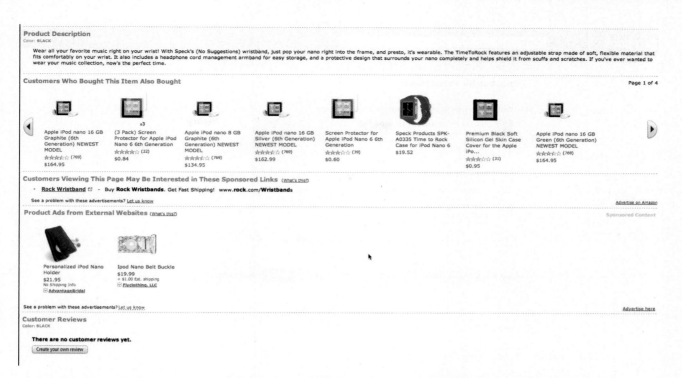

Figure 6.21 Amazon.com and other online shopping sites uses social media and past behavior to provide more relevant advertising to their customers.

that data with the behavior patterns shown by other shoppers. Social media sites rely heavily on personal data such as location, age, sex, hobbies, preferences, favorite stores, and all of that data for a person's best friends as well. All that information and more is typically provided by social network users in exchange for free access to the service, in the form of an account registration form and profile page.

By increasing the chances that people will act favorably to ads, online retailers are more likely to make sales, and online ad hosting sites can charge their advertisers a higher price than sites that simply provide random, less-effective advertising. People who respond favorably to advertising in general may find that this form of targeted advertising provides a more fun experience when shopping or using online social tools. Those who find advertising to be intrusive and unwanted may react even more negatively to the reminder that their actions are being monitored, and that the "free" access they have to Web 2.0 sites is being purchased with information rather than cash.

Unfortunately, just as e-commerce is a big business, so is fraud, and there are unethical practices in online advertising to support that endeavor as well. Advertisements themselves can be used to deliver malware payloads by enticing users to click on the ad, thus unknowingly agreeing to install the malware on their systems. Though there are an endless variety of

ways this can happen, there are two common types of ads that you should always avoid: ads or pop-up windows that claim to have found malware or system problems on your computer; and ads that have no real purpose other than to get you to click on them.

Malware protection should always be obtained and installed directly from a trusted and major source. Accepting a free malware scan (or variations such as, "This tool will fix registry problems and make your computer run twice as fast!") will most likely install the malware you were hoping to avoid. Ads such as, "You are the 100,000th visitor—click to receive your prize!" or "Punch the monkey and win!" may install malware, or they may simply be trying to unethically drive traffic to a Web site; either way, it's best to avoid them.

The unethical use of personal data is as great a concern for users as is malicious advertising. Filling in your name, address, phone number, and e-mail address in order to access a site may not seem important, but an unethical Web service can use that information to make a great deal of money. Many bulk advertisers and telemarketing firms highly prize personal contact information that is voluntarily given and are willing to pay dozens or even hundreds of dollars per name to acquire that data.

Many legitimate online sites have strict privacy policies to demonstrate that they will not sell your information, but others do not. When faced with a

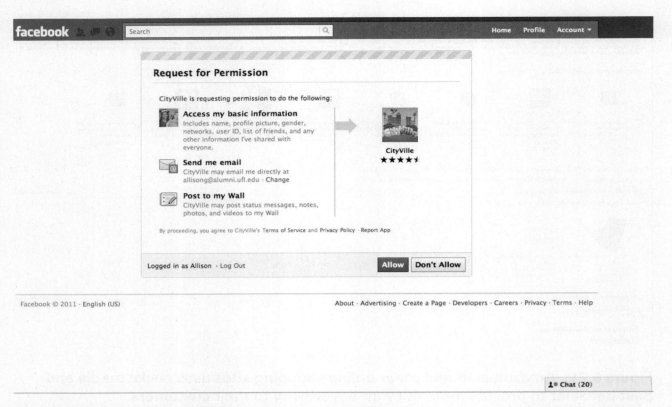

Request for Permission

CityVille is requesting permission to do the following:

Access my basic information
Includes name, profile picture, gender, networks, user ID, list of friends, and any other information I've shared with everyone.

Send me email
CityVille may email me directly at allisong@alumni.ufl.edu · Change

Post to my Wall
CityVille may post status messages, notes, photos, and videos to my Wall

CityVille
★★★★⯪

By proceeding, you agree to CityVille's Terms of Service and Privacy Policy · Report App

Logged in as Allison · Log Out   **Allow** **Don't Allow**

Facebook © 2011 · English (US)   About · Advertising · Create a Page · Developers · Careers · Privacy · Terms · Help

👤● Chat (20)

Figure 6.22   Facebook apps often request or require access to your personal data in order to run. Be cautious; not every app is guaranteed to treat your data with respect.

form for personal data, consider the source that is asking. When an online retailer needs your name and address, it makes sense; how else will they know where and to whom to send the products you purchase? But when a free IQ test (that you found by clicking a Web site ad) wants your e-mail address and cell phone number in order to mail you the results, think twice about providing that sensitive information. Better still, think once and then quit the test without providing the requested data.

Even reputable social networking sites may not fully control the safety of your data. Facebook apps—the programs that you find and run in order to play social games and take quizzes—commonly ask you for permission to access your personal data so they can personalize your play experience and notify your friends of your in-game deeds and needs. Though the apps run within Facebook and therefore seem legitimate, Facebook cannot verify and monitor the contents of all Facebook apps. It is very easy to cross ethical boundaries and invite people to send snuggly teddy bear pictures to their friends in exchange for large amounts of personal data that can be mined and sold, and a great deal of information can be obtained before the app is caught and removed.

SEARCH ENGINE OPTIMIZATION

As people first turned to the Web to produce and seek information on practically every subject, search engines were developed to find and catalog as much information as possible. People quickly learned to rely on search sites as those sites demonstrated that they could effectively gather and sort most of the content being produced for the Web.

For their part, search engine companies developed complex methods to interpret and return the raw data found on the Web. By itself, a request for "leather shoes" might relate to a hundred shoe manufacturers around the world, ten thousand online stores that sell shoes, a thousand articles in newspapers about the new U.S. president's favorite brand of shoes, and a hundred sites with copies of an audio file of a blues song called, "Old Leather Shoes." Search companies had to find ways to prioritize all these different resources and meanings so that their users would be more likely to quickly find what they were seeking. To accomplish this, search companies considered many factors, including the popularity of competing sites, the amount of information on various Web sites, and what people clicked on when presented with similar searches in the past.

It didn't take long for Web site owners to realize the importance of appearing at the top of the list of a search engine's results. People use search engines not to find hundreds of possible sites to visit, but rather the one or two sites that will give them what they want, whether what they want is a new pair of shoes or an online dictionary. The best shoe store in the country may struggle to find customers if their site fails to appear on the first page or two of search engine results; conversely, if they could guarantee the first-place spot in the search results every time, they would always get the first chance to impress and sell shoes to customers who are looking for that product.

In order to get better placement in search results, Web site owners needed to know what factors were being considered and used by the search engine companies. However, the search companies had no interest in revealing their methods, so they provided little assistance beyond general suggestions that Web site owners should make their sites useful to visitors and rich in content.

In the absence of specific information from search companies, the practice of **search engine optimization (SEO)** was born. SEO is the process of analyzing Web site contents and search results, and determining the ideal configuration for a Web site that will raise its position in search results. SEO analysts look at sites that consistently appear at the top of search results, and compare their structure and contents both to each other and to sites that are not ranked as high. The goal is to identify specific structures, patterns, and relationships that cause a site to be well regarded by search engines, as well as to identify contents or structures that the search engine actively distrusts or avoids. With that knowledge, Web designers can modify sites to make them more appealing and therefore, hopefully more visible to users who make relevant search requests.

Search engines are constantly being modified to better identify useful sites and ignore malicious or poorly constructed sites. This is due in part to a continuous evolution in the type of information being added to the Web. For example, the Web 2.0 practice

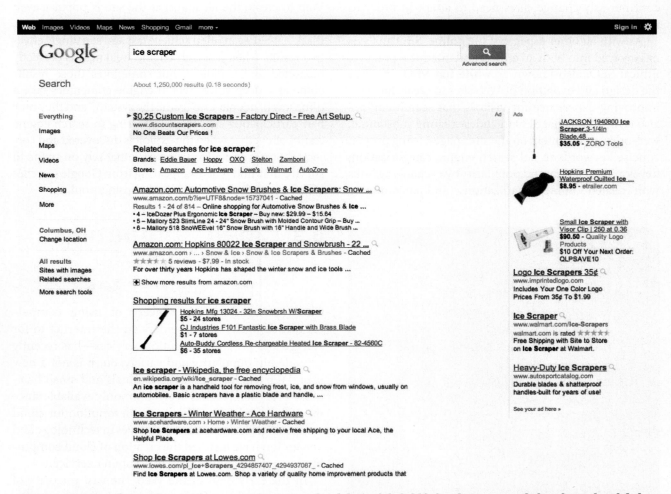

Figure 6.23   Search engine results can decide which Web sites are visited and which are overlooked; site owners have good reason to make their content appealing to search engines.

of user-provided recommendations for certain sites and pages creates a valuable opportunity for search engines to correlate site popularity and the recommendations within a specific user's community.

Modifications are also added to counter attempts to manipulate search engine results. If the search company determines that results are being deliberately or unwittingly skewed to favor sites because of their appeal to the search engine rather than their actual content, it may modify the engine's behavior to compensate.

SEO analysts, therefore, are generally in demand not just once during site creation, but as a permanent part of an online enterprise. As search engines continuously change, sites need to adapt in order to remain well placed.

As with all other aspects of life online, SEO analysis has evolved into both an ethical and unethical practice. Ethical SEO, also known as **white hat SEO**, involves the design and evolution of Web sites to create an ever-improving experience for visitors that search engines also favor. White hat SEO includes creating substantial, well-organized content on the site's pages; using proper, concise keywords to aid search engine categorization; developing visibility and popularity by exchanging links with related online organizations; and encouraging

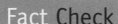

Figure 6.24   White hat SEO analysts may not look like heroes, but they work hard to make Web sites appealing without crossing tempting ethical boundaries.

visitors to independently link and recommend the site. As a general rule of thumb, white hat SEO has less immediate effect on search engine results, but over time it will result in a more favorable and more consistent search rating.

Black hat SEO, the unethical side of optimization, creates structures on Web sites designed to exploit search engine preferences or weaknesses. If a search engine prefers to see many links on a Web site, for example, black hat methods may create thousands of links at the end of a site's main page that are only visible to the search engine. If the search engine changes its preference to sites that are heavily linked by others, the site maintainer can place thousands of referring links around the Web to create the illusion that the site is popular even though none of the referrers are real users of the site. Black hat SEO can often achieve fast and startlingly effective results when a search engine weakness is correctly identified and exploited, but sometimes those results come at a steep price. Search engine companies take a dim view of people who "game the system," and they may ban participating sites from appearing in search engine results altogether when the exploit is discovered and corrected. Stores and advertising sites that rely on traffic to survive may find that disappearing from Google searches effectively ends their ability to do business online.

Fact Check

1. What is the usual way to calculate the price charged for Internet advertising?
   a. The number of Web pages on the advertiser's Web site
   b. How often Internet users click on the advertisement
   c. The size of the advertisement relative to the size of the Web page
2. White hat SEO is a term that describes
   a. an operating system that competes with Red Hat Linux.
   b. ethical practices for improving a Web site's search engine ratings.
   c. a Wild West themed computer game.

6.3 Cloud Computing for Individuals and Businesses

Cloud computing—the concept of using computers owned by service providers on the Internet to for storage and program execution services—has recently exploded in popularity and variety, but it is not a new idea. Web site hosting for individuals and small businesses, for example, has been commonly available since the 1990's, and it handily fits the description for cloud computing. However, recent changes in technology and perception have justified the creation of cloud computing as an independent class of computer service.

In the early days of the Web, the vast majority of users accessed the Web and other Internet services by way of a modem that transmitted data by using sound across telephone wires. Such connections were made at speeds that were orders of magnitude slower than the high-speed cable and fiber optic links that are common today; they were also fairly unreliable, with disconnections in mid-transmission being a fairly common occurrence. Such connections were at worst unsuitable, and at best inefficient, for supporting the continuous transfer of large amounts of information back and forth between a user's computer and a server residing on the Internet.

Now, however, with fast, reliable connections from practically anywhere, and computing devices from PCs to smart phones that are designed specifically to move data back and forth, computer hardware, networks, and operating systems are far better suited for high-volume data traffic. Along with the improved environment, more people than ever use multiple computing devices in multiple locations, creating substantial pressure to provide better ways to have one copy of data and software that can be accessed by a user no matter where they go.

STORING YOUR DATA IN THE CLOUD

As you learned in Chapter 4, cloud services can be used for storing data both for individuals and organizations. Cloud-based data storage generally serves one or more of the following three needs: backing up

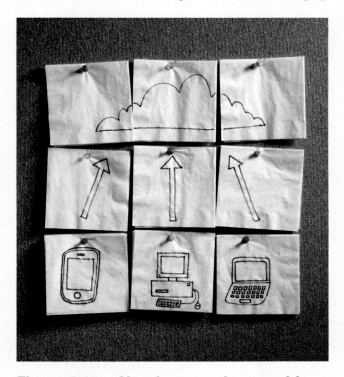

Figure 6.25 Cloud computing provides the ability to store data and run programs in a central location so users everywhere can access the same data and software.

and archiving data, providing a central location for data retrieval, and enabling the collaborative creation and modification of information.

Most people understand that backing up documents and data to keep them safe is an important process. Despite that understanding, however, many people and businesses do not actually perform data backups on a regular and comprehensive basis. Ideally, new data should be backed up shortly after it is created, and backups should be stored in a remote location. Failing to make backups leaves data vulnerable to loss in the event of something as simple and ordinary as a hard disk fault; even if regular backups are performed, theft and natural disasters can cause locally stored backup disks to disappear or become ruined and useless.

Cloud-based storage can provide a simple and effective way to accomplish this task. Services like Carbonite, as discussed in Chapter 4, and Mozy (http://mozy.com) provide the ability for individual users and businesses to regularly and automatically back up their data to a cloud-resident location. The services provide strong encryption for stored data to ensure that even if sites are hacked, user data cannot be exploited. Data centers are maintained to always be available, and services let users retrieve data on any machine at any time.

Prices range greatly between services, but most services have some kind of sliding scale that increases with the amount of data being stored. Users can save money by restricting backups to include only the data that is necessary to recover in the event of a local loss; backing up a complete hard drive will archive many unnecessary files, including the operating system, program files and temporary data files such as the Web browser cache. Users can also reduce file size with compression utilities, for large file libraries that are meant to be saved simply as archives.

While data backup services focus simply on saving copies of files and allowing users to retrieve the data if needed, companies like DropBox provide an additional synchronization service. DropBox uses cloud-based storage to archive files that its subscribers upload. When new data arrives for storage, the service saves it and then distributes copies to a list of desktop and mobile devices supplied by the user. DropBox also allows user-specified friends or co-workers to share and modify the data, exporting changes to the device list as they are saved.

Google Docs stores documents on its servers, but its focus is on collaborative work rather than data storage. Google imposes low limits on document size and overall storage space, though additional storage can be purchased on a sliding scale.

Figure 6.26   Cloud storage companies can use strong data encryption to ensure that user data cannot be used even if stolen from their sites.

After signing up to participate on Google Docs, users have the ability to create new documents such as text files, spreadsheets, slide presentations, and data entry forms. Users can also upload existing files from several common applications, such as Microsoft Word and Adobe Illustrator, and view those documents online in a Google–supplied viewer. Existing files whose format is recognized by Google can be converted to Google Docs' own format and edited directly within a browser window by extensions that are automatically supplied by Google when a user opens a document.

Documents that are uploaded or created within the service are assumed to be private, meaning that only the owner can see and change them. At the user's direction, Google can make specific documents visible to people, whether or not they are Google Docs subscribers, and allow those additional users to view and modify the documents. As with most collaborative editing services, multiple users can view and change a document at the same time; Google receives changes from each user, coordinates the changes and updates all participants' view of the document so that everyone's changes are visible within seconds of being made. Along with editing documents, readers can attach comments and review tags to a document, providing suggestions and asking questions without actually changing the contents of the document.

Though Google Docs does not provide DropBox's facility for distributing new files to multiple loca-tions, any user with access to a document can retrieve it manually from Google's storage.

RUNNING APPLICATIONS IN THE CLOUD

Traditionally, software for PCs has been distributed one copy at a time to one user at a time. The user installs the software and then has a local copy to run. While this model, with some changes, has worked well, there are some circumstances for which it is less than ideal; for example:

Software updates.   It is inevitable that after software is created and released to users, it needs to be updated with bug fixes and new features. Many software companies now check for and update software versions over the Internet, but even when done automatically, software sellers may not be able to guarantee that all users have precisely the same software version. Even if the software version is the same for every user, each user can have a different environment on their PC, creating challenges for support specialists and programmers trying to track down the source of a software-related problem.

Collaboration compatibility.   Multiple users sharing documents must all use software that can work with a common document format. If one person on the team has old software, they may not be able to work with newer document formats in use by the rest of the team, requiring extra accommodation or expense to find common ground.

Software piracy.   Some software companies lose a great deal of money when programs are shared between users. Copy protection schemes and methods are strictly temporary measures for protecting software; they do not reliably guard against software piracy, and in some cases, they can interfere with the ability of legitimate software owners to run their programs.

Installation inefficiency.   Most people who use tax software use it once at tax time and don't think about it again until the times comes to buy the latest software version for the next round of taxes. Yet those users must still download or purchase the software take the time to install it, and allocate another chunk of hard drive space for it, just as they would for a program that they planned to use all year long.

Multi-computer access.   Some software companies do not allow a legitimate owner to install their copy on more than one computer, preventing that

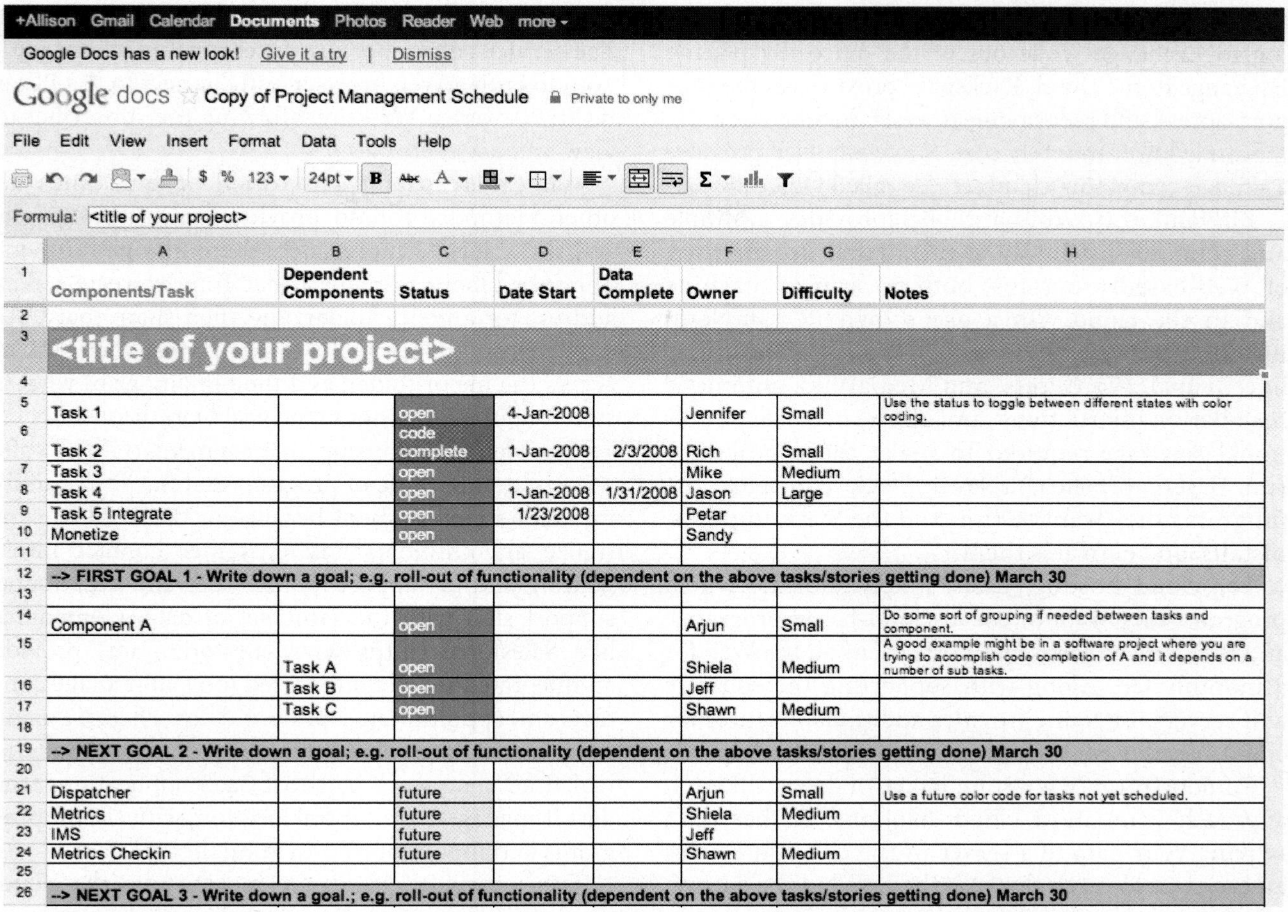

	A	B	C	D	E	F	G	H
1	Components/Task	Dependent Components	Status	Date Start	Data Complete	Owner	Difficulty	Notes
2								
3	<title of your project>							
4								
5	Task 1		open	4-Jan-2008		Jennifer	Small	Use the status to toggle between different states with color coding.
6	Task 2		code complete	1-Jan-2008	2/3/2008	Rich	Small	
7	Task 3		open			Mike	Medium	
8	Task 4		open	1-Jan-2008	1/31/2008	Jason	Large	
9	Task 5 Integrate		open	1/23/2008		Petar		
10	Monetize		open			Sandy		
11								
12	--> FIRST GOAL 1 - Write down a goal; e.g. roll-out of functionality (dependent on the above tasks/stories getting done) March 30							
13								
14	Component A		open			Arjun	Small	Do some sort of grouping if needed between tasks and component.
15		Task A	open			Shiela	Medium	A good example might be in a software project where you are trying to accomplish code completion of A and it depends on a number of sub tasks.
16		Task B	open			Jeff		
17		Task C	open			Shawn	Medium	
18								
19	--> NEXT GOAL 2 - Write down a goal; e.g. roll-out of functionality (dependent on the above tasks/stories getting done) March 30							
20								
21	Dispatcher		future			Arjun	Small	Use a future color code for tasks not yet scheduled.
22	Metrics		future			Shiela	Medium	
23	IMS		future			Jeff		
24	Metrics Checkin		future			Shawn	Medium	
25								
26	--> NEXT GOAL 3 - Write down a goal.; e.g. roll-out of functionality (dependent on the above tasks/stories getting done) March 30							

Figure 6.27 Google Docs provides document storage and browser-based programs for people to edit and change their documents.

user from running the program at their desk and then shifting to their laptop to continue working while commuting home. There may also be installation restrictions on one computer; some companies do not allow their employees to install additional programs beyond what the company provides, preventing the user from adding the program to a work computer.

High-speed Internet connections and powerful servers have made practical the development of cloud-based software. Also called **software as a service (SaaS)**, companies now provide a wide array of programs for users that are run on the service company's computers instead of the user's PC or mobile device. The SaaS program uses a standard PC program like a browser to display output and receive user commands and data, performing all the data storage and processing work on their own servers.

Cloud-based software handily addresses the problems with traditional software distribution listed above. The cloud software company can then have one version of the software running on one type of server environment, making software updates and diagnosis vastly simpler. Since they control access to the software, piracy is no longer an issue. Users of cloud software do not use extra installation and disk space resources. And any program that can run the user interface can access the cloud-hosted software, even in restricted installation environments.

As you may have already guessed, services like Google Docs are examples of SaaS and cloud computing. Documents are created, edited, and stored on Google's servers, using organization and editing tools that are provided as part of the browser window that is loaded when users visit the site. Any computer that can run a browser can access the information on the server, making both the data and the software independent of the hardware.

Many other services exist to provide SaaS. The Web hosting company Rackspace (http://www.rackspace.com) provides support for a Microsoft Exchange server for a monthly fee. Exchange is a program that handles employee e-mail, calendar, and contact information. In the past, Exchange would normally be run on a company's own servers, requiring support for those computers as well as security and support for employees connecting to Exchange while out of the office. By placing Exchange in the cloud, Rackspace provides all the support, access, and security measures, potentially at a significantly lower monthly cost. Microsoft itself provides a similar, competing cloud service called Office 365.

BitNami (http://bitnami.org) provides a simple and comprehensive way to install and use an array of Web-based programs, both on a local machine and in the cloud. On a user's own PC, BitNami installs a BitNami Stack, which is a set of programs like Drupal, WordPress, and MediaWiki, automatic installation instructions, and all the necessary additional software required to make those programs run. Users of the BitNami Stack can pick the programs they want to run, and the Stack unpacks, installs, and activates them.

For cloud hosting, users simply indicate which programs they want to use as cloud-based programs, and BitNami activates and hosts them on the Web for a monthly fee. Along with supporting the software and servers, BitNami provides additional features for cloud-based users such as automatic data backups.

Tonido (http://www.tonido.com) takes a different approach from most cloud solutions. Rather than moving your data to a server in the cloud, it creates an easy way to reach through the cloud to the data on your computer.

The company provides software that catalogs files and folders on a user's PC, and manages an Internet

connection from the PC to the online Tonido service. The service subscriber can access their account with Tonido with a Web browser and connect to the PC as if the PC were a Web site, allowing the subscriber to view and use their files.

While this capability has existed for some time with other methods, Tonido provides an easy interface, and the ability to more safely share files with others. The subscriber can request that Tonido create a Web address for a file or folder, and then share that URL with others. The invited users simply use that URL to access the file or folder, and the remainder of what is stored on the PC is not made visible to the visitors.

Customer relationship management (CRM) software is another type of program that has fit naturally in a cloud environment because of the need to centralize appointments and customer contact information, and to support mobile sales and deskbound support staff with the same set of data. Companies like Salesforce (http://www.salesforce.com) provide an integrated set of cloud-based tools to manage contacts and appointments, price and data sheets, e-mail, notes and data gathered during lead generation, and real-time chat. As with most SaaS applications, the data is managed in a central location, with simple programs and mobile apps providing the interface.

Even computer games are moving into the cloud. Services such as Gaikai and OnLive are working to develop reliable, cloud-based services that allow anyone with any computer or TV to immediately play games that normally would require a dedicated console or high-end PC. The game itself is run at the host's server facility, with only the final display and user control input residing at the user's computer. A high-speed, reliable Internet connection provides a play experience that many users find enjoyable, though there is still much work to be done to provide a delay-free experience for all users.

PLACING YOUR BUSINESS IN THE CLOUD

As cloud computing becomes more and more common, all sorts of technology-using companies are exploring the viability of moving most or all of their data management and business-related computing tasks from their desks and into the cloud. There are

Figure 6.28 High-speed Internet connections, even for mobile devices, make cloud computing a viable choice practically everywhere.

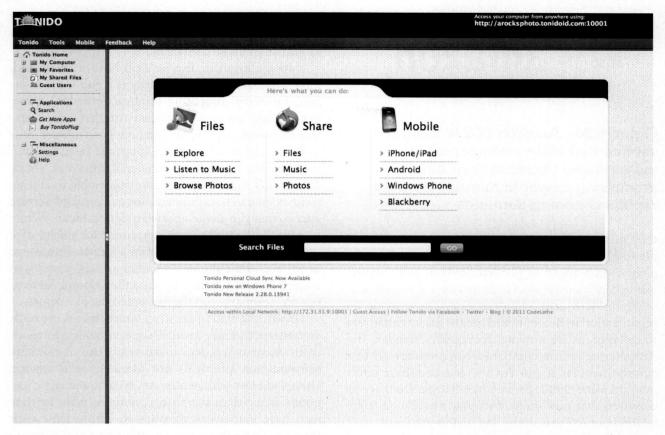

Figure 6.29 Tonido allows a user to connect to their computer through the cloud to use and retrieve data; users can assign Web URLs to files and folders and share them safely with friends.

advantages and disadvantages in all cloud-based solutions; ultimately, each user and business must decide on the most effective solution.

One of the compelling arguments in favor of cloud-based computing is cost. Purchasing computers to act as servers and full-fledged workstations can be expensive; and once purchased, they must be put somewhere and powered. People must be hired (or existing people must take time) to maintain software and repair and replace hardware when it breaks. Expensive software packages may need to be purchased each time a new employee is hired, and software usually requires upgrading from time to time. If workers are sharing data, then some kind of central storage hardware may be required, and companies may need to pay to archive and store data as time goes by.

Worse still, hardware is sometimes needed only for a short while. A company may hire interns or temporary contractors; if computer hardware is required for them, it may sit idle after the temporary job is done.

By using cloud services, a company can exchange its own up-front and maintenance costs for a monthly or annual subscription for similar online services.

Servers can be replaced by cloud storage, and the company's floor or desk space can be used for something else. Instead of employing local support technicians, the cloud company provides a 24/7 data center and is under contract to restart and repair systems as needed. By switching to cloud-based document systems, the company no longer needs to purchase individual copies of software. Companies that have seasonal or cyclic work can adjust their subscription for more storage and performance when times are busy, and then reduce their cloud costs when projects are complete.

Amazon, with its Amazon Web Services (http://aws.amazon.com), provides a wide array of cloud computing services for small companies and large corporations, and makes an especially compelling case for e-commerce and other types of business that are vulnerable to activity spikes tied to specific events or times. The Amazon Elastic Compute Cloud (Amazon EC2) provides a way to scale processing power up and down in minutes by adding or removing servers in minutes in response to increasing or decreasing demand. A company selling widgets online cannot afford to have their servers become overloaded and crash when

Figure 6.30 Amazon EC2 is a cloud service that allows companies to increase and decrease their online processing power in minutes to meet rapidly changing demands.

they are featured on an evening TV program and people rush to the Web to buy one. Conversely, the company cannot afford to run hundreds of extra servers just in case their product is shown on TV someday.

Along with cost, cloud services can provide an organization with a standard means for its employees to collaborate. By moving document, calendar, and data sharing online, companies can provide a no-fuss environment for employees to create and share information; some cloud services like Google Docs are so common that new employees may already be fully-trained in their use on the day they begin work.

Cloud solutions also provide a disciplined and comprehensive approach to data archival that many companies and individuals lack. Many people simply do not bother to back up their data; of those who do, a good portion do not do it automatically and regularly, nor do they maintain off-site copies of data for disaster recovery. Most cloud-based storage and collaboration services provide some kind of automatic backup and recovery service, and often back up changes as they are being made rather than once every day or two.

As with all things, cloud computing cannot solve every technology problem a business might have, and there are disadvantages and risks in cloud computing as well.

One of the biggest liabilities in cloud computing is the need to connect to the Internet. If you want to bring documents with you on a weekend trip into the wilderness to work in peace, it is relatively easy to plan ahead and download what you need to your tablet before you head into the desert where the Internet cannot be found. But if you are sitting at work and your Internet modem malfunctions, the connection to your cloud service and that document you needed to finish within the hour similarly vanishes. If you are using Tonido to access files on your home computer and your computer loses power and switches off, then you will likely find yourself without access to your data until you get home and turn your computer back

on. The advantage of moving data offsite to a central location can become a major liability if that central location cannot be contacted.

Data security can also be a problem in the cloud, though realistically data security is a risk to be managed for every computing solution. Storage facilities that do not encrypt their data (or that use easily-compromised encryption methods), no matter how well they claim to be protected against intruders, put sensitive data at extreme risk. Even if data is encrypted, storage and sharing services are vulnerable to at least some degree to hacker intrusions or denial-of-service attacks that can make accessing data difficult. While keeping out intruders, extra security for offsite data can occasionally cause trouble for a forgetful employee or worker, as the storage site refuses to allow access to a user's own documents because they cannot remember the new password they invented the day before.

Finally, the cloud may simply not possess the tools or features that are needed for a company to move there. Some companies make heavy use of specialty software that simply is not available as a service. Others are low-tech enterprises that do not use computers other than for an occasional e-mail, or they may have employees who are so comfortable with their existing regime that changing to cloud software would prove an unacceptable disturbance. But cloud technology provides such a compelling solution for so many people and companies that eventually, most users may rely on some form of cloud service for at least part of their computing needs.

Fact Check

1. Cloud computing provides which of the following?
   a. Software you can run without an Internet connection
   b. Data storage and software execution hosted by Internet service companies
   c. Convenient weather forecasts on your smart phone
2. Software as a Service (SaaS) provides computer programs
   a. that run much faster than conventional software.
   b. that are free to install and run.
   c. that are hosted on an Internet server, with the local computer used only for input and output.

IN
Summary

- The term social media defines online services and sites that allow and encourage people to share their thoughts and activities with others via create text, audio, and visual contributions.

- Social media encompasses several subcategories of services that include social networking for sharing all manner of information; social bookmarking for expressing preferences about Web content; blogging for primarily text-based communication; wikis for collaborative information gathering; media sharing for publishing audio, picture and video files; social reviews for providing opinions of goods and services; and social events for using online services to organize face-to-face events.

- Web pages are created using a language called HyperText Markup Language (HTML). HTML uses special tags to tell browser software how to display the text elements of a Web page. A cascading style sheet (CSS) can be used to provide additional layout and design information for the Web page.

- Social networking sites like Facebook provide users with a way to build groups of people with which to share thoughts, ideas, pictures, and links to Web sites. Users can play games with each other, comment on the things that others post, and express preferences for things they see.

- Social bookmarking allows users to tag Web pages that they like, build lists of their favorite pages, share their favorites with others, and see what sites are popular with the bookmarking community.

- A blog is a special kind of Web site that specializes in providing essays and articles to readers. Blog entries can be reviewed chronologically or retrieved based on keywords that the author assigns to them. Micro-blogging services like Twitter encourage users to broadcast short, single-thought expressions.

- A wiki is a Web site that contains special software for cataloging, updating, and displaying information in a uniform way. Wikis are created by companies, organizations, or communities of people who want to accumulate and share information about a specific theme. A wiki contains a set of pages, each of which discusses a single, specific topic related to the overall theme of the wiki.

- Electronic commerce (e-commerce) means doing business online. E-commerce can be conducted between consumers and businesses, or among businesses or other organizations with no consumer involvement.

- Advertising products and services via the Internet has become commonplace. Advertisers commonly use one or more of the following types of ad delivery: e-mail messages containing advertising, a banner or other advertising box displayed as part of a Web site, or search engine advertising that is displayed as part of search results.

- Search engine optimization (SEO) is the process of adjusting the layout and contents of a Web site to make major search engine companies view it more favorably, giving the site greater prominence in search results provided to searching users.

- Cloud computing refers to services that provide data storage, collaboration, and software execution hosting services via the Internet. Cloud storage allows users to archive data to servers at a data center and to retrieve them from any computer or location for updating. With documents stored on the cloud company's servers, users can often create and edit the same document simultaneously for greater efficiency. Software programs can be executed on cloud computers, freeing users from the need to purchase and install copies of the software on individual machines.

Key Terms

auction sites, 242
automatic payments, 243
banner ads, 244
black hat SEO, 248
business-to-business (B2B)
    transactions, 243
cookies, 241
electronic commerce
    (e-commerce), 240
following, 234
friends list, 229

like button, 230
news feed, 229
one-step checkout, 241
online banking, 242
online payment companies, 241
online shopping, 240
pay-per-click, 244
pop-up ad, 244
pop-up blockers, 244
search engine optimization
    (SEO), 247

shopping cart, 241
skin, 235
software as a service (SaaS), 251
tweet, 234
vandalism, 235
Web content management system
    (WCMS), 228
white hat SEO, 248
wiki, 235
WYSIWYG (what you see is what
    you get) editors, 228

Key Terms QUIZ

Complete each statement by writing one of the terms listed under "Key Terms" in each blank.

1. Facebook encourages its users to click a(n) _____ as a way of expressing approval or a preference for a comment, picture or Web page link.

2. _____ are tiny files used to hold information about how and where people visit Web sites.

3. _____ allows people to check bank balances and shift money from one account to another.

4. A(n) _____ is a special kind of Web site used to collect and store information in a collaborative manner.

5. _____ editors show the user what their Web documents will look like as changes and additions are made.

6. _____ is the practice of analyzing search engine behavior and tuning the content of a Web site to achieve better placement in search results.

7. E-commerce transactions between two businesses are known as _____ transactions.

8. Online shopping selections are stored in a(n) _____ so consumers can shop for multiple items at a time.

9. Cloud computing companies may provide _____, which lets subscribers run software programs on hosted machines instead of their own computer.

10. Advertisers sometimes make a(n) _____ agreement with Web site owners to pay for advertising only when site visitors click on their ads.

Review QUESTIONS

In your own words, briefly answer the following questions.

1. What is e-commerce? Why is it attractive to businesses and consumers?

2. What is pay-per-click advertising?

3. Describe three ways businesses can advertise via the Internet.

4. Suppose you have decided to create your own Web site. Describe some software products that help people author Web pages. Which would you try first? Why?

5. Explain what a blog is for. How would you go about creating a blog?

6. Briefly summarize five software-related problems that SaaS can solve.

7. Suppose you work for a company that sells products for organic and natural gardeners. Gardening retailers and home gardeners come to you for expertise in preventing and solving a wide variety of gardening problems, from choosing the best plants for their area to combating pests. Already, your employees are experts in particular areas, but everyone needs to be continuously learning. Discuss how a wiki might meet this need. Would you recommend making your wiki public or private? Why?

8. Give an example of a change one could make to a Web site that might qualify as black hat SEO? Give an example of a white hat SEO change.

9. Describe two kinds of common Web advertisements that one should never click, and why they should be avoided.

10. Besides sales transactions, what activities are involved in business-to-business e-commerce?

Complete the following exercises as directed by your instructor.

1. Do some shopping. Visit the Web site of a popular online merchant, such as Zappos.com, Amazon.com, Dell.com, or a site selected by your instructor. Without purchasing anything or providing any personal information, inspect the site. What products does it sell? How does its catalog function? Is it easy to navigate the site and find products? Check the site's customer service and help options. Describe your findings in a one-page report, to share with the class.

2. Compare cloud storage prices online. Visit three cloud storage companies such as Google.com, Carbonite, and DropBox. You can also search online for "cloud storage," or pick favorite companies you might already have. At each site, find the price per year for 50 gigabytes of storage. Investigate each service for their offerings regarding encryption. List your findings and be prepared to discuss the results in class.

Employers often forbid the use of computer and Internet tools for personal matters. Personal e-mail, social network pages, computer games, and news sites can distract employees from their work, lower productivity, introduce computer viruses and other malware from questionable sites, and even create an uncomfortable environment for customers and coworkers. Still, many employees point out that they have good judgment, work hard for long hours, and benefit the company when they are well informed and able to communicate fully with their network of friends and colleagues. Often when companies face a complex issue such as limits on computer use, they form a team to consider the problem from many angles and arrive at a recommended solution.

Team
EXERCISE
Ethics

To practice taking part in such a team, divide into groups of three or four. Imagine that you and your teammates are your company's new Productivity Task Force, charged with finding ways to reduce the liability of using work computers for nonwork activities. Discuss the following questions, with the aim of arriving at a policy:

- What kind of controls or restrictions, if any, should be placed on computer use at work? (For example, should employees be denied access to certain Web sites?) If you don't have limits, how will you protect the company from harm resulting from misuse?

- How will the company enforce any limits? For example, should it monitor computer use, such as Web traffic and e-mail?

- What kind of penalties or sanctions should be imposed if rules are violated? Should different standards apply to shopping online, sending emails to one's mother, and surfing for the latest celebrity news?

List your recommended actions, and be prepared share those results with the class.

LESSON 6B:
Computer Security and Online Privacy

Most people store some sort of personal information on their computer. Many people use computers to purchase items online, for example; others write e-mails about private family matters or confidential projects at work; still others use computers to store important projects, reports, or research. Imagine what it would be like to have your financial information stolen, or your personal correspondence made public, or months of hard work on projects damaged or destroyed. Safeguarding your computer and its valuable information is important.

You are aware that cars are stolen every day, so you probably take measures to reduce the risk of losing yours, such as locking the doors, parking in a garage, or using a car alarm. In the same way, you should be aware of the threats facing your computer and data, and take measures to protect them as well. By taking some precautionary steps, you can safeguard not only your hardware, software, and data but also yourself.

The first step to good computer security is awareness. You should understand *all* the dangers that specifically threaten your computer system. You need to know how each threat can affect you and prioritize the risks accordingly. This lesson introduces you to some of the most common threats to your privacy, data, and hardware. The following lesson shows you how to protect yourself and your system.

6.4 Basic Security Concepts

Any discussion of computer security is likely to use certain terms. Thus, a basic understanding of security needs to include definitions of *threats, vulnerability,* and *countermeasures,* as these terms are used in the computer industry.

The entire purpose of computer security is to eliminate or protect against threats. A **threat** is anything that can cause harm. In the context of computer security, threats can be as varied as a burglar, virus software, an earthquake, or a simple user error.

By itself, a threat is not harmful unless it exploits an existing vulnerability. A **vulnerability** is a weakness—anything that has not been protected against threats,

making it open to harm. For instance, the presence of a car thief is a threat, but if there are no cars on the street to steal, the threat is meaningless to those in the neighborhood. Similarly, a vulnerability is relevant only if a threat is likely to be present. Your freshly planted flower garden is vulnerable to being crushed beneath a herd of stampeding elephants, but unless you live near a lot of elephants, that vulnerability is not a concern.

Those absolute examples aside, we gauge the danger of a threat by a combination of factors:

- The probability of a threat
- The degree of vulnerability
- The penalty or injury that may occur if the threat succeeds in causing harm

Threats that are very likely to cause harm, or threats that cause very painful consequences if unchecked, are much more likely to be guarded against. Most people wear a seat belt when driving their car, not because we are all so likely to crash, but because the threat of severe injury in that unlikely event makes us cautious. Most people make an effort to stop properly at red lights with photo enforcement, not so much because the penalty will ruin our lives, but more because the probability of getting a ticket for violating the law is extremely high.

We guard against threats when their danger is high enough that it warrants our attention. Sometimes, our

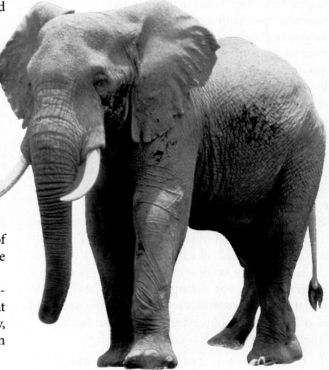

Figure 6.31 Not all threats are close enough to cause harm.

best-laid plans still do not keep us safe, but often, if we are affected by a threat, it is because we did not properly assess its degree of danger. This is true for computer systems just as much as for cars and flower gardens. When people think of the ways their computer systems can be damaged, they may think only of damage to the hardware or the loss of data. In reality, computer systems can be damaged in many ways. And remember, as you learned in Chapter 1, you (the user) are part of the computer system. You, too, can suffer harm of various kinds, from the loss of important data, to the loss of privacy, to actual physical harm.

When protecting your computer system, it pays to think in the broadest possible terms about the types of harm that could affect you, to better assess the risk. A nasty virus or hacker can wipe out your programs as well as your data, but the risk may be greater than just that incident. If your PC is connected to a network, other systems on the network could suffer similar problems. Damages to your home or office—such as a fire or flood—can easily extend to your computer, everything stored on it, and possibly even backup copies of data.

A practical and accurate risk assessment is critical to being able to guard against danger to a computer system. Unfortunately, assessing risks is complicated. Sometimes a pet fear might lead us to overprotect against a minor problem, ignoring other risks that are more critical. Worrying about an identity thief breaking into your basement office in order to steal passwords from your computer system might not be your greatest risk, especially if you always use your last name as your password. Other times, solutions to problems can lead to greater problems. Requiring that your company's users change their passwords every few days might sound like a great idea, until you realize that half of the employees will write their password on a sticky note attached to their monitor, so they won't forget the ever-changing secret. When it's time to assess risk, consider as many factors as possible, and try to be realistic about where the biggest threats lie.

For any threat, there is some action or plan you can employ to guard yourself against the risk. Any step you take to ward off a threat—to protect yourself, your data, or your computer from harm—is called a **countermeasure**. For example, regularly backing up your data is a countermeasure against the threat of data loss. A firewall is a countermeasure against hackers.

There are two classes of countermeasures:

1. One type of measure shields the user from personal harm, such as threats to personal property, confidential information, financial records, medical records, and so forth.

2. The other type of safeguard protects the computer system from physical hazards such as theft, vandalism, power problems, and natural disasters or attacks on the data stored and processed in computers.

The choice of countermeasures will vary according to the types of computer system threats that are of concern.

6.5 Safeguarding Your Hardware

While many of the threats to computer systems are malicious and willful, threats to computer hardware—incidents that affect the operation or maintenance of the computer—are much more likely to be environmental in nature. They can, of course, involve malicious acts such as theft or vandalism, but more commonly they range from routine problems such as system breakdown and misuse or disasters such as fire and flood.

POWER PROBLEMS

The electricity supplied to computer hardware is critical to its operation. Power problems affect computers in two ways:

1. **Power fluctuations** may cause the strength of your electrical service to rise or fall.

2. **Power failure**, meaning power is lost altogether, causes systems to shut down. Both power failure and fluctuations can result in a loss of data.

Power levels that rise and fall can produce unpredictable behavior in, or cause damage to, sensitive

Figure 6.32 Consistent, constant power is essential for running computers safely. What comes from the wall can sometimes be anything but that.

Loss of power altogether when service is interrupted may not cause component failure, but it can cause the loss of unsaved work when the failure occurs. A power failure can also cause social or career problems if the user was in an online meeting, giving a videoconference presentation, or even simply chatting with friends.

There are a couple of common countermeasures for the threat of lost or uneven power. If your budget is extremely tight or the hardware you need to protect is nonessential (some people would consider a printer in this category), a **surge suppressor** is an inexpensive product that guards its appliances against large power spikes or surges that may infrequently occur. It doesn't provide protection against reduced or total loss of power, however. Surge suppressors are common products available at electronics and hardware stores and sometimes even supermarkets. Check the packaging carefully to make sure you are actually buying a surge suppressor and not a many-to-one extension cord that looks the same but lacks protection against power surges.

computer components. The computer system unit has its own power supply that is designed to strictly regulate the power feed to the motherboard, CPU, and other internal parts. But the power supply itself is vulnerable to problems with incoming electricity, and other devices outside the computer such as network hardware, printers, and external storage devices may be at risk from inconsistent power. Also, when a system unit's power supply malfunctions, it can simply shut off (causing a power failure), or it can go out with an acrid eruption of electrical smoke and a massive power surge that melts and ruins delicate components on the motherboard.

Power problems can arise for many reasons. People commonly think electrical storms are the primary cause of power interruptions, but storms are actually one of the least likely causes. A more likely source is the house or building itself. Disturbances from high-demand equipment such as air conditioners, space heaters, dryers, and copy machines produce fluctuations, for example. Old wiring in houses may also produce an inconsistent power feed.

Problems with both power fluctuations and power failure can be minimized by adding another kind of hardware, an **uninterruptible power supply (UPS)**. A UPS functions as a battery backup and power conditioner for your computer. The unit delivers a consistent supply of power to your computer components, regardless of spikes, and sags in power may occur in the electricity before it gets to the UPS. When the power fails completely, the battery contains enough power to run a complete

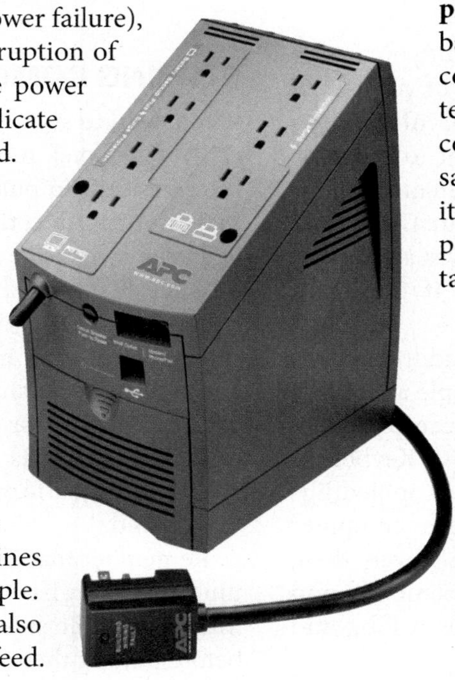

Figure 6.33 An uninterruptible power supply unit can provide peace of mind in the form of reliable electricity for computer and network hardware.

desktop PC from a few minutes to the better part of an hour, depending on the size of the computer components and the capacity of the UPS. If you include a UPS unit for your network hardware (your routers and Internet modem, for example), you can keep on working, surfing, or gaming even when the lights go out. Many UPS models are able to communicate with a PC to provide status information and shut down the PC when battery power falls too low. The battery recharges when the power returns, so it's ready for the next power failure.

THEFT AND ACCIDENTS

Though perhaps less common than electrical failures, theft or vandalism can result in the total loss of the system and the data it stores. While this fact may seem obvious, very few homeowners and students take precautions to protect their PCs from intentionally destructive acts.

In principle, hardware is simple to secure from theft and vandalism. The best way to keep thieves and vandals at bay is to keep your system in a secure area. If it is difficult to get to the hardware or carry it off without being noticed, the computer hardware is safer. At home, keeping your home secure protects everything in your house including the computer. At work, you can use special locks that attach a system unit, monitor, or other equipment to a desk, making it difficult to move. These lock sets can also be used to keep a system unit from being opened, which guards against an office thief opening computer cases and removing expensive CPUs, memory sticks, and video cards.

If your computer is stolen, the loss of your hardware is potentially just the beginning of your trouble. If you have stored sensitive personal information on the computer, the thief could use it to compromise your financial, professional, or personal safety. The section, "Restricting Access to Your Data" later in this lesson has tips for keeping thieves away from your data, rendering it useless even if they gain access to it.

Accidental harm is much harder to address, but it is no less of a threat. Something as simple as spilling a cup of coffee into your system unit can provide a spectacular example of an accidental loss. Keyboards are especially vulnerable to failure from spilled liquids; immediately powering down the computer can sometimes save the keyboard, but even then, depending on what was spilled, disassembling and cleaning sticky cocoa from the keys is a long and tedious exercise.

There are so many ways a computer can be destroyed by human accidents and environmental disasters that it is pointless to attempt to list them all. In any case, it doesn't really matter whether a computer was destroyed by a cup of hot soup, a building fire, or falling furniture after an earthquake. The protection process is the same for every possible issue: try to keep the hardware reasonably safe from harm, and have recovery plans in place in the event that the countermeasures did not fully protect the computer.

HANDLING STORAGE MEDIA

You may think of your CDs as sturdy little objects; they just lie around, and even with a scratch or two, they still seem to work fine. Even so, keep those CDs and DVDs in their jewel cases, storage sleeves, or binders when you aren't using them. A deep enough scratch in the wrong place, enough scratches, or even heat damage from that coffee cup you put down on the disk last night when you were intent on studying can suddenly turn your data CD into a permanent coaster for that coffee cup. Minor abrasions can sometimes be smoothed down and repaired, but if disks don't get scratched, you won't have to find out if they are repairable.

Solid-state storage like USB flash drives won't get harmed from scratches, but they are easy to lose or sit on. Consider attaching them to something easy to spot, if you have a habit of losing things. Keep them out of extreme cold and hot areas, and away from liquids.

STORING COMPUTER HARDWARE

If you need to store your computer equipment, especially flat-panel monitors with their delicate surfaces, it's best to put it back in the original boxes. If that's not possible, then store hardware in a way that will keep it dry, safe from thieves, and as dust-free as possible. Keep hardware away from large electrical equipment such as refrigerators or generators. Avoid storing hardware in damp, humid environments, and if there's the slightest chance of water running across the floor (for example, if there's a water heater or plumbing pipes nearby), put the hardware on shelves or a platform that's at least a few inches off the ground.

Remember that if you are storing computer system units, they may have hard drives that contain valuable information. Be sure to back up data from the drives before putting them into long-term storage.

KEEPING YOUR COMPUTER CLEAN

Although it appears robust, the computer is a precision instrument and should be kept spotless. Computers have three major enemies:

1. *Liquid* can cause fatal electrical faults for a computer. It can come in many forms, including spilled beverages, heavy rain coming through a window, or flooding on the floor.

2. *Dust* can clog cooling systems and, in extreme circumstances, also cause electrical faults. Cigarette smoke can also be highly toxic to computer systems over time.

3. *Heat* can cause sensitive electronic components to melt beyond repair, most commonly because of faults and failures in hardware cooling systems.

Keep liquids away from computers to the greatest degree practical, especially from the system unit. Keyboards, the most commonly liquid-damaged parts, are cheap and usually easy to replace. If hardware gets wet, turn it off or unplug it immediately and leave it off until it is completely dry.

Regularly remove dust from your system unit—once a month if your computer lives in a very dusty or smoky environment, a few times a year if the air is clean. With the computer unplugged, use a compressed-air can to whisk away dust from fans and anywhere else it has accumulated. You can use a vacuum cleaner to catch the resulting dust cloud, but avoid poking at the sensitive electronics with the vacuum hose. Flat-panel monitors can be gently dusted with a microfiber cloth, but never use glass cleaner, degreaser spray, or wood-fiber cloths like facial tissue or paper towels.

Figure 6.34   A can of compressed air helps keep fans and cooling towers free of dust and working properly.

The hardware of many computers, especially desktop computers built for high-performance graphics, contains diagnostic systems that monitor CPU temperature, fan speeds, certain electrical voltages, and other measures of hardware health. These systems are specialized tools, and, though they could be useful or fun to learn more about, most users will not need to adjust any of the settings or limits in the systems. With luck, you will never know they are there, but if a hardware fault such as a broken fan occurs, they may save your computer from extensive damage by shutting down your system before it overheats.

6.6 Keeping Your Data Secure

The purpose of a computer is to process data in some way to create information. The goal of computer security is to protect this process. Because data and information are intangible, this mission is difficult. Despite this, you should try to protect everything of value from every threat you can identify.

MALWARE: VIRUSES, WORMS AND TROJANS

As you learned in Chapter 1, malware is a type of software that is designed to cause your system harm. Malware is the most common threat to your data and security. The exact goals of malware vary greatly, but most of the time it attempts to steal information, destroy data, harm the flow of data through a network, or **hijack** (meaning to take over some or all control of a computer's functions) computers in order to attack other users.

One stereotypical assumption about malware is that it announces its installation and activity loudly, flashing warnings or contemptuous messages to the user as it wipes the hard drive clean. In reality, the last thing that most forms of malware want is recognition. Your computer is very valuable to a cyber criminal while it is silently hosting a data-stealing invader. Even malware that pops up annoying advertisement windows does what it can to misdirect your attention, making it look like your browser is responsible for the unwanted ads. The malware philosophy is often "What you don't know about, you won't try to remove."

In addition to operating in the background, malware is often written in a way that disguises its presence or purpose on the computer, making it very difficult for the average user to find all of its components. It may install itself in separate parts, with one part responsible for spying on or damaging its environment and other parts designed to quietly detect removal attempts and repair itself when attacked. It may perform certain operations only during system startup or shutdown, to avoid being seen by the user. It may also attempt to disable protection software on the host computer, to reduce its chances of being detected.

Malware has several subcategories, depending on the behavior and purpose of the software. It's common to refer to all malware types as viruses, but that term actually defines only a very specific kind of program. A **virus** is software that is attached to a host, such as a file or e-mail message, and has the ability to **replicate**, or copy, itself from one computer to another (see Figure 6.35). For example, a virus can be sent through e-mail as part of a word processor document. When a recipient opens the file with the word processor, the virus can activate, find more word processor documents on that system, and add itself to those documents to increase the chances that it will be sent to other systems.

Similar to a virus, a **worm** program is one that self-replicates, but it is a fully contained program and is not attached to a host file or service. A worm

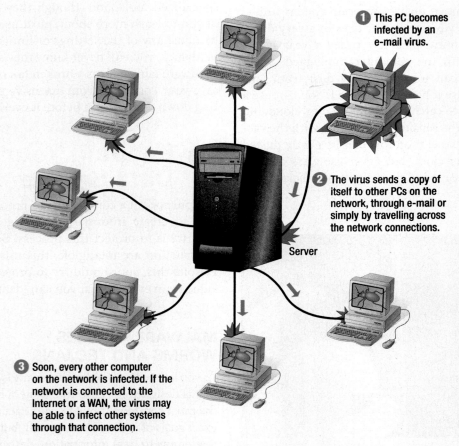

① This PC becomes infected by an e-mail virus.

② The virus sends a copy of itself to other PCs on the network, through e-mail or simply by travelling across the network connections.

Server

③ Soon, every other computer on the network is infected. If the network is connected to the Internet or a WAN, the virus may be able to infect other systems through that connection.

Figure 6.35 Viruses copy themselves from one computer to another. Unchecked, an infection on one computer can quickly infect all other computers on the network.

may copy itself to multiple locations on a computer that it infects and then use e-mail or direct network connections to deliver itself to new computers.

A **Trojan horse** (sometimes just **Trojan**, named for the Trojan horse full of Greek soldiers that was delivered as a secret weapon during the ancient siege of Troy) is a program that cannot self-replicate and must rely on other methods for delivery. Similar to the ancient wooden horse, a software Trojan horse disguises itself as something interesting, useful, or desirable in order to gain access to your system. The user plays the part of the citizens of Troy, welcoming the software or data file onto his or her computer, only to have it install dangerous instructions.

Trojan horses are very commonly attached to downloaded files of questionable legality, such as media files and pirated software. They are often found on sites delivering pornographic media. They can also be delivered in subtler ways, such as a seemingly-innocent popup message on a Web page that asks a question or invites the user to view a funny or outrageous video.

Malware can perform practically any kind of action once installed, but a few general behaviors are most common.

The most benign form of malware—at least when considering threats to computer data—is software that exists simply to copy itself to elsewhere. Those programs can cause headaches for network administrators because, unchecked, they can consume a great deal of network resources by sending itself everywhere repeatedly, but the computer data on infected machines is left untouched.

Malware that is used to display unwanted advertising on a computer is known as **adware**. Adware programs are sometimes unknowingly downloaded as Trojan horses, but they are also commonly bundled into game and utility software download packages. Some peer-to-peer file sharing programs also include adware in their configuration. In some cases, the adware is included as an alternative to paying for a desired software utility; the adware can usually be deactivated by paying for and registering the software.

One type of malware that has rapidly grown in use is **spyware**, which is designed to report activity on

Figure 6.36 Trojan horses are loaded when unsuspecting users follow an intriguing link or invitation, installing toxic software on their systems.

your computer to another party. Spyware can record individual keystrokes, Web usage, e-mail addresses, personal information, and other types of data. It can sift through data files on your computer and look for names, addresses, passwords, and other sensitive information. Once it has data to report, the program transmits the collected data via e-mail or directly across the network to another computer on the Internet.

Malware sometimes opens communication ports, even bypassing firewalls, and quietly makes the host computer available for control by human intruders. Computers infected and compromised in this way are known as **zombies**, because they are under external control, in many cases without the computer owner's knowledge. Massive networks of zombies, known as **botnets**, can be used to spread new Trojan horse infections, e-mail spam, and conduct carefully orchestrated network attacks at large, popular Web sites in attempts to shut them down. This type of attempt to shut down or block access to a Web site is known as a **distributed denial-of-service (DDoS)** attack.

PROTECTING AGAINST MALWARE

As with other aspects of computer security, effectively dealing with malware attacks requires a combination of avoidance, defense, and mitigation when the first two efforts fail.

If you don't visit sites where malware is typically hosted, the chances of infection are greatly reduced. Malware is extremely common on sites that deliver erotic or pornographic content and on sites that offer free downloads of illegal software. Other questionable sites—for example, sites offering amazing weight-loss secrets or get-rich-quick schemes—can be sources of infection. If you are an online gamer, Web sites that illegally sell in-game cash and items or advertise game-hacking software are notorious for loading malware onto the systems of visitors. Even some sites that offer to helpfully install driver software and other utilities on your system may be hosting malware.

No category of site is guaranteed to download malware to your system, of course. In every category of content, there are some sites that will not attempt to compromise your system. Conversely, once in a while, even everyday, fully legitimate sites that host advertising accidentally let a malware-containing ad or link to slip past. Your best bet is simply to be cautious. Learn to avoid the worst places, understand the neighborhood where your electronic feet are walking, and be aware of your surroundings.

Infections via social network sites are also extremely common. When we see one of our friends post a link to a video or wacky Web story, we naturally assume that they are sharing something safe. We click it to share in the fun, only to discover too late that the friend hadn't posted the link on purpose; the link was posted by their malware-infected computer, and the Web site contained advertising for great deals on prescription drugs, along with a Trojan horse that infects our computer as well.

The best countermeasure is to think about what you're seeing as you surf. Would your grandmother really send you a link with a caption, "OMG did they rly do that in public??? Check it out!!!"? Does your best friend usually bother to use a link-shortening service like Bit.ly (which hides the final destination site) when forwarding you links on Facebook? Avoid the questionable links, or at the very least post a comment asking if the link is real.

Malware defense for your computer comes most typically in the form of anti-malware software. Many major companies, such as Symantec, McAfee, Avast, and Check Point, offer products ranging from special-purpose to very comprehensive. The more comprehensive packages attempt to block malware from all sources and include antivirus scanning, spyware detection and removal tools, and firewall software. Some packages are free to download and use; others require some form of purchase.

Though all of these tools are constantly updated with new rules to handle new types of malware, no one tool is capable of preventing every form of malware attack on the Internet. Some repair solutions are programmed better by some companies than others. Some programs will miss a given type of malware attack more often than others.

Your best bet is to carefully review the features and opinions of others and decide what type of protection solution is best for you. You may be more comfortable with a complete program that protects your computer in every possible way. You may prefer a more

Figure 6.37 Would your grandmother send you photos of a wild party? If not, don't open the e-mail attachment that seems to be from her.

specialized setup that guards against fewer types of threats but does it more reliably and consumes less of your computer's resources.

Finally, if your wise-surfing efforts and anti-malware software fail, and strange advertising appears on your screen or your friends report that you are unwittingly sending e-mail or Facebook spam, fear not. Several freeware and shareware software utilities exist that are designed to detect and remove invaders that the defender programs missed. Malwarebytes' Anti-Malware software (http://www.malwarebytes.org/) is a comprehensive cleanup tool that removes many forms of malware. AVGFree Anti-virus (http://free.avg.com) and Alwil's Avast (http://www.avast.com) both provide virus protection and infection-scanning utilities. If your computer is infected with malware, using more than one cleanup utility is highly advised.

You may also consider enlisting the aid of anti-malware support Web sites, such as Bleeping Computer (http://www.bleepingcomputer.com/). Help at such sites is not always immediate, as they are often inundated with requests to assist, but if your infection requires expert attention, this is a good resource if you have the time to wait. Your local computer store may also have resources for disinfecting your computer after a malware attack. Above all, be especially vigilant when disinfecting or protecting your system. Be sure to use commonly-available protection software that is provided directly from the software developer. Never rely on protection solutions from unknown companies, and never download protection software from secondary locations unless they are mirror sites specifically authorized by the software company.

CYBERTERRORISM AND OTHER CYBERCRIMES

Computer crime is aimed at stealing the computer, damaging information, or stealing information. Computer crime is not necessarily the work of technical experts. Most criminal acts against computers do not directly involve technology; most crimes involve simple hardware theft.

At the international level, computers are actively used in cyberterrorism. Unlike conventional wars that attack a population directly, **cyberterrorism** is a new form of warfare, attacking the critical infrastructure systems of a nation through the technology it uses. The conventional goal in the case of cyberterrorism is to harm or control key computer systems or digital controls. It is done to accomplish an indirect aim such as to disrupt a power grid or telecommunications. Typical targets are power plants, nuclear facilities, water treatment plants, and government agencies. However, any site with network-based monitoring and control systems is vulnerable if it is hooked to the Internet.

Cyberterrorism is not a new phenomenon. In 1996, the threat was so credible that the federal government created the Critical Information Protection Task Force, which later became the Critical Infrastructure Protection Board (CIPB). The Information Security Management Act of 2002 set basic security requirements for all government systems; at the same time, the White House issued the first coherent national strategy to secure cyberspace.

The use of a computer to carry out any conventional criminal act, such as fraud, is called **cybercrime** and is a growing menace. Cybercrime is growing so rapidly, in fact, that the federal government has created a handful of agencies to deal with computer-related crimes. More than 336,000 complaints of Internet-related crime were reported to the Internet Crime Complaint Center (IC3) in 2009, a 22 percent increase over the previous year, and a twenty-fold increase over the 16,755 complaints made in 2001. Cybercrime can have wide-ranging purposes, from stalking and intimidation to fraud. However, **hacking**—the practice of accessing computer systems in an unauthorized way—is rapidly gaining as a crime in its own right, and as a way to accomplish other crimes.

HACKING

A **hacker** is someone who uses a computer and network or Internet connection to intrude into another computer or system to perform an illegal act. This may amount to simple trespassing or acts that corrupt, destroy, or change data. Hackers' activities are usually categorized by their intent, as shown in Table 6.1.

There are two general ways that hackers can gain access to a computer or network: by exploiting some kind of system vulnerability, and by obtaining passwords or other access information from a legitimate user.

TABLE 6.1 CATEGORIES OF HACKER ACTIVITY

Recreation attacks	Typically involve attempts by hackers to prove their abilities without doing any damage.
	Invades privacy but is usually relatively harmless.
Business, financial, or intelligence attacks	Typically take the form of data diddling—forging or changing records for personal gain, or attempting to copy the data from the penetrated system.
	Potentially more damaging than recreational attacks.
Grudge attacks	Attacks by hackers with a grievance against an individual or organization. Frequently destructive.
Terrorist attacks	Attacks by terrorists targeting the industrial world's dependence on computers.
	A potentially catastrophic tool of warfare.

Focus on the Issues

Stuxnet: Cyberterrorism or anti-terrorism?

Much of the attention given to hackers and cyberterrorists centers around either a model of anarchistic hackers breaking into companies for fun and profit; or of rogue terrorist organizations seeking to disable or destroy critical national infrastructure. Those hackers and terrorists certainly exist, but not every cyberattack originates from an independent source. Sometimes, the attacks appear to be mandated and funded by national governments to further their own interests.

In the summer of 2010, a security company detected the appearance of a new malware program: a worm named Stuxnet. Curiously, though Stuxnet rapidly spread from computer to computer, it did little harm to the host machines. In fact, the worm appeared to be looking for a specific kind of target computer, and if it arrived in a computer that failed to match its target, it made itself inert after copying itself a few times.

Examination of the worm's program code revealed it to be extremely complex, well beyond the scope of the type of malware typically encountered around the world. As experts dug deeper, they found that the worm's target hardware was actually a specific model of industrial centrifuge manufactured by Siemens, used by Iran as part of their nuclear weapons program.

When landing in the right hardware's computer controller, the worm's sophisticated programming began a series of actions that appear to be designed to destroy the centrifuge. It speeds and slows the centrifuge's rotor in a specific way to cause damage, all the while feeding false operating data to systems monitoring the centrifuge to hide its destructive activity. The worm contains the ability to mutate, disguise itself in different ways and continue replicating itself in other machines, making it extremely difficult to completely eradicate.

Did it work? In a limited way, it seems to have had an effect. Though all sides playing the game of international espionage are cagey about their actions, Iran did announce that they had been infected by Stuxnet, and eventually that the worm had affected a limited number of their centrifuges. Though the worm did not seem to have caused a major loss of progress to their program, it appears to have created an ongoing disruption to the use and maintenance of their centrifuge equipment.

Not surprisingly, Stuxnet's creators remain a mystery. The complexity of the worm causes many to believe that it was created a large development team, funded by a government and possibly even working with Siemens. Plausible whispers have suggested involvement by the United States and Israel, but so far, no one has taken credit for the program.

As is often the case, it can be difficult to tell the difference between superhero and villain in the realm of international intelligence. That governments might develop tools to destroy each others' infrastructure is disturbing, yet it is worth noting one bright spot: while Stuxnet is incredibly devious and sophisticated, it was nevertheless detected and brought to light by an independent, private security company. International vigilance may turn out to be a force that helps keep cyberwarfare in check.

Computer networks are complex sets of hardware and software. Often, computer networks allow a variety of different ways for users to connect in order to access Web pages, data files, databases, e-mail, and centrally installed programs. It can be a challenge to secure all access points properly such that hackers cannot gain entry. Sometimes, browser and database programs themselves contain errors or unintended gaps that hackers can find and exploit.

It is also possible for hackers to be legitimate users of a system who can access vulnerabilities that exist inside the strict security keeping unauthorized intruders out. For example, a hacker might be a customer at a bank and log into the online banking system via their browser. Once inside, the hacker may be able to find improperly protected Web locations or databases that allow him or her to find passwords, account numbers, or other sensitive information for other bank customers.

Instead of searching for security holes, hackers may instead gain system access by stealing account information from legitimate users. There are many specific ways to accomplish such theft, but there are two basic methods for obtaining user names and passwords: sniffing and social engineering.

Sniffing refers to any of various ways that hackers can steal or guess passwords. **Password sharing** is a form of sniffing where a victim simply discloses his or her password to a hacker. Since nobody willingly gives away their password to known hackers, the process often requires multiple iterations: a password is shared with a friend, who either carelessly transmits it to a hacker or shares it with someone else, in which case the process repeats until it is discovered.

Password guessing is done exactly as the term implies: a hacker tries to guess a user's password and keeps trying until he or she gets it right. In some cases, users help the process a great deal by using a ridiculously easy password to discover, such as their last name, a simple sequence such as "123456," or even the word "password." In other cases, users select short or simple passwords that sophisticated software programs can discover quickly, sometimes in under a minute.

In **password capture**, passwords are detected as a user enters them. Trojan horses can be used for this purpose; once installed on a user's computer, they can capture login information to any number of sites and services, and transmit the password data to the hacker for use. Trojan horses are especially useful because they may sit on a user's computer undetected for a long time, patiently recording a user's various activities, even identifying password changes that a user dutifully enters in attempt to protect their personal data.

Password capture software often takes the form of **keyboard logging**, or **keylogging**, where each key typed by the user on the keyboard is saved. Keylogging software is commonly available, and it is designed to operate undetected by the system's user. Keylogging programs can be used not just by hackers, but also by companies and individuals that want to monitor the detailed activity of people using computers that they own.

Social engineering is the practice of gaining a person's confidence through misrepresentation or fraud, in order to convince that person to divulge private information. While sniffing focuses on obtaining passwords via technological means, social engineering convinces people that it is safe to relay sensitive information.

There are many ways social engineering can be employed to steal passwords and user data. In some cases, automated systems use social engineering to attempt to trick large numbers of people; for example, e-mail messages that appear to be from a bank, credit service, or government agency can be sent to millions of people, requesting that users log in unknowingly into a hacker-run duplicate site to confirm a password.

In other cases, hackers may target a specific person or set of people at an organization, and make

Figure 6.38 Sometimes the best passwords are rendered useless when they are unwittingly shared with others.

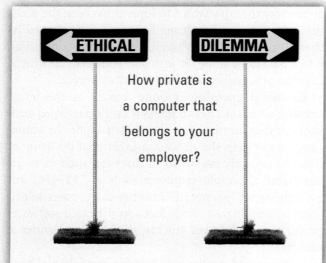

ETHICAL ← → DILEMMA

How private is a computer that belongs to your employer?

At an all-hands meeting at work today, the head of your 100-person company complained that recreational computer use on company time was creating an unacceptable loss of productivity. You've heard this story from management before, but this time the story had a different ending: your CEO told the assembled employees that starting next week, every computer would be outfitted with keyboard logging and Web page analysis software, and that everything done on a company computer would be actively monitored. Any non-work activity such as surfing the Web, checking personal e-mail, or viewing Facebook pages would result in warnings, and repeated warnings would be grounds for termination.

In your opinion, does the company have the right to monitor your every keystroke while online on company time? Are there any times when you have an absolute right to privacy when using company resources? What if you were asked to submit while working to online monitoring on your own personal devices such as an iPad that you bring to work? Would it be acceptable for the company to forbid workers to bring their own Internet–ready devices to work?

and sending Facebook status updates that contain an irresistible link for others to click, or asking people for personal data in order to receive details of a personality test. Any means of convincing a user to reveal sensitive data to an entity they mistakenly view as trustworthy qualifies as social engineering.

RESTRICTING ACCESS TO YOUR DATA

It doesn't take a professional hacker to ruin all the data on your PC. A member of your own family can do it just as well, if unintentionally. Ideally, if you are the only user of your PC, then you are the only person who can accidentally download malware to your system, and you do not have to worry about the wrong eyes reading the wrong file. The more people who have access to your computer, the more people who can unwittingly damage your data and operating environment, and the more careful you need to be about protecting sensitive information.

If you want to allow others to occasionally use your computer, make sure you keep track of what they do. Set very clear rules about what sites may be visited and what—if anything at all—may be downloaded or installed. If at all possible, keep yourself available to look at any download or update requests that may occur during the other person's session.

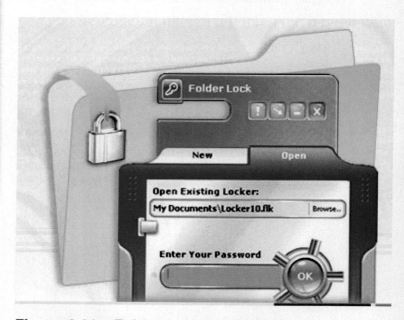

Figure 6.39 Folder Lock is a popular program that allows you to easily encrypt files and folders on your PC, so that you are the only person who can access their data.

one-to-one contact via e-mail or telephone. A hacker could call a technology support desk at a company and identify himself as an executive who has forgotten their password. They could send authentic-looking e-mail to the executive's secretary and request similar information. Unsuspecting workers may give away passwords and other sensitive information, especially if the hacker already knows key data, such as a Social Security number, of his or her target.

Sometimes, social engineering is accomplished as simply as compromising a computer with malware

If you have to share your PC with other users, you still may be able to limit their ability to find your data. Most newer operating systems allow users to set up "accounts" on a shared PC. In his or her account, each user can set up a unique set of preferences, such as the desktop's appearance, passwords, and more. Your operating system may allow you to hide folders and files or make them private so that no one else can open them while using your computer. Note, however, that you may still be vulnerable to systemwide malware that someone else may have installed; a program to record a user's keyboard activity will most likely install itself in the operating system, not simply in the user environment of one account.

Some applications can lock files so they can be opened only with a password. If others frequently use your computer, you may want to take advantage of these features. If your PC is part of a network, you can turn off sharing of entire disks or of individual files and folders.

You also can encrypt data so no one else can use it via a network connection. Data encryption is an ideal solution for keeping your information safe from all eyes but your own because it changes the data to make it completely undecipherable to anyone who does not have the exact key required to decrypt and restore the data. Naturally, encryption will also prevent you from accessing your own data if you forget the master key, so if you use an encryption program, make sure you can retrieve the password somehow, or keep unencrypted backups of your data in a secure location.

There are many free or inexpensive programs, such as Folder Lock, that provide encryption. TrueCrypt (http://www.truecrypt.org/) is an open-source encryption solution ideal for securing data on everything from a pocket flash drive to a PC's hard drive. TrueCrypt provides its encryption in such a way that the storage device shows no evidence of organized storage at all, encrypted or otherwise, where the secure data is stored.

If other people have physical access to your computer but you don't want them to use it at all, configure your operating system to require a password when starting up. This task requires different instructions depending on your operating system. In Windows 7, you can access the User Accounts window from the Control Panel and choose from a list of choices that includes setting or changing your account password.

As an extra precaution, set up a password-protected screen saver, so that the screen saver will ask for a password before going away; this way, no one will be able to use your system if you leave it running. In Windows 7, right-click the background of your desktop and select *Personalize*; from the resulting window, select *Screen Saver*. In the screen saver window, check the box to display the login screen when the computer resumes operation.

USING A FIREWALL

A firewall's main purpose is to prohibit unauthorized access to your computer via the Internet. A functioning firewall is your best defense against hackers or anyone else who might try to reach your PC via the Internet. There are various kinds of firewalls—both hardware and software—and they can use different methods to keep intruders away from your system. Many firewalls work, for example, by effectively "hiding" your computer from other computers on the Internet. The only computers that can find your computer are the ones with which you have initiated communications.

If your PC connects to the Internet through an **always-on connection**—that is, a connection that is always active, such as a cable modem or DSL connection—then you should use a firewall. Without one, your computer is virtually unprotected from intruders, who can easily find your system and break into it. Most broadband routers contain firewalls, so if you have a home network, you may already have a firewall to protect all the computers on the network. Check the features of the router to be sure. Some operating systems also provide software firewalls to guard against intrusions to the computer; nowadays, Windows is normally by default installed with this feature—and other security measures—active.

BACKING UP DATA

You never know when or how data may be lost. A simple disk error can do just as much damage as a hacker might do. And even the most experienced computer user occasionally deletes a file or folder by accident. When such events happen, you'll be in the clear if you keep your data backed up.

You can use a backup copy of your data to restore lost files to your PC. Backups are useful for many reasons. If you save changes to a file but later decide the changes should not have been made, you can return to the previous version of the file by using the backup. If you buy a new computer, having a complete backup makes it easy to move your data.

You can also use utility programs such as Symantec Software's Norton Ghost that save a complete hard disk image, including all files, drivers, programs, and device configurations. If your hard drive becomes corrupt and you cannot boot your system, regular

Fact Check

1. What is a virus?
   a. A program that attaches to a host file and replicates itself
   b. Any type of program that causes damage to computer data
   c. A program that replicates itself without the need for a host file
2. What does spyware do?
   a. Displays advertising
   b. Searches for sensitive data or records user activity and reports its findings to an unauthorized person
   c. Tracks terrorist activity
3. What type of operation could become a target of cyberterrorism?
   a. Nuclear power plants
   b. Any government-run operation
   c. Any site with network-based monitoring and control hooked to the Internet

data backups will preserve your information, but those backups will not help your system start up again. You can reload a disk image onto your hard drive (or a new hard drive, if your old one is broken), restore your data from your most recent backup, and be up and running with all your programs already installed.

More and more people are turning to cloud-based storage solutions for backing up data, as you learned in Lesson 6A. Cloud backup services often provide encrypted, secure storage for data, and a variety of features for retrieving and distributing files.

6.7 Protecting Yourself and Your Identity

Networks and the Internet have created limitless possibilities for people to work, communicate, learn, buy and sell, play games, and interact with others around the world. These possibilities come from the openness of networks—especially the Internet, which is available to virtually everyone, for virtually any kind of use. However, the very openness that makes the Internet so valuable also has made it a conduit for many types of threats.

We cannot blame the Internet for all computer-related problems. Some issues, such as identity theft, are still best accomplished with little or no help from a computer. Others, such as injuries stemming from computer use, are often the fault of poor design or poor work habits.

IDENTITY THEFT AND HOW TO AVOID IT

If someone impersonates you by using your name, Social Security number, or other personal information to obtain documents or credit in your name, you are a victim of **identity (ID) theft**. With the right information, an identity thief can effectively "become" the victim, obtaining a driver's license, bank accounts, mortgages, and other items in the victim's name.

Identity theft cost the U.S. economy $54 billion in 2009. That year alone, more than 11 million Americans became victims of ID theft. Beyond monetary losses, however, victims of ID theft pay in other ways, spending many hours trying to repair the financial damages and regain their good reputation.

Identity thieves can use several methods—low-tech as well as high-tech—to obtain the information they need:

- **Shoulder surfing.** A trick known as **shoulder surfing** is as simple as watching someone enter personal identification information for a private transaction, such as an ATM.
- **Snagging.** In the right setting, a thief can try **snagging** information by listening in on a telephone conversation while the victim gives credit card or other personal information to a legitimate agent. As

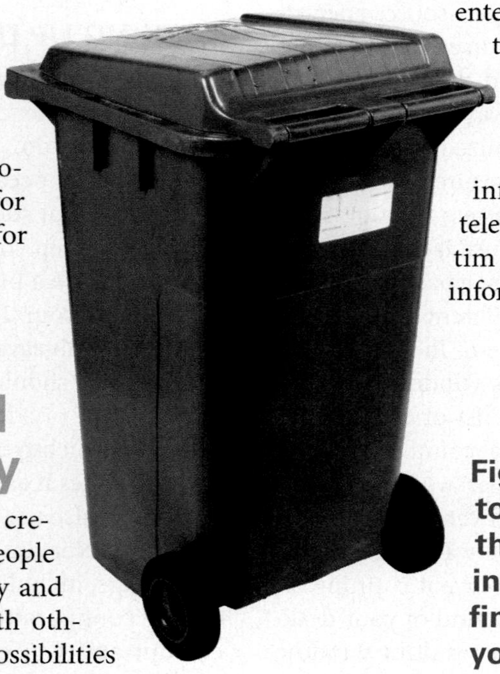

Figure 6.40 Be careful not to throw away documents that contain valuable information. An ID thief may find what he or she needs in your own trash can.

more and more people carelessly hold loud, private conversations on their cell phones in public areas, snagging is easier than ever.

- **Dumpster diving.** A popular low-tech approach is **dumpster diving**. Thieves can go through garbage cans, dumpsters, or trash bins to obtain canceled checks, credit card and utility statements, or bank account information that someone has carelessly thrown out. They win when they find items that have account numbers or personal information. Some ID thieves are brazen enough to swipe documents right out of your mailbox.

- **Social engineering.** Thieves can use social engineering tactics both by pretending to represent your bank, utility company or even the government; and by pretending to be you when contacting your bank or utility company. Their goal is to convince someone with private information about you that they have a legitimate purpose to receive that information.

- **High-tech methods.** Sophisticated ID thieves can get information using a computer and Internet connection. For instance, Trojan horses can be planted on a system or a person's identity may be snagged from unsecured Internet sites. Users providing private financial data via an unsecured "HTTP" Web page are especially vulnerable to the theft of that data.

Victims of identity theft stand to lose large sums of money, suffer damage to their credit and reputation, and can possibly even lose possessions if the situation is not handled properly. It's important to remember that, even if you don't make transactions yourself, you may still be held responsible for them unless you take action quickly.

Because ID thieves mainly use nontechnical methods to get the information they need, most of the precautions you can take against ID theft are low-tech. Further, they all are matters of common sense; you should do these things anyway, even if ID theft were not even possible.

From the moment they enter your mailbox until they reach the landfill, valuable documents such as account statements, financial records, bills and credit card applications are vulnerable. By handling them wisely, you can keep them out of the hands of an ID thief:

- **Guard your mail.** Pick up your mail as soon as possible after it arrives. Never allow mail to sit for a long time in your mailbox. If ID theft is a problem in your area, get a P.O. box and have sensitive documents delivered there. Also, put important outgoing mail in a public mailbox or take it to the post office, where no one can steal it.

- **Check your statements immediately.** Open and check your bank and credit card statements as soon as you get them. Look for suspicious charges, ATM transactions, or checks you did not write. If you find one, report it immediately. The sooner you report suspicious activity, the greater the chance that the company will be able to help you. Some financial institutions place a time limit on reporting unauthorized transactions; after the time limit, your bank or credit card company may require you to pay for the charge.

- **Discard important documents wisely.** When you are ready to get rid of any important document, do it right. Shred any document that contains sensitive information such as your Social Security number, account numbers, or passwords.

In the course of a normal week, you probably give away all sorts of information about yourself without even thinking about it. It pays to be careful when

Figure 6.41 Many threats to your privacy are low-tech, and require awareness more than a high-tech solution.

sharing personal information to make sure it doesn't fall into the wrong hands:

- Never give anyone an account number over the phone unless you are sure he or she is a legitimate agent. Remember, a bank or legitimate business will never call you and ask for an account number. They should already have this information; if they need it, they will notify you by mail.

- Never give out account numbers, passwords, or other personal information via e-mail. E-mail is not a secure way to transmit data. It can be intercepted, or the recipient can forward it to someone else. Banks and legitimate businesses won't ask you to provide such information via e-mail.

- When buying something online, make sure the Web site is secure before entering any personal information into a form. Secure Web pages start their URL with "HTTPS", and the browser will display a lock icon, change the color of the title bar, or in some other way indicate that a secure connection has been made.

You can take additional steps to protect your credit as well as your personal information:

- Check your credit report at least once a year. A **credit report** is a document that lists all your financial accounts that can be a source of credit or that you can use for making purchases or for other transactions. These include bank accounts, mortgages, credit cards, and others. Under certain circumstances, you may be entitled to get a free copy of your credit report one or more times a year. Even if you need to pay for a copy of your credit report, you should get one from each of the three major credit reporting bureaus (Equifax, Experian, and Trans Union) at least once each year. Check each report not just to learn your overall credit rating but to find and report any errors they may contain.

- Maintain a good filing system. Carefully file all important papers, and keep them for at least three years. You may need them to dispute errors on a credit report or when reporting unauthorized activity to your credit card company or bank.

- Check with your bank and credit card company and make sure you are protected against unauthorized charges. In most states, your liability is limited if someone else accesses your bank account or uses your credit card without your knowledge. But you may be required to report the incident quickly.

PROTECTING YOUR PRIVACY

While legitimate companies do not use your personal information for identity theft, they nevertheless find those details about you to be extremely useful. Did you know that your buying habits are tracked electronically, in a range of commercial systems? This doesn't apply just to online transactions either. Any time you use a "store loyalty" card to rent movies or buy groceries, the purchases are logged in a database. Your medical, financial, and credit records are available to anybody authorized to view them.

Many of the companies you deal with every day—from your local supermarket to your insurance company—maintain databases filled with information about you. You might expect these firms to know your name and address, but you might be surprised to learn that they know how many times each month you put gas in your car or buy a magazine. And a lot of companies do not keep this information confidential; they may sell it to other companies who are interested in knowing about you.

Personal information is a business commodity that supports a huge shadow industry called **data mining**. Data mining is a business-intelligence-gathering process that every large organization, from banks to grocery stores, employs to sift through computerized data. Companies spot useful patterns in overall behavior to target individuals for special treatment. Companies often use data mining to more efficiently target consumers with products, offers, and discounts that are more likely to interest and attract them.

Some parts of your personal information are available to anybody who has the few dollars required to buy it from

Figure 6.42 A shredder is an excellent and affordable way to destroy sensitive documents in your home or office.

commercial public record services. For a minimal price, companies such as Intelius will give you detailed reports about most people. These reports contain such detailed information as:

- Criminal records, including sex offender registry, felonies, misdemeanors, and federal and county offenses.

- Background information, including marriage records, divorce records, adoption records, driving records, credit history, bankruptcies in the past 20 years, tax liens, small claims, past address history, neighbors, property ownership, mortgages, and licenses.

Records such as marriage licenses and divorce records are **public records**. This means that they, along with many other kinds of legal records, are available to anybody who wants to view them. A number of companies collect public records, package them, and sell them to anyone who wishes to purchase them.

As with other forms of data collection, information providers serve people regardless of their underlying intentions. There are many situations when it can be very useful to have comprehensive background information available. If you are considering a business partnership, for example, it might be helpful to know if your potential new associate has a set of past problems that would make you question the wisdom of such an arrangement. Matters of public record can be used by unscrupulous individuals, but that is an artifact of the user, not the information provider.

Legal records are not the only things that become visible to the public. When using the Internet, you should be aware that your interests and habits are being monitored automatically. The monitoring activity can be carried out by programs running on your own computer or a connected server. This might not seem to be a problem if your motto is "I'm not doing anything wrong, so I have nothing to fear." However, the interpretation of why you visit a particular site is

Figure 6.43 Many of the purchases you make are logged in corporated databases.

in the eye of the beholder. You may not be aware of how your browsing habits are interpreted by others. A single visit to one of the ubiquitous advertiser banner ads at the top of your browser identifies you as someone with an interest in related products.

Data about when you visited, what you looked at, and how long you stayed is used by most commercial Web sites. Use of this data is called "online profiling" and is done to build a profile of your interests and habits. It is analyzed to learn more about you. There are commercial profiles for most people in the United States based on the browsing activity at a specific Internet connection address. This address is tied to the name of the owner of that address no matter who is doing the actual browsing. The reports contain information about browsing habits and may contain accompanying marketing conclusions, called psychographic data. This data makes guesses about who you really are based on your surfing behavior and elaborate inferences are drawn about your interests, habits, associations, and other traits. These guesses are available to any organization willing to pay for access to the profile. Online marketers, commercial information service providers, and, in some cases, federal agencies may have access.

If you take precautions to guard against ID theft, you'll be going a long way toward protecting your privacy in general, but there are a few other steps you should take to keep your private information out of the wrong hands.

Figure 6.44 Marriage licenses and real estate transactions are matters of public record.

One of the main reasons for guarding your personal information is to avoid the attention of marketers, who want to know as much about you as possible so they can target marketing campaigns to people of your demographic status or interests. Helping them understand your interests can reduce the amount of irrelevant marketing messages you receive, but it may also greatly increase the number of demands for your money overall because of your willingness to share data. The following tips can help you keep them off your back:

- Be wary about filling out forms. Whenever you fill out a form on a Web page, send in a subscription card for a magazine, or submit a warranty card for a product, you give out information about yourself. Some of these forms ask for much more than your name and address. As a general rule, don't submit such forms (either online or by mail) unless you have read the company's privacy policy. This policy will tell you how the company handles private information and what it will do with your information. Many companies provide an **opt-out option** on their registration or warranty forms. If you select this option, the company promises either not to share your information with anyone else or not to send you advertisements.

- Guard your primary e-mail address. As you will read later in this lesson, you can avoid spam by having two e-mail addresses. Give your primary address only to people you trust, and use the second address for everything else. The secondary address will receive most of the spam, leaving your main inbox relatively clean.

You can protect yourself further by knowing your legal rights. Consumers have the right to control access to their information. The control is based on a set of laws that have evolved over the past 50 years:

- In 1966, the **Freedom of Information Act** (5 U.S.C. § 552) allowed each individual to view and amend personal information kept about him or her by any governmental entity.

- The **Privacy Act of 1974** (5 U.S.C. § 552a) places universal restrictions on sharing of information about you by federal agencies without written consent.

- The **Fair Credit Reporting Act** (1970) mandates that personal information assembled by credit reporting agencies must be accurate, fair, and private. It allows you to review and update your credit record as well as dispute the entries.

- The **Electronic Communications Privacy Act** (1986) prevents unlawful access to voice communications by wire. It originally regulated electronic wiretaps and provided the basis for laws defining illegal access to electronic communications, including computer information. It is the basis for protection against unreasonable governmental intrusion into Internet usage, stored electronic communications, and e-mail.

- The **Right to Financial Privacy Act of 1978** and the **Financial Modernization Act of 1999** (Gramm-Leach-Bliley) require companies to give consumers notice of their privacy and information-sharing practices.

In response to terrorist attacks on September 11, 2001, the federal government took actions aimed at modifying these protections. Specifically, the Uniting and Strengthening America by Providing Appropriate Tools Required to Intercept and Obstruct Terrorism Act was enacted. It is commonly known as the **USA Patriot Act** and extends the authority of law enforcement and intelligence agencies in monitoring private communications and access to your personal information.

Figure 6.45 An efficient filing system can help you properly keep what you need, and destroy sensitive documents when appropriate.

Not everyone is proficient with computers, and not everyone wants to be. It's Karen Koenig's job to make sure that the students she's working with leave her classroom not only more knowledgeable about computers but also more confident in their ability to use them in daily life.

"Once in a while I'll get a student who is afraid to touch the computer, for fear that he or she may delete files or mess something up," says Koenig, a computer training specialist in the Professional and Community Education area of Bowling Green State University's Continuing & Extended Education program located in Bowling Green, Ohio. "It's very rewarding when that same person walks out of my classroom feeling much more comfortable using technology."

Comfortable, and safer too. Users who have more understanding about their computers, software, and environment are less likely to become a security risk or a victim of malicious activity.

A graduate of Bowling Green State University, Koenig earned her degree in business education and is a certified Microsoft Office User Specialist (MOUS). She began her career teaching a sole computer class and later became a full-time instructor. Koenig spends her time teaching both day and evening classes of university faculty/staff and other adult students on how to use computers and specific applications like Microsoft Excel and Microsoft Word. Along the way, she's mastered applications such as HTML for Web site building and university-specific programs, such as a calendar-scheduling application used by faculty and staff.

Koenig sees future opportunities for computer trainers as good, based on how integrated computers are in our everyday lives. "It's amazing just how many people know nothing about computers, even though they've been around for so long," says Koenig, who is continually updating her own skills to meet her students' needs.

A successful trainer needs a strong background in general computer hardware and software. This means that a trainer should have a solid understanding of how a computer system functions and a mastery of current operating systems and common application software. Often, trainers must get additional instruction or certification if they want to teach others to use certain programs. Companies such as Microsoft and Oracle, for example, offer trainer-certification programs that ensure employers that a trainer has mastered certain products and is qualified to teach others how to use them.

The Bureau of Labor Statistics reported the 2009 mean annual wage at $55,000 for training and development specialists, with a wide overall range of $30,000 to $85,000 for that type of work.

"It's very rewarding when that same person walks out of my classroom feeling much more comfortable using technology."

ONLINE SPYING TOOLS

Software developers have created a number of ways to track your activities online. While such profile building can be done for legitimate and helpful reasons—for example, helping webmasters determine who visits their sites most often—the software tools used for this purpose are also being used in ways most consumers do not appreciate.

One of the best-known tracking methods is the use of *cookies*. As discussed in Chapter 4, a cookie is a small text file that a Web server asks your browser to place on your computer. The cookie contains information that identifies your computer (its IP address), you (your user name or e-mail address), and information about your visit to the Web site. For instance, the cookie might list the last time you visited the site, which pages you downloaded, and how long you were at the site before leaving. If you set up an account at a Web site such as an e-commerce site, the cookie will contain information about your account, making it easy for the server to find and manage your account whenever you visit.

Despite their helpful purpose, cookies are now considered a significant threat to privacy. This is because they can be used to store and report many types of information. For example, a cookie can store a list of *all* the sites you visit. This data can be transferred to the site that placed the cookie on your system, and that information can be used against your wishes. For example, the cookie's maker might use the cookie to determine what kinds of advertisements will appear on your screen the next time you visit the Web site. Many web-masters use information from cookies to determine the demographic makeup of their site's audience. Even worse, cookies can be used as the basis of hacker attacks. At any time, your PC may be storing hundreds or thousands of cookies. If you could examine them, you probably would decide that you didn't want to keep many of them on your system.

Another tracking method is to use a **Web bug**, a small image file that can be embedded in a Web page or an HTML-format e-mail message. A Web bug can be as small as a single pixel and can easily be hidden anywhere in an HTML document. Behind that tiny image lies code that functions in much the same way as a cookie, allowing the bug's creator to track many of your online activities. A bug can record what Web pages you view, keywords you type into a search engine, personal information you enter in a form on a Web page, and other data. Because Web bugs are hidden, they are considered by many to be eavesdropping devices. Upon learning about Web bugs, most consumers look for a way to defeat them.

While *spyware* is mostly considered to be a tool of hackers, similar technology is sometimes used by legitimate companies to gather information about how their products are being used. For example, when you install and register a program, it may ask you to fill out a form. The program then sends the information to the developer, who stores it in a database. When used in this manner, spyware-type programs are seen as perfectly legitimate—although perhaps more aggressive than many people prefer—because the user is aware that information is being collected. In some cases, consumers are given the ability to opt out of the collection process.

SPAM, PHISHING, AND SPOOFING

As you learned in Chapter 5, e-mail spam has flooded the Internet's mail system and is very costly in time and money to keep it at bay and then process what gets through the gates. If you begin to receive spam e-mail messages—and chances are good that eventually you will—it means that your e-mail address has been found by spammers. This commonly occurs through harvesting e-mails from Web posts (finding your e-mail address in the text of messages in for-sale or chat forums, for example); purchasing e-mail lists from brokers who have been harvesting on the Web or finding ways to get you to voluntarily reveal your information to them; or by randomly creating e-mail address names in an attempt to find legitimate addresses.

Along with spam, e-mails containing a form of social engineering called **phishing** are

Figure 6.46 Sometimes more malicious than delicious, computer cookies can turn a Web site into a powerful data-gathering tool, for both helpful and harmful purposes.

Figure 6.47 Phishing scams appear to warn you of a security problem, but they are fake sites designed to steal passwords.

very common. Phishing (an alternate spelling of the word "fishing") e-mails are designed to look like official messages from banks, government agencies, and online services such as PayPal or eBay. The messages almost always contain a warning that a problem has occurred with your account or its security, and requests that you log in to correct the problem, verify security data, or change your password. The e-mails vary greatly in sophistication, appearing as anything from an obvious, clumsy fake to an exact duplicate of the graphics and layout the actual company uses in its e-mails.

Phishing e-mails contain links directing you to Web pages, but while the link's user-visible text may say "http://www.ebay.com," the actual link to follow inside the e-mail will send the user to a completely different, hacker-operated malicious site. Unwary users will then be prompted to enter account names and numbers, passwords, and other sensitive information; because the Web site looks superficially correct, users are sometimes fooled into providing the data.

Avoiding the phishing trap is fairly simple with three basic concepts. First, be aware that very few online services, banks, utility companies, or government agencies will send you an e-mail and ask you to enter a password. If a problem has been detected at the company or agency, problems will certainly be communicated in a more professional way than a clumsily-worded message. As a general rule, assume that any surprise announcement is fake until proven otherwise. Some services use a special identifier in their messages, the absence of which is a sure sign of phishing; PayPal, for example, writes the user's account name in the salutation, so a PayPal message that begins simply, "Dear Valued PayPal Customer," is a scam.

Second, never respond to an unsolicited e-mail request by clicking one of the e-mail links. If you get a strange message from your bank and you want to verify that everything is okay, start a browser yourself and travel to the bank's Web site in order to log in. Chances are, the bank's home Web page will contain a warning against a recent phishing scam.

Third, do not use your public, disposable e-mail address for trusted sites and services. Any security alerts that arrive on your spam-catching address can then be safely ignored along with the rest of the junk.

Phishing is part of a more general category of hacking known as **spoofing**, which is an attempt to deceive a computer user or system by providing false information in some way. Along with phishing, spoofing includes a variety of ways that e-mails and network requests to computers can be altered.

For example, e-mail and network messages contain headers—data not usually visible to the user that relate to the source and destination of the messages—that can be manipulated to make those messages appear to be from a different person or location. Spammers often alter the headers of their e-mail messages so that they appear to come from legitimate sources, bypassing filters that weed out junk mail from known spammer locations. They may also alter the "reply" fields in the message header so that if you try to reply to spam e-mail, you find a useless return address.

Other than phishing scams, most forms of spoofing are done in ways that are invisible to the average user. E-mail and Web hosting companies frequently handle spoofing problems on behalf of their customers; and spoofing that is local to a user's PC was likely delivered via malware that can be removed once detected.

MANAGING COOKIES, SPAM, AND SPYWARE

Unlike most of the countermeasures you have read about previously, high-tech methods are required to deal with privacy threats such as cookies and spyware. Fortunately, many privacy management systems are already active in the software you use for Internet services.

Most Web browsers feature built-in settings that give you control over how cookies are handled. You can elect to refuse them altogether, allow them from certain sites, allow certain kinds of cookies, or simply allow them all. Refusing all cookies will prevent many Web sites from functioning properly (especially online shopping sites, which usually rely on cookies to store shopping cart and other vital information). You also may become unable to use browsing preferences that make your Web experience more pleasant, such as bypassing a rule-acceptance page after your first visit to a Web site. At the other extreme, accepting all cookies leaves you vulnerable to an invasion of your machine and your privacy by people you normally would not allow inside your home or office.

Most browsers create default cookie settings that seek a balance between security and a functional browsing experience. They generally accept **session cookies** (cookies that last only for your current browser session and typically act as helpers for navigating through the site) and **first-party cookies**, which are cookies placed by the Web site you are visiting. They may refuse certain kinds of **persistent cookies**, which stay on your system after your browsing is done, and **third-party cookies**, which come

Along with cookie handling, most browsers now provide the ability to block pop-up advertisements, the creation of new browser windows by Web sites, and the execution of certain kinds of browser program instruction scripts. As with cookies, these features are initially set in the browser to provide a balance between functional browsing and privacy protection, and they can be modified if desired by the user.

Browsers will typically alert you when they have blocked a pop-up window or a script and give you the option of allowing it to proceed. Sometimes, legitimate companies will use these tools to provide you with a service you want, so you can enable that function on their sites.

Unlike browser security, e-mails and e-mail spam cannot be so easily configured and evaded. Web sites exist in a single place and deliver content only when requested; if you don't trust a site or don't want to see it, you simply don't navigate to it. E-mail, in contrast, is delivered whether you want it or not, and spammers are uninterested in stopping their activity no matter what you might tell them.

Most Internet service providers are already doing what they can to filter and remove unwanted e-mail content. To deal with what remains after their efforts, you can take several countermeasures against spam, all of which are simple.

> ## "Unlike browser security, e-mails and e-mail spam cannot be so easily configured and evaded."

from a different Web site than the one you are viewing (which commonly means they are provided by an advertiser on the site you are viewing).

Browsers provide the ability to view the current cookie rules and alter them if the current values are unacceptable. If you wish, you can build lists in the browser's tool for cookie preferences of sites that are specifically allowed to use cookies and sites that must not be allowed to use cookies. Browsers also provide the ability to delete existing cookie files at the request of the user. It is not a bad idea to delete them periodically, but keep in mind that, if you delete them all, you will get rid of the ones that are helping you, not just the ones that are helping the advertisers.

As mentioned earlier, you should never give your primary e-mail address to any person or business you don't know. (Your **primary e-mail account** is the one you set up with your ISP as part of your Internet access package.) Instead, give that address only to people and businesses you trust, and ask them not to give it to anyone else. Then, set up a **secondary e-mail account** using a free, Web-based e-mail service such as Gmail, Hotmail, or Yahoo. If you own and host your own domain, you can create another e-mail address for general-purpose use (for example, spamforjack@jackstravels.com). Use this address when you must provide an e-mail address when making a purchase or registering for a service. The secondary address can collect the spam, while your primary address stays out of the hands of spammers.

Figure 6.48 Most e-mail programs use spam-filtering software and may send messages identified as spam into a separate folder.

Make sure your ISP is indeed working to block incoming spam. If it isn't providing that service, consider switching to support an ISP that does. Look at the offerings of various e-mail programs, and find one that provides **spam filtering** functions; many of the newer versions can toss a good percentage of spam e-mail into a Junk Mail folder as it arrives. For the messages that aren't filtered, you can delete them by hand or create new rules to handle recurring messages. For example, you can tell the program to ignore messages from a specific sender or to automatically store certain messages in a specific folder (see Figure 6.48).

Finally, never respond to a spam message, even if it includes a link that purports to remove you from the sender's address list. Most such "remove me" options are phony and do nothing more than alert the spammer that your e-mail address is valid and that someone is actually reading the messages that arrive. This, unfortunately, makes you a prime target for even more spam than before.

To get onto the Internet equivalent of a "do not spam" list, you may choose to opt out of any kind of legitimate targeted advertising by going to http://www.networkadvertising.org/. This site is operated by the Network Advertising Initiative (NAI) and is the advertising industry's voluntary response to consumers' objections to secretive tracking and spamming of Internet users.

Fact Check

1. How can you reduce threats related to paper documents?
   a. Read your statements immediately, and discard unneeded documents wisely.
   b. Accumulate all mail in a box, and open it once a month.
   c. Put old bills and documents in a recycling bin rather than the trash can.
2. Privacy settings for cookies, pop-up windows, and program scripts can often be set within
   a. e-mail programs
   b. Web browsers
   c. power management utilities

- With regard to computer security, a threat is anything in the environment that can cause harm; a vulnerability is any unprotected element of a computer system that is not protected from harm; and a countermeasure is an action or device put into place to prevent a threat from causing harm.

- To secure your data, you must keep other people away from it. This means limiting physical access to your computer so other people cannot get to your data. It also means using a firewall to prevent hackers from accessing your system via the Internet.

- Take care when handling computer hardware and storage media to avoid damaging them. If a disk becomes damaged, the data it stores may be lost.

- Computer data may be vulnerable to malware, which is software designed to harm a computer system or user's personal security. In addition, hackers may compromise data by illegally accessing computer systems, altering and destroying data, and overloading networks to prevent access to information. Any system linked to the Internet is also at risk of cybercrime.

- Regular data backups are an effective countermeasure against threats to your data. Should any of your data become lost or damaged, you can restore it to your computer by using a backup copy.

- By protecting your hardware, you are also protecting your data and avoiding the expense of replacing your PC. Make sure others cannot get to your PC and damage or steal it.

- Another way to protect your PC hardware and data is by keeping the system clean and avoiding exposure to magnetism or extreme temperatures. Dust can also cause system components to fail, so it is important to keep your PC clean.

- You can protect your privacy and avoid identity theft by handling important documents carefully—especially those that contain personal information such as your Social Security number or account numbers.

- Another important step to protecting your privacy is to be careful about giving out personal information. Never give out account numbers or passwords via e-mail. Check your credit report once a year to look for suspicious transactions and errors. The report can provide clues if someone else is making transactions in your name. Learn more about the laws that exist to protect your personal information from being misused. Shred documents that contain personal information such as account numbers and financial records.

- Web browsers commonly provide tools for managing cookies, pop-up advertising, and browser scripts. A cookie management utility will offer more options for identifying and removing unwanted cookies from your PC.

- Spyware and other forms of malware can usually be detected and removed by anti-malware software. Consider installing more than one of these programs to find and remove problems. If do-it-yourself methods fail to fix your PC, local computer stores and online anti-malware forums may provide valuable assistance.

- To avoid receiving spam, avoid giving out your e-mail address. Otherwise, you can reduce spam by setting up a secondary e-mail account and using e-mail filters.

Key Terms

Key Terms QUIZ

Complete each statement by writing one of the terms listed under "Key Terms" in each blank.

1. A(n) _____ will protect your computer hardware against power spikes but no other electrical supply problems.

2. A(n) _____ is anything that has not been protected against threats, making it open to harm.

3. A firewall is highly advised for users with a(n) _____ to the Internet.

4. _____ occurs when someone impersonates you by using your name, Social Security number, or other personal information.

5. If you select the _____ on a company's Web page or warranty form, the company promises either not to share your information or not to send you advertisements.

6. A low-tech ID thief might resort to _____, searching for personal information in garbage cans.

7. A(n) _____ cookie is temporary; it is automatically deleted when you close your browser.

8. A(n) _____ cookie comes from a different Web site than the one you are viewing.

9. Unwanted advertising is produced on a user's computer with malware called _____.

10. By creating a(n) _____ in your e-mail program, you can tell the program to ignore messages from a specific sender.

Review QUESTIONS

In your own words, briefly answer the following questions.

1. When is it especially important to use a firewall? How does it help?

2. By itself, is a threat to a computer system harmful? Why or why not?

3. Choose three of the threats described in this lesson, and compare them in terms of their likelihood and the seriousness of the damage they can cause. Which of the risks you chose is the most serious to you as a computer user? Which would you expect to be most serious to your phone company?

4. Why should you tell your bank or credit card company about suspicious transactions or charges immediately?

5. Describe two circumstances for sharing passwords that you should avoid in order to keep your data private.

6. How can you avoid spam by having two e-mail addresses?

7. What is phishing? How can it be avoided?

8. Define four types of cookies that can be placed on your computer by a Web site. Which, if any, of these would you allow?

9. What is the best way to deal with spyware and other forms of malware?

10. What is spam filtering? Where would a computer user obtain this function?

LESSON LAB

Complete the following exercises as directed by your instructor.

1. How much personal information do you give away? Do a self-survey to answer this question. In the past six months, have you given away any information about yourself? Think about purchases you've made online, over the phone, and in stores. You also may give out information when registering at a Web site, setting up an account, registering a product, or subscribing to a magazine. List all the personal information you've given out, and estimate the number of times you have willingly released it.

2. Find a backup power supply solution. Use your browser to visit APC Corporation's UPS product selection tool at http://www.apc.com/tools/ups_selector/index.cfm. Fill in the information about your current computer, as best you can determine, in the fields provided on the Web page, and click the Show UPS Solution button. Review the products provided, and note the retail cost required to keep your computer running for the desired amount of time. When you are finished, close your browser.

Employees in any field need to apply critical thinking skills to observe, interpret, and analyze information from a variety of sources, such as reports, customer complaints or ideas, and situations in the workplace. In this exercise, you will practice critical thinking by evaluating a real-world situation and making recommendations about computer security.

In groups of three or four, visit a nearby public location where computers are in active use, such as your school's library or computer lab. Pretend that you have been appointed as a security evaluation team to assess the security measures taken in the work area you visit. By observing the environment and the computers themselves, identify what kinds of threats exist to the proper functioning of the area and equipment, as well as to the safety of the people and data in the area.

Agree on five security threats to the people or equipment, and list them on a sheet of paper. For each threat, summarize any measures that have been taken in the work area to counter the threat. Finally, recommend any additional measures that should be taken to protect the hardware and people. Bring your list to the next class meeting.

[*Chapter* LABS]

Complete the following exercises using a computer in your classroom, lab, or home.

1. Learn more about anti-malware programs. Visit at least one Web site for an active software solution that protects your system in real time, such as Avast Antivirus. Then visit at least one Web site for cleaning and repair software, such as Malwarebytes' Anti-Malware or SUPERAntiSpyware. Identify the ways that each type of software works to keep your system free of malware. Summarize the comparison in a one-page report, and be prepared to present your findings to the class.

2. Back up a folder. Use your operating system's Help system to find out if your OS has a built-in backup utility. If so, launch the utility, and learn how it works. With your instructor's permission, use the program to back up at least one file or folder. You may be able to back up the data to a network drive, another hard drive in your computer, or a recordable CD. Next, use the program's Help system to learn how to restore the backed-up data, in case it were accidentally deleted from the hard disk.

3. Learn more about CAN-SPAM. Go online and research the CAN-SPAM law, which took effect at the beginning of 2004. What measures does the law take to limit the amount of spam messages that consumers receive? What penalties does it assess spammers who violate the law? What recourse does the law give to consumers who continue to receive a lot of spam? Your instructor may ask you to focus on one aspect of the law or to work with a group. Compile your findings into a one-page report, and be prepared to share it with the class.

[*Think* AND DISCUSS]

As directed by your instructor, discuss the following questions in class or in groups.

1. Laws such as CAN-SPAM hope to curb the amount of junk e-mail by imposing restrictions on spammers. Do you think these laws go far enough? Should unsolicited commercial e-mail messages be banned altogether? Why or why not? How might the United States go about enforcing domestic spam laws against criminal spammers in other countries?

2. Before you read this chapter, what steps (if any) were you taking to protect your personal information? How will you change your approach to guarding your privacy? Compare your thoughts and ideas with those of your classmates.

[*Fact check* ANSWERS]

6A:

LO6.1 Making Your Mark on the Web

1: **a.** to make an outline of the information to include

2: **b.** For regularly sharing a person's thoughts about a particular subject

3: **b.** A Web site that collects information and uses a standard format for displaying it

LO6.2 Online Income and E-Commerce

1: b. Based on how often Internet users click on the advertisement.

2: b. Ethical practices for improving a Web site's search engine ratings.

LO6.3 Cloud Computing for Individuals and Businesses

1: b. Data storage and software execution hosted by Internet service companies.

2: c. that are hosted on an Internet server, with the local computer used only for input and output.

6B:

LO6.4 Basic Security Concepts

1: b. Anything that has not been protected against threats

2: a. Anything you do to protect yourself and your computer from harm

LO6.5 Safeguarding Your Hardware

1: b. A battery backup and power conditioning unit for computer hardware

2: a. Liquids

LO6.6 Keeping Your Data Secure

1: a. A program that attaches to a host file and replicates itself

2: b. Searches for sensitive data or records user activity and reports its findings to an unauthorized person

3: a. Nuclear power plants

LO6.7 Protecting Yourself and Your Identity

1: a. Read your statements immediately, and discard unneeded documents wisely.

2: b. Web browsers

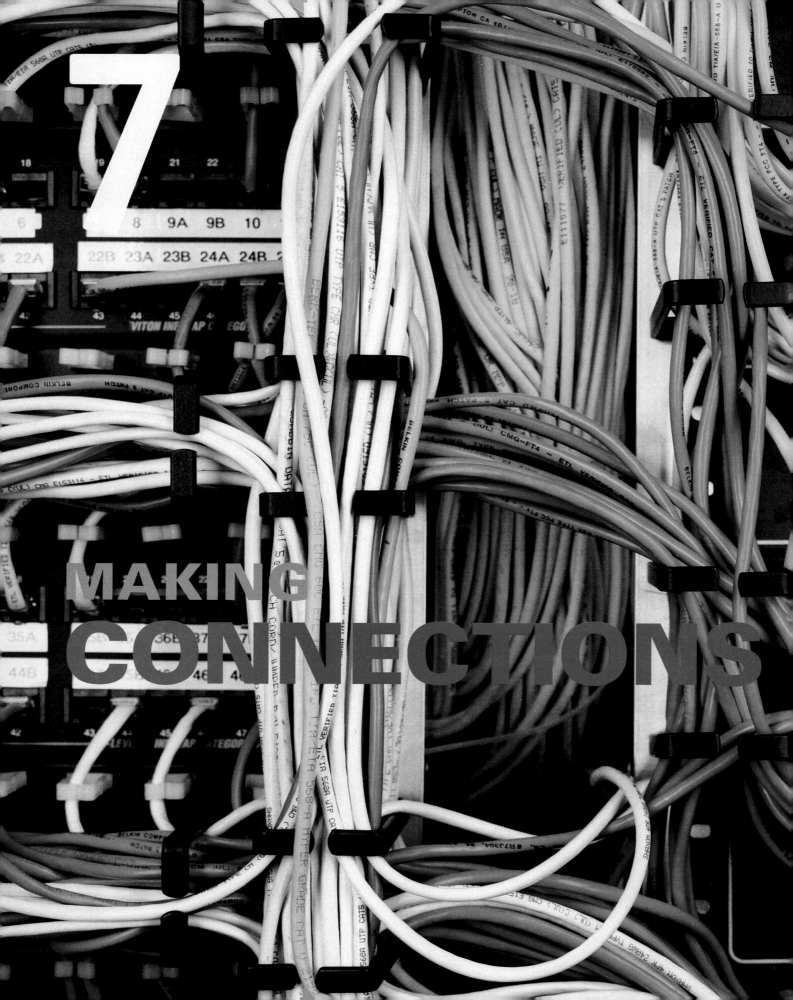

7

MAKING CONNECTIONS

Chapter Overview

One of the most powerful aspects of computing is the ease with which people make connections and stay in contact. Whether at work, at home or out on the town, we stay in constant touch with the people in our lives via the vast computing network that surrounds us. Along with that power and convenience, however, comes the need to understand how our computer-related actions and decisions affect our reputations and the lives of those around us. Have you ever shared music with other computer users? Have you thought about the degree of harm, if any, that might come from that kind of sharing?

LESSON 7A:
Networking and Information Systems

When PCs first appeared, software was designed for a single user. There were few obvious advantages to connecting many PCs together, and the technology was not adequate for doing so. People who had computers either worked on their own or shared files via "sneakernet"—a term coined to describe people bringing data disks and tapes from place to place on foot.

As the use of personal computers spread, developers began offering complex software designed for multiple users. Organizations quickly learned the importance of connecting PCs. Home users discovered an appetite for an ever-increasing volume and variety of information, from news to entertainment. In response to the universal demand for more and better access, data communications technology has become an explosive area of growth in the computer industry. Now businesses and people alike take advantage of near-instant delivery of video, sound, documents, pictures, and news, and the state-of-the-art data transmission continues to rapidly evolve.

Not surprisingly, the ease of sharing and storing information has led to an explosion of ways that business, governments and individuals make use of that technology. Online shopping companies like Amazon.com combine a wealth of information about products, customers, shippers and reseller partners to offer comprehensive catalogs of products for sale. Hospitals need to store, find and retrieve information about their patients' records and appointments; and they also use complex information networks to manage employee data, inventories, payment and billing records, and more. Governments must maintain massive financial and document databases, and manage a heavy, constant inflow of new rules and paperwork.

Networks go hand in hand with software systems to connect users and distribute computing power and storage. Together, the software and network hardware create information systems to properly serve both provider and user.

In this lesson, you'll learn more about the basic hardware and software needed to create and configure computer networks. You will also take a look at several types of information systems and what they do.

7.1 Computer Networks

A **network** is a set of hardware, software, and media systems used to connect computers together, enabling them to communicate, exchange information, and share resources in real time.

Networks come in many varieties. When most people think of a network, they imagine several computers in a single location sharing documents and devices such as printers. But a network can include all the computers and devices in a department, a building, or multiple buildings spread over a wide geographic area. The Internet is an example of a massive global network that interconnects many individual networks, allowing people around the world to share information as though they were across the hall from one another.

BENEFITS OF USING NETWORKS

Networks let multiple users access shared data, programs, and hardware devices almost instantly. Along with the ease of sharing resources, networks open up new ways to communicate that were not practical or possible in the past.

Figure 7.1   Networks allow many users to share the same resources from their own computer.

In any business, several workers may need to use the same data at the same time. In addition to using many of the same data files, office workers can use the same programs when they are on a server. In contrast, if PCs are not networked, a separate copy of each program must be installed on every computer. This setup can be costly. Companies can lower that cost somewhat by purchasing a **site license**, which is an agreement to buy a single copy of a program and then pay the software developer a fee for the right to copy the application onto a specified number of computers. However, installing and configuring a program on many different computers still requires time and labor, and maintaining many separate installations of a program is an ongoing expense. Many organizations therefore connect users' computers to a network server and enable users to share a **network version** of a program. In a network version, one copy of the application is stored on the server, with a minimum number of supporting files copied to each user's PC (see Figure 7.2). For the users, the program runs as if it were on their computer.

One of the best reasons for small businesses to set up a network is the ability to share peripheral devices (like printers, scanners, and storage devices). Peripheral devices are not normally in constant use by every person working on a computer; documents are normally printed now and then, and backups are typically made on a daily schedule. Many organizations purchase a few peripheral devices and make them available via a network.

In business, data is extremely valuable, so it is important that employees back up their data. One way to ensure that data is backed up is to keep it on a shared storage device that employees can access through a network. Often the network manager makes regular backups of the data on the shared storage device. Site managers can also use special software to back up files stored on employees' hard drives from a central location. With this method, files do not have to be copied to the server before they can be backed up.

As more and more people connect to the Internet, the world's largest computer network, an ever-growing array of communication methods and programs is being produced. Some of the early modes for personal communication are still going strong, while others have faded or disappeared completely in favor of new methods. Here are just some of the ways that networks connect people as well as computers:

- **Electronic mail.** These systems, which allow a user to deliver messages and data files to others on the network, are common and heavily used, serving as one of the primary communication methods for people of all ages, and businesses around the world.

- **Real-time chat programs.** Years ago, real-time chat was limited mostly to "chat rooms" formed with Internet Relay Chat (IRC) software. Chat channels were formed with specific names, and people could join channels for discussing an endless variety of topics. While IRC still exists, its popularity has waned in favor of modern chat programs. Chat software is provided both as a standalone program like AOL's Instant Messenger; and as an integrated feature of other programs such as Facebook, Skype, or even as part of a company's customer support Web site.

- **Social media.** Social networking sites like Facebook and LinkedIn, and microblogging services like Twitter rely heavily on computer networks to keep their "people networks" actively sharing information. Many social media programs extend their support to smart phones and other mobile computing devices.

- **Business conferencing.** With the ability to stream video, pictures, and sound in real time, high-speed networks have made it possible to conduct business in new ways. Companies frequently set up videoconferencing

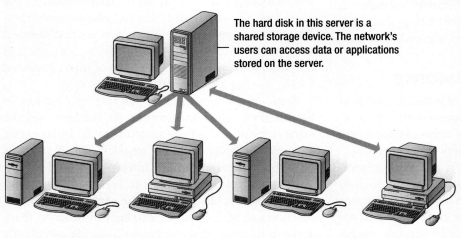

The hard disk in this server is a shared storage device. The network's users can access data or applications stored on the server.

Figure 7.2   A computer network lets users share access to data and/or applications.

sessions between distantly located offices or groups, so presentations or face-to-face meetings can be conducted via webcam, microphone, and screen. Webinars, which are sales or education meetings that commonly feature either voice, presentation slides and live video, or sometimes prerecorded information, have become a popular and cost-effective way to generate interest in a company's offerings.

- **Voice over Internet protocol (VoIP).** VoIP is a method of efficiently and reliably transmitting voice across a computer network, turning a computer into a telephone. Software and services like Skype allow users to make calls from their computer both to other computers running Skype and to regular telephones. The reverse is also possible: Telephone users can call a number purchased by a Skype user, and the telephone call "rings" the Skype-running computer anywhere in the world so long as it is connected to the Internet.

- **PC sharing.** Software exists (for example, via the GoToMyPC service on the Internet) to allow one user to access another user's PC as if it were his or her own. One part of the program runs to send data on one PC to the other; another part of the software runs on the receiving computer to interpret the sender's data. The receiving computer creates a program window that is an exact copy of the sending PC's desktop. The receiving user can control the mouse, start and stop programs, and type data into files on the sender's computer. Some people use this service as a way to access their home or office computer when they are away. PC support staff use it as a way to diagnose problems or educate new users with live demonstrations. Security modules in both parts of the software ensure that only those authorized to access a PC are allowed to do so.

COMMON TYPES OF NETWORKS

To understand the different types of networks and how they operate, you need to know how networks are structured. There are two main types of networks: local area networks (LANs) and wide area networks (WANs).

A **local area network (LAN)** is a data communication system consisting of multiple devices such as computers and printers. This type of network contains computers that are relatively near each other and are physically connected using cables or wireless media. Any network that exists within a single building, or even a group of adjacent buildings, is considered a LAN. It is often helpful to connect separate LANs

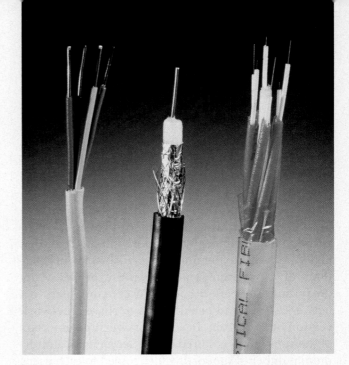

Figure 7.3   Twisted pair, coaxial and fiber-optic cable are all common network media in use today.

together so they can communicate and exchange data. Though a LAN can make a connection to other networks in the public environment (such as the Internet), that public connection itself is not part of the LAN.

A **wide area network (WAN)** is the connection of two or more central computers or LANs, generally across a wide geographical area. For example, a company may have its corporate headquarters and manufacturing plant in one city and its marketing office in another. Each site needs resources, data, and programs locally, but it also needs to share data with the other sites. To accomplish this feat of data communication, the company can attach devices that connect over public utilities to create a WAN. Though it is common for a WAN to be made up of interconnected LANs, it is not a requirement.

Some organizations offer an internal version of the Internet, called an **intranet**. An intranet uses the same software and service structure as the Internet (for example, Web sites and file transfer), but it contains only the company's private information, and it usually limits access to employees and selected contractors having ongoing business with the company. The organization can also create an **extranet** in order to share some of its intranet resources with people outside the organization. You can access an extranet only if you have a valid username and password, and your identity determines which parts of the extranet you can view.

NETWORK MEDIA

The means used to link together a computer network's **nodes**—the processing location that can be a PC or some other device such as a networked printer—is called **media**. The network uses the media to carry data from one node to another. Network media may take the form of wires, or in a wireless network the atmosphere itself acts as the medium because it carries the wireless signals that nodes and servers use to communicate. Following are a few of the most common types of wire-based media:

- **Twisted-pair cable** normally consists of four pairs of wires. The individual pairs have two wires that are separately insulated in plastic, then twisted around each other and bound together in a layer of plastic. Except for the plastic coating, nothing shields this type of wire from outside interference, so it is also called unshielded twisted-pair (UTP) wire. Some twisted-pair wire is encased in a metal sheath and called shielded twisted-pair (STP) wire.

- Like the cabling used in cable television systems, **coaxial cable** has two conductors—a single wire in the center of the cable and a wire mesh shield that surrounds the first wire—with an insulator between. Coaxial cable's main advantage is that it is less susceptible to signal interference, so compared with twisted-pair wire, it allows for more distance between the devices being connected.

- A **fiber-optic cable** is a thin strand of glass that transmits pulsating beams of light rather than electric current. Fiber-optic cable is immune to the electromagnetic interference that is a problem for copper wire, so distances between nodes can be greater than with coaxial or twisted-pair wire. Besides being extremely fast, fiber-optic cable can carry an enormous number of messages simultaneously and is a very secure transmission medium. However, it is much costlier than other cables and somewhat more vulnerable to damage in installation.

Wireless networks use radio or infrared signals that travel through the air to transmit data. Office LANs can use radio signals to transmit data between nodes in a building. Notebook computers are now commonly equipped with an antenna and transmitter for connecting to LANs and public Internet access points, called **wireless hotspots**. Corporate WANs often use microwave transmission to connect LANs within the same metropolitan area. WANs that cover long distances often use satellites and microwave communication.

What kind of media should you use to assemble a network? In wired network communications, the relative quality of media is compared using two factors. The first is the maximum distance between nodes that data can reliably travel without **attenuation**, which is the loss of intensity and clarity of the data signal being transmitted. The second factor is **bandwidth**, or the amount of data over time that the media can carry, typically measured in either megabits per second (Mbps) or gigabits per second (Gbps).

For wired networks, twisted-pair wire is by far the most common medium in use today in home and many business environments. Different wire specifications have been developed over the years; currently, Category 5e (sometimes known as Cat5e) is the most common of in use. Category 6 and 6a wires, designed to carry data at a higher frequency with less signal degradation between wires than Cat5e, is slowly gaining greater acceptance. The latest twisted-pair standard, Category 7, has not yet achieved mainstream acceptance. Table 7.1 gives a brief comparison of bandwith and transmission distances for the popular types of wired media.

NETWORK TOPOLOGIES

A well-designed network will move data efficiently. Data moves though the network in a structure called **packets**, which are pieces of a message broken down into small units by the sending PC and reassembled by the receiving PC. Different networks format packets in different ways, but most packets have two parts:

1. The **header** is the first part of the packet and contains information needed by the network: the node that sent the packet (the source) and the address of the node that will receive the packet (the destination). The network reads each packet's header to determine where to send the packet and, in some cases, the best way to

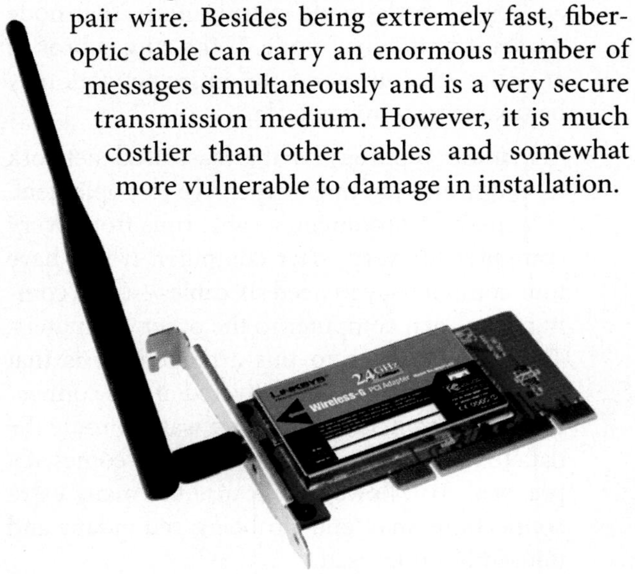

Figure 7.4 A wireless interface card enables a desktop PC to join a wireless network.

TABLE 7.1 BANDWIDTH AND DISTANCE LIMITS FOR WIRED NETWORK MEDIA

Type of Media	Maximum Transmission Distance	Bandwidth
Category 5e twisted-pair	100 meters	up to 1 Gbps
Category 6 twisted-pair	100 meters	At least 1 Gbps
Coaxial cable	500 meters	100 Mbps
Fiber-optic cable	10 kilometers or more	1 to 100 Gbps

get it to its destination. The header also contains control data that helps the receiving node reassemble a message's packets in the right order.

2. The **payload** is the actual data being transmitted between the two nodes.

Messages are broken down into packets in order to increase transmission efficiency. Smaller packets reduce the chances for a lost or broken transmission. Because a message's packets do not have to be received in any particular order, individual packets can be sent separately through whichever paths in the network are most efficient at the time of transmission.

The efficiency with which packets move through a LAN depends on its **topology**—the logical layout of the cables and devices that connect the nodes of the network. One way a network's topology improves efficiency is by reducing collisions, which occur when multiple nodes try to transmit data at the same time. If two packets collide, they are either discarded or returned to the sender to be retransmitted in a timed sequence.

Network designers consider several factors when deciding which topology or combination of topologies to use: the type of computers and cabling (if any) in place, the distance between computers, the degree of reliability needed, the speed at which data must travel around the network, and the cost of setting up the network. Figure 7.5 illustrates basic topologies that are used for computer networks:

- A network with a **bus topology** arranges the network nodes in a series, linking one node to the next via a single cable. A special device, called a **terminator**, is attached at the cable's start and end points, to stop network signals so they do not bounce back down the cable. This topology's main advantage is that it uses the least amount of cabling. However, extra circuitry and software are used to keep data packets from colliding with one another. Also, a broken connection can bring down all or part of the network.

- With a **star topology**, probably the most common topology, all nodes are connected to a hub (a type of linking device, described in the next section) and communicate through it. Data packets travel through the hub and are sent to the attached nodes, eventually reaching their destinations. In a star topology, a broken connection between a node and the hub does not affect the rest of the network. If the hub is lost, however, all nodes connected to that hub are unable to communicate.

- The **ring topology** connects the network's nodes in a circular chain, with each node connected to the next. The last node connects to the first, completing the ring. Each node examines data as it travels through the ring. If the packet is not addressed to the node examining it, that node passes it to the next node. If the ring is broken at or between one node, the entire network may be unable to communicate.

- The **mesh topology** is the least-used network topology and the most expensive to implement. In a mesh environment, a cable runs from every computer to every other computer. If you have four computers, you need six cables—three coming from each computer to the other computers. The big advantage to this arrangement is that data can never fail to be delivered; if one connection goes down, there are other ways to route the data to its destination. That advantage comes at a practical cost, however, because the many extra connections may end up being redundant and unused or underused.

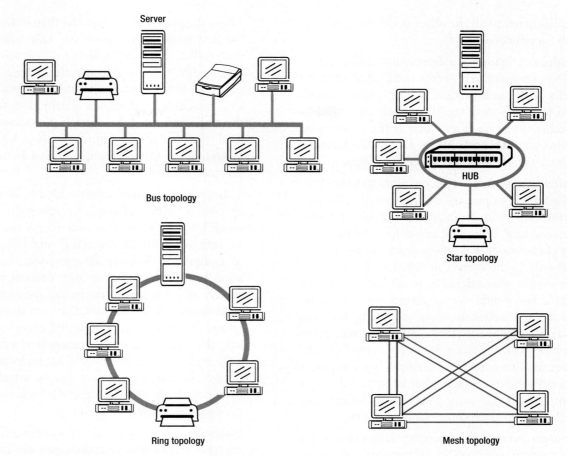

Figure 7.5 Network topologies.

Remember that the network topology describes a logical layout, not a physical one. If you hook up four PCs and a printer with a bus topology, the network wiring will connect those nodes one after the other in series. Even so, you don't have to have them actually placed in a straight line on the desk; what matters is the way they are connected, not the way they sit around the office.

NETWORK HARDWARE

A transmission medium is necessary to make a network, but wires alone are not enough. Hardware must be present at each node to translate data to and from packets and to send and receive the packets. In most network configurations, more hardware must be in place along the way to act as mail carrier and traffic cop for the packets that are being sent.

The device at each node that performs translation and transmission is the network interface card (NIC), also known as a network adapter card or network card. In some cases, the NIC is a circuit board that must be installed in or attached to the computer or device. Much more commonly now, the NIC hardware is included as a subsystem on computer motherboards and in network-ready printers. NICs for wired networks have a port where data cables can be connected. Wireless NICs provide an antenna and transmitter instead of a cable port, and, in some cases (especially in modern laptops), those parts are not visible to the user because they are integrated into the case of the device. The NIC's tasks of sending and receiving packets are overseen and controlled by special network software that coordinates its actions with the computer's operating system.

Unless the network has an exceptionally simple configuration, linking devices need to be added to ensure that data gets to the right place (and without attenuation when long distances are involved). These linking devices include the following:

- **Repeaters.** A **repeater** is used to prevent attenuation when packets are traveling long distances. It receives each packet, ensures that it is intact, and retransmits it down the line toward the next node at full-signal strength.

- **Hubs.** A **hub** provides multiple ports for connecting nodes. When it receives a packet from one port, it transmits the packet without modification to all the other nodes to which the hub is connected.

- **Bridges.** A **bridge** is a device that connects two LANs or two segments of the same LAN. A bridge looks at the information in each packet header and forwards data traveling from one LAN to another. In some cases, such as the connection between a LAN and a WAN such as the Internet, routers are often used in place of bridges.

- **Switches.** A **switch** is a packet-routing device, typically with multiple port connections, that is aware of the exact address or identity of all the nodes attached to it. Because it can determine the identity of each node, it is able to send packets directly and only to the correct destination. Because it is not merely rebroadcasting in all directions, as a simple hub would do, the chance for packet collisions and retransmission is greatly reduced, increasing network efficiency. It can also allow multiple conversations between nodes to take place simultaneously (for example, two computers can deliver data to each other while two different computers do the same), because it can keep the packet flow of each conversation separate.

- **Routers.** A **router** is a complex device that stores the routing information for networks. A router looks at each packet's header to determine where the packet should go and then determines the best route for the packet to take toward its destination. A router will not allow unknown data traffic to pass through the device unless modified to do so; a packet must be addressed to a specifically identified destination to pass through the router. A router is connected to at least two networks, commonly two LANs or WANs, or a LAN and the network of its Internet service provider.

Routers commonly come with a built-in hub or switch, which also allows computers on a small LAN to share files and access the WAN or Internet without requiring multiple pieces of equipment. Routers also provide increased security for the LAN they link. Because routers receive all packets and transmissions in order to send them to LAN devices, they can detect and ignore attempts by unauthorized users to break into the local network. By refusing to acknowledge inquiries and attempts to access local computers, the router both prevents the attacks and provides no confirmation that the local computers even exist beyond the router.

- **Gateways.** To create a connection between different types of networks, you need a gateway. The term has two meanings within the networking environ-

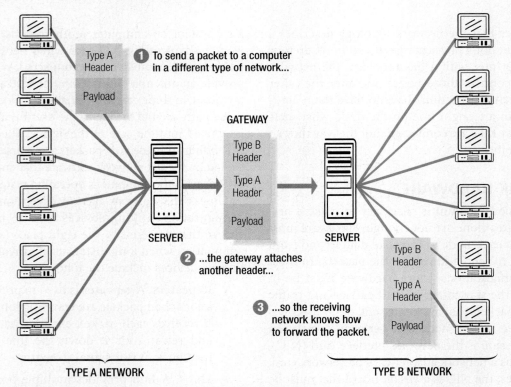

Figure 7.6   How a simple gateway sends a packet from one type of network to another.

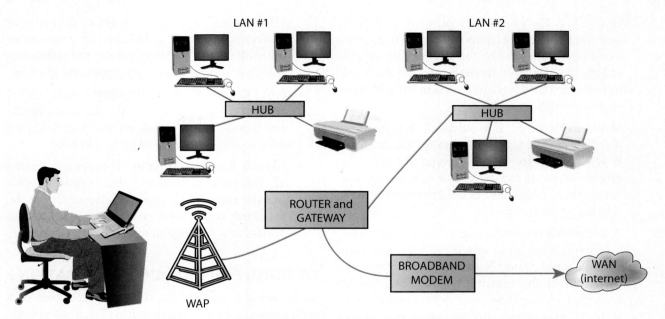

LAN #1

LAN #2

HUB

HUB

ROUTER and
GATEWAY

WAP

BROADBAND
MODEM

WAN
(internet)

Figure 7.7   A router links to separate LANs together, allowing them to share resources. The router also provides wireless connectivity, and access to the Internet.

ment. In its simplest form, a **gateway** is a node on a network that serves as an entrance to another network. In the small-business or home network, the gateway is the device that routes data between a local PC and an outside network such as the Internet. Gateways are needed because packets from different types of networks have different kinds of information in their headers, and the information can be in various formats. The gateway can take a packet from one type of network, read its header, and then add a second header that is understood by the second network (see Figure 7.6). The gateway also handles the configuration and maintenance of the various WAN or Internet addresses required to connect and relay information outside of the LAN. Each PC on the LAN can simply point to the gateway's network address without needing to know exactly where to find things on the Internet.

Figure 7.7 shows how these elements can tie together a network of computers and even link one network to other networks.

Though many kinds of network hardware are available for different situations, the typical home user has a much simpler set of requirements to create a home network. A typical installation would center around a broadband wireless router. Assuming that a high-speed Internet connection was present from a local provider, the user would install the router near the broadband modem and create a simple Internet connection. Wireless computers and smart phones could then connect throughout the house. Any computers located near the router—desktop PCs in the home office, for example—could be connected by wire to the back of the router for faster and more reliable data transfer.

In many cases, the broadband router is the only extra piece of hardware required to create a home network. Modern consumer-oriented routers and computer operating systems are designed to be fairly graceful when creating and connecting to a new network; often, simply following installation instructions and prompts is all that is required to get the network up and running.

NETWORK PROTOCOLS

Each LAN is governed by a **protocol**, which is an agreed-upon message format for transmitting data between two devices. This is done to ensure that both the sending and receiving computers on a network will transmit and receive data in exactly the same way.

There are many standard protocols, each with advantages and disadvantages. To effectively communicate, all network nodes must have the same protocol installed and active. A single LAN may utilize more than one protocol. The following protocols are most widely used today:

- TCP/IP, originally used with host computers running UNIX software, is the protocol of the Internet, so it is required on any computer that must communicate across the Internet. It is the default networking protocol of Windows, Macintosh OS, and many other operating systems.

- IPX/SPX is the proprietary protocol of Novell and used in most versions of the NetWare network operating system for networking offices worldwide. However, its use has largely declined in favor of TCP/IP (newer versions of NetWare support both).

- NetBIOS/NetBEUI is a relatively simple protocol with no real configurable parameters. It sends messages to every computer that can receive them. It can be useful for networking small offices or homes but does not expand well into larger environments.

- A token ring transmits a special message called a *token* in a sequence around a ring.[1] Network nodes cannot transmit data until they receive the token. Nodes transmit by attaching data to the token and sending it for delivery. The hardware is expensive, and transmission speeds are relatively slow, so it has now mostly been replaced by Fast Ethernet networks.

Protocols are typically implemented in both the network hardware and software and, in some cases, in the network node's operating system as well. The pieces of the protocol tell the computer exactly how to break up, format, send, receive, and reassemble data. Computers and peripheral devices without the necessary protocol hardware and software cannot participate in the network.

PHYSICAL TRANSMISSION STANDARDS

Just as a network protocol sets a standard for the structure of the data to be transmitted across a network, standards must exist for the hardware as well. This ensures that all the hardware, from NICs to media to linking devices, can all properly connect to each other. A number of physical transmission standards have been developed over the years. Of these, the following standards—all of which are variations of Ethernet—are most common:

- **Ethernet.** Once the most common form of network, Ethernet's dominance is being supplanted by Fast Ethernet, described next. The original implementations of **Ethernet** used coaxial cable and were called 10Base-5 and 10Base-2. The most popular implementation of Ethernet—called *10Base-T*—can achieve transmission speeds up to 10 Mbps. Most network installations use an

Ethernet star topology with either twisted-pair or fiber-optic cables. With Ethernet, if two nodes transmit data at the same instant, the collision is detected, and the nodes retransmit one at a time.

- **Fast Ethernet.** Fast Ethernet (also called *100Base-T*) is available using the same media and topology as Ethernet, but different NICs are used to achieve speeds of up to 100 Mbps.

- **Gigabit Ethernet. Gigabit Ethernet** is a version of Ethernet technology that supports data transfer rates of one gigabit per second or more. Standards are currently complete or in process for 1-, 10-, and 100-gigabit transmission standards.

OPTIONS FOR DATA COMMUNICATIONS

So far, we have covered the construction of networks with media (cables or wireless links) that are specifically set up for transmitting digital signals around the network. An alternative to using dedicated media is to use the telephone system—called the **plain old telephone system (POTS)**—for data communications. Telephone lines may offer both analog and digital communications access.

Using Modems with Telephone Lines Once the primary means of connecting PCs around the world to the Internet, the simple telephone line is far less popular than it once was as a network tool. It is often viewed as a method of last resort in places where no digital access is available. Some personal computers no longer include telephone connectivity hardware as part of their standard features. Nevertheless, the technology is still in use, so it is worthwhile to gain a basic understanding of its function.

Regular phone lines are not very well suited for carrying data. They transmit data at a much, much slower rate than a typical digital network. The telephone system was originally designed to carry the sound of voices, which are analog signals. Because computers are digital machines, they require special hardware to translate their data from digital to analog, so the information can be carried across the telephone lines. The hardware is known as a *modem*, which is short for "modulator/demodulator." Its name identifies the two operations it performs: modulation and demodulation. In its modulation mode, the modem turns the computer's digital signals into analog signals, which are then transmitted across the phone line. The reverse takes place during its demodulation phase.

As with other network devices, the transmission speed of a modem is measured in bits per second. The fastest modems available for PCs are limited to

[1] B. Mitchell (2010), Token ring, *About.com*. Retrieved May 22, 2010, from http://compnetworking.about.com/od/networkprotocols/g/token-ring-networks.htm

a maximum speed of just 56 kilobits per second, roughly 2,000 times slower than the digital Fast Ethernet connection that is often found in homes and businesses.

Access Several broadband technologies are offered today. The term **broadband** is used to describe any data connection that can transmit data faster than is possible through a standard dial-up connection using a modem, by using a wider band of frequencies than those used to carry human voice.

Some broadband connections, such as integrated services digital network (ISDN), T1, and T3 service, combine multiple data channels along the same wires in order to increase their transmission rates. Another type of digital telephone service—called digital subscriber line (DSL)—transmits data at a higher frequency than what is used for voice transmission. Cable modem service is a technology that enables users to connect to the Internet through their cable TV connection with higher speeds than those offered by dial-up connections. Communications companies sometimes also offer a service called **asynchronous transfer mode (ATM)**. ATM is a protocol designed by the telecommunications industry as a more efficient way to send voice, video, and computer data over a single network.

Wireless Networks Wireless networks are favored for convenience and user mobility. Wired networks are fine when wires can be easily run from node to node, and when each user will use his or her hardware in the same place all the time. In circumstances where adding wires would be an expensive, unsightly, or awkward alternative, a wireless network can bypass the problems. Users with notebook computers and smart phones want Internet and company network access no matter where they go. A wireless network allows them to roam, and it allows new users to enter the area and access the network without requiring a fresh wired connection (see the "Ethical Dilemma" feature for one implication of this ability).

The overwhelmingly popular standard for wireless networking is called 802.11 or **Wi-Fi**. The latest version of the standard, **802.11n**, describes specifications for wireless speeds up to 600 Mbps, which is faster than earlier forms of Ethernet (at 10 Mbps) but still substantially slower than Gigabit Ethernet (1 Gbps). Unlike wired networks, achieving the maximum wireless transmission rate is often either impractical or impossible for most installations,

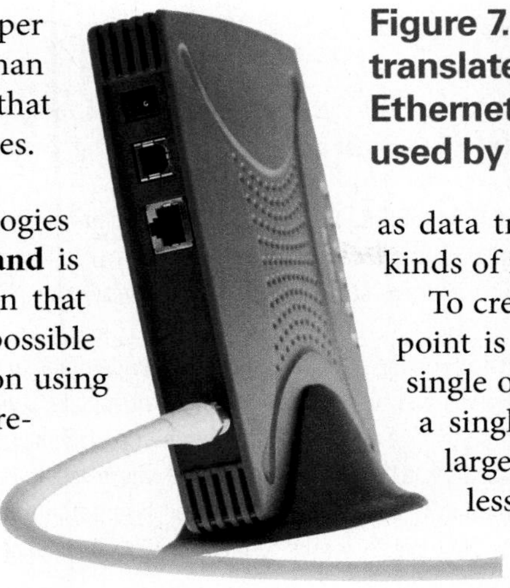

Figure 7.8 A broadband modem translates data between the local Ethernet protocol and the protocol used by the Internet service company.

as data transmission is susceptible to many kinds of interference.

To create a wireless LAN, a wireless access point is needed. In a wireless environment, single or multiple PCs can connect through a single **wireless access point (WAP)**. In larger wireless topologies, multiple wireless machines can roam through different access points and stay on the same network domain with the same level of security. If the network must grow to handle more users or expand its range, extension points can be added.

The WAP connects to an Ethernet LAN like any other device and allows computers with wireless NICs to function in the Ethernet LAN environment. In addition, some wireless access points come with built-in routers, firewalls, and switches so that you do not have to buy multiple hardware devices. The WAP typically also contains password and other security settings to prevent unauthorized network access.

A PC or laptop needs a wireless NIC that meets 802.11 standards to make contact with the WAP. Many wireless NICs come with utility software that allows you to monitor signal strength and download speeds.

Fact Check

1. Twisted-pair cable
   a. carries data on just one of its two wires
   b. is best for carrying sound files and not documents
   c. normally consists of four pairs of wires
2. With a star topology
   a. data moves in five directions simultaneously, in the shape of a star
   b. all nodes are connected to a hub and communicate through it
   c. computers are far less likely to crash
3. Which of the following is a requirement for creating a wireless LAN?
   a. A wireless access point
   b. A special government license
   c. Ability of all nodes on the network to support wireless communication

With the increased attention to national and corporate security in the United States, Michael French is well positioned for a long and successful career in computer networking, particularly when it comes to protecting those systems from hackers.

As a senior security consultant for IBM, French has conducted and managed projects for leading firms in the insurance, banking, investment, and educational industries. A typical workday will find him on the road at a client's location or working to improve security on company networks, SUN Solaris servers, or PCs running Microsoft Windows.

French is living proof that networking professionals have a wide range of career paths to choose from. Before joining IBM, for example, French ran his own consulting firm focused on mobile computing and voice/data networks and previously served as vice president of e-commerce for Bank of America.

A graduate of Brown University and Long Island University, where he earned a master of science in management science, French is IBM certified in IT security, was awarded two patents for electrical designs, and was a co-inventor on four other patents. He typically works 10-hour days, with much of it spent assessing network security for individual IBM clients.

Keeping up to date on the latest developments in the networking space is French's biggest job challenge—one he overcomes by reading, studying, and attending trade conferences and seminars. "There's a constant need to upgrade your knowledge," says French. "The current buzzword, for example, is Voice over IP and it's unleashing a flood of new products and problems that we never knew we had."

Most rewarding about the IT networking field, says French, is that it's always interesting and never boring. The job also comes with a degree of autonomy, since many networking professionals manage their own projects and are considered competent and capable of making decisions and attaining goals.

Other careers relating to networking and data communications include the following:

Customer service support. Many entry-level jobs are coming from the customer support areas of software, operating systems, and telecommunication systems industries. This involves troubleshooting issues with customers over the phone or sometimes providing mobile on-site support.

Network administrators. These individuals are responsible for managing a company's network infrastructure. Some of the jobs in this field include designing and implementing networks, setting up and managing users' accounts, installing and updating network software and applications, and backing up the network.

Information systems (IS) managers. IS managers are responsible for managing a team of information professionals, including network administrators, software developers, project managers, and other staff. Jobs in the IS management field differ according to the needs of the company.

Data communications managers. These managers are responsible for setting up and maintaining Internet, intranet, and extranet sites. Often they are also responsible for designing and establishing an organization's telecommuting initiative.

The Bureau of Labor Statistics reports median annual earnings of network and computer systems administrators were $67,710 in 2009, with the middle 50 percent earning between $52,940 and $85,830.

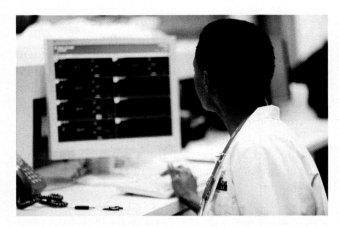

Figure 7.9 Hospitals use information systems to manage everything from patient records to medical supply and food inventories.

7.2 Information Systems: What and Why

Network hardware and software provides an unparalleled vehicle for making connections between users, whether they are in the same room or around the world. Along with those connections, networks provide an ideal platform on which to build systems that actively collect, manage and share information. An **information system (IS)** is a complex system for acquiring, storing, organizing, using, and sharing data and information. The basic purpose of any information system is to help its users get value from the information in the system, regardless of the type of information stored or the type of value desired. Information systems, therefore, can be designed to help people harness many kinds of information in countless ways.

Though we will focus only on computer-based information systems, an information system does not by definition require a computer system. A small consulting business with a handful of employees could create an information system with notebooks to hold policies and procedures, filing cabinets to hold proposals and contracts, and trays on desks to organize documents the consultants share. Because computers are so adept at storing and sharing information, however, they can improve the efficiency of even small information systems.

As you study information systems, remember that they do much more than store and retrieve data: they help people *use* information, whether that involves sorting lists, running a factory's computer-controlled machining system, or matching a single fingerprint against a national database of millions of prints.

Though the details of an information system's structure can be very complicated, all information systems consist of four basic components:

1. The physical means for storing data, such as a file cabinet or hard disk. For many businesses, data storage is an enormous requirement that involves many terabytes of disk space.

2. The physical means, methods, and procedures for distributing and sharing information with others.

3. Procedures for handling information to ensure its integrity. Regardless of the size of the information system, its users must follow data-management rules to eliminate errors in data and the loss of important data.

4. Rules regarding data use and distribution. The rules of the information system govern what information should be distributed to whom, at what time, and in what format. In any organization, data is meant to be used for specific purposes in order to achieve a desired result. An organization improves the security of its information by limiting access, ensuring that information is only given to those who need it. Limited access can also improve efficiency, as workers are given only what they need to do their job and are not distracted or encumbered by large amounts of irrelevant data.

Most of today's information systems also include tools for validating, sorting, categorizing, and analyzing information. These additional tools increase a system's complexity, but they make the system much more useful.

Fact Check

1. What is the basic purpose of any information system?
   a. To harvest knowledge from other databases and collect it in one location
   b. To help its users get value from the information in the system
   c. To fully automate human processes
2. Which of the following components is required for any information system?
   a. The physical means, methods, and procedures for distributing and sharing information
   b. A minimum of 10 terabytes of data storage
   c. An Internet connection

7.3 Types of Information Systems

As more and more business functions have become automated, information systems have become increasingly specialized. One of a company's systems, for example, may help users gather and store sales orders. Another system may help managers analyze data. Still others exist to support the company's day-to-day operations. These specialized systems can operate alone or can be combined to create a larger system that performs different functions for different people.

OFFICE AUTOMATION SYSTEMS

In organizations of any size, basic office work such as maintaining project schedules, keeping records of meetings, and handling correspondence can become extremely time consuming and labor intensive. Collaborating with coworkers, serving customers, and dealing with suppliers require the sharing of accurate information as varied as phone numbers, meeting minutes, work schedules, and the promises and ideas spelled out in volumes of correspondence. Especially when these types of information are scattered about the office on pieces of paper, it is easy to make mistakes, lose a key piece of information, or fall behind on recordkeeping or filing tasks.

For gathering, storing, and making available the kinds of information needed in an office environment, many organizations set up a type of information system

Figure 7.10 Office automation systems allow sales employees to stay up to date on appointments, and access information to support their sales efforts.

known as an **office automation system**, which uses computers and/or networks to perform various operations, such as word processing, accounting, document management, or communications. Office automation systems are designed to manage information and—more important—to help users handle certain information-related tasks more efficiently.

An office automation system can link key information together and allow each person in the system to enter and retrieve what he or she needs. Suppose the system supports a small insurance office. A cold caller who reaches an interested prospect can enter basic contact information into a database and indicate that the prospect would be open to hearing from the agent serving that territory. Working from that information, the office assistant calls the prospect, sets up an appointment, and updates the agent's online schedule, attaching a link to the latest price spreadsheet created by the company's marketing department. The agent receives e-mail via his or her smart phone, informing the agent that a new appointment has been made. The agent reviews the contact information and can open the spreadsheet to check the pricing details before the meeting.

Using office automation tools frees workers at all levels from performing redundant and mundane tasks, allowing time for handling more mission-critical jobs such as planning, designing, and selling. Because office automation systems integrate different functions, information can be shared across applications (in the previous example, a customer database, scheduling software, and a spreadsheet), reducing the errors and time spent copying data from one program to another.

Office automation systems are commonly built using **off-the-shelf applications**, software that is available for purchase by anyone, not requiring custom design and development. Popular office software suites are Microsoft Office, IBM's Lotus Symphony, and Oracle's open-source OpenOffice.org. Each of these includes several applications, such as a word processor, a spreadsheet program, a presentation program, an e-mail client, and a database management system. The programs can be used interchangeably to facilitate office tasks.

TRANSACTION PROCESSING SYSTEMS

A **transaction** is a complete information operation. Transactions can be one-step events like adding a new piece of information to a database, or they can be more complex and require many steps (for example, the entire process of purchasing an online product can be considered a transaction from the buyer's perspective). Although you may conduct business transactions frequently, you may have never considered the steps that make up a typical transaction. All these steps can be processed through an information system. A system that handles the processing and tracking of transactions is called a **transaction processing system (TPS)**.

Consider the process of withdrawing cash at an automated teller machine (ATM). From your perspective, this involves a single transaction: you put in your card and take your money, with the understanding that the $60 in your hand has been removed from your account. However, this transaction is actually a series of smaller, linked transactions:

- Before any money is transferred, the ATM verifies your identity by reading your ATM card's magnetic stripe, requesting a password from you, passing that information to your financial institution, and receiving authorization to proceed.

- When you select an amount to withdraw, the ATM forwards that amount to your bank and requests authorization to dispense the cash.

- Your bank verifies the amount in your account and (assuming your balance is sufficient) places a hold on the funds in the amount of the withdrawal. It then authorizes the ATM to dispense the cash.

- The ATM counts out the requested cash, makes it available to you, and internally records its operation.

- The ATM notifies the bank that the cash was successfully distributed.

- The bank changes the hold on your funds to an actual debit, and the amount in your account is reduced.

The single transaction to your eyes is broken down into this longer behind-the-scenes list because it allows the overall transaction (you getting your money) to be monitored and, in the event of an error, identifies precisely what went wrong and where. If the ATM's power goes out before it can dispense your cash, the bank will eventually release the hold on your funds because it will be able to determine that the ATM never gave it to you. If the ATM dispenses cash but its communication network crashes immediately afterward, the bank will be able to compare the ATM's log with the unfinished transaction and properly debit your account.

A transaction processing system is designed specifically to work with completing the basic transactions

Figure 7.11   Withdrawing money from an ATM is simple for the user, but a complex information system manages the operation.

and monitoring the overall transaction for success and failure. Some transaction processing systems have sophisticated abilities to undo the unfinished parts of a failed transaction, correcting databases and performing other tasks to bring information back to the state it was in before the broken transaction began.

MANAGEMENT INFORMATION SYSTEMS

Within any business, workers at different levels need access to the same type of information, but they may need to view the information in different ways. At a call center, for example, a supervisor may need to see a daily report detailing the number of calls received, the types of requests made, and the production levels of individual staff members. A midlevel manager, such as a branch manager, may need to see only a monthly

Figure 7.12   Management information systems analyze data to give managers better information about company operations.

summary of this data shown in comparison to previous months, with a running total or average.

Managers at different levels also may need very different types of data. A senior manager, such as a vice president of finance or chief financial officer, could be responsible for a company's financial performance; he or she would view the company's financial information (usually in detail) regularly. But a front-line manager who oversees daily production may receive little or no financial data, except when it specifically affects his or her area of responsibility. Ultimately, the challege in each scenario is the same: To get the right information to the right person at the right time, and in a format that is useful and appropriate.

A **management information system (MIS)** is a set of software tools that enables managers to gather, organize, and evaluate information about a work group, department, or entire organization. These systems meet the needs of three different categories of managers—executives, middle managers, and front-line managers—by producing different kinds of reports drawn from the organization's database. An efficient MIS summarizes vast amounts of business data into information that is useful to each type of manager. Since different people have different ways to express and understand information, a good MIS will allow the same data to be displayed in a variety of ways, such as columns of numbers, line graphs, and bar graphs. That allows digital thinkers to see the numbers, while 3-D visual analysts can see a picture of how those numbers relate.

DECISION SUPPORT SYSTEMS

Some questions in business or management can be easy to identify but much more difficult to answer without some kind of assistance. Of the four colors of T-shirts that a shirt company produces, how many of each should they make in their latest production run? How many salmon should the local fishery controller allow fishers to catch before halting the season's activity? Without useful information, perhaps including rules for how to interpret and apply data, answers to these questions are simply guesswork.

A **decision support system (DSS)**, a special application that collects and reports certain types of data, can help managers make better decisions. The shirt manufacturer can collect and analyze buying trends, not only of its own T-shirts but of the marketplace in general, and look for guidance for forecasting what current products will sell in the near future and what new product opportunities might be profitable. The fishery manager can collect data such as estimates of the current salmon population, historical population trends, the number of applications for fishing licenses, and so forth, in order to predict what level of fishing will be sustainable.

Figure 7.13 Decision support systems can assemble sets of information from many sources to help manage inventories efficiently.

Decision support systems can combine and correlate information from multiple locations. Business managers often use decision support systems to access and analyze data in the company's transaction processing system. In addition, these systems can include or access other types of data, such as stock market reports or data about competitors. By compiling this kind of data, the decision support system can generate specific reports that managers can use in making mission-critical decisions.

Decision support systems are useful tools because they give managers highly tailored, highly structured data about specific issues. Many decision support systems are spreadsheet or database applications that have been customized for a certain business. These powerful systems can import and analyze data in various formats, such as flat database tables or spreadsheets, two-dimensional charts, or multidimensional "cubes" (meaning several types of data and their interrelationships can be graphically shown). They can quickly generate reports based on existing data and update those reports instantly as data changes.

Decision support systems can be active or passive:

- A passive system simply collects and displays data in the format requested.

- An active system collects the data but also makes recommendations as to the best decision; in this regard, an active DSS resembles an *expert system*, described next.

Because few people are willing—rightly so—to blindly trust the recommendations of a software program, active-decision support systems are often used cooperatively, where users review the recommended decisions along with the data.

EXPERT SYSTEMS

Some types of analysis, though complex, follow the same sequence of questions and answers to arrive at a decision or solution. For example, diagnosing a computer's faulty network connection may require that you check the cable connections, the functioning of the computer's interface hardware, the state of the network's router, the proper connection of other hardware on the network, and the state of various settings in the computer's operating system. In theory, this kind of analysis could be done in any order, but it is often practical to start with the simplest of questions—for example, "Is it plugged in?" and "Is the power on?"—before moving on to more complex and less obvious tests. Arriving at a solution by asking a series of questions is something a computer can be programmed to perform (or to direct a person to perform).

An **expert system** is a type of information system that performs analytical tasks traditionally done by a human,

Figure 7.14 Medical professionals sometimes use expert systems to help them interpret patient data and arrive at a diagnosis.

using sequences of questions to ask and actions to take based on the responses to those questions. The system begins its analysis with an initial set of data (for a failed network connection, it might begin with, "Is the Ethernet cable plugged into the proper port of the computer?"). Based on each piece of information it receives, it may take new avenues of analysis. If the Ethernet cable is plugged in and the connection is detected, an expert system may move on to test the router. If the Ethernet cable is plugged in but cannot be detected, the expert system may begin to diagnose the hardware in the computer itself.

An expert system requires a large collection of human expertise in a specific area. Detailed information is compiled from the human experts on the ways that problems are considered, the actions that are taken to diagnose problems and find solutions, and the decisions and explanations that the experts give as a result of discovering new information through their analysis. This information is entered into a highly detailed database, called a **knowledge base**. A program called an **inference engine** accepts information about the problem or question being analyzed and uses the knowledge base to select the most appropriate response or follow-up question (see Figure 7.15).

Basic expert systems are typically little more than preset question-and-answer sequences, using simple yes or no answers to move along its list. Sophisticated expert systems may use new information to reevaluate the problem from the start. They also contain a feedback process that refines the data in the knowledge base, so as users report success and failure during the diagnostic process, the expert system can learn more efficient diagnostic paths. For example, an expert system diagnosing network faults may over time discover that most of the faults involve malfunctioning network adapter cards in employees' personal computers, so it changes its analysis path to focus first on testing those parts.

Sometimes, expert investigators piece together clues or bits of information about a difficult problem and then—without really understanding how or why—leap to a new understanding of the problem that suggests a creative solution. Although expert systems mimic the routine decision-making process of experts, they do not innovate, because they are simply machines following instructions. Consequently, expert systems are most useful in situations where a given set of circumstances always calls for the same kind of response.

Some expert systems are empowered to make decisions and take actions, especially when the conditions for action can be fully defined or when lives or critical resources are at stake. An example is an expert system that monitors inventory levels for a grocery store chain. When the system determines that inventory of a product

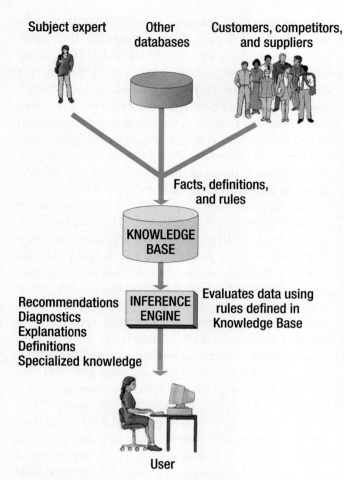

Subject expert **Other databases** **Customers, competitors, and suppliers**

Facts, definitions, and rules

KNOWLEDGE BASE

INFERENCE ENGINE

Evaluates data using rules defined in Knowledge Base

Recommendations
Diagnostics
Explanations
Definitions
Specialized knowledge

User

Figure 7.15 An expert system distills human expertise into rules and definitions, and provides a software interface that works with non-expert users to aid in diagnosing problems or providing explanations.

falls below a given level, it can automatically order a new shipment of the product from a supplier. In air traffic control, if the expert system detects that two aircraft are on a collision course or flying too near one another, it can issue a warning without human intervention.

7.4 Networks, Hardware, and Data Management

Computer-based information systems use much of the same hardware as any other application: personal computers, servers, mainframe computers, and networking

Figure 7.16 Financial exchanges rely extensively on computers; failure of those computers would be far worse than inconvenient.

hardware. Some information systems, such as office automation and expert systems, may even comfortably reside in a conventional computing environment. Many organizations provide office automation in the form of software suites that employees can use without the need for special hardware or customized applications.

Other information systems, such as complex transaction processing systems, often have additional requirements such as the need to be available without fail every moment of every day or the ability to store and quickly access hundreds of terabytes of information. Such needs require additional hardware, network, and software solutions beyond what is available from a garden-variety PC.

NETWORKS FOR INFORMATION SYSTEMS

As you learned in this lesson, organizations sometimes create intranets and extranets, which provide the same tools and services as the Internet but with restricted access. Many information systems benefit from this structure, especially when the services provided by the company involve Internet-based transactions.

With an intranet, users within the organization can access and maintain the information system using the same types of tools as the organization's customers. For example, an online shopping site's database, which is accessed via a Web browser by shoppers, can also be accessed within the company using Web browsers in order to check order and inventory status. This has the advantage of using standardized software within the organization, which can greatly reduce development, support, and training costs.

When different organizations all use common tools within their intranet, it makes it much easier to share limited amounts of information with each other via extranets. An online store selling machine tools, for example, might have access to the tool manufacturer's extranet so it can check wholesale prices and place orders without assistance from the manufacturer.

Because both the online store and the manufacturer have Internet-based software, they have a common means to share information and also a very convenient intermediate network: the Internet itself. Many organizations connect to each other's extranets via **virtual private networks (VPNs)**.

REDUNDANT AND FAULT-TOLERANT HARDWARE

With a typical computer, most hardware failures cause the computer to crash. If the hard drive malfunctions or the CPU overheats after a cooling fan fails, the computer stops running, and whatever it was doing is lost. If network hardware such as a router breaks, network traffic is disrupted, either by slower operation or by an outright disconnection.

This kind of event is frustrating. After all, we buy a computer so we can use it, not so we can leave it for days or weeks at the repair shop. But while losing files or opportunities to work and play can be distressing, consider that if computers running life-support systems crashed, the consequences could be far worse than inconvenience. Even small amounts of downtime

> **"With a typical computer, most hardware failures cause the computer to crash."**

at a major stock exchange or in an air defense system are unacceptable. These types of systems are called **mission-critical**, meaning they must run without failure or with nearly instant recovery from failure.

Because it's simply not possible to construct computer hardware and software that can never fail, mission-critical hardware and software systems have been designed so that, when components and programs fail, the computer is able to continue without interruption. Such systems are known as **fault-tolerant** computers, because they are able to continue their operation even when problems are present.

One of the ways fault tolerance is accomplished is via redundancy. **Redundant** computers are ones that have multiple hardware systems performing the same task at the same time. A fully redundant computer will have multiple complete system units—motherboard, CPU, and memory—and multiple hard drives. The computers execute software instructions in **lockstep**, meaning all CPUs and attendant hardware execute the same instruction at the same time. Special hardware and software monitor program execution for differences, and when one of the CPUs produces a different result (or no result, if it breaks), it is declared to have failed. The remaining hardware systems continue to operate without the failed unit until it can be fixed.

Even in computer systems that aren't mission-critical, extra disk drives are sometimes used as a way to provide a countermeasure against data loss. A **redundant array of independent disks (RAID)** is a storage system commonly found in PCs that links any number of disk drives (a disk array) so that they act as a single disk.

RAID's capabilities are based on many different techniques, but there are three basic ones:

1. **Striping**, or RAID 0, gives the user rapid access by spreading data across several disks. Striping alone, however, is used to boost data access performance and does not provide redundancy. If one of the disks in a striped array fails, the data is lost, because it is not being duplicated on any of the other disks.

2. In a **mirrored** system, called RAID 1 data is written to two or more disks simultaneously, providing a complete copy of all the information on multiple drives in the event one drive should fail.

3. **Striping-with-parity** most commonly implemented as RAID 5, is a more sophisticated

RAID configuration in which data is spread over multiple disks. It provides the speed of striping with the safety of redundancy because the system stores parity information that can be used to reconstruct data if a disk drive fails.

SCALABLE AND INTEROPERABLE SYSTEMS

Most businesses plan to grow and expand over time, and computer systems need to be able to grow with the organization. Many company directors find it unacceptable to start from scratch with new computer and software systems every time the company outgrows its current system, and many information systems cannot practically be redesigned and replaced. **Scalable** systems address this need because they can be incrementally expanded as the need occurs. **Scalability** is the capability to provide increasing amounts of computing power, storage, and software (for example, more and faster CPUs, more hard drives to store data, more and faster network connections, larger databases to organize more information). Scalable systems allow organizations to buy affordable systems that meet their current computing needs and gradually increase their computing capability only as needed.

Many information systems need to interact with other systems. The efficiency of a tool manufacturer's accounting system, for example, can be greatly enhanced if it has access to the company's inventory and order-entry systems. **Interoperability** is the ability of each organization's information system to work with

the other, sharing data and services. Interoperability also is required of information systems to allow partnership and customer–vendor relationships between organizations using a variety of systems. Though interoperability is often viewed at a software level, as in the example of the tool manufacturer, hardware interoperability is just as critical. If the accounting system is owned by an accounting company and runs on completely different computer hardware and operating systems from the tool manufacturer's inventory system, there needs to be a common interface so those systems can effectively communicate.

DATA WAREHOUSING, DATA MINING, AND DATA SCRUBBING

A massive and growing amount of data is required today to do business and create records for reporting and transaction history. To add to the burden, the data must be available when needed. If data is not available—or worse, is lost—a company can lose money and may even be breaking laws.

Huge data warehouses can supply the data requirements for tens of thousands of users in a large organization. They also are used to store and support thousands or millions of transactions per day on active Web sites, such as the popular electronic auction and retail Web sites. Data Warehouses also make hardware management simpler; locating hundreds or thousands of hard drives and data servers in one place makes it easier for a single support team to diagnose and fix hardware faults and ensures that all of the hardware is in a proper operating environment.

Large databases to support information systems can also provide an ideal environment for data mining. Businesses can tap their customer and sales data to find trends, new sales opportunities, and signs of waning interest in their customers' behavior. Internet service providers can use data mining techniques on e-mail and other massive types of communication traffic to analyze data flow, search for spam, and optimize data delivery. Governments can correlate and analyze data from many different areas to track needs and spending for citizens, as well as monitor public behavior for security threats.

Figure 7.17 Scalable systems can add new or upgraded hardware as an organization grows, in order to keep up with increasing information and processing demands.

Figure 7.18 Data scrubbing reduces accidental errors by preventing obvious entry mistakes, and finding inconsistent data.

Sometimes, data scrubbing can be accomplished by specifying format or range requirements at data entry. For example, a form for entering a shipping address may require that a zip code contain exactly five numeric characters, or a field for a birth year may require information that is a four-digit year in the recent past. Requests to submit incomplete or incorrect information are rejected.

Another way to accomplish data scrubbing is to compare information with what is typical. For example, services that provide historical financial data, such as tick-by-tick stock prices, use data scrubbing methods to find data errors. If a stock's daily trading activity shows many trades at $10 per share and one trade at $10,000 per share, the scrubbing program can either simply eliminate the mistake or flag it for a person to review and take action.

While data scrubbing can assist with unintentional errors in data entry, it is far less effective for eliminating deliberately misleading data. Requesting that you enter your e-mail address twice, into two separate fields, is a form of data scrubbing. People often make typos in an e-mail address, and if you enter it wrong the first time, this requirement helps you or the data entry system to notice and correct the problem. But suppose you want to read an online article posted on a Web site whose privacy protection you don't trust, and it requires you to enter an e-mail address before it will display the article. Some users might deliberately enter an incorrect e-mail address in both fields. Data scrubbing will not prevent this deliberate error of a fake e-mail address.

Like most other forms of data analysis, data mining can be helpful or intrusive depending on the intent of the miner. A social media site can be helpful by tailoring friend suggestions and news articles for its users according to patterns that show up in user-expressed preferences and behaviors. That same site can cross ethical boundaries by selling those preferences without permission to businesses to help fuel advertising campaigns and sales efforts.

In order for data mining and the use of information systems in general to be effective, the databases that support them must be as free of errors as possible. One method for checking and improving the reliability of data is called data scrubbing. **Data scrubbing** or data validation is the process of safeguarding against erroneous or duplicate data by checking what is entered and, in some cases, placing restrictions on how the data is entered.

Figure 7.19 Search engines are complex, massive storage companies that provide information organization and prioritization for their users.

From the point of view of Web site operators, this type of deliberate error poses its own risks: the fake e-mail address could come from a zombie computer taking part in a malicious attack. Therefore, some organizations require that, before they will display an article or provide some other service, you must first respond to an e-mail message, as a way to validate that you are a real person with a legitimate address. But in many cases, these intentional data errors are unavoidable because the organization is asking people to disclose information that users would rather keep private. When we want to provide information, we willingly participate in the process of making sure it is complete and correct; when we are suspicious of the organization's motives, we are

At your best friend's insistence, you've agreed to sign up on his favorite social networking site. The signup screen wasn't really a problem; it wanted a screen name, a password, and your e-mail address. You made up a screen name, picked a password, and provided your usual public e-mail address at gmail.com, which you use for this sort of thing.

But instead of letting you into the network, the site has given you a second page, titled "You're Almost There—Fun Is One Click Away." On that page, you are required to enter your name, address, home and cell phone number, and birth date.

This is absolutely not the kind of information you like to give away, yet you promised your friend you would finally join him online.

ETHICAL ◄   **DILEMMA** ►

Does it harm anyone to gain access to a social networking site using false personal information?

QUESTIONS

What do you do? Disappoint your friend? Give away your private, sensitive data? Or is it OK to just fake up a crazy name, a bogus address, random phone numbers and your dog's birthday? Is it harming anyone to gain access to the site by providing junk instead of data?

more likely to look for ways to keep our distance, as discussed in the Ethical Dilemma box.

ORGANIZING DATA FOR SEARCHING

Finding what you need in a massive collection of information can be simple or complicated, depending on what you need. Using a search engine such as Google or Bing in your Web browser is a good example. Sometimes, all you have to do is type in a search phrase, and the search engine delivers precisely what you need on the first try. Other times, you may need to try many search phrases and sift through a great deal of information that wasn't what you wanted.

Most information systems attempt to organize data and information in ways that make it easier for users to find what they need. Databases, as described in the next lesson, are a fundamental building block for organizing much or all of the data in an information system. Creating a framework for storing the information makes retrieving information must easier, whether you need the phone number for the coffee maker repair shop, the phone number for every client your company serves, or a complex analysis of whether the type of coffee you serve at sales meetings influences the number of new deals you close.

DATA TRANSACTIONS WITH ELECTRONIC DATA INTERCHANGE

Sending a document or an e-mail to a client or cooperative business is a way to share information, but by itself, that type of sharing is unstructured. E-mail as a technology can certainly support the ordering of new machine parts or providing an invoice; you simply start the e-mail program, type in your request or attach the invoice file, and send it to the recipient. A great deal of business around the world is conducted in exactly that manner. But it's not very efficient; imagine if a major auto manufacturer like Toyota sent an e-mail to every parts supplier and car dealer in its corporate network to order parts, transfer invoices, and collect sales figures. The amount of paperwork to process manually would be staggering.

Electronic data interchange (EDI) is a standardized electronic transfer of information between companies over networks, usually in a format that complies with a standard defined by one of the several international standardization and conformity assessment organizations. EDI can occur between companies over extranets or the Internet. Though EDI is specifically not a way to transfer funds, it is a form of e-commerce because the concept supports the delivery of business-related information. EDI data can contain anything from purchase orders and invoices to very sensitive patient medical records.

EDI transfers are different from the ones you've come to expect. Typical data transfers are made outside of the original software. If you e-mail an invoice to your customer, the invoice arrives as a document file attached to the message; that document must be opened and viewed by the person receiving it. If you send someone a spreadsheet of sales figures via FTP, the FTP client (not the spreadsheet program) delivers the file to the destination system, and the person receiving the file must open it and view or integrate it with his or her own spreadsheet information.

EDI data is delivered electronically in a predetermined format between applications running in each organization. The data is transferred directly from software in one company's network to software on another company's network. For example, rather than sending an invoice as a text document, an EDI invoice would move directly from the seller's accounting system to the buyer's accounting system. The buyer's accounting staff would see the invoice in their system without having to enter it by hand.

Fact Check

1. Redundant computers are ones that have
   a. software stored in multiple locations in case one copy is lost
   b. access to separate types of network connections
   c. multiple hardware systems performing the same task at the same time
2. How does data scrubbing reduce errors in data entry?
   a. By performing hardware-level integrity checks on hard-drive media
   b. By checking what is entered and, in some cases, placing restrictions on how the data is entered
   c. By encrypting data so it cannot be altered once it is verified

IN Summary

- A local area network (LAN) consists of computers that are relatively close to one another. A LAN can have a few PCs or hundreds of them in a single building or several buildings. A wide area network (WAN) results when multiple LANs are connected through public utilities such as phone lines or microwave systems.

- When used in the context of networks, the term media refers to the wires, cables, and other means by which data travels from its source to its destination. The most common media for data communications are twisted-pair wire, coaxial cable, fiber-optic cable, and wireless links.

- A topology is the logical layout of the cables and devices that connect the nodes of a network. Topologies get their names—such as bus, star, or ring—from the logical shape of the network they create.

- A protocol is an agreed-upon format for transmitting data between two devices. Some popular protocols include TCP/IP (the Internet protocol), IPX/SPX, and NetBIOS/NetBEUI.

- Consumer wireless technology follows a standard called 802.11. The two most popular standards in use are 802.11g and 802.11n. In addition to other requirements, each governs the standards for wireless speeds. The 802.11n standard describes specifications for data transfer rates of up to 600 Mbps, though the data rate in practical applications is commonly much lower. To gain access to an Ethernet LAN wirelessly, you need a wireless NIC, and a wireless access point (WAP) needs to be added to the Ethernet LAN.

- An information system is a complex combination of hardware, software, data, and networks that is used to acquire, store, organize, use, and share information.

- Though information systems vary considerably in their structure, any information system will contain a physical means for storing data, a physical means for distributing and sharing information with others, procedures for ensuring the integrity and safety of the data, and rules to govern the use and access of the data.

- Office automation systems improve the efficiency with which office workers create and share documents of various types. Transaction processing systems facilitate and track the completion of processes that move information, goods, or money from one place to another. Management information systems gather and analyze information to aid management in understanding business operations. Decision support systems collect information and make recommendations and decisions based on underlying data. Expert systems diagnose problems and make recommendations based on a combination of knowledge provided by experts, information provided by users or diagnostic systems, and the history of solutions.

- Fault-tolerant computing is the combination of redundant or backup hardware and software modules to create an operating environment that can experience hardware failures and data errors and still continue to operate correctly without the loss of system or data availability. Information systems can use fault-tolerant computers to help ensure that they are always online and available for accepting and sharing data.

- Electronic data interchange is a concept and set of standards for transferring e-commerce information directly from one organization's software to another organization's software, allowing the two entities to share vital information without requiring intervention by people to distribute and then retrieve the information.

Key Terms

asynchronous transfer mode
  (ATM), 299
attenuation, 293
bandwidth, 293
bridge, 296
broadband, 299
bus topology, 294
coaxial cable, 293
data scrubbing, 309
decision support system
  (DSS), 304
electronic data interchange
  (EDI), 310
Ethernet, 298
expert system, 305
extranet, 292
Fast Ethernet, 298
fault-tolerant, 307
fiber-optic cable, 293
gateway, 296
Gigabit Ethernet, 298
header, 293
hub, 295

inference engine, 305
information system (IS), 301
interoperability, 308
intranet, 292
knowledge base, 305
local area network (LAN), 292
lockstep, 307
management information system
  (MIS), 304
media, 293
mesh topology, 294
mirrored, 307
mission-critical, 307
network version, 291
nodes, 293
off-the-shelf applications, 302
office automation
  system, 302
packets, 293
plain old telephone system
  (POTS), 298
protocol, 297
redundant, 307

redundant array of independent
  disks (RAID), 307
repeater, 295
ring topology, 294
router, 296
scalability, 308
scalable, 308
star topology, 294
site license, 291
striping, 307
striping-with-parity, 307
switch, 296
terminator, 294
topology, 294
transaction, 302
transaction processing system
  (TPS), 303
twisted-pair cable, 293
Wi-Fi, 299
wide area network (WAN), 292
wireless access point, 299
wireless hotspots, 293
wireless networks, 293

Key Terms QUIZ

Complete each statement by writing one of the terms listed under "Key Terms" in each blank.

1. Many office automation systems can be built with _____, like those found in any computer store.

2. Managers commonly use _____ to assist in their decision-making processes.

3. A(n) _____ analyzes data and produces a recommended course of action.

4. A(n) _____ combines knowledge from an expert and an inference engine to make diagnostic recommendations.

5. A(n) _____ is a network of computers that serves users located relatively near each other.

6. _____ computers have multiple hardware systems performing the same task at the same time.

7. RAID disks are configured as _____ when the same data is written simultaneously to two separate hard disks.

8. Organizations that plan to grow prefer _____ computer systems that can add storage capacity and computing power as needed.

9. The logical layout of wires and devices that connect a network's nodes is called the network's _____.

10. Two organizations can directly share e-commerce information with each other via _____.

In your own words, briefly answer the following questions.

1. Describe the main differences between a LAN and a WAN.

2. List three different network topologies, and explain the layout of each.

3. Describe three types of network media commonly used in data transmission.

4. What are the basic components of an information system?

5. Define a transaction, and provide a basic example of a type of transaction involving your school library or a public library.

6. Explain the function of a decision support system, and compare a DSS with an expert system.

7. Describe how the information in an expert system's knowledge base is collected.

8. What does it mean for computers to be executing in lockstep? Why do some information systems use this type of process?

9. Explain the concept of interoperability. One challenge facing those who provide medical care to service members returning from military deployment has been a lack of interoperability among the information systems containing medical records in the Department of Defense, Department of Veterans Affairs, and civilian medical systems. Why would interoperability be important in this situation? What are some issues you would need to consider in planning for interoperability of these information systems?

10. Define electronic data interchange, and explain how it is different from simply sending someone a document via e-mail. Why might a manufacturer want to use electronic data interchange with its suppliers? How might its suppliers benefit from electronic data interchange?

Complete the following exercises as directed by your instructor.

1. Investigate two different office automation systems. Visit the Web site for Microsoft Office at http://office.microsoft.com/en-us/products/. In the Programs section, choose Learn More to get a list of the various programs that make up the Office suite. Select See More for several of the applications, to learn more about what they do and how they share information between each other. Then, visit OpenOffice.org's site at http://www.openoffice.org/ and select "I want to learn more about OpenOffice.org." Read through the tabs of information on that page. How are OpenOffice.org and Microsoft Office the same and different? Does one seem to do a better job than the other at integrating information, or are they similar?

2. Test out an expert system. Go to the Whale Watcher demonstration run by Acquired Intelligence at http://www.aiinc.ca/demos/whale.shtml. Click the button that says Run Whale Watcher. Answer the questions that appear in any way you like; you can also click on the Back button on your browser if you want to back up and change your answers. Pay attention to how your answers lead the system to providing different solutions. Does there appear to be any way for the system to refine its information or to acquire new information that would allow it to expand or improve its diagnostic ability?

Team
EXERCISE
Organizational
Skills

Developing information systems is a complex effort that generally requires teams of employees working together. When you are a team member, and even as an individual employee, choices you make about how you use your time will affect others. How do you balance your personal desires, ambitions, and responsibilities against the goals and needs of your team? When your decisions can help or hurt others, those decisions have an ethical component.

To apply these ideas, divide into groups of three or four, and consider the following scenario:

Three months ago, you were hired as a junior programmer at a company that develops custom e-commerce software for national retailers. The latest project is a complex software suite. At a morning staff meeting today, the team manager announces that the lead software designer was in a car accident and will be out of work for two or three weeks to recover. The project is in a critical phase, so all the team members must step up and take on extra work to see the project completed.

Your dilemma is that for the last month, you and your three best friends have been planning to call in sick this week and take a long-weekend trip to the beach. If you call off the beach trip in order to support the work team, your friends will be angry and disappointed, and you will have a seven-day workweek instead of a weekend of fun. Also, because you are inexperienced at this point in your career, you have not yet been able to make major contributions to the software. Even with the team in crisis mode, you doubt whether you will be a tremendous help.

As a group, discuss this scenario and arrive at a recommendation for what the junior programmer should do. Be prepared to compare your recommendation (and the reasons behind it) with the other groups' ideas in a class discussion.

LESSON 7B:
Computing Ethics

The advent of personal computing technology has undeniably taken the world by storm. In just a few short decades, personal and mobile computers have affected the way people interact almost everywhere on the planet. Where once our actions might affect a few dozen people around us, our online behavior can affect—or at the very least be visible to—thousands or even millions of people around the globe.

It is no surprise that the ethical use of computing technology is a pressing issue everywhere from the kitchen table to the boardrooms of multinational corporations. This lesson will discuss and clarify some of the unethical computing practices that are common in the digital world, as well as some of the penalties that exist for violating computer-related laws.

And yet, though our new computer technology does pose some fresh questions, the issues and dilemmas of computer-related ethics are the same in many ways to those found in distinctly un-technical places such as elementary school playgrounds. In this sense, a discussion of computing ethics should seem very familiar and serve as a reinforcement of lessons that were hopefully learned long ago.

The idea of ethics itself involves much more than just the consequences of being caught doing something wrong. For example, most people will never try to rob a bank. We understand that there are large

Figure 7.20   Ethical computing behavior has many parallels to the rules of conduct we begin learning as children.

penalties for doing so, of course, but the penalty itself is not what prevents most of us from committing the crime. Conversely, though it is illegal to drive a car faster than the posted speed limit, and steep fines and penalties may be waiting for those who are caught, many people occasionally or routinely break speed laws knowing full well that they are doing so.

Ultimately, what governs our actions is a complex combination of factors that includes—along with the fear of being punished—a sense of what is right and wrong. For most people, robbing a bank is clearly wrong; hence, our population in general does not engage in that activity. However, for many people, driving a car a bit faster than the speed limit simply doesn't seem very wrong, even knowing that a law forbids it; is it any wonder that so many people on the streets routinely drive faster than they are allowed?

Computer-related behavior mirrors this situation. Hacking into a bank's database and stealing millions of dollars is clearly wrong, and most people, even if they had the necessary expertise, would not do such a thing. Yet many people routinely share copyrighted music and software with each other, even if they know that it is illegal to do so, in part because it seems like a minor and harmless exercise.

One of the factors that can significantly affect a person's ethical outlook and behavior is **empathy**, the ability to recognize, understand, and share the feelings of others. For example, suppose you pass a colleague's desk at work and see that he has left himself logged into Facebook when he left for lunch a few minutes ago. It seems like harmless fun to post an outrageous status message on his behalf, and even though you are potentially violating laws by pretending to be your colleague when writing the message, it still seems far more funny than wrong.

Consider what might be the outcome of faking that post. For sure, the message might generate some embarrassment on his behalf, but what if it caused genuine harm in his life? What if his family or relatives saw him saying something rude or incendiary and decided not to believe his protests that his account had been compromised? What if other colleagues saw a message that they deemed to be highly unprofessional and complained to his boss?

It may be easy to shrug and say, "Well, that's his problem; I don't care. It was just a joke." But those who express that perspective are not truly being empathetic; they are not understanding and sharing the stress that they caused.

Empathy requires that we practice that exercise we have been given since children: "How would you feel if that happened to you?" If we were honest rather

Figure 7.21 An unattended PC still logged in to a social site might be a great opportunity for a prank, but at what cost to the people involved?

than defensive, most of us would have to admit that a demotion or being fired would be a traumatic experience. A big argument at home would leave us feeling emotionally wounded and unfairly treated.

Applying this honest empathy to ethical situations can help sharpen how we feel about them, whether they are high- or low-tech questions, and this may modify our behavior. Perhaps that joke Facebook status should be toned down to something mild and silly, or avoided altogether. Given the risk of ruining lives by hitting someone when speeding in a car, perhaps driving laws should be obeyed more closely, at the very least in residential areas where the risk to others is higher.

Throughout this lesson, take time to not just understand the mechanical aspects of unethical behavior and the legal penalties, but also to practice being empathetic. Ethics can involve many gray areas and unanswered questions, but you may be surprised at how often a gray area resolves into clearer situations that seem right or wrong when you understand the perspective of others.

7.5 Digital Piracy

One of the most widespread forms of unethical computer use is piracy. Though the word has many definitions and applications, with regard to the world of computing **piracy** means acquiring copies of protected digital creations such as software, music, or writing, and redistributing that work to others without the permission of the creator. Such actions need not involve profit in order to be illegal; sharing digital products without consent is considered piracy whether the copier is paid or not.

Examples of piracy are commonplace and varied. Popular songs are frequently traded either directly or via computer communications from one person to another. Software programs can be found and downloaded from Internet sites that are not authorized to distribute the programs, in many cases slightly altered to disable copy protection and authenticity checks. Many people record TV shows and live performances and upload their recordings to social media sites like YouTube to share, even though the artist or show owner had prohibited such actions.

Piracy is a different crime from **forgery**, which is the process of making copies that appear to be real and selling those copies to unsuspecting buyers as legitimate products. Posting a copy of Microsoft Windows to one's Web site and encouraging people to download it is a form of piracy. Creating one's own DVDs that look just like authentic Windows products and advertising them online as genuine Microsoft software is forgery.

In a forgery, only the perpetrator is considered to be the criminal. If caught, the forger may go to jail, but the buyer is considered to be a victim of the crime. With piracy, however, both provider and receiver are generally considered to be part of the crime. People have been caught and prosecuted both for sharing material online and for copying it from a pirate site.

The volume of computer users around the world makes piracy both an extremely important issue and a difficult one to pursue. Media companies claim that billions of dollars in revenue are lost annually to piracy, though quantifying lost revenue is an inexact and speculative process; regardless of the exact amounts, the impact is substantial, especially for

Figure 7.22 Whether on CD or on the Web, digital piracy distributes unauthorized copies of creative works, and the creators get nothing in return.

products such as music that could be easily affordable by many of the people sharing with each other for free.

Finding both uploaders and downloaders to prosecute can be difficult as well. Many countries that host pirate Web sites have little or no interest in sharing information about pirates with the United States and other media-producing nations. Without evidence that specific people are sharing data without permission, legal authorities cannot proceed with lawsuits and charges; and in cases where lawsuits are successful, they are individual victories in a sea of continuing violations.

WHAT IS INTELLECTUAL PROPERTY?

It can be a bit challenging to understand the products over which the piracy battle is being fought. It is much easier to picture the theft of a television from a store than software from Microsoft. The television is a real item that was manufactured, shipped to a store, and placed on a shelf to be sold. When a thief breaks in and removes it from the shelf, it is obvious that the television has been taken; a big empty space is now present where a TV once sat. Moreover, video surveillance cameras may have footage showing a person coming into the store and leaving with the television. When the police visit the suspect's house, they may very well find the TV inside.

In contrast, digital software and music do not take up shelf space. If someone makes a copy of a music file online, the original file is still in the same place, making it less obvious that a theft has occurred. Even if digital traces of the download are found, there may not be direct evidence that the owner of the computer was the actual person who performed the download. And if the police look at the contents of the suspect's computer, they may not find the copied file.

Even so, legal concepts have been created and refined to help protect products of the mind. While ideas, designs, and expressions of creativity may not have much (or any) physical form, they can be quite valuable. **Intellectual property (IP)** is the term that is used to designate ideas, trade secrets, inventions, technical diagrams, writing, music, art, and other kinds of mind-based products that are intended to be used in a commercial way. IP laws identify the criteria that are used to define intellect-based products and the protections that are afforded to such products.

Intellectual property laws are not new; the origins of modern IP law can be traced to the 17th and 18th centuries. The digital age, however, has brought a flurry of new challenges and decisions, as many IP laws have proven understandably inadequate to define and enforce protection of intellectual property in a world where millions of violations could occur anywhere in the world. The revisions and extensions to IP law concerning online rights and protections are ongoing, and it will likely be quite some time before online IP law is considered settled.

IP law is often written in language that is open, suggestive, or in some ways unspecific. This is usually done purposefully in order to avoid writing rigid laws that are easily skirted when a slightly different kind of idea or expression is created that is not covered by the law. The disadvantage of that flexibility is that it can on occasion be difficult to definitely determine ahead of time whether using protected intellectual property will or will not violate laws. Most of the time, however, it is fairly clear whether IP use is legitimate or infringing.

COPYRIGHT AND FAIR USE

One of the foundation blocks of intellectual property law is the **copyright**, a legal concept that grants rights and control to the owner of any published work. A creative product such as a book, song, or photograph is generally considered to be published when it is made available to the public for consumption. If you write a song and sing it just for your family with specific instructions that they not re-transmit it to others, then it is likely not published. If you release it to YouTube, it would most likely at that point be considered published.

A copyright allows the author of a story, song, or other form of expression to preserve the right to declare how and by whom that product may be legally used. So long as the copyright is in effect, the author has legal control over the work. Authors commonly control the distribution of their product via licenses

Figure 7.23 You can't put intellectual property on a table or in a bag, but it is still a legitimate product that can be sold.

that define the rules for distribution, and the compensation due to the author for the sale of copies of the work.

Though copyright protects the specific song, book, program, or picture, it does not protect the ideas contained in the product. If someone writes a catchy little song about the virtues of orange juice, they can control the distribution and use of that particular song, but they cannot prevent others from writing new songs about orange juice, so long as the new songs are original and not simply a copy or extension of the first author's song.

As a general rule, if a work is copyrighted, people may use it for their own enjoyment as long as they acquire it legally (for example, by buying a copy of a song, book or software program, or by visiting an artist's free Flickr site or YouTube channel). But if people intend to reproduce part or all of that work, either to share it or include it in their own new creation, they must first ask for permission from the author. Failing to do so usually violates the copyright.

Downloading the latest song from your favorite artist from iTunes is an example of how to legally acquire that copyright-protected music. Once you have the song, you can listen to it as often as you like, and you can also play it for your friends and family, all without violating the copyright. If you want to give copies of that file to your friends, doing so without first getting permission from the author violates copyright law because the author's publishing license did not give you permission to become a distributor of the music.

But what if you want to write a review of the song on your blog and include a small audio clip of the song to illustrate an important point in the review? Must you ask for permission even for that small piece?

Figure 7.24   If you're reviewing music, a book, or a movie on a blog, fair use may allow you to use snippets of the creative work without first securing the owner's permission.

Copyright law contains an exception for this, called **fair use**, which provides for a limited set of circumstances where others can use copyrighted material without first obtaining permission. The fair use exception, for the most part, covers two basic categories of use: commentary and criticism, and parody. People can use small excerpts from a larger work in reviews and observations, so long as the review is genuine and not just a disguised means of unauthorized reproduction. Parody—poking fun at the original work—is also generally allowed.

Fair use is a common concept in copyright law, but it is by no means clear-cut. Each copyright dispute involving a fair use claim must be individually evaluated and decided by a judge, and often take into consideration a range of factors that include the way the copyrighted text is used, the benefits to the public of the new use, and the financial impact of the new use on the original author.

There is an additional limited exception granted to teachers who wish to use copyrighted video materials in their face-to-face teaching in the classroom. A teacher, therefore, may show a movie to the class as part of their in-classroom lessons. However, that same teacher must obtain special permission to show that same movie to the class as part of an end-of-year trip to a local pizza restaurant.

The same restriction applies to individuals who purchase music or video products. You can play music and movies for yourself, your friends, and your family in your home. However, if you want to show the movie outside your home, or if you want to invite a large group of strangers and friends to your house for a dance party where movies or MTV videos are shown, you should first secure special permission in order to comply with copyright law.

Copyrights do not last forever. For new works that are created and published today, the copyright lasts for the life of the author and for 70 years after the author's death. Anything published prior to 1923 in the United States is also considered to be uncopyrighted. Once the copyright expires, the work is considered to be in the **public domain**, which means that anyone can use part or all of the work without first obtaining permission from anyone. So, if your big backyard dance party were relying only on music published between 1910 and 1920, you would not need to ask permission to play any of that music, although you may find yourself with a smaller crowd than you had originally intended.

Figure 7.25 Paying for a song is no different from paying for a television, even if the song doesn't sit on your coffee table at home.

The reasoning behind copyright law is simple, even if the laws and their application are not. Authors of creative work want to share the result of their efforts with others and in most cases, receive compensation for their work. In that regard, they are no different than a television manufacturer, who wants to receive payment for the time, effort and materials required to construct the TV; or the retail outlet that sells the television, which wants to receive compensation for the costs involved with running the store and working with customers.

Unlike the television manufacturer, however, an author's work can often be easily recreated by others, and often for their own profit. A popular song from one band is very likely to be performed by others; without any legal protection, other bands would keep all the proceeds from their playing, giving nothing to the original author even though the author's work enabled them to profit from playing the song. Without copyright protection, a photographer's work could suddenly appear in magazines and on Web sites, without any compensation for his effort.

Even with copyright laws in place, many artists and authors struggle with the rapid and uncontrolled distribution of their work, seeking to find the balance between ways to profit from the products they produce and trying to control the illegal and harmful aspects of unauthorized distribution.

Figure 7.26 A site or enterprise license makes it convenient for a large office to legally own many copies of the same program.

SOFTWARE LICENSING AND PIRACY

Just like music and books, software is a type of intellectual property that can be subject to copyright laws. And just like music and books, software is heavily shared and distributed in ways that violate copyright laws.

Software that is copyrighted is typically distributed either with a personal license or with a multi-user license. Like its name implies, a **personal software license** is one that grants a single person the ability to use the program, and it may impose terms and conditions that limit the program's use. A multi-user license may simply authorize the software buyer to install and use the program on up to a certain number of different computers. Larger organizations may negotiate a **site license**, which allows the software to be installed and used on any computer in a building or corporate campus; or an **enterprise license**, which grants installation and use privileges on any computer within the company.

The term *license* conveys a critically important distinction that many people do not realize, which is that software purchasers are buying only the right to use the software; they do not own the software itself when they buy it. Microsoft is happy to sell you a copy of Office to make your work more productive, but you do not gain ownership of the software by making that purchase. Since only the owner can legally decide to distribute or sell a program, Microsoft is very careful not to give away ownership of the software to others.

Some software is specifically intended by its creators to be distributed freely to anyone who wants to install, use, study, and modify it. Known as open-source software, while such programs are free they are usually published with specific conditions and restrictions to the public. Open-source software developers may require that everyone using the program agree to acknowledge the creator's ownership of the

program, to not restrict others' access to the software, nor to charge fees for its use. In some cases, users are required to agree to the open-source license in order to acquire the software; in others, the software simply comes with a notification that its use is subject to a license agreement that is published on the Web.

Software piracy can occur in several different ways. **End-user piracy** occurs when a legitimate purchaser of a program makes unauthorized copies, either for other computers that they own or in order to share with others. If a program's license specifically prohibits its sale to another person once purchased, a legitimate purchaser may violate the license by selling the product on an auction site like eBay, even if they have uninstalled the program before selling it. **Internet piracy** describes the use of Web and Internet resources to host and distribute software copies to anyone who can gain access to the files. **Manufacturer piracy**, a less common form, involves a computer manufacturer installing unauthorized copies of programs onto their new computers for sale in order to make them more attractive to consumers.

Barring a fundamental change in the way computers and software are created, software makers focus more on mitigating the damage caused by piracy than on eliminating the practice altogether. This is at least partly because piracy simply cannot be stamped out, despite every effort made to protect the software.

Early forms of copy protection, especially for more expensive software products, used a **dongle**, which is a hardware device that plugs into one of the ports of a computer. If the program failed to detect and communicate with the dongle, it would simply not run. Though dongles are occasionally still used, they add an extra expense for the producer and an inconvenience for the user; in any case, if pirated software is altered to no longer check for the presence of the dongle, then the dongle's value as a piracy deterrent drops to zero.

Many versions of software-based copy protection have been created, involving everything from serial numbers to be entered by the purchaser during installation, to encrypted data tracks hidden on installation disks. In every one of these cases, hackers have quickly written counter-agents to defeat the copy protection; in the more difficult cases, the program is edited to remove or shut down the copy-protection check.

Most recently, software companies have turned to Internet-based copy protection, requiring that users activate and validate their software with a security server on the Internet. This method can be effective in some situations, such as for online games that require a paid account to play, but for many single-user programs, hackers have been able to counteract the online checks, either by removing them from the

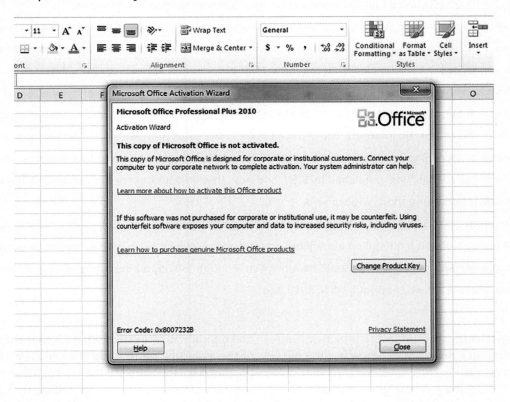

Figure 7.27   Many software manufacturers are now using Internet-based activation to reduce piracy.

Focus on the Issues

software or by tricking the program into thinking that a local computer program is actually the company's security server.

The reality about piracy protection is that any protective measure done by one person can be undone by another. Software companies, therefore, develop innovative ways to protect their software largely to make piracy inconvenient enough that some or most of the would-be pirates find it more attractive to simply purchase the software they need. Mass-distributed software simply cannot be protected well enough to completely prevent copies from being stolen, but many people would rather buy a legitimate copy of a game or utility than risk a nasty Trojan horse infection from an online piracy site, or follow complex instructions for changing (and possibly destabilizing) their computer environment to defeat a program's online validation.

DOWNLOADING AND SHARING MUSIC AND OTHER MEDIA

In the days before computers and CDs, music was sold on vinyl records and cassette tapes. Individual consumers might copy songs onto a tape to share with friends, but wholesale copying and distribution was left to a small number of people with the resources, time, and equipment necessary to create and distribute counterfeit tapes.

With the advent of computers, writeable CD media, and the Internet, the mass redistribution of copyrighted material became simple for anyone and everyone who wanted to participate. Making a copy of a music CD for a friend has effectively the same impact on the marketplace as copying a cassette tape in decades past; but uploading those music files to a sharing service can turn every uploader into a high-volume distributor. When thousands of people share with thousands of others, it does not take long for millions of copies of songs and movies to be produced, without a penny in revenue being given to the artist that created the song.

One of the most prominent services created during the early years of online music sharing was Napster. Released in 1999, Napster provided users with a convenient way to offer files for sharing, browse a catalog of what was currently shared by all users, and download files from other users. The service was a huge success; at its peak a year later, 25 million users were sharing 80 million songs.

Unfortunately, the bulk of what was shared among users were copyrighted music files whose owners had not granted permission to share them. Music companies and individual artists quickly filed lawsuits against Napster, and by 2001, the service had shut down in order to restructure its business to a legitimate, fee-based download system. That new business model met with far less success, and Napster was eventually acquired by another media company.

Though Napster faded quickly into the shadows, other services and sharing methods were designed to replace it. Today, the fight against illegal media sharing continues without a clear winner on either side. There are a number of reasons for the stalemate, both technical and social. On the technical

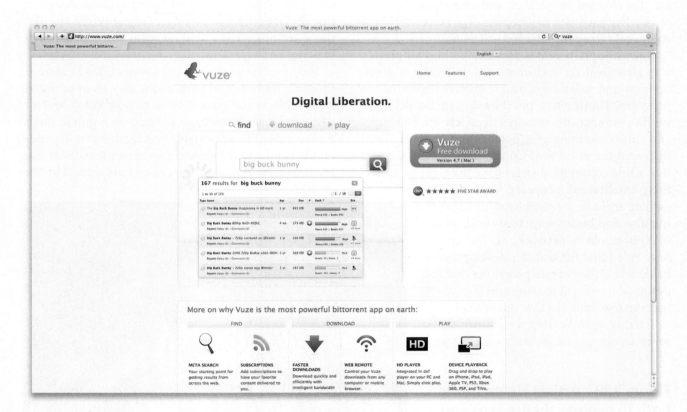

Figure 7.28   bitTorrent programs like Vuze can be used for fast and efficient downloading of both legitimate and pirated software.

side, decentralized sharing and the legitimate value of data sharing contribute to the persistence of illegal media sharing.

If music, movies and software for sharing were contained in a central location or offered by one online entity, it would be relatively easy to shut the site down. But most media sharing systems are based on peer-to-peer networks, where each contributor stores the data on their own computer, and each copier forms an independent connection with a contributor in order to make their copy. There is no central entity or service that stores and controls the connections of others, so there is no single point of control that can be disabled.

Another avenue of protection might be to sue and shut down developers of sharing software. To an extent, this has been and continues to be attempted, but success is limited in part by court decisions affirming that file sharing designs can also serve a beneficial purpose. For example, one of the most popular and effective methods for sharing pirated software, movies, and other large packages is the **bitTorrent** protocol, which links dozens or hundreds of users together to cooperatively and simultaneously contribute small pieces of the complete file to the copier. Transmission time is generally greatly reduced through bitTorrent connections because pieces are downloaded in parallel, and users can share the pieces they have with new copiers even before they have completely assembled the entire data file.

But while bitTorrent is an ideal method for pirates, it is also ideal for legitimate online software development and sales companies. Digital copies of the program, legitimately purchased, can be delivered to the customer much more effectively via bitTorrent and similar technologies; patches and updates can be delivered the same way. Courts have upheld the idea that while copyright owners have the right to protect their intellectual property, that defense cannot include a prohibition on designing new and better ways to transfer information across a network. So far, courts have ruled that file transfer developers are liable when they create programs that are designed for illegal sharing and encourage users to use them for that purpose.

Further complicating the picture, while some artists and music companies aggressively pursue legal action against copyright violators, others have done the opposite, embracing file sharing via peer-to-peer and social networks as a way to gain visibility and popularity in a crowded field. Those artists claim success stories in the same sharing environment that others claim a substantial loss of profits.

While it is clear that the legal owner of any product, whether a television or a song, is the only entity that can decide whether to sell it or give it away, the ethical framework for many people is closer to speeding in a car than robbing a bank. It can be difficult for an average person to pinpoint the harm that is done from a single act of file sharing; and it can be difficult to find instances of bands, music companies, and movie studios that have gone out of business or fired thousands of people because profits have been ruined by piracy. A decision to share or not share may become ethically clearer by considering not the side issues (for example, whether or not record companies already make too much money) but simply a central one: if a song or a product is good enough or enjoyable enough to own, should its producer and owner be paid for creating that value?

It is usually fairly clear when professionally-created music, video, and images are copyright-protected; such products are often distributed with advisory text that declares them to be subject to copyright law. But there are other risks to those who share media that may not be so obvious.

For instance, parks and city venues often host summertime festivals and fairs, and it may seem perfectly reasonable to use your iPhone to take video footage of an awesome blues band playing on a public stage. It may indeed be reasonable and legal, but it depends on the band and the venue. If an agreement exists that the broadcast rights for the concert are owned by the

Figure 7.29 Artists create music both to express themselves and also to make a living through the sale of their songs.

city or the band, you may also be violating a copyright by recording that video and uploading it to YouTube.

You may also run into trouble if you post pictures of people on a commercial image site, even if the pictures were originally just snapshots or for your own personal use. If you use the appearance of others in pictures or video as a way to make money, those people may be able to sue you for damages or a share of the profits if you didn't sign a contract or agreement with your subjects.

OTHER LEGAL AND SOCIAL RISKS

Along with copyright violations and financial liability, there are other risks inherent in sharing media, especially videos and photographs. Early in this lesson, you considered the consequences of creating a fake status message on a colleague's Facebook page. While the example dealt with impersonating them on their own page, those same risks to others might arise in information that you post on your own page.

A person posting pictures and video of compromising situations at a recent party will surely cement the wild reputation for everyone who appears in them. Often, however, employers take a very dim view of inappropriate behavior on the part of their employees because they fear that the company's reputation may be compromised, especially if the business presents a formal, professional appearance to their clients or customers. Like it or not, employers sometimes search (or hire search firms) to look for precisely those kinds of photographs and descriptions, often as part of an interview and hiring process. Depending on the circumstance, those party pictures could cost the subject their job or a job offer.

Many social media users feel spied upon or feel that they have a right to privacy that is being violated by companies or individuals combing through Web and Internet data looking for evidence of unacceptable behavior. Unfortunately, this is more of a misunderstanding on the part of the user than a legitimate concern.

Though Facebook allocates resources to each user and allows that user to participate in controlling access to the data that is stored on the system, nothing posted to Facebook—or anywhere else on the Internet, for that matter—should be considered private. Facebook itself may include conditions for using the service in which each user grants Facebook permission to use their page information in certain ways. Friends who can see pictures and status messages can copy, store, and forward that information to others. Automated software programs called **spiders** or **Web**

crawlers are run by search engine and other companies to constantly sift through, catalog, and in some cases store information that they find.

Even if one were to delete everything on their Facebook, YouTube or Flickr account and close the account, there is no assurance whatsoever that the information once stored there is completely gone. One of the most important online rules of thumb is this: *What goes on the Internet, stays on the Internet forever.*

The only means to keep information private is to truly keep it private. Compromising photographs should not be posted to social media sites if they could be devastating to the lives of oneself or others. Personally identifying information should be minimized and kept as safe as possible. Incendiary opinions and hateful speech might come back to haunt the writer a few years down the road; care in how and where thoughts are expressed is advisable for everyone.

Privacy can also be compromised for children as well as adults. Posting pictures of minor children with identifying information to Facebook, Flickr, or other public locations may put them at risk. Major companies can also be the culprit in privacy breaches. Google, for example, ran afoul of privacy issues when their Google Maps Street View images captured faces of people on the street as their cars drove past. In response to criticism, Google began to blur the faces in photographs and simplified the process for people to request the removal of photographs related to them or their private property.

Figure 7.30 Though it may not feel comfortable for everyone, companies often closely monitor their employees' online activity while at work.

Figure 7.31 Our first online experiences rarely begin with coaching and mentoring by others; most people learn as they go.

Ultimately, ethical, legal, and social risks in the distribution of music and visual media of all kinds can be distilled to a very simple evaluation. If the product is one that you own, you may decide what to do with it. If you do not own the product, be it the latest song from your favorite band or a copy of a picture your best friend took last week, you need to think carefully about whether you have the right to reproduce it and whether you might do harm somewhere by sharing it.

7.6 Personal Computing Ethics

From the moment we are able as toddlers to begin following rules, the world hands us a long list of them to learn. We learn to take turns, follow directions, stand in line, and hand in our assignments on time. We learn to stop at red lights, let older people have our seats on the bus when it is crowded, and be on time to work. There are countless hundreds of manners, regulations, rules, and conventions that we absorb and follow, with varying degrees of commitment. We do this both to live more effectively and also to help large numbers of people coexist with a minimum of fuss and trouble.

When we begin to use computers and the Internet for the first time, we do not generally go through the same process of mentors and supervisors coaching us on the conduct that is most expected. Most people simply join in and participate, whatever their age, and either learn as they go or simply do whatever they want.

That last approach—to do whatever one wants without regard for consequences—can cause a great deal of harm to one's own social, professional and online reputation. It can also cause harm, inconvenience, and distress for others. While the Internet can accommodate many different styles of behavior and points of view, there are some actions that are undeniably unethical and should be avoided without exception.

COMPUTER MISUSE AND ABUSE

The average computer user will most likely never learn how to perform common hacking tasks and attacks. In addition to requiring a fair amount of time and risk to put into practice, such activities for most people fall into an obvious, seriously unethical category of behavior. No hacking technique is discovered and employed by accident.

For instance, in order to initiate denial of service attacks against Web sites, hackers must deploy and

Figure 7.32 Hackers typically keep the emotional consequences of their actions at arms' length.

use tools that flood Web servers with excessive traffic. Configuring, using, and disguising the source of traffic from such tools is not impossible to learn, but it requires a specific effort to gain the required knowledge. In order to co-opt other systems, programmers of Trojan horses and other malware must actively learn about security gaps and errors in programs, networks, and business processes, and then create applications that exploit those loopholes. Social engineering tactics, such as sending e-mails or making phone calls that are designed to trick recipients into giving out secret information, are only employed by people attempting to gain unauthorized access to systems and information that they should not see.

As with any other kind of serious lapse in ethical judgment, decisions to join hacking groups is often accompanied by a significant lapse or absence of empathy. Hackers often express that for them, breaking into systems and stealing or corrupting information is either simply a game, or it's just plain funny to see the distress that is caused. Both of those sentiments suggest that no genuine consideration for the damage being done is really being made. It would be nothing short of sociopathic to carefully understand and internalize the plight of people who have lost savings, privacy, and in some cases their personal safety, and still gleefully continue to cause that kind of distress.

Though the chances are low that you will find yourself presented with a tempting opportunity to join up with a hacking group, should that happen at some point, do some research into some of the social consequences of those actions and gain an understanding of the pain and loss those acts will likely cause.

NETIQUETTE

The term **netiquette** is a concatenation of *Internet etiquette*; in other words, it refers to the set of online behaviors that are considered polite and proper. By and large, the behaviors that find their way onto netiquette lists are the same ones that we regard highly in our non-technical society and interactions: politeness, courtesy, and respect are highly prized, while abusive speech and rude behavior are discouraged. Interacting with others online insulates us to some degree from having to see the consequences of our negative actions, but those consequences are still very real.

There are many Web sites and articles devoted to netiquette, just as there are for conventional etiquette. Use your favorite search engine and search on terms like "netiquette" and "web etiquette" to find varying perspectives on the subject.

Beyond the rules of common courtesy, netiquette can includes cautions and suggestions about situations as well as behavior, such as:

- **Angry words will outlive your anger.** When you write furious and hurtful e-mails, Facebook wall posts, Twitter tweets, or chat forum posts, you will never have a chance to take back those words when you are no longer angry. Remember, *what goes on the Internet, stays on the Internet forever*. When you are full of rage and hurt feelings, grab a Notepad document, and write everything you want to say there. Save the document, and go away. When you are calmer, go back to that document, and send only the useful part of it to the intended recipient. By

Figure 7.33 A computer makes it easy to spiral out of control when participating in controversial online forums; usually, losing control just makes you look ridiculous to others.

and large, you will end up with much less to regret as the months and years pass.

- **Your indignation is not very interesting to others.** Mixing it up with others in political chat rooms is a great way to feel like you are winning arguments. Joining chat threads about incendiary topics in order to set the record straight on the subject feels like fighting the good fight. The truth is, however, that most of the time none of the other participants are really listening to you; they are there only to shout down those who disagree with them. If you leave those sessions feeling aggressive or anxious, reduce your participation.

- **If sand bothers you, stay out of the sandbox.** Some forums and services provide no-holds-barred access to all manner of subjects. For example, Omegle and Chatroulette are two services that pair up two random strangers using the service for chat and video sessions. Neither service restricts the actions of either participant, and as one might guess, the topics and antics are often raw and offensive to many. If you are bothered by the content you find on services or sites, don't spend extra time there to rail against the actions of the participants; your own mood will suffer, and the long time residents will take delight in your criticisms. Simply ignore the services and the people that use them.

- **Humor requires the right audience to be funny.** Sending e-mail containing funny jokes to the people at work is more risky than it sounds; if somebody takes offense, the sender's standing in the company could suffer. Sending e-mail containing racist or sexist jokes to anyone at work is not only unethical, it is just plain stupid; even if no one takes offense, the sender risks being fired simply for having put the company in danger of litigation. Before you send a joke, make sure that everyone on your distribution list will like it, and make sure that you will not regret sending it tomorrow.

- **If you have cautious instincts, trust them.** If you have ever thought, as you finish an e-mail, status update or wall post, "Oh, I probably shouldn't send this, but..." then you are right. You shouldn't send it, whatever it is. Don't send it.

ONLINE STUDENT NOTES AND ESSAY DATABANKS

The Web has provided great opportunities to students both for legitimate collaboration with peers and mentors and for accessing resources useful for cheating; a little Web surfing can quickly discover sites that can help users to either forge greater success or simply to create an illusion of accomplishment.

There are many sites that provide local, national, or international communities for sharing insights and seeking help with learning. From junior high to graduate school, services exist to connect tutors and students and provide raw information for research.

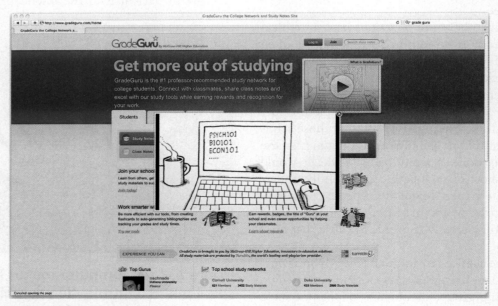

Figure 7.34 **Student help sites like GradeGuru encourage legitimate knowledge sharing to help students ethically complete assignments.**

Services can be provided by local school districts, libraries, or for-profit enterprises.

At the college level, sites such as GradeGuru (http://www.gradeguru.com/) provide services to aid student collaboration. Students are invited to contribute notes and study aids for others, earning reputation points and in some cases payment for materials that are rated as exceptionally helpful within the community. The site also offers a pathway to business recruiters, allowing contributors to transform helping others into job opportunities. Users of the site gain access to relevant materials and assistance to help them overcome the hurdles they encounter in challenging courses.

Cheating is a common temptation for anyone in any endeavor, and that includes students of all ages. The Web serves those needs just as handily as for legitimate workers in college. Some sites sell access to answers for standardized tests or practice questions for tests whose questions are supposed to be a surprise. Other sites sell class notes and pre-written essays, while still others offer to ghost-write fresh essays for students for a fee.

Technology in some cases serves both the cheater and the institution. Many schools are now requiring that students submit their work to services like Turnitin (http://www.turnitin.com/). Turnitin compares each essay to a vast database of essays, Web pages, and other published resources in an attempt to detect plagiarism. The submitted essay is then added to the database to be used for future searches. Professors can also individually submit writing that they are given to Turnitin when they suspect plagiarism, even if students are not required by policy to use the service.

Penalties for being caught cheating, depending on the institution, are often severe; students are commonly expelled altogether if they are found to have cheated, plagiarized text, or submitted an essay that they did not write themselves. Yet despite the high risk, cheating is not uncommonly regarded as an ordinary practice that contains little ethical damage.

Part of this casual acceptance may stem from a misunderstanding about what is being measured when an essay is requested. The student may simply see an assignment to be completed and a grade to be received, at which time another work assignment will be made. In that sterile, "the end justifies the means" view, it is no surprise that cheating seems unimportant. Web sites that present the means to cheat in a bland, businesslike manner only help to enhance the belief that the practice is ordinary and reasonable.

Figure 7.35 Cheating is easy to do, but cheaters can't honestly claim to be as good as their test and essay results may indicate.

The practice becomes better defined as a problem if the perspective changes to focus on the process as well as the final product. What is truly being evaluated is not the essay, but the ability of the student to produce the essay; it is the same idea as a race testing a runner's ability to run from start to finish, not simply to cross the finish line. When students (or runners, or business people) cheat, they have lost sight of that critical aspect. And similar to a marathon runner who takes a taxi to the finish line and jogs triumphantly across hours before the other runners arrive, cheaters in education and business display an embarrassing lack of sophistication to those who measure the complete process of producing work.

ACCEPTABLE USE POLICIES (AUP)

As computer and network technology brings new aspects and environments to the challenge of ethical behavior, many organizations have created policies and guidelines specifically to address these new areas. Often referred to as an **Acceptable Use Policy (AUP)**, this type of document attempts to encode and formalize the practice of ethical computer use for an institution or company.

AUPs generally cover topics such as copyright violation, plagiarism, and information privacy, along with listing prohibited unethical behaviors such as various kinds of hacking, identity theft, or using computer resources in a way that blocks or harms other users. They may also define obligations and limitations of the institution with regard to providing services such as data storage and Internet access.

Some AUPs are simply a comprehensive statement of policy so that the institution's point of view is made clear. Others are framed as an agreement or contract that people are required to sign in consent before being given access to computer-related resources. They can be useful tools for creating a legal framework for punishing wrongdoers; as a method for improving ethical behavior, an AUP's effectiveness is dependent as much if not more on the willingness of the participants than on the completeness of its coverage.

For examples of AUPs for universities, see Queen's University's Computer User Code of Ethics at http://www.queensu.ca/secretariat/senate/policies/codes.html, and a contract-style AUP and code of ethics developed at the University of Illinois at http://lrs.ed.uiuc.edu/students/mickley/ethicsnew.htm.

7.7 Professional Computing Ethics

Much of the discussion so far in this lesson has focused on ethical computer use as an individual and as a student. Ethics on the job shares much in common with those categories. It is just as illegal to download pirated copies of Microsoft Office for one's business as it is for oneself at home. It is no more ethical to take credit for someone else's idea or presentation at work than it is to submit an essay at school that was provided by an online service. But just as with school and home, our workplace provides additional aspects to ethical behavior to consider.

COMPUTING ETHICS IN THE WORKPLACE

Much of the time, an employer's perspective on employee behavior is very simple when stripped of long explanations, policies, and exceptions: For the time an employee is being paid, that employee should focus solely on producing work and value for the business. It is a rare employer who would declare that they are unconcerned with whether their employees are producing the products or services necessary to make the business thrive. It is, however, extremely common to find employers who are deeply interested in extracting more work and productivity out of the same work force.

With that in mind, it should be unsurprising to discover that many employers whose workers use computers in office settings are nervous about the negative impact that those computers might have on worker productivity. The same Internet that can be used to run cloud-based business programs, share documents, and back up data can also be used to chat with friends, post to Facebook, and surf pornography. For an employer who micro-measures work and productivity, each employee who spends half an hour of

Figure 7.36 What companies want most are employees that work hard when on the clock; computer monitoring is one way to encourage or enforce that ideal.

company time browsing YouTube, eBay, or Amazon poses a major threat to corporate progress.

Along with lost productivity, online personal time at work can create risk and liability for the company. Workers caught in illegal activities such as downloading copyrighted files can create reputational and financial risk for the firm. Public statements and comments made by employees at work could, depending on the situation, be construed as being made by the company, even when they were not being made in a place or manner sanctioned by the company. And employees visiting high-risk sites or clicking through on banner ads not related to work may download malware to company computers, compromising internal security and increasing the flow of spam and junk mail onto corporate e-mail servers.

Some companies react to the risk of intrusion and lost privacy by enacting AUPs for their employees, identifying behaviors and practices that are forbidden and allowed. Still others implement computer-resident monitoring devices that track keystrokes and Web activity, checking activity logs periodically for unacceptable use by employees. Company e-mail may be monitored, both between people in the same company and in communications to the outside world, to ensure that appropriate work standards are not being violated.

Workers often complain about the lack of fairness or legality of employer monitoring of computer and e-mail use. While there is a great deal of room to debate the ethics and efficacy of AUPs and key loggers, the legality of such measures is not so ambiguous; court cases have demonstrated that much of the time, employers are within their rights to restrict free Internet access at work and monitor employee use of computer resources.

INFORMAL AND SOCIAL CODES OF CONDUCT

Much of the focus on workplace computer-related ethics centers around communication rather than resource use. It is less common to have a corporate crisis centered around the amount of hard drive storage used by one person or another, but far more common to deal with objections to the way that employees conduct themselves via e-mail.

Ethical electronic communication at work follows familiar rules of thumb that are found everywhere: think before speaking, and treat others with respect. Even so, in many cases trouble can be avoided by realizing that workplace communication almost always requires a higher and more limited standard than is practiced at home and in social forums online.

People generally cross ethical boundaries in work communication in one of two ways: by becoming careless in sharing non-professional material, and by using e-mail to express opinions that should absolutely remain private and confidential.

When one grows comfortable at work, communication with colleagues becomes understandably less formal; after all, the typical worker spends a good portion of their life with their co-workers, and it is natural to share anything and everything with the people around you. This sometimes includes sharing opinions and thoughts in sensitive areas such as politics, religion, and relationships. This, of course, is not unique to the workplace; many families, for example, have an annoying cousin or uncle who is especially good at ruining Christmas Day dinners with loud, racist jokes. The difference is that at Aunt Martha's house, such jokes might result in discomfort and injured feelings; but at work, those same jokes can result in official reprimands, lost opportunities, a damaged reputation, and in some cases, the loss of the job altogether.

E-mail is also often used to complain about policies and people at work that are causing trouble for someone. E-mail can be a perfectly valid way to express and document concerns within a company, but it is essential to read each negative e-mail while

Figure 7.37 Whether online or in-person, extra care must be taken at work to behave with respect. An offensive joke or remark can swiftly result in termination.

considering that it might be read by anyone from the CEO to the receptionist, no matter how private one believes the communication might be. Sensitive communication, especially about other people, may be better handled face to face than by a document storage system, which in this case is what e-mail can be.

Of course, there are times when identifying a risk or problem is something that one specifically does want to document, whether to protect one's integrity as an employee or to build a case for wrongdoing within the company. The process of pointing out a major internal problem, called **whistleblowing**, is quite often both a demonstration of high ethical standards and also a major test of endurance for the person identifying the problem.

Many state and federal governments have laws that protect the job and safety of whistleblowers, preventing them from being fired for identifying illegal or unethical behavior within the company. Even so, retaliatory action is often a real consequence for the whistleblower, whether it manifests itself as reassignments to lower-priority roles in the company or simply being frozen out socially by other workers who no longer wish to associate with the whistleblower.

Because of the high risk, whistleblowers should take extreme care to fully document both the illegal or unethical behavior that they witness, and each and every communication regarding the problem that they make to others within the company. In this case, e-mail is an ideal format for communication both because it can be saved by the employee as paper copies, and because it normally is saved on corporate mail servers, allowing the whistleblower to corroborate their communication claims with the electronically-stored copies.

FORMAL CODES OF PROFESSIONAL RESPONSIBILITY

Just as universities and companies often produce AUPs and codes of conduct, many professional societies and organizations also publish ethical standards of their own for their members to follow. Though societies for engineers and architects may not have any legal standing to prosecute violations to their codes, membership is in some cases a necessary badge of honor in order to do business within the industry; at the very least, being unable to declare membership in

Figure 7.38
Whistleblowers may not use a whistle, but they can still attract plenty of attention to a severely unethical or illegal practice in their workplace.

a prominent trade organization may raise questions when a prospective client is seeking those professional services. Active, publicly declared membership in those organizations is generally viewed as an agreement to follow the ethical guidelines promoted by those organizations.

The exact rules and principles in a professional code of ethics vary from group to group, of course, but the overarching principles of working to benefit the client, and avoiding harmful and deceitful practices, are consistent throughout the various groups. For examples of professional codes, view the Institute of Electrical and Electronics Engineers (IEEE) Code of Ethics at http://www.ieee.org/about/corporate/governance/p7-8.html, or the Software Engineering Code of Ethics & Professional Practice at http://www.computer.org/cms/Computer.org/Publications/code-of-ethics.pdf.

Fact Check

1. Keystroke loggers and Web surfing monitors are sometimes used by companies
   a. to search for employee account numbers and passwords
   b. to enforce rules against personal online activity when at work
   c. to hack into competitor Web sites
2. Whistleblowers may find e-mail communication desirable because
   a. e-mails can effectively document the whistleblower's communication attempts
   b. they don't have to have uncomfortable face-to-face meetings
   c. they can send messages to managers anonymously

- Empathy, the ability to understand and care about the problems and situations of others, is at the root of ethical behavior. Genuinely considering the impact our actions will have on others can significantly change the ways that we decide to behave.

- Intellectual property, products, and creations of the mind are in many cases protected by copyright. Copyright protects the owners of intellectual property and gives them the right to determine the terms for how and by whom their creation may be used and distributed.

- Fair use is a term that describes exceptions to copyright protection. Fair use generally means that in certain limited ways, such as when reviewing or making a parody of a work, a person may use copyrighted material for their purposes without permission from the owner and without liability.

- Copyright violations are extremely common. Software, music, and image files are routinely copied and shared, either directly from one person to a friend, or via massive peer-to-peer sharing networks. Many people violate copyrights by posting music and image files without consent to social media sites like Facebook and YouTube. It is also common to violate copyrights for movies by sharing them online, and also simply by showing them in public places without permission for parties and large gatherings.

- Netiquette describes the wide variety of ways that people should engage in courteous and respectful behavior while online. Just as with rules of etiquette in the non-technical world, rules for netiquette are highly individual and can cover practically any online situation. Examples of good netiquette are toning down extreme emotions when communicating; staying clear of endless and pointless polarized fights over sensitive subjects; refraining from beginning fights and extended criticisms of undesirable online behavior that is limited to a forum established for that purpose; and carefully considering one's audience before posting humor, religious, or political commentary, or other potentially sensitive material.

- Online student resources can be valuable, but they are sometimes unethical. Sites that encourage students to learn from each other and contribute teaching and mentoring materials are ethical and are often funded or otherwise supported by faculty and universities. Unethical sites provide and seek material to aid students in cheating, such as confidential test questions and answers, and essays that students can claim as their own work.

- Beyond the general ethical principles of computer use, employers sometimes impose additional restrictions and conditions on the use of corporate electronic resources. This may include the prohibition of personal online activities while at work; restricting access to certain kinds of social media even for work purposes; and enforcing ethical standards in e-mail communication between employees.

Key Terms

Key Terms QUIZ

1. Computer _____ is the acquisition and redistribution of protected digital creations such as software, music, or writing without the permission of the owner.

2. _____, the ability to recognize, understand, and share the feelings of others, is a critical component of how we choose between what is right and wrong.

3. Collections of polite and proper online behaviors are often referred to as _____

4. Unlike physical products, _____ is a category of ideas, writing, music, and other kinds of mind-based products that are intended to be used commercially.

5. _____ provides a limited set of exceptions where others can use copyrighted material without first obtaining permission.

6. The practice of _____ is the process of pointing out a major internal problem at a company, institution, or government agency.

7. A(n) _____ is a legal concept that grants rights and control to the owner of any published work.

8. A published work that is not controlled by a copyright is considered to be in the _____.

9. A(n) _____ allows software to be installed and used on any computer in a building or corporate campus.

10. Organizations will sometimes formally define the practices and behaviors it deems acceptable in a(n) _____.

Review QUESTIONS

1. Explain the difference between piracy and forgery.

2. What is intellectual property (IP)? List at least three examples of types of IP.

3. What is the purpose of a copyright?

4. How does fair use allow the use of copyrighted material without permission?

5. List three different types of software piracy that commonly occur.

6. Give three examples netiquette guidelines.

7. Explain the ethical difference between sharing class notes in an online forum and purchasing an essay from a Web site.

8. What is an Acceptable Use Policy?

9. Give two examples of ethical considerations for the workplace.

10. What is whistleblowing? What are the benefits of taking that kind of ethical stand, and what are the risks that might be involved?

LESSON LAB

1. Look into whether your school has an AUP or other online ethical guide. Visit your school's Web site and search for the phrase "acceptable use policy." Whether you are reading the policy for the first time or were required to acknowledge it before taking classes, read the AUP keeping in mind the ethical lessons you have just completed. Does the AUP seem adequate, too brief, or too excessive in your opinion to adequately define the ethical use of school computers? Be prepared to explain your opinion. If your school does not have an AUP, discuss with the class and instructor whether such a document would be useful; if possible, use specific examples to identify any ethical risks that currently exist in the school's computing environment.

2. Compare and contrast different opinions on what makes up "netiquette." From your favorite engine, search on "netiquette rules." Identify three sites that in your opinion do a good job of explaining courteous and ethical online behavior. Record the three sites you chose. Do the sites concentrate on rules for a specific type of online activity, such as social networking or e-mail; or are the rule lists comprehensive and general for any type of activity? Along with the sites you chose, record your five favorite rules from all of the ones you read. Bring your list of sites and your top five netiquette rules to class to share.

Team EXERCISE
Ethics

Companies of any size and type can face significant risk from copyright violations. Companies that rely on the sale of intellectual property are vulnerable to piracy; but even companies that do not distribute creative works can be vulnerable to lawsuits and judgments against them if employees are found to be using pirated software or the trade secrets of other organizations.

You and three or four of your classmates, for this exercise, have been appointed as a company's Copyright Safety Team. Your job is to formulate a plan with your teammates to identify copyright- and piracy-related risks. Your company is a small but established accounting firm, with around 100 employees total. Each worker uses computers for their jobs, producing documents, filing tax forms, prospecting for new clients, and working with government regulatory agencies.

Working together, build a list of five important risks based on copyright infringement, piracy, breaches of confidentiality, or other similar unethical behaviors. For each risk, list one or more ways that the company can monitor or be informed about employee activity that might cause problems, and list any steps the company should take to handle evidence of unethical actions.

[*Chapter* LABS]

1. Working either alone or with one or two classmates, design a basic network solution for the Half Full Mug, a busy, local coffee shop. The shop has the following layout:

   - three desks in a back room for administrators and managers, each of which has a desktop computer;
   - one file server, also in the back room, for backups and central document storage;
   - and an L-shaped interior customer seating area (the shop is on a street corner), with each side of the L being large enough to hold around ten customer tables.

   The shop has given you the following networking requirements:

   - the three back office computers and the file server should be in a LAN, and they should be connected to the Internet;
   - customers should have access to free wireless Internet;
   - the customer Wi-Fi and the back office LAN must not be connected together, and the customers must not be able to see or access the LAN.

   Create a basic explanation of the components, wired or wireless, that you would use to create the networks, taking into consideration the requirements above. If it would help to design or explain, create a sketch of what the shop might look like and where the network components would be placed. When complete, be prepared to share your design with the class.

2. Practice considering an event in order to develop empathy. First, select a non-technical crisis or serious event that has meaning for you; it could be a local event like a house fire or domestic dispute, or a more national or global circumstance. It should not be an event in which you were directly affected or involved. Spend some time and think about those who experienced distress as a result of that event. Briefly record the event you have chosen, and list one or more things you thought about that would be difficult for those affected by the event to experience.

   Now, choose an unethical computer-related behavior to consider; if you wish, you may use one of the situations discussed in Lesson 7B. Repeat the exercise of thinking about those affected and identifying one or more things that would be distressing or painful to experience as a result of the unethical behavior.

   Once you have completed both analyses, think about your experience. Were you able to feel any kind of connection in each case? Was there a significant difference in the ease with which you could empathize with one type of victim versus another? Be prepared to discuss your experience and observations in class.

3. Working in groups with two or three of your classmates, create ideas for a new early elementary school program designed to teach kids from age five to eight about empathy and taking responsibility for their actions. First, list a number of difficult situations or problems that could arise in the environment of young children, such as name-calling or having toys taken away. Then, discuss ways to engage the children in analyzing those types of situations from both the perspective of the aggressor and victim. List and organize the methods you decide to use, and at the end of the exercise, review your decisions and ideas with the class.

[*Think* AND DISCUSS]

1. Many online shopping sites track the things you browse and buy as a way to make additional suggestions, sometimes in the form of alternate but similar products, and sometimes

providing you with unrelated products that other shoppers matching your browsing or purchasing behavior have responded to in a positive way. If you've visited these types of sites, do you notice those additional suggestions? Is it helpful for you to see sections beginning, "Shoppers who looked at this product also viewed …"? Is it fun to think that your own shopping habits can be a guide for others, or is that worrisome?

2. The ongoing dispute between the music industry and people who illegally share music online shows no sign of being resolved in anyone's favor. Some industry participants pursue aggressive lawsuits against thousands of individuals to recover lost income; yet people who share music have little or no interest in ceasing their activity. What do you think should be done in this situation? Can you think of ways that artists can publish their music that would encourage people to pay rather than steal the songs? Are there ways to make music sharing be something other than a copyright violation, and the artist and publisher can still benefit?

[*Fact Check* ANSWERS]

7A:

LO7.1 Computer Networks

1: **c.** normally consists of four pairs of wires
2: **b.** all nodes are connected to a hub and communicate through it
3: **a.** A wireless access point

LO7.2 Information Systems: What and Why

1: **b.** To help its users get value from the information in the system
2: **a.** The physical means, methods, and procedures for distributing and sharing information

LO7.3 Types of Information Systems

1: **c.** word processing, accounting, document management, or communications
2: **a.** E-commerce
3: **b.** The knowledge base that selects solutions or more questions to answer

LO7.4 Networks, Hardware and Data Management

1: **c.** multiple hardware systems performing the same task at the same time
2: **b.** By checking what is entered and, in some cases, placing restrictions on how the data is entered

7B:

LO7.5 Digital Piracy

1: **b.** the ability to recognize, understand and share the feelings of others.
2: **a.** music, software, secret recipes and patents.
3: **b.** a software owner making unauthorized copies of software for himself or others.

LO7.6 Personal Computing Ethics

1: **c.** the set of online behaviors that are considered polite and proper.
2: **b.** to formalize an organization's requirements and limitations for computer use.

LO7.7 Professional Computing Ethics

1: **b.** to enforce rules against personal online activity when at work.
2: **a.** emails can effectively document the whistleblower's communication attempts.

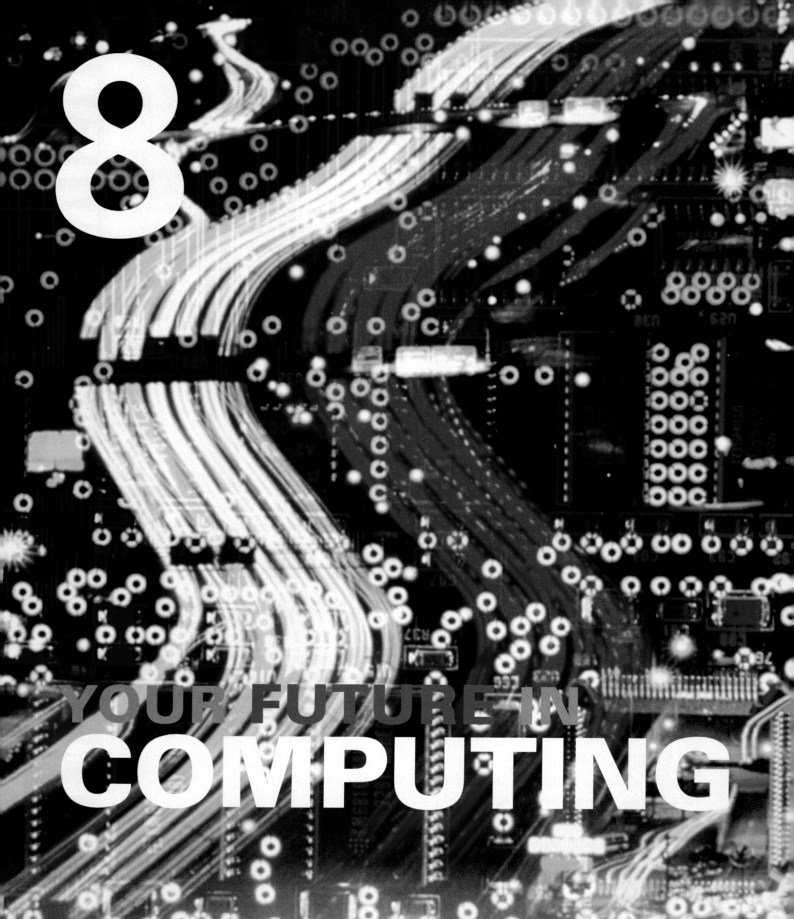

8

YOUR FUTURE IN COMPUTING

Chapter Overview

Our reliance on computers in one way or another has grown so nearly universal that no matter what type of career you choose, it is highly likely that you will actively use computing hardware and resources at least part of the time. In this lesson, you will explore the ways that computers are used in some of today's careers. You will also take a peek at the possible future of computing by examining emerging computer technologies. Do you have a specific job in mind for your future? Can you think of different ways that computers are used in that field?

LESSON 8A:
Computing and Careers

Just a few short decades ago, the use of computers in business was limited and rare. From architects to zoo veterinarians, people in business relied on analog methods for solving problems, building products, and providing services.

Now, architects use computers for creating drawings, doing calculations, and making 3D presentations for clients. Zoo veterinarians use computers to research symptoms and diseases, order supplies, and collaborate with other doctors around the world. And chances are good that both the architect and the zoo vet have a social networking page to share their latest office story with friends and family.

Industrial employees are no less involved with computers, whether they are using computer-aided machinery on a manufacturing floor or working in the administrative office. Service businesses rely on computers for administrative support and to reach out to find new customers and maintain existing relationships. Retail companies track sales and inventory levels with computers, and in some cases run their entire business on the Internet.

Figure 8.1 With the arrival of design software, the drafting table has mostly become a thing of the past for architects.

8.1 Computing in Your Field

As the computer revolution began, people sometimes wondered if their job might someday require computer expertise. Already, the question for nearly any worker in any job has become, "So what hardware or programs will I need to use at work?" An exhaustive survey of all the ways computers are used in any field, much less all careers in the world, is impractical for any textbook. Even so, let's take a look at a few examples of how computers can be used in the workplace.

COMPUTING IN EDUCATION

Computers are a very common sight in classroom settings, from elementary schools to universities. College students often combine their own hardware, software and online services with those provided by their school as they pursue their education. But beyond that superficial starting point, computers continue to be a major contributor to the efficiency and effectiveness of both student and teacher.

Consider a university-level course in any subject, no matter how non-technical. Typically, the students spend at least part of their time in a lecture hall or classroom. The professor teaching the class probably uses some sort of computer technology to deliver the lectures and lessons; LCD projectors and portable computers are common tools for displaying slides to assist in information delivery. As part of the course, the students may be required to access or contribute documents via collaborative services such as Google Docs; or, depending on the professor's preferences and the requirements of the class, a wiki may be provided to collect, organize, and share information.

Naturally, computer-based presentations and collaboration systems must be created ahead of time with the assistance of some kind of software, but the same is also often true for the content of the lectures and student assignments that together define the course.

To develop lectures, professors may search the Internet for new ideas and supporting documentation. Where this was once limited to using search engines to browse academic sites and online databases, professors may also rely on Twitter and special-interest forums, using their network of mentors and professional colleagues to find pointers to fresh articles and studies as they are first published and discussed. Professors may also use online resources to help create work assignments for students; textbook

Figure 8.2 Slides and handouts are created by the professor to support the information presented in lectures.

concepts, requiring the instructor to be proficient with those software tools.

Looking still closer, there are a number of other computer-supported functions related to delivering the course that the student may see only peripherally. The professor, possibly in cooperation with administrative staff, must also perform classroom management tasks. Calendar and appointment programs can be used to schedule meetings with students and colleagues. The college probably provides online services for distributing class registration lists and accumulating grades for completed assignments and tests. If grade processing is not handled at a central site, then the professor may use a local solution such as Microsoft Excel or another spreadsheet in order to track student performance over time.

Along with managing the course itself, professors are increasingly turning to computers to help monitor student performance. Instructors may use anti-plagiarism database services to scan essays and original writing for evidence of copying. Some even use statistics to compare their current class' performance to

publishers may provide digital resources for developing labs and homework tasks; and discussion forums can provide a way to explore ideas and ask for suggestions from others.

With the required information available, word processing software is used to create lesson plans, course outlines, and sets of notes or other student materials that can be either printed and distributed in class, or posted online for students to retrieve on their own time. Presentation software is employed to create the various slides and multimedia content that are used in lectures.

More technical courses may directly employ computers as part of the teaching process. Programming classes most likely provide a standard development environment for the students to use in creating their programs. The instructor must therefore teach not only the syntax and style of the programming language, but also the mechanics of building and testing software within that development environment. Specialized classes in engineering and architecture will likely provide training in specific types of programs along with the study of more theoretical

Figure 8.3 Along with developing materials for classes and lectures, professors use computers for grading and other administrative tasks.

the marks earned in classes taught in previous years to find evidence of cheating on tests and assignments.

COMPUTING IN HEALTH CARE

As a whole, the health care industry is a vast, multi-disciplined collection of professions. Researchers, doctors, engineers, manufacturers, caregivers, accountants, and administrators all play a major role in providing new and better ways to help people thrive and survive. As a patient in a doctor's office, most of that is hidden from view, but even from that limited perspective, computers seem to crop up everywhere.

A patient's first contact with a computer very likely comes even before the visit begins. Many doctors and hospitals allow patients to make appointments online for routine and non-emergency visits. Even if patients must call for an appointment, the appointment center or front office receptionist is probably using a computer and an appointment program to pick a time for the patient's visit. Sometimes, the appointment system is part of a comprehensive data management system that integrates appointments, staff information, and patient records, allowing administrators and doctors alike to view a more complete picture of the patient's ongoing history of care.

In the examination room, the doctor or nurse and visiting patient may very well share the space with a computer terminal. The doctor can call up the patient's medical history in order to review past issues and immediately enter new notes and infor-

mation provided during the current visit. If drug prescriptions are needed, the doctor may be able to order them via the computer and have them delivered straight to an onsite pharmacy for filling. Tests at an onsite lab and referrals to specialists can be handled the same way, reducing the processing time for such requests as well as reducing the chances for miscommunication; fewer administrative people and steps lie between the doctor's decision and the next person who needs to take action.

At the conclusion of the visit, the record system can be used to print a summary of the visit for the patient, along with reminders about prescribed treatment and tips for future care. Generic fact sheets and suggestion lists relevant to the patient's condition may also be available for selecting and printing, so that they can be given to the departing patient with the visit summary.

Before and after doctor visits, many online facilities exist to help patients validate and consider the advice they receive from doctors. Databases and discussion forums exist for researching symptoms and comparing notes on treatments. Support sites and forums can help people with serious illnesses find companionship, motivation, and insight. Patients can use these types of services to become better educated about their health and problems, which can in turn help them work more effectively with doctors to find good treatments.

Behind the scenes, doctors and nurses can go online to access symptom and drug databases, retrieving the latest information from research facilities and drug manufacturers. They can access forums and online sites at other facilities to stay connected with their colleagues, requesting assistance when a circumstance lies beyond their expertise. And of course, computers provide all manner of means for the doctors and nurses to communicate with each other and with patients, allowing patients to receive answers to questions via e-mail and chat systems.

COMPUTING IN SALES AND MERCHANDISING

Computer technology has revolutionized retail business in many ways, from the customer experience all the way to the fundamental business model on which many businesses operate. Fully online stores rely completely on computers to market products to customers and provide support, of course, but even small retail stores

Figure 8.4   Computers can help doctors immediately record relevant patient information during a consultation.

Figure 8.5   Computers can help storeowners track the parts they have in stock.

can have a need for computing technology in many different areas of their operations. Let's take a closer look at a local computer store and the steps required to deliver a new PC for one of their customers.

The storeowner works with the customer to identify the exact set of required components for the new machine. With list in hand, the owner can begin the process of acquiring those parts. Some of them may already be in the shop; for example, to save money the owner may buy several units at a time of power supplies, computer cases, and other fairly generic components that customers rarely want to specify. She can check the shop's inventory on the office computer to see what's currently in stock and what wholesale prices were paid for the various parts.

For unusual or expensive parts that are not in stock (this particular computer build, for example, calls for two high-end video cards and a motherboard that can support them both), she can go online to various component stores and search for the best deals on those parts. The storeowner adds those parts, wholesale prices, and shipping cost to the complete list. The owner may use a spreadsheet to create a detailed parts list, apply a percentage or fixed markup to the prices for profit, and create a formal quote sheet for the customer.

She may also decide to check her quoted price against published prices for similar systems at online stores to see how competitive her offer will look. If her prices are too high, she may reduce the price or

sweeten the deal with extra software or hardware. If the prices are lower than her competitors, she can print the less favorable competitor's offer and include it with the quote sheet.

With approval received from the customer, the owner places the online parts orders. At the supplier's warehouse, an integrated set of computer systems receive the order, process payment, and provide instructions to the warehouse workers to package and ship the parts to the computer store. More computer technology is used by the overnight shipping company to track the package at each transfer point and to confirm the next day's delivery of the parts at the store.

Once the parts are received at the store, the owner pulls the rest of the parts from the in-store inventory, notes their use in her own inventory control program, and assembles the parts into a sleek, new computer for the customer. When assembled, the computer is loaded with the Microsoft Windows operating system, and the owner uses the Internet to access Microsoft's automatic update facility to ensure that the new operating system is fully updated and ready to go.

To complete the transaction, the storeowner takes a credit card payment either in the store or online. The customer's name, address, and other information is saved in a computer database along with the items that were bought and the date of purchase; this information helps the store owner track the customer's purchasing habits, and it creates warranty and replacement information in the event that problems occur in the future.

When not building computers and ordering parts, the storeowner still puts the office computer to good use. Payroll programs can keep track of employee hours and wages. Payroll and sales data can feed into an integrated accounting program, allowing the

Figure 8.6   Hosting computer-related events is a good way to stay visible within the local computing community.

storeowner to trade her technology hat for her business manager hat and focus on sales trends, accounts payable, and receivable, and ways to improve operating efficiency.

Sales and marketing can also be greatly improved by computer technology. Social networking pages and Twitter can generate visability, interest in weekly specials, in-store seminars, and how-to classes for new computer users. The store's Web site can be used to provide deeper details about product offerings and advantages over competitors that this particular store provides. E-mail and Web forms can both be used to receive questions and requests for quotes. And a couple of display tables, some chairs, power cords, and LAN hardware creates a great way to host game competitions and make connections within the local gaming community.

COMPUTING IN TOURISM AND HOSPITALITY

Large hotels and restaurants, as you might expect, put computers to good use in many ways. Hotels use computers to create and track customer reservations, improve the speed of the check-in and check-out processes, serve movies and other services to guest rooms, manage back-office administrative tasks, and even provide morning wake-up calls for guests. Restaurants use computers for inventory, employee, and facility management; they are also often used to relay orders and special requests from the wait staff to the kitchen.

Computer use in the hospitality industry is not only for large operations, however; even the owner and sole proprietor of a bed-and-breakfast inn can use computers to improve efficiency and customer service.

While some B&B proprietors might still take reservations by phone and write them in a book on the desk, computers can tie telephone and online reservations together. The owner can use a cloud-based calendar or reservation system to capture people searching for accommodations via search engine, travel site, or local chamber of commerce Web site. When people call to book a room, the owner simply uses that same reservation system while on the phone to check room availability and make the requested reservations. If there are special needs or requests from the guests, the proprietor can either make notes in the reservation system or keep those notes on the local computer.

Since many travelers today carry mobile computing devices, the proprietor can do the same and give guests an e-mail address, VoIP phone number, or online chat screen name to aid in communication. If guests are delayed or need to change plans, they can send text messages or e-mails, or call via smart phone app and reach the owner right away; the owner can roam around on the B&B property as needed without worrying about missing an inquiry, request, or notification.

As with practically any small business, computers can serve as the B&B's central means for performing administrative tasks. The owner can use a computer for printing breakfast menus, lists of local attractions, and invoices for customers. He can track expenses and prepare annual tax and financial reports. He can order supplies online for maintaining and improving the property, check for Web reviews and comments made by past visitors, and even check the online presence of competitors to fine-tune his marketing strategy.

Gaining visibility and popularity is critical for the survival of a B&B business, and social media can play a large part in that effort. Twitter provides a convenient and effective way to send occasional reminders and suggestions to past guests, such as giving people last-minute chances to book empty rooms at reduced rates. Facebook and other social networks can be used to provide more detailed reminders and keep guests engaged in conversation even when they are not in the area. Review site monitoring keeps track of what people are saying, and in some cases gives the owner a chance to respond and offer to correct problems mentioned in reviews, improving future service as well as the innkeeper's reputation. Social networking can also cement relationships with other local service providers and create opportunities to help market each other's services through referrals and cooperative offers.

Figure 8.7   Small bed & breakfast inns can use the Web to take reservations, market themselves, and connect with guests via social media links.

8.2 Telecommuting

As you learned in Chapter 5, telecommuting is the process of working for a company without being physically present at the company's office. The term describes a wide variety of remote work practices, from working at home now and then to permanently living halfway around the world from the company's main office. In addition, though freelance and independent contractors who provide online services might not strictly be considered telecommuters since they work for themselves and not a remote company, they have most of the same challenges and use the same services as the traditional telecommuters.

A telecommuting worker's needs fall into two basic categories: practices and processes, and computing technology. In order to be effective as a telecommuter, a worker needs to be able to follow processes that are either required by the employer or are simply required by the worker in order to complete work efficiently. A worker must also have the computer hardware, software, and services required to get the job done properly. It is easy to concentrate on just one or the other

(for example, tracking down the perfect computer without considering the work environment). It is also easy to let popular assumptions about telecommuting replace realities that are sometimes quite different.

TELECOMMUTING: PRACTICES AND PROCESSES

One of the first skills to test as a potential telecommuter is the ability to assess and estimate a project's success. Telecommuting can provide a tremendous sense of independence and freedom, but it also provides significant risks if the independence from a formal workplace causes the worker to do a bad job.

A prospective telecommuter should first perform a self-assessment. Not everyone has a lifestyle or personality that is suited to working independently.

Figure 8.8 Not everyone is suited for telecommuting; an honest self-assessment can help determine your chances for success.

One may hate their office job, but switching roles to remote work may not always fix that state of discontent, and the stresses of the workplace can be replaced or magnified if one is ill-equipped to working away from the office. A self-assessment should include carefully and honestly considering factors such as the following:

- One's ability to set and clearly understand short-term goals as well as longer term expectations.

- One's ability to set one's own pace for getting work done. If a goal is clearly defined for the day's work, does it get done almost every time?

- The value in face-to-face interaction. If one thrives on chatting in the lunchroom and poking a head through cubicle doorways, how likely is telecommuting to lead to a sense of isolation?

- One's ability and level of comfort for self-promotion and self-marketing. If a telecommuter works with a core group that shares office space, they are at risk for being less noticed within the organization. The telecommuter may need to have a knack for staying visible with the right people in order to ensure that they are considered valuable employees.

The telecommuter-in-planning should also assess the potential work environment, considering factors both physical and emotional such as the following:

- Will the necessary work environment be available every workday? Whether a café table or a home office, the workplace must match the worker's needs, and it must be ready to go when work time begins. If the home office on Monday morning is still full of luggage and relatives from a weekend visit, the telecommuter's career or family life could suffer.

- Is the designated workplace safe for the work that is being performed? A public location might be a terrible place to work on sensitive, confidential information. Sharing your work computer with kids who might unwittingly download keyloggers and other malware could jeopardize the security of the work data, along with creating vulnerabilities for the employer's privacy.

- Are the necessary services available and affordable in the exact work location? Internet, cell phone, and cable TV service are often required for telecommuting; if they are not already functioning in the remote office, their availability should be checked. Keep in mind that wireless service can be unpredictable, and that cell and Wi-Fi connections that work in one room may be totally absent in another.

- Is one over-optimistically planning to combine work with other major demands for attention that would not normally be present in an office? Working from home can be a nightmare if small children constantly need the company's Chief Information Officer to become Mommy or Daddy instead.

- Are there other people who need to understand and support the role of the telecommuter? Will a spouse or roommate come home at the end of their work day and criticize the telecommuter's lack of progress on household chores or shopping, not comprehending that the at-home job is a serious, full-time effort?

- Is the telecommuter able to effectively end the workday if other demands are present? Are there risks that the work phone will ring even after hours? Will that cause trouble for relationships and families?

- Will the job involve early or late phone calls? Is the remote office situated so those calls will not wake or annoy others nearby?

Assuming that the employee and the environment seem acceptably suited for telecommuting, it can be helpful to test those assumptions before formally beginning remote work. If possible, working remotely on a couple of weekend or other days off can sometimes identify successes and failures in the remote environment without impacting the new telecommuter's work schedule. Some amount of changes or adjustments are inevitable, since it's a rare business process that works perfectly the first time, but it can be good to discover connectivity and peace-and-quiet problems when the worker is not under deadline pressure.

Figure 8.9   If your work requires you to be on the phone from a home or public office, make sure you have the privacy you need.

TELECOMMUTING: COMPUTING TECHNOLOGY

Along with figuring out how to establish and run a remote office, the telecommuter will be faced with a number of technical challenges as well. In some cases, companies may supply remote employees with hardware and software to get their job done, but even in those cases setting up hardware and network connections will likely need to be done by the remote worker.

If the telecommuter is responsible for supplying the remote computer hardware, then ideally the remote worker should try to match the hardware to both the work environment and the job to be done. Desktop PCs, notebooks, tablets, and handheld devices all have value; however, an ill-fitting choice of hardware can seriously impact the worker's efficiency. If multiple devices are required in order to be effective, cloud storage solutions may help keep data synchronized for all of the various computers.

Most telecommuters will rely on Internet services for communication. Employees of a company may be given access to a VPN so that the telecommuter can access corporate computers at the central office. In such cases, the remote employee will most likely work with an IT employee in the company to set up and test the VPN connection.

Figure 8.10 Make sure remote office hardware matches the needs of the job. More than one device might be required.

As part of evaluating a new remote operation, the telecommuter should identify all programs that are used to perform their work. Some programs, especially cloud-based software, are not tied to a specific computer; cloud-based software can be installed without issues on the remote hardware. Other programs that might be installed at the main office, such as word processors and spreadsheets, may have been installed with a site license; a remote worker may not be considered to be part of that corporate site, requiring the purchase of an extra copy for the remote computer.

Technology support can be a burden that catches new remote workers by surprise. When networks, programs, and computer hardware fail to work as expected, it is not uncommon for the support tasks to fall on the shoulders of the remote worker. If one works for a large company, the IT department may not be particularly helpful in diagnosing what is wrong in your home office. If the remote worker is self-employed, then "Infrastructure Support" is just one of many job titles that the worker will need to assume.

One of the best ways to prepare for technology support is to keep a notebook handy to contain support information. Though it can be tempting to simply use computer documents and contact lists to keep track of support people and topics, those computer records won't help much if the computer is the thing that is broken.

As software is installed, note the titles that are installed along with serial numbers that might be required for installation. If one uses online services and cloud-based applications that require a user ID and password, consider writing down the user ID. Never write both the user ID and password together in the notebook, as this creates a severe security risk; however, cryptic hints for unusual passwords might be safely included in the notebook. A password like "fakin823it" is difficult to randomly guess, and writing down a hint like, "Rhymes with bacon" won't pose much additional risk.

Most importantly, the remote worker should write down the e-mail addresses and phone numbers of critical business and online support contacts. If the cable Internet service clicks off unexpectedly, the telecommuter won't be able to go online to ask what went wrong. If the computer's power supply fails in a cloud of sour, electrical smoke, the freelance writer won't be able to call a client to reschedule a meeting if Skype was the only place where the client's phone number was recorded.

As part of preparing for a loss of service at the office, the remote worker should develop a plan for how to continue working when connectivity or computer

Figure 8.11 A paper record of support information is essential in order to get help when the computer or Internet connection fails.

hardware does fail. In some cases, more hardware can help; for instance, a good UPS unit can help mitigate the trouble caused by a power outage in the office. If the telecommuter relies on a desktop PC as the main office computer, a backup laptop computer can help a great deal if the computer, the power, or the Internet connection fails. If the problem cannot be quickly resolved, the user can switch computers—and if needed move to a new location where the required services are still operating—and resume work while waiting for a resolution to the loss of service.

The backup laptop, of course, must be able to run the same programs using the same data that was present on the desktop PC. Depending on the kind of work that is being done, cloud-based software and storage can make switching computers a snap. Storing work documents on a flash drive rather than the main computer hard drive can also speed the process of resuming work on a backup system. It's critical to test the backup system and the process of switching before a crisis occurs; take a day every now and then and work from the backup computer just to make sure everything is working, fully charged and up to date.

In the same way that a remote employee must evaluate the ongoing flow of work and relationships with an eye for improvement, the telecommuter should also pay attention to the hardware and software systems that are in use. If efficiency or comfort is suffering because computer hardware is too slow, or because something is set up ineffectively in the office, see if there are solutions. Both high- and low-tech solutions to problems can boost a telecommuter's productivity and mood. Sometimes, something as simple as bringing in a better footstool or moving the office desk to a new location can create better focus and work output; other times, a more reliable Internet connection is needed to fix lagging or lost network requests.

8.3 Emerging Careers

It is extremely unlikely that computer-related changes in the world are beginning to subside. All indications, rather, point to continuous and rapid changes in our society for many years to come as the computing revolution shifts the way we communicate, work, and think about the world around us.

Already, careers and in some cases entire industries are either struggling to survive or have been made obsolete by the arrival of the computer. Central online shopping portals, for example, are replacing many retail stores; the print newspaper industry is struggling to stay relevant as more and more people seek their news, information, and entertainment from a screen instead of sheets of newsprint on the dining room table.

Computers have made many tasks easy enough that we no longer seek assistance in completing them. Tax software and the electronic filing of returns with the government have reduced tax-preparation customers by millions. The ease of booking airline and hotel reservations online have deeply affected the travel agency field. Even local computer repair stores now struggle to make ends meet. What was once a lucrative enterprise before the turn of the 21st century is already now a victim of dramatically lower computer prices; fewer people are interested in paying a repair bill that's half the cost of a replacement computing device, and few of the increasingly-popular mobile devices we use are intended to be repaired and reconfigured outside the factory.

While this may sound bleak—and to be sure, it can be a grim circumstance for the people who lose jobs and opportunities during such changes—this process of career replacement is hardly a new one. In every case where new technologies are developed, old jobs are made obsolete as new ones spring up. No longer does the iceman deliver blocks of ice around the neighborhood in order to keep food cool, for example; refrigerators have replaced that service. Lamplighters, who were once hired to travel through neighborhoods every evening and lit gas streetlights were long ago replaced by electric light bulbs.

Figure 8.12 Some workers, like tax preparers, find their jobs threatened when computers reduce the need for people to seek their help.

In exchange for those lost jobs, refrigerator manufacturers and appliance repair shops were created; people were hired in light bulb factories instead of gas lamp factories, and electrical engineers were trained to effectively design the power grids for cities. Improving technology causes change, and though that change can be painful for some, it also provides opportunity for others.

21ST CENTURY SKILLS AND BEYOND

In the 21st century, the details of technological change in our world are different from those of a hundred years ago, but the lesson remains the same. The key skills for surviving change are not specific to a type of computer or program; rather, they are the life skills of flexibility and adaptability.

One of the hallmarks of the computer revolution is the speed with which things change. New hardware designs are created to increase processing and communication speed every several months. New programs and ways to use computers are released to the public every day of the year. It's not too uncommon to see emerging technologies superseded and discarded in favor of something better even before they are fully developed and deployed.

Trying to pick an emerging career or hot employment sector is sometimes therefore an exercise in trying to hit an elusive moving target. While some careers are fairly stable and will likely be around no matter what happens with computers in the future, others may come and go in years or a decade or two. An exciting career in writing applications for mobile computing platforms may look promising today, for example, but the few short years of training required to learn those skills might be enough to saturate the app-programming field with millions of new programmers; suddenly that hot demand could be gone.

What aids career hunters better than targeting a hot sector is to pick a career field that looks interesting and shows promise, and then change goals as needed to keep up with what is going on in the industry. Those mobile-app programming skills in the example above may not be worth much if the market is saturated with apps, but perhaps there are other places where those programming skills and knowledge of wireless network communication could be put to use. The new app programmer might instead be employed working to create wireless links for manufacturing systems in an industrial company.

As innovation drives more and faster change, it is often no longer enough to pick a career before college and expect to begin that career once a standard education is complete, especially in fields where computing technology is heavily or primarily used. The flexible students will keep an eye on their target industry as they learn and practice their required skills, shifting their educational focus or goals if needed to fine-tune them to changes that they see. With their education completed and their work begun, those same people can stay alert and be ready to adapt as technology-driven changes continue to alter the field in which they work.

Figure 8.13   Flexibility in business is more about being able to respond quickly to changes than about reaching your laptop in unusual ways.

EMERGING CAREERS IN HEALTHCARE

One of the most enduring and often growing fields of employment is healthcare. There is no shortage of people in the world who require treatment for ailments and injuries, and as life expectancy increases, there is a corresponding increase in the elderly population.

Figure 8.14 Doctors can use tele-medicine to share information with remote colleagues to improve local care.

Computing technology has spread throughout the healthcare industry, providing boosts in efficiency, skill and understanding for facility management, patient treatment, and research. In most cases, the new technology has not made jobs obsolete as much as providing more effective ways to do the same jobs and to provide access to new medical methods that were impractical or impossible to achieve without computing assistance.

Medical research, while hardly an emerging career by name, is nevertheless one of the best places to work to be involved with computer-assisted discoveries. Research into some of the thorniest medical problems such as cancer, autoimmune diseases, and even the aging process, have recently yielded surprising and encouraging results. Researchers use computers for mundane office tasks, just as in any other professional field, but they also use computer technology to analyze massive amounts of data to help gain a better understanding of diseases and biological processes work. They can also use computers to run elaborate simulations and tests on ways that chemicals and living beings interact, improving testing efficiency and reducing the risk for live test subjects.

For patient care, computers can be used for **telemedicine**, which allows doctors to practice and advise in patient diagnosis and treatment from a remote location. With **teleradiology**, for example, X-rays and other internal body scans can be collected in one facility and then sent anywhere in the world via computers and secure networks for analysis. It is much more cost-effective to send data to a diagnostic expert on another continent than to send the patient, and it may be safer for the patient as well. Such collaboration with experts can improve care for people around the world that might otherwise not have access to the specialists they need.

Computers are also present to assist with surgical procedures. They can monitor a patient's vital signs during a procedure, and they can also control robotic assistants for a surgeon, moving or targeting surgical equipment with fine precision in response to input from the surgeon. In some cases, the combination of robotic devices and virtual reality hardware have even allowed doctors to perform complete surgical operations from hundreds of miles away, by using the virtual reality interface to remotely guide the robot's actions.

Support roles exist not only for patients and facilities, but also for the information technology in use throughout the medical industry. **Health informatics** combines computer technology and healthcare disciplines to manage the acquisition and use of health-related information. The health informatics field designs databases, software, and specialized programming languages for automating tasks and managing data in dental and medical offices. Though health informatics has been around for decades—widespread use of computers in medicine began to take hold in the 1950s—the field continues to grow and change rapidly as new types of technology and medical practices are established.

OTHER EMERGING CAREER OPPORTUNITIES

As mentioned earlier, chasing an emerging career or technology can carry the risk of arriving a bit too late to be a part of the new wave, or arriving along with millions of others who all had the same idea. Even so, it's unusual for a new field to simply vanish without a trace, and agile, adaptable workers may be able to use their existing knowledge and experience as a springboard to find work as emerging technology and careers evolve.

If your career interests point to jobs that are not directly technical, such as programming or online work, you may still find that a solid understanding of computers and software makes you a more valuable employee, or at the very least that some parts of your dream job will be easier to perform than if you lacked those technical skills.

Figure 8.15 With social media exploding in prominence and importance for business, social media strategists are in high demand to keep businesses properly engaged in those areas.

If your future job lies in a technical arena, and if you are interested in the cutting edge of the computer industry, you might consider some of the following types of jobs:

- **Mobile platform programmer/designer.** The mobile computing industry has been expanding rapidly, and competent, trained programmers for these platforms can be hard to find. While much attention is paid to the creators of a few wildly successful apps, there is a larger demand created by companies who want to expand their online presence to include support for mobile devices.

- **Social media strategist.** Companies face challenges in successfully adopting social media technologies. A social media expert can help design strategies for using Facebook, Twitter, and the next new communication tools effectively. Customer service skills and marketing know-how are critical skills to have along with an understanding of social media tools for this type of job.

- **SEO expert.** Search engine visibility can make or break companies that rely on attracting their customers online. As search engine behavior changes, companies must shift and change their Web site contents and marketing approach to stay visible. Being able to decipher and ethically cooperate with search engine expectations is a full-time and highly sought-after skill.

- **Video journalist.** As multimedia continues to play an increasing part in the online experience, skilled workers able to produce effective and interesting clips are in demand, whether as part of a public relations company or a promotion or advertising firm. Especially prized are video specialists who can produce creative and original work on a tight budget.

- **Online security specialist.** Security threats will always be present, and as hacker activity targets more and more corporations of all sizes, the demand for security analysis and threat mitigation is likely to continue to grow rapidly.

- **Network architect/support specialist.** Companies everywhere rely on networks. Network architects design and in some cases install networks for new buildings and companies of all sizes. Network support specialists are responsible for maintaining the proper function of existing networks. Though these types of jobs have been around for a long time, new communication technology is constantly being developed and deployed, requiring that professional network specialists stay up to date.

Fact Check

1. Two life skills that can help you stay ready for new opportunities in your career are
   a. aggression and a single-minded focus
   b. flexibility and adaptability
   c. caution and hesitation
2. A good way to prepare for an emerging technology job is to pick a field that looks interesting and promising, and then
   a. only apply for jobs in that field
   b. make sure to get a college degree in that exact field
   c. pay attention to the field as you study, making changes to your goals or education if needed as the technology changes

- Computers are useful tools in a wide variety of occupations and fields. In education, computers can be used to help plan, produce, and deliver lectures; connect professors to colleagues and resources; and provide administrative support for managing grades and appointments. In healthcare, computers drive appointment and patient record systems, allow doctors to review records and take notes during consultations, order prescriptions and make referrals, and act as a research portal for both doctor and patient. In retail sales, computers can be used to maintain inventory and sales records, purchase parts and supplies online, provide payment methods to customers, and serve marketing and customer outreach functions. In hospitality, computers can drive reservation systems, provide tools for developing marketing materials, provide business management programs, and provide social media access between guest and proprietor.

- Telecommuting can be an effective way for employees to work from remote offices, but the skills and discipline required to work independently and alone are not always present. Prospective telecommuters should assess their suitability, specifically considering his or her ability to successfully work on a task-driven schedule; to maintain positive, valid professional relationships with remote colleagues and managers; and to manage their professional image, visibility, and perceived value within the organization.

- Along with their own strengths and weaknesses, prospective telecommuters should evaluate their work environment, identifying whether the appropriate hardware, software, and network connections are available; considering whether work data can be kept secure and safe; ensuring that remote office work will not harm personal relationships; and ensuring that work will be able to be done with a minimum of distractions and conflicts.

- When a telecommuter sets up the remote office, they should check that all systems and human processes are working as expected by testing out the practice of working from the remote office during off-hours. Problems with hardware, communication, or the work environment can then be addressed without impacting the ongoing work schedule.

- To maximize the chances of benefiting from opportunities in emerging and rapidly changing careers, workers should stay alert to the changes that are occurring and be flexible and adaptable to those changes, shifting study or career goals if needed to stay aligned with the new directions that they see.

- The healthcare industry provides a wide array of job opportunities in patient care and technology, and the field is expected to continue to experience considerable demand for the foreseeable future. Other fields that concentrate on emerging technology include those related to social media, such as social media strategists and SEO experts, video journalists and multimedia developers, mobile platform programmers, online data security specialists, and network architects and support specialists.

Key Terms

health informatics, p. 351

telemedicine, p. 351

teleradiology, p. 351

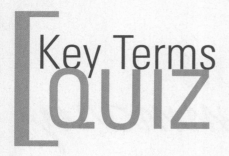

Key Terms QUIZ

1. Doctors sometimes practice _____ by providing opinions and care via computer network to patients in a remote location.

2. _____ connects X-ray and other investigative technicians to radiology specialists via computer network.

3. The application of computer science to manage medical information is sometimes known as _____.

Review QUESTIONS

1. How might college professors use the Internet to support their work to create and teach a class?

2. List three different tasks a doctor could perform with a computer while visiting a patient in an examination room.

3. Explain how a retail storeowner can use a computer to track and replenish the store's inventory items.

4. Identify three ways that social media can help a small B&B innkeeper promote his or her business.

5. Explain why it's important for a person considering a telecommuting job to carefully estimate their chances for success before starting.

6. Give an example of a personal ability that factors into telecommuting success, and describe how a strength or weakness in that ability could impact a remote employee's job performance.

7. List at least three aspects of the remote office or other work environment that should be evaluated as part of the telecommuting setup process.

8. Explain the importance of flexibility and adaptability for workers, especially those in rapidly changing industries.

9. Define telemedicine, and give an example of a way that doctors might use that approach for consultation or treatment.

10. List at least three technology-related careers that are in high demand.

1. Investigate the employment outlook for the health informatics field. Visit the career assistance Web page for the American Health Information Management Association at http://careerassist.ahima.org. Select the *View Jobs* link on that page, and find at least two job descriptions that appear interesting to research further via following these steps:

   - Browse and then select a job category in the Job Function dropdown menu.
   - Search for jobs in all U.S. states.
   - Select a job to investigate from the resulting list.

   For each job opening that you choose, record the name of the job and the state in which it is offered. Note the compensation that is offered, and the basic education and experience that are required. Are there certifications or extra educational requirements for the jobs you chose? What specific information, if any, is given as to the technology knowledge required in order to do the job? Be prepared to discuss your findings in class.

2. Research the current offerings for your dream job (or simply one that sounds interesting, if you are not yet pursuing a career). Visit Monster at http://www.monster.com, and search on the job title of your choice from the main page of the site. How many listings appeared? If the job list is large, try refining your search by a location in the USA—either your own location or the place you would prefer to work. Select one of the jobs from the list, and for this job, note down the same facts as you did for the first Lesson Lab: the job name and state, the compensation, the education and experience required, and any computer-related requirements that may be specified. Compare your preferred job with the ones you researched in health care. How is the pay in your field compared to health care? Which career path currently seems to provide more opportunity in terms of job variety and the number that is available? Once again, be prepared to discuss your findings in class.

Many companies, in order to survive, must be alert to changes in their industry and respond in an agile way to stay well positioned for the future. Companies that can identify new trends and opportunities before they are fully exploited by others stand a better chance of profiting from them.

Divide into teams of three or four people. For this exercise, your team will be part of a creative startup company that has just received new investment capital sufficient to fund one or two new positions. Your task is to work together to identify the newest, most cutting-edge type of job you can think of, and create a job description so that a person can be interviewed and hired. The job need not be strictly computer-related, though that is allowed if desired; but some reliance on technology is essential.

First, meet as a team and brainstorm about new jobs you can create, drawing on your own life, work, and online experiences. It may be helpful to combine existing jobs in order to create an interesting hybrid; for example, combining nursing and social media to create the job of Online Care Specialist, a medical professional who actively moderates an online support forum to empathize with and offer coping strategies for people with chronic illness. Refine your brainstormed ideas and agree on one or two jobs to define.

Together, write a basic description for each job; then, list the responsibilities and educational and experiential requirements, and set a starting salary. When you are done with the exercise, the instructor will lead a discussion so that each team can share their emerging career ideas with the class.

LESSON 8B:
The Future of Computing

It's clear beyond a doubt that computers are here to stay as an integral and critical part of our society. They have become indispensible throughout almost every part of our world, whether helping us to communicate, solve problems, or simply have fun.

Twenty years ago, no one had a complete understanding of how computers would be used today and how they would shape our activity and careers. Some of those guesses still remain the stuff of science fiction, while others were brought into reality only to be quickly bypassed by better ideas. Nevertheless, evaluating the present and predicting the future of the computer industry was a valuable exercise twenty years ago, and it is just as useful today.

At the very least, imagining the future is something that many people simply find fun to do. We wonder about all kinds of things that are yet to be, from the outcome of a sporting event to how our lives and the lives of our children may turn out. All the fiction on the shelves of the local library is in some way a product of an author thinking, "What if...?"

In a more practical vein, predicting the future of an industry can to a certain extent help us to see problems and hazards before they occur. Though human endeavor is arguably not at its best when it comes to predicting and analyzing future trouble, there is still value in having a hypothetical scenario to analyze in order to find problems both small and large that could occur within that scenario.

From the perspective of the college student preparing for a career, predicting the future can provide guidance as to ideal subjects to study. As you learned in the last lesson, identifying emerging technologies and occupations can be a good way to make sure one is at the forefront of the new opportunity, rather than arriving at the end with millions of other identically-trained latecomers.

But most important of all, future predictions actually help to drive the innovations and inventions that are made. Today's crazy idea and wild imagining can become tomorrow's breakthrough product more often than one might think. Even if those ideas fail, or turn out to be mere springboards for even greater innovation, the constant supply of "What if..." questions creates a fertile field for product developers.

Figure 8.16   Imagining the future can be fun, and there are some practical benefits as well.

In the previous lesson, you learned about how computers are used in various careers, and you explored some of the new technology-based careers that are being created today. This lesson will focus more on the technology itself and what the future may hold for computers and the people that use them.

8.4 Advancements in Computing and Technology

From the arrival of the first personal computer, large improvements in computing speed, storage capacity, and communication rates have been commonplace. Some types of performance doubled again and again with each passing half year. Along with this rapid progress, competition, and improvements in manufacturing efficiency led to falling prices, bringing computers into the easily affordable range for many consumers around the world.

However, speed, capacity, and efficiency are not the only ways that innovation occurs in the computer industry. Along with improving existing technology, engineers and inventors have continually created new ways to use computers; and software designers have created an ever-changing array of programs for us to use.

INNOVATION: EMERGING VERSUS CONVERGING TECHNOLOGIES

Just as you have read about emerging careers, the same process of development and improvement is occurring with the technology itself. Think about the first digital computers that were invented in the 20th century. Clumsy and slow by today's standards, they occupied an entire room and produced limited computing power.

Though it may seem unlikely, those first digital computers are the ancestors of the tiny computer that sits in the family car, regulating fuel use and accumulating diagnostic data to aid in future repairs. At some point, computing engineers took what they knew about digital computer technology and spawned a new and separate industry. While mainframe computers continued to evolve and improve, the emerging automotive computers took their place as a new use for computer technology and began their evolution as well.

With regard to computers, the term **emerging technology** refers simply to any new way of using computers that is separate from what is established. The next version of Windows or Mac OS will probably

not constitute an emerging technology; though they will likely be full of useful new features, they will not herald an entirely new way of using computers. Solid-state data storage, however, qualified when it first arrived as an emerging technology because it provided a new way to store data that was different from the magnetic, spinning floppy disk. The business of producing flash drives is still very active, and new solid-state products continue to arrive in parallel with other forms of data storage.

Though it is difficult to concisely identify what technologies are currently in an emerging state, many people consider that there are four broad categories of study that will yield major developments in the near to medium-term future: **nanotechnology**, involving the manipulation of matter and creating machines at the molecular scale; **biotechnology**, an application of biology that uses living organisms to manufacture new products; **information technology**, methods and tools for managing and distributing information; and **cognitive science**, which studies the processes of the mind, in part to seek ways to artificially reproduce them. These categories are sometimes grouped together under their acronym, **NBIC**.

There are many other fields and areas of study that will produce emerging technology, of course; for example, it is entirely likely that the explosive growth of the mobile computing industry will spur the invention of new technologies to manage the proliferation of devices and communication that continue to increase exponentially. The current state of mobile technology, however, has arisen from more than just emerging technology.

Before the iPhone, many people carried PDAs, which managed appointments, ran spreadsheet programs, and allowed people to take notes with a stylus. PDAs were ideal for a wide range of business and casual users on the go. From their first primitive versions, they proved to be innovative and popular.

Along with the PDA, more and more people began to carry cell phones once their designs shrank from briefcase- to pocket-size. As cell phone engineers refined and improved their designs, they found ways to add more complex display screens to the phones, which in turn led to the creation of small programs that could run on the cell phones.

At that point, the next logical step in the evolution of both of those products

Figure 8.17 Solid state storage like this thumb drive was an emerging technology in the not-too-distant past; it has surpassed and made obsolete several kinds of magnetic storage devices like floppy disk drives.

was to combine them. After a brief period of adjustment during which each type of manufacturer experimented with ways to adopt the other machine's technology, the smart phone companies emerged as the primary providers for the combined technology. Today, if one searches one can find an old-style PDA to purchase, but they are rare in contrast to the dozens of different smart phone styles, operating systems and computing power. This process of blending separate concepts to create a single, unified solution is known as **technological convergence**.

Not every new innovative product produces this effect, even if its function is relatively close to that of another product. For example, the microwave oven was heralded by some as the doomsday machine for the conventional oven. Able to cook foods in a fraction of the time as an ordinary oven and without the long delay for preheating, microwave ovens became a common—and in some cases required—element in kitchens around the world. However, despite its popularity, the microwave never replaced the conventional oven in the typical kitchen. Many foods simply do not turn out as desired when cooked in a microwave, and the technology used for a conventional oven (radiant heat in a metal box) is incompatible with the technology used in a microwave (high-intensity radiation that, among other things, super-heats metal). The microwave oven was eagerly given its place alongside or atop the conventional oven, but their technologies and results precluded their convergence.

In some cases, the process of technological convergence can combine several products together. Today's smart phone is quite possibly the ideal example of converging technology. Along with the PDA and smart phone, many consumers also had a portable music player (either to play CDs or MP3 files), a video-playback device, a digital camera, a document scanner, a GPS device, and a computer with which to access the Web. Today, all of these devices and more can be found in a single, garden-variety smart phone.

Technological convergence may or may not remove the individual components from the market. An iPhone has a very nice screen and digital music output, but its movie-showing capability is no match for a 60-inch home theater system with surround-sound speakers. The smart phone's digital camera is great for snapshots and quick video clips, but professional photographers continue to buy precision cameras with multiple lenses in order to satisfy their artistic needs. Even so, the converging technologies for video, audio, and digital communication have created a unique and extremely powerful device that can satisfy the needs of millions of consumers.

PERVASIVE AND UBIQUITOUS COMPUTING

When we think of computers, we likely think of some sort of device in a box that receives input from a human user and produces some form of audiovisual output. Whether in the palm of a hand, on a desk or in a giant air-conditioned room, it's extremely common for a computer to be a machine that waits for us to make a request, and then responds with our answer.

As you've learned through lessons in this book, computers surround us in many other places we sometimes don't consider, in part because they perform their work without direct requests from a user. New cars nearly always contain some kind of computer, for example, to accumulate diagnostic information and help keep the engine using fuel at optimal levels. Smart refrigerators and other appliances contain simple computers to manage their functions, and post alerts when something goes wrong.

This second kind of computer—working behind the scenes without our help and in some cases without our knowledge—is related to a field of investigation and invention called **ubiquitous computing** or **pervasive computing**; as the name implies, ubiquitous computing involves integrating computer and communication technology into the objects that make up our everyday environment, autonomously controlling and

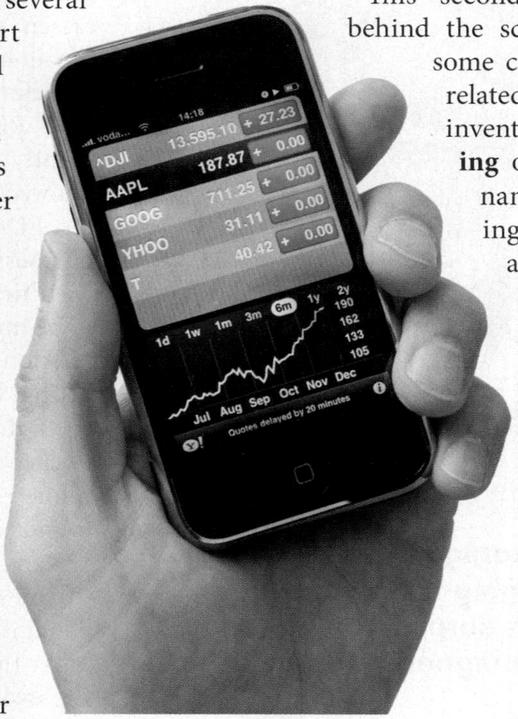

Figure 8.18 Smart phones are an example of technological convergence; they contain many features that were once only available as separate devices.

Figure 8.19 **Pervasive computing can be used to control environments without human intervention, such as dimming the living room lights when the movie starts.**

assisting with the maintenance of that environment. First formally conceived in the late 1980s, the goal of ubiquitous computing is to explore the concepts of machines integrated into objects and materials in a transparent or invisible way, providing benefit to the users without attracting their attention.

A house, for example, could use ubiquitous computing to combine sensors, controls, communication, and programming to control the electric lights in a house. Wireless sensors could be installed to monitor the amount of light in each room. Motion or heat sensors could detect the presence of people in a room. Lamps or recessed lighting could be fitted with dimmer switches that could respond to computer commands. A central computer could monitor data from sensors and light levels, and issue commands as needed.

As afternoon turned to evening, the light sensors would relay the darkening state of the rooms to the computer. The computer could issue commands to turn on lights in rooms where people are present, gradually increasing the intensity of the lighting to counter the loss of light from outside. As people depart from rooms, the computer could switch off lights behind them in order to save power and activate lights in their direction of travel. The computer could even be programmed to dim lights in the living room when someone turns on the TV, or when someone sitting on the couch stops moving for a while in order to make that evening nap more pleasant.

The user would be unaware of the sensors and computing decisions being made; after a while, many people would simply stop thinking of nighttime lighting as something that required consideration. With the addition of some kind of override mechanism—a receiver for spoken commands, perhaps—it would be easy to forget that one once had to use switches to turn lights on and off in one's home.

The above example is quite achievable with readily available hardware, as long as one had the budget and know-how to install and program such a system; but that type of control system isn't something that would be installed in a typical home today. There are, however, many products that are in use around the world that are related to ubiquitous computing. Many smart phones now contain GPS tracking, and the combination of the positioning system and the unique user ID of the cell phone makes it easy (for good and bad purposes) to see the places that large communities of people go as they move about during the day. Wireless game controllers worn by players can seamlessly translate motion into in-game decisions. Even many newer models of candy and soda vending machines have computers that provide sales and inventory data via phone connection or wireless network, so the vending company can efficiently dispatch people to keep the machines stocked.

While more and more products do use computers in an unobtrusive way, much of what is envisioned and discussed with regard to ubiquitous computing is still firmly in the realm of science fiction. You cannot yet go to your local hardware store and buy little jars of **smart dust**—sub-millimeter sized particles that are actually tiny sensors—to sprinkle on windowsills to warn of intruders. It is not yet possible to head to the mall and buy a leather jacket that contains smart phone circuitry, an antenna, a flexible screen in the cuff, and a microphone in the collar. Your home theater system cannot yet detect the presence of specific people in the room and offer different movie choices to watch based on the people in the audience.

Though such ideas might seem crazy or impossible, they are actually not implausible to create, and in some cases they are already actively being developed or researched. Regardless of whether those concepts do become products on a local store's shelf, ubiquitous computing research is still in its infancy, and it is one place where science fiction and reality are very close together.

AUGMENTED AND VIRTUAL REALITY

While ubiquitous computing can help control our environments from behind the scenes, computer technology can also change the way we see our environment or provide entire alternate environments for us to explore.

Sometimes, computing devices can help us better understand or interpret our environment by highlighting key features of the things around us or by reducing what we see to simpler elements. The term **augmented reality** refers to the process of computers providing enhancements to our environment. Some examples of augmented reality are quite commonplace and have been a familiar site for a very long time. For example, computers are responsible for managing and delivering facts and statistics to the TV screen when we watch sporting events. The extra information, delivered in real time, deepens and expands our understanding of the game or race we are watching.

Augmented reality can also be used to overlay extra computer-generated elements on a real-life scene in order to increase comprehension. When

Figure 8.20 Augmented reality adds statistics, graphics, and other computer-generated information to real images to make them more meaningful.

watching a race on TV whose finish seems too close to call, viewers at home can sometimes determine the winner of the race faster and more accurately than the people in the stands by watching slow replays of the race complete with enhanced finish-line markings provided and positioned by a computer. In other sports, broadcasters can enhance the game play itself to make it easier to watch, for example by adding a computer-generated trail following a fast-moving hockey puck. They can also use it to make money by displaying billboard-style advertisements around a stadium; since the advertising is added to the TV picture by a computer instead of actually being placed in the stadium, the broadcaster can show ads for local businesses no matter where the game is being shown.

Augmented reality systems are sometimes used with vehicles. Military pilots flying high-performance fighter jets have critical information displayed on the visors of their helmets to remove the need for looking at indicators within the cockpit. Some visors are even designed to completely block out the actual view, replacing it with images provided by cameras mounted on the outside of the airplane, allowing the pilot to look fully around the aircraft with nothing to interfere with the view. Some car manufacturers, borrowing the military heads-up display concept, have integrated information displays on the driver's side windshield, displaying the car's speed and other operating data above the steering wheel instead of on the dashboard.

In contrast to augmented reality, **virtual reality** systems are designed to replace our real environment with one that is computer-defined. By providing complex, computer-rendered scenes either through special hardware or simply via an ordinary desktop PC, such programs open up new worlds, experiences, and personal connections for their users.

Many PC-based games provide a virtual reality experience. Sony's Everquest 2 is an example of a fantasy game that provides a massive online world to explore. The combination of huge wilderness and city areas filled with sights and challenges, complex environmental elements and the semi-realistic motion of animals; people can quickly immerse players in a world that seems somehow genuine. Even though the activity takes place on a screen rather than hardware that completely blocks out the real world, it is not unusual for players to view the actions of their in-game character as temporarily real.

Other games, such as Linden Labs' Second Life, provide an online experience that is more

Figure 8.21   3D worlds in online games can draw players into the experience, even though they appear only on a PC screen.

player-controlled. Instead of elves and trolls fighting dragons, Second Life players create (with a few exceptions) human character representations called **avatars**. Through their avatars, they join millions of others in an online world that is almost entirely player-built, complete with roads, parks, businesses, and houses. The game hosts a complete and complex economy in which players design, manufacture, and sell virtual products, services, and real estate to each other using an in-game currency.

Virtual reality systems commonly provide an **immersive** experience, meaning that they create a feeling within user that the artificial environment or actions are in some way real. Immersive virtual systems can accomplish this feat either through technology or storytelling.

To create **tactical immersion**, where the user believes that they can physically feel and alter things in the virtual world, virtual systems use various types of technology to replace the real environment's presence with digitally rendered information. Users can wear headgear to supply the digital world's sights and sounds; and gloves, boots, and clothing can be worn that contain sensors both to detect user motion and to provide haptic feedback. With the real environment successfully blocked and the digital world effectively rendered, the user can quickly become

engaged in the digital world in ways that feel convincingly real. Tactical immersion can be a fun and intense way to play a game, and it can also be used for more serious pursuits, allowing surgeons and engineers to precisely control remote robotic hardware.

Virtual environments can supply compelling characters in a story that is challenging, triumphant, or simply relevant and familiar. Such experiences can create **narrative immersion**, in which the user closely identifies with the avatar or protagonist in the story. Movies and TV shows sometimes create this effect, as do many modern games that rely heavily on story and character development over an extended period of time.

Though virtual environments have been around for many years and immersive environments in computer games have become commonplace, there is still a great deal in this area of technology that is yet to be explored and developed. Motion sensor technology continues to improve, providing new ways to apply increasingly sensitive and sophisticated responses. Advances in artificial intelligence allow for the creation of characters in a story that can react spontaneously and differently each time the game

Figure 8.22   Virtual reality systems can achieve tactical immersion by replacing real-world sensory input with computer-generated substitutes.

is played, providing a startlingly realistic simulation of unpredictable human behavior. And little by little, the technology to sense input and provide immersive output continues to approach the budget requirements of the typical consumer, increasing the opportunity to deliver more and more products to a mainstream audience.

8.5 Impact of Emerging Technologies

Predicting the next new development in computer technology can be difficult. Predicting the full effect that an emerging technology will have on its users and society in general can be an exercise in futility, given the number of variables that can affect a technology's reception and the way it is put to use.

However, much can be learned from considering the early changes that we see as an emerging technology is accepted by the public. By viewing the improvements that occur along with unintended consequences, we can analyze, discuss, and make changes for the future. As you'll see, every new invention can be a catalyst for both positive and negative change in our lives; computing technology, after all, is simply a tool, and the way we decide to use the tool in large part determines the effect that it has.

EMERGING TECHNOLOGIES AND THE ENVIRONMENT

As the years pass, our society finds itself increasingly concerned with the effect we have on the global environment. Every participant in the ecosphere contributes to its health or malaise, and humanity is no exception. As the human population has grown over the millennia, our impact on the health of the planet has become a critical factor for the survival of the balance of life on the planet as we now know it.

To be sure, technology has accelerated our use of resources and the increase in pollution, both by creating tools to make our lives easier and last longer (increasing the world's population) and by focusing on creating tools and technology in expedient rather than Earth-friendly ways.

Figure 8.23 Satellites and computers can work together to help scientists measure climate change.

But lately, technology has also helped us to better understand the problems we now face. Satellites orbiting Earth are providing us with a wealth of data about air and water pollution. Data stations on the planet's surface as well as in orbit allow us to measure changes in climate and global temperature with unprecedented precision. Computers now provide sophisticated simulations to test what-if climate change scenarios, along with heavy-duty data analysis that aid scientists in developing new ways to mitigate climate damage and reverse some of the atmospheric imbalances that now exist.

One of the emerging technologies that provides a significant boost to the environment is green computing, which concentrates on reducing the environmental impact of computer hardware and use. The designs for modern digital computers initially focused on their speed and capability, rather than the environmental impact of their presence in the world. They consume a great deal of electricity to operate; are manufactured with power-hungry processes that sometimes produce toxic chemical waste; and like other metal-and-plastic creations, do not disappear very quickly in a landfill.

Over time, as hundreds of millions of people put computers into use—and sometimes replaced them with new models every several months—the cost to the global environment began to become apparent. The same technology used to measure adverse pressure on our global ecosystem had also become a significant contribution to resource use and pollution.

Green computing has emerged as a new way to consider the manufacture and operation of computers to make their environmental impact lower. Given the number of computers in use around the world, a new design that yields only a fractional reduction in a computer's power consumption can cause a substantial reduction in the global demand for electricity. Less toxic batteries in mobile devices produce less toxic waste leaching into groundwater near landfill sites.

Currently, green computing follows the "reduce, reuse, recycle" model that has been promoted for decades in environmental initiatives. Computers and monitors are being developed to run on less power, either by powering down unused components, running them at slower speeds when high performance is not required, or by finding ways to more efficiently manage heat output. Smaller devices can use solar cells to provide power, reducing or eliminating the need for wall electricity. Research is ongoing to develop less toxic alternatives to the lead in batteries and the chemicals used to produce silicon wafers

Figure 8.24 Computers can be constructed in more eco-friendly ways to reduce their own environmental impact.

and chips. And in some cases, cloud computing can reduce the amount of hardware required because users share central hardware resources.

Some local and international programs collect old computers to be refurbished and redistributed to local low-income residents or to people in third-world countries that would otherwise not have access to computers at all. Most population centers now have a municipal or private program that encourages the recycling of old and broken computers and peripherals. Those centers can resell working parts; strip and sell scrap gold from CPUs and other components that contain that metal; and properly recycle and dispose of the scrap metal and toxic components, reducing the volume and toxicity of what is sent to the landfill.

As with many other green initiatives, green computing is a mixture of high- and low-tech solutions. There is still much to be done to gain control over our impact on the ecosystem, but brilliant new inventions will need to work hand-in-hand with good old dumpster diving and garbage collection in order to be maximally effective.

EMERGING TECHNOLOGIES AND YOU

Individuals around the world have already been profoundly affected by the personal computing revolution, and there is no evidence that this process has begun to mature. Indeed, the surge in mobile computing activity seems to be accelerating the change.

Desktop PCs brought simplified tasks to some users, but to many others they instead brought brand new capabilities that were not previously available. Complex tax forms could be easily and accurately completed; vast libraries and online etiquette mavens became equally and instantly available for consultation; and games allowed us to while away hours that once had to be spent on gardening and laundry chores.

Laptop computers provided access to business, fun, and information on the go, but the focus for the user was not much different from the desktop PC. However, with the arrival and universal availability of the handheld computer, millions of people suddenly found themselves able to instantly broadcast and receive information about any subject, anywhere they happened to be.

New—and in some cases startling and unintended—uses for these devices sprang up. Tools that were created to share a quick thought, online link, or image suddenly became fuel for revolution and social action. Uprisings against governments have been started by and chronicled with Twitter updates and video clips posted to YouTube. Rebels have used mobile devices and social media to coordinate their actions and receive information to aid their cause. Oppressive governments have been caught by surprise by the rapidity with which socially sensitive information can spread through these channels and have had a difficult time finding a way to restrict access to social media tools without creating an angry and disillusioned populace.

The same tools can be used both to create and prosecute trouble. In 2011, riots in London were aided by social media networks, allowing rioters and looters to track the movements of police. In the aftermath, however, many of the comments and videos posted to social media sites proved to be useful evidence in tracking down and arresting those who had been involved.

From a humanitarian perspective, mobile computing can aid in rescue efforts following major disasters. The 2011 tsunami in Fukushima, Japan created terrible devastation in the coastal cities where it struck. Many people both in and out of the area had no access to conventional communication after the disaster, but they were still in some cases able to find wireless Internet signals and could use their mobile devices to access Facebook and other social media sites. Such connections allowed people to reach out for help and understanding to others beyond the range of the disaster itself.

At present, much of the focus on new technology for individuals focuses on providing services and information tailored specifically for each user. New application designers are working to find better ways to learn what each user values and then provide information that matches what each user prefers. Currently, companies like Google and Facebook look both at the preferences that a user expresses when viewing Web pages and other content; and at the preferences and information habits of a user's friends, family, and colleagues.

Despite the progress that has been made, however, the "customized Internet" is still far from a reality. There is much work to be done, not just to create new programs to serve each user's needs, but also to simply understand what users really want in their computing environment, and whether there is a cost-effective way to produce what users crave. As users simultaneously demand more information, better information, and free access to information, the challenge for the next wave of new technology may very well involve both new ways of modeling behavior and new ways of making a profit.

Figure 8.25 Texting, tweeting, and media sharing have quickly become a part of revolution and disaster recovery efforts.

$\mathcal{Focus}$ on the Issues

Help from Everywhere

Some data analysis tasks are so complex that supercomputers sporting tens of thousands of processors are required to complete the job. Not everyone has the budget necessary to build and buy a supercomputer, however, and even renting processing time from a supercomputer owner can be prohibitively expensive.

Sometimes, too, even a supercomputer is inadequate for the job at hand, even if the necessary money is in the bank to afford the use of one. In some cases, the volume of data to be analyzed is simply impractical for a single computer to complete; in others, the problems require intuition and leaps of comprehension that a brute-force linear calculator like a computer cannot provide.

What to do, when faced with budgetary constraints or a problem that defies a computer's best efforts? Some researchers turn to people and PCs in the world around them.

SETI, short for Search for Extraterrestrial Intelligence, is a field of science related to discovering evidence that other intelligent species exist in the universe. One aspect of SETI involves the use of radio telescopes to scan the heavens for special types of radio signals that would not occur in nature, possibly indicating the presence of extraterrestrial technology.

The more computing power available to analyze the radio signals, the more refined the scans can be. The SETI@home project, started at UC Berkeley in 1997, decided to recruit volunteers with home computers to essentially create a distributed supercomputer that could help process data. Since its inception, millions of volunteers around the world have connected to the project via the Internet, using their otherwise-idle computers to process radio data and return results.

The BOINC project (http://boinc.berkeley.edu) took the SETI@home project in a more general direction, providing a central place for large-scale data processing projects to request volunteer help. Visitors are invited to sign up, download BOINC software, and join in the efforts to find new astronomical phenomena, cure diseases or study global warming. The secure platform provides an easy way for anyone to use their PC to help advance science.

In another novel approach, the University of Washington reached out to the gamer population in 2011 when it needed help solving a complex chemical problem related to protein structures that cause the AIDS disease. After more than a decade of being stymied by the difficult problem, researchers created a game called Foldit (http://fold.it/portal) that provided tools and a mechanism for deciphering the protein, and made the game public. More than 200,000 players signed in to try their hand at solving the puzzle, and ten days later the crystal mystery became a closed case.

Computers sometimes amaze us with their computational ability; yet sometimes, they provide us with ways to collaborate that far transcend simple computing power.

EMERGING TECHNOLOGIES AND THE LAW

In the United States and many other countries, the legal system is based on the accumulation of centuries' worth of ideas, traditions and procedures. When new situations arise or when existing laws seem incomplete or unfair, governments initiate extensive debate and consideration regarding the best way to proceed. Politics, science, community standards, and existing laws are examined by legislators and regulators, and eventually changes and additions are made to the legal framework within which we live.

Unfortunately for this model, digital technology and new computer-aided sciences are moving forward both literally and figuratively at the speed of light. New ideas around the globe are conceived, designed, and brought into production in months rather than decades. Each new idea spurs further new imagining and new development. New controversial technologies are made available long before legislators even think to consider how to adapt to them; and new products based on those technologies are in laboratories, businesses, or homes long before the regulators fully understand them.

In the absence of regulation, lawsuits are brought to the courts by technology providers and users alike, demanding resolutions to thorny problems of liability and ownership. Without specific regulations to reference, judges, and juries find themselves in the position of setting policies and creating regulations by setting precedents in court. Governments must then do their best to catch up and either affirm or undo the decisions that the courts first made.

Technology will not slow its emerging pace in the near future, and the speed of our governmental system is not likely to increase much. We are faced with difficult decisions going forward, either to accept the inevitable, ineffective lag that regulation will continue to have, or to develop new legislative and regulatory practices that are far more nimble and can better keep up with technology.

There are many complex legal issues brought on by emerging technology; in addition, there are a number of legal issues with common and accepted technology that still have yet to be fully considered and regulated. As a consumer, we might hear "legal issue" and automatically think, "copyright violation," and indeed there is a great deal of legal wrangling in process over how to properly defend against copyright infringement. Some of the other problems currently being considered include:

- **Genetic research.** It is already possible for an average—albeit somewhat wealthy—consumer to have their DNA structure analyzed for susceptibility to certain diseases and for adverse reactions to drugs. Because this is an emerging technology, it is still expensive and rarely covered by health insurance. If a patient dies from a disease or drug reaction that DNA screening could have warned against, can the doctor, hospital, or health insurance company be sued for not employing that experimental test?

- **Cell phone tracking.** Cell phones have since their creation acted as positioning devices, allowing service providers to track the movements of the phone with surprising accuracy and detail. Police can be greatly aided in finding suspects and witnesses for crimes by using cell phone records; unfortunately, stalkers and criminals can also use cell phones and GPS trackers to harm their victims. Is it legal for police to follow your movements without a warrant? Can people sue to be allowed to move about in privacy? Do police or government officials have the right to require cell phones to track citizens?

- **Lie detection.** New MRI and other brain scan technology can detect lies by scanning brain activity. The accuracy of such methods can approach 90 percent. Given that degree of accuracy, are there types of situations where such scans should be allowed or required?

Figure 8.26 Technology regulation is often slow to arrive, putting courts on uncertain ground when deciding the legality of many technological issues.

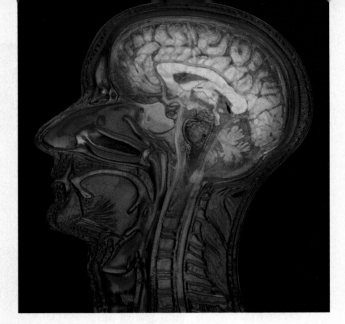

Figure 8.27 Brain scans are able to detect lying with a higher degree of accuracy than a polygraph test, but they are still not perfect.

What about court testimony, job interviews, political debates, or even casual traffic stops by police? Since such scans are not 100 percent effective, who will be in charge of determining success versus failure, and how?

- **Online economies.** Second Life, the game where players provide services and products to each other, and accumulate property and resources, uses a fictitious currency called Linden dollars. However, Linden dollars can be exchanged for real-world money according to an exchange rate set inside the game, allowing people to assign a real-money value to their transactions and holdings in the game. Can governments tax that in-game wealth, even though it is a digital fiction, because it has a real-life value? How can financial regulators control fraud and theft inside the game, where they have no jurisdiction? If two in-game avatars "marry" and accumulate assets like property and a house, and one real-life player dies, who inherits the in-game property, the real-life spouse or the in-game spouse?

Along with such thorny problems comes the issue of jurisdiction. While laws and regulations are mostly local or national, technology is a global phenomenon. Many things are legal in one country but strictly forbidden in another. There are some obvious candidates such as gambling and sexually explicit material, of course, but even things like Twitter and simple e-mail systems run afoul of governmental regulations in some countries.

Many governments want to specifically control the types of things their citizens can access electronically. But while a government might want to prosecute a company like Google and its employees for producing material that is illegal in its country, they have no legal standing to prosecute the people of another country whose actions are perfectly legal where they live and work.

The problem manifests itself in the other direction as well. Music companies in the United States would love to shut down sites in other countries that host and distribute copyrighted material in violation of American copyright laws, but those countries have no interest in cooperating with or abiding laws they did not make, leaving the music companies without recourse.

To further complicate matters, actions and events are sometimes said to have taken place "in cyberspace," when involving images or concepts transferred from one Internet location or device to another. Cyberspace has no specific geographic location—at least, not yet—and at this time no court or agency can claim jurisdiction over that realm.

Going forward, regulators and courts alike will find themselves under greater pressure to keep up as emerging technology provides an increasing array of troublesome issues, and as existing technology such as the Internet continues to create emerging conundrums as new uses are discovered and new populations are reached. It may be necessary to find

Figure 8.28 The Internet is a global system that is unregulated as a whole. National governments have little success applying their laws to the Internet outside their own borders.

new ways to regulate technology and the products it creates, perhaps by creating nimble super-national regulatory agencies that have the expertise and perspective to monitor specific technologies, along with the efficiency of being charged by governments to regulate without answering directly to any one country. But no matter what the specific solution, emerging technology is demanding rapid work and creative thinking to create emerging policy.

THE DARK SIDE OF EMERGING TECHNOLOGIES

Up to now, we have focused primarily on the practical and beneficial aspects of computing technology. Our world and our understanding of the universe has forever changed because of the incredible helper that the digital computer has become. And yet, computers are simply tools, and it is a pragmatic reality that the same tool can achieve very different results depending on the one who wields it. We can both build and destroy with computers. We can set ourselves free and allow ourselves to become enslaved. We can lift up the human spirit, and we can cause great pain and misery.

Since computers are simply tools, and technology is simply a workshop for transforming ideas into reality, it is critically important that we all work to identify both the benefits and dangers that exist in computing. If we do this, we can better see warning signs that a problem is growing, and we can better work to change the outcome. If we assume that somebody else will make sure we are kept safe from the harmful use of technology, then we will more likely become hapless victims.

Some of the negative aspects of computing are the same as for the arrival of any new technology. Computers can do certain things much faster and better than people; as computers are put in place to do those jobs, the human employees find themselves out of work. While this process is a gradual one in most cases, it can create difficult times for people that find their expertise and abilities are no longer needed anywhere. Some governments may provide retraining; others may simply shrug, count the net positive effect on business revenue and move on.

Whether educating young people or retraining older workers for computer-related jobs, there is a risk that computer technology will widen rather than narrow the gap between the rich and poor members of our society. If computer knowledge is essential for finding a good job, and computer knowledge requires extra money in school and expensive equipment out

Figure 8.29 As computers are adapted to new jobs and industries, many people find themselves out of work, their skills no longer needed.

of school, many poor people will be shut out from participating in education; and since they are denied the education, they will also be denied the better jobs. Governments and charitable organizations can provide help to bring computers and resources to low-income areas, but without a long-term commitment to addressing the problem, it will continue to get worse.

There are many social risks and consequences that computers bring us; indeed, the same social media tools that give us the opportunity to stay connected can also drive us apart. Social networking systems like Facebook have been used again and again to engage in concerted bullying attacks within school populations, with one person or groups of people working together to destroy the reputation of somebody they don't like. Forged posts, altered photographs, and poisonous, aggressive status messages have all been used to painfully ostracize others. Occasionally, people have taken their own lives to escape the pain of cyber-bullying, yet some participants in the bullying community show no particular sense of remorse or responsibility for the death they help to cause.

There is also growing concern that the pervasive use of opinion forums throughout the Internet may be helping to reinforce aggressive and divisive behavior, while dramatically reducing empathy and understanding. Thirty years ago, a racist comment or a bitter, thoughtless reaction to tragedy would either go unheard, or it would fall on the ears of a tiny community. That same comment or reaction at the end of a story in *The New York Times*, however, is seen by many thousands of people. Though many may disagree, the comment's author will also get a handful (or dozens, or hundreds) of responses in support of that opinion or reaction. The author is encouraged to post more mean and thoughtless comments, as are readers of the first post who feel emboldened to take a harsher stand of their own in the future.

Frequently, comment posters deliberately write incendiary reactions to a post not because it is what they believe but because they know it will produce a strong reaction. This behavior is called **trolling**, named for the style of fishing that slowly drags a lure through the water in the hope of enticing a fish to bite. People who troll for reactions in this manner find it funny, and there are times when the humor is clearly evident. Yet trolling is also encouraging people to react strongly and practice lashing out in anger at controversial statements; in that sense, trolls (the people doing the trolling) are teaching other posters how to care less for the people with which they converse and how to take delight in causing distress for others.

Rivaling our growing lack of concern for others is the growing threat to privacy and certain kinds of freedom. We provide more and more information about ourselves and our personal lives to a wide variety of people, companies, and agencies, and the more we give, the more we are encouraged to give. Some of this sharing provides us with great benefits, as you've already seen in discussions about social media and Web 2.0 concepts, but we ignore the risks of the information-sharing world at our peril.

When we buy products from Web sites and register with online sites in order to gain access to site contents, we reveal a variety of personal information, from e-mail addresses to credit card numbers. Naturally, it is important to make sure that e-commerce companies are legitimate, and most of us are at least fairly careful about shopping online with well known companies. But as hacker activity has recently shown, our financial and personal data may not always be safe even when held by reputable companies. For instance, in 2011 some of Sony's internal systems were compromised by hackers, who stole large numbers of names and e-mail addresses, along with smaller amounts of financial information like credit card and bank account numbers. Though Sony itself did not misuse its subscriber information, it failed to protect that data adequately against intrusions by others.

Social media companies face a challenge that is different from simply protecting data from unauthorized access. Facebook, LinkedIn, and many other massive social networking sites are the custodians of vast amounts of personal information for hundreds of millions of people. That information, when used with strategies to sell products and services to users, can be worth billions or trillions of dollars in revenue. Users have willingly provided the networking companies all of this information for free, but very few users did so with the understanding and hope that their information would be used for marketing and sales.

Figure 8.30   We post many personal and financial details to online sites, yet we may not always have assurance that our data will be treated with care and respect.

This presents a delicate dilemma for a social media company. The company is in business to turn a profit, and it possesses a gold mine in personal information that was provided by people who agreed—in many cases without thinking—to allow that data to be used by the company. Yet if the company aggressively markets the personal data to advertisers, opening the floodgates to sales pitches to users at every turn, the user community could very well revolt and discontinue use of the service, destroying the company's revenue source. So far, ideas for making money from subscriber data have in large part been cautiously pursued, but extra vigilance on the part of the user community is well advised when the company charged with data safekeeping is also the same company that can make a handsome profit by distributing it.

Of even greater concern than media companies profiting from voluntarily-given data, is the degree of self-monitoring that users provide to governments. As we increasingly rely on computing devices at all hours of all days, we provide an increasingly detailed and complete picture of our lives for others to monitor. From morning to night, we carry cell phones that track and store our location, and the routes we traveled from place to place. Cell phones and social media provide records of the people we visit and the things we talk about. Our smart phones and desktop computers provide a record of the Web sites we visit and the search engine terms we've used to find information. Some cars contain their own link to a monitoring company that can track a car's location and shut down its operation.

Figure 8.31 Mobile technology keeps us in touch with our friends; it can also leave us exposed to unwanted tracking and surveillance.

All of these functions have good and valuable purposes. If your laptop or car are stolen, it's a great feeling to know that a monitoring company can find it and alert police to its exact location. It's fun to broadcast your location to all your friends, so they can join you at a restaurant or at the very least react with envy that you're having the best steak in town. If a crime is committed, it's good to know that the police can use cell phone records to track the suspect's movements and prove that they were at the scene of the crime.

Unfortunately, all of these abilities are also ideal tools for a oppressive government to monitor its citizens and crack down on activity it finds dangerous. Political dissidents could be tracked from place to place. People found to have spent time in the same place as a government suspect could be rounded up and questioned, even if they were one room away from a secret meeting and had no knowledge it was taking place. Visits to inappropriate Web sites could be identified, and offending users could be tagged by automatic surveillance systems and referred to the police for further investigation.

This kind of micro-monitoring sounds like something better suited to George Orwell's "1984," and in most places it remains nothing more than fiction. However, citizens of open societies and democratic governments have a responsibility to remain vigilant against intrusions on the personal liberties that they prize so highly. The shift to a totalitarian form of government is often gradual, with ground given up bit by bit by a willing populace; it is vital to firmly draw the line between keeping the population safe and spying on citizens to search for opposition. Without pressure, governments and companies will not avoid or discontinue practices that benefit them, even if they are harmful to the freedom of their citizens or users.

Cell phone tracking is an ideal example. The technology to do so has been around for as long as the cell phone, though recent years have seen an increase in tracking accuracy. Yet cell phone manufacturers and companies have been reluctant to share details of how much data is kept, and for how long, and to whom that data may have been given. Smart phone companies have proven further reluctant to provide convenient ways to switch off data collection, because the data aids their development of better phones, and also because there are many ideas in development that involve ways to make billions of dollars by sending advertisements to phone users for nearby products and services. Users are effectively being told to endure their loss of privacy because it would be inconvenient or unprofitable to allow them to be untracked; those users must decide for themselves whether the manufacturer's needs outweigh their own.

ETHICAL **DILEMMA**

Is it okay to download and use software without paying for it?

As a software developer specializing in apps for mobile phones and computers, you've recently created a new, breakthrough technique that can alter the positioning data collected by these devices. Your program doesn't erase or corrupt the tracking data; rather, the data is cleverly altered to show the phone traveling all over the place at all hours of the day.

This program could be an ideal solution for people wishing to preserve their privacy and prevent unwanted surveillance. You realize, however, that some of the people wanting to avoid monitoring are criminals; so your tool could be used both to secure personal liberty from governmental intrusion and to help lawbreakers avoid detection. Altered data, still uploaded by the phone, might also eventually call into the question the validity of non-altered data, since it could be difficult to prove that location records for any phone had not been tampered with.

Will you release the software for distribution, knowing that it could both help shield innocent people and aid criminals? Is there an alternative to this type of program that you would prefer? Explain your reasoning either way.

Fact Check

1. At present, much of the focus on new technology for individuals focuses on
   a. improving the features and color selection for new smart phones
   b. providing services and information tailored specifically for each user
   c. providing faster download speeds to home computers
2. Cell phone location tracking can be helpful and fun, but major risks to personal rights may occur when
   a. you speak loudly in public
   b. you fail to shield your phone's display when entering a number to call
   c. police and government agencies track and monitor your movements without some kind of prior legal process and authorization

Our best weapon against the misuse of technology, whether by government, corporation, or classroom bully, is awareness. That awareness starts with ourselves; we are the best police and regulators of our own behavior. If we are using computer technology to cause harm, sadness, or financial cost to others, then we are part of the dark side of computing; the good news is that it takes very little to change our own actions for the better.

Beyond our own behavior, we should be extremely careful about putting our personal data in harm's way, and we should make sure to carefully consider whether calls against decreasing privacy are in everyone's best interest. "I have nothing to hide, so I don't care," is a very easy perspective to adopt, but remember that it does not require much to change before one is suddenly detained or restricted not because one has something to hide, but merely because someone believes that one might.

8.6 What's Next?

Short-term, the future of computing can be guessed with some degree of accuracy by considering new developments currently in progress in various areas of the field. Longer-range estimations for any kind of future, technological or otherwise, often fall wide of the mark. It is hard enough to estimate what new inventions will arrive, as innovation and invention occur both in a linear, logical way and also by serendipitous discoveries and unpredictable new ways to think about old problems.

But even though the aerial highways filled with flying cars we were promised 50 years ago have not yet come to pass, thinking about the short and long term future of technology is fun, and it can help fuel the imagination of the inventors who will bring the real discoveries our way.

As you've learned earlier in this lesson, the NBIC technologies—nanotechnology, biotechnology, information technology, and cognitive science—are four broad fields of research that are likely to produce changes in our world in a magnitude similar to the computer revolution that is still emerging around us. Many of the current discoveries and future hopes in these areas require background explanations and education beyond the scope of this textbook; however, let's consider the present and possible future of a few familiar technological areas.

ROBOTICS

It has been a long time since Robby the Robot showed up in the 1956 movie *Forbidden Planet,* bringing to life the mechanical, benevolent servant that could do more than humans, yet was content to assist us in the tasks of our daily lives. Digital technology has so far brought forth a number of limited impostors to follow in Robby's footsteps, and the future of robotics may very well at some point achieve or surpass the benchmark that Robby's movie illusion created.

Robotic research had initial success in a very limited scope; namely, teaching a machine to perform a single and specific task with consistency and precision. Robotic arms, for example, could be taught to

Figure 8.32   Once the stuff of pure science fiction, a humanoid multi-function robot may someday be just as likely to be found in a store as a movie screen.

position themselves over an object, grasp that object, move it to a new location, and set the object down. By applying precise motion and force, such an arm could gently move a glass of water from one place to another without spilling a drop.

While that accomplishment may not seem like much in retrospect, it required the development of machinery that could be manipulated in exacting ways, and it required creating methods to store and repeatedly retrieve those motion instructions.

From the beginning of their development, single-purpose robots grew rapidly in popularity. Robotic welding arms are used for industrial applications such as automobile assembly, where they can position metal and fuse the same joints at the same place on every single car to be created, without distractions or sick leave. Mobile robots can help the military and police investigate dangerous situations, and recover and detonate explosive devices. Robots can analyze objects and sort them into different piles based on their appearance or encoding. Robots are even common at the consumer level; many people have little autonomous vacuum cleaners that crawl around the floor on their own, chasing down dust mice without a human to help.

As robots have gained in sophistication and precision, the complexity and delicacy of their tasks have increased. A company called Intuitive Surgical, for example, has created a robotic surgery assistant called the da Vinci Surgical System. Instead of holding a scalpel, the surgeon sits at a console away from the patient, holding controls that attach to the surgeon's hands and fingers. The view of the operation is transmitted to the surgeon's console, where he or she sees a 3D, magnified view of the activity and incision site. At the patient, an array of robotic arms move in response to the surgeon's motions, bringing various tools to bear as required by the operation. The combination of precise control, magnified view, and surgeon comfort allow surgeries to be completed with less invasion and greater success than by people alone.

The future of robotics is likely to be as varied as the ways they are used today; however, one of the key areas of research and development is focused on the future version of Robby the Robot. In the 1950s, Robby's ability to answer questions and do practically anything were nothing more than movie magic. But already, multi-purpose humanoid robots are beginning to make the transition from science fiction to science reality.

New technology in robot construction is exploring ways to simulate human muscles and organs,

Figure 8.33 Multi-function robots aren't quite ready to live with us, but robots like Honda's ASIMO are making surprising progress.

animating humanoid shapes with artificial muscles; environmental sensors in place of eyes, ears and skin; and computer controlled balance and motion. Some humanoid robots, like Honda's ASIMO, can already walk and run, recognize both stationary and moving objects, and sense and understand certain kinds of human input such as spoken words and gestures such as a hand extended for shaking.

As sensor and motion technology continues to improve, the notion of a housekeeping robot that cleans and cooks seems more in the realm of reality than fiction. We may find robots as affordable elder care helpers, providing 24/7 oversight that patients may not get even in a nursing home; or as companions and caretaker for developmentally disabled people who might otherwise need to be institutionalized. And in the absence of medical problems, it may not be long before we eat dinner that our robot made, be reminded that we still need to go for a jog afterwards, and have the robot accompany us down the street to keep us on pace for that upcoming 10k run.

ARTIFICIAL INTELLIGENCE

Just as robotics has intrigued us in both science and popular culture for many decades, our fascination with artificial intelligence, or AI, continues unabated as well. Though the science of AI and robotics are very different, some of the futuristic products and accomplishments we envision involve contributions from both of them.

Artificial intelligence is the science of creating machines that possess a version of intelligence similar to what is found in humans and certain other animals. Mathematicians, programmers, behavioral scientists, and many others have struggled for decades to create artificially intelligent machines, and the target continues to remain elusive in no small part due to a lack of a precise definition of *intelligence*.

Superficially, intelligence can be defined as the calculating processes that are used in order to achieve goals; essentially, this means the processes of observing, learning, predicting, and understanding when working to accomplish a task or acquire something desirable. Creating exact definitions of what constitutes intelligence within those basic categories, however, is a subject of ongoing debate. Inevitably, both philosophy and science pose challenges when evaluating intelligence; even if a standard model for human intelligence were created, the model might not cover the behavior of other species also nominally considered to be intelligent.

People have created many types of programs that attempt to simulate or imitate intelligence. Expert systems, which receive input regarding conditions or problems, compare the input to a database of known conditions, and return a best-guess result based on how closely the known conditions match the input, can sometimes seem intelligent. They will often produce the "right" answers to questions and can be useful tools for encoding an expert's expertise for others to access in a digital form. However, expert systems are simply mechanical processes; they are not truly intelligent, and they lack the ability to generalize and expand their knowledge beyond their narrow purpose. Chess programs are similarly mechanical; though they can be formidable opponents in chess, computers achieve their skill not through intelligent reasoning, but by brute-force calculation.

One intriguing AI project is Cleverbot, which can be found on the Web at http://cleverbot.com. Cleverbot is a type of program known as a **chatterbot**, which simulates conversation with human participants. Visitors to the site begin the conversation by typing anything at all into a text box; Cleverbot reads the input, and then selects and displays a response.

Figure 8.34   Cleverbot isn't truly artificially intelligent, but now and then its responses can be funny and relevant.

Cleverbot's responses are accumulated from past conversations, rather than being part of a static database, so the more conversations it has, the more diverse its responses can become. At times, conversations with Cleverbot can seem authentic and real, as if a human was typing the answers; other times, the answers are strange and irrelevant. Though Cleverbot itself is still simulating rather than actually displaying intelligence, it is nevertheless positive progress in creating a mechanical partner for small talk.

The future of AI research is uncertain. Some people believe that artificial intelligence will be achieved when computer processing power reaches a substantially faster level; others point out that today's computers can produce enormous amounts of computational power yet still cannot achieve anything that approaches real intelligence. Some people have suggested that a new, fundamental way to think about and design intelligence is required in order to teach machines to understand and learn. Though the industry has yet to produce its first definitive breakthrough, it is entirely possible that new ways of considering human and animal intelligence will arrive on the heels of new computer-aided discoveries in biology and cognitive science.

THE FUTURIST'S VIEW

The futurist's job, among other things, is to make calculated predictions about the future of our society and technology. That job, while fun, is not dissimilar to being asked to guess what the weather will be like in twenty years' time. There are a dizzying number of variables that govern the course of the future, including technology, global politics and economics, human nature, and an infinite array of unpredictable events.

In addition, all of us, futurists included, begin with what we know and have experienced when thinking about new problems. Sometimes, we do indeed make new discoveries and inventions by moving along a single path of inquiry from a known starting point; but other times, a new perspective and idea can appear from nowhere. Serendipity, that unexpected flash of discovery and understanding, can take us decades ahead with a single "Aha!", while its absence can hold us helplessly entangled in problems that seem unsolvable.

Though there are as many possible futures for us as there are people to imagine them, some seem to have more potential than others. For example:

Mobile technology.   Mobile computing devices are already exploding in popularity. The future will bring even smaller devices, especially for communication, integrated into eyeglasses, jewelry, or clothing. Larger devices may be made with new, flexible plastics and nanomaterials, allowing users to open a small tube and unroll a fully-functional desktop PC complete with large monitor for output and voice, motion, and fingertip input mechanisms. Alternatively, wireless heads-up displays could be embedded into eyeglass-sized units for both input and output, condensing that desktop PC into one fashion accessory.

Power production and storage.   As we use more mobile devices, we will see the invention of new power storage technologies that will provide those mobile devices with enough electricity for weeks' worth of continuous, active use. As fossil fuels run out and prices for conventional power continue to rise, we will begin to implement new forms of energy based on renewable or always-available sources, and we may increasingly rely on locally produced and stored power from home solar power plants. Over time, the use of overhead electricity wires will fade and become nothing more than a memory.

Communication.   Facebook, LinkedIn, Twitter, Skype, AIM, Flickr, e-mail, cell phone, and many

Figure 8.35 As power costs rise and mobile device popularity increases, demand may increase for better power storage and cheaper power sources that don't require a municipal power grid to provide.

other services currently make up the hodgepodge of our online presence. We will eventually replace this unwieldy mess with a single, secure, high-capacity storage and identity chip. Similar in size to a cell phone SIM card, the "me" chip will store personal information, financial data, and digital files and media. A single, unified online service will provide one point of contact for connecting to the community, and the chip will be able to communicate with point-of-sale devices to effortlessly make purchases and pay bills. Data transfer will take place wirelessly, almost instantaneously and at rates large enough that the old "cloud computing" model of storage and computing will be made obsolete, returning control and security of data to the user.

Medicine. Nanotechnology and biological research will create new cures for viral, autoimmune, and cancerous diseases. Burns and limb damage will be easily treated with artificial tissue infused with regenerative nanomaterials. With many diseases and traumas eliminated, humanity will struggle to find solutions to the biological damage caused by the

overuse of the nanomaterials to counteract those diseases, both in our bodies and in nature. Advances in genetic understanding will allow us to correct our DNA structures to slow the aging process, extending a human's theoretical lifespan tenfold or more. With our planet already straining to support our population, bitter debates and conflicts explode over who among us is to be given near-immortality.

Physics. Ongoing research into particle and quantum physics will result in new technology that will allow us to instantly transmit digital data and small amounts of matter to anywhere in the world or universe. Though people will not be able to teleport, many consumer products will be shipped around the world by teleportation; and the ancient wired and Wi-Fi networks of decades past will be replaced by the instant transfer of files and information from one computer to another. The same quantum transportation system will lead to the creation of data-gathering space probes, which will be deployed around the universe to learn, investigate, and search for other signs of life. The discovery of habitable planets, with or without existing life, will be considered as a possible solution to Earth's overcrowding and craving for extended life spans.

Social structures. With advancements in data security and transmission, and with the sharply increasing costs of travel, the central office will become a thing of the past for most white-collar jobs. In place of physical office space, virtual office buildings will allow remote employees to interact as 3D avatars while they are on the job. The ongoing trend to

Figure 8.36 A breakthrough in quantum physics may allow us to instantly shuttle rovers and probes to distant parts of the galaxy in search of habitable planets.

speak a local language plus English has proceeded to the point where now the world speaks English, unless conversing with old people; individual languages are gradually becoming absorbed into a single, global language. Rapid advances in technology and unstoppable global communication will constantly collide with national customs and laws; in order to remain as separate nations while being globally competitive, governments will participate in the creation of limited bodies who will oversee and regulate global technical advances and data transmission. For the foreseeable future, this will continue to create much tension between nationalists and globalists in every country, as people struggle to stay connected both with a global computer society as well as their cultural roots and identity.

Will any of these possibilities come to pass in the near future? They may indeed, or there may be surprises that send our technology and society in new directions. But forward progress depends not just on scientists and entrepreneurs. Scientific discoveries and human advancement are at their best only when the human condition and political climate are willing and able to support the new developments. Computers can file our taxes and run an international stock exchange, but they cannot prevent deep, global economic problems or a social backlash against scientific inquiry and research.

Computers are merely calculating tools that help us create what we imagine. It is up to each of us to use our tools wisely and to work whenever possible toward promoting a society that can use technology of all kinds to improve and advance rather than repress and regress. In an open and nurturing environment, the future of computers and humanity has very few limits.

Fact Check

1. What major future product is being researched in the robotics industry? create a single, unified solution is known as
   a. The creation of an adaptable multi-purpose companion robot
   b. The development of a computer that follows you from room to room
   c. An oven that will hand you food on a plate when it is ready
2. Cleverbot is an example of a chatterbot, which is
   a. a robotic squirrel
   b. a program that imitates human conversation
   c. a sophisticated humanoid robot that is programmed to deliver television news

- Emerging technology is a term describing the development of major new ways to use computers and other technologies. Converging technology refers to the process of different types of existing technology with similar characteristics or goals, merging together to create a single device or process that encompasses the originally separate ancestors. Smart phones can be used both as an example of emerging technology because they are rapidly evolving and are making major changes to our world; and as converging technology because they represent the combination of cell phones, music players, digital cameras, and PDAs, all of which originally existed as separate, standalone devices.

- Pervasive or ubiquitous computing involves integrating computer technology into buildings, clothing, and other objects, allowing the computers to perform their designated functions without the user's awareness of their existence.

- Augmented reality systems blend computer output with real-life information in order to enhance that information. Virtual reality systems replace real life sensory information with digital alternatives, allowing the user to see and participate in an environment that is artificially created.

- Emerging technologies are helping people measure and understand the impact that we are having on the planet's ecosystem, as well as helping us to model possible ways to mitigate the negative aspects of that impact. For individual users, emerging technologies are helping to manage increasing amounts of information in our lives; monitor and manage cars and appliances for trouble; and assist in the creation of new types of products that do everything, from keeping our pants stain-free to replacing human tissue that has been damaged by injury.

- Emerging technologies create tremendous legal pressure for governments around the world because advances in technology happen so frequently and so rapidly that they outpace the processes in place to regulate that technology.

- People can use technological tools both for good and to harm others. Hackers can destroy data and release sensitive information that harms the lives and livelihood of others. Cyberbullies can use social networks to ostracize and cause endless misery for their school peers. Sitting behind a screen makes it much easier to be cruel and aggressive when discussing current events with others; and positive feedback received by such commenters may encourage them and others to increase that activity. Mobile computing tools make it easy to track people's movements and whereabouts, providing fertile opportunities for stalkers and intrusive governments to track people against their will.

- The future of computing, as with any technology, is extremely difficult to predict. It is likely that advances will continue in computer, molecular, and quantum sciences, producing advances in cures for disease; significantly faster and more powerful computers; advances and simplifications in our ability to manage and control our personal data online; and improved ways to generate and store electricity.

Key Terms

augmented reality, p. 360
avatars, p. 361
biotechnology, p. 357

Chatterbot, p. 373
cognitive science, p. 357
emerging technology, p. 357

immersive, p. 361
information technology, p. 357
nanotechnology, p. 357

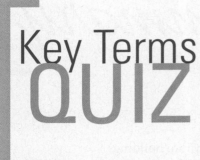

Key Terms QUIZ

1. People in 3D online games use game-generated figures called _____ to represent them.

2. _____ describes the development of major new ways to use computers and other technologies.

3. Adding statistics displays or a shimmering aura around a ball to a sports broadcast are examples of _____ technology.

4. In a _____ system, real-life sights, sounds, and other sensory input are replaced by computer-created substitutes.

5. Posting comments to online forums that are designed specifically to make others upset or angry is an activity known as _____.

6. _____ or _____ can be used to control the lighting in a room or house, as computers sense what is needed and make adjustments without user intervention.

7. A _____ is a kind of artificial intelligence program that simulates human conversation.

8. _____ occurs when multiple separate, parallel designs or devices are merged into a single device that incorporates the features of the separate units.

9. A virtual reality system may use gloves or a body suit to create _____, where the user's tactile sense is manipulated by computer input.

10. _____ is a product of nanotechnology, consisting of sub-millimeter-sized particles that are actually tiny sensors.

Review QUESTIONS

1. Explain the difference between emerging and converging technology. Give an example of each.

2. Explain the concept of pervasive or ubiquitous computing, and describe a scenario where pervasive computing might be used.

3. Define augmented reality and virtual reality, and use an example for each to illustrate how they can be used.

4. Explain tactical and narrative immersion, and how they can be used as part of a virtual reality system.

5. Provide an example of how green computing is reducing, reusing, and recycling to reduce environmental impact.

6. List three ways that mobile technology has advanced a political cause or aided people in distress.

7. Describe four areas where the legal system is struggling to keep up with emerging technologies.

8. Explain why legal jurisdiction causes problems for controlling and regulating computing technology.

9. Briefly explain why it is difficult to accurately predict the future of technology or our society.

10. List four breakthroughs or technologies of your own—not ones in this lesson—that you think will be present 50 years from now.

1. Find the latest news for ways that nanotechnology is being used to advance regenerative medicine, which creates ways to replace or regenerate human cells in order to repair wounds and make human organs function normally. Power up your favorite search engine, go to the News category, and search for current events related to "nanotechnology regenerative medicine." Browse stories until you find one that is interesting; take notes on the development so you can share it in class.

2. Learn more about ASIMO, Honda's ongoing project to create a humanoid, multi-purpose robot. Visit the ASIMO home page at http://world.honda.com/ASIMO/ and browse the latest news, and read descriptions of the technology used by the robot to operate. You can also visit YouTube and search on "ASIMO," and retrieve many video clips of the robot's activity, including an occasional less-than-stellar moment. Think of the various functions and actions that the robot can perform, and be prepared to briefly explain what you find most interesting or intriguing about the project.

As part of a growing marketing and media company, you and two co-workers have been chosen to create a pervasive computing solution for your company's suite of offices. Your office area is in a high-rise building, taking up the corner of one floor. It consists of a large conference room in the corner, six window offices on either side of the conference room for management and the creative directors, and a big bullpen area to house workstations for a dozen creative staff and the receptionist. Your task is to create environmental and lighting controls for the office in a way that is fun and at times responsive to staff and customer requests. For this exercise, unlike in the real world, you will have an unlimited budget.

You must work with two of your classmates to create the system's design. First, discuss the overall plan. You must create a way to monitor the lights and temperature in the company area. Since this is a marketing and media company, you should consider that everyone from the CEO to prospective customers may be open to interesting or artistic effects along with simple, pragmatic controls. You may want to consider controlling music, colored lighting, or other interesting effects. You may also, if desired, separate the areas of the office and assign different behaviors in each.

Sketch out a basic floor plan, and brainstorm some of the ways you could implement pervasive controls in this kind of creative environment. Then, list the tasks to be accomplished, and divide them evenly between team members. Working separately from that point, each team member should sketch or describe their contribution to the overall plan, showing how and where controls will be placed, and what they will do. Don't worry about whether ideas for sensors, controls, and communication are actually available as products.

As directed by your instructor, meet in class and compare how your pervasive system has come together. Be prepared as a team to explain to the class your overall design and the steps you took to accomplish it.

[*Chapter* LABS]

1. Learn more about the da Vinci Surgical System. Visit the Intuitive Surgical Web site at http://www.intuitivesurgical.com. Read through the marketing materials in the Products section of the site, and explore other areas of the site if you'd like. You can also check YouTube for promotional videos and the news section of your favorite search engine for reviews, stories, and opinions about the system. As you explore, consider and note down your opinions for the following questions, and be prepared to discuss your answers in class.

   a. Think of the surgeon and how they would normally position themselves to operate on the patient. How does the da Vinci system change how they work? What would be positive and negative aspects of those changes?

   b. How steep do you think a surgeon's learning curve would be to make the transition to a robotic system?

   c. Do you think it would be difficult to switch back and forth from robotic to manual surgery? If so, would that require a hospital to have separate robotic specialist surgeons on staff?

   d. If you found news stories related to this system, were those stories primarily supportive or critical? Briefly highlight the opinions you found.

2. Compare and contrast Cleverbot with ELIZA, one of its ancestors. ELIZA is an early, natural-language processor that was written in the 1960s. There are a number of ELIZA implementations on the Web. You can either find one at http://psych.fullerton.edu/mbirnbaum/psych101/Eliza.htm, or you can use a search engine; if you must search, use the phrase "Rogerian ELIZA" to narrow your results.

   a. Run the ELIZA program and have a few conversations with it. Note down as you converse how long ELIZA is able to seem real and carry on a genuine conversation. Also note whether ELIZA becomes repetitive, or simply ceases to answer in a genuine way, when the program fails to emulate a real conversation.

   b. Now, visit Cleverbot at http://cleverbot.com. Go through the same exercise, noting the same information as you did for ELIZA.

   c. When you are done, compare the two programs. Did one seem more genuine and believable than the other? If they both failed to stay consistently relevant, which one seemed to get off track more quickly? What kind of responses made it seem more real, and less real, during the conversations? Be prepared to discuss your findings in class.

3. Investigate the current state of cell phone privacy issues. From your favorite search engine, use the News section and search for the phrase "cell phone privacy." Note what issues are being reported, if any, regarding device tracking and call monitoring. Read through some of the news stories, and pick three that you find relevant. Note the parts of the stories that you find important. Are you pleased or unhappy with the activities being reported in these stories? In each case, be prepared to discuss the story and your opinions of it with the class.

[*Think* AND DISCUSS]

1. Often, new technology developers have scheduling constraints that require them to release a product before every feature and design nuance is in place. Sometimes, developers must choose whether to concentrate on adding new features or to emphasize aspects of a product that make it easier to use. Imagine that you were designing a new generation of smart phone and had to make a similar choice. Would you choose to pack the phone full of new features, or would you concentrate on making it easier to use? Explain your choice; if possible, use examples of what you would add, leave out, and why.

2. Web 2.0 represents the idea that users should see information that has been tailored to their needs. Whether for search engine results, shopping sites, or in a social networking program, the user's past activity and expressions of preference are ideally used to select information that closely matches what the user wants to see. How can you verify that your needs are the ones being favored, rather than those of the data provider? For example, how will you know if the list of restaurants you requested represents your preferences as opposed to the advertising premiums paid to the search or review company? How can you tell that all of your friends' "like" selections on Web pages and products are being impartially used as opposed to being selectively applied according to the social network's favorite pages or products? Would you want a way to "un-2.0" certain kinds of information so you have unfiltered access to data, and if so, when would you want to take that kind of action?

[*Fact Check* ANSWERS]

8A:

LO8.1 Computing in Your Field

1: a. providing the doctor with a way to deliver prescription requests to an on-site pharmacy.

2: b. ordering new computer parts online from the store's suppliers.

LO8.2 Telecommuting

1: c. a self-assessment of strengths and weaknesses, to determine whether a decision to work alone and independently is likely to succeed.

2: a. the information in the notebook will always be available, even if the electronic hardware fails.

LO8.3 Emerging Careers

1: b. flexibility and adaptability.

2: c. pay attention to the field as you study, making changes to your goals or education if needed as the technology changes.

LO8.4 Advancements in Computing and Technology

1: a. technological convergence.

2: b. computer equipment that senses temperature and moisture in a nursery, and autonomously controls temperature and plant watering as needed.

3: b. replaces real-life content with computer-generated imagery and feedback.

LO8.5 Impact of Emerging Technologies

1: b. providing services and information tailored specifically for each user.

2: c. police and government agencies track and monitor your movements without some kind of prior legal process and authorization.

LO8.6 What's Next?

1: a. The creation of an adaptable multi-purpose companion robot.

2: b. a program that imitates human conversation.

HISTORY OF COMPUTERS

1837

Charles Babbage first describes plans for his **Analytical Engine**, a mechanical, programmable computer that relies on punched cards for input and includes output concepts such as a printer and a curve plotter. Though Babbage will work on the idea for the rest of his life, his computer design—advanced even compared with some of the first computers of the 20th century—will never be fully created, an unfortunate result of a lack of funding and political support.

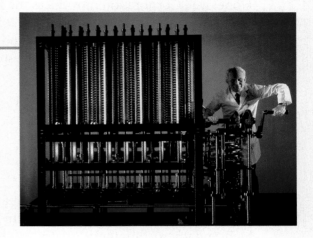

1944

The Colossus Mark 1, designed by the British to break German encrypted messages during World War II, is put into operation, establishing itself as the first programmable, digital electronic computer.

1946

ENIAC, the first general-purpose programmable electronic computer, is unveiled and put into operation, two and a half years after the start of its construction. Other than shutdowns for maintenance, ENIAC remains in active operation until 1955.

1951

The first commercial computer produced in the United States, UNIVAC I, is delivered to the U.S. Census Bureau.

1965

Honeywell Corporation introduces the **H316 "Kitchen Computer,"** the first home computer. It is offered in the Neiman Marcus catalog for $10,600 and includes a two-week programming course for the price. Despite the advertisements, no record of any sales exists.

1970

Ken Thompson and Dennis Ritchie create the UNIX operating system at Bell Labs. UNIX will become the dominant operating system for critical applications on servers, workstations, and high-end microcomputers.

1971

In 1971, Dr. Ted Hoff puts together all the elements of a computer processor on a single silicon chip slightly larger than one square inch. The result of his efforts is the Intel 4004, the world's first commercially available microprocessor. The chip is a four-bit computer containing 2,300 transistors (invented in 1948) that can perform 60,000 instructions per second. Designed for use in a calculator, it sells for $200. Intel sells more than 100,000 calculators based on the 4004 chip. Almost overnight, the chip finds thousands of applications, paving the way for today's computer-oriented world and for the mass production of computer chips now containing millions of transistors. Steve Wozniak and Bill Fernandez create a computer from chips rejected by local semiconductor companies. The computer is called the Cream Soda Computer because its creators drank Cragmont cream soda during its construction.

1972

Dennis Ritchie and Brian Kernighan create the C programming language at Bell Labs. The UNIX operating system is rewritten in C. C becomes one of the most popular programming languages for software development. **5.25-inch floppy diskettes** are introduced, providing a portable way to store and move data from machine to machine.

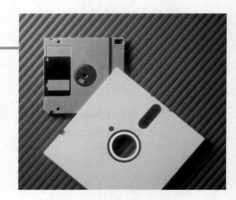

1973

IBM introduces new mass storage devices: the eight-inch, two-sided floppy disk that can hold 400 kilobytes of data and the Winchester eight-inch, four-platter hard drive, which can hold an amazing 70 megabytes.

Bob Metcalfe, working at Xerox PARC, creates Ethernet, a methodology to connect computers.

1974

Intel announces the 8080 chip, a two-megahertz, eight-bit microprocessor that can access 64 kilobytes of memory using a two-byte addressing structure. One chip contains more than 6,000 transistors and can perform 640,000 instructions per second.

Motorola introduces the 6800 microprocessor, another eight-bit processor. It is used primarily in industrial and automotive devices. It will become the chip of choice for Apple computers, sparking a long-running battle between fans of Intel and Motorola chips.

1975

One of the first commercially successful microcomputers, the **Altair 880**, is also one of the first machines to be called a "personal computer." It has 64 kilobytes of memory and an open 100-line bus structure. It sells for $397 in kit form or $439 assembled. The name "Altair" was suggested by the 12-year-old daughter of the publisher of *Popular Electronics* because Altair was the destination that evening for the *Enterprise*, the *Star Trek* space ship.

Two young college students, Paul Allen and Bill Gates, unveil the BASIC language interpreter for the Altair computer. During summer vacation, the pair formed a company called Microsoft, which eventually grows into one of the largest software companies in the world.

1976

Steve Wozniak and Steve Jobs build the **Apple I** computer. It is less powerful than the Altair but also less expensive and less complicated. Users must connect their own keyboard and video display, and they have the option of mounting the computer's motherboard in any container they choose—whether a metal case, a wooden box, or a briefcase. Jobs and Wozniak form the Apple Computer Company together on April Fool's Day, naming the company after their favorite snack food.

1977

The **Apple II** computer is unveiled. It comes already assembled in a case, with a built-in keyboard. Users must plug in their own TVs for monitors. Fully assembled microcomputers hit the general market, with Radio Shack, Commodore, and Apple all selling models. Sales are slow because neither businesses nor the general public know exactly what to do with these new machines.

Datapoint Corporation announces Attached Resource Computing Network (ARCnet), the first commercial LAN technology intended for use with microcomputer applications.

1978

Intel releases the 8086 microprocessor, a 16-bit chip that sets a new standard for power, capacity, and speed in microprocessors.

Epson announces the MX-80 dot-matrix printer, coupling high performance with a relatively low price. (Epson from Japan set up operations in the United States in 1975 as Epson America, becoming one of the first of many foreign companies to contribute to the growth of the PC industry. Up until this point, it has been U.S. companies only. According to Epson, the company gained 60 percent of the dot-matrix printer market with the MX-80.)

1979

Intel introduces the 8088 microprocessor, featuring 16-bit internal architecture and an eight-bit external bus.

Motorola introduces the 68000 chip; it contains 68,000 transistors, hence the name. It will be used in early Macintosh computers.

Software Arts releases **VisiCalc**, the first commercial spreadsheet program for personal computers. VisiCalc is generally credited as being the program that paved the way for the personal computer in the business world.

Bob Metcalf, the developer of Ethernet, forms 3Com Corp. to develop Ethernet-based networking products. Ethernet eventually evolves into the world's most widely used network system.

MicroPro International introduces WordStar, the first commercially successful word-processing program for IBM-compatible microcomputers.

1980

IBM chooses Microsoft to provide the operating system for its upcoming PC. Microsoft purchases a program developed by Seattle Computer Products called Q-DOS (for Quick and Dirty Operating System) and modifies it to run on IBM hardware.

Bell Laboratories invents the Bellmac-32, the first single-chip microprocessor with 32-bit internal architecture and a 32-bit data bus.

Lotus Development Corporation unveils the Lotus 1-2-3 integrated spreadsheet program, combining spreadsheet, graphics, and database features in one package.

1981

Adam Osborne creates the world's first "portable" computer, the **Osborne 1**. It weighs about 22 pounds, has two 5.25-inch floppy drives, 64 kilobytes of RAM, and a five-inch monitor but no hard drive. It is based on the z80 processor, runs the CP/M operating system, and sells for $1,795. The Osborne 1 comes with WordStar (a word-processing application) and SuperCalc (a spreadsheet application). It is a huge success.

IBM introduces the IBM-PC, with a 4.77-megahertz Intel 8088 CPU, 16 kilobytes of memory, a keyboard, a monitor, one or two 5.25-inch floppy drives, and a price tag of $2,495.

Hayes Microcomputer Products introduces the SmartModem 300, which quickly becomes the industry standard.

Xerox unveils the Xerox Star computer. Its high price eventually dooms the computer to commercial failure, but its features inspire a whole new direction in computer design. Its little box on wheels allows the user to interact with objects on the screen, making it the first commercial computer to provide a mouse and graphical user interface.

1982

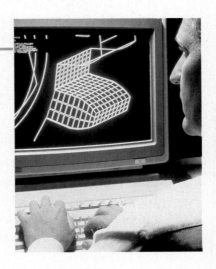

Intel releases the 80286, a 16-bit microprocessor.

Sun Microsystems is formed, and the company begins shipping the Sun-1 workstation.

AutoCAD, a program for designing 2D and 3D objects, is released. AutoCAD will go on to revolutionize the fields of architecture and engineering.

Work begins on the development of TCP/IP. The term *Internet* is used for the first time to describe the worldwide network of networks that is emerging from the ARPANET.

1983

Time magazine features the computer as the 1982 "Machine of the Year," acknowledging the computer's new role in society.

Apple introduces the Lisa, a computer with a purely graphical operating system and a mouse. The industry is excited, but Lisa's $10,000 price tag discourages buyers.

IBM unveils the IBM-PC XT, essentially a PC with a hard disk and more memory. The XT can store programs and data on its built-in 10-megabyte hard disk.

The first version of the C++ programming language is developed, allowing programs to be written in reusable independent pieces, called objects.

The **Compaq Portable** computer is released, the first successful 100 percent PC-compatible clone. (The term *clone* refers to any PC based on the same architecture as the one used in IBM's personal computers.) Despite its hefty 28 pounds, it becomes one of the first computers to be lugged through airports.

1984

Adobe Systems releases its PostScript system, allowing printers to produce crisp print in several typefaces, as well as elaborate graphic images.

Richard Stallman leaves MIT to start the GNU (GNU's Not Unix) free software project. This project will grow, adding thousands of programs to the library of free (open-source, available under a special license) software. This movement is supported by the Free Software Foundation, an alternative to expensive, closed-source software.

Apple introduces the "user-friendly" Macintosh microcomputer, which features a graphical interface.

IBM ships the IBM-PC AT, a six-megahertz computer using the Intel 80286 processor, which sets the standard for personal computers running DOS.

IBM introduces its Token Ring networking system. Reliable and redundant, it can send packets at four megabytes per second; several years later, it quadruples that rate. Several years after that, Token Ring's popularity fades, replaced by new standards and designs in Ethernet.

Satellite Software International introduces the WordPerfect word-processing program.

1985

Intel releases the 80386 processor (also called the 386), a 32-bit processor that can address more than 4 billion bytes of memory and performs 10 times faster than the 80286.

Aldus releases PageMaker for the Macintosh, the first desktop publishing software for microcomputers. Coupled with Apple's LaserWriter printer and Adobe's PostScript system, PageMaker ushers in the era of desktop publishing.

Microsoft announces the Windows 1.0 operating environment, featuring the first graphical user interface for PCs to match many of the interface elements found the previous year on the Macintosh.

Hewlett-Packard introduces the LaserJet laser printer, featuring a resolution of 300 dots per inch.

1986

IBM delivers the PC Convertible, IBM's first laptop computer and the first Intel-based computer with a 3.5-inch floppy disk drive.

Microsoft sells its first public stock for $21 per share, raising $61 million in the initial public offering.

The First International Conference on **CD-ROM** technology is held in Seattle, hosted by Microsoft. Compact discs are seen as the storage medium of the future for computer users.

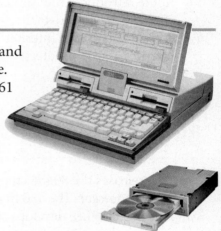

1987

IBM unveils the new PS/2 line of computers, featuring a 20-megahertz 80386 processor at its top end. This product line includes the MicroChannel bus but is not a great success because consumers do not want to replace industry-standard peripherals with alternatives that work only with the PS/2.

IBM introduces its **Video Graphics Array (VGA) monitor** offering 256 colors at 320 × 200 resolution, and 16 colors at 640 × 480.

The Macintosh II computer, aimed at the desktop publishing market, is introduced by Apple Computer. It features an SVGA monitor.

Apple Computer introduces HyperCard, a programming language for the Macintosh, which uses the metaphor of a stack of index cards to represent a program—a kind of visual programming language. HyperCard allows linking across different parts of a program or across different programs; this concept will lead to the development of hypertext markup language (HTML).

Motorola unveils its 68030 microprocessor.

Novell introduces its network operating system, called NetWare.

1988

IBM and Microsoft ship OS/2 1.0, the first multitasking desktop operating system. Its high price, a steep learning curve, and incompatibility with existing PCs contribute to its lack of market share.

Apple Computer files the single biggest lawsuit in the computer industry against Microsoft and Hewlett-Packard, claiming copyright infringement of its operating system and graphical user interface.

Hewlett-Packard introduces the first popular inkjet printer, the HP Deskjet.

Steve Jobs's new company, NeXT, Inc., unveils the NeXT computer, featuring a 25-megahertz Motorola 68030 processor. The NeXT is the first computer to use object-oriented programming in its operating system and an optical drive rather than a floppy drive.

Apple introduces the Apple CD SC, a CD-ROM storage device allowing access to up to 650 megabytes of data.

A virus called the "Internet Worm" is released on the Internet, disabling about 10 percent of all Internet host computers.

1989

Intel releases the 80486 chip (also called the 486), the world's first million-transistor microprocessor. The 486 integrates a 386 CPU and math coprocessor onto the same chip.

Tim Berners-Lee develops software around the hypertext concept, enabling users to click on a word or phrase in a document and jump either to another location within the document or to another file. This software provides the foundation for the development of the World Wide Web and is the basis for the first Web browsers.

The World Wide Web is created at CERN, the European Particle Physics Laboratory in Geneva, Switzerland, for use by scientific researchers.

Microsoft's Word for Windows introduction begins the Microsoft Office suite adoption by millions of users. Previously, Word for DOS had been the second-highest-selling word processing package behind WordPerfect.

1990

Microsoft releases **Windows 3.0**, shipping 1 million copies in four months.

A multimedia PC specification setting the minimum hardware requirements for sound and graphics components of a PC is announced at the Microsoft Multimedia Developers' Conference.

The National Science Foundation Network (NSFNET) replaces ARPANET as the backbone of the Internet.

Motorola announces its 32-bit microprocessor, the 68040, incorporating 1.2 million transistors.

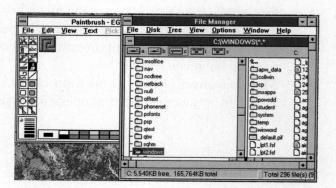

1991

Linus Torvalds releases the source code for Linux 0.01 (a clone of UNIX for the 80386 personal computer) on the Internet. It quickly becomes the base operating system of the open-source movement. Linux will grow to become one of the most widely used open-source PC operating systems.

Apple Computer launches the PowerBook series of battery-powered portable computers.

Apple, IBM, and Motorola sign a cooperative agreement to design and produce RISC-based chips, integrate the Mac OS into IBM's enterprise systems, produce a new object-oriented operating system, and develop common multimedia standards. The result is the PowerPC microprocessor.

A fully working Difference Engine mechanical computer, based on Charles Babbage's 1849 design, is completed by the London Science Museum.

1992

With an estimated 25 million users, the Internet becomes the world's largest electronic mail network.

IBM introduces its **ThinkPad** laptop computer.

In Apple Computer's five-year copyright infringement lawsuit, Judge Vaughn Walker rules in favor of defendants Microsoft and Hewlett-Packard, finding that the graphical user interface in dispute is not covered under Apple's copyrights.

Microsoft ships the Windows 3.1 operating environment, including improved memory management and TrueType fonts.

1993

Mosaic, a point-and-click graphical Web browser, is developed at the National Center for Supercomputing Applications (NCSA), making the Internet accessible to those outside the scientific community.

Intel, mixing elements of its 486 design with new processes, features, and technology, delivers the long-awaited Pentium processor. It offers a 64-bit data path and more than 3.1 million transistors.

Apple Computer expands its entire product line, adding the Macintosh Color Classic, Macintosh LC III, Macintosh Centris 610 and 650, Macintosh Quadra 800, and the Powerbooks 165c and 180c.

Apple introduces the Newton MessagePad at the Macworld convention, selling 50,000 units in the first 10 weeks.

Microsoft ships the Windows NT operating system.

IBM ships its first RISC-based RS/6000 workstation, featuring the PowerPC 601 chip developed jointly by Motorola, Apple, and IBM.

1994

Apple introduces the Power Macintosh line of microcomputers based on the PowerPC chip. This line introduces RISC to the desktop market. RISC was previously available only on high-end workstations.

Netscape Communications releases the Netscape Navigator program, a World Wide Web browser based on the Mosaic standard but with more advanced features.

Online service providers CompuServe, **America Online**, and Prodigy add Internet access to their services.

After 2 million Pentium-based PCs have hit the market, a flaw in the chip's floating-point unit is found by Dr. Thomas Nicely. His report is made public on CompuServe.

Red Hat Linux is introduced and quickly becomes the most commonly used version of Linux.

1995

Intel releases the Pentium Pro microprocessor.

Motorola releases the PowerPC 604 chip, developed jointly with Apple and IBM.

Microsoft releases its Windows 95 operating system with a massive marketing campaign, including primetime TV commercials. Seven million copies are sold the first month, with sales reaching 26 million by year's end.

Netscape Communications captures more than 80 percent of the World Wide Web browser market, going from a start-up company to a $2.9 billion company in one year.

A group of developers at Sun Microsystems create the Java development language. Because it enables programmers to develop applications that will run on any platform, Java is seen as the future language of operating systems, applications, and the World Wide Web.

Power Computing ships the first-ever Macintosh clones, the Power 100 series with a PowerPC 601 processor.

eBay, the premier online auction house, is formed.

1996

Intel announces the 200-megahertz Pentium processor.

U.S. Robotics releases the **PalmPilot**, a personal digital assistant that quickly gains enormous popularity because of its rich features and ease of use.

Microsoft adds Internet connection capability to its Windows 95 operating system.

Several vendors introduce Virtual Reality Modeling Language (VRML) authoring tools that provide simple interfaces and drag-and-drop editing features to create three-dimensional worlds with color, texture, video, and sound on the Web.

The U.S. Congress enacts the Communications Decency Act as part of the Telecommunications Act of 1996. The act mandates fines of up to $100,000 and prison terms for transmission of any "comment, request, suggestion, proposal, image or other communication which is obscene, lewd, lascivious, filthy, or indecent" over the Internet. The day the law is passed, millions of Web page backgrounds turn black in protest. The law is immediately challenged on constitutional grounds, ultimately deemed unconstitutional, and repealed.

Sun Microsystems introduces the Sun Ultra workstation that includes a 64-bit processor.

1997

Intel announces MMX technology, which increases the multimedia capabilities of a microprocessor. Also, Intel announces the Pentium II microprocessor. It has speeds of up to 333 megahertz and introduces a new design in packaging, the Single Edge Contact (SEC) cartridge. It has more than 7.5 million transistors.

AMD and Cyrix step up efforts to compete with Intel for the $1,000-and-less PC market. Their competing processors are used by PC makers such as Dell, Compaq, Gateway, and even IBM.

The U.S. Justice Department files an antitrust lawsuit against Microsoft, charging the company with anticompetitive behavior for forcing PC makers to bundle its Internet Explorer Web browser with Windows 95.

Netscape Communications and Microsoft release new versions of their Web browsers. Netscape's Communicator 4 and Microsoft's Internet Explorer 4 provide a full suite of Internet tools, including Web browser, newsreader, HTML editor, conferencing program, and e-mail application.

Digital video/versatile disc (DVD) technology is introduced. Capable of storing computer, audio, and video data, a single DVD can hold an entire movie. DVD is seen as the storage technology for the future, ultimately replacing standard CD-ROM technology in PC and home entertainment systems.

1998

Microsoft releases the Windows 98 operating system. Seen mainly as an upgrade to Windows 95, Windows 98 is more reliable and less susceptible to crashes. It also offers improved Internet-related features, including a built-in copy of the Internet Explorer Web browser.

Netscape announces that it will post the source code to the Navigator 5.0 Web browser on the Internet. This is a major step in the open-source software movement.

The Department of Justice expands its actions against Microsoft, attempting to block the release of Windows 98 unless Microsoft agrees to remove the Internet Explorer browser from the operating system. Microsoft fights back, and a lengthy trial begins in federal court, as the government attempts to prove that Microsoft is trying to hold back competitors such as Netscape.

Intel releases two new versions of its popular Pentium II chip. The Pentium II Celeron offers slower performance than the standard PII but is aimed at the $1,000-and-less PC market, which quickly embraces this chip. At the high end, the Pentium II Xeon is designed for use in high-performance workstations and server systems, and it is priced accordingly. Both chips boost Intel's market share, reaching deeper into more vertical markets.

Apple Computer releases the colorful **iMac**, an all-in-one system geared to a youthful market. The small, lightweight system features the new G3 processor, which outperforms Pentium II–based PCs in many respects. The iMac uses only USB connections, forcing many users to purchase adapters for system peripherals, and the computer does not include a floppy disk drive.

In response to concerns that the rapidly growing Internet will soon exhaust all available IP addresses, the new Internet Protocol, version 6 (IPv6), draft standard is released by the Internet Engineering Task Force. Despite the concerns, at the time of the new protocol's 10-year anniversary, IPv6 will be used by approximately 1 percent of the Internet hosts around the world.

1999

Intel unveils the Pentium III processor, which features 9.5 million transistors. Although the Pentium III's performance is not vastly superior to that of the Pentium II, it features enhancements that take greater advantage of graphically rich applications and Web sites. A more powerful version of the chip (named Xeon) is also released, for use in higher-end workstations and network server systems.

With its Athlon microprocessor, Advanced Micro Devices finally releases a Pentium-class chip that outperforms the Pentium III processor. The advance is seen as a boon for the lower-price computer market, which relies heavily on chips from Intel's competitors.

Sun Microsystems acquires Star Division Corporation and begins free distribution of StarOffice, a fully featured alternative to Microsoft Office and other proprietary office productivity products.

Apple Computer introduces updated versions of its popular iMac computer, including a laptop version, as well as the new G4 system, with performance rated at one gigaflop, meaning the system can perform more than 1 billion floating-point operations per second.

The world braces for January 1, 2000, as fears of the "Millennium Bug" come to a head. As airlines, government agencies, financial institutions, utilities, and PC owners scramble to make their systems "Y2K compliant," some people panic, afraid that basic services will cease operation when the year changes from 1999 to 2000.

Peter Merholz coins the term *blog,* a contraction of "Web log." In early 1999, there are already 50 recognized blog sites on the Web. By 2009, nearly 200 million people around the world will have started a blog, with millions producing regular content for a regular audience.

2000

Shortly after the New Year, computer experts and government officials around the world announce that no major damage resulted from the "millennium date change," when computer clocks rolled over from 1999 to 2000. Immediately, a global debate begins to rage: had the entire "Y2K bug" been a hoax created by the computer industry as a way to reap huge profits from people's fears? Industry leaders defend their approach to the Y2K issue, stating that years of planning and preventive measures had helped the world avoid a global computer-driven catastrophe that could have brought the planet's economy to a standstill.

Microsoft introduces Windows 2000. It is the biggest commercial software project ever attempted and one of the largest engineering projects of the century, involving 5,345 full-time participants, more than half of them engineers. The final product includes almost 30 million lines of code.

Advanced Micro Devices (AMD) announces the shipment of a one-gigahertz version of the Athlon processor, which will be used in PCs manufactured by Compaq and Gateway. It is the first one-gigahertz processor to be commercially available to the consumer PC market. Within days, Intel announces the release of a one-gigahertz version of the Pentium III processor.

In April, U.S. District Judge Thomas Penfield Jackson rules that Microsoft is guilty of taking advantage of its monopoly in operating systems to hurt competitors and leverage better deals with its business partners. Soon after the finding, the Department of Justice recommends that the judge break Microsoft into two separate companies: one focused solely on operating systems, the other focused solely on application development. Microsoft quickly counters by offering to change a number of its business practices. The judge rules to divide the software giant into two companies.

IBM announces that it will begin selling computers running the Linux operating system. As with other Linux vendors, the IBM version of Linux will be open source.

2001

Microsoft releases the Windows XP operating system, with versions for home computers and business desktops. The XP version of Microsoft Office also is unveiled.

After blaming digital music pirates for lost revenue, the Recording Industry Association of America (RIAA) files lawsuits against purveyors of MP3 technology—most notably Napster, an online service that enables users to share MP3-format files freely across the Internet. The suits effectively shut down Napster but do not stop individuals and other file-sharing services from exchanging music, text, and other files.

Apple introduces OS X, an operating system for Macintosh computers that is based on BSD (Berkeley Software Distribution) Unix with a beautiful graphical interface. It is an immediate success.

Several versions of recordable DVD discs and drives hit the market. Users instantly adopt the devices to store digitized home movies, data, and software. Even though movie pirates soon begin copying and distributing movies on DVD, most users simply find the large capacity discs a wonderful storage and backup medium.

Apple introduces the iPod, the premier music player with a 5-gigabyte internal hard disk that will store 1,000 CD-quality songs.

2002

The wireless networking boom continues with an emphasis on enabling handheld computers and telephones to access the Internet via wireless connections. Products such as digital two-way pagers, wireless phones, and combination telephone/PDAs sell at unprecedented levels.

XML (eXtensible Markup Language) and Web-based applications take center stage in many businesses. Microsoft releases Windows XP Server Edition and the .NET Framework.

OpenOffice.org announces the release of OpenOffice.org 1.0, a free, full-featured suite of productivity applications compatible with the file formats used by Microsoft Office and many other office suites. An open-source alternative to expensive application suites, OpenOffice.org runs under Windows, Solaris, Linux, the Mac OS, and other operating systems.

2003

The National Center for Supercomputing Applications announces that **Mike Showerman** and **Craig Steffen** have created a supercomputer based on 70 Sony PlayStation 2 gaming systems. The supercomputer cost about $50,000 to build, uses the Linux operating system and a Hewlett Packard high-speed switch, and can perform 6.5 billion mathematical operations per second.

The SQL Slammer worm, one of a continuous parade of malware programs, causes substantial service interruptions and slowdowns across the Internet.

Microsoft releases Office 2003, the latest in the Office suite series.

Intel and AMD release 64-bit processors targeted for the home computer market.

Apple introduces the Power Macintosh G5, a 64-bit processor.

In a continuing attempt to control file sharing, the Recording Industry Association of America begins suing individuals who share files.

Apple opens an online music store, iTunes, offering more than 200,000 titles at $0.99 each.

Wi-Fi (Wireless Fidelity) or 802.11b/g comes to the consumer market, with hot spots springing up both in home networking and in some commercial locations such as coffee shops.

2004

By March, Apple's iTunes store has sold 50 million songs.

The MyDoom malware program achieves (and still holds) the record as the fastest-spreading e-mail worm.

Google announces the availability of its Gmail free e-mail service.

The first version of the Firefox Web browser is released. It quickly becomes a popular and free alternative to Microsoft's Internet Explorer.

IBM announces plans to sell off its computing division to Lenovo Group.

Social networking site Facebook is launched as a limited project to create social connections among college students.

2005

Microsoft announces plans to release its next version of Windows, Windows Vista. (The actual first release to the general public will not occur until a year and a half later.)

Intel and AMD both release their first dual-core microprocessor for desktop PCs, continuing their ongoing struggle for dominance in the CPU marketplace.

The video-hosting service YouTube begins operating. Less than a year after opening to the public, tens of thousands of videos are being added every day, and tens of millions of people are watching them.

Bluetooth-enabled devices allow sharing of files, text, data, images, and music across a wide range of personal devices, allowing users to play tunes from an iPod, on a cell phone, or as background on a PDA.

IBM announces that it will no longer sell or support its OS/2 operating system.

2006

Intel releases the first quad-core microprocessor for the PC market, the Core 2 Extreme QX6700. Several months later, AMD follows through with its own first, the quad-core Phenom product line.

Blu-ray optical disc technology, which allows for up to 10 times more storage than a conventional DVD drive, is announced.

Wikipedia, the online collaborative encyclopedia, sees the creation of its millionth article.

Apple releases Boot Camp, a utility that allows users to install and execute Windows and Windows-based programs on Macintosh computers.

Skype, the VoIP phone company, crosses the 100-million-user threshold.

The Twitter service introduces microblogging. Initially, the service hosts a few hundred thousand short messages—called tweets—per calendar quarter.

2007

Apple debuts its new smart phone, the **iPhone**, selling its first units to customers who lined up in droves outside stores in anticipation. During the first five quarters after release, more than 6 million units are sold.

The Kindle, a portable electronic book reader, is released for sale by Amazon.com.

Google releases Android, an operating system designed for mobile platforms such as smart phones. By 2010, Android will be found on more than a third of the smart phone devices that are sold.

2008

The Blu-ray optical storage system triumphs over other competing high-capacity storage standards. HD DVD, its primary competitor advanced by Toshiba and NEC, throws in the towel to leave Blu-ray standing as the future standard for optical storage.

Cloud computing, which provides Internet services and resources to users on demand, explodes in popularity and moves from abstract concept to common buzzword.

Smart phones extend their popularity with the release of Apple's iPhone 3G the Google G1, and RIM's Blackberry Storm.

Netbooks arrive to fill a market niche for people seeking low-power, inexpensive computers to use for simple tasks and online access.

2009

Clearwire Corporation begins the rollout of broadband-speed wireless coverage in Portland, Oregon, using the 4G WiMax microwave network standard.

Microsoft releases the Windows 7 operating system, gaining favorable attention from both legacy Windows XP users and those who not too long ago had upgraded to Windows Vista.

Apple completes and distributes its own new latest operating system version, Snow Leopard.

Microsoft releases **Bing**, a search engine designed to compete with Google. Bing incorporates search results with other related information that it predicts may be of additional interest to searchers.

By year end, Apple's App Store has more than 100,000 applications available for download to its iPhone smart phone. Google, RIM, and Palm respond to the explosion of smart phone use and interest by launching their own stores to serve their operating system and hardware platforms. According to Apple, the iPhone apps that receive the highest ratings included SmackTalk, a voice-altering app that features an animated animal repeating what you say in real time; and Smule, music software that lets the user create music and play duets with other Smule players.

2010

Apple's tablet computer iPad is released to long lines of waiting customers; 3 million units are sold less than three months after release.

Facebook surpasses 500 million users around the globe. At the same time, Facebook is subjected to intense and increasing criticism of its privacy policies, and the company finds itself facing large groups of users who want to use the service without their personal details made freely available to searchers and advertisers.

Firefox, the free Web browser running on Windows, Mac OS X, and Linux, supports more than 70 different languages and is the browser of choice for nearly a quarter of Web users.

YouTube's video hosting continues to grow; users view billions of amateur and professionally crafted videos each month.

Twitter delivers approximately 65 million tweets from celebrities, politicians, businesses, and friends each day.

Though the Blu-ray optical storage standard stands unopposed as a new storage solution, its progress in replacing conventional DVD drives is slow, and its market share has risen to just over 10 percent.

Mobile communication has moved from novelty to commodity, with more than 4 billion people using mobile devices around the world. Mobile computing is rapidly following suit as cell phones increasingly take on the role of smart phone and companies introduce more varieties of tablets, notebooks, and netbooks.

2011

A study reveals that the average smart phone user now spends more time running apps than talking via the cell phone service.

The technology world mourns the loss of two major contributors: Steve Jobs, who founded Apple Computer and championed a vision of consumer-oriented computing; and Dennis Ritchie, who created the C programming language and with others, the UNIX operating system, putting in place a broad foundation for the development of computers and software around the world.

IBM unveils experimental semiconductors called cognitive chips, creating a new design with processing and memory functions integrated rather than separated. The chips are designed to emulate certain kinds of human brain activity that process patterns rather than linear streams of data.

Not to be outdone, researchers in California create a quantum computer, using molecular particles to represent the zero-or-one bits of a digital computer; but unlike a conventional computer, these quantum bits (called "qubits") can represent zero, one, or both at the same time, and large numbers of calculations can be performed simultaneously.

A

3-D modeling software special type of graphics software that lend realism and dimension to subjects   (p. 125)

Acceptable Use Policy (AUP) a type of document that attempts to encode and formalize the practice of ethical computer use for an institution or company   (p. 329)

Activate to tell the operating system that you want to use a resource that a shortcut or button represents by clicking on it   (p. 38)

Active matrix LCD screens that assign at least one transistor to each pixel, which are turned on and off individually   (p. 61)

Active-matrix organic LED (AMOLED) screens that use significantly less power than conventional LED screens   (p. 164)

Address a unique numeric identifier that each byte of a computer's RAM has   (p. 94)

Address books contact lists in e-mail programs and PIMs   (p. 119)

Adware malware used to display unwanted advertising on a computer   (p. 265)

All-in-one peripherals devices that combine printing, scanning, photocopying, and faxing capabilities; also called "multifunction peripherals"   (p. 67)

Alphanumeric keys the area of the keyboard that looks like a typewriter's keys and arranges numbers and letters the same way on almost every keyboard   (p. 43)

Always-on connection a connection that is always active, such as a cable modem or DSI   (p. 271)

American Standard Code for Information Interchange (ASCII) an eight-bit code that specifies characters for values from 0 to 127; by far the most commonly used character set in computers of all types   (p. 89)

Application software tells the computer how to accomplish specific tasks, such as word processing or drawing, for the user   (p. 27)

Arithmetic logic unit (ALU) performs processes involving comparing numbers or carrying out mathematical operations   (p. 92)

Arithmetic operations include addition, subtraction, multiplication, and division   (p. 93)

ARPANET the seeds of the Internet developed in 1969 by the Advanced Research Projects Agency of the U.S. Department of Defense—a large computer network with multiple paths that transferred data through telephone lines   (p. 180)

Asynchronous transfer mode (ATM) a protocol designed by the telecommunications industry as a more efficient way to send voice, video, and computer data over a single network   (p. 299)

Attenuation the loss of intensity and clarity of the data signal being transmitted   (p. 293)

Auction sites allow sellers to auction new and used goods, provide an avenue for selling unusual services, and allow buyers to bid on and purchase these goods and services—all online   (p. 242)

Augmented reality the process of computers providing enhancements to our environment   (p. 360)

Automatic payments once the customer creates an online account and provides required account information, companies can automatically deduct monthly bills from the customer's bank account   (p. 243)

Avatars human character representations in online games such as Second Life   (p. 361)

B

Backbones central network structures that several telecommunications companies built after NSFnet was created   (p. 181)

Backup utility helps you copy large groups of files from your hard disk to another storage medium   (p. 100)

Backward compatible designed to work with most or all of the program sthat were created for the old version   (p. 94)

Band printer an impact printer that features a rotating band embossed with alphanumeric characters   (p. 68)

Bandwidth the amount of data over time that the media can carry, typically measured in either megabits per second (Mbps) or gigabits per second (Gbps)   (p. 293)

Banner ads thin rectangular advertising boxes commonly placed across the top of a Web page   (p. 244)

Bar codes patterns of printed bars that appear on product packages to identify the product   (p. 49)

Bar code reader a device that emits a beam of light—frequently a laser beam—that is reflected by the bar code image in order to identify the product labeled by the bar code   (p. 49)

Biometric scanners analyze physical patterns in humans, such as the fingerprint scanner   (p. 50)

Biotechnology an application of biology that uses living organisms to manufacture new products   (p. 357)

Bit a single binary unit in a computer   (p. 88)

Bitmap a grid whose cells are filled with one or more colors that makes up graphics files   (p. 120)

BitTorrent one of the most popular and effective methods for sharing pirated software, movies, and other large packages; a protocol that links dozens or hundreds of users together to cooperatively and simultaneously contribute small pieces of the complete file to the copier   (p. 324)

Black hat SEO creates structures on Web sites designed to exploit search engine preferences or weaknesses; the unethical side of search engine optimization   (p. 248)

Block a contiguous group of characters, words, lines, sentences, or paragraphs in your document that you mark for editing or formatting   (p. 110)

Blu-ray disc the latest advance in optical storage technology, named after the blue-spectrum laser that drives uses and able to store more data than DVDs   (p. 26)

Bluetooth wireless protocol that provides short-distance radio communication between devices; an accessory to cell phones and smart phones   (p. 165)

Boot sector contains a program that runs when you first start the computer as well as information that the operating system needs to access data on the disk   (p. 98)

Booting the startup process in the boot sector where a program determines whether the disk has the basic components necessary to run the operating system successfully, and then begins loading the operating system from the disk   (p. 98)

Botnets massive networks of zombies that can spread new Trojan horse infections and e-mail spam, and can conduct carefully orchestrated network attacks at large, popular Web sites in attempts to shut them down   (p. 265)

Bridge a device that connects two LANs or two segments of the same LAN; looks at the information in each packet header and forwards data traveling from one LAN to another   (p. 296)

Broadband any data connection that can transmit data faster than is possible through a standard dial-up connection using a modem, by using a wider band of frequencies than those used to carry the human voice   (p. 299)

Buddy list a list of other users with whom you would like to chat   (p. 186)

Bus the electronic path in a computer that is used to transfer data between components   (p. 90)

Bus topology arranges the network nodes in a series, linking one node to the next via a single cable   (p. 294)

Business-to-business (B2B) transactions takes place between companies, and consumers are not involved; account for most of the money spent online   (p. 243)

Byte the amount of memory it takes to store a single character, such as a letter or numeral   (p. 24)

C

Cache a smaller, faster memory subsystem than in the main RAM in a computer; usually located physically closer to the part of the computer that uses it   (p. 91)

Cards circuit boards that are used to provide a specific ability (ie. sound, video) in the computer   (p. 23)

Carpal tunnel syndrome one type of repetitive stress injury that is common among computer users that injures the wrists and/or hands due to using a keyboard for long periods of time   (p. 53)

Cathode ray tube (CRT) a type of monitor that used to come with most desktop computers; they are relatively inexpensive and their pictures are bright and sharp, but they are heavy, bulky, and energy-inefficient   (p. 60)

CD-Recordable (CD-R) allows you to create your own CDs, but data on these cannot be erased or reused   (p. 25)

CD-ReWritable (CD-RW) allows you to write and erase data multiple times on the same disk   (p. 25)

CD-ROM drive the most common type of optical storage device recently surpassed by the use of DVD drives   (p. 25)

Cell addresses unique identifiers of cells in a spreadsheet defined by the column letter and the row number   (p. 112)

Cell pointer indicates the active cell in a spreadsheet by making the cell's borders look bold   (p. 112)

Cells (in a battery) the sections in the battery that hold power to be distributed   (p. 159)

Cells (in a spreadsheet program) the intersection of any column and row in a spreadsheet   (p. 112)

Central processing unit (CPU) the main processor for the computer that organizes and carries out instructions that come from either the user or the software; like the brain of the computer   (p. 23)

Character formatting settings that control the attributes of individual text characters such as fonts, font size, and type style   (p. 111)

Chat communicate in real time using software   (p. 184)

Chatterbot a program that simulates conversation with human participants   (p. 373)

Circuit board a thin, rigid piece of plastic or other material onto which a computer's electronic parts and subsystems are mounted   (p. 22)

Click to move the pointer to an item on the screen, then press and quickly release the primary mouse button once   (p. 46)

Clip art generic art in either bitmat or vector format that is provided in many software programs to enhance digital documents   (p. 122)

Clipboard a temporary holding space in the computer's memory for data that is being copied or moved   (p. 85)

CMYK printers Color inkjet printers that produce their palette of output colors from four color tanks: cyan, magenta, yellow and black   (p. 66)

Co-working a central workplace that provides a desk, phone, and copier access; meeting rooms; and a community feeling, all for a daily or monthly fee   (p. 208)

Coaxial cable a cable with two conductors—a single wire in the center of the cable and a wire mesh shield that surrounds the first wire—with an insulator between; its advantage is that it is less susceptible to signal interference than a twisted-pair cable and it allows for more distance between the devices being connected   (p. 293)

Cognitive science the study of the processes of the mind, in part to seek ways to artificially reproduce them   (p. 357)

Color monitor can display between 16 and 16 million colors   (p. 60)

Commercial software any software program that requires or requests payment   (p. 106)

Communications devices connect one computer to another; usually are hardware devices—either a modem or network interface cards (NICs)   (p. 25)

Compact discs (CDs) a type of optical storage identical to audio CDs   (p. 25)

CompactFlash (CF) one of the two major formats for memory (SSD) cards currently in use for portable devices (p. 26)

Compatible when a program can be used in any file format (p. 121)

Computer a machine that accepts some kind of input, performs actions and calculations according to a set of instructions, and returns the result of its calculations (p. 4)

Computer system includes hardware, software, data, and the user (p. 20)

Computer-aided design (CAD) computerized version of the hand-drafting process that used to be done on a drafting table; also called computer-aided drafting or computer-aided drawing (p. 123)

Computer-generated imaging (CGI) an outgrowth of the 3-D explosion that allows users to create animation more quickly than ever and to create photorealistic scenes (p. 125)

Contact managers see "personal information manager (PIM)" (p. 119)

Contact-management software see "personal information manager (PIM)" (p. 119)

Contrast ratio measures how close the monitor can get to perfect black and white; the bigger the ratio, the better (p. 62)

Control unit manages all of the computer's resources (p. 92)

Convergence the process where devices or applications with very different initial purposes become more and more alike as they share features (p. 158)

Convertible tablets contain a keyboard attached by a special hinge, allowing the tablet screen to be rotated and flipped up (p. 162)

Cookies a special kind of data packet that stores information in small files on your system; short for "magic cookies" (p. 278)

Copy command makes a copy of data (rather than deleting it from the original document) and stores it on the Clipboard (p. 85)

Copyright a legal concept that grants rights and control to the owner of any published work (p. 318)

Countermeasure any step you take to ward off a threat—to protect yourself, your data, or your computer from harm (p. 260)

Credit report a document that lists all of your financial accounts that can be a source of credit or that you can use for making purchases or for other transactions (p. 274)

Cursor a mark on the screen indicating where the characters you type will be entered; also known as "insertion point" (p. 43)

Cursor-movement keys allow users to move around the screen without using a mouse (p. 43)

Customer relationship management (CRM) software that includes PIM-style features like contact data for customers and meeting calendars, and adds a host of other features for managing ongoing customer relationships (p. 119)

Cut command removes data from a document and places it on the Clipboard (p. 85)

Cybercrime the use of a computer to carry out any conventional criminal act (p. 267)

Cyberterrorism a new form of warfare that attacks the critical infrastructure systems of a nation through the technology it uses (p. 267)

D

Data individual facts or pieces of information specific to the task at hand or a given context (p. 20)

Data area the part of the disk that remains free after the boot sector, the file allocation table, and the root folder have been created; this is where data and program files are actually stored on the disk (p. 98)

Data mining a business-intelligence-gathering process that every large organization, from banks to grocery stores, employs to sift through computerized data (p. 274)

Data scrubbing process of safeguarding against erroneous or duplicate data by checking what is entered and placing restrictions on how the data is entered; also called data validation (p. 309)

Database management system (DBMS) software that allows users to create tables and relationships, fill them with data, and answer complex questions; for example, Microsoft Access (p. 116)

Decision support system (DSS) a special application that collects and reports certain types of data, thus helping managers make better decisions (p. 304)

Deselect clicking elsewhere in a document to not select text anymore (p. 111)

Desktop computer a personal computer designed to site on (or more typically under) a desk or table (p. 6)

Desktop metaphor the background of the GUI that shows graphical tools and that stores users' work (p. 38)

Digital camera portable, handheld devices that capture still images electronically (p. 52)

Digital light processing (DLP) a display method that uses a special chip on which a grid of thousands of microscopic mirrors are mounted (p. 70)

Digital pen see "stylus" (p. 7)

Digital video disc (DVD) can be used for permanent, removable storage or viewing movies (p. 25)

Directory see "folder" (p. 98)

Disk drive the complete device that holds a disk (p. 25)

Distributed denial of service (DDoS) attack a carefully orchestrated attack that attempts to shut down or block access to a Web site (p. 265)

Docking station allows a device such as a notebook or smart phone to hook up to other devices, such as full-sized keyboards, large monitors, and local networks (p. 6)

Docking station allows the notebook computer to hook up to devices and services like full-size keyboards, large monitors, and local networks (p. 6)

Document a file that a user can open and use (p. 29)

Document area where users can view documents using software; also called "document window" (p. 110)

Document formatting includes the size of the page, its orientation, and headers or footers   (p. 111)

Document window see "document area"   (p. 110)

Dongle a hardware device that plugs into one of the ports of a computer   (p. 321)

Dot matrix printers impact printers commonly used in workplaces where physical impact with the paper is important   (p. 66)

Dot pitch the distance between the like-colored phosphor dots of adjacent pixels   (p. 62)

Dots per inch (dpi) a measurement of image quality; the higher the dpi, the higher the image quality   (p. 69)

Double-clicking to move the pointer to an item on the screen, then press and quickly release the primary mouse button twice in rapid succession   (p. 46)

Drag and drop see "dragging"   (p. 46)

Drag-and-drop editing see "dragging"   (p. 46)

Dragging positioning the mouse over an item, pressing the primary mouse button, and holding it down as you move the mouse; also known as "drag and drop" or "drag-and-drop editing"   (p. 46)

Draw programs vector-based graphics programs that are well suited for work when accuracy and flexibility are as important as coloring and special effects   (p. 123)

Drivers programs that allow the operating system and other programs to active and use—that is, "drive"—the hardware device; one type of driver would be a program for working with printers   (p. 87)

Dumpster diving a low-tech cybercrime where thieves go through garbage cans, dumpsters, or trash bins to obtain canceled checks, credit card and utility statements, and bank account information that someone has thrown out   (p. 273)

Dye-sublimation (dye-sub) printers produce realistic quality and color for photo images for desktop publishers and graphic artists; a ribbon containing panels of color is moved across a focused heat source capable of subtle temperature variations   (p. 68)

E

E-mail a system for exchanging messages through a computer network; the only Internet service used more frequently than the Web   (p. 184)

Editing changing an existing document   (p. 110)

Edutainment programs that are both educational and entertaining   (p. 194)

Electroluminescent displays (ELDs) similar to LCD monitors but use a phosphorescent film held between two sheets of glass   (p. 62)

Electronic commerce (e-commerce) doing business online   (p. 240)

Electronic Communications Privacy Act (1986) prevents unlawful access to voice communications by wire; originally regulated electronic wiretaps used by the government to protect citizens from unreasonable search and seizure   (p. 276)

Electronic data interchange (EDI) a standardized electronic transfer of information between companies over networks   (p. 310)

Electronic mail see "e-mail"   (p. 184)

Emerging technology any new way of using computers that is separate from what is established   (p. 357)

Empathy the ability to recognize, understand, and share the feelings of others   (p. 316)

Emulator software program designed to recreate the exact environment of the older program   (p. 95)

End-user piracy when a legitimate purchaser of a program makes unauthorized copies of media   (p. 321)

Enterprise license grants installation and use privileges on any computer within the company   (p. 320)

Ergonomics the study of the physical relationship between people and their tools   (p. 53)

Ethernet network that was once the most commonly used; older versions (10Base-5 and 10Base-2) used coaxial cables; the most popular version (10Base-T) achieved transmission speeds up to 10 Mbps and used star topology with either twisted-pair or fiber-optic cables   (p. 298)

Executing see "running"   (p. 27)

Execution cycle occurs after the instruction cycle; consists of executing and storing: during executing, the CPU carries out the instructions in order, and during storing, the CPU stores the results of an instruction in memory   (p. 93)

Expert system a type of information system that performs analytical tasks traditionally done by a human, using sequences of questions to ask and actions to take based on the responses to those questions   (p. 305)

Extended ASCII an eight-bit code that specifies the characters for values from 128 to 255 with the first 40 symbols representing pronunciation and special punctuation and the remaining symbols as graphic symbols   (p. 89)

External bus connects external devices, such as hard drives, keyboards, mice, video cards, printers, and so on, to the CPU; also called the expansion bus   (p. 90)

Extranet an external version of the Internet used by organizations that require users to have a valid username and password to view   (p. 292)

Eyestrain fatigue of the eyes caused by focusing on the same point for too long; one of the most frequently reported health problems associated with computers   (p. 63)

F

Fair Credit Reporting Act (1970) personal information assembled by credit reporting agencies must be accurate, fair, and private   (p. 277)

Fair use copyright law that provides for a limited set of circumstances where others can use copyrighted material without first obtaining permission   (p. 319)

Fast Ethernet network that uses same media and topology as Ethernet, but different NICs are used to achieve speeds of up to 100 Mbps; also called 100Base-T   (p. 298)

Fault-tolerant systems that are able to continue their operation even when problems are present   (p. 307)

Fiber-optic cable a thin strand of glass that transmits pulsating beams of light rather than electric current; immune to electromagnetic interference that is a problem for copper wire, extremely fast, able to carry an enormous number of messages simultaneously, and very secure transmission medium   (p. 293)

File a set of data that has been grouped together and given a name   (p. 29)

File allocation table (FAT) a file system used by older versions of Windows   (p. 98)

File format a standardized method of encoding data for storage that tell the program what kind of data is contained in the file and how the data is organized   (p. 121)

File system a logical method for managing the storage of data on a disk's surface   (p. 98)

File transfer protocol (FTP) a collection of files, including data files and/or programs, housed on an FTP server; often called archives   (p. 186)

Financial Modernization Act of 1999 require companies to give consumers notice of their privacy and information-sharing practices; also called Gramm-Leach-Bliley   (p. 277)

Firewall hardware on an Internet connection that examine and block traffic coming from and going to the Internet   (p. 101)

FireWire see "IEEE 1394"   (p. 90)

Firmware software that is embedded on microchips and placed on the hardware device it controls, such as keyboards, hard drives, and memory cards; can be found inside and outside computers   (p. 27)

First-party cookies placed by the Web site you are visiting   (p. 280)

Flash drives small storage sticks that plug into USB ports; can be used to transfer files between computers or store files   (p. 26)

Flat-panel display a much lighter-weight and thinner alternative monitor   (p. 60)

Folder a tool for organizing files on a disk that can contain files or other folders, enabling users to create hierarchical systems; also called "directory"   (p. 98)

Following each user chooses a set of people from which they wish to receive messages on Twitter   (p. 234)

Font a named set of characters that have the same characteristics   (p. 111)

Force feedback the application of a motion to a controller in conjunction with a visual event   (p. 72)

Forgery the process of making copies that appear to be real and selling those copies to unsuspecting buyers as legitimate products   (p. 317)

Formatting the process of mapping a disk; also called "initializing"   (p. 97)

Formula bar where you can create and edit data and formulas in a worksheet   (p. 112)

Formulas special cell contents that perform calculations or logical tests using the values in other cells as input for their tasks   (p. 113)

Frames special resizable boxes for graphical elements   (p. 114)

Freedom of Information Act (1966) each individual can view and amend personal information kept about him or her by any governmental entity   (p. 276)

Freeware any software made available to the public for free   (p. 107)

Friends list a list of connected people on Facebook   (p. 229)

Function keys allow users to input commands without typing long strings of characters or navigating menus or dialog boxes; they are usually labeled F1, F2, and so on, and arranged in a row along the top of a keyboard   (p. 43)

G

Game controller an input device for a computer game   (p. 49)

Game pad a small, flat device with an array of buttons, triggers, and thumb-driven joysticks that enable the user to send complex commands to the game system using both hands   (p. 49)

Gateway a node on a network that serves as an entrance to another network; takes a packet from one type of network, reads its header, and then adds a second header that is understood by the second network; also handles the configuration and maintenance of various WAN or Internet addresses required to connect and relay information outside of the LAN   (p. 296)

Gigabit Ethernet a version of Ethernet that supports data transfer rates of one gigabit per second or more   (p. 298)

Gigabyte (GB) one billion bytes   (p. 24)

Graphical user interface (GUI) enables user to issue commands to the computer by using visual objects instead of typing names of commands in order to launch programs and make choices   (p. 38)

Grayscale monitor display varying intensities of gray against a white or off-white background and are essentially a type of monochrome monitor   (p. 60)

H

Hacker someone who uses a computer and network or Internet connection to intrude into another computer or system to perform an illegal act   (p. 267)

Hacking the practice of accessing computer systems in an unauthorized way   (p. 267)

Handheld personal computer, or **handheld PCs** computing devices small enough to fit in your hand   (p. 7)

Haptic feedback see "haptics"   (p. 72)

Haptics the communication of vibration, motion, or physical resistance to a user; also called "haptic feedback"   (p. 72)

Hardware the physical devices—both electronic and mechanical—that make up the computer   (p. 20)

Header the first part of the packet containing information—the node that sent the packet (the source) and the address of the node that will receive the packet (the destination)—that is needed by the network to determine where to send the packet   (p. 293)

Health informatics combines computer technology and healthcare disciplines to manage the acquisition and use of health-related information; involves designing databases, software, and specialized programming languages for automating tasks and managing data in the health care industry   (p. 351)

HFS+ file system used by Mac OS X, which supports a similar directory structure to Windows, but it provides a different method from NTFS for finding data within its directories, and it separates program data and visual element data   (p. 98)

High-Definition Multimedia Interface (HDMI) a port in many laptops that sends a signal to digital television   (p. 159)

Hijack to take over some or all control of a computer's functions   (p. 263)

Hot swap removing and replacing batteries while the computer is running and active   (p. 159)

Hub provides multiple ports for connecting nodes; receives a packet from one port and transmits the packet without modification to all other nodes to which the hub is connected   (p. 295)

Hyperlink see "hypertext link"   (p. 189)

Hypertext a special kind of text used for Web page documents that is able to respond to user input and link to other objects   (p. 189)

Hypertext link a word or picture users can click on to immediately jump to another location within the same document or to a different Web page   (p. 189)

Hypertext markup language (HTML) a formatting language that organizes hypertext and contains special text flags and instructions for browsers to interpret; these text flags—called tags—identify links to other documents, display information such as font types and colors, etc.   (p. 189)

HyperText Transfer Protocol (HTTP) a detailed standard of electronic communication defining an exact way that data is formatted and transferred back and forth between browser and server   (p. 189)

HyperText Transfer Protocol Secure (HTTPS) HTTP that has data encryption and Web site identity verification to the rules for transmitting data for added security that many online retailers use   (p. 189)

I

Icon a tiny picture representing an object   (p. 38)

Identity (ID) theft when someone impersonates you using your name, Social Security number, or other personal information to obtain documents or credit in your name   (p. 272)

IEEE 1394 a serial bus commonly known as FireWire and typically used to transfer video and audio data   (p. 90)

Image scanner convert any printed image into electronic form by shining light onto the image and sensing the intensity of the light's reflection at every point; also known as scanners   (p. 50)

Immersive creating a feeling within the user that the artificial environment or actions are in some way very real   (p. 361)

Impact printer creates an image by striking an inked ribbon against paper with some physical instrument such as metal pins or hammers   (p. 66)

Incompatible when a program cannot be used with or by other programs because they are not totally supported by other programs   (p. 121)

Inference engine a program that accepts information about the problem or question being analyzed and uses the knowledge base to select the most appropriate response or follow-up question   (p. 305)

Information processing cycle the series of steps the computer follows to receive data, process the data according to instructions from a program, display the resulting information to the user, and store the results   (p. 21)

Information system (IS) a complex system for acquiring, storing, organizing, using, and sharing data and information   (p. 301)

Information technology methods and tools for managing and distributing information   (p. 357)

Initializing see "formatting"   (p. 97)

Inkjet printers nonimpact printers that create an image directly on the paper by spraying ink through tiny nozzles   (p. 66)

Input/output (I/O) device a device that receives input and produces output the same way each time   (p. 9)

Insertion point see "cursor"   (p. 43)

Installed the program is written into the computer's permanent storage   (p. 27)

Instant messaging (IM) a type of chat software that restricts participation to specific users   (p. 186)

Instruction cycle consists of fetching and decoding: during fetching, the control unit retrieves a command or data from the computer's memory, and during decoding, the control unit breaks down the command into instructions that correspond to those in the CPU's instruction set   (p. 93)

Instruction set list all the operations that the CPU can perform   (p. 92)

Integrated pointing device two buttons that perform the same function as mouse buttons just beneath the spacebar and are pressed with the thumb; also known as a 3-D point stick   (p. 47)

Intellectual property the ideas, trade secrets, patents, and confidential operating practices of the company   (pp. 206, 318)

Interactive involving the user in a media by accepting and responding to input from the user   (p. 126)

Internal bus connects the CPU to memory modules and subsystems that reside directly in the motherboard; sometimes called the system bus   (p. 90)

Internet a network of networks—a global communications system that links together thousands of individual networks   (p. 180)

Internet piracy the use of the Web and Internet resources to host and distribute software copies to anyone who can gain access to the files   (p. 321)

Internet Relay Chat (IRC) one of the early methods used to chat   (p. 184)

Internetworking the process of connecting separate networks   (p. 181)

Interoperability the ability of each organization's information system to work with the other, sharing data and services   (p. 308)

Interrupts requests for attention by some part of the computer system   (p. 87)

Intranet an internal version of the Internet containing only the company's private information and limiting access to employees and selected contractors having ongoing business with the company   (p. 292)

IP address a unique set of numbers that identifies the router of the network   (p. 167)

K

Key a column uses its values to uniquely identify each record in the table in Microsoft Access   (p. 117)

Keyboarding the ability to enter text and numbers with skill and accuracy; also known as typing   (p. 43)

Keyboard logging password capture software that saves each key typed by the user on the keyboard; also called "keylogging"   (p. 269)

Keylogging see "keyboard logging"   (p. 269)

Kilobyte (KB) one thousand bytes   (p. 24)

Knowledge base a highly detailed database   (p. 305)

L

Labels text in worksheets that serve as names for data values   (p. 113)

Landscape mode using a horizontal display rather than a vertical one   (p. 164)

Lanes data pathways within a bus   (p. 91)

Laptop computer see "notebook computer"   (p. 6)

Laptop see "notebook computer"   (p. 6)

Laser printer nonimpact printer that relies on a laser to print   (p. 67)

Latency the delay between the request and the completed task   (p. 143)

LED monitor a new monitor design that uses liquid crystal design and is list by a grid of tiny electronic lights called light emitting diodes (LEDs); compared with LCD screens, a more consistent brightness can be achieved   (p. 61)

Like button a Facebook-generated link that tags an item with a user's approval   (p. 230)

Line printer special type of impact printer that works like a dot matrix printer but uses a special wide print head that can print an entire line of text with a single strike   (p. 68)

Liquid crystal display (LCD) most common type of flat-panel monitor that contains a light source and a screen of special crystals placed in the monitor between the user and the light source   (p. 61)

Local area network (LAN) a data communication system consisting of multiple devices such as computers and printers   (p. 292)

Lock disable a device's ability to be used and to connect to other networks   (p. 166)

Lockstep when all CPUs and attendant hardware execute the same instruction at the same time   (p. 307)

Logical operations include comparisons, such as determining whether one number is equal to, greater than, or less than another number   (p. 93)

M

Machine cycle the completed series of steps in an instruction in the CPU   (p. 93)

Magnetic disk the most common type of computer storage   (p. 25)

Mainframe computers large, powerful systems used in organizations such as insurance companies and banks, where many people frequently need to access the same data   (p. 9)

Malware a generic term to describe various kinds of software programs that are designed to harm a computer's data or operating system, or compromise the security of a computer; different types of malware include viruses, worms, Trojans, and adware   (p. 100)

Management information system (MIS) a set of software tools that enables managers to gather, organize, and evaluate information about a work group, department, or entire organization; summarizes vast amounts of business data into information useful to each type of manager   (p. 304)

Manufacturer piracy when a computer manufacturer installs un-authorized copies of programs onto their new computers for sale in order to make them more attractive to consumers   (p. 321)

Mechanical mouse contains a small rubber ball that protrudes from a hole in the bottom of the mouse's case and uses sensors attached to the ball to detect the speed and direction of the location; then the computer adjusts the location of the pointer on the screen accordingly   (p. 45)

Media the means used to link together a computer network's nodes   (p. 293)

Megabyte (MB) one million bytes   (p. 24)

Memory one or more sets of chips that store data and/or program instructions either temporarily or permanently   (p. 23)

Menu bar provides lists of commands and options for this specific program   (p. 40)

Mesh topology a cable runs from every computer to every other computer; the least-used and most expensive network topology, its advantage is that data can never fail to be delivered   (p. 294)

Microcode a series of basic directions that tell the CPU how to execute more complex operations   (p. 92)

Microcomputer see "personal computer" (p. 5)

Microprocessor a specialized chip that integrates several different processing functions into a single chip and functions as the CPU in a PC (p. 23)

Midrange computers see "minicomputers" (p. 9)

Minicomputers computers released in the 1960s that were relatively smaller than other computers of the day; also called "midrange computers" (p. 9)

Mirrored a system called RAID 1 where data is written to two or more disks simultaneously, providing a complete copy of all the information on multiple drives in the even one drive should fail (p. 307)

Mission-critical systems that must run without failure or with nearly instant recovery from failure; examples include systems for a major stock exchange or air defense system (p. 307)

Mobile computer a category of devices including the notebook PC; systems small enough to be carried by their user (p. 7)

Modem converts in both directions between digital data the computer understands and analog signals that are transmitted over telephone or cable television wires (p. 25)

Modifier keys SHIFT, ALT (Alternate), and CTRL (Control), which modify other keys' input in some way if you hold down the modifier key while pressing another key (p. 43)

Monochrome monitor display only one color (such as green, amber, or white) against a contrasting background, which is usually black (p. 60)

Motherboard the largest circuit board in a personal computer containing connectors and ports for hooking up all the other parts of a computer, from the CPU to the webcam on top of the monitor (p. 23)

Multi-user/multitasking operating system an operating system that allows multiple users to use programs that are simultaneously running on a single network server (a terminal server) (p. 84)

Multifunction peripherals see "all-in-one peripherals" (p. 67)

Multimedia using more than one type of medium at the same time (p. 126)

N

Nanotechnology the manipulation of matter and creating machines at the molecular scale (p. 357)

Narrative immersion the user closely identifies with the avatar or protagonist in a story (p. 361)

NBIC an acronym grouping together nanotechnology, biotechnology, information technology, and cognitive science (p. 357)

Netbooks small, compact computers with reduced processing power and often without extra devices such as DVD drives (p. 6)

Netiquette a concatenation of "Internet" and "etiquette" referring to the set of online behaviors that are considered polite and proper (p. 327)

Network a set of hardware, software, and media systems used to connect computers together, enabling them to communicate, exchange information, and share resources in real time (p. 290)

Network interface cards (NICs) digital-to-digital hardware components that allow communication and uniquely identify the computing device on the network (p. 25)

Network operating system allows computers to communicate and share files and device resources across a network while controlling network operations and overseeing the network's security (p. 27)

Network server a powerful, central computer with special software and equipment that enable it to function as the primary computer in the network (p. 8)

Network version when organizations connect users' computers to a network server, the copy of the application is stored on the server with a minimum number of supporting files copied to each user's PC (p. 291)

Networking the process of connecting to and sharing data between devices and locations (p. 5)

New Technology File System (NTFS) a newer file system used by current Windows versions that offers better security and overall performance (p. 98)

News feed a list of other users' posts on Facebook (p. 229)

Nodes the processing location that can be a PC or some other device such as a networked printer (p. 293)

Nonimpact printer use other means to create an image, applying ink to the page without physically striking a ribbon on the page (p. 66)

Nonvolatile memory that never loses its contents (p. 25)

Notebook computer approximately the size of a notebook and sized to easily fit inside a briefcase; also called "laptop" (p. 6)

NSFnet in the mid-1980s, the National Science Foundation created a new, higher-capacity network and connected it to ARPANET, establishing the Internet (p. 181)

Number system any regular structure for counting (p. 88)

Numeric keypad resembles a calculator's keypad and is usually located on the right side of the keyboard (p. 44)

O

Object Linking and Embedding data that is copied to and from the Clipboard retains a link to the original document so that a change in the original document also appears in the linked data; also called "OLE" (p. 85)

Off-the-shelf applications software that is available for purchase by anyone, not requiring custom design and development (p. 302)

Office automation system a type of information system that uses computers and/or networks to perform various operations—word processing, accounting, document management, and communications—to manage information efficiently (p. 302)

OLE see "Object Linking and Embedding" (p. 85)

One-step checkout an option to purchase the contents of your shopping cart simply by clicking on a button on the screen, bypassing the need to fill out and confirm shipping and payment options (p. 241)

Online banking customers can log in to bank Web sites, check rates and balances, and perform financial transactions online (p. 242)

Online payment companies pay for a product online and link to the customer's bank account or credit card as a way of protecting the bank account and credit card information; the largest is PayPal (p. 241)

Online shopping the process of buying a product or service through a Web site (p. 240)

Open-source software whose source code is available to users in editable formats (p. 107)

Operating system (OS) a software program that controls the system's hardware and that interacts with the user and application software, ensuring that the results of a program and user actions are displayed on the screen, printed, and so on (p. 38)

Opt-out option customers can choose to have companies not share their personal information with anyone else and/or not send them advertisements (p. 276)

Optical character recognition (OCR) software translates an image into text that you can edit (p. 50)

Optical mouse a non-mechanical device that uses a sensor and special image processor to track the motion of the mouse; then the computer adjusts the location of the pointer on the screen accordingly (p. 45)

Optical storage devices that use lasers to read data from or write data to the reflective surface of an optical disc (p. 25)

P

Packets pieces of a message broken down into small units by sending the PC and reassembled by the receiving PC (pp. 211, 293)

Pages per minute (ppm) measures printer speed (p. 69)

Paint programs bitmap-based graphics programs that allow users to "paint" and that range from the very simple to the very complex (p. 123)

Paper-white displays sometimes used by document designers such as desktop publishing specialists, newspaper or magazine compositors, and other persons who create high-quality printed documents (p. 62)

Paragraph any text that ends with a paragraph mark (p. 111)

Paragraph formatting includes settings applied to one or more entire paragraphs, such as line spacing, paragraph spacing, indents, alignment, tabs, borders, or shading (p. 111)

Parallel bus a bus that sends its information in parallel lines across multiple wires (p. 90)

Passive matrix LCD relies on transistors for each row and each column of pixels, thus creating a grid that defines the location of each pixel (p. 61)

Password capture passwords are detected as a user enters them (p. 269)

Password guessing a hacker tries to guess a user's password and keeps trying until he or she gets it right (p. 269)

Password sharing a form of sniffing where a victim simply discloses his or her password to a hacker (p. 269)

Paste command places data from the Clipboard onto a document (p. 85)

Pay-per-click payment model where advertisers pay for their ads only when a Web site visitor clicks on the ad to go to the advertiser's Web site (p. 244)

PC video camera enables users to transmit live, full-motion video images to a limited number of recipients on a network or the world on the Internet (p. 52)

PCI Express (PCIe) was created to replace the PCI bus because its data transfer design is more efficient and it offers scalability (p. 91)

Peer-to-peer (P2P) a transfer service that uses a distributed network that does not require a central server to manage files (p. 187)

Peripheral Component Interconnect (PCI) bus a type of bus designed by Intel to integrate various hardware devices into a computer (p. 91)

Persistent cookies stay on your system after your browsing is done (p. 280)

Personal computer (PC) computer that is meant to be used by only one person at a time; also called "microcomputer" (p. 5)

Personal digital assistant (PDA) handheld PCs with intuitive and shortcut-rich user interfaces with colorful displays (p. 7)

Personal information manager (PIM) software that is designed to keep track of many different kinds of contact information for many different people; also known as "contact managers" or "contact-management software" (p. 119)

Personal software license grants a single person the ability to use a program and may impose terms and conditions that limit the program's use (p. 320)

Personal VPN services that provide users with access to a VPN server that allows them to securely connect to the Internet for a monthly or annual fee (p. 212)

Pervasive computing see "ubiquitous computing" (p. 358)

Photo printers print photos for users and can use inkjet technology of dye-sublimation technology (p. 68)

Photo-editing programs allow users to edit images at the pixel level and control precisely how a picture will look (p. 123)

Photorealistic computer-generated images that look so realistic that they could be mistaken for a photograph of a real-life object (p. 125)

Pipelining the control unit begins a new cycle before the current cycle is completed, enabling newer microprocessors to execute more than two dozen instructions simultaneously; also known as pipeline processing   (p. 93)

Piracy acquiring copies of protected digital creations such as software, music, or writing   (p. 317)

Pixels tiny dots on a display screen, each with its own unique address that the computer uses to locate it and control its appearance   (p. 60)

Plain old telephone system (POTS) an alternative way to transmit data communications using the telephone system; may offer both analog and digital communication access (p. 298)

Plasma displays created by sandwiching a special gas between two sheets of glass   (p. 62)

Plotter a special kind of output device similar to a printer but used to print large-format images, such as construction drawings for architects; table (or mechanical) plotters use robotic arms and are being replaced with thermal, electrostatic, and inkjet plotters   (p. 68)

Podcasts radio broadcasts suitable for downloading to a portable music player; the term combines part of "iPod" and "broadcast"   (p. 191)

Pointer an on-screen object, usually an arrow, that is used to select text; access menus; and interact with programs, files, or data that appear on the screen   (p. 45)

Pointing the process of moving the pointer to a location on the screen with your mouse   (p. 45)

Pointing device allows users to interact with the computer; usually a mouse for PCs   (p. 45)

Points measurement of font's size in height   (p. 111)

Pop-up ad an online advertisement window that "pops up" to cover the content of the Web site, forcing the site visitor to view the ad   (p. 244)

Pop-up blockers utilities that intercept and deny requests to create pop-up windows while a user is surfing the Web (p. 244)

Port an interface socket on a personal computer through which other devices connect   (p. 42)

Portable computers self-contained units, with keyboard, monitor, and system unit combined   (p. 158)

Power failure when power is lost altogether, causing systems to shut down   (p. 260)

Power fluctuations cause the strength of your electrical service to rise or fall   (p. 260)

Power plan allows you to list various settings for the computer to use depending on whether it is on the battery or wall power   (p. 160)

Presentation a series of slides displayed in a specific order to an audience   (p. 113)

Presentation programs allow the user to design slides on colorful backgrounds and create presentations   (p. 113)

Primary e-mail account users set this up with your ISP as part of your Internet access package   (p. 280)

Print head creates shapes and alphanumeric characters in a printer; contains a cluster of short pins arranged in rows and columns   (p. 66)

Privacy Act of 1974 places universal restrictions on sharing information about you by federal agencies without your written consent   (p. 276)

Processing transforming raw data into useful information (p. 23)

Processors the computer components responsible for this procedure   (p. 23)

Profile a personal information layout page on a social networking site that users can customize   (p. 191)

Program any piece of software   (p. 20)

Protocol an agreed-upon message format for transmitting data between two devices that governs each LAN   (p. 297)

Public domain anyone can use part or all of a work without first obtaining permission from anyone after a copyright expires   (p. 319)

Public domain software software that is free to the public and in addition, the source code is free for anyone to use for any purpose   (p. 107)

Public records available to anyone who wants to view them, such as marriage licenses and divorce records   (p. 275)

Q

QR Code short for Quick Response; a new format for storing data visually that uses a square filled with dots and lines that can be read and interpreted by various optical scanners (pp. 49, 202)

Quad-core processor a high-end CPU with four cores that enables users to process many different tasks at once   (p. 142)

Queries information requests that a user makes to a database   (p. 117)

R

Random access memory (RAM) a set of chips mounted on a small circuit board that allows the computer to store and retrieve data and instructions very quickly; a volatile, nonpermanent form of memory that needs a constant supply of power to hold its data   (p. 23)

Read-only memory (ROM) permanent data storage for computer instructions and hardware information; a form of nonvolatile memory   (p. 24)

Read/write heads read data from the disk or write data onto the disk   (p. 25)

Real-time applications programs and hardware that respond instantly to input; frequently used in running medical diagnostics equipment, life-support systems, machinery, scientific instruments, and industrial systems   (p. 84)

Real-time operating system a very fast, relatively small operating system designed to respond to hardware and program requests almost instantly   (p. 84)

Record all of the values on each row associated with each other in a spreadsheet   (p. 117)

Redundant computers that have multiple hardware systems performing the same task at the same time   (p. 307)

Redundant array of independent disks (RAID) a storage system commonly found in PCs that links any number of disk drives (a disk array) so that they act as a single disk   (p. 307)

Refresh rate the number of times per second that the monitor draws its visible image   (p. 62)

Registry a special file that contains detailed information for the operating system about the locations and purposes of programs, files, and utilities   (p. 108)

Removable media can be separated from computers and are used both for easily transferring files from one computer to another and for creating portable sets of programs that can be run on different computers   (p. 147)

Repeater prevents attenuation when packets are traveling long distances by receiving each packet, ensuring that it is intact, and retransmitting it down the line toward the next node at full-signal strength   (p. 295)

Repetitive stress injury (RSI) ailments resulting from continually using the body in ways it was not designed to work   (p. 53)

Replicate copy   (p. 264)

Resolution the number of pixels that are displayed on the screen   (p. 62)

Response rate the amount of time in milliseconds that it takes for a pixel to change from black to white   (p. 62)

Ribbon a style of menu where options are displayed horizontally across the top of the work area   (p. 40)

Right to Financial Privacy Act of 1978 require companies to give consumers notice of their privacy and information-sharing practices   (p. 277)

Right-clicking pointing to an item on the screen and then pressing and releasing the right mouse button   (p. 46)

Ring topology connects the network's nodes in a circular chain with each node connected to the next   (p. 294)

Root folder the "master folder" on any disk   (p. 98)

Router a complex device that stores the routing information for networks; looks at each packet's header to determine where the packet should go, then determines the best route for the packet to take toward its destination   (pp. 167, 296)

Rulers show you the positions of text, tabs, margins, indents, and other elements on the page   (p. 110)

Running when a computer uses a particular program; also called "executing"   (p. 27)

S

SATA see "Serial ATA"   (p. 91)

Scalability the capability to provide increasing amounts of computing power, storage, and software, allowing organizations to buy affordable systems that meet their current computing needs and gradually increase their computing capability only as needed   (p. 308)

Scalable systems that address the need to grow computer systems by incrementally expanding as the need occurs   (p. 308)

Screen savers popular utilities that automatically appear when a keyboard or pointing device has not been used for a specified period of time in order to hide what would otherwise be displayed on the screen   (p. 101)

Script a special program that runs to place files in various folders on the hard drive as required by the software being installed   (p. 108)

Scroll bars allow users to view parts of the program or file that do not fit in the window   (p. 40)

Scrolling moving a list of information up and down   (p. 46)

Search engine optimization (SEO) the process of analyzing Web site contents and search results and determining the ideal configuration for a Web site that will raise its position in search results   (p. 247)

Search engines complex and sophisticated combinations of hardware and software that constantly crawl through the Web's contents to find new sites and information and to verify the contents of what was previously known   (p. 190)

Secondary e-mail account uses a free, Web-based e-mail service such as Gmail, Hotmail, or Yahoo   (p. 280)

Sectors smaller parts into which tracks are divided during the creation of a hard disk   (p. 97)

Secure Digital (SD) one of the two major formats for memory (SSD) cards currently in use for portable devices   (p. 26)

Select to choose text or images by dragging your mouse across it, clicking on it with your mouse, or by using keyboard combinations   (p. 110)

Serial ATA the current bus standard for connecting hard drives to the computer; also known as "SATA"   (p. 91)

Serial bus a bus that sends its information one bit at a time in series   (p. 90)

Service set identifier (SSID) identifies a wireless router to the nearby area   (p. 167)

Session cookies last only for your current browser session and usually act as helpers for navigating through the Web site   (p. 280)

Shareware software whose developers encourage users to share it with one another and to try out the software before purchasing, sometimes for a fee   (p. 106)

Shopping cart an electronic holding bin where customers can place items they want to purchase while they shop (p. 241)

Shortcut small object on the desktop representing links to resource on the PC or network (p. 38, 99)

Short-throw projector a projector designed to be used very close to the display area (p. 71)

Shoulder surfing watching someone enter personal identification information for a private transaction, such as an ATM (p. 272)

Single-user/multitasking operating system an operating system that allows a single user to perform two or more functions at once (p. 84)

Single-user/single-tasking operating system an operating system that allows a single user to perform just one task at a time (p. 84)

Site license an agreement to buy a single copy of a program and then pay the software developer a fee for the right to copy the application onto a specified number of computers (pp. 291, 320)

Skin formatting instructions for wiki sites that create a standard browser layout for displaying the information (p. 235)

Slides single-screen images that contain a combination of text, numbers, and graphics (such as charts, drawings, or photos) often on a colorful background (p. 113)

SMART Board a digital version of the analog whiteboard (p. 71)

Smart dust sub-millimeter sized particles that are actually tiny sensors that can be sprinkled on windowsills to warn of intruders (p. 359)

Smart phone a multi-function device that combines a personal digital assistant and a cell phone (p. 7)

Snagging listening in on a telephone conversation while the victim gives credit card or other personal information to a legitimate agent (p. 272)

Sniffing any of the various ways that hackers can steal or guess passwords (p. 269)

Social media software programs and utilities that make it simple for people to share common interests and information (p. 191)

Social networks Web sites that connect people directly together, provide users with a standard structure for Web page organization so it is easy for anyone to create a profile (p. 191)

Software as a service (SaaS) programs for users that are run on the service company's computers instead of the user's PC or mobile device; these programs use a standard PC program like a browser to display output and receive user commands and data, performing all the data storage and processing work on their own servers (p. 251)

Software a set of instructions that makes the computer perform tasks (p. 20)

Software suites packages of software programs that are very commonly that are sold together (p. 106)

Solid state drive (SSD) a memory subsystem that relies on special kinds of ROM to permanently store data (p. 26)

Sound card a circuit board that converts sound from analog to digital form, and vice versa, for recording or playback (p. 64)

Spam filtering functions on e-mail programs that place junk e-mail into a Junk Mail folder as it arrives (p. 281)

Speech recognition translating voice into text; also known as "voice recognition" (p. 51)

Spiders automated software programs that are run by search engine and other companies to constantly sift through, catalog, and sometimes store information that they find on the Web; also called "Web crawlers" (p. 325)

Spoofing an attempt to deceive a computer user or system by providing false information in some way (p. 279)

Spreadsheet a software tool for entering, calculating, manipulating, and analyzing sets of numbers (p. 111)

Spyware malware that reports activity on your computer to another party; can record individual keystrokes, Web usage, e-mail addresses, personal information, and other types of data (p. 265)

SSID Broadcast when a wireless router shows its SSID to the nearby area (p. 167)

Stand-alone program an application that performs only one type of task, such as a word processing program (p. 106)

Star topology connects all nodes to a hub through which they communicate; probably the most common topology (p. 294)

Start page a document on the Web that the user has selected as the first one to load upon being launched (p. 188)

Status bar displays information related to your position in the document, the page count, and the status of keyboard keys (p. 110)

Storage permanently holding data, even when the computer is turned off (p. 25)

Striping gives the user rapid access by spreading data across several disk; also called RAID 0 (p. 307)

Striping-with-parity a more sophisticated RAID configuration in which data is spread over multiple disks, providing the speed of striping with the safety of redundancy; most commonly implemented as RAID 5 (p. 307)

Stylus the special pen used to input information directly to a tablet PC; also called "digital pen" (p. 7)

Subscriber identity module (SIM) a card in a cell phone that identifies the user and subscription owner of the phone and is usually provided and configured by the company that provides the user with cellular service (p. 169)

Supercomputers the most powerful and physically some of the largest computers that can process huge amounts of data quickly (p. 9)

Surge suppressor an inexpensive product that guards its appliances against large power spikes or surges that may infrequently occur (p. 261)

Switch a packet-routing device, typically with multiple port connections, that is aware of the exact address or identity of all the nodes attached to it; determines the identity of each node, sends the packet directly and only to the correct destination; can handle multiple conversations between nodes at once and keep each packet flow conversation separate (p. 296)

System calls built-in instructions in computer programs that request services from the operating system (p. 85)

System software any program that controls the computer's hardware or can be used to maintain the computer in some way so it runs more efficiently (p. 27)

System unit the case that houses the computer's critical parts, such as its processing and storage devices (p. 6)

T

Tables two-dimensional row and column sheets that users of Microsoft Access use to build databases (p. 117)

Tablet PC the newest development in portable, full-featured computers offering all the functionality of a notebook but lighter (p. 7)

Tactical immersion the user believes that they can physically feel and alter things in the virtual world; virtual systems achieve this by using various types of technology— such as headgear providing sights and sounds; or gloves, boots, and clothing that detect user motion and provide haptic feedback—to replace the real environment's presence with digitally rendered information (p. 361)

Technological convergence the process of blending separate concepts to create a single, unified solution (p. 358)

Telecommuting practice of having employees work remotely (p. 205)

Telemedicine allows doctors to practice and advise in patient diagnosis and treatment from a remote location (p. 351)

Teleradiology X-rays and other internal body scans are collected in one facility and then sent anywhere in the world via computers and secure networks for analysis (p. 351)

Template a predesigned document that already has coordinating fonts, colors, a layout, and a background; presentation programs often provide dozens of built-in templates (p. 114)

Terabyte (TB) one trillion bytes (p. 24)

Terminal a device through which each user accesses the mainframe's resources (p. 9)

Terminal client software that allows each user's applications to run with their user session on the server separate from all other user sessions on a multi-user operating system (p. 85)

Terminal server a single network server connecting multiple users working on programs simultaneously (p. 85)

Terminator a special device attached at the cable's start and end points to stop network signals sot hey do not bounce back down the cable (p. 294)

Text boxes special resizable boxes for text (p. 114)

Text code a list of text characters and an associated number for each character (p. 89)

Thermal-wax printers are primarily used for presentation graphics and handouts; they use bold colors and have a low per-page cost for printouts (p. 68)

Thin-film transistor (TFT) technology that employs four transistors per pixel that is used in active matrix LCD (p. 61)

Third-party cookies come from a different Web site than the one you are viewing (p. 280)

Threat anything that can cause harm (p. 259)

Toner a powder composed of tiny particles of ink used in printers (p. 67)

Toolbars contain buttons that let you issue commands quickly (p. 40)

Topology the logical layout of the cables and devices that connect the nodes of the network (p. 294)

Touch screens Computer monitors that, along with displaying video output, accept input from the user via fingertip or stylus touch (p. 47)

Touchpad see "trackpad" (p. 47)

Trackball a pointing device that works like an upside-down mouse (p. 46)

Trackpad a stationary pointing device that many people find less tiring to use than a mouse or trackball; also called a "touchpad" (p. 47)

TrackPoint the name for the integrated pointing device on the Lenovo ThinkPad line of notebook computers (p. 47)

Tracks concentric rings on each side of the disk that a disk drive creates during formatting (p. 97)

Transaction a complete information operation; can be one-step events like adding a new piece of information to a database, or they can be more complex, requiring many steps (p. 302)

Transaction processing system (TPS) a system that handles the processing and tracking of transactions (p. 303)

Transistors tiny electronic switches that are in either an on or off state and that make up the CPU (p. 87)

Trojan horse a program that cannot self-replicate and must rely on other methods for delivery; also called "Trojan" (p. 265)

Trolling posting deliberately incendiary reactions to a post because they know it will produce a strong reaction; teaches other posters how to care less for the people with which they converse and how to take delight in causing distress for others   (p. 369)

Tunneling a method that VPNs employ where each piece of data (packet) from the sending computer is encapsulated within another packet before being sent over the Internet (p. 211)

Tweet a message sent on Twitter that all of a user's followers can read   (p. 234)

Twisted-pair cable consists of four pairs of wires; can be unshielded (UTP—unshielded twisted-pair wire) or shielded (STP—shielded twisted-pair wire)   (p. 293)

Type styles effects applied to characters such as boldface, underline, or italic   (p. 111)

U

Ubiquitous computing integrating computer and communication technology into the objects that make up our everyday environment, autonomously controlling and assisting with the maintenance of that environment; also known as "pervasive computing"   (p. 358)

Unicode Worldwide Character Standard character set that provides up to four bytes—32 bits—to represent each letter, number, or symbol; can represent more than 4 billion different characters or symbols and is compatible with ASCII codes   (p. 89)

Uniform resource locator (URL) a specific format used by hyperlinks on the Web to uniquely identify every single object on the Web   (p. 189)

Uninterruptable power supply units containing a battery backup system along with power delivery that is much more consistent than a simple surge protecting power strip (pp. 151, 261)

Universal Serial Bus (USB) a popular bus found on all modern computers and supported by a host of devices including keyboards, mice, webcams, flash drives, and digital cameras   (p. 91)

Unsecured a connection where anyone within range of the router can simply connect his or her mobile device and gain access   (p. 168)

USA Patriot Act extends the authority of law enforcement and intelligence agencies in monitoring private communications and access your personal information   (p. 276)

USB port a specific type of interface socket designed to accept any kind of input or output device—such as cameras, printers, and some keyboards and mice—that makes use of the USB connector   (p. 42)

User interface the on-screen elements with which a user interacts   (p. 38)

User session when a single user has a complete environment on a server with a multi-user operating system   (p. 85)

Users people who operate computers   (p. 21)

Utilities programs that enhance or extend the operating system's capabilities or offer new features not provided by the operating system itself   (p. 27, 100)

V

Value any number or text that is considered spreadsheet data, not a label; can be entered by the user or the result of a calculation that the spreadsheet has been directed to perform   (p. 113)

Vandalism making maliciously incorrect modifications to a wiki   (p. 235)

Vectors mathematical equations describing the size, shape, thickness, position, color, and fill of lines or closed graphical shapes   (p. 121)

Video capture card device that allows user to transmit images from other video devices, such as DVD players and camcorders, to the PC, and vice versa   (p. 52)

Video card contains videos on a computer; also called video controller or video adapter   (p. 63)

Viewing angle measures how far to the side a user can be before the picture fades or blurs   (p. 62)

Virtual office a work arrangement in which the company sets up minimal office services so employees can visit the space as needed for meetings with managers and colleagues (p. 206)

Virtual private network (VPN) allow organizations to connect to each other's extranets   (pp. 211, 307)

Virtual reality systems designed to replace our real environment with one that is computer-defined   (p. 360)

Virtual teams members are geographically dispersed and use technology to communicate and collaborate in real time (p. 204)

Virus software that is attached to a host, such as a file or e-mail message, and has the ability to replicate itself from one computer to another   (p. 264)

Voice over Internet Protocol (VoIP) translates analog voice signals into digital data and uses the Internet to transport the data; can connect to telephone networks and digital sources such as PCs   (pp. 165, 187)

Voice recognition see "speech recognition"   (p. 51)

Volatile memory that loses its contents when the computer is shut off   (p. 24)

Vulnerability a weakness—anything that has not been protected against threats, making it open to harm (p. 259)

W

Web 1.0 the state of the World Wide Web from its creation through the early 2000s; focused on providing information to users; short for "The Web, version 1.0"   (p. 183)

Web 2.0 the state of the World Wide Web from the mid-2000s into the short-term future; focused on user-generated content, sharing information, and social networking sites; short for "The Web, version 2.0"   (p. 183)

Web 3.0 the expected next phase of activity of the World Wide Web that will increasingly focus on user expression of preferences, interests, and activities; short for "The Web, version 3.0"   (p. 183)

Web bug a small image file that can be embedded in a Web page or an HTML-format e-mail message that can track user's online activities   (p. 278)

Web content management system (WCMS) a software service that provides storage, usually in a database, of the information to be displayed on a Web site   (p. 228)

Web crawlers see "spiders"   (p. 325)

Web pages documents for Web browsers that are used to distribute news, interactive educational services, product information, catalogs, live audio and video, and other kinds of information   (p. 188)

Web-based Distributed Authoring and Versioning see "WebDAV"   (p. 99)

Webcam a popular, inexpensive type of PC video camera that can sit on or near a computer so that users can capture images of themselves near the computer   (p. 52)

WebDAV a structure for managing access and changes to files stored on the Web that are created and modified by multiple users in different locations; stands for Web-Based Distributed Authoring and Versioning   (p. 99)

Whistleblowing process of pointing out a major internal problem, often an ethical one   (p. 332)

White box computers constructed by the store rather than by a major manufacturer   (p. 149)

White hat SEO the design and evolution of Web sites to create an ever-improving experience for visitors that search engines also favor; also known as ethical SEO   (p. 248)

Wi-Fi the most popular standard for wireless networking; also called "802.11"   (p. 299)

Wi-Fi Protected Access (WPA2) the encryption method that provides better protection than WEP; the router owner gives the router a passphrase to require network users to provide in order to log in   (p. 168)

Wide area network (WAN) the connection of two or more central computers or LANs, generally across a wide geographical area   (p. 292)

Wik software that collects, organizes, and updates information in a simple, standard way; the most popular example is Wikipedia   (p. 235)

Windows 7 Starter a reduced-feature version of the Windows 7 operating system that consumes less of the system's limited resources and lacks many of Windows 7's personalization features   (p. 161)

Wired Equivalent Privacy (WEP) an encryption method included in router setup to support old networks, but its encryption is fatally flawed and can be defeated in minutes   (p. 168)

Wireless access point (WAP) connects single or multiple PCs in the wireless environment   (p. 299)

Wireless hotspots public Internet access points   (p. 293)

Wireless networks use radio or infrared signals that travel through the air to transmit data   (p. 293)

Word processing program provides tools for creating all kinds of text-based documents; also called "word processor"   (p. 110)

Word processor see "word processing program"   (p. 110)

Workbook a place where you can collect related worksheets; also called a notebook in some programs   (p. 112)

Worksheet a sheet in a spreadsheet program   (p. 112)

Workstation a specialized, single-user computer that typically has more power and features than a standard desktop PC   (p. 6)

World Wide Web in 1989, researchers at CERN created a way to link documents stored in different locations on a single computer or on different computers on a network; also known as the Web or WWW   (p. 182)

Worldwide Interoperability for Microwave Access (WiMAX) a rapidly emerging telecommunications protocol that supports a data transfer rate competitive with other broadband methods and can provide wireless coverage across a much wider area than a Wi-Fi antenna   (p. 166)

Worm a program that self-replicates, is a fully contained program, and is not attached to a host file or service   (p. 264)

WYSIWYG (what you see is what you get) editors Web site construction programs that show you how a Web page actually looks while you build it; pronounced "whizzy-wig"   (p. 228)

Z

Zombies computers infected and compromised by malware and under external control, often without the computer owner's knowledge   (p. 265)

Chapter 7

Chapter 8

Appendix

INDEX

A

Acceptable Use Policy, 329–330
Access to Internet, 182
Accidents and hardware, 262
Activating shortcuts, 38
Active matrix LCD, 61
Active-matrix organic LED, 164
Active windows, 40
Address books, 119
Addresses, 94
Adobe
    Director, 127
    Dreamweaver, 228
Advanced Research Projects
    Agency (ARPA), 180
Advertising
    to cell phone customers, 211
    on Internet, 243–246
    targeted, 183–184, 244–245
Adware, 265
All-in-one peripherals, 67–68
Alphanumeric keys, 43
Altair 880 computer, 384
Always-on connections, 271
Alwil Avast, 266
Amazon.com, 241
Amazon Web Services, 253–254
AMD processors, 142
America Online, 391
Analog computers, 4
Analytical Engine, 382
Android operating system, 97, 398
Animation, 125
Anti-malware programs
    for cell phones, 210
    companies offering, 266
    description of, 100–101, 202
    e-commerce sites and, 245
Apple
    Apple I computer, 384
    Apple II computer, 385
    App Store, 203, 399
    iMac, 393
    iPad, 138, 163
    iPhone, 164, 398
    iTunes, 396
    Newton MessagePad, 164
    Safari browser, 188
Application software
    acquiring, 106–108
    categories of, 28
    description of, 27
    installing, 108, 110
    running in cloud, 250–252
Archives, 186–187
Arithmetic logic units, 92
Arithmetic operations, 93
ARPANET, 180–181, 386
Artificial intelligence (AI), 373–374
ASCII (American Standard Code for Information
    Interchange), 88–90
Asynchronous transfer mode (ATM), 299
Attenuation, 293
Auction sites, 242
Audio editing and production, 126
Audio input devices, 50–52
Augmented reality, 360
AutoCAD program, 386
Automated teller machine (ATM), 303
Automatic payments, 243
Autonomous acoustic recording devices, 65
Avatars, 361
AVGFree Anti-virus, 266
Awareness of mobile users, 200

B

Backbones, 181
Backing up data, 249, 254, 271–272
Backup utility, 100
Backward compatibility, 94–95
Band printers, 68–69
Bandwidth, 293, 294
Banking, online, 242–243
Banner ads, 244
Bar code readers, 49
Base 10 and Base 2, 89
Battery life, 159–160
Binary system, 88
Bing search engine, 190, 399
Bioacoustic research, 65
Biometric scanners, 50
Biotechnology, 357
Bit.ly, 266
Bitmaps/bitmapped images, 120, 122
BitNami, 252
Bits, 88
Bit size, 94, 141
BitTorrent protocol, 187, 324
BlackBerry, 164
Black hat SEO, 248
Blades of network servers, 8
Bleeping Computer Web site, 266
Blizzard Corporation, World of Warcraft, 193
Block of text, 110
Blogger.com, 233
Blogging, 225, 233–235
Bluetooth wireless protocol, 165, 397
Blu-ray
    discs, 26, 397, 398
    optical drives, 146–147
BMP format, 122
BOINC project, 365
Bookmarking sites, 225, 231–233
Booting, 98
Boot sector, 98
Botnets, 265
Bowling Green State University, 277
Brain Communicator, 14
Bridges, 295–296
Broadband technologies, 299
Browsers, 186, 188–190
Buddy lists, 186
Building computers, 148
Bullying, 368
Bus, 90–91
Business conferencing, 291–292
Business model. *See also* e-commerce
    cloud-based, 252–254
    description of, 204
Business to business (B2B) e-commerce, 243
Business to consumer (B2C) e-commerce,
    240–243
Business uses of mobile devices
    locations for meeting job requirements,
        208–209
    overview of, 204–206
    responsibilities of remote employees,
        207–208
    supervision of remote employees, 206–207
Bus topology, 294, 295
Butterscotch mobile page, 204
Buying pre-built computers, 148–149
Bytes, 24

C

Cables for networks, 293, 294
Cache memory, 91–92

Cameras, digital, 52–53, 122
Canvas Systems, 19
Carbonite, 170
Cards, 23
Careers
    in data communications, 55
    emerging, 349–352
    as game designers, 193
    in healthcare, 350–351
    in multimedia, 125
    as network and systems administrators,
        154
    in networking, 55, 300
    as telecommuters, 347
    as training and development specialists,
        277
Carpal tunnel syndrome, 53
Cascading Style Sheets (CSS), 228
Cases, 144
Cathode ray tube (CRT) monitors, 61
Cathode ray tubes, 60
CD-Recordable (CD-R) disks, 25
CD-ReWritable (CD-RW) disks, 25
CD-ROM drives, 25, 388
Cell addresses, 112
Cell phones. *See* smart phones
Cell phone tracking, 366, 370
Cell pointers, 112
Cells
    of battery capacity, 159
    of spreadsheets, 112
Central processing unit (CPU), 23, 92–93, 141,
    142
CERN, 182, 389
Character formatting, 111
Chat, 184, 291
Cheating, 329
Chrome operating system, 97
Circuit boards, 22–23
Classes, online, 195–196
Cleaning
    computers, 151, 153, 263
    monitors, 153, 263
Cleverbot, 373–374
Clicking with mouse, 46
Clients
    FTP, 186
    terminal, 85
Clip art, 122
Clipboard feature, 85
Cloud computing
    description of, 248–249
    Google Docs as, 108
    placing businesses in, 252–254
    running applications, 250–252
    for storing data, 162, 249–250
Cloud service companies, 170–171
Coaxial cable, 293
Codes
    of conduct, informal and social, 331–332
    of professional responsibility, 332
Cognitive science, 357
Color monitors, 60–61
Command-line interfaces, 41–42, 96
Command Prompt (Windows), 41–42
Commercial software, 106
Communication, future of, 374–375
Communication devices, 25. *See also* mobile de-
    vices; smart phones
Communication with remote
    employees, 207
Compact discs (CDs), 25
CompactFlash (CF) cards, 26, 147
Compaq Portable computer, 387
Compatibility of file formats, 121
Compressed air, 263

Integrated services digital network (ISDN), 299
Intellectual property, 206, 318
Intel processors, 142
Interactive media, 126
Internal bus, 90
Internet. *See also* electronic mail; social media
  advertising on, 243–246
  browsers, 186, 188–190
  chat and instant messaging, 184, 186
  cloud computing and, 254
  as education helper, 194
  File Transfer Protocol, 186–187
  games, 192–194
  history and structure of, 180–181
  online classes and universities, 195–196
  online research, 194–195
  ownership of, 181–182
  Peer-to-Peer (P2P) data transfer services, 187
  radio and television, 190–191
  searching, 190
  services carried by, 182
  spam, 185, 278, 280–281
  Voice over Internet Protocol, 165, 187–188, 292
  World Wide Web, 182–184
Internet piracy, 321
Internet2 project, 182
Internet Protocol version 6 (IPv6), 322
Internet Relay Chat (IRC), 184, 291
Internet service providers, 167, 182
Internetworking, 181
Interoperability, 308
Interrupts, 87
Intranets, 292, 307
Intuitive Surgical, da Vinci Surgical System, 372
IOS (iPhone OS), 96, 162
IP addresses, 167, 322
IPX/SPX, 298

J

Jenny Craig Inc., 154
John J. Lothian & Co., 347
Jokes in workplace, 328
JPEG format, 122

K

Keyboarding, 43
Keyboard logging/keylogging, 269
Keyboard-related injuries, 53–54
Keyboards, 43–45
Kilobytes, 25
Knowledge base, 305

L

Labels in cells, 113
Landscape mode, 164
Lanes, 91
Laptops, 6–7. *See also* notebook computers
Laser printers, 67
Latency, 143
Law and emerging technologies, 366–368
The Learning Company, *Reader Rabbit* software series, 194
LED monitors, 61–62
Licenses
  site, 291, 320
  for software, 109, 320–323

Licensing work for conditional online distribution, 227
Lie detection, 366–367
Like buttons, 230
Linden Labs, Second Life, 360–361, 367
Line printers, 68
LinkedIn, 230–232
Linux, 96, 390
Liquid cooling systems, 152
Liquid crystal display (LCD) monitors, 61, 70
Livescribe Echo Pen, 48–49
Local area networks, 292
Locking cell phones, 166
Lockstep, 307
Logical operations, 93

M

Machine cycle, 93
Mac OS X, 95–96
Magnetic disks, 25
Mail, guarding, 273
Mainframe computers, 9
Maintaining system, 29–30
Malware, 100, 201, 263–265
Malwarebytes, Anti-Malware software, 266
Malware protection, 153, 245, 265–267
Management information systems, 303–304
Managing
  cookies, spam, and spyware, 279–281
  files, 29
  mobile employees, 206–207
Manufacturer, selecting, 148–150
Manufacturer piracy, 321
Manufacturing, computer-aided, 73
Massachusetts Institute of Technology OpenCourseWare, 196
Mechanical mouse, 45
Media sharing, 225–227, 237–239
MediaWiki software, 236, 237
Medicine, future of, 375
Medium, 125
Megabytes, 25
Memory, 23–25, 141, 142–143
Menu bars, 40, 110
Mesh topology, 294, 295
Micro-blogging, 233–235. *See also* Twitter
Microcode, 92
Microcomputers, 5
Microphones, 51–52
Microprocessors, 23
Microsoft. *See also* Windows
  Access, 116–118
  Bing, 190, 399
  Excel, 117
  Exchange, 251–252
  Expression Web, 228
  Internet Explorer, 186, 188
  legal ruling against, 394
  operating system, 142
  Outlook, 118
  PowerPoint, 114, 115
MIDI (musical instrument digital interface) ports, 52
Midrange computers, 9
Minicomputers, 9
Mirrored systems, 308
Mission-critical systems, 307
MMORPG (massively multiplayer online role play game), 193
Mobile access to data, 169–171
Mobile computers, 7, 140. *See also* mobile devices
Mobile devices. *See also* notebook computers; smart phones
  choosing, 165–166

  courteous use of, 212–214
  effective business using, 204–209
  future of, 374
  handheld, 162–165
  netbooks, 6, 161–162, 200–201
  privacy issues of using, 210–212
  safety and courtesy using, 209–214
  social risks of, 200
  software for, 200–204
  using while driving, 209–210
Mobile networking
  providers, 166–168
  users, 168–169
Mobile phone number identification, 202
Mobile platform programming/designing, 352
Modems, 25, 159, 298–299
Modifier keys, 43
Monitoring by governments, 370
Monitors
  categories of, 60–61
  choosing, 143–144
  cleaning, 153, 263
  comparing, 62
  ergonomics and, 63–64
  types of, 61–62
  video cards, 63
  Video Graphics Array, 388
  viewing slides on, 115
Monochrome monitors, 60
Mosaic Web browser, 390
Motherboards, 23, 145
Motorola Xoom, 163
Mouse, 45–46
Mozilla Firefox, 186, 188, 399
Mozy, 249
Multifunction peripherals, 67–68
Multimedia authoring software, 127
Multimedia careers, 125
Multimedia software, 125–127
Multi-user computers, 5, 8–10
Multi-user/multitasking operating system, 84–85
Music
  downloading and sharing, 323–325
  inputting, 52

N

Nanotechnology, 357, 375
Napster, 323, 395
Narrative immersion, 361
National Science Foundation (NSF), 181
NBIC, 357, 372
NetBIOS/NetBEUI, 298
Netbooks, 6, 161–162, 200–201
Netiquette, 327–328
Network access passwords, 168
Network and systems administrator careers, 154
Network architect/support specialists, 352
Networking. *See also* networks
  careers in, 55, 300
  definition of, 5
  hardware and support, 144
  mobile, 166–169
  providers, 166–168
  users, 168–169
  wireless, 159, 293, 299
Network interface cards, 25, 295
Network operating systems, 27
Networks. *See also* networking
  benefits of using, 290–292
  data communication options, 298–299
  hardware for, 295–297
  for information systems, 307
  physical transmission standards, 298

protocols for, 297–298
topologies for, 293–295
types of, 292
wire-based media for, 293
Network servers, 8
Network versions of programs, 291
Neural interface devices, 14
Neural Signals, Inc., 14
News feeds, 229, 231
New Technology File System (NTFS), 98
Nonimpact printers, 66
Nonvolatile memory, 25
Notebook computers
description of, 6–7
features of, 158
flexibility of, 141
operating systems for, 140
power management for, 159–160
software for, 200–201
NSFnet, 181, 389
802.11n standard, 299
Number systems, 88
Numeric keypad, 44

O

Object-oriented programs, 123
Office automation system, 302
Off-the-shelf applications, 302
OLE (Object Linking and Embedding), 85–86
One-step checkout, 241
Online banking, 242–243
Online classes, 195–196
Online economics, 367
Online games, 192–194
Online payment companies, 241–242
Online profiling, 275
Online research, 194–195
Online retailers. *See* e-commerce
Online security specialists, 352
Online shopping, 240
Online student notes, 328–329
OnLive, 252
Open Handset Alliance, 97
OpenOffice.org
Calc, 112
suite, 395
Writer, 111
Open-source software, 107
Operating system (OS)
Android, 97, 398
choosing, 141
Chrome, 97
description of, 27, 38
DOS, 96
enhancing with utility software, 100–101
finding data on disks, 98–99
iOS, 96
Linux, 96
Mac OS X, 95–96
for smart phones, 165
terminology, 94–95
types and functions of, 84–87
Unix, 96
Windows, 95
Windows 7 Starter, 161
Opinion forums, 368–369
Optical character recognition software, 50
Optical drives, 146–147
Optical input devices, 49–50
Optical mouse, 45
Optical storage, 25
Optimizing disk performance, 99–100
Opt-out option, 276

Organizing disk storage, 97–98
Osborne 1 computer, 386
Output, 21–22
Output devices
computer-aided manufacturing, 73
description of, 25, 60
haptic feedback, 72
monitors, 60–64
printers, 66–69
projectors, 69–71
SMART Boards, 71
sound systems, 64, 66
Overtype mode, 44
Ownership of Internet, 181–182

P

Packets, 211, 293
Pages per minute (ppm), 69
Paint programs, 123
PalmPilot, 392
Paper-white displays, 62
Paragraph formatting, 111
Parallel bus, 90
Parts of computer system, 20–22
Passive matrix LCD, 61
Password capture, 269
Password guessing, 269
Passwords
for installing wireless routers, 167, 168
setting, 271
Password sharing, 269
Paste command, 85
PAUSE key, 44
Payload, 294
PayPal, 241–242
Pay-per-click, 244
PBWorks, 237
PCI Express, 91
PC sharing, 292
PC video cameras, 52
Peer-to-Peer (P2P) data transfer services, 187
Pens for data input, 7, 48–49
Performance of disks, optimizing, 99–100
Peripheral Component Interconnect
(PCI) bus, 91
Peripheral interfaces, 144
Persistent cookies, 280
Personal computers (PCs), 4, 5, 28
Personal data
protecting, 273–274, 371
social media companies and, 369
unethical use of, 245–246
Personal digital assistants (PDAs), 7, 163–164,
357, 392
Personal finance software, 12
Personal information managers, 118–119
Personal software licenses, 320
Personal VPN, 212
Pervasive computing, 358–360
Phishing, 278–279
Photo-editing software, 120, 123
Photo printers, 68
Photorealistic scenes, 125
Photos, sharing, 238–239, 324–325
Physics, future of, 375
PICT format, 122
Pipelining, 93
Piracy
copyright, fair use, and,
318–319
description of, 317–318
intellectual property and, 318
legal and social risks of, 325–326
of software, 109, 250, 320–323

when downloading and sharing music
and media, 323–325
Pixels, 60
Plagiarism, 329
Plain old telephone system, 298
Plasma displays, 62
Plotters, 68
PNG format, 122
Poaching wireless signals, 213–214
Podcasts, 191
Pointers, 45
Pointing and pointing devices, 45, 47
Points, 111
Pop-up ads, 244
Pop-up blockers, 244, 280
Portable computers, 158
Portable media devices, 147–148
Portable software, 108
Ports, 42–43
Post-purchase support, 150
Power
fluctuations in or failure of, 260–262
management of for notebook computers,
159–160
production and storage of, 374
Power plans, 160, 201
Power supplies, 144
Presentation programs, 113–115
Primary e-mail accounts, 280
Printers, 66–69
Print heads, 66
PRINT SCREEN key, 44
Privacy Act, 276
Privacy issues
with emerging technologies, 369
with mobile devices, 210–212
protecting personal privacy, 274–276
with social media, 226, 325
Processing, 23
Processors, 23–25
Productivity software
database management programs,
115–117
personal information managers, 118–119
presentation programs, 113–115
spreadsheet programs, 111–113
word processing programs, 110–111
Profiles for social media, 191
Programs. *See also* anti-malware programs;
application software; graphics software;
productivity software; software
computer-aided design, 123, 125, 386
definition of, 20
edutainment, 294
Folder Lock, 270, 271
FTP client, 186
network versions of, 291
object-oriented, 123
presentation, 113–115
running, 27, 29
sharing data between window
and, 85–86
social networking, 11, 225
spreadsheet, 111–113, 385
stand-alone, 106
synchronizing, 202
warranty, 150
WordPress blog development, 233
word processing, 110–111
Projectors, 69–71, 115
Prompts, 41
Protocols, 297–298
Psion Organiser, 164
Public domain software, 107
Public domain works, 319
Public record services, 275